ECONOMICS OF TRANSITION

p. 13 top

To my wife
Suzan M. Davran Kızılyallı

Economics of Transition

A new methodology for transforming a socialist economy to a market-led economy and sketches of a workable macroeconomic theory

HÜSNÜ KIZILYALLI
Professor of Economics

Ashgate

Aldershot • Brookfield USA • Singapore • Sydney

Published by
Ashgate Publishing Ltd
Gower House
Croft Road
Aldershot
Hants GU11 3HR
England

Ashgate Publishing Company
Old Post Road
Brookfield
Vermont 05036
USA

British Library Cataloguing in Publication Data
Kızılyallı, Hüsnü
Economics of transition : a new methodology for transforming a socialist economy to a market-led economy and sketches of a workable macroeconomic theory
1. Economic policy 2. Privatization
I. Title
338.9'25

Library of Congress Catalog Card Number: 97-76936

ISBN 1 84014 135 2

Printed in Great Britain by The Ipswich Book Company, Suffolk.

Contents

Chapter 8 High inflation problem

Chapter 9 Dollarization

Chapter 10 Demise of CMEA and collapse of CMEA trade and inter-republican trade of the former Soviet Union

Chapter 21 Phillips curve trade-off 413

Chapter 22 A review of country experiences 443

List of Tables

Preface

Judging from economic and political results, the transformation process in Eastern Europe and the former Soviet Union has not been successful in general. Partial, ad hoc or 'big bang' type approaches applied without even roughly estimating the implications of reform measures have yielded unsatisfactory results.

Transformation experiences in general have resulted in big drops in output, high or hyper inflation, high and rising unemployment, large balance of payments (BOP) deficit or extreme foreign exchange shortage, slow pace of enterprise restructuring and privatization, unsatisfactory growth in private sector and foreign direct investment, grand uncertainty about economic and political prospects and pessimistic expectations.

Even under the 'big bang' approach, with open and free trade and exchange regime and with zero or near-zero tariffs, importation of world prices has not materialized, either because of the foreign exchange shortage (overly undervalued domestic currency and inadequate import penetration as a consequence, despite a liberal trade regime on paper) or because of monopolistic market structure, despite and along with an overvalued currency (when external aid inflow was sufficient). Moreover, when the economy is in a state of flux and every market is in disequilibrium, with high-or hyper-inflation and grossly negative real interest rates, it is not possible to claim that the market rate of foreign exchange (either reflecting extreme shortage of foreign exchange or used as a nominal anchor to reduce the rate of inflation) is the true market clearing rate. The market rate of exchange on one hand reflects still distorted domestic relative prices, and on the other it is either clamped down by additional external borrowing (the Polish case) or inflated by the government to raise extra revenue (the Russian case).

The market socialism experiments have not been successful because the process of economic planning was abandoned, while an inadequate market system (partial price reforms affecting commodity markets only, absence of money, and capital markets, and proper taxation systems, without private property rights and entrepreneurship) was instituted. Although this experiment probably helped Hungary perform better in relation to other reforming countries, after the 1990 reforms, while also compared with Poland. In the 1990 reforms, the gradual approach also have possibly yielded better results (examples of Hungary, Czechoslovakia and China) compared with the 'big bang' approach which rather proved to be less successful (example of Poland) or chaotic (Russian example). Contrast between Russian and Chinese experiences is striking; China achieving almost 10% real economic growth and reduction in poverty in the last decade under gradual dual track approach, and Russia ending up in hyperinflation and with impoverishment of large masses and large output/employment losses.

A new method developed herein allows estimating the correct exchange rate based on world prices and under conditions of macroeconomic equilibrium. It also provides a planning methodology for sequencing market reforms, so that macro balances are kept throughout. The method, along with giving the estimate of foreign exchange rate, will provide forecasts of possible outcomes of reform measures, and hence enables planning accordingly. It adopts a comprehensive approach and provides both price and trade reform with immediate effect, but also allows sequencing the reforms in a coordinated manner and in the light of economic, social and political realities. It combines the 'big bang' approach (to price and trade reforms) with gradualist approach to enterprise reform and privatization. Its prerequisites are establishment of a market infrastructure with its basic institutions, banking reform and creation of an effective taxation mechanism with sales and income taxes.

In the second part of the book basic reform issues, such as market socialism experience, the soft budget constraint, enterprise reform and restructuring, privatization, high inflation, dollarization, etc. are reviewed in separate chapters or sections. The reform experiences of the former socialist countries, particularly of Poland, Hungary, East Germany, China and the former Soviet Union are reviewed and evaluated.

In the third part of the book, in the context of the theoretical foundations of the reform programs, developments in the macroeconomic theory in the last 2-3 decades are reviewed, from the viewpoint of reforming and developing countries, particularly in addressing their inflation, unemployment and growth problems. In particular, the neoclassical and new Keynesian theories, the Phillips curve hypothesis and crowding-out effect of government budget deficits are looked into, both as a theory (their economic logic, causal relationships, validity of their assumptions in the real world, etc.) and in practice, i.e., outcomes of policies shaped under these theories, and empirical findings in macro-and micro-economic studies, related to their economic rationale or assumptions. It is concluded that both neoclassical and new Keynesian theories fail to provide an economically meaningful framework for analysis of current economic and unemployment problems, nor for their cure. These theories and their assumptions are not confirmed and validated by empirical findings or outcomes of policies prescribed under them. On the contrary, there is ample empirical evidence to reject these hypotheses and/or their basic assumptions. Despite these facts and failure of these theories in the analysis and explanation of modern economies and their problems, all policy recommendations, particularly those recommended to the reforming or developing countries are still based on these unproven theories or hypotheses, such as the Phillips curve trade-off, supply-side economics, laissez-faire policies of monetarism or neoclassical theory, etc.

It is shown that the Phillips curve does not exist both in theory and practice. The empirical evidence suggests that the Phillips curve not only does not exist, but is positive in the long run, i.e. wage/price inflation reduces output and employment in the long run. Paradoxically, the trade-off may emerge, when strict price stability record is attained, but even then expansionary policy leads to more output increase than employment increment and which might well be explained by the aggregate demand increase under the standard Keynesian analysis, without recourse to the Phillips curve hypothesis. It is empirically observed that the real wages do not change over the business cycle, wage increases do not lag behind price increases and that the aggregate demand increase when leading to the inception of night shift operations rather affects output than employment. All these facts refute the basic premises of the Phillips curve trade-off.

It is also observed that the crowding-out effects of sizeable and systematic budgetary deficits (particularly on current account) on output, saving and investment are negative and significant. It turns out that the budgetary deficits do not promote but retard economic growth.

For developing and the reforming socialist countries (even tentatively for the industrialized countries), it is concluded that the best policy in addressing unemployment and growth issues, is to observe strict price stability, balanced budgets and reducing consumption, if necessary by additional tax effort. A new Marshall plan both to assist in the transformation of reforming former socialist countries and help with the unemployment problem of the industrialized countries would achieve this aim if financed by sound means, i.e. mainly by additional taxation, since capital is and will be in short-supply worldwide in foreseeable future despite a virtually stagnating world economy in the last decade.

The potential output is an illusory concept, based on the unemployment rate rather than on the actual capacity of existing production facilities. The latter reflects the correct potential output (because part of output decline in a recession or stagflation could be explained by a drop in the competitive productive capacity due to declining industries, competing imports and de-industrialization), variation of output around the former or change in the number of shifts worked in the manufacturing industry is construed as physical evidence of output fluctuations and business cycles. While with rising costs, etc., overutilization of capacity cannot continue indefinitely, its ending may coincide with disinflation policy and then it will be interpreted as the stagflation costs of disinflation; whereas it means returning to the normal level of output.

Moreover in overutilization of capacity and night-shift operations, it is empirically verified that output increase far outweighs employment increase and it is not the wage inflation or any wage-cost advantage inherent in it (in fact overtime and night premiums paid to labor rather constitute a wage-cost disadvantage) that induces firms to operate late shifts, but rather considerations of utilizing the existing production facilities better and thus possibly reaping economies of scale, that entice firms to overutilization of capacity.

The flexible exchanges rates have increased instability and uncertainty worldwide. Volatile movements of exchange rates have increased risks of capacity creation in exporting sectors. Increase in domestic interest rates, to curb inflationary tendencies by leading to capital inflow, have caused appreciation of the currency, which in turn leading to lower exports and higher imports, eventually have resulted in a lower output than originally planned. Hence output might decline even below the potential level, as a result of disinflation policy, because of flexible exchange rates; and this would not have been possible under pegged or stable exchange rates.

The flexible exchange rates have become a major source of instability, by allowing countries with inflationary tendencies and policies, to abandon fiscal and monetary discipline and rely on exchange rate to redress BOP problems by successive devaluations (i.e. through floating the rate). In case of high inflation economies, this policy has accelerated the inflationary process through continuous supply shocks (cost-push effects) generated. The other extreme opted for is to maintain the rate stable for long periods, irrespective of the domestic price developments, to control and check the cost-push effects and thus reduce the inflation rate. This alternative is more destabilizing, because it leads to accumulation of sizeable short-term external debt and generates expectations of devaluation at a higher rate in the future. Along with developing countries, the reforming countries as well are now employing either policy. Both of these policies are just palliatives, since they don't address the real causes of domestic inflation by means of fiscal and monetary discipline.

The aim of this book is to study the economic problem (transition, inflation, unemployment, growth and development particularly), without any preconceived idea or prejudice and recommend solutions accordingly. The author subscribes to no general school of thought, new Keynesian, neo-classical or Austrian, but believes that under certain conditions (in certain periods of certain countries) one of them may hold true.

Moreover the book attempts to look into the current economic problems combining both the short-run (stability) and the long-run (growth and development) aspects. Although 'in the long run we are all dead', the seeds of future are sown today. In reality, it is not possible to separate and isolate the long run from the short run. This obvious fact, however, deliberately or by ignorance is overlooked by governments in general and they try to solve the current apparent problem by sacrificing the long run (at a huge future cost). However the long-run and the short-run are interwoven and interdependent; and ignoring the long run implications of short-term economic decisions has, in fact, become the main cause of the current economic problems.

Except for a general war or a major technological breakthrough like the discovery of a cheap source of energy, it is possible roughly to predict economic prospects of developing and industrialized countries, in the next 5-10 years, under the present policies (except for major, drastic policy changes). On the basis of current policies and prevailing stagnating or declining trends, one can safely claim that, except for Far East, (which would be better off), these countries would not be better off in general and some would be worse off; and the unemployment problem will definitely get worse. Although all this is quite obvious, and shows that today shapes the future and there is no other future than the one which is the result (function) of current trends and policies, policy-makers and economists alike still distinguish between the short run and the long run. An economic policy prescription or package should not divorce the long run from the short run; preoccupation with the short run, however, seems to be the standard practice during the last 2-3 decades and nowadays.

As a matter of fact, in government decisions, the long-run considerations are either not weighed properly or completely ignored. A way out of this dilemma might be setting up an independent or autonomous economic administration mechanism, although financial system (taxation and budgets) would still be shaped and decided upon by the executive and legislative branches of the government. In practice, such a mechanism could be put in place by an independent central bank and a charter for financial/economic affairs and a semi-autonomous economic planning (indicative) machinery (in countries where politically it is admissible); this mechanism will see to it that the long-run considerations also count in current economic decisions.

Since the subject matter of this book is applied economics, consistent unequivocal positions have to be taken on specific issues, even risking error, provided that the real economic world is firmly identified, validity of assumptions are verified and acceptability/admissibility of basic hypothesis are firmly established; because in policy-making and economic planning ambiguity and vagueness complicate issues, lead to inconsistencies and frequent policy reversals, and cause uncertainty or even chaos. Nevertheless, policies and measures that turned out to be harmful or useless, should be corrected in good time and in a consistent manner.

The correct approach in economic policy making requires proper diagnosis of the economic problem to be dealt with, and identification and verification of actual conditions surrounding it. Whereas in most instances, particularly in developing and even in certain reforming countries, policy package derived from the standard or novel theory is readily applied, without making sure that the hypothetical conditions assumed are valid for the case to be treated. In this sense, it is still not understood that there is no unique solution to even the most common current macroeconomic problems. E.g., nowadays in high inflation countries it is fashionable to use privatization proceeds in financing the budgetary deficits on current account with a view to checking inflationary growth and a lower inflation rate thus achieved (which is a short-term phenomenon anyway) is treated as a big success, while the real remedy, the genuine tax reform is being only paid lip service.

The first four chapters of this book were drafted in November 1990, were circulated to a limited audience in 1991 and were submitted for publication in early 1992 to the Boğaziçi Üniversitesi Ekonomi ve İdari Bilimler Dergisi, and its first part was published in its 1992 issue.

Hüsnü Kızılyallı
Istanbul, November 1997

Acknowledgements

I thank gratefully the authors, editors publishers and agents for their kind permission to reproduce extracts from their works: "Growth and Trade Prospects for Central and Eastern Europe" by J.M.C. Rollo and J. Stern, in *the World Economy*, 1992, pp. 645-668, published by Blackwell Publishers, 108 Cowley Road, Oxford OX4 IJF, "Dollarization in Latin America: Greshains Law in Reverse?" by Pablo E. Guidotti and Carlos A. Rodriguez, in *IMF Staff Papers*, 1992, pp. 518-544, published by International Monetary Fund, 700 19th St, N.W., Washington DC 20431, *Project Appraisal R Planning for Developing Countries* by I.M.D. Little and J. A. Mirrlees, published by Heinemann, Halley Court, Jordon Hill, Oxford OX2 8EJ, Copyright I. M.D. Little and J.A. Mirlees 1974 and OECD, Paris, 1968, reprinted in 1977 by permission of Heinemann Educational publishers, a division of Reed Educational R Professional Publishing Ltd of Quadrant House, The Quadrant, Sutton, Surrey, SMZ 5AS; *Economics* 9th edition, by R.G. Lipsev, P.O. Steiner, D.D. Purvis and P.N. Courant, published by Harper Collins Publishers, 10 East 53 rd Street, New York, NY 100222 and Addison Wesley Longman, One Jacob Way, Reading, Massachusetts 01867-3999, which bought Harper Collins' educational publishing dirisions; "Stabilization and Economic Reform in Russia" by S. Fischer in *Brookings Papers on Economic Activity,* 1 : 1992, pp. 77-126, published by Brookings Institution Press, 1775 Massachusetts Avenue, N.N. Washington, D.C. 20036-2188; *Macroeconomics* (1990) by R. Dornbusch and S. Fischer, published by Mc Graw-H.H, 1221 Avenue of the Americas, New York, NY 10020-1095; *World Tables, Wored Development Reports, Wored Bank News*, and Bank's Wored, published by the Wored Bank, 1818 H Street N.W., Washington, D.C. 20433; "Polish Economic Reform, 1990-91 : Principles and Outcomes" by Stanislaw Gomulka in *Cambridge Journal of Economics,* September 1992, published by Academic

Press Ltd, 24-28 Oval Road, London NW1 7DX and Copyright by Academic Press Inc, 6277 Sea Harbor Brive, Orlando, Florida 32887; *Economics* by John Sloman, published by Harvester Wheatsheaf, Campus 400, Maylands Ave, Hemel, Hempstead, Herts, HPZ TEZ; and "Economic Crisis in a Shortage Economy" by Kent Osband in *Journal of Political Economy*, 1992, Vol. 100, no. 4, pp. 673-690, published by University of Chicago Press, 1126 East 59th street, Chicago, Illinois 60637.

My special thanks go to Prof. Dr. Z. İlsem Önsan, Prof. Dr. Metin Balcı, Gül Tuncel, Muhittin Salih Eren and Linda Mercan for their kind assistance in connection with the preparation of the manuscript for printing and regarding reprinting.

Proposed methodology for transforming a socialist economy to a market-led economy: summary

Proposed methodology for transforming a socialist economy to a market-led economy: summary

1 Introduction

1.1 The proposed methodology is applied to the design of a model which allows immediate transition into an open free market system for a small-to-medium size country, after a preparatory phase of 6 months. It assures, with immediate effect, a free price mechanism, a stable foreign trade balance and an open economy with moderate (rate to be chosen) protection (tariffs and some import quotas). Under the model exchange rate, wage rates and protection levels are selected, taking into account their alternative consequences in terms of lost jobs, incomes and closed-down plants.

1.2 The model is most suited for short-to-medium term planning of the industrial sector during transition, with a down-to-earth approach with respect to responses of economic agents (firms and households), based on the estimated responses of goods producing sectors, to the new system. It is a macro model based on the aggregation of micro economic decisions. The basic approach is by planning in stages and carrying out computations by an iterative process.

2 Scope

2.1 Household and Government sectors can be treated as exogenous or included as endogenous variables.

2.2 The model forecasts the worst possible outcomes (shock effects) to start with, of moving into an open and free market system (beneficial future effects of this change will improve the outcome over time; labor efficiency, use of better imported inputs and machinery, technology, allocative efficiency of free price mechanisms). In this sense the model is realistic; society might choose better if the worst possible outcome was known.

2.3 It assures free price mechanisms and balance in foreign trade, as well as foreign exchange stability, and gives estimates of factory shut-downs and the unemployment that will emerge thereafter.

3 Outputs

3.1 The model determines the exchange rate, wage rate and level of protection in a discretionary manner. In that sense the exchange rate and wage rate are selected (determined) considering the consequences in terms of unemployment and closed plants and loss of income. The system could be completely open with some tariff protection and no import restrictions or with a predetermined temporary level of import quotas for certain products, depending on export and balance of payments prospects and the competitive strength of international sectors (import substitution in particular).

3.2 The model gives estimates of total output, GDP, total profits and the wage bill, exports and imports. It allows determination of the fate of import substitution industries (identifies plants to shut down, plants to be given subsidies for adjustment and rehabilitation) in a discretionary manner.

3.3 In view of the fact that (with no or little protection and import restrictions) consumers might initially prefer high-priced foreign products to lower priced even if better-quality local products, or just to slowdown the initial import shock, some temporary import restrictions (not bans but quotas) might be resorted to, taking into consideration the effects of lost incomes and jobs.

4 Conclusions

4.1 The scheme will lead to early recognition and acceptance of socialist countries as market economies by the international economic and financial community and organizations, and open up possibilities of concessionary loans therefrom. In fact such a program could be designed in such a manner that IMF stand-by credits and IBRD structural adjustment loans would be made available with the launching of this program.

4.2 In order to maintain price and foreign exchange stability after the transition, however, it is imperative to introduce corporation (profit) income and expenditure (sales or value-added) taxes or any other revenue system which upholds budgetary balance, along with the launching of the program.

4.3 Import quotas might also be essential, because the reaction (response) of households to the new system [the most difficult part of estimation (projection)] is difficult to predict, regarding the level of consumption and its breakdown between local and foreign goods and services.

4.4 The totally integrated approach to moving into a market-led economy, as against the piecemeal approach which presently seems to be exercised, enables a country to enjoy the benefits of a free market mechanism in the short run. The country may therefore qualify in principle for IMF and IBRD credits and GATT membership with immediate concomitant benefits.

4.5 Although the proposed methodology launches a market mechanism with immediate effect, transition is orderly and smooth and shocks can be phased out over subsequent years as deemed appropriate by decision-makers.

Chapter 1

Need for a new approach in transforming the socialist economies

Need for a new approach in transforming the socialist economies

1 Economics of transition

It is sad to observe in the Eastern Europe and Soviet Union the turmoil, in the form of shortages, inflation, unemployment and declining output, caused by political and economic changes taking place in a disorderly fashion. It is sad because this chaos to a great extent could have been avoided, if their policies during the transition period were right and aimed at salvaging (not destroying) what could have been rescued from the old regime.

It is observed world-wide that the science of economics does not lend much assistance during transition periods (when major changes in economic policies take place with a view to altering income distribution, resource allocation and pace of economic and social development drastically or as a result of an external shock like an oil price hike) and practice shows that these drastic policies and changes cause major disruptions in the economies concerned (shortages, inflation, unemployment, capital flight, balance of payments problems, etc.).

The crux of the issue in transition economics is to maintain, not to disrupt economic equilibria by observing the balance between resources and their use through reliable macro-economic forecasts and appropriate policies (budgetary and monetary discipline).

The economics of transition, dealing with economic equilibria in moving from one economic order into another, is not a well trodden path. Examples of such transitions are post-independence African economies, periods of socialist/social democrat policies being pursued in developing or even developed countries (Chile under Allende, Turkey in the late 1970s pursuing fast growth policies without adjusting to the petroleum price shock, the early years of the Mitterrand era pursuing socialist economic policies in France, the welfare policies of Carter etc.).

The most common outcome of this type of transitional economic policy was inflation, and a decline in economic and employment growth rates. When wrong policies were sustained for longer periods, shortages of basic goods and balance of payments problems also emerged.

When there is a major change in the economic order (system), as from an open market-oriented economy into a closed socialist-oriented one or public investment (sector) dominated one or vice versa, from a stagnant economy to a fast-growing one, or in the form of drastic change in income distribution or sectoral composition of investments (public versus private, productive versus un-productive infrastructure, housing), it is imperative that a comprehensive analysis should be made to judge its overall impact; and it should be noted that a partial analysis focusing on direct, generally beneficial effects often misses critical aspects.

The prerequisite for success is keeping a free market/price mechanism to signal shortages and to maintain economic equilibrium. Targets set for quick changes in income distribution, consumption pattern and size and composition of investments and level of public expenditures result in increases in inflationary gap/pressures, and balance of payments difficulties. Governments have to tread cautiously on these paths and accurately estimate their inflationary impact. One should not analyze and estimate first-round effects only, but also effects of further rounds and long-term effects as well.

Here the most crucial problem is how to avoid inflation which is commonplace in transitional situations. Avoiding inflationary ways of financing (deficit financing) and aiming at balanced budgets (increasing taxation to fund increased public expenditures and investments) are the bare minimum for financial and economic stability. But even in cases where increased public expenditures and/or transfer payments are financed by sound means (say taxation), they might still be inflationary if private savings are reduced by a greater amount and if there is an increasing outflow of capital abroad, which during transition periods might well be the case.

This analysis should also include other adverse, side effects. Increases in public sector investments and public expenditures, increased regulation (of the economy) and income re-distribution policies will have repercussions on private investments (disinvestments included), outflow of funds overseas, savings (decisions) by households and business, which have to be taken into account in the final analysis.

2 Transformation attempts in Eastern Europe: a critique and remedies

It is in the interest of all countries for the transformation process to succeed. Because successful and orderly transformation of socialist countries into a market system and their integration into the world economy, with eventual higher efficiency and productivity, will help world peace, prosperity and welfare.

Transformation attempts in Eastern Europe so far failed because of *inadequate forecasting techniques* and planning ahead, *lack of a comprehensive approach* and inappropriate policies resulting therefrom.

The Eastern European countries erred in following areas of economic policy:

1 Establishment of *sound financial and monetary structures* in line with the requirements of a market economy, was not given due priority. Economic equilibria could not be maintained if taxation and banking systems are not restructured with a view to gearing it to the market mechanism.

Introducing a modern income, corporation, import and expenditure (sales tax or VAT) taxation system, with immediate effect when the free market system is launched, to yield adequate revenue to meet current expenditures and subsidies to be paid, carries highest priority. Central bank and commercial banks should be restructured accordingly. These systems and institutions will establish and assure financial discipline and monetary stability.

2 These measures would have enabled creation of a sound and stable national currency. If need be a new currency could have been issued. In the context of the privatization program, sale proceeds of houses, shops, and farms to interested nationals even on credit terms, by *mopping up excess liquidity of the banking system* (saving deposits of nationals), would have and still could help the cause.

3 In lieu of establishing a sound local currency, *dollarization* was opted with dire consequences. Dollarization in Turkey and Poland has not led to monetary stability and growth. On the contrary, in these countries in 1980s inflation was rampant with little growth. Free purchase of foreign currencies by itself could not bolster a weak local currency, on the contrary it exposes its weakness. Similarly, a floating exchange rate by itself is not a cure (on the contrary it is a damaging factor), if the domestic

inflation rate is high and then is not accompanied by classical (orthodox) anti-inflationary budgetary and monetary measures. Flexible exchange rates help the adjustment process, if domestic instability is of minute magnitude and only then obviates the need for domestic fiscal and monetary adjustment. Otherwise, as revealed by the Turkish experience, it exacerbates inflationary process, when not coupled with fiscal and monetary measures and discipline.

Moreover Turkey, Poland and Latin America with high inflation and external debts and low growth rates, should not be taken as examples. Rather the exemplary precedents set by Far Eastern countries such as South Korea and Taiwan who succeeded brilliantly through guidance provided by economic planning, export drive, high saving propensity and some protection, should be followed.

4 *The East German experience* also shows that replacing a weak local currency by a convertible one and immediate open economy (full and complete integration with West Germany) is not a panacea, rather they are culprits of the unification aftermath. Proper policies for East Germany would not have been an immediate political union, but a phased economic union (integration). Such an approach, for which a planning methodology is described below, would have averted many disruptions now experienced and might well have enabled full integration in some 5 years, in lieu of the 10 years now expected.

5 Dollarization in the form of *duty-free dollar-shops* in the Eastern Europe is another damaging factor. It is not possible to understand its real 'raison d'être'. At these shops foreigners and some (or all) nationals can buy imported goods paying in convertible currencies. The apparent aim is to earn foreign exchange whatever the source. Depending on the free market price of these imported goods in the country concerned, black market exchange rate for dollar is determined, which becomes outrageously high and enables foreigners to live luxuriously at 10-20 dollar a day. This measure could hardly increase (on the contrary decreases) net foreign exchange earnings of the country through tourism.

Even when a realistic dollar rate, based on purchasing power of local currency, is 10 units of local currency, the said black market rate could go up to 70-80 units depending on the domestic scarcity of imported goods sold at these shops. This out-of-proportion black market rate of foreign exchange, being the only free market rate, of course has many adverse consequences on the economy and the economic decisions.

In lieu of this system, if these import goods (tea, coffee, tinned food and luxuries) are offered to the general public at highly taxed-prices and similarly foreign exchange for foreign travel is sold at corresponding (higher) rates, the bulk of local demand for black market foreign exchange will vanish and the free market rate of foreign exchange will come down substantially.

6 *Privatization* and private entrepreneurship are important and essential for moving the socialist economies to the free market system. But the former is not the top-most economic priority, even though it is a must politically. In other words, free market mechanism could and should be launched before privatization is accomplished and complete, and it should not be delayed awaiting privatization.

Nevertheless, foreign partners, if they can be found on reasonable terms and conditions, should be welcomed and advantages over technology and marketing should be reaped. The problem, however, is attracting reliable foreign partners under the circumstances, which proves to be rather difficult. Because, when the whole economy is in a flux, only adventurers, to reap quick profits, will be interested in investing or participating in old-technology plants with insurmountable problems. Similarly sectoral and project-based attempts to improve technology, efficiency and marketing are bound to fail, because the overall economic outlook is a big unknown.

These uncertainties will vanish and economic prospects will be clarified and be bright when the *comprehensive economic plan approach*, explained below, is adopted. Then it will be possible to attract local and foreign entrepreneurs for privatization of existing plants and establishment of new ventures.

7 It seems that these countries after long experience with mandatory central planning, dumped or degraded any *economic planning* notions. Whereas for orderly and successful transition *indicative economic planning* as used in the Western Europe and Far East is a must.

8 Recent immediate *dismantling of COMECON* will have significant adverse effects. The neighboring countries, during the interim period, should rather have mutually tried to keep whatever trade going on between them. (Some COMECON goods with reasonable quality would still have been preferred by customers because of familiarity, if their prices were low, as they should.) This intra-regional trade could be promoted by a *Multilateral Payments Mechanism or Union* (outstanding

balances to be periodically settled in hard currencies), otherwise many what-used-to-be export plants will be shut down, without being given a chance to adapt, transform and survive. (When payment in hard currencies is required, these East European plants can hardly compete with the world's most efficient plants which they are bound to face.)

Such a multi-lateral payments mechanism assures that whatever net hard currency earnings to materialize under the normal free trade system from regional trade, still accrue to relevant members, except for credit limits of chronic creditor countries.

3 A new planning methodology

Economic forecasting and planning is a difficult proposition during transition periods. The conventional macroeconomic forecasting, based on econometric techniques or input-output analysis fails, because many parameters assumed fixed, change drastically during transformation.

An unconventional type forecasting and planning methodology is developed herein for transforming a socialist economy to market led economy. This methodology allows immediate transition into an open free market system. It assures with immediate effect free price mechanism, stable foreign trade balance and open economy with moderate (rate to be chosen) protection (import tariffs and some import quotas). Under this methodology exchange rate, wage rates and protection levels are determined and selected, taking into account their alternative consequences in terms of lost jobs, incomes and closed-down plants. It is a computer model based on aggregation of microeconomic decisions.

It gives, by sectors and plants, estimates of total output, gross domestic product, profits and wage bill, employment, exports and imports, subsidies to be given to industries for adjustment and rehabilitation. The methodology while ensuring immediate transformation of socialist economies into free market system, allows orderly transition and maintenance of producing units and plants which could survive and rehabilitated.

The other alternative, widely exercised in the Eastern Europe, is plunging into unknown seas of market economy with partial analyses and reforms, high-priority privatization, ad hoc measures and establishment of priorities and institutions of market economy in a haphazard manner. This alternative has caused major disruptions, declining outputs and great uncertainty. Even in East Germany, with total financial and economic backing of West Germany, the same phenomena have emerged and it is now estimated that the process will take l0 years to succeed.

The proposed alternative, based on the immediate creation of basic requirements and institutions of a market economy, is a comprehensive and gradual approach, which allows the advantages of a market mechanism to be reaped with immediate effect, but cushions, postpones and alleviates adverse and disruptive effects through appropriate planning and measures.

This methodology, based on international prices (plus/minus local transport costs) adjusted by moderate tariff protection and subsidies (in cases where the industry can survive or flourish in the medium run), will enable the economy move to open and free market system right away.

During the planning stage, which may require 6 months to 1 year, alternative exchange rates, wage rates, tariff and subsidy levels will be investigated in view of their consequences (benefits and costs) in terms of production, GDP, employment by sectors and plants, balance of payments, and government budget and forecasts. At this stage required policy decisions could be reached by consensus; this could be relatively easy in view of the absence of divergent vested-interest groups, which will emerge later. Still at this stage an action program will be drafted and market institutions and structures (tax laws, import regime, banking system included) will be set up with immediate effect and with a view to efficient implementation after the action program is launched.

The method can be repeatedly employed to make new forecasts thereafter say every year. All endogenous variables can be re-estimated, including exchange and wage rates, with little effort. It will provide revolving plan and estimates (macro, sectoral and for individual plants), until transformation is completed and a competitive free market economy is achieved. (And then it will be possible to employ conventional macroeconomic models and plans.)

Transition under this methodology is smooth and orderly, and everything is under control. Every economic variable will be forecast with reasonable accuracy, including decline in sectoral outputs, unemployment and closing plants. There will be a major adjustment and shock when the action program based on international prices is launched, but even then everybody will know his/her role in the new competitive world, which will be determined by negotiation and consensus. Tariffs, subsidies and training programs will cushion and phase out shocking effects. It will be easier to maintain financial and monetary discipline and economic equilibria thereafter, provided the initial consensus and deal is realistic and considered satisfactory by the majority.

Chapter 2

The proposed methodology

The proposed methodology

1 Institutions/schemes required by the methodology

The method, particularly at the preparatory stage, requires collaboration or four institutions, namely (i) the Central Plan Bureau (CPB), (ii) establishments, (iii) policy making body and (iv) fiscal and monetary institutions.

CPB operates under indicative planning approach, provides initial 2-3 estimates of foreign exchange rate, customs tariff rates, wage categories; feeds in a computer data and information gathered from establishments; prepares alternative scenarios for policy decisions.

Establishments or plants, taking account of their international competitive strength or weakness, individually estimate their export/local sale prospects, and determine whether they will be industries exporting, import substituting or closing down, when international prices are exercised at the initial exchange rates provided by CPB.

At the preparatory stage fiscal and monetary institutions and schemes required in a market economy should be introduced and be in place before implementation under the method starts. Basic requisites are a Central bank, commercial banks and an efficient taxation system and mechanism.

Policy making body, on the basis of alternative scenarios worked out by CPB, determines exchange rate, level of tariff protection, average wage rate, etc. considering the consequences of alternative scenarios in terms of shut-down plants, lost jobs and incomes, and external borrowing requirements.

Limited number of establishments in the former socialist countries (8,000 in Hungary, some 100,000 in the former USSR) are mostly public enterprises which enables the method to work. Existing private enterprises can participate in the exercise on a voluntary basis, but this is not essential, on the assumption that they can survive in an open free market system.

The model is a very simple one, in view of the limited reliable information available during transition and requires a central computer at CPB with terminals at major centers and establishments. All data and information from establishments will be loaded in to the computer, including international prices compiled and supplied by enterprises and definite selling prices of establishments. Establishment should have access to certain computer data, such as international prices and finalized selling prices of other establishments.

2 Prices

The methods uses international prices, adjusted for transport and customs tariff. Hence export prices are fob and import prices are cif, plus/minus local transport charges and customs tariffs applicable to get ex-factory or ex-warehouse prices. International prices are those relevant for the country and establishment (or plant) concerned.

In deriving export values, establishments will determine prices their goods will fetch in relevant world markets, considering quality of their goods, international competition prevailing, etc.

Calculations of the method are based on a relevant foreign currency unit, say $. At the final stage of the exercise (transactions) it can be converted into local currency, applying the exchange rate determined in the process.

3 Production costs

Goods producing plants using the relevant international prices for their output and inputs in the tradeable category (it does not matter whether tradeable goods concerned will in fact be exported/imported or sold/purchased domestically), calculates value/cost of their output/inputs in $. Inputs comprise raw materials, other material inputs, internationally procured services. Unit prices of utilities and domestic services in $, will be calculated beforehand separately (as shown below) and supplied to establishments by CPB.

4 Depreciation charges

Depreciation charges for fixed capital invested (buildings, plant and machinery) are omitted as a cost element. Royalties to be paid in foreign exchange and service of external debt (principal repayments and interest payments in the year concerned) contracted or used by establishments, however, could be included in the cost.

Exclusion of depreciation charges from cost are justifiable since they represent 'capital sunk', which could not be utilized otherwise, considering many plants in Eastern Europe are out-moded, inefficient, old-technology plants. This treatment will introduce a bias in favor of consumption against saving in the aftermath of transformation, which could be justified on grounds of saving bias exercised in the past under communism.

In cases where plants could be utilized for purposes other than originally designed, through diversification, introduction of new technology, joint-ventures with foreign concerns, still it is better to exclude depreciation in costing. The beneficial effects of better utilization of fixed-capital assets planned, however, will be included in output (higher, diversified or better quality output priced accordingly).

In case of planned new capital investments, since capital is not sunk yet, depreciation charges should be included in the cost. Depreciation rates will be applied to values based on international prices, whether the goods are to be imported or locally procured. In case of locally manufactured capital goods, realistic prices, taking account of required discounts from international prices to make them competitive, should be used.

5 Labor costs

Labor Costs will be shown by two indicators: (i) Number employed (ii) total wages paid expressed in an index using minimum wage as a base. E.g. a plant employing 100 and paying 20,000 in local currency p.a., will have a labor index of 1,000, if minimum wage is 200 (wage index = total wage bill/minimum wage).

2-3 exchange rates *or* wage rates in $ will be provided to establishments in order to enable them calculate manufacturing costs in $.

In this exercise actual level of wage bill is not important, rather strata of wages reflecting different kinds of skills required for production process feature in. In this estimate economizing in labor cost, the elimination of feather-bedding is expected.

6 Domestic sectors

In case of non-tradeable goods and services (transport, communication, utilities, trade, etc.) prices will be based on production costs (material inputs, services and labor). All material inputs whether of import or local origin should be valued at international prices (cif plus local transport).

Calculation of unit costs for domestic sectors in $ is the first step of the whole exercise. Minimum wage rate and unit local transport costs in $ will however, precede this very first step.

Any customs tariff on imported inputs will be taken care of by a percentage increase (at the planned advalorem rate of tariff) of international prices.

Domestic sectors (non-tradeables, utilities) are prerequisites of any economic activity. A service cannot be shut down even if not profitable, provided user industries or consumers need it, unless its alternative is more economic. Hence they have to be profitable and their prices should include a comfortable profit margin to make them viable. Economies of scale prevailing in the sector can be accounted for by assuming normal, optimum capacity utilization. (Cost increase due to below capital operations is to be subsidized, particularly for transport and utilities.) This calls for a strong Government budgetary position to full stop inside braclat accommodate this kind of eventualities. Assumption of normal capacity operation when not materialized, will lead to lower imports than forecast, however.

7 Stages of calculation for non-tradeables

(i) A preliminary minimum wage in $ will be calculated using commodity base of consumer price index (wage basket) and international prices. Some adjustment to international prices could be made for local transport and customs tariff, if any. In case of pricing housing, utilities and services some guesses can be made. Effect of errors in these estimates is marginal. These estimates, however can be revised in a further round. But then this will require, going back to domestic service establishments a second time. In case of rent, it can fixed as a certain percentage of minimum wage during transition.

(ii) A preliminary unit local transport cost in $ for rail, road and naval transport and air cargo will be estimated for adjusting international prices to local transport requirements.

(iii) New wage levels for different skill categories based on present strata and/or planned changes in them, as multiples of minimum wage are determined, for/by domestic sectors.

(iv) Using the preliminary minimum wage strata, labor costs of domestic sectors would be calculated in $. This will make possible domestic sectors to estimate unit costs of goods and services produced.

(v) The relation between the present minimum wage in local currency and new minimum wage in $, will give the new exchange rate. In practice this rate or a depreciated version of it (for balance of payments considerations) could be employed. Applying this exchange rate to local transport tariff (making any adjustment for subsidy, undervalued input, etc.) will give an indication regarding local transport rates in \$. These might be used to check transport rates calculated under (ii) above.

Minimum wage and transport tariff estimates in \$ could be improved by iterative process, using first-round estimates in the second round of calculations.

Unit production costs for domestic sectors, will be calculated using the minimum wage rate and its two variants (say 20% lower and 10% higher rates). It is deemed that minimum wage could not be below subsistence (poverty) level and it should not be too high (even when seems feasible) to cushion many surrounding uncertainties.

In transportation of export goods, subsidized rates can be envisaged and used in the exercise.

Tariff protection also should not be too high, if integration into world economy is aimed at and hence it can be predetermined for various commodities. Critical sectors (like agriculture, some manufacturing subsectors) can be protected by higher than normal customs duties. Exchange rate will be used for balance of payments equilibrium. Import quotas can be applicable to take care of further, eventualities or unanticipated disruptions, as exercised even in EC, Japan and USA.

8 Tradeable sectors

Given minimum wage, prices of utilities, domestic services and goods in \$, establishments producing tradeables (manufacturing, mining, agriculture) and in tourism, etc. sectors, gathering relevant international prices for their output and input, can estimate their costs. On the basis of their costs they can determine sales prospects (local and export markets), output and prices.

Firms in reporting to CPB will specify whether their inputs will be purchased locally or imported and indicate value of main items which used to be procured locally, but now planned to be imported. The latter aspect will vary in line with minimum average wage rate in \$ terms.(*) A loss incurring enterprise can also determine whether in the medium run with subsidy payments from the Government budget and modernization investment, it can be a viable operation, and make a proposal along these lines. If this proposal is approved by the relevant ministry, then the establishment concerned will operate under agreed terms; otherwise this enterprise has to close down.

(*) This information is not necessary for calculations of the method; it will give an estimate of import increase due to transformation.

The establishments whose production costs and prices are less than international prices will be exporting. If costs and prices are greater than international prices by a margin less than the tariff protection, then they will be substituting imports. Establishments, whose cost and prices are greater than international prices, after tariff protection face the prospect of close-down.

For import-substitution industries, international prices will only serve as a reference point; because of lower cost and quality, and competition from imports, actual domestic prices might be set lower. This should be planned by the enterprise during the planning phase and included in estimates accordingly.

In case of export industries also, discounts to be offered because of quality, lack of credit terms, etc. considerations, have to be taken into account. Transport, production etc. subsidies planned or called for have to be taken into consideration in calculations and if deemed necessary requested by enterprises concerned.

Enterprises producing several products would estimate costs, sales, profits, employment, etc. by products, and report CPB separately, particularly if their competitive position differs substantially among products (some for export, others for import substitution and those resulting in loss whatever exchange/wage rate is employed).

9 Government expenditures

Government departments after estimating their budgetary expenditures in current local prices will provide commodity and service breakdown of them. On the basis of this breakdown, expenditure values in $ terms will be estimated, using minimum wage rate, international prices and given utility, service rates. Imports (specifying items and their breakdown which used to be locally purchased, but now planned to be imported), and labor (wage) index will also be provided to CPB.

10 Private consumption

Private consumption will be estimated using total wage bill and private savings deposits as explanatory variables. Consumption pattern as revealed by the latest input/output table could be starting point in deriving commodity breakdown of private consumption. Availability and new prices of consumer goods will, however, change the said pattern. Nevertheless, consumption pattern of a country can not change dramatically overnight. Although there will be a shift to motor cars, consumer durables and new or better packaged import items. Hence excise duties, VAT or sales tax and customs duties should be in place to curb these expenditures. Import quotas for some consumer goods could be applied to protect local industries and achieve foreign trade balance, as a last resort.

Total private consumption estimate is called for achieving macro-economic balance (available resources and their use). The import component of consumption expenditures must be estimated for balance of payments equilibrium purposes in this exercise. Commodity-service breakdown of consumption is not, however, a basic input for this exercise.

11 Investments

Except for modernization investments, projects for which external financing secured and investments which cannot be postponed due to any reason in the first year of the program, no new public investment should be planned. Valuation of investment in $ terms will be by its building, machinery, labor, utility and service components, in the manner already described. And its import component will also be calculated.

12 Imports

Firms, inter alia, would report imported raw material, etc. requisites under (i) non-competing imports and (ii) competing imports categories. Imported input requirements of competing nature, would be classified by commodities (indicating local source as well).

CPB on the basis of the new status of import substitution industries, i.e. taking account of close-downs and decline in these industries, would estimate import demand. Estimation of competing imports, hence, would require further rounds in calculation to take care of plant shut-downs and declining output in this sector. The margin of error in import estimate might still be high even after several trials in estimation. Moreover set-backs in plan implementations below expectations might also result in higher import demand. Hence need for import quotas might arise.

13 Central Plan Bureau (CPB)

CPB on the basis of reported possible outcomes by establishments will calculate and estimate under alternative wage/exchange rates, output, national income, exports, imports (of inputs for industrial use, consumer goods, due to phased-out import-substitution industries will be shown separately), employment and unemployment due to the program, wage bill and labor index, total profits, tax revenue, etc. and will see to it that internal and external macro-economic equilibrium is achieved, under the scenario selected.

Effects of shut-down import-substitution as foreseen in the program on import demand for intermediary and final goods should be taken into account. The import estimate might further be raised to take care of errors and omissions in estimation, and of preference by producers and consumers of imported goods over locally supplied varieties (by ongoing viable import substitution industries).

Data and information format described above allows CPB to work out alternative scenarios, (changing wage/exchange rate, tariff protection and subsidy rates for ailing industries, critical ones or whose productivity can improve over time), promotion schemes for export industries and focus on possible problem areas, such as unemployment and industries likely to be phased out.

14 Monetary and fiscal measures

Exchange rate determined through wage rate, will assure survival and well-being of labor, which is by far the largest population group in these countries. This rate will also maintain equilibrium in balance of payments. Exchange rate, subsequent-years might be based on monetary, foreign trade and general economic developments.

Price changes due to launching of the program cannot be termed as inflation, as all wages, incomes and prices will change simultaneously to move into a new world. Provided budgetary balance and discipline and moderate monetary expansion is sustained, there will be no inflation or inflationary expectations. Also it is essential that estimation and expectations at macro and micro (firm) level are realistic, and no substantial relapses arise behind expectations in implementation. Establishments, should beforehand understand that they have to live with their estimation, whatever the actual outcome and no relief, subsidy should be provided unless agreed upon in advance. Autonomy and profit sharing of workers will be a useful device in better management of enterprises, when privatization is not imminent or likely in the short-run.

Government budget and monetary system will be employed with a view to maintaining macro-economic equilibrium. To this end, income, corporation, VAT (or sales) taxes and modern import duties have to be introduced before launching the program.

Central Bank and commercial banks should be restructured to function in a market economy. An unemployment insurance scheme for workers laid-off is also a must, and its cost should be included in budgetary and macro balances.

15 Equations of the method

Let for i the establishment

x_i= exports

s_i= domestic sales

a_i= material inputs purchased locally

m_i= imported inputs

$e_i=$ employment
$w =$ minimum wage
$\bar{e}_i=$ labor index (wage bill/w)
$\bar{e}w=$ wage bill
$d_i=$ depreciation charges, if any
$b_i=$ other inputs and utilities from domestic sectors
$R_i=$ profit/loss

Then

(1) $R_i= x_i+s_i- (a_i+m_i+\bar{e}_i w+d_i+b_i)$

Let for j'th domestic sector output, under normal capacity utilization, a_{hj}, m_{hj}, b_{hj}, $\bar{e}_{hj}$ stand for items as defined above, f_j is profit margin (mark up as a ratio of total costs), q_j quantity of output, P_{hj} its price. Then,

$$P_{hj}= (1+f_j)\,(a_{hj}+m_{hj}+b_{hj}+\bar{e}_{hj}w)/q_j$$

(2) $P_{hj}= A_j+B_j w$

where $A_j= (1+f_j)\,(a_{hj}+m_{hj}+b_{hj})/q_j$
$B_j= (1+f_j)\,\bar{e}_{hj}/q_j$
are constants.

Domestic sectors set their prices on the basis of their costs; whereas, import substitution industries determine their prices on the basis of market conditions (international prices, customs tariff rate and competition in the local market).

Export and import substitution industries first determine their selling prices, taking into consideration market conditions, quality of their products, discounts to be offered, secondly estimate their sales and then work out costs, etc.

There will arise a *discrepancy* from the fact that while import-substitution industries might value their output below international prices, user industries will evaluate the same at international prices. This will give rise to higher profitability in user industries in practice than forecast. This discrepancy can be avoided in major cases, in the second round (when establishments are given final wage rate after preliminary evaluations or when import-substituting industries are able to fix their selling prices definitely, to which information establishments will have access through a central computer from their terminals). Otherwise, as bias is towards underestimation of favorable outcome, the error (discrepancy) can be tolerated.

Let

q_{hji} = quantity of j'th domestic sector's output used as input in i'th industry.

P_{hj} = price of j'th domestic sector's output
then, substituting from (2).

$$(3) \quad b_i = \sum_j q_{hji} P_{hj} = \sum_j q_{hij} (A_j + B_{jw}) = \bar{a}_i + w\bar{c}_i$$

where

$$\bar{a}_i = \sum_j q_{hji} A_j \text{ and } \bar{c}_i = \sum_j q_{hji} B_j$$

are constants.
Plugging (3) in (l):

$$(4) \quad R_i = x_i + s_i - (a_i + m_i + d_i + \bar{a}_i) - (\bar{e}_i + \bar{c}_i)w$$

Similarly unit cost of i th firm's output P_i is given by

$$(5) \quad P_i = (a_i + m_i + d_i + \bar{a}_i)/q_i - (\bar{e}_i + \bar{c}_i)w/q_i$$

where q_i is quantity of i th firm's output.

Profit and unit cost equations are crucial in determining the changing status of industries (between import substitution, exporting and closing-down). Through these changes balance of payment position is determined.

Balance of payments (B) equation is

$$(6) \quad B = \sum_i x_i - \sum_i m_i - \sum_j m_{hj} - m_g - m_c + F$$

where F is net invisibles balance and foreign capital inflow, m_g government imports, m_c consumer goods imports.

Gross domestic product (Y) equation is

$$(7) \quad Y = w \left(\sum_i \bar{e} + \sum_j \bar{e}_{hj} + \bar{e}_g\right) + \sum_i R_i + \sum_j f_j P_{hj} q_j + \sum_i d_i$$

where $\bar{e}_g$ is government labor index. Interest and rental income could be included when significant.

Government budget equation is

$$(8) \quad G + S = t_l w \left(\sum_i \bar{e}_i + \sum_j \bar{e}_{hj} + \bar{e}_g\right) + t_2\left(\sum_i R_i + \sum_j f_j P_{hj} q_j\right) + T_l + D + F_g$$

where S= subsidies (for losses, exports, unemployment insurance scheme), T_l= import duty and VAT revenue, D=domestic borrowing, F_g= foreign borrowing by government, t_l= income tax rate, t_2=company tax rate.

All establishments might be required to estimate import duties and VAT they will pay on their imports and purchases (and sales) and the income tax on their wage bill.

Total employment E will be given by

$$(9) \quad E = \Sigma e_i + \Sigma e_j + e_g + e_p$$

where e_j is employment in the domestic sectors, e_g government employment, e_p self employed, employed in domestic services and employees of private sector. The establishments would report to the CPB the number of workers to be laid off under each scenario.

Chapter 3

Benefits of a systematic methodology for immediate transformation of socialist economies into free market systems

Benefits of a systematic methodology for immediate transformation of socialist economies into free market systems

The approach is a macroeconomic one, based, however, on actual (expected) response of economic agents (firms in particular and households) to new economic conditions, i.e. it is a macroeconomic model based on microeconomic decisions and their aggregation.

It requires a preparatory phase of planning the transition, which might require 6-12 months depending on the efficiency of Central Plan Bureau, itself and its communication with firms, and on the speed of political decision making.

This phase determines exchange rate, wage rate, tariff protection required, employment and output levels, imports and exports, etc. i.e. all consequences of the move is known beforehand.

Upon implementation of this program, the socialist economies will immediately move into a situation where free market mechanism will prevail with desired level of tariff protection (some quantitative import restrictions for some items might be required), which will in turn determine exchange and wage rates.

The move is into the worst situation (rock-bottom), in the sense, over time things can only change for the good.

This aspect is politically appealing, since the public will know that gradually things will get better through:

(i) introduction of modern technology, management and marketing processes,

(ii) access to international markets and finance and concomitant increase in productive investments and output,

(iii) increase in production of consumer goods.

All inflationary impacts (change in living standards) through wage declines and price increases), unemployment, reduction in output (through plants that will close down) will take place during the move (at the transition).

These adverse effects, however, can be scaled down, cushioned and lessened to a level acceptable to the public and policy makers.

Decisions regarding how open the economy would be to start with (on the degree of openness of the economy) and level of protection will determine the outcome in wages, output and employment, exports, etc.

After the move, there will be no inflationary effect provided that budgetary balance is maintained and excessive monetary expansion is avoided, (except for major crop failures or drastic change in international prices concerned).

The system presupposes existence of a Central plan mechanism and its efficient functioning until the move.

The approach assures orderly transition into market mechanism, knowing all its consequences in output, employment, wages, exports. It may require some import restrictions (in countries where there is chronic or excessive BOP deficit or high expenditure propensities and resistance to lowering living standards of workers. Otherwise, with the transition, it is possible to move into convertible currency.

It is *total controlled* approach as against total opening up the economy with a *'wait and see'* approach (the case of East Germany, without realistically estimating aftermath) or partial opening up here and there in a haphazard or chaotic manner or groping its way; with total opening up the economy in principle, with completely free price mechanism and liberalized imports and at the same time a gradual approach (phasing out all adverse effects to acceptable levels over time) and with realistic estimation of aftermath based on reactions of economic agents to the new economic world.

In this context the methodology could provide subsidies for ailing industries, for foodstuffs and other essentials.

The methodology tells about what would be produced or manufactured, and where. Computations would require a medium-capacity computer.

Chapter 4

Conclusion

Conclusion

The method aims at simulating the outcome which will result by an immediate move into an open free market system. International prices of tradeable goods which are bound to prevail with some adjustment, after the transition, form the basis of the exercise. The firms, given international prices and wage rate in a foreign currency unit (say $), will estimate their output, sales (to local or export markets), profits, etc. in $ terms, the following year and a year after. Alternative wage rates will give different outcomes, and with the help of Central Plan Bureau (CPB), the policy making body will choose the best feasible scenario.

It does not matter whether the country has already taken some measures in the direction of free market. Under the prevailing policies in former socialist countries, however, these changes are, rather exercised in a haphazard manner. As a consequence:

(i) They have not yielded relative prices that will prevail under free market mechanism (because some prices are controlled, import regime and external payments are not transformed into regular mechanisms, with unsystematic restrictions and rampant inflation), hence allocation of resources is not efficient; whereas, the opposite will materialize under the proposed scheme.

(ii) They have given rise to uncertainty for short-and medium-run, which will not be the case under the proposed method.

(iii) They have resulted in shock effects, which are bound to be repeated in the foreseeable future, whereas under the proposed method although a move into an open free market system is immediate, there are comprehensive systematic cushions against shocks in the form of selection of appropriate exchange/wage rate, customs tariffs (to allow ailing industries to adapt and improve) and subsidy schemes to suit the same and all these safety measures will be in place in good time.

The method *allows open and free market mechanism to be launched immediately* with all its concomitant allocative efficiency, free competition etc. effects without causing inflationary expectations, *without awaiting finalization and realization of other reform measures,* like privatization and joint-ventures.

The methods *maps out worst possible shock* (short-term), adverse effects of immediate move into open free market system and provides a mechanism to cushion these adverse effects by appropriate choice of exchange/wage rate, level of tariff protection, transitory subsidy scheme to support problematic key import substitution industries (for adjustment and rehabilitation on a discretionary basis). It is a comprehensive approach to transition process and allows to foresee every major aspect of transformation and to plan against any eventuality in these fields.

The scheme will lead to early recognition and acceptance by international economic and financial community and organizations and bilateral donors, former socialist countries as market economies and generate a larger volume of concessionary long term financing. Launching of such a program should increase availability of stand-by credits and structural adjustment loans by international financial organizations such as IMF and IBRD.

Chapter 5

Points of clarification

Points of clarification

1 'The method', its merits and shortcomings

In this book basic framework of the methodology is presented; many details are deliberately omitted because these could better be worked out in the real world conditions and solved on a case-by-case basis, depending on availability of data and political preferences, rather than on hypotheses.

'The method' aims at estimating market prices, after an open market economy is installed and becomes operational, and predicting the response of enterprises and consumers to market forces.

The method does not aim at estimating real or shadow prices of goods and services at the CPB level. It is up to enterprises to estimate prices they will confront, when all prices are set freely; relevant international prices, however, will serve for a basis for these estimates, since domestic prices in foreign currency terms will be in line with export prices or the prices of competing imports prevailing at the location/area concerned, if the economy is open.

The methodology is not a *panacea*. It is, however a useful device, since it

(i) yields an estimation technique during the transition period, when all conventional forecasting methods break down,

(ii) provides for an orderly transition mechanism by coordinating all reform measures and allowing simultaneous action on all fronts,

(iii) and allows open market economy conditions prevail with immediate effect, along with launching forth on the program.

The following intractable problems, however, would still remain to be tackled: enterprise reform and hardening the budget constraint, privatization, tax reform and its enforcement, banking reform and monetary discipline, establishment of all other market institutions and implementing other reforms, and starting the economic growth process.

2 The role of Central Plan Bureau (CPB)

It might be questioned whether the method entails the comeback of command-economy style compulsory economic planning from backdoor or lead to centralization of decision-making in lieu of decentralization and devolution.

Basically the method is an estimation procedure for macro economic forecasting during the transition period when conventional forecasting techniques breakdown due to continuous change in parameters. The method, as a side product, also provides a comprehensive framework and policy package for a successful transformation process, as a tool of indicative economic planning.

In view of the fact that the present governments of the socialist countries are averse to any kind of central planning, convincing authorities in these countries of the usefulness of the method is a difficult proposition. Without some indicative economic planning (macroeconomic management), however, the reforming countries could not successfully complete transformation, unless transition is very gradual.

After the transition period, these countries can either opt for consumption-oriented policies of US, UK, Turkey and Latin America, dismantling CPB or the saving/investment oriented fast growth policies of Japan, Korea and Taiwan with some form of indicative planning.

The method aims at simulating the probable outcome, after transforming a socialist economy to market economy and determining exchange and wage rates that will prevail and lead to equilibrium in all markets, and estimating, output, income, employment/unemployment, foreign trade gap, etc. levels, which are feasible and acceptable. This task will be carried out at the *preparatory stage* of the method.

At this stage the data for this exercise by CPB will come from firms. In fact firms, collecting relevant international prices, estimating their costs, and given exchange, minimum wage and interest rates, rates of customs tariffs, taxation and subsidy rates, if any, will determine their output, sales, imports, etc. At the *implementation stage*, after launching the transformation program, firms will make their decisions according to the market they face and shoulder the consequences. All this has nothing to do with the command economy.

To summarize, the processing under the method by CPB produces as its main products, exchange rate, minimum and average wage rates, profitability of economic activities carried out by firms; and as side products, macroeconomic magnitudes such as national income, exports, imports, wage bill and employment, tax revenue, etc. Determination of prices of individual goods and services are not the concern of CPB.

3 Prices and microeconomic decisions

All relevant international prices and production costs will be collected and estimated by enterprises concerned, not by CPB. (Although CPB computer might well store prices for use by other enterprises). Enterprises, given the exchange and minimum wage rates, tariffs and taxes, utility prices, subsidies if any, will decide what to produce and sell at what prices or close-down. The task of CPB is of indicative-planning nature and mainly during preparatory stage with the main purpose of determining exchange and minimum wage rate and assist the Government in determining policies on customs tariff, taxation and subsidies. 'The method' has nothing to do with large-computer models of 1960s.

The aim of this exercise is not to transfer any microeconomic decision or even data to central authorities, other than necessary for macroeconomic management. The method does not aim at or entail replacing market mechanism or create a surrogate for it after the orderly transformation process starts; on the contrary, since decentralized decision-making is the backbone of the method, establishment of a genuinely free and open market economy is the main goal and private-initiative and privatization is welcome (market reforms, however, should not await privatization or the speed of the latter should not be accelerated unduly to this end).

4 Use of 'the method' for command economy and economy with ongoing transition

Some might presume that the method might well serve the needs of a command economy, with compulsory central planning. This presumption is not valid, since the method is designed for orderly transition to market economy and eventual market test is essential, to make this exercise meaningful. Also, otherwise reporting by firms to CPB will be biased and useless and aggregate welfare and economic efficiency will not increase as a consequence.

Moreover estimation process of the method can be repeatedly employed say every year, during transition period, even when market economy is functional.

The method can even be employed in countries where disorderly transformation process is already in progress, with partial market reforms and rampant inflation, with a view to setting the house in order and completing and speeding up the reform process.

Even the method provides a useful short-term estimation procedure, enables determination of equilibrium exchange and minimum wage rates, and identifies problem plants and sectors correctly for further attention.

It will be a much simpler exercise then. It will, however, require some modifications in the methodology. Hence, any argument that the method aims at replacing market mechanism is ill-founded.

5 Trial-and-error method of the market and the method

One can argue that in the market the number of informations is infinite and changes quickly, and hence any simulation of market would be erroneous. And hence the method will lead to hypothetical equilibria and prospects which might prove to be completely out of line with the actual outcome.

In these changing markets, however, many irrevocable decisions on industrial and agricultural production, employment, investment, etc. are taken and plans are prepared by firms. In similar fashion, firms, knowing the consequences, will react to this simulation exercise, in the same manner as they respond to actual market signals. Because after launching the transformation program, firms will confront the real market and have to live with their choices.

It is true that any simulation can not substitute real market conditions and outcomes, no simulation can be more efficient than the trial-and- error method of the market. In the absence of any other reliable forecasting technique during the transition period, however, the method might provide a useful and satisfactory second best.

It should also be noted that the same economic agents, on whose reactions, decisions and projections the method is based during the preparatory stage, will shape the actual outcome during implementation.

6 Consequences of the trial-and-error method

Without observing the chaotic outcome which partial ad hoc reform measures will lead to, it may be difficult to acknowledge usefulness of the method.

Even in China, which is pursuing gradualist reform approach, chaotic price increases are experienced and objected.

Zhao Minshan et al (1992) maintain that the, "Chinese prices are irrational mainly because price ratios are irrational. 'Round Robin' raising of prices will not straighten out the price system. Unstable raw material prices are most unfavorable to improving management and economic performance".

They therefore recommend "strengthening price control, stabilization of raw material prices and imposing ceilings on [production of] processed goods and prohibiting 'round–robin' price rises" which would be self-defeating from the viewpoint of price reform (Minshan, et al, 1992).

The present piecemeal approach in the former socialist countries is bound to fail, because it ends up in chronic high inflation (two-or three-digit), increasing unemployment and declining welfare expectations of the public in general. Lifting price controls, liberalizing trade regime and deregulation accompanied by ad hoc reform measures (privatization, property rights, fiscal and banking, etc.) if not carried out under a comprehensive approach with reasonably good estimates of implications are bound to result in high inflation and unemployment, and declining output and incomes. Remedial measures in the form of wage increases, or incomes policy, restoring price controls, import restrictions and subsidies, then follow these partial reform measures, which in turn worsen inflationary pressure and distortions.

In a two-or triple-digit inflation environment, no sound economic decision can be made because of increasing uncertainty and widespread economic distortions. Even market prices and exchange rate, being the result of prevailing conflicting policies, subsidies, restrictions and distortions, would not reflect the correct prices and exchange rate which would have prevailed if stable open market economy conditions (free pricing, liberal trade regime except for some import quotas, reasonable tariff protection, inflation rate in the range of 15-45% or less the first year and single-digit inflation thereafter) were valid.

Wrong exchange rate, distorted market prices and surrounding chaotic economic environment will not allow many enterprises sufficient time to learn by doing, at a time when drastic change in working habits and ethic, managerial conduct and orientation to market conditions are called for, all of which require extra time to adjust. Many of these enterprises will be insolvent, need government subsidies or close down, some of which might have survived and even flourished under orderly transition with some marketing and technical assistance and improvement investments.

Under these circumstances, no reliable forecasting of macro-and even micro-economic variables is possible, and one has to grope its way. In a triple-digit inflation situation, economic growth and future prospects are set aside anyway. Main goal of economic policy becomes short-term survival and this process goes on indefinitely, because partial market reform process has a built-in high inflationary nature.

In a high-inflation economy, the calculation of taxable income, profits, interest income correctly becomes troublesome and requires elaborate techniques. Decision-making by enterprises on production and investment will be extremely difficult. In this environment tax evasion will be widespread.

Under high inflationary conditions, consumption and waste increase, savings and productive investments decline, external debt and budgetary deficits increase, capital flight speeds up and growth rate vacillates and declines, as observed in Turkey (1976 on) and in Latin America. Experience of Poland, over a decade, shows that partial lifting of price control and ad hoc reform measures, increase inflation and external debt, and reduce growth rate of income.

Problems associated with the transformation of a socialist economy to a market economy are much more severe than the problems associated with liberalization of high-inflation cum high-protection market economies such as

Turkey and Latin America, where there exists an operational market, albeit an inefficient one.

The budgetary estimation problem encountered in Poland during the 1990 reform process and its aftermath, is just an example of possible complications under conventional reform approach: Gomulka (1992) has observed that, large price increases under a price reform leads to "inflation-induced, extraordinary profits of enterprises" and then to a large budget surplus. "If reformers underestimate them, as they did in Poland" then an excessive recession results in. This risk is high if price liberalization, price correction and convertibility are all combined in one package (Gomulka, 1992, p. 367). Under 'the methodology', since all reform measures are combined, reliable estimation of enterprise profits and the budgetary items is crucially important, which in fact what the method aims at.

An evaluation of the outcome of the Russian reform process and recommendations by the World Bank exemplify the issues raised heretofore and indicates the need for a new comprehensive reform approach, as suggested by 'the method'.

A top World Bank official[1], toward the end of 1992 stated that *the former Soviet Union need to adopt comprehensive reforms in order to reverse sharp drops in economic output,* after *a 'traumatic experience' in 1991.* Output declines of 15-25% have hit the 15 new republics. *"The declines in output already are large* and the cost of transition is high. It is urgent that stabilization be achieved and growth restored". In view of the progress to date, *transformation* (which is profound and complex), *will take more time than originally anticipated, "will be fraught with frustration and reversals, errors in pace and sequence will be inevitable". "In order to stem the economic deterioration"*, the 15 republics will need to *adopt comprehensive programs of macro-economic stabilization, structural reform* and sectoral development aimed at *encouraging a supply response.* The structural and sectoral reforms by leading to a growing private sector (free to allocate resources and respond to market signals) will increase productivity, growth, employment and incomes.

7 Start with initial equilibrium versus disequilibrium: the case of the 1990 Polish reform program

The reform programs in Eastern Europe, like the 1990 Polish program start from a disequilibrium situation and evolve another kind of disequilibrium with intermittent reform measures, stop-go-stop process and the system is unlikely to end up in equilibrium. (Whereas the method aims at starting with equilibrium and maintaining it.)

---

(1) Ernest Stern, Managing Director of World Bank, at the Tokyo Conference on Assistance to the Newly Independent States, Oct 29, 1992 *World Bank News* (WBN), Nov. 5, 1992.

A brief description of the 1990 Polish stabilization measures will enlighten the contention :According to IBRD at the beginning of 1990 Poland was in a hyperinflation situation and on the verge of massive default on its international obligations.(2) Achieving price stability, however, was not the priority; neither stability of exchange and wage rates in 1990 was considered (Gomulka, 1992). In fact inflation rate shot up to 585% in 1990 as against 250% in 1989. According to Commander and Coricelli (1992), wage drift and exchange rate changes were the two causes of high inflation. During 1988-90, wages had been de facto indexed to prices. In 1990 there were a series (of devaluations (Gomulka, 1992). A large fall in wages, increased profits of firms, and hence tax revenue.

Money supply being the only nominal anchor in 1990, macro economic policy became restrictive in the first half; in the second half financial policies were relaxed which in turn increased wages, prices and imports rather than domestic output.

The stabilization program was expected to lead to initial expansion, since new prices were not lower than new average costs; but on the contrary it resulted in a deep recession (Calvo and Coricelli, 1992). In fact GDP fell by 12% in 1990 and 7% in 1991 and expected to decline by 1-2% in 1992; and according to IBRD long term growth prospects depend on the speed of integration into EC. It is expected Poland to grow at rates higher than those of Western Europe, if the international economic prospects are favorable.(3)

The 1990 Polish reform program has essentially stayed on course for 3 years, so far over this period GDP has declined by 20%, consumer price index rose by 586% in 1990 (1989 rate was 251%) and in 1992 the labor strife became critical.

8 If 'the suggested method' were employed in Poland

Compared to the 1990 Comprehensive Polish transformation program, the method has the advantage that initial impact (on prices and output) would have been disregarded psychologically (to this end a new currency could well be launched at the same time): Because it means starting with a clean slate; enterprises and households will be well-informed about the initial price level and incomes, with the onset of the program. This initial jump in the price level would not be treated as inflation, since incomes are already adjusted accordingly. Hence the onset of the program will not lead to inflationary expectations by itself; on the contrary, if accompanying fiscal/monetary/ credit measures were credible, then stability would be anticipated. In order to avoid a credit squeeze as experienced in Poland (Calvo and Coricelli, 1992), credit

(2) *World Bank News* (WBN), Sept 10, 1992.
(3) *World Bank News* (WBN), Sept 10, 1992.

ceilings could be arranged to circumvent such an outcome and stagflation (i.e. enterprises will plan not only their production, but its financing, as well and credit ceilings are imposed accordingly in advance).

If with the 'big-bang' the exchange rate was set at a higher level to make sure generation of export surplus, the wage rate commensurate to it at a lower level and prices by enterprises were set at possible equilibrium levels (from the very beginning), a social safety net (unemployment insurance, social welfare programs, retraining schemes and reformed pension scheme) were initiated, predetermined production and consumption subsidies, a liberal foreign trade regime with moderate protection scheme were in place in advance, the following advantages would have been reaped:

(i) Labor, unemployed and poor could have been convinced that they are at the worst possible/rock- bottom level and that their lot would improve over time and that they have to be patient for some time; a once-for-all sacrifice is better than permanent/indefinite uncertainty.

(ii) Subsequent inflation rate would have been modest, since there would be no need for major upward exchange, wage and interest rate adjustments.

(iii) Any balance of payments (BOP) and budgetary surplus (due to income tax revenue on increased profits) could have been utilized to fund stand-by programs and investment projects, depending on price stability.

(iv) Low inflation rate and interest rate commensurate with it, would have encouraged economic activity and investments, and avoided the costly stop-go-stop sequence of economic monetary/financial policies.

9 Calculation of equilibrium rates of exchange and wage, etc.

(i) Calculation rounds

Steps of the calculation process at the CPB and enterprise levels have to be designed according to the outcome of first step and the size of economy concerned; depending on this once or twice going back to enterprises might be sufficient to obtain the equilibrium exchange/wage rates.

Every enterprise, even in a market economy, has to prepare its production program and projections for next year anyway. Estimates required by the method has to be by output categories, which could be produced independently (i.e. in products whose production can be suspended or stopped without affecting production of other goods). CPB will be supplied with material, wage and utility costs, sales and profit figures for each product group; CPB will not deal with prices because they are not needed by CPB. Effects of change in the exchange rate (even rate of protection) will be readily obtained by CPB, by changing material and utility costs, sales, wage bill figures at that rate. The capacity of central computer will be the limiting factor and even there will be no need to review computer printouts by firms and product groups at initial rounds, since the computer can be programmed to give totals deleting unprofitable activities (items). In these simulation exercises there is no need to go back to individual firms.

It will be useful to go back to enterprises with new exchange rate or with its new range, supplying also them with macroeconomic estimates (national income, etc.) for next year. And enterprises should have final say in deciding on their final production plans with or without subsidy. This iterative process might take a third round. And it might look like a lot of paperwork, both at the side of central authorities and enterprises. This, however, is useful because, in lieu of deciding on policies in vacuum central government will know the effects of alternatives policies (protection, subsidies, taxation, import regime, privatization, etc.) on national income, employment and foreign trade. Enterprises also will learn a lot about domestic and foreign market conditions, their cost structure, alternative production plans and corporate strategy, response to market signals, albeit in simulation manner, during the preparatory stage, in lieu of confronting hard facts of market economy overnight.

Calculations regarding *import-substitution industries* might turn out to be intractable, this however, could be overcome by further iteration covering only relevant producer and user industries. It is possible that after the second round firms might lose interest in the exercise.

The method by using a wage-bill index and international prices denoted in a foreign currency enables CPB to carry out simulations without reference to enterprises to determine exchange and wage rates and other macro economic variables and magnitudes. Alternative policies can be tested in the course of simulations and shaped accordingly, including the amount of subsidies to be paid to certain enterprises and for certain goods.

Going back to enterprises will only refine and improve estimates depending on the size of error considered permissible. The second and third rounds will be required to take care of effects of closing plants (reduced priced import substituting input will be replaced by normal priced imported input, direct effects on incomes, employment and imports), to get necessary adjustments in estimates made as required by consistency checks made by CPB. This interim round could also be handled by asking only the enterprises, whose profitability is significantly affected by planned shut-downs of plants, to revise their statements.

A final round before launching the program will be useful to give enterprises the opportunity to update and improve their estimates on the basis of macroeconomic estimates for the next year.

(ii) Prices to be stored at CPB

Except for major import substitution industries, whose output is used as input in other producing sectors, CPB need not compile and store any prices. In this case discounts to international prices might be applied for standard, quality, etc. differences and it is necessary that producers and users use the same discounted prices in their calculations for the sake of consistency. This also can be achieved by instructing and ensuring that these enterprises (selling to a domestic producer or buying from a local supplier) consult and agree on the discount percentage.

On the other hand to cater for this need and assist some enterprises in obtaining export prices and required discounts on them, the CPB computer, can store international prices of important export and imported goods collected and used by enterprises, with a view to passing them on to enterprises asking for them and even ensuring consistency in case of significant discrepancy.

"The *quality of East European* and Soviet *goods* are acknowledged to be below the levels of Western goods" (Rollo and Stern, 1992)

(iii) Exclusion of private sector firms

For the private sector enterprises, participation in the exercise is voluntary, possibly except for large-scale plants. This necessary omission will not affect the results, as explained before. Moreover, Hare (1987) points out that conventional, one sector, constrained equilibrium model of the state sector of a centrally planned economy does not yield misleading results and inclusion of the private sector in the model does not matter.

10 Truthfulness of enterprise response

It can a priori be maintained that enterprises will be biased towards their interest in their reporting to CPB. This, however, will not be the case under the method. Because if enterprises make optimistic plans, they know that no subsidy will be forthcoming when they fail and then they can blame only themselves. If they make pessimistic plans, then they run the risk of shut-down if relevant authorities can't be convinced for subsidy and protection; moreover their reporting will be double checked in this case.

Hence the method would compel managers and owners of enterprises to make careful estimates and plans, and be realistic. The method is superior, in this respect, to the present transition approach, since enterprises facing rising prices and costs, increasing competition from imports and dwindling exports could now blame others for their own faults.

Reports by firms will reflect their planned/desired/feasible degree of learning by doing/change/performance. It is true that public enterprises are not profit-maximizers and it will take longer than 1 year, even years to change their behavior. This, however, will not affect estimation under the method, provided enterprises report realistically their expected performance.

11 Periods of preparation and implementation

It should be noted that the 6-12 monthly period is for preparatory/planning stage, after which transformation program is launched with free pricing mechanism and open economy, with immediate effect, which is the major advantage of the method. Actual transition period with production and consumption subsidies, temporarily high tariffs for critical sectors, quantitative import restrictions for ditto, sizeable foreign aid and privatization in progress might take 3-5 years or longer, depending on the pace of restructural adjustment.

Adoption of marketing techniques and management principles of market economy, development of new export markets, completion of privatization, successful implementation of fiscal/banking reforms might take longer, the latter, however, is crucial for fiscal/economic stability and hence should be given due priority.

Provided estimates are realistic and reforms are implemented effectively and efficiently, there will be relative price stability, no severe savings/ BOP gaps and hardships suffered by masses will be bearable with better expectations for future.

It can be argued that, the method might produce a nice action plan, but little action and its implementation might not be satisfactory, because of the lack of political will, incompetency on the execution side. It might give unjustifiable breathing space to some old institutions and enterprises which should rather be phased out rightaway, and might delay some reforms. Nevertheless, unless all accompanying measures and reforms called for an open market economy are taken and implemented during the preparatory stage, the method can not be employed, since then its assumptions will not hold true. Hence, it can safely be maintained that if the method is adopted, it will speed up the reform process.

In contrast, the present approach produces many uncoordinated, almost chaotic, actions and apparently irrevocable reforms, with the possibility of dangerous backlash (political and economic).

12 Coordination, estimates versus performance

The method calls for coordinated action on all fronts, failure in one field in planning or implementation stage might jeopardize the whole program. One can still maintain that, this exercise might still be superior to pursuing uncoordinated, sometimes contradictory policies.

To be on the safe side against any eventuality, CPB might determine exchange and minimum wage rates, increasing cost figures and decreasing sales figures by certain percentages, to ward off estimation errors and performance shortfalls.

Changing the behavior and conduct of enterprises geared to command economy to market led economy, is crucial in this respect. Performance of public enterprises, however, might turn out to be much worse than the most conservative estimates.

Required managerial change in firms to act according to market signals will take years. Those enterprises, however, which have not forecast foolishly and rather predicted realistically and took into account all their deficiencies, should manage well in the first year, which is crucial. In the following years their performance should improve in every respect through learning by doing.

13 Aim of 'the suggested method'

(i) Internal and external equilibrium and stability

Vegh (1992) expects that high inflation and structural changes are likely to coexist in Eastern Europe and the former Soviet Union in the foreseeable future.

The aim of 'the method' could be achieving at most an inflation rate of 30-40% a year, a budget deficit equivalent to 4-5% of GDP and the current account deficit is covered by orderly external financing as suggested by Fischer (1992, p. 77) in the first year or two during transformation.

(ii) Possible outcome of 'the suggested method' compared with the optimistic scenario of Rollo and Stern (1992)

The suggested method would make possible achievement of many aims simultaneously and its prospective outcome compares favorably, with what Rollo and Stern (1992) call 'best' or 'optimistic scenario', which assumes attainment of following:

(i) Macro-economic stabilization is successful and inflation falls [to OECD levels],

(ii) Currency convertibility is achieved and sustained,

(iii) Initial downward pressure on real living standards is politically acceptable and that living standards begin to rise before the political pressures become intolerable,

(iv) Privatization, demonopolization and liberal trade regimes introduce competition,

(v) Price liberalization and competition lead to significant domestic supply response,

(vi) Domestic saving, aid and debt relief... are not constraints on growth,

(vii) Infrastructure deficiencies are not a significant constraint on supply at any given point in time,

(viii) The existing capital stock can be applied to new uses, i.e. incremental capital-output ratios are low,

(ix) Foreign trade restrictions are not a significant constraint on exports,

i.e. association with EC offers access to EC markets. In fact the method assures attainment of items (i)-(v), readily or in the medium-run, particularly item (i) and also (viii), because the initial aim to keep economy afloat allowing enterprises some time for adjustment (as little destruction of the existing productive capacity as possible); and success in these items will pave the way for success in other items.

Rollo and Stern note that the optimistic scenario simulates "The experience of Korea since 1970 or of Spanish performance since the death of Franco".

14 Temporary protection of some industries during transition

Nontariff barriers in socialist economies are prevalent. They include not only formal quantitative restrictions but also the implicit restrictions, "associated with the dominant role of state-owned foreign trade organizations and with the centralization of the distribution system. Tariffs have replaced such quantitative restrictions in the countries that have proceeded furthest with market-oriented reforms". Hungary, Yugoslavia and Poland undertook market liberalization measures during 1970s and 1980s (Dinopoulos and Lane, 1992).

Fischer (1992) prefers *uniform tariff structure* over reducing all tariffs proportionately (under which the ratio of domestic-to-foreign prices approaches unity gradually), because the latter is liable to manipulation under pressure.

Poland in 1990 and Russia in 1992 reduced customs tariffs below 5% on the average and abolished completely respectively. It is important to keep open the doors of international competition, limit protection to industries in need of *temporary* protection during the transition period or to genuine cases of infant industry, and prevent the overly common degeneration of the infant industry cause into inefficient protection lobbies, by clearly specifying and announcing a fixed duration for such protection.

However, there is a need for protecting some industries during transition period for giving breathing space for restructural adjustment, setting up proper management, technological/marketing/organizational improvements The Chinese experience sheds light on the case.

At the end of 1986 China had 422,000 industrial enterprises doing independent accounting at and above the village level; of which 56,000 incurred losses in 1986. Losses concentrated in six major industries, namely coal mining, machine building, petrochemicals, food, building materials and textiles (Minshan, et al, 1992).

The Chinese chemical fertilizer industry has become quite developed after considerable technical renovation. Because of excessive imports, however, many plants were forced to stop production in 1985. Similarly excessive importation of cars and TVs led to inventory piling up and losses in local industries. Due to importation of $8.7 billion production equipment in 1986, the machine-building industry suffered losses despite rapid growth in fixed investments and technical renovation funds in recent years (Minshan, et al, 1992).

15 Market prices versus calculated prices

Market clearing prices are determined by the behavior of consumers and the trade regime. *With quota,* the price of imported goods equal the black market price, through an adjustment of price; *with tariff,* the quantity of imports is adjusted so that the black market price becomes equal to and maintained at the world price plus the tariff; i.e. if imports were restrained only by tariff, the difference between the black market and official price would depend only on the tariff (Dinopoulos and Lane, 1992).

The gap between world and domestic prices can be considered as an implicit tariff.

The issue is to what extent actual market price will diverge from prices used in the exercise. It can be maintained that some domestic prices might be higher than the calculated prices of competing imports, namely sum total of CIF import price, customs tariff, local transport and profit margin (mark-up), because of local scarcities, imperfect market conditions and demand pressures.

It is well-known that the calculated price, which implies cost-plus pricing, will lead to the maximization of profit, if based on marginal cost and if the markup equals [1/(1-1/e)]-1 where e is the price elasticity of demand. Nevertheless, market prices would be above the calculated prices, if quantitative import restrictions (which would be exceptional if the suggested methodology is employed) and market imperfections (monopoly or oligopoly in production and/or distribution) do exist.

If the goods concerned are consumer goods, higher prices than expected will reduce consumption and increase producers' and distributors' profits and income taxes; the latter two will improve macroeconomic outcome. If measures are taken to ensure competition prevails and quantitative import restrictions are not imposed on basic consumer goods (which should be the case), a rise in the consumer price index, due to these factors, would be negligible.

If the good concerned is an input used by producers, rise in price would undermine the methodology; this, however, could be prevented if producers or their associations/cooperatives are entitled to import required inputs directly.

As for price increases arising from inflationary demand pressures, the method aims at obviating any inflationary gap and if accompanying fiscal/monetary measures are successfully implemented, there would happen no significant inflation. Moreover, under inflationary conditions all prices tend to increase by the same percentage, hence real (relative) prices (or prices in foreign exchange) are not expected to vary.

Under the method, it is also assumed that, at the implementation stage, exchange rate would be determined by market forces or would be raised at the rate of domestic inflation.

16 Estimated wage bill versus actual

Wage increases after launching out the program might not be in line with the wage strata submitted by enterprises or wage bill estimates, if certain ground rules are not set.

Public enterprises can rightfully be compelled to live with their original estimates. Considering the fact that the wage bill estimate is derived by ignoring the cost of capital sunk, existing enterprises will be able to offer wages competitive with those offered by new enterprises (which would most likely be private or privatized ones) which have to include the cost of capital investments in their calculations.

Some restraint on wage increases by the public sector has to be exercised anyway, during the transition period.

Moreover private or privatized firms offering higher wages, do not damage the system, provided they can afford it without government subsidy, which will indicate that they are in equilibrium. In the first year of implementation, the share of this sector in the economy might be small anyway.

17 Equilibrium in balance of payments: 'the method' versus the trial-and-error method of the market

The former socialist countries were in extreme shortage of convertible foreign exchange. Even in German Democratic Republic, there was a chronic shortage of foreign exchange. Export prices were out of touch with the world prices; they were above or below the world market prices (Claus and Taake, 1992).

"Early export growth is essential for [the reforming socialist] countries if they are to modernize and refurbish their capital stock. There is *a huge, pent-up demand for hard currency imports both on investment and consumption goods...."* (Rollo and Stern, 1992).

Hence attainment of equilibrium in BOP should be a top priority in the reform process and under the suggested method, observing the BOP constraint and determining the equilibrium rate of exchange are of crucial importance.

The exchange rate calculated by the suggested procedure should achieve equilibrium in the overall BOP and vice versa (i.e. maintenance of equilibrium in the overall BOP will yield the same rate), if necessary by lowering the minimum wage rate below poverty line or through wage-controls (e.g. fixing average wage for public sector. Kornai (1990) points out the danger of excessive wage increases during the transition period and recommends some discipline be enforced in this respect), except for temporary imbalances due to timing of receipts and payments which could be tided over by short-term borrowing.

If the exchange rate selected yields a comfortable surplus in the overall BOP position and other estimates used by 'the method' are reliable, disturbances arising from repayment of short-term debt, capital movements, etc. will not prevent achievement of equilibrium in BOP.

In countries where export potential and prospects are limited, the method might give a too high exchange rate and a too low minimum real wage, which might not be socially acceptable. This outcome, however, will point out the need for sizeable foreign aid or economic union/integration with the neighboring country or countries.

Regarding the trial-and- error method of market, one should note that, chronic high-inflation economies and present socialist economies in transition are in continuous disequilibrium on domestic and external fronts, as evidenced by rising prices and exchange rates, and sizeable savings and BOP gaps. In the former socialist economies disequilibrium problem is further worsened by continuous partial or half-hearted reform measures, their reversals and gloomy expectations.

If the present trial-and-error system employed by the former socialist economies, provided for

(i) free setting of prices under market forces (complete abolition of price controls),

(ii) removal of widespread open and hidden subsidies,

(iii) a liberal foreign trade regime,

(iv) and relative price stability,

simultaneously, it would have been more efficient than the proposed methodology. Many of these conditions, however, are not met in practice in these countries, e.g. price controls on essential goods are kept or restored, foreign trade regime is not liberal (maybe on paper, but not in practice) and inflation is rampant.

It would have been useful to make this exercise in chronic high-inflation economies with significant distortions originating from market structure and government intervention (subsidies, tax evasion, huge short-term borrowing, etc.), with a view to determining correct exchange and minimum wage rates, and efficiency of resource allocation. This, however, is not possible because of the existence of a large private sector.

18 Need for reform and 'the suggested method'

Can one argue that if the method is feasible, then there would be no need to transform, privatize and decentralize? Although this question misses the essence of the method, since the method rests on decentralized decision-making and after the transition program is launched, enterprises confront market conditions, have to live in it and stew in their own juices, it has to be elaborated, however, in order to dissipate any misunderstanding. First of all one does not sacrifice the end (market economy) to the means (the method). The method is not and cannot be a surrogate for the market mechanism; it merely aims at simulation of market conditions during the preparatory stage.

This question also ignores the well-known fact that the socialist economies failed because of (i) the absence of market mechanism and (ii) the lack of private initiative, entrepreneurship and ownership, and that through the latter formidable equilibrating and development force were left idle and demobilized, which also prevented the development of political democracy and freedom.

These deficiencies further led to centralized decision-making and allocation of resources (without market mechanism, desired level of decentralization could never be attained even when the political will is there). All this resulted in (i) the absence of a built-in stabilization mechanism for market disturbances, which had a devastating effect on agricultural performance (without private ownership any agricultural system is bound to fail) and (ii) limited growth prospects particularly in consumer goods industries and services (without market mechanism and private initiative, demand-supply balance and growth in these sectors are out of the question).

The methodology could not and does not claim to remedy all these deficiencies of a socialist economy. On the other hand it enables enterprises to learn by doing, hence to survive. Successful privatization will increase, if transition is orderly and if more plants are kept operational during transition. It considers privatization is necessary, but not sufficient for successful and irreversible transformation, especially if it ends up in economic chaos and too much human misery (through asset-stripping, irresponsible management under ownership by the public at large, increased unemployment, etc.).

19 Treatment of depreciation charges for capital sunk

Under 'the suggested method', to allow a higher minimum wage level, exclusion of depreciation charges on the fixed assets considered capital sunk (i.e. could not be redeployed for more efficient use) has been recommended. This procedure, also bypasses intractable problem of valuation of fixed assets during transition, and reduces, both losses of public enterprises and (hence) number of plant close-downs, and takes into account technically and economically obsolete nature of the existing capital stock in the reforming countries.

In socialist economies *because of central allocation of capital* and absence of well-functioning capital markets, *capital is not mobile across sectors* and sector-specific capital assumption is valid (Dinopoulos and Lane, 1992).

Gomulka (1992, p. 367) recommends that, in transition, in order to reduce recession through price shock, *sharp upward pricing of the capital stock should be avoided,* in order to keep depreciation costs low.

When the cost of capital is taken into account in *profit calculations,* profitability of the former Soviet Union industries declines dramatically (Senik-Leygonie and Hughes, 1992).

"Much of the existing capital stock in the reforming countries has become economically obsolete": Capital stock is old-fashioned and not suitable for adjustment to the factor proportions of a high-wage economy, and a sizeable portion is in sectors or industries which are unviable. Borensztein and Montiel estimated that half to three-quarters of investment in the Czech and Slovak republics, Hungary and Poland was wasteful; and concluded that "a large portion of the currently existing capital will be of little value in the context of a market economy. In the past, investment decisions were not made on the basis of profitability but instead were determined by central plan objectives, by the bargaining power of different enterprises, and other non-market criteria".This evaluation is more valid for manufacturing capital stock than for housing and infrastructure (Dornbusch and Wolf, 1992).

Description of the Chinese experience in inefficient capital stock and resulting depreciation problems by Minshan et al (1992) is self explanatory. For a long time Chinese industry has expanded rapidly in scale, while technical progress has been relatively slow. Low-priced raw materials and manpower, massive investment injection and the expanding scale of production were the main factors which contributed to the relatively high rate of growth.

Excessive investment of this kind, however, would cause demand inflation and could not be sustained for long. Moreover, when the rate of rate of industrialization slows down, the *increased fixed expenses* (depreciation of fixed assets, overhead and management costs, etc.) would result in *a high cost of production.* A lot of *duplicative and blind investment in nonproductive projects* have been made (Minshan, et al, 1992).

In the course of reform in China in 1980s fixed asset *depreciation rate was raised, which led to losses* in industries which were barely profitable. In China enterprises *used to get allocation of working capital free of charge; in reform process,* these allocations *were converted into loans* on which enterprises have to *pay interest.* This was one factor which increased losses of enterprises (Minshan, et al, 1992).

It should, however, be pointed out that, this measure is for the transition period. When transformation with monetary and fiscal stability and discipline is underway, depreciation rules should be changed and working capital requirements should be financed by loans, not by interest-free allocations or grants.

Because as experienced in Yugoslavia in 1980s and in Poland in 1990s, labor and management is able to extract more than their share from public enterprises. As Dinopoulos and Lane (1992) observe "bargaining over the wage creates a capital market distortion by reducing the rental of capital below its productivity; this distortion arises essentially because labor is able, through bargaining, to appropriate some of the returns to capital in the public sector".

20 Distorting effects of dollar shops

The dollar shops not only give a wrong idea about the purchasing power of national currency by indicating an overly undervalued currency, but also affect wage demands. Commander and Coricelli (1992) observe that workers in Poland are concerned with the purchasing power of wages, not only in terms of domestic goods but also of dollar goods. This is explained by the presence of dollar shops. Contrary to wage illusion theories, the perception of a greater availability of goods in the market may have caused higher wage demands.

21 Operation of inter-firm credit market and commercial bank lending with 'the method': reduced uncertainty and creditworthiness of enterprises

'The method', by identifying enterprises that have to close down or phase out certain activities, will provide sufficient *information about the creditworthiness of enterprises* (clarifying the most critical factor) seeking inter-firm credit or loans from commercial banks. The lack of this crucial information during the 1990 Polish reform program has impeded efficient functioning of the interfirm credit market in Poland, and was one of the factors leading to a sharp decline in interfirm credits from March to November 1990 (Calvo and Coricelli, 1992).

In fact, in Poland the interfirm credit market dried up in mid 1990 because the central bank withdrew its role as lender of last resort with the January 1990 program (before this institutional change, interfirm credit market had the implicit full backing of the central bank). One other reason for the interfirm credit market's failure to meet the credit demand of deficit firms was unavailability or scarcity of information on creditworthiness of firms, also intensified by the lack of knowledge of the survival or closure possibilities of enterprises in the early phase of reform process (Calvo and Coricelli, 1992).

22 Currency convertibility and dollarization

(i) The issue

The currency convertibility with dollarization in a high-inflation country is a wasteful luxury, because it does not reap any of the major advantages of convertibility, while paying its cost. By not imposing any trade or exchange restrictions on a current account of BOP transactions, the country loses jobs and incomes in services, entertainment, luxury goods, etc. sectors, and by legalizing dollar holdings of households and firms and by switching into foreign currency balances out of local currency balances, it frustrates monetary policy. Moreover, increase in non-monetary holdings of foreign currency is in general realized by increased external borrowing. Increase in interest rates to reduce non-monetary holdings of foreign currency discourages growth and investment, whereas convertibility with economic and price stability does not entail most of the above mentioned costs and induces external credibility and reduces foreign currency holdings of firms and households.

(ii) Experiences of Poland and Russia in dollarization

The 1990 Polish program was not launched at equilibrium levels of prices, exchange, wage and interest rates; it has not achieved stability and economic growth and has not significantly reduced foreign currency balances of households, although these were the main goals.

The foreign currency holdings of the household sector in Poland constituted 80% of its total deposits at the end 1989 (more than 45% of GDP and almost 3 times the stock of domestic money and amounted to more than 60% of the M3 money supply) and gradually declined to 65% in August 1991.

The foreign currency deposits of the enterprise sector comprised 66% of its total deposits at the end 1989 and declined to 12% in August 1991, possibly also due to surrender requirement (of foreign exchange receipts) to the central bank, and the credit squeeze (Calvo and Coricelli, 1992).

The large dollar deposits of households represent a threat to the sustainability of the convertibility of the currency at any time and reduces the effectiveness of monetary policy instruments.

Because of the fact that nearly 60% of the total money supply was dollar-denominated in December 1989, the Jan 1990 devaluation increased real money supply than it increased prices (normally devaluation increasing the price level of tradeables reduces the real money balances, like a contractionary monetary policy) (Gomulka, 1992).

In Poland and Russia dollarization has increased at unprecedented rates, replacing the national currencies, pushing up the dollar rate e.g. in Russia from 150 rubles in Aug. 1992 to close 600 rubles in Jan 1993. As admitted by the Russian Prime Minister Cheromyrdin in Parliament in Feb. 1993, of increased credit supply, while only 20% were spent to sustain manufacturing capacity, the rest was used for wage increases and on the foreign exchange market. According to press reports the Government actively supported dollarization and has a vested interest in jacking up the dollar exchange rate and in a weak ruble.

Benefits of dollarization, alias 'Gresham's Law in Reverse', in these countries is an open question; whereas benefits accruing to USA, in terms of financing its unparalleled external deficit and debt at low low rates of interest, from dollarization in Arabia, Latin America, Turkey and Poland, and now in the former socialist economies are clear-cut and enormous.

(iii) Conclusions

It is obvious that stop-gap measures, partial remedies, partial reforms, such as dollarization and partial price reforms create more problems than they solve. In particular, partial price reforms generate a wage-price spiral, and dollarization engender a process in which national currency becomes useless within the economy and as a macroeconomic policy tool. Aside from the heavy short-run costs of holding billions of dollars in banknotes without any interest income, and the capital outflow involved (from transferring the required sums abroad out of monetary reserves, export receipts or through external borrowing) the long-term implications of dollarization on capital accumulation and formation and economic growth are much more costly, persistent and continuous.

While the best solution, a stable convertible national currency option could have been attained, spreading resources on divergent partial goals could only be termed irrational.

The only economic solution to dollarization is achieving zero inflation rate, which is impossible under piecemeal reform approach. The other solution, namely compulsory de-dollarization, on the other hand, is again costly, since it will entail capital flight. This issue is taken up, with Latin American experiences, in Chapter 9 of the book.

(iv) Dollarization and hyper-inflation: averting the worst crisis and hence precluding the permanent solution to high-and hyper-inflation

One effect of dollarization is prevent domestic currency lose all its functions through hyperinflation process and thus avert returning to barter economy before the final collapse; and as a consequence makes high-or hyper-inflation endemic and chronic. In other words, worst crisis is averted at the cost of increase in external debt and chronic inflation.

If legal constraints or constraints on external borrowing have precluded a hard currency to replace some functions of money, then a hyperinflation is bound to end up in a catastrophe finale, in which households and firms dump all their money holdings in exchange for goods, increasing prices and velocity of money as a consequence, while monetary institutions are increasing money supply to finance government expenditures and to sustain the level of real stock of money for transactions purposes, as happened in the both post-war hyperinflation.

Dollarization or currency substitution allows economic agents to dump (substitute) domestic currency for hard currency, without necessarily increasing domestic prices of commodities and velocity of circulation on impact.

In this process some of the functions of domestic currency (store of value, unit of account, and even in some cases medium of exchange) are partly or fully taken over by the hard currency, hence, real demand for domestic currency declines which also limits domestic money supply growth. As a consequence money supply and velocity increases could not become too excessive, hence further escalation of hyperinflation to a crisis is avoided. This process can continue indefinitely, provided that the extent of inflationary pressure (gap) is geared to the availability of foreign *financing*.

23 Use of international prices

(i) Advantages of importing the world price system

Use of the relevant international prices by enterprises in valuing their tradeable output and input constitutes the basis of the suggested method. The aim is to base simulations and estimations on the relative price structure that will prevail with launching forth the trade liberalization (with moderate, preferably uniform tariff protection) and current account convertibility, because the latter would eventually import the world price system, subject to the effectiveness of foreign competition and competition conditions in domestic markets.

Trade liberalization allows the country to import international price system; along the same lines, as Fischer (1992) puts down current account convertibility allows the country to import the appropriate, world price system, because essentially convertibility is the same thing as trade liberalization.

However, in case of excessive devaluations of the domestic currency (as Rodrik observed in the Eastern European experience), trade liberalization through helping import a price system, has not achieved its aim of disciplining domestic price rises by introducing foreign competition (Fischer, 1992).

Import of "the world price system would provide much more appropriate relative prices for guiding resource allocation" than those that currently exist in the reforming socialist countries (Fischer, 1992).

Dinopoulos and Lane (1992 pp. 484, 489) also suggest the use of world prices in evaluating effects on national income of reform measures, in former socialist countries.

(ii) Difficulty in calculation of true profitability of enterprises

Under the existing distorted relative prices of commodities and factors in the reforming socialist countries, it is not possible to judge correct economic profitability of any enterprise or activity; hence any decision to close down or subsidize an enterprise is bound to be arbitrary.

Gomulka observed that, in Poland in 1990, due to the *poor quality of the price system, shortages and distortions, it was not possible to determine which enterprises were really profitable.* Hence it was decided to keep some price regulations, but use the key market signals in determining the structural changes, including the closure or restructuring of loss-making enterprises and activities, to be on a sound economic basis (Gomulka, 1992).

(iii) Negative value-added measured at world prices

A recent study by *Hare and Hughes* suggests that "*the immediate adoption of world prices* for tradeables by the countries in transition would result in a significant part of their manufacturing sector *producing negative value-added.*

The proportion is *20% for Poland, the former Czechoslovakia and Hungary,* and about *30% for the former USSR"*.

Gomulka (1992, p. 367) maintains that

> the Hare and Hughes evidence, if true, may be taken to *suggest the need to adopt world prices gradually*, ... [but the latter course] depends on whether and how fast producers would switch, if given a chance, to products and processes which economize the use of newly-expensive inputs. On the other hand, *a gradual transition to world prices risks allowing social resistance to emerge* and, consequently, it may never progress sufficiently.

Gomulka (1992, p. 358) adds that *"if initial conditions are those of a crisis", it is better to introduce the liberalization measures all at once.*

'The suggested method' while, introducing the liberalization reforms immediately, provides temporary cushions against some painful aspects of the initial shock.

Senik-Leygonie and Hughes (1992) employing *input-output tables valued at world prices,* find out that many industries in the former Soviet Union are currently unprofitable; some such as food processing lead to reduction in value-added and some industries with *positive value-added do not cover long-run costs.* (A critical appraisal of this study is made in Chapter 7 of the book.)

These negative value-added estimations for some sectors based on input-output tables (could only be taken as rough indicators due to aggregation involved in compiling these tables), (a) show the extent of price distortions compared to the world price system, which calls for immediate introduction of comprehensive price liberalization reform (as Gomulka, 1992, suggests), and (b) also underpin the value of the suggested method by identifying problem areas on enterprise basis and allowing solutions under pre-determined criteria and principles, in lieu of crisis-management type ad hoc solutions under pressure, without fully understanding and evaluating implications.

(iv) Effects of import of the world prices

(a) Experience in Poland and Hungary. In Poland the trade liberalization aimed at importing international prices and a new price structure; this led producers in exposed sectors (consumer goods) to lower markups; markups for producer goods were sustained longer (Commander and Coricelli, 1992).

For Hungary and Poland it was found that in propagation of inflation during the reform process, although foreign prices matter, developments on the cost side, however, are crucial (Commander and Coricelli, 1992). This outcome was the result of a monopolistic market structure and an undergoing wage drift, and also of excessive devaluations noted by Rodrik (Fischer, 1992).

(b) Danish case. The Danish experience shows that for an open economy with competitive market structure world prices and exchange rate determine movement of domestic prices, as indicated by economic theory.

Juselius (1992) employing cointegration analysis, empirically verified that Danish prices are affected by changes in the exchange rate as well as changes in foreign prices. Empirical support was found for purchasing power parity between the countries as well as for interest rate parity; and it was verified that both prices and exchange rates adjust to deviations from purchasing power parity. The external theories of inflation prescribe a transmission mechanism via input prices in foreign currency and/or via depreciation of the exchange rate. It was found that in the long run "the adjustment primarily took place in the exchange rates rather than in prices, consistent with the notion of sticky nominal prices". For the short-run, it was found that "about half of German inflation feeds into Danish inflation within a quarter" and that "prices do adjust, contrary to the hypothesis of nominal price stickiness".

For an open economy, Denmark, Juselius (1992) concludes that *"external effects dominate* the determination of consumer price inflation" (domestic influence on the price level is modest compared to the external influence) and that being within EEC, Danish prices are *"directly influenced by the price developments" in Germany,* which may represent "the foreign influence since it is by far *the most important trading partner for Denmark"*.

Surrey and Juselius empirically verified that "commodity prices within the industrial countries are basically determined by some common international commodity price level. Considering the dominant role of Germany within the EEC, it seems reasonable to assume that German commodity prices are indicative in a broader context of the European price level" (Juselius, 1992).

(c) Conclusion. These findings also identify the major *source of foreign influence* i.e., the dominant trading partner. The suggested method also advise each enterprise to use relevant world price; i.e., market prices in their import sources and /or in export destinations.

24 Privatization

(i) Ground rules

The issue of public enterprises should be approached not by *ideology* but by *pragmatism* during transition. The crux of transformation is creating *viable* operations out of state firms as quickly as possible and in whatever manner possible, by restructuring, privatizing, phasing out, and introducing the required incentives and discipline. And this is not a matter of *conviction,* but *practicability.*

More important and urgent than privatization of existing medium and large-scale enterprises, in the short-and medium-run, is their restructuring and reform. *And as important and urgent as the enterprise reform is privatization of small-scale enterprises* (industry, services, etc.) *housing and agriculture,* and *development of private property rights, genuine private entrepreneurship and initiative, new private firms, private banking and financial institutions and foreign direct investment.*

Oscar Lange (1938) was of the opinion that "private property of means of production and private enterprise may well continue to have a useful function by being more efficient than a socialized industry might be".

As observed by Bardhan and Roemer (1992), the root cause of problems with many inefficient, white-elephant type public firms or parastatals lies in their being monopolies than being publicly owned. "There are many examples of efficient public firms in competitive environments around the world. Empirical evidence of significant efficiency differentials between public and private firms, after adjusting for market structure (and regulatory policy) is quite scanty. Competition, rather than ownership per se is the key to efficiency."

(ii) Practical problems and constraints

Price liberalization in Poland was placed before privatization deliberately, but it was also inevitable. Small-scale privatization, involving lower transition costs, however, was promoted and has been nearly completed (Gomulka, 1992).

In the former Soviet Union *the large size of the enterprises and the concentration of industries* create both advantages and problems for restructuring. The large firms are also vertically integrated, with a wide range of ancillary services, machine tool shops, etc. Viable parts of these activities could readily be privatized. Many of these firms are *monopolies that hold most of the country's technical know-how* to produce a commodity, which will give them a chance to survive in the market economy (Fischer, 1992).

In the absence of a fully developed stock market, its concomitant financial institutions (which is the case in reforming socialist countries) and hence lacking the discipline exercised on firms through stock market, *there is no reason to expect the former state firms readily converted into joint-stock companies to operate efficiently.*

Carlin and Mayer (1992) observe that, *ironically the absence of initial government restructuring necessitates significant government intervention after privatization,* i.e. initial concern to avoid centralization of control ultimately results in more state involvement. Moreover, "the attempt to encourage immediate sales of assets to foreigners is itself discouraging inflows of foreign direct investment"

Private buyers of loss-making enterprises might indulge in *asset-stripping* (Senik-Leygonie and Hughes, 1992).

The deficiency of Eastern European privatization is *institutional,* namely *inadequate managerial and financial resources in both the private and the public sector.* This deficiency can be corrected by purchasing management and finance; hence the ultimate constraint on the speed of privatization is the size of Western resources available for this end (Carlin and Mayer, 1992).

(iii) Russian privatization dilemma

(a) Privatization through cooperative enterprises in the Soviet Union

> Soviet industrial enterprises were very large and industry was correspondingly monopolized.... In 1988, 47,000 industrial enterprises operated in the Soviet Union. In the first half 1990, enterprises owned by local authorities and republics accounted for 35% of value added. The private sector was not significant, and nearly 90% of employment was in state enterprises, 8% was on collective farms, and less than 4% was in private sector, including cooperatives (Fischer, 1992).

Cooperative enterprises started to re-emerge in 1986, when the Soviet leadership became tolerant toward individual and cooperative forms of production, in order to reverse the economic stagnation prevailing during last few years. By mid-1990, some 200,000 cooperatives were operational, employing close to 5 million people, producing an output of about 60 billion rubles, mainly in construction, consumer goods production and provision of scientific and technical goods and services (Jones and Moskoff, 1991).

According to Fischer the number of cooperatives increased towards the end of Soviet rule, exceeding 250,000 (of which nearly 40% in construction sector) in mid-1991, employing more than 6 million people and accounting for 5% GDP. "However, 80% of these cooperatives were operating within existing enterprises-a process that can be viewed either as the beginning of industrial restructuring through the spinning off of viable components of firms or simply as the ripping off of state assets" (Fischer, 1992).

Cooperatives in general paid higher prices than state enterprises for material and capital inputs; wages paid by them were substantially higher than the average nominal wage in the state enterprise sector. Despite these higher costs, they could compete with the state sector on product quality and arbitrating goods across markets (Jones and Moskoff, 1991).

There were more than 1,000 legislation applying to cooperatives and 1988 Law on Cooperatives which aimed at codifying legislation, created more legal and economic ambiguity and confusion than it cleared; and as a consequence many cooperatives went underground or out of business or tried to survive via linking up with state enterprises. Cooperatives dealing with arbitrage caused much grievance and animosity, and as a consequence their pricing practices were closely monitored (Jones and Moskoff, 1991).

(b) Corruptive privatizations in the former Soviet Union and a remedy

> Stories about spontaneous or nomenklatura privatization of larger firms [are] abound. ... [It seems that] firms managers' have generally strengthened their control and their residual property rights during the period since 1988, but that they have not obtained de jure ownership of firms. ... Johnson and Kroll emphasize the part played by management and downplay the role of the nomenklatura. ... [The role of bureaucracy is emphasized in other reports, regarding corruption in the transfer of property. Fischer argues that] in many cities and regions, property rights are being passed from the state sector to others, to the benefit of the nomenklatura (Fischer, 1992).

In order for the larger firms to be moved quickly into the private sector, both existing management and workers have to support privatization schemes; hence it would be helpful if *the scheme gave existing workers and management significant shares of the privatized firm.* For example, a rule specifying that shareowners could receive dividends only after privatization, would induce and encourage management to accept and speed up privatization (Fischer, 1992).

(c) Gradual versus rapid approach. Russia in privatization cannot adopt China's gradualist approach, since the state and the state order system have collapsed and government has been losing control over the enterprise sector; and hence the ownership status of firms and the rules of operation have to be clarified (the new rules and strategy must be developed and implemented) quickly and enterprises must be moved out of the state control as early as possible. For example in the New Economic Policy (NEP) in the 1920s, large firms, which were kept under state ownership, were required to behave like commercial enterprises, and they formed themselves into large trusts and presumably maximized profits as monopolists. However, *enterprise reform has to be gradual, since privatization of large firms will take time*, perhaps up to a decade, in order "to implement a strategy in which the state will be responsible for a significant, but diminishing part of industry for years and not for months"(Fischer, 1992).

(d) Evaluation by the World Bank. World Bank President Lewis Preston(4) points out that even though stabilization is important in the former Soviet Union, "the overriding issue is the need for structural and sectoral reforms" and simultaneously "help halt, and then reverse, the precipitous economic decline", through rehabilitation loans, which will support enterprise reform (aiming at breaking monopolies, privatization of old enterprises and encouragement of new businesses) and through an overhaul of trade relations among republics.

The World Bank (1992/E) is of the opinion that without sustained progress in enterprise reform in the former Soviet Union the stabilization program cannot hold as the state becomes hostage to the pressures from the enterprise sector. The Russian government, however, is constrained in implementing reforms by its institutional capacity.

(iv) Creation of new private firms versus privatization

Nordhaus observes that, contrary to the expectations of Chicago School, private economic activity will not quickly spring up when state restrictions are withdrawn. Fischer maintains that "within a few years, the Russian private sector will grow more through the creation of new firms than through privatization." Therefore, developing the legal, financial and educational systems and infrastructure to support new enterprises, should form an essential element of the enterprise reform strategy (Fischer, 1992).

In view of existing economic chaos and zero protection import duties (Nordhaus notes that Russia is the only major country in the world that has no duties on imports), it is very unlikely that genuine private sector could develop in Russia, in the foreseeable future, except for cooperatives or firms set up by plundering state assets, unless drastic measures are taken to halt decline and establish stability.

(v) Privatization of housing, small business and agriculture

Housing is one area where privatization could have a high payoff; but it has progressed slowly in Eastern Europe (Fischer, 1992). Housing privatization could progress rapidly and establishing private property rights concretely paves the way to market reform, and restores private saving motive.

Privatization and expansion of the service sector would add to employment and it could be quickly realized.

Dornbusch and Wolf (1992) however, observe that, expansion of the service sector would add to employment, but its productivity is low; whereas improvements in technology and investment in plant and equipment and in human capital formation would increase productivity.

(4) Speech at June 15, 1992 Meeting of the Bretton Woods Committee, WBN, June 19, 1992.

The latter, however, would call for privatization of industry or joint ventures with foreign direct investment.

Fischer (1992) with respect to the former Soviet Union notes that improving the agricultural sector should be one of the highest reform strategies. Improving the availability and quality of food, could also bring political support to the reform process. However, many farmers on collectives do not want privatization. The development of private ownership of land and the extension of private areas, could progress rapidly and would have a high pay-off.

(vi) Need for banking reform

> Creation of a viable private sector depends on the availability of financing both to purchase existing firms and to create new firms. ... The development of new firms depends more on the development of the banking system through restructuring of existing balance sheets and the creation of new banks or units within existing banks (Fischer, 1992).

25 Forecasting difficulty for economies in transition

(i) General

Many economists point out extreme difficulty in forecasting developments in the former socialist economies in transition. *Huang*(5) observes that, *because of the uncertainty in Russia economic forecasts can be made only for the next few months.*

Ron Duncan(6) observes that it is hard to predict *worldwide trade effects of recent changes in Eastern and Central Europe and in the countries of the former Soviet Union*, although there is potential for a large impact on world trade patterns.

Rollo and Stern (1992) note that it is *impossible to predict the longer term outlook* for Eastern Europe and the former Soviet Union. *Impossibility of prediction stems from*

> (a) the massive scale of changes underway,
> (b) The probability of serious policy mistakes en route from communism to democracy and the market economy, ...
> (c) the lack of experience in the region or anywhere else of how best to structure and sequence such a massive change in regime, [and]
> (d) the serious lack of reliable data. ... In trying to assess the future course of the economies of the region therefore *the methodologies are limited. Extrapolation of past trends is of no value* in the face of major structural

(5) of World Bank, WBN, Aug. 7, 1992.
(6) of the World Bank (Chief of the International Trade Division) WBN, Feb. 20, 1992.

change. ... [On these grounds Rollo and Stern employ a] *judgmental approach to a problem* which *approaches intractability*, ... [and] *construction of [alternative] scenarios* is the basis of [their] approach. ... *These scenarios depend on* the interaction of political and economic pressures which lead to the expected *success or failure of reforms.*

(ii) The Polish reform experience

Gomulka (1992) observes that *"modern economies are so complex that, even if uncertainty were not present, which it is in large measure, no one can predict all the economic implications of any policy decision"*. In case of the potential impact of the reform measures on economic activity much larger uncertainties prevail. In the 1990 Polish reform program, policies aimed to be "more rather than less restrictive in the first few months following the big bang" were reversed to an "excessively expansionary policy" in the second half of 1990 (Gomulka, 1992) to which output response was much less than to the credit contraction of the first half of 1990, according to Calvo and Coricelli (1992) due to the sharp rise in real wages. And as a consequence price increase reached 585% in 1990 far above the expectations.

It was expected that the exchange-rate-based heterodox program in Poland would initially lead to output expansion, whereas the initial effect was stagflationary, the inflation rate accelerated sharply, industrial output fell and a deep recession set in. In January 1990 the inflation rate overshot the officially expected rate of 35% and reached 79%, and industrial production declined by about 30%. The inflation rate declined to 24% in Feb. 1990 and oscillated around a monthly 4-5% throughout the rest of 1990; and because of a new round of increases of administered prices, inflation rose to double digit monthly rates from Jan 1991 on. For 1990 as a whole, industrial output was about 25% below its level in 1989 (Calvo and Coricelli, 1992).

GNP per capita(7) (in 1987 US $) declined from $1,740 in 1989 to $1,470 in 1990 and $1,370 in 1991 (21% decline from the 1989 level); consumption per capita after declining from $1,040 in 1989 to $860 in 1990 rose to $930 in 1991, while domestic investment per capita declined from $560 in 1989, to $410 in 1990 and $310 in 1991.

GNP declined by 15% in 1990 and 6.4% in 1991, and GDP by 12% in 1990 and 8% in 1991.(8) In 1991 instead of the anticipated recovery in GDP by some 3-4%, a further fall of some 7% occurred (Gomulka, 1992).

All this confirms the view that in transition economies, using conventional macroeconomic forecasting methods, it is impossible to estimate the effects of any major change (even its direction), even if it is of a partial-reform nature.

---

(7) Source: 1992 IBRD World Tables.

(8) World Tables, IBRD, 1992.

(i) Marketization of socialism

The classic Lange model of market socialism concentrates on the primacy of the role of prices in resource allocation. Managers of public firms *do not maximize profits,* but rather *apply soft administered prices,* often involving *cost-plus pricing,* "under the built-in expectation of the *soft budget constraint*" and with political interference "with the harsh exit mechanism of the market and the state remains the ultimate rescuer of losing concerns"; political accountability prevails over financial accountability as observed by Kornai (Bardhan and Roemer, 1992).

The 1990 reforms in Eastern Europe are *not the Marketization of Soviet-type socialism as those of the 1960s, 1970s, and early 1980s* (i.e. not a change within the system), but a change of the system, with re-modelling of institutions, skills and attitudes, privatization, which will take a number of years. "The transformation, in this first stage, may be described as one from a modified centrally regulated economy of the Hungarian type, 1968-1989, to *a market-oriented socialist economy,* the latter to be changed within the 1990s, into a fully fledged market economy of the Western type" (Gomulka 1992).

"In theory, market socialism was means of seeking the best of both worlds, the efficiency of the market and the social justice of socialism." "Unfortunately, efficiency is a fact and justice is a slogan." Optimistic views, however, are extended about "the possibilities of combining socialism with the efficiency of a market economy" (Hillman, 1992). For example, Julian Le Grand and Saul Estrin (1989) tried to show that markets can be used to achieve socialist ends or that the fundamental problems of socialism could be tackled with a *decentralized economic mechanism;* e.g., through assuring individual liberties, equalizing initial endowments, nondistorting lumpsum taxes and protecting consumers by *the simulation of competitive markets* and by consumer representation on the boards of natural monopolies; other than Yugoslavia and Hungary, Algeria, Mozambique, Laos and China practice market socialism.

(ii) Transition: neither plan nor market

"The economic transformation currently being undertaken in Eastern Europe, is often described as a '*leap to market*'. However a switch to a full-fledged market economy and building new institutions cannot be made overnight." Moreover in many countries (Hungary, Poland and Yugoslavia in the 1980s and the former Soviet Union in the early 1990s) *reforms have been undertaken gradually,* while the basic structures of a socialist economy have been preserved. As a result, in the interim there existed a situation of *'neither plan nor market',* in which no central economic plan is implemented but in which the state continues nominally to own a substantial part of the enterprises. A reforming socialist economy may also have a substantial nonsocialized sector (industries never nationalized, newly established private firms and privatized enterprises). "*Despite the absence (or irrelevance) of a central plan, the state frequently continues to influence enterprises*" wage, employment, and output decisions through a variety of channels (Dinopoulos and Lane, 1992).

(iii) Experiments with market socialism

Two experiments of market socialism (in Yugoslavia and Hungary) have failed. The aim was to achieve market efficiency, while avoiding distributional consequences of private ownership. *Yugoslav social ownership of capital with labor management in a market setting failed because of politicization and cross-subsidization;* behavioral predictions derived from the theoretical models have not materialized in practice and the system have not succeeded in duplicating the efficiency of a competitive market economy. The same outcome happened in *Hungary's version of market socialism, launched when central planning ceased in 1968, with no accompanying privatization;* when the system formally came to an end in 1990, the socialist enterprises were technologically backward and in need of restructuring (Hillman, 1992).

(iv) Dilemma of market socialism: prevalence of imperfect competition, ineffective central planning and soft budget constraint

Views of *Newbery and Kattuman* (1992) regarding the failure of market socialism could be summarized by simultaneous prevalence of imperfect competition (domestic entry and imports restricted), ineffective central planning and soft budget constraint. Different countries in Eastern Europe differed in their degree of central planning and control, Czechoslovakia with the most rigid and Hungary with the most market-oriented and flexible. Despite these differences all these economies performed poorly in the 1980s.

In Hungary, *quantitative central planning was replaced* in 1968 by a more *decentralized system of guidance*. This, however, reduced both the quality of information flows to the center and the ability of the center to commit to future performance-related rewards and penalties, which in turn led to inefficient outcomes. Despite a clear recognition of the unsatisfactory performance of the economy neither the *soft budget constraint* was hardened in order to compel enterprises to improved efficiency, *nor competition by domestic entry or imports was introduced,* which would have removed the root cause of the problem (i.e. monopolization). Because of the poor quality of information supplied by enterprises to the center, the authorities lacked objective measures of the efficiency of the enterprise and resources were not allocated on the basis of profitability. There was no correlation between investment and profitability in Hungary (Newbery and Kattuman, 1992).

According to Bardhan and Roemer,

> what the Eastern European experience has shown is that *a system of pervasive state control of firms, plus the absence of markets, does not work. Competitive markets are necessary* to achieve an efficient and vigorous economy, *but full-scale private ownership is not necessary* for the successful operation of competition and markets. Contrary to popular impression, this claim has not yet been disproved by either history or economic theory.

Failure to disentangle the concepts of private ownership and the competitive market has led to the premature obituaries for socialism (Bardhan and Roemer, 1992).

Some variants of market socialism have been tried in Eastern Europe (e.g. in Hungary since 1968) and have failed. And Kornai has stated that 'the principle of market socialism' should be abandoned. Kornai himself, however, admits that

> *whatever has been tried was at best piecemeal; market socialist reform in some integrated pattern, with institutional restructuring to address the various incentive and agency problems, has never been tried, and certainly not with* any measure of *political democracy or market competition.* Quite often the crucial decisions on the entry and exit of firms and the selection, promotion and dismissal of managers have remained in the hands of the all-powerful party nomenklatura (Bardhan and Roemer, 1992).

(v) Absence of money and financial markets in market socialism experiments

Nuti (1989) observes that "*the role of money and financial institutions under market socialism*" has been neglected. "The original experiments with market socialism in Eastern Europe restricted the operations of the market to product markets and left investment under central control." The failure of market socialism in Eastern Europe was the result of its failure to incorporate capital markets.

Brus and Laski (1989) note that the market-oriented economic reforms, *without a capital market, has failed to bring about the desired change from bureaucratic to market regulation.* Bowles and White (1992) point out that a capital market enables the central authorities to control the macro-economy without intervening directly in the decisions of enterprises (microeconomic decision-making) regarding investment plans, entry and exit of firms. Hence in its absence market socialism cannot work.

Banking reforms were introduced in Bulgaria and Hungary in 1987, in Poland in 1989 Financial markets for bonds were opened in Soviet Union, Yugoslavia, Hungary and Poland (the latter two countries also introduced both bond and stock markets) (Bowles and White, 1992).

(vi) Why market socialism failed: an overview

The experiences of market socialism in Yugoslavia and Hungary failed because of following reasons, identified by Hillman (1992)

(a) "Economic decision making remained politicized and subject to political monopoly", "in order to ensure that market outcomes did not contradict the objectives of socialist equality" (Hillman, 1992).

(b) Factor markets did not exist (simply were *absent*) and *product markets were non-competitive.* "Domestic barriers to competition assured workers security by precluding the functioning of capital markets that would have facilitated competitive investments" (Hillman, 1992).

(c) "Foreign competition was ruled out by a highly protectionist system of international trade" (Hillman, 1992).

(d) Lack of private property rights and absence of private entrepreneurship: In these experiments of market socialism, market is characterized by the *lack of private property rights* and the political regime can be described by political monopoly rather than democracy; there is, however, no example of "a democratic nonpoliticized system that has denied private property rights". Hence evidence shows that, socialist markets without property rights cannot attain efficiency of capitalist markets. Property rights provides basis for value-maximization of assets. And in the absence of private property rights, and consequent lack of profit maximization, decision makers do not have any incentive to monitor production and use resources efficiently. In fact, under socialism absence of efficiency was not of much concern, since the task of management was "to manage social property in a socially responsible manner" (Hillman, 1992).

(e) Soft-budget constraint, which did not allow closure of inefficient enterprises through bankruptcy. The soft-budget constraint precludes success of macroeconomic stabilization policies, since these are linked to enterprise efficiency. "In the absence of privatization no one has responsibility for capital,

and capital is not efficiently utilized. In fact, management and labor capture capital and use it for self-advantage. Even there is incentive to incur loss and evoke subsidies, in order make higher wage payments" (Hillman, 1992).

Bankruptcy is virtually ruled out, "because of political and ideological implications or because the enterprise is the sole supplier of a particular good". Enterprises lend each other money through accumulating arrears and thereby create "a chain indebtedness" wherein the bankruptcy of one enterprise would lead to a series of bankruptcies, which would be politically unacceptable to the government.

Required subsidy payments from the government budget to loss-making enterprises, undermine the budgetary discipline and effective implementation of macroeconomic stabilization policy. Stabilization could only be effective if the government can credibly commit itself and enterprises to observe hard-budget constraint, by letting loss-making enterprises go bankrupt. Hence Hillman (1992) along with Hinds concludes that *for an effective conduct of stabilization policy privatization is essential.*

Along these lines Berend (1990) observes that after the 1968, reform which created market for commodities only, but with central price and wage controls and with central distribution of investment funds, there was not any substantial new development of the Hungarian economic model even in the 1979-87 period.

(vii) The suggested method versus market socialism

One should add to this list by Hillman (1992) the absence of money and capital markets, specifically (though included under factor markets and closely linked to the soft-budget constraint) as revealed by negative real interest rates, and segmented money and capital markets observed in Poland by Calvo and Coricelli (1992), and widespread price fixation by government in existing markets, and the absence of foreign exchange markets.

In view of the absence of these markets and lack of competition, denial of free entry and pervasive fixed prices in existing markets, it is difficult to understand how these experiments in Hungary and Yugoslavia could be termed as market socialism. The suggested methodology has nothing in common whatsoever with these experiments as can be readily seen by comparing the two.

One referee has alluded that the suggested method implies market socialism even with administrative price fixation (formation) by the central planning authority. Under the method, it is suggested that (i) all instruments and market institutions should be set up during the preparatory stage (so that they should be in place at the onset of the program). This includes the establishment of private property rights, private entrepreneurship, privatization of small businesses and housing, removal of restrictions on free entry and competition, setting up banking and financial institutions, and the taxation system of a market economy. (ii) With the launching of the program, free price formation for commodities (elimination of subsidies in principle), free determination of exchange and interest rates (some form of wage restraint would be necessary during first few years), hardening of budget constraint for enterprises (the suggested mechanism now under new credible threat of close-down would force enterprises to make realistic estimates and live up to their estimates and act efficiently and with economy), and an open (moderate tariff protection and in principle liberalized trade and exchange regime) competitive market economy would all come into force. Even in preparatory phase, simulations are based on enterprises' own pricing and decisions, and the role of economic planning agency is limited to aggregation of these microeconomic decisions and estimates and forecast possible outcomes of alternative scenarios. With the launching of the program all prices will be freely determined; even in case of subsidized (on production or consumption) goods, there is no need for administratively fixed prices.

27 Gradualism versus 'big bang'/shock therapy approach, piecemeal/partial versus comprehensive reforms and sequencing and pacing reforms

(i) Introduction

A lot of discussion took place on issues titling this section. Salient points are summarized below.

While *China* adopted *a gradual,* two-tier system more than a decade ago and became remarkably successful, *Russia* ended up with hyperinflation and political instability under the *'big bang'* approach. Israel succeeded in liberalizing trade through a gradual program over 2 decades. Various authors (Kadar and Terdos, Csaba) recommend *gradualism in liberalization, restructuring, and privatization and caution against too much haste. Sachs* is in favor of rapid transition along the lines of the *Polish Big Bang of Jan 1990 (Koves and Marer, 1991).*

Under the *Polish 'big bang' approach,* during 1990 and 1991 "the costly *stop-go-stop sequence of policies" could not be avoided* (Gomulka, 1992) and in fact there were frequent policy reversals.

Creating the institutions of market economy is a monumental task, it takes time and resources. Hence it is necessary to adopt a *comprehensive* rather than a *partial* approach to the transition process (Koves and Marer, 1991).

"The capacity for reform is limited by political uncertainties" and "the lack of institutions that can design and carry out market-oriented policies".[9] This will obviously affect the pace of reform process.

Alexeev (1992) maintains that "even in the presence of developed parallel markets, *partial reforms lead to economic instability* and that a full-fledged conversion to a market economy is a matter of great urgency". According to Commander (1992), "*piecemeal price reforms* have tended to be strongly inflationary, when fiscal correction was insufficient. Piecemeal economic reforms that weakened centralized controls on both prices and wages tended to expose the latent inflationary pressures."

Osband (1992/A) *claims that failure and crisis in reforming* socialist economics *is brought about by improper sequencing of reforms. Relaxation of wage controls in the absence of hard budget constraints on enterprises and flexible prices for consumer goods have been dangerously destabilizing.* When prices are fixed, global wage increase benefits middlemen/ speculators more than workers and can discourage work effort. If workers continue to strike for higher wages and the government gives in, wage/price spiral and output decline (stagflation) result in. Because, the difference between market-clearing prices and official prices (the shortage rent) accrues to those who can buy deficit goods at official prices. Impact of a general wage increase, in such an environment, would be further shrinkage of output, increased shortages and market prices of deficit goods outpacing wages.

(ii)Sequencing the Polish reform program: macroeconomic equilibrium versus microeconomic efficiency considerations

The 1990 Polish program was deliberate, with the aim of avoiding "a catastrophe of the East German type: large-scale bankruptcies and large scale unemployment at the start of the reform" (Gomulka, 1992).

The Polish program's implicit *sequencing* was

> to deal first with macro problems, such as the budget deficit, inflation, international reserves and foreign debt, and only later with the more fundamental, difficult and time consuming problem of microeconomic efficiency. *Structural adjustment* can be slower or faster, but it must always *gradual.* So far the only exception to this rule is East Germany, where jumping all at once into a completely open system with highly competitive markets has destroyed much of the existing economic structure. However, the large human and capital resources of West Germany are available there to create a new system rapidly in its place

---

(9) Yukon Huang of World Bank, (interview) WBN, Aug 7, 1992.

and, in the meantime, to provide adequate social safety nets (Gomulka, 1992).

> In contrast to such structural adjustment, stabilization and liberalization measures are easy to devise and implement. Moreover, a case can be made for introducing the measures all at once. The case is particularly strong if initial conditions are those of a crisis, such as the situation of Poland in the second half of 1989. *Strong measures are then needed anyway to avoid a collapse.* ... [In conditions of crisis, the population is also] more inclined to accept a large dose of sacrifice in exchange for a prospect, however distant and unclear, of an improvement (Gomulka, 1992, p. 358).

These views reflect the essence of a correct reform strategy and sequencing ; and conditions of Russia in early 1993, are just of a nature calling for such a strategy; and under 'the suggested method', prospect of improvement is clear and not distant, and sacrifice is minimized, as well.

All this indicates the necessity and desirability of an approach just provided by the suggested methodology, which makes possible immediate implementation of an overall price and trade regime reform, but at the same time allows a gradual approach to more painful aspects of structural adjustment (unemployment, protection of critical sectors).

In fact in Poland, "still, selective industrial policy was pursued through direct subsidies and new institutions created for that purpose". However, as a proportion of GDP, subsidies were reduced from 15% in 1989 to 6% in 1990. "While concern to avoid large-scale bankruptcies was paramount, there was also a desire to allow some closures to underpin the break with the old paternalistic attitudes" (Gomulka, 1992, p. 361, 366).

Freely determined agricultural producers, industrial producers and consumer prices comprised 100%, 88% and 83% respectively of the total in the early 1991. "Administered prices apply only in the case of alcohol, electricity, gas, heating and hot water, rents in the state housing sector, postal services and communications, and state rail and road transport" (Gomulka 1992, p. 366).

(iii) The world experience with structural adjustment programs and sequencing and pacing reforms[10]

The World Bank has learned from experience over the last decade that the structural adjustment is extremely difficult and costly; that *realistic estimates of the short-run cost and long-run benefits of adjustment are needed;* that

(10) Speech by Attila Karaosmanoğlu, World Bank Managing Director, at a IBRD/IMF Seminar for International Trade Union leaders on Nov. 3, 1992, WBN, Nov. 5, 1992, before the World Economic Forum in Davos, Bank's World, March 1993.

adjustment cannot be avoided, although it can be deferred (through sequencing and adjusting pace of reforms) and as a consequence "adjustment programs have evolved considerably over the last decade" and *"the 'second generation' programs of* recent years *go well beyond issues of stabilization, fiscal balance, foreign exchange and trade reform,"* and *"focus on the sequencing and pacing of reforms according to circumstances in individual countries."*

Karaosmanoğlu further points out in the second generation adjustment programs, restructuring of public expenditures (in order to protect social service spending), reversing the bias against agriculture (which promotes labor-intensive, poverty-reducing growth), and elimination of anti-employment biases in highly protected industries (where overvalued exchange rates and subsidized interest rates has supported a capital-intensive pattern) has become important.

(iv) Gradualism versus shock-treatment/ 'big bang' approach and sequencing reforms: Russia and China

In making a choice between gradualism and shock treatment in transition to a market system, it is often argued that because of the initial massive macro disequilibrium existing in the former socialist economies, rapid stabilization and price liberalization are essential. Fischer (1992) suggests *that gradualism in trade liberalization and privatization is a viable option.*

Allowing tariffs for a limited period could provide needed *temporary protection* to domestic producers while the economy is reorganizing (and still allow a foreign price system to be imported), and would also provide *much needed revenue* to the government. He suggests that *tariffs be uniform,* to minimize pressures for special treatment, starting as 30 to 40% and declining over a period of years to low levels.

Fischer (1992) points out that rapid price liberalization is essential *"when shortages are pervasive,* as they were in Russia, and also some elements of a social safety net must be put in place immediately to ensure that stabilization does not cause excessive hardship".

Regarding *privatization,* China's policy of gradualism is often contrasted with the proclaimed preference *in Eastern Europe for rapid privatization.* Fischer, however, notes that,

> *in practice, privatization has proceeded slowly in Eastern Europe* and has been disappointing, particularly for medium-and large-scale firms. In *China, gradualist reforms* started in agriculture and have not yet involved the sale of state farms to private individuals; *yet an essentially private sector has developed in both agriculture and industry.*

Fischer maintains that China's gradualist "reforms have been extremely successful by any economic measure. " The situation in *Russia* differs from that in China because *the state and state order system have collapsed.* In this situation Fischer argues that there is an urgent need for the government to "*clarify the ownership status of firms and the rules* under which they are to operate" (Brainard and Perry, 1992; Fischer, 1992).

Fischer (1992) argues that while *Russia* must quickly develop and implement a new strategy and new rules of games regarding enterprises, *the enterprise reform and privatization have to be gradual, a strategy similar to those being carried out in practice, although not in rhetoric, in Eastern Europe.*

(v) Absence of a long-term perspective

In studies, recommendations and prescriptions regarding the reforming socialist economies, short-term issues (price adjustments, trade liberalization, inflation, declining outputs, unviable state enterprises addicted to soft budget constraints, setting up market institutions, etc.) are focused on without due attention to longer-term implications and without a long-run perspective. Experience in these countries show that with reform measures high-inflation and declining-output are commonplace. Beneficial effects of privatization and foreign investment are not significant in the short- and medium-run to check these adverse developments and that the reform process is rather of a long-term nature, while focus is on short- run, mainly.

Whereas internal and external stability in the short-run, is only a small part of the whole transformation process, which will soon confront low income level (living standards), large unemployment and sizeable foreign debt, which are consequences, inter alia, of the present short-sighted reform policies. Long-term growth, however, could materialize only if short-term economic/monetary stability is achieved quickly, and if the price/wage spiral and frequent currency devaluations and significant dollarization are avoided, and short- and medium-run policies conducive to entrepreneurship, genuine private enterprise, technology transfer, productivity increase, increased investment, etc. are pursued presently. The gimmick is that all this could be achieved on a significant scale only after short-term stability is realized.

Experience in high-inflation countries world-wide with declining or stagnating output and rising external debt (it seems that the reforming economies are on the road to join this club) in general shows that these problems are intractable even in the long-run. The apparent solution of extensive quick privatizations, block sales and influx of foreign capital to this end are mere short-run palliatives, (which now almost universally concede to be an unrealistic target). They are not a long-term permanent solution, because in the medium-run when readily available saleable assets are exhausted, the government budget would still continue to run deficits. Throw-away type privatizations will possibly end up with dismemberment of production facilities, unemployment and low growth rates would persist, and under the circumstances new foreign investment would not be attracted, rather repatriation of foreign capital, profit transfers and debt service would put a heavy burden on balance of payments (BOP).

28 Price liberalization (an overview), stabilization programs and the economic policy of the 1990s

(i) Price liberalization (an overview) of recent experience

In pre-reform socialist economies prices were fully controlled from the center.

In Poland during 1953-82, consumer prices broadly reflected movements in total costs. Prices of basic items (food, transport, rent, and energy) lagged behind the overall price index. Monetary growth outpacing price growth in the 1970s and 1980s led to a large premium of the black market exchange rate over the official exchange rate (Commander and Coricelli, 1992).

In partially reformed socialist economies, with progressive price liberalization, *dual pricing systems* emerged where monetary stance was basically passive (accommodating). Endemic shortages induced excess demand in goods and factor markets (due to fixed or *sticky prices* and wages) and resulted in *repressed inflation.* Hence rationing for both households and enterprises were exercised (chronic sellers' markets). Excess demand translated into excess liquid balances or excessive inventories.) *Exogenous price shocks tended to widen the gap between domestic and international prices* because of widespread price controls, creating a distorted relative price structure (Commander, 1992).

The soft budget constraints of the enterprise sector and the banking system mean increased subsidy payments. Centrally planned and partially reformed economies in 1980s responded to external shocks by depressing investment, raising subsidies to enterprises (through the budget, negative interest rates, and preferential credits) and maintaining stable real wages (Commander, 1992).

Selective price liberalization in 1980s led to rising open inflation. Recent price reforms led to high inflation in Poland (250% in 1989 and 1990), Yugoslavia (220% in 1987, 290% in 1988, 1,340% in 1989 and 130% in 1990), Bulgaria (65% in 1990, 330% in 1991) and Soviet Union (100% in 1991, estimate); in all these cases causal link between inflation and budget deficits was strong, when money financing is opted. Accommodating monetary policy stems from subsidy policy arising from price controls and pervasive soft budgets of the enterprises. Piecemeal price reforms have tended to be strongly inflationary when fiscal correction was insufficient (Commander, 1992).

The optimal pace of price reforms and their dynamic effects are controversial issues nowadays. Recent experience with price liberalization schemes in Eastern Europe have ended up in *jumps in the price level that translated into accelerated inflation, large declines in recorded output and* slow, but accelerating increase in the rate of open *unemployment. Decline in output preceded the dismantling of COMECON and the oil price shock of 1990.* Unemployment rose to a range of 6-12% and is estimated to accelerate. Output has declined more sharply than unemployment has risen; hence *labor productivity has fallen.* Stabilizing inflation requires fiscal correction, reforms to the tax system and incomes policy (as a complement, not as a substitute for budget balancing), (Commander, 1992).

The *Stabilization programs* put in place in most of the socialist economies in transition since January 1990, envisage *generalized price revisions* (large upward shifts in the price level), *large contraction in subsidies, fiscal correction* and *tight monetary policy.* In order to provide anchor to stabilization, the *exchange rate has been fixed* and *wage cuts* have been enforced ex ante to avert price-wage spiral (in Czechoslovakia and Poland). The exchange rate has been floated (Bulgaria) or a dual exchange rate system was established in 1990 to be unified in 1991 (Romania) with money and wages providing *the anchors. Current account or internal convertibility has been established* (except for Bulgaria and Romania) with trade opening (Commander, 1992).

Large jumps in the price level eliminated monetary overhang and shortages. Prices however, cannot jump to equilibrium values quickly. Even with trade opening, *domestic prices adjusted slowly to international prices,* while prices of sensitive goods (housing, transportation) need periodic revisions/shifts. Lags in relative price adjustment and 1990 oil price and COMECON shocks explain the persistence of inflation (Commander, 1992).

High inflation in Poland and Yugoslavia was preceded by flight from domestic money. The accelerated dollarization was the characteristic of these cases which reflected great uncertainty in the expectations of economic agents. In Yugoslavia high inflation was traced back to currency depreciation, de facto wage indexation and quasi-fiscal deficit (despite balanced central government budget) and accommodating monetary stance. Wage indexing and cost-plus pricing rule provoke a ratchet effect which raises the inflation rate, with accommodating monetary policy. In Poland, with indexation, currency depreciation fed through pricing and the budget into accelerated high inflation (Commander, 1992).

Controlling inflation is a difficult problem which lies at the heart of the reforms in the former socialist economies, given the need for price liberalization and a new relative price structure. The microeconomic features of the economies and the legacy of the past (ownership, wage setting, financial system, allocative mechanisms) nullify or distort the effects of conventional macroeconomic policies (Commander, 1992).

(ii) Current views on economic policies of 1990s(11)

During the postwar era, world opinion on the role of state in the economy changed from decade to decade, 1960s and 1970s were decades of intervention and of macroeconomic fine-or gross-tuning to maintain full employment output, in 1980s marketplace was dominant and 1990s would be the decade of "*balance between respective roles of governments and markets.*" The emerging *'market-friendly' approach* which stresses that *competition* is "essential to spur growth, employment and technological progress" and that *environment must be conducive to entrepreneurship and private sector development.* At the same time it is recognized that *"markets alone are not enough."*

> *Governments must also play a positive role*, making the tangible and intangible investments that underpin rapid growth and a healthy private sector-and that ensure social and economic justice with efficiency. Governments must intervene to *establish legal and regulatory frameworks,* and to provide essential public services: Social safety net, investments in infrastructure, environmental protection and so on.

But there are "things that governments should not do." As Keynes put it down in his work *'The End of Laissez Faire'*:

> *The important thing for the government is not to do things which individuals are doing already*, and do them a little better or a little worse; but to do those things which at present are not done at all.
>
> Practical experience also suggests that it is better *government not to micro-manage economic development.* [In Sub-Saharan Africa, while government] pricing policies, taxes and marketing boards in agriculture have contributed to two decades of economic decline in 1970s and 1980s; paradoxically, the 'informal economy' has shown remarkable dynamism. ... Government *policies which protected and isolated industries have also proven disastrous* in many parts of the world. The former Soviet Union is probably the most extreme case... When governments has *interfered with prices and retarded competition, it has proven counterproductive.*
>
> On the other hand government investment in social sectors has... had high returns. It is no coincidence that China's average economic growth rate of

(11) Speech by Attila Karaosmanoğlu, Managing Director of World Bank, before the World Economic Forum in Davos, Bank's World, March 1993.

about 8% over the last decade has been accompanied not only by increasingly *open and 'market-oriented' policies*, but also by increased *public investment in education and health.*

(iii) Lessons from the East Asian miracle

Japan, the four dragons (South Korea, Taiwan, Hong-Kong and Singapore) and Indonesia, Malaysia and Thailand continued to grow steadily at high rates, unaffected by the oil shock. These countries pursued free-market oriented economic policies based on openness to market forces, export orientation, monetary and fiscal discipline, on one hand; and as well exercise infant industry protection and selective credit policies (interest subsidies), and take advantage of guidance provided by indicative economic planning, on the other.

Attila Karaosmanoğlu,(12) while pointing out that interventionist policies (selective credit and industrial policies) are not different from those of less successful countries; adds that "strategic interventions in industries in Korea and Singapore,... were much more effective than in Malaysia or Indonesia". He summarizes the lessons that can be drawn from the East Asian Economic Miracle as follows:

(1) Macroecomomic and stabilization policies and economic fundamentals were set right. Relative prices were not distorted unduly; bias against exports arising from protection policies was successfully neutralized; capital formation and savings rates were boosted e.g. Singapore increased domestic savings rate from zero in 1965 to 40% in 1992.

(2) Government interventions were constantly measured and disciplined against the yardstick of international and domestic competition; a failed action was removed, not ideology but market performance mattered and ruled.

(3) These countries had "high-quality management and policy making capabilities", implemented 'best practices', and had strong public institutions and independent civil services.

(4) High level of investment in human resources was realized, which had a high economic and social pay-off; the proportion of people in poverty was reduced from 30% in 1970 to 10% in 1990.

---

(12) Managing Director of World Bank, speech before the World Economic Forum in Davos, Bank's World, March 1993.

(5) There was economic and "political stability, and a development 'vision', regardless of the democratic or authoritarian complexion of various regimes." "Authoritarian regimes are not necessary for growth"; "empirical evidence suggests that growth proceeds at about the same rate in democratic and non-democratic regimes."

(6) Foreign aid and development assistance was made available in a timely manner and was used effectively; on per capita basis East Asia has received much less aid than Africa, but used it much more efficiently.

(7) East Asia approached intervention/'laissez-faire' issue by pragmatism, and with the concept of public/private partnership.

Karaosmanoğlu asserts that "intervention is essential for development-but intervention must be based on market-friendly principles", and that three basic guidelines should apply:

(1) *Intervene reluctantly*: Let markets work and intervene only when it is absolutely clear that they are not working.

(2) *Intervene flexibly*: "Policies must reflect economic and political realities"; failed policies have been reversed quickly; policies were adapted to suit different times and circumstances.

(3) Intervene openly: "Make interventions transparent and subject to rules rather than discretion"; "the most important intervention a government can make is to protect and maintain the rule of law in economic life-creating a level playing field on which everyone can compete."

(iv) Theoretical background of policy/reform packages

In applied economics and particularly in shaping policy proposals, one should not subscribe to any theory (Keynesian, structuralist, monetarism, etc.) on faith (abstract argumentation over superiority of this or that theory) and then reverse the course when expectations are not materialized, and opt for the other extreme, which appears to have occurred e.g. in Poland in 1990, and as in the early 1980s in the US and UK. One should rather determine the validity of assumptions of any theory inherent in the policy package considered or investigate thoroughly in advance implications of any policy move to be initiated.

The policy should be a mixture of measures designed to overcome structural bottlenecks without causing macroeconomic disequilibrium. An inflation rate exceeding 5-10% could not be attributed to structural factors since they would be due to demand-pull factors or a combination of demand-pull and cost-push factors. Incomes policies, monetary and fiscal discipline should be rather always geared to maintaining macroeconomic balance during the initial phases of transition period, and temporary balance of payments (BOP) improvements or stagflation arguments should not provide pretext for disequilibrating expansion.

If a careful balance in the 'big-bang' package, between price reform, minimum real wage and exchange rate is secured and the financial viability of the enterprise sector under hard-budget constraint assuming realistic performance targets is guaranteed, along with BOP and the budgetary equilibrium, then there would be no reason for cost-push effects through wage increases or currency devaluations or demand-pull effects of budgetary deficit or of additional enterprise subsidies; because in these estimates structural problems are accounted for and possibilities of cost-push or demand-pull effects are eliminated in advance.

Regarding the structuralist view on the transformation of Eastern Europe, which predicted 'the deep, long and inevitable recession' because of sector-specific capital and fixed assets, rigidities in redeployment of productive resources and factors, one can point out following view: *These countries have provided minimum living standards, at the least for masses and achieved high education/health standards, under the worst economic mechanism conceivable and allocating huge resources to defense, wasteful investments and bureaucracy and internal repression. Now to argue that these countries could not provide that minimum living standard for majority of people because of structural rigidities and transition, only means that the transformation is not building on existing though inefficient and obsolete productive capacity, but destroying it before replacing it by its efficient substitutes, which is now expected to be realized in an ever increasingly far distant future. Granting the effects of CMEA dismantlement which should be more than compensated by a cut in defense and internal security expenditures, and despite no significant change in foreign-aid inflow (at least from virtual moratorium on external debt) and more favorable treatment of exports in the western markets, the sharp decline in living standards of low-income group, successive output declines and resulting high inflation could not be attributed to structural rigidities or this outcome could not be described as stagflation calling for expansionary fiscal, monetary and exchange rate policies; because otherwise it becomes a too simplistic modelling of the real world since a permanent decline in the short-run potential output is the real cause of the problem.*

This outcome arose because of the wrong policies pursued, as explained in this book. In a similar pattern, while Korea and Taiwan (which were on a par with Turkey in 1970 and below in 1960, on a per capita income basis), attained developed status in the last 30 years, Turkey, many Latin American and Middle Eastern countries are still underdeveloped, because of unwise inflationary, wasteful economic and fiscal policies, and wrong investment decisions.

Except for 1923-1940 1946-53, and 1961-68 period, Turkish per capita income, under wasteful, consumption-oriented and inflationary policies, ever increasing government expenditures economically and financially unviable, low-or negative-return large-scale investment projects and programs, excessive investment in infrastructure, inefficient, wasteful and corrupt state enterprises (maximizing employment, rather than profits) and wrong economic and foreign exchange policies (encouraging consumption, speculative and real-estate investments), blind faith on Phillips trade-off between inflation and employment, as well as on merits of supply-side economics (overgenerous subsidies), excessive short-term external borrowing relied on as a permanent source of finance, from 1980 on achieving BOP equilibrium by frequent devaluations without exercising fiscal and monetary discipline, overvalued currency/exchange rate policy, belief in merits of dollarization which recently increased at excessive proportions. etc.) increased slightly after 1975, and Turkey at end 1992 is a country with $1600 per capita income, 5 million open and another 5 million disguised unemployment, chronic inflation running at 60-70% p.a., $56 billion external debt and with one of the worst income distribution and unjust taxation system, (heavy taxation of wage income and low or zero tax rates on profits, interest income and capital gains). The outcome is definitely the result of policies pursued, not of supply rigidities or fast population growth (2.5% p.a.) as many claim in Turkey. (On the contrary casual observations suggest that with fast economic growth the population growth rate declines to about 1%, and the reverse relationship does not work or exist.)

This subject will further be dealt with in Chapter 22.

29 Price formation after price liberalization

Certain aspects of this topic were dealt with in section 23 of this chapter.

(i) Cost-plus (markup) pricing

"Cost-plus pricing is a characteristic of socialist economies in transition"; in these countries enterprises explicitly pursued cost-plus routine. The pricing routine is related to the absence of any strong, market-based restraint on prices or wages, hence a *simple markup pricing system,* in which price movements (through government controls or behavior of monopolistic firms) reflect cost movements, describes well the pricing mechanism in a *partially reformed socialist economy.* As a consequence price and wage controls are called for the stability of the system. Prices are restrained by permissible markup margins and wages by the rate of expected inflation and productivity (Commander and Coricelli, 1992 Commander, 1992).

(ii) Polish experience in cost-plus pricing

Following price liberalization, most prices would follow the cost-plus principle, with supplies being adjusted to demand at these prices. Therefore, e.g. in the 1990 Polish reform, the anti-inflationary policy aimed to restrict the growth of unit nominal costs, in particular wage costs, and "the incomes policy was the primary instrument for controlling wages, especially in the state sector." It was, however, thought that incomes policy would not survive long and be sufficient unless supported by monetary, fiscal and exchange rate policies, with a view to hardening the budget constraint and increasing competition. "*Profit margins did vary significantly among enterprises and whole sectors,* as well as over time, indicating that *demand factors and market structure were also important." The relaxation of financial policies* in the second half of 1990 *led to wage, price and import increases, rather than domestic output,* as expected.(Gomulka, 1992).

In Poland many critics of the reform package have claimed that *the acceptance of 'cost-plus' pricing principle "rather added to inflation than restricted it"* and have preferred tough *administrative credit rationing rather than positive real interest rates* to control inflation. Gomulka (1992) points out that positive interest rates were needed "to prevent massive transfer of money from zloty to dollar accounts, to protect convertibility and to encourage savings."

(iii) Evaluation of Polish experience

Demand-pull versus cost-push causes of inflation argument in transition economics is not much meaningful, because both effects would coexist and reinforce each other, unless an orderly simultaneous comprehensive transformation is achieved. Because a partial or general price reform would lead to both input price (unit cost) increases and higher wage demands (cost-push inflation), subsequent accommodating monetary policy and softened budget constraints would entail demand-pull inflation.

In fact, prices, wages and monetary aggregates in Poland (1983-1990) moved together in the long run as result of *monetary accommodation,* not because of a causal relation running from money to prices. The role of wages in the transmission of inflationary impulses, during 1988-90 was important, while wages have been de facto indexed to prices (Commander and Coricelli, 1992).

Regarding a positive real interest rate policy, on top of Gomulka's remarks, one can add that the credit rationing can't achieve efficient allocation of investment funds. Moreover, if the two most important prices (interest rate and exchange rate) are not freely determined and fixed by the government, and do not reflect underlying market conditions, then market reform will proceed under grand distortions.

It is true that with high-inflation, real rates of interest become exorbitant (in Turkey 30-50% lending rates are normal) also due to high risk premiums and to effects of high compulsory reserve requirements), which in turn (i) cause public debt service payments to be an unbearable burden on the budget and (ii) prevents loan-financing of any productive investment, unless an interest subsidy is granted; the latter two factors increasing the budgetary deficit further fuel inflation. There is no other appropriate solution to this vicious circle other than stopping inflation quickly by appropriate measures.

Moreover dollarization of high-inflation open economies could not be stopped by positive real interest policy alone, if high inflation becomes chronic (see. e.g. Guidotti and Rodriguez, 1992), and uncertainties about economic prospects increase. In Turkey despite positive real interest rates, foreign exchange deposits as a percentage of money supply (M2) increased from 23% at end 1990, to 65% at end 1992.

The cost-plus or mark-up pricing rule is of old standing and employed by both manufacturing concerns and retail business in market economies in profit maximization and is helpful when precise cost and demand data are not available. Profit maximization is achieved by changing the mark-up percentage in line with sale performance; hence the cost-plus prices are adjusted according to the price elasticity of demand (see, e.g. Mansfield, 1990, pp. 416-422). As a consequence limitations imposed on mark-up pricing in transition economies, implies restoring price control and explicit or implicit subsidization.

On the other hand it is maintained that in Poland state enterprises following a *fixed markup rule, did not lower prices in 1990 when faced with excess supply* (Calvo and Coricelli, 1992, p.75). This, however, implies that prices are not freely determined in relation to demand changes in the state sector *obeying a rigid pricing rule. The mistake is not in the rule, but in its application.*

(iv) Propagation of inflation during transition and basic features of stabilization programs for reforming socialist countries

Inflation will surge when prices are decontrolled, because of monetary overhang, excessive money supply increase and wage increases (Osband, 1992/B).

Commander and Coricelli (1992) estimated dynamic price and wage equations for Hungary and Poland, using quarterly data that cover the reform period (Hungary: 1981-89; Poland: 1993-90) to analyze the role and weight of foreign prices and domestic factors in propagating inflation. In a partially reformed economy, the relationship between prices, wages and the role of the exchange rate in determining domestic inflation were analyzed. They found that foreign prices matter, but developments on the cost side are critical. They recommend that *any stabilization program adopted by reforming socialist economies, should include nominal anchors, wage restraints* in particular, in view of the absence of endogenous market based, equilibrating mechanisms (given full employment and an absence of conventional relation between output and prices). This fact shows the importance of incomes policy in any stabilization program (Commander, 1992). "By itself translation of repressed inflation into open inflation cannot explain the acceleration and persistence of inflation in reforming socialist economies" (Commander and Coricelli, 1992).

(v) Commander and Coricelli remedy for stabilization versus 'the suggested methodology'

Commander and Coricelli found that in socialist economies in transition, *increased reliance on price adjustments* to redress macroeconomic imbalances (Poland) *further destabilized the system and failed to address the sources of imbalances* (wage drift and cost increases due to currency devaluations). Countries employing administered prices and wage restraints to stabilize the system, (Hungary) were more successful in achieving stability. This is because of the absence of conventional equilibrating mechanism and the presence of *monopolistic pricing* behavior (Commander and Coricelli, 1992). Wage and price controls, however, only repress inflation and distort the price mechanism.

Under the *suggested methodology, since cost-side pressures* (price/wage spiral) *are minimized* by selecting equilibrium exchange rates and sustainable wage levels, the likelihood of macroeconomic stability is much greater than that of any other stabilization program.

30 Relative price distortions: effects of superficial remedies

Wrong relative prices in shortage economies *generate waste, distortion and inefficiencies (e.g. queuing)*, (Rollo and Stern, 1992).

(i) Rationing, queuing and corruption

According to Osband,

> wage workers are better off under *rationing* than under queuing or corruption. The wealth effect of rationing increases workers' demand for leisure, so that output is less than under corruption, but the more efficient use of labor leaves output higher than under queuing. As wages rise, rations grow both absolutely and in relation to wealth,

thereby increasing leisure. Wage hikes beyond a certain threshold, will cause both workers and the state to suffer. From a broader perspective, rationing is part of the problem and shortage economies need more not less flexible distribution and pricing. For any given wage, rationing is strictly better for workers than corruption, which is better than queuing. *Maximization of output or insiders'* welfare favors corruption over rationing and rationing over queuing. These rankings neglect the administrative costs. Rationing, which is the fairest, is the most costly to administer and the least fair corruption is cost free (Osband, 1992/A).

(ii) Food subsidies versus price hikes

Osband maintains that social justice argument against price increases are not quite valid, in particular in the former Soviet Union, since the real benefits of price controls to the poor are often meager (e.g. when differences in the amounts of meat purchased are taken into account, higher-income families received three times the meat subsidies of lower-income families) and the costs of shopping congestion may outweigh the superficial benefits even for the poor (Osband, 1992/A).

(iii) Black market and rents

"A transitional socialist economy may also be characterized by *shortages*. The government may continue to exert an influence over prices, and price controls may be associated with shortages, queues, and black market activity. In many socialist economies, the shadow economy is highly developed." It may be assumed that *black market activity exhausts the rents associated with the controlled price* (Dinopoulos and Lane, 1992). The latter conclusion, however, assumes that everybody is engaged in black market activity, which could not be universally true, hence some goods are simply wasted in consumption, industrial use or hoarding.

(iv) Increased supply of deficit goods without price change

"An alternative to official price increases is improved supply through redirection of state production, expansion of nonstate domestic production or import of foreign goods" (the latter sold at market clearing prices rather than at the low prices for domestic substitutes). In Poland in the 1980s the Pewex network of state stores, sold western goods virtually at domestic shadow prices (black-market prices). "Attempts in the former Soviet Union to improve the supply of consumer goods were of limited help." With a view to increasing labor productivity, a campaign was launched in May 1985 against alcohol consumption, but proved to be counterproductive by depriving the state of significant tax revenue and aggravating shortages of other goods (Osband, 1992/A).

(v) Underground economy: a necessary evil?

Parallel (black) market, underground economy (informal sector), which will develop with partial price reforms has now emerged in many countries in transition (e.g. in Hungary, Russia). There are arguments that governments should tolerate the illegal underground economy and avoid from criminalizing its participants, since it is a means of survival at times of economic collapse and it will surface gradually.

The black market economy is not a necessary evil, since it can be avoided with full-fledged price reform under the suggested methodology. The assumption that the underground economy would surface over time is a false premise, because the underground economy wherever emerged never vanishes; on the contrary it flourishes over time as experienced in Italy and Turkey; and aside from its damaging ethical and social effects, it continues to undermine fiscal, monetary and economic stability, at an increasing rate through tax-free and illegal activities. The Italian underground economy which used to be estimated at close to 25% of total gross national product (Lipsey et al, 1984, p. 513) is now estimated at 30% or more.

The underground economy becomes a necessary evil, if strict bureaucratic rules and regulations unduly hamper emergence and growth of small business, e.g. as in the Republic of South Africa, in the immediate post-Apartheid period, strict regulations against small black business could not be relaxed rightaway, and tolerating the illegal activity became a stop-gap measure in transition period. A similar tolerant attitude would pay off in the reforming socialist countries, in the short- to medium-run, for obvious reasons; in the long run, however, the policy should be reversed.

Because in many countries, e.g. in Turkey and Italy, underground economy has flourished because it has developed into a haven for illegal and tax-free activities ; and employment and small business opportunities created by it, is at the expense of tax-paying employment and small or medium-scale business (it merely substitutes for them). The simple solution is to weed out unnecessary bureaucratic entanglements against small business, which are never applied anyway, because of well-established vested interests which take roots with the tolerated emergence of illicit activities.

31 Exchange rate policy

(i) Difficulty of selecting the right exchange rate

Fischer agrees that it would be desirable to have fixed exchange rate and a convertible currency, but stresses *the difficulty of choosing the level at which to fix the rate.* "He agrees that fixing the rate would help stabilize the price level by controlling the price of imports and helping to stabilize inflationary expectations. Furthermore, he believes that at the microeconomic level, convertibility, *by introducing the world price system, would provide much more appropriate relative prices for guiding resource allocation"* than those that currently exist in the reforming socialist countries. "However, it is difficult to know what exchange rate to choose." Using the current black market rate, with its very low value for rubles, would produce an inflationary shock and would not provide much competition from imports.

> Fischer suggests setting a higher rate, one that would put Russian wages in the vicinity of $50 to $100 per month, but sustaining this rate in the next few years would require a stabilization fund, external financing, and the ability of authorities to prevent capital flight by exporters (Brainard and Perry, 1992).

The suggested method selects realistic rate that achieves BOP equilibrium, hence solves all these problems.

(ii) Undervaluation or overvaluation of the domestic currency

Large undervaluation of the exchange rate at the outset of the program would provide cushion and give some price rigidity in sectors (capital goods) where competition was restricted (Commander, 1992). However, as experienced in Eastern Europe, and observed by Rodrik, excessive devaluations of the domestic currency have prevented disciplining domestic price rises through foreign competition, i.e. despite trade liberalization the world price system has not been imported (Fischer, 1992).

According to Fischer (1992) the most important objective of exchange rate policy is to avoid significant overvaluation of the currency.

(iii) Effects of excessive undervaluation of the domestic currency

Gomulka notes that, any substantial devaluation creates a large gap between international and domestic prices for tradeables, which in turn causes domestic producers to pass any cost increases onto prices; and this outcome neither enhances competition, nor restrains inflation. Moreover "any devaluation has a chance to stimulate exports, if it increases prices and therefore reduces the real money balances in the economy, similar to a contractionary monetary policy" (Gomulka, 1992, p.365) and hence may lead to a recession.

Whereas under the suggested method, all prices will initially be set at their equilibrium levels, given the new exchange rate and initial real money balances could be estimated and determined accordingly, not to cause any disturbance; moreover no excessive cushion (protection) will be provided to domestic tradeable producing sectors, since the exchange rate will be realistic and tariff protection moderate; hence foreign competition will be definitely introduced and the world price system will be imported.

(iv) Effects of overvalued currency on inflation

In Poland the "massive use of the exchange rate and low tariffs to reduce inflation during most of 1991" was a controversial issue (Gomulka, 1992, p. 370).

Lowering the rate of inflation through overvalued currency and low tariffs (in Turkey even at zero rate) is a costly palliative since inflation could not be stopped unless its root causes are routed, as economic rationale suggests and the Turkish experience during 1980s shows. Moreover, in such a framework there exists an inconsistency, while increased foreign competition compels enterprises to structural adjustment and improved efficiency, continuing inflation albeit at lower rates provides room for waste and inefficiencies through passing on any cost increases to prices, in particular in sectors where foreign competition is not significant or effective, because of imperfect competition (particularly in the distribution channels).

This policy also would discourage private and direct foreign investment in Poland, as against high levels of private investment achieved in Hungary and former Czechoslovakia, until 1991 (Pfeffermann and Madarassy, 1993).

(v) Feasibility and benefits of wage and exchange rate anchors

Unless monetary and fiscal discipline and stability are to a great extent secured, anchoring exchange rate becomes very wasteful and wage anchor is not politically, etc. sustainable; and indexation of wages creates a built-in inflationary mechanism within the economy.

(vi) Effects of trade liberalization while anchoring exchange rate in a high-inflation economy: the case of Turkey in the 1980s

Turkey in the early 1980s liberalized the foreign trade regime and dismantled the foreign exchange control system. Equilibrium in balance of payments (BOP) was maintained by floating the exchange monetary rate (virtually continuous devaluations), generous export rebates and huge external borrowing. The floating exchange rate mechanism, being designed for and helpful with redressing minor disturbances to BOP, without resorting to fiscal and monetary measures, exacerbated the inflation running at 5% monthly rates, as should have been expected, unless accompanied by measures exerting fiscal and monetary discipline.

From early 1980s on generous export rebates (including on fictitious exports) and huge increase in net foreign indebtedness, (from $14.7 billion at end 1978 to about $56 billion at end 1992, excluding the foreign exchange deposits of $14 billion with the banking system and the debt from military credits).

Using exchange rate as nominal anchor, in a high-inflation open economy to control inflation has dangerous consequences, as indicated above. Survival and emergence of import-substituting and infant industries would be jeopardized; imports, profit transfers abroad, capital outflow and industries with high imported input requirements would be encouraged; and as a consequence productive investments and growth rate are bound to slow down.

Actual outcome confirmed these expectations. Import dependence of the Turkish economy increased in 1985 twofold compared with 1973 and 1979 and 2.5-3 times compared to 1968, according to various criteria employed (Şenesen, 1990). Share of productive investments (agricultural, mining and manufacturing investments) in GNP declined from 7.4% in 1984 to 5% in 1990. During this period while the productive investments of public sector declined as a consequence of the government policy to reduce the share of public sector in the economy, it was observed that productive private investments also declined simultaneously (Yeldan, 1990). While Turkish industrialization followed the growth pattern of countries such as South Korea and Portugal until 1980, after 1980 it diverted from that pattern concentrating on small-scale light industries, with an increasing share of the food and beverages and textile sector (whose share was declining until 1980, as in the said countries) and manufacturing investments in 1989 declining to 55% of the 1975 level (Özmucur and Özötün, 1990).

In parallel to these developments Turkish income growth rate in the 1980s was relatively small in contrast with the huge infusion of foreign capital over the period. Turkish per capita income grew at annual rate of 3.1% during 1950-60 and 3.8% during 1962-70, with moderate external borrowing (in fact total external debt was less than $2 billion in 1970). Per capita income growth rate (measured in 1987 US dollars) was 2.1% during 1970-80 and 2.75% during 1980-90. In this outcome, excessive increase in consumption as a result of various factors, policy measures and chronic inflation and inflationary expectations and unsatisfactory performance of investments played a role. Over the 1980-89 period, against 5.1% annual increase in GDP, consumption increased by 5.6% and gross domestic investments by 3.7% in real terms. Gross domestic investment per capita declined from $300 in 1988 to $250 in 1991.

32 Wage and incomes policy, wage drift and wage price spiral, and need for wage restraint

(i) Need for incomes policy and tax on excessive wage increments

In reforming socialist economies, so long as the *ownership of enterprises is ambiguous,* firms will tend to pay out excessive amounts to workers and other stakeholders, which may result in *decapitalization of the firm.* In order to control inflation wage increases have to be curbed, say by *taxing excessive wage increases* as in Poland. Since wage setting in state-owned firms is not determined by market forces, as in Poland *the tax should only apply to the public sector and private firms should be exempt,* which would provide an incentive to privatize (Fischer, 1992).

According to Gomulka, in Poland *not this tax,* but the substantial deterioration in the *liquidity position* of state-owned enterprises in early 1991 due to new supply and demand shocks related to foreign trade and a non-accommodating monetary policy, have contributed to the relative wage restraint (Gomulka, 1992). Moreover since tax collection is a problem in Russia, it is not clear how successfully this tax could be enforced, also because evasion will be widespread.

Furthermore, *tax arrears* and their payment would be blamed for job losses and would be used as a pretext for *unfair competition from private firms,* and hence would be a contentious issue with the government.

Instead, *fixing the average wage level for state enterprises* (or setting ceilings on the average level) with penalties to be specified, could be more effective and also could improve efficiency (observing the average level, key personnel could be given higher wage increases according to their marginal productivity). This is the *routine adopted by the suggested method.* Kornai (1990) also recommends wage restraint.

Paying the tax still higher wages could be paid, defeating the purpose of the stabilization program. This would be the case *when the profitability or liquidity position of enterprises improves* because of macroeconomic, sectoral or other reasons (not related to better management or performance of the enterprises); and then one really needs binding wage restraints.

(ii) Wage subsidy and high wage policy

"*Sustained subsidization on the job is undesirable* because it demoralizes workers and retards the urgent task of modernization and restructuring. A better approach is to pay *unemployment compensation,* provide education and *training premiums,* and create financing vehicles for *small business.*" A wage policy linked to productivity is essential (Dornbusch and Wolf, 1992).

Views on effects of higher wages on productivity growth are divergent. In relation to the eastern German transition, while Akerlof and Yellen argue that higher wages induce greater work effort and rise in productivity; Charles Murray claims that, simultaneously raising wages and unemployment benefits would have little effect on productivity (Dornbusch and Wolf, 1992, Comments and Discussion). The other reforming countries, should not opt for higher wages, during initial phases of transition; in order to curb consumption, generate funds for modernization and restructuring and attract foreign investment, and later align wage increases to productivity increases.

(iii) Wage drift and wage regulation

Commander cautions against *wage drift* because of uncertainty over ownership and future profitability, in view of the dominance of labor-dominated (worker-controlled) firms in these economies, i.e., where wages and employment are jointly maximized, workers will not be directly constrained by labor demand curve but by the firms' profit level. Wages will tend to be equal to average rather than marginal product, depending on government aversion to bail-outs (i.e. the soft budget constraint), (Commander, 1992).

Wage regulation is called for in view of the institutional legacy and tendency for wage drift emanating from decentralization and uncertainty. Wage regulation implies efficiency loss and impedes the appropriate adjustment of relative wages, its opportunity cost (the macroeconomic cost of abandoning wage control), however, justifies it. As a consequence incomes policies (various types of wage control) have been applied in Poland, Czechoslovakia, Hungary and Romania in regulating the wage bill (Commander, 1992).

How long these wage controls should be maintained is an open question, in view of the emerging private sector and efficiency loss related to relative wage structure, labor allocation and aggregate employment.

(iv) Wage policy in a shortage economy

Osband shows the danger of nominal wage increases in an economy with fixed official prices, which will reduce labor productivity, exacerbate social inequality (and even harm workers if shortages are sufficiently widespread) and concludes that "the *central lesson* for policymakers in reforming shortage economies is the need to *keep wage liberalization from outpacing price liberalization,* preferably through acceleration of the latter" (Osband, 1992/A).

Osband maintains that, in reforming socialist economies relaxation of wage controls without hardening budget constraints on enterprises or freeing consumer goods prices, can be dangerously destabilizing. Higher wages tend to exacerbate shortages and lead to waste and corruption. Economy wide wages hikes, beyond a certain level, will also worsen worker welfare (Osband, 1992/A).

As a remedy for the economic crisis in reforming shortage economies, Osband recommends

> *reduction in the official real wage, through higher official prices for deficit goods.* In a queuing equilibrium, higher official prices will shift effort from shopping to material production. In a corruption equilibrium, higher official prices will reduce the purchasing power of insiders. In a rationing equilibrium, higher official prices will shift income from rations to wages, which will induce more productive effort. In all three cases, shadow prices will fall and the range of deficit goods will shrink. If *all prices are allowed to float,* there will be *no deficit goods* and *nominal wage increases* will leave *real variables unchanged, apart from money balance effects.*

Official price hikes, however are extremely sensitive politically and "stormily protested regardless of the net social gain, because the losses are concentrated and the benefits diffused" (Osband, 1992/A).

(v) Wage policy episode in Poland during 1990/1991, complications which arose, wage/price spiral and appraisal of policy

In the first half of 1990, wages remained significantly below the ceiling levels specified, because of the liquidity squeeze experienced by enterprises, as a result of the sharp decline in real money balances, which in turn was a consequence of a much higher inflation in the first quarter than estimated.

In the second half of 1990, as a consequence of relaxation of fiscal and monetary policies, which turned out to be greater than planned, enterprises could increase wages above the ceiling levels specified by the incomes policy for the second half of 1990. Therefore "it was necessary for enterprises to reduce nominal wages at the start of 1991, just at the time when inflation accelerated owing to a new wave of increases in administrative prices, which caused 'a near-mass revolt against the policy'."

However, due to a substantial deterioration in the liquidity position of state enterprises, low-wage policy could be maintained in early 1991. The latter was because of loss of exports to the former CMEA area, increase in import prices from that area, lower profitability of exports to the West and increased competition from Western imports, the latter two due to continuing fixed exchange rate. Moreover a non-accommodating monetary policy was initiated to fight inflation. These new pro-recessionary supply and demand shocks caused grave problem for the budget, and are bound to increase bankruptcies and unemployment. These, however, is considered the necessary cost of structural adjustment (Gomulka, 1992, pp. 366-67).

In fact the root causes of these complications are:

(a) failure to estimate correctly the price effects of reform measures and adjust wages accordingly initially, in order to avoid wage/price spiral thereafter and frequent policy course reveals;

(b) and conducting an overly unrealistic exchange rate policy, without properly taking into account effects of immediate creation of an extremely open economy on the competitiveness of producing sectors (quantitative import restrictions and exchange control were abolished, average tariff protection was lowered to 4%) and continue with the fixed exchange rate for almost two years (to fight against inflation), at the cost of substantial export losses and thereby enhancing the competitiveness of western imports and lowering profits of enterprises and employment.

Although an alternative policy of devaluation to a realistic exchange rate would not have reduced real money balances on impact due to large proportion of dollarization (Gomulka, 1992), (households' wealth however in real, dollar terms would not have changed to induce a rise in consumption) relative prices of domestic and imported tradeables would have been changed in favor of domestic production and exports, and imports would have been curbed. And labor might have preferred a decline in real wages to impending unemployment (The latter phenomenon has already been observed in Poland; see Gomulka 1992, pp. 369-70). As a consequence, there would have been some slow-down in structural adjustment, but this should have been acceptable, in view of the major breakthrough (price reform and extremely open economy) already accomplished.

(vi) Dollar wage rate (the Russian case) and exchange rate and the current account convertibility

The following arguments by Fischer (1992) that are related to the wage rate and exchange rate tie in perfectly with the suggested method; the latter providing the mechanism for determining an average wage rate for Russia possibly at $50-100, at any rate a realistic wage and exchange rate.

According to Fischer (1992), "one attraction of convertibility at a fixed exchange rate is that there would then be a clear monetary policy rule: to conduct monetary policy so as to maintain the exchange rate". This would help, but is not sufficient; "the nominal anchor of exchange rate would have to be supplemented by a nominal anchor on, say, domestic credit, so that domestic inflation would not first erode competitiveness and then force a devaluation, as often has happened-including in Poland in 1991".

But Fischer adds that

> *the exchange rate should not be hold fixed no matter what. The exchange rate anchor is most needed in the early stages of stabilization and reform* and may have to be moved to a *crawling peg* or other system after some time. *The most important objective of exchange rate policy must be to avoid significant overvaluation of the currency* (Fischer, 1992).
>
> The usual argument for a fixed exchange rate rule *during stabilization* is that it ensures that the supply of money will adjust automatically to relevant *demand shifts at a time when shifts in the demand function are difficult to predict.* However this argument assumes that there are no capital controls

and hence would not apply to reforming socialist economies (Fischer, 1992).

Convertibility allows the country to import the appropriate, world price system, because:

> essentially current account convertibility is the same thing as *trade liberalization.* ... Current account convertibility is not consistent with widespread quantitative restrictions on trade or foreign exchange licensing, but could be *consistent with tariffs* and export subsidies or taxes. In most reforming Eastern European countries, tariffs have been reduced to lower and more uniform levels than was typical in the reforming countries of Latin America (Fischer, 1992).

Nordhaus observes that, given the current exchange rates at between 80 rubles to 140 rubles to the dollar as of April 1992, external convertibility of the ruble is a long way off. Hence Nordhaus and Summers have found Fisher's recommendations of an exchange rate of 10 rubles to the dollar implying very substantial appreciation, as unrealistic (Fischer, 1992).

The fixed rate will determine the course of subsequent inflation.

> Setting the initial exchange rate at about the current market rate (120 rubles per $ in early 1991) would create an inflationary shock and would not provide any competition from imports. *Rodrik, in reviewing the Eastern European experience,* has found that *trade liberalization through helping import a price system,* has not achieved its proclaimed aim (i.e. *foreign competition has not disciplined domestic price rises), because of the excessive devaluations* of the domestic currency (Fischer, 1992).

The current free market rate could not provide a useful yardstick, because the market is thin (most trade is not conducted at that rate) and the rate can be moved by small amounts of foreign exchange (Fischer, 1992). E.g. on March 23, 1993 when rate was 684 rubles per US dollar, total sales amounted to $60 million, including intervention by the Central bank.

This is the recent indication of the absurd 'dollar shop' syndrome explained above. This market rate does not reflect the purchasing power of ruble, but the dramatic decline in Russia's export receipts and imports, and the much more restricted supply to this free market (E.g. Nordhaus notes that Russia ran out of hard currency in the 1991/92 winter, Fischer, 1992).

According to *Summers, relative wages at current market exchange rates are well below levels likely to prevail if the currency stabilizes.* At the current exchange rates, wages are in the $10 to $20 range. Nordhaus observes that

> at an exchange rate of 100 rubles per dollar, in the first quarter of *1992 wage rate was $10 per month, and at this rate, Russia ties Ethiopia as the world's second poorest country.* The under-valued exchange rate results in such *absurdities* in the price system as gasoline selling at 4 cents a gallon, bread selling at 3 cents a loaf, and subway costing 0.5 cent a ride, along with restaurant meals that cost Russians several months' salary and a *total Russian GNP less than Hong Kong's (at current exchange rates),* (Fischer, 1992).

Fischer (1992) prefers *setting of the initial exchange rate at level, which allowing some subsequent inflation, would put dollar wages in the vicinity of $50 to $100 per month.* Feasibility of this depends on the availability of a stabilization fund and other external financing, and on the extent of preventing capital flight. Summers observes that Fischer's proposal leading dollar *wages to increase from $10-20 range to $100 per month,* world entail *a dramatic appreciation,* which he considers *unrealistic.* In view of the fact that *the monthly Polish wage was at $75*; he suggest $50 for Russia. Summers also adds that *"any kind of fixed exchange rate is not a viable option until some control on macroeconomic fundamentals is achieved"* (Fischer, 1992).

33 Output and productivity effects of switch to market-led economy

With market reform, *output in the short run is likely to contract* because of adjustment costs, monopolistic behavior, credit constraints, liquidation of previously hoarded inventories and uncertainty about the new economic environment (Osband, 1992/B).

(i) East German experience

Initial impact of transition to a market economy, with a new set of prices and techniques is an immediate reduction in GDP because of (i) tougher environmental standards and (ii) economic obsolescence (including no demand for some products at any price) and (iii) a very sharp rise in real wages. In Eastern Germany, the initial impact was 40% decline in GDP per capita. High and rising wage level, also played an important and singular role in this outcome, (rising real wages in Eastern Germany is a peculiarity of German economic union, and will reduce output and growth effect of investments due to increasing capital intensity (Dornbusch and Wolf, 1992). Lastly, closure of inefficient plants also led to initial output decline, unless their value-added were negative.

In Eastern Germany "most of the adjustment has and will take the form of job displacement. However, a good part of that unemployment and underemployment is resolved by emigration and commuting, and the rest will provide ample labor supply for investment-led output growth" (Dornbusch and Wolf, 1992).

The shift to market economy improves *productivity*, in the first phase by means of eliminating the worst inefficiencies (by closing down highly inefficient operations), reducing labor hoarding and restoring incentives through market mechanism. In this first phase, the movement is from the interior to the frontier of the production possibilities set, for given factor supplies and technologies. In the following stages productivity increase will result from the adoption of better technologies (replacement of existing factor supplies with state-of-the-art technology) and increased factor supplies, particularly the productive capital stock (Dornbusch and Wolf, 1992).

Privatization by selling to foreign firms, is an important vehicle for rapid technology transfer and capital accumulation. Availability of a large pool of educated and generally skilled labor (which guarantees that capital accumulation will not run into bottlenecks due to a shortage of skills for a long time) and the less 'green' attitudes of the population and administration should attract foreign investment (Dornbusch and Wolf, 1992).

Moreover if productivity grows rapidly, unemployment will increase sharply in the short-run, which makes quick productivity increase a mixed blessing for reforming socialist countries (Dornbusch and Wolf, 1992).

"All the Eastern European *transition economies should reap a one-time productivity gain that derives from their unusual isolation.* The more easily a country can gain access to and implement foreign knowledge [technology] and can attain an efficient international division of labor, the larger these gains will be" (Dornbusch and Wolf, 1992).

Lewis Alexander, has pointed out that, the inefficiencies of the old socialist system did not only manifest themselves in fixed capital and the lack of appropriate incentives but also caused resources other than capital to be used inefficiently. The elimination of these other inefficiencies through the introduction of the incentives of a market system, will increase productivity, without further investment (Dornbusch and Wolf, 1992, Comments and Discussions).

(ii) Output and productivity under 'the suggested method'

At the first phase, productivity gains are most easily achieved by closing down highly inefficient operations. There is a conflict between achieving high productivity and achieving high employment (Dornbusch and Wolf, 1992). Under the comprehensive approach of the method, at the first stage the main aim is to implement a full price reform and liberal trade regime, with low inflation and unemployment rates and viable macroeconomic balances; productivity gains through major plants close-downs should get priority at the next phase. By lowering real wages and raising customs tariffs, and paying subsidies, socially/politically undesirable major plant close-downs could be postponed at this stage, depending also on the fiscal and monetary balance. It is better to align job displacements through closure with job-creation in the private sector and with investment-led output/employment growth over time and also take into account the burden on the budget of the social safety net system to be redesigned. Exercises conducted under the method, in the preparatory stage, would provide enough evidence to convince enterprise managements and labor unions of the necessity for strict obedience to the hard budget constraint and low real wages.

Chapter 6

Some further thoughts, remarks and observations

Some further thoughts, remarks and observations

1 Price formation and resource allocation under Soviet-type socialism

In a classic Soviet type economy, *wages and prices are fixed by central plan bureau, through which production and wholesale trade are directly regulated.* The wastefulness of this system is now almost universally conceded (Osband, 1992/A).

The socialism experience brought is downfall by setting up an artificial pricing system without regard to supply and demand functions in the markets and by imposing a central allocation of resources. Command-type central planning employing material input-output balances, sophisticated mathematical tools and shadow (scarcity) prices aimed at solving resource allocation problem through centralization. Oscar Lange (1970, 1971) had pointed out that cybernetics had great potential as a scientific tool of management in the socialist economy.

An attempt was made in USSR to improve the pricing formula and mechanism under *Liberman reforms.* Liberman (1966) proposed that the planned or actual prices should include entire cost of production (not only labor cost) and a profit margin as well. And a new planning and incentive system was introduced in 1967-68, along with introduction of new wholesale prices for industrial goods. Under the new system, wholesale prices were to be determined such that, enterprises would be able to recover their production costs (*recoupment of full costs) plus a profit margin* (Sharpe, 1966/A).

Reforms of wholesale prices were to be carried out without any rise in retail prices. Retail prices could only be revised downward. The wholesale prices should correspond to the economic interrelations between industry and agriculture. Costs should include *geological* prospecting outlays for extracting industries, *amortization of assets* (depreciation charges for fixed assets) and social security contributions.

Prices should be fixed for branches and specific products. All enterprises of a given branch, should establish *uniform prices. Outlays* should form the basis of *planned prices.* Opinions differ regarding socially necessary labor outlays. Planned prices should reflect the relative capital-output ratios of different products (Sharpe, 1966/B).

The planned prices (pricing formula) comprise (i) production cost (material outlays per unit, including amortization), (ii) wages and social security contribution, (iii) a profit margin on production assets, (iv) rent payments and turnover tax. Territorially differentiated prices were acceptable.

Prices calculated at enterprise or sector level were checked by means of a mathematical-economic model of planned prices *at the State Planning Committee.*

There was a dual system of prices, (i) some for the consumers, (ii) others for the producers (accounting prices). The wholesale prices of industry and the accounting prices of enterprises were uniform or zonal for consumers (Sharpe, 1966/B).

Nemchinov (1962) argued that, planned prices should be improved; by improvement of planned prices and selection for the enterprise of appropriate assortment of output, it would be possible to *liquidate money losing operations* of many enterprises and plants.

In the socialist system it was assumed *excess demand and overproduction* to lead to required changes in production and investment without changing prices. Any change in prices (also wages, interest rate and rent) is made by the central authority (Miesczankowki, 1969). *Prices in a socialist economy are tools only.* The Central Plan Bureau sets prices and incomes (Zielinski, 1969).

"There is not *clarity* in the fundamental issues of the *theory, methods and techniques of proper price fixing for capital and consumer goods."* Even *equilibrium in markets* (demand=supply) in socialist economy does not really *mean that supply equals demand;* because consumers buy some commodities because there is no other choice (Zielinski, 1969).

Chichocki obtains *optimum resource allocation strategy* and optimum value of the net national product which *is a parametric function of prices,* i.e. depends parametrically on prices. *Proper selection of prices is a most difficult job.* Prices should provide for market equilibrium (Chichocki, 1979). Even when *the price and cost system reflect the marginal rate of transformation,* market equilibrium at a constant price will be achieved when there exist *adequate stocks* and reserves (in *productive capacity* as well), (Zielinski, 1969). In the socialist planning the *prices of products reflect the amount of labor required in production and there is no reason that these should lead to equilibrium between demand and supply* (Nemchinov, 1964).

Scarcity prices for raw materials and fuel and other prices were based, in theory and practice, on labor input (marginal-cost pricing) (Nemchinov, 1964). *Planned prices (accounting prices) diverged from market prices for consumer goods;* for producer goods no such market existed (Maksimovic, 1969).

2 Soviet economic theory and practice

(i) Development of the Soviet economic theory

The Soviet economic theory began with NEP, continued with the Stalinist political economy of Socialism, followed by Kantorovich's mathematical approach and the system of optimally functioning economy and finally Popov, Shelev and Shatalin in Perestroika; which shows a move from central planning to market economy, i.e. as reform develops more features of a market economy are incorporated into socialism. The first stage of reform attempted to *rationalize the 'single factory model'*; the second stage devolves some economic power to enterprises; the third stage is Brus's planned economy with built-in market mechanism tried in Hungary (Sutela, 1991) and the last stage will be transition to full market economy (Sutela, 1991).

The Soviet planning was not democratic; and Sutela (1991) is of the opinion that *Soviet economics can not provide the basis for a successful reform.*

(ii) From Kantorovich to Gorbachev

Kantorovich's linear optimization method, aimed at *maximization of a politically pre-determined product mix* (Sutela, 1991).

Gorbachev's reform policy, until 1987 was based on *dual-track planning* idea, (which originates from the former system of optimally functioning economy) and was doomed to failure, because *markets are regarded as a technical device* which can be used at will (Sutela, 1991).

Mikhail Gorbachev made a losing campaign to save the 'Communist experiment' which collapsed in the wake of the August 1991 coup. Gorbachev has not started with any grand design, but wanted to tackle with the country's problems realistically and *pragmatically. Piecemeal reform approach* in economy, however called for more sweeping measures; economic disruption and desperate cures only worsened the crisis (White, 1991).

(iii) Perestroika and gradualism

White (1991) suggests that *despite the inconsistencies and limitations of perestroika, the Soviet Union might have been better in every respect if the coup had not occurred and the gradualist reform process had continued.*

The Enterprise Law of 1988, worsened the problem rather than solving it (White, 1991). *"Enterprises in localities run in a personal way almost as 'suzerainties' by local bosses"* ; devolution of central power led to a situation which *contradicts both a free market and the rule of law. Coupons and barter* have replaced the ruble and orders from central authorities and a vacuum of political and legal power have emerged which led to the emergence of local autarchies. Goods and services are distributed by the local bosses, and the 'suzerainties' of the other republics through the 'mafia connection' (Merridale and Ward, 1991). Forsyth [1] notes that corruption and the local mafias, and even the narcotics trade were widespread even in 1986.

3 Reasons for the collapse of socialism

(i) Failure of partial reforms: wage rises lead to universal shortages

Spending on surplus goods can be partly identified as savings, and sum of the surplus goods not sold to consumers may be directed to export, consumption of non-workers or domestic investment (Osband, 1992/A).

All these including change in inventories, are automatically investment by definition. Hence increased production of surplus goods, under centrally planned economies might have been the result of a deliberate policy to increase private savings (monetary overhang) by reducing private consumption, and to increase exports and investments and to record greater capital accumulation performance even by inventory increase in surplus goods. Conversely, creation of shortages in consumer goods could have been a means of repression policy in the form of (forced savings and humiliation of queuing) not only the result of the absence of market mechanism and mistakes of central planning. This factor (policy) may partly explain too high gross investment/GDP ratios in the socialist economies and the failure of the 1980 reforms. In fact Cottarelli and Blejer (1992) observe that, "the persistence of shortages would enhance *social discipline*", e.g. social tensions "could be eased by allowing temporary increases of the supply of consumer goods at the most appropriate moment."

In such a policy framework, however, nominal wage increases along with partial price reform, as observed in 1980s, would have caused the collapse of the economy. Osband (1992/A) shows that with fixed output proportions determined by central planners, extra wages will always have to be spent on surplus goods and shadow prices for deficit goods also rise further. As wages continue to rise, the range of surplus goods narrows (possibly with discrete jumps) and vanishes ultimately, and once the shortage becomes universal the economy collapses.

---

(1) James Forsyth, "Review on Simon (1991)" , Soviet Studies, Vol.44, No.4, 1992, pp. 719-720.

(ii) Increased reliance on imported technology and capital

According to Dembinski (1991), at the core of planned socialism was Marxist social theory combined with Bolshevist political and social institutions. Material (input-output) balance is at the core of the central planning of socialist economies. Allocation of resources (resource requisitioning) and the valuation of labor were plagued with problems; accounting was ineffective and money was never allowed to play its full role. Planning, requisitioning and valuation dilemmas were exacerbated by the arms race and external dilemmas, namely the chronically poor performance of foreign trade due to administratively fixed prices. In lieu of generating a process of improving technical methods(2) and organization of the economy, the planned economy *increasingly relied on imported technology and foreign capital*, with the result of mounting debts. All this ultimately brought about the collapse of socialism, according to Dembinski (1991).

Huge external debts and large debt service payments have exposed the weaknesses of the Soviet-type socialist system, and thereby helped to bring about its downfall (Gomulka, 1992).

(iii) Final phase

Reasons for the break-up of the Soviet Union include (a) unsatisfactory social conditions, (b) the spiritual vacuum left by official ideology (Simon, 1991), (c) economic decline, (d) hypocrisy and cynicism which characterized the pre-perestroika Soviet Union, (e) corruption, the local mafias and the narcotics trade.(3)

(iv) Bardhan and Roemer analysis

According to Bardhan and Roemer (1992), the socialist economic experiment failed because of "(a) state ownership of the means of production, (b) non-competitive, non-democratic politics and (c) command/administrative allocation of resources and commodities". Negating (b) and (c) they maintain that "a feasible economic mechanism of competitive socialism" is possible without necessarily replacing state or public ownership of the means of production with traditional private ownership. Public ownership is redefined "to mean that the

(2) E.g. the plant and machinery being used for sugar processing in the former Soviet has not changed since before the 1917 revolution, (Speech by A.Karaosmanoğlu, Managing Director of the World Bank, before the World Economic Forum in Davos, Bank's World, March 1993).

(3) James Forsyth, "Book Review on Simon (1991)", *Soviet Studies*, Vol.44, no.4, 1992, pp. 719-720.

distribution of the profits of firms is decided by the political democratic process" while the firms might be controlled by private agents.

Bardhan and Roemer (1992) maintain that the problem with the traditional public ownership of firms, is the failure to separate political from economic criteria in decision-making concerning firms, as revealed by the soft-budget constraint. They propose a system by which firms are removed from "the state's orbit" and placed under a "bank-centric insider monitoring" (the final discipline in monitoring managements is administered by banks responsible for financing the firms' operations). They prefer this system to Western-style capitalism on grounds that, (a) the institutions of Western capitalism evolved over a long period, hence they could not be readily duplicated in reforming socialist economies. They observe that the underdevelopment of capital markets in late 19th century Germany gave rise to its present system of heavy bank involvement in the financing and management of industrial companies. (b) Such a system would have a more egalitarian form of income distribution. It would be more sensitive to social needs such as education, health care and environmental protection (Bardhan and Roemer, 1992). An evaluation of this proposal is made in Chapter 12.

4 Individuals' behavior in ex-socialist countries: 'Homo Sovieticus'

The analyses of transforming socialist economies rather focus on "macroeconomic management, developing institutions, property rights and a legal system appropriate to a free market economy. But many observers are concerned that *people who had lived for so long under communism are now ill-equipped to operate in a market economy*". Hence it is essential that individuals' behavior must change in order the transition to succeed; Shiller, Boycko and Korobov (1992) attempted to find out

> what shapes the economic behavior of the people of the ex-communist countries; ... [and whether individuals from these countries hold] fundamentally different attitudes and views of the economy than people who live in market economies, ... [and] whether the observed differences are so deeply ingrained that they will not change for a long time, or whether differences in people's perceived situations are responsible for differences in behavior. If the latter is the case, behavior might change readily when those situations (along with the expectations they engender) are changed.

Shiller et al (1992) suggest that "the speed with which individuals' behavior can change will affect the speed of adjustment that can be expected in these economies. If situational influences predominate, reforms can proceed quickly.

By contrast if attitudinal factors predominate, policymakers may need to be cautious about the transition to a market economy". Shiller et al found out that 92% of the responses obtained on 2670 interviews, most of them on telephone (in Russia, Ukraine, eastern Germany, USA, Japan and Western Germany) *show "greater, and statistically significant, situational problems in the ex-communist countries* compared to advanced capitalist countries. By contrast, questions about *attitudes reveal no consistent pattern of differences* between ex-communist and advanced capitalist countries".

Shiller et al (1992) comparing attitudes between eastern and western Germany found that market-oriented attitudes are more prevalent among the eastern Germans. Comparing Russia and Ukraine, no significant difference in attitudes appeared, and only a slight suggestion that situational factors were more favorable in Ukraine than in Russia.

The *prevailing situations* in the ex-communist countries would lead people to *take a relatively short-term view and to avoid making long-term commitments.*

Shiller et al conclude that

> *it is quite misleading to refer to homo sovieticus as a distinct breed of person, defined by deep-seated attitudinal differences.* Rather, situational factors appear to be much more important in shaping behavior, so that behavior can be expected to change noticeably as situations and expectations are altered. ... [They] don't see greater timidity, fear of change, or lack of ambition among people in the ex-communist countries as impediments to privatization and movement to a market-based, incentive-driven economy, ... [but] believe that the *situational problems are important,* ... [and] find that *people trust current institutions relatively less in the communist countries and are more likely to believe that the government creates problems that will undermine their own efforts* (Brainard and Perry, 1992).

Shiller et al

> suggest that the situational problem might constitute a *bad expectations equilibrium* in which a vicious circle of poor expectations keeps people from investing in the system, which in turn causes the system to fail, justifying poor expectations ...; [and] believe that *such perceptions might be altered by visible changes in laws, regulations and property rights* (Brainard and Perry, 1992).

One can conclude that the suggested method's comprehensive, radical, fresh and once-and-for-all approach will greatly enhance overcoming the "situational problems", removing "bad expectations" and changing people's attitude of aversion from "making long-term commitments", and promote rapid transformation.

5 Growth prospects in the reforming socialist countries

(i) Growth prospects

Rollo and Stern (1992) even under optimistic assumptions regarding reform and restructuring, foreign aid and exports, in the reforming socialist countries, expect output declines in the short run and point out that "in general, all current forecasts suggest substantial falls in output until at least 1993" and some countries (e.g. former USSR) can not resume positive growth until 1996.

The World Bank view [4] is that,

> if the [Russian] government moves forward with reforms as planned, the decline in production nationwide could be stabilized within a year or two, with growth resuming by 1994 or 1995. ... Inflation could drop to more normal levels-about 20% p.a. by 1994 [and] significant private flows of capital could materialize by the middle of this decade.

On the basis of the standard UNESCO and ILO *human capital* indicators (enrollments in various level of education and proportion of higher grade occupations in the workforce, which suggest that the former Soviet Union and East Europeans are on par with the rest of Europe), Rollo and Stern suggest that "levels of productivity at market exchange rates on a par with Greece or Portugal are attainable." Cohen, also on the basis of human and physical capital considerations, estimates the long term growth potential of Eastern Europe and the former Soviet Union at around 4% per year. However, *before growth resumes in these countries, output will continue to fall as a result of structural adjustment and stabilization.* In fact in 1990 and 1991 output fell between 20-30% in many of these countries (except for Hungary where decline was 12%); and *"yet there is no sign of significant bankruptcies and restructuring in Central or Eastern Europe".* The reform process has not yet taken off fully in Bulgaria and Romania; "the Soviet Union and Yugoslavia in such political flux that serious reform is in abeyance"; hence output will continue to fall in 1992 and 1993 in Central Europe, and for longer in other countries. Given the current performance, under optimistic assumptions Poland, Hungary and Czechoslovakia can start positive growth by 1993 and other countries by 1995; and achieve 1988 levels of GDP by the turn of century. "Chinese experience in the 1980s demonstrates that large countries in the process of liberalization can

---

(4) Interview with Huang, WBN, Aug 7, 1992.

grow fast, suggesting that the former Soviet Union could also potentially achieve growth rates of [10% p.a.]", (Rollo and Stern, 1992).

Under Rollo and Stern's 'pessimistic scenario' the reforming socialist countries do not reach 1988 levels of GNP even by the year 2010, and only Hungary and Czechoslovakia attain that level by the year 2000 (Rollo and Stern, 1992). For eastern Germany, a much higher growth rate is expected and the catch-up with western Germany is estimated at 15-30 years (Dornbusch and Wolf, 1992).

(ii) Are the 1990 reforms successful so far?

According to Fischer, a stabilization policy could be considered "reasonably successful in Russia if the inflation rate is reduced to less than 30 to 40% a year", the budget deficit is at about 4-5% of GDP or less and the current account deficit is covered by orderly external financing (Fischer, 1992).

In 1991, in the former Soviet Union inflation rate was 100% and the budget deficit 20% of GDP; respective rates were 223% and 1.4% in Romania; 60% and 5.7% in Poland; 33% and 3.9% in Hungary 54% and 2.1% in former Czechoslovakia (Fischer, 1992, p.79).

The actual outcomes of reforms in the former socialist countries have many common features with *the pessimistic scenario of Rollo and Stern* (1992), whose salient features are reproduced below:

> The pessimistic scenario assumes in essence that the reforms do not work. *Stabilization fails and these countries suffer stop/go cycles at high average levels of inflation.* A combination of protectionism and subsidy maintains domestic monopoly and stifles any supply response to price liberalization. Privatization maintains the current monopolistic structure of industry. Foreign markets-in particular the EC-remain effectively closed to competitive exports from the region.

If itemized, the pessimistic scenario comprise:

(a) "*Ineffective macro-stabilization with a political business cycle,* as policy is first loosened and then tightened in response to resistance to cuts in living standards,"

(b) "The failure of structural reform leading to continuing monopoly power as demonopolization and import competition are stifled in response to pressure groups, and *privatization leads only to a redistribution of monopoly rents under price liberalization; supply fails to respond* significantly to reform",

(c) *"failure to achieve effective and sustained convertibility"*,

(d) *"Inadequate levels of domestic saving and aid,* and insufficient debts relief, *restricting investment,* with *recurrent balance of payments crises and hard currency shortages"*,

(e) *"Protectionism in foreign markets"*.

In short, unsuccessful scenario (outcome) indicates *"a system of incomplete price liberalization, continuing monopoly and no import competition, high budget deficits and high inflation* alternating with periods of austerity." The examples are Brazil and Argentina or Hungary and Poland in the 1980s "when there was incomplete price liberalization and out-of-control fiscal policies."

Many reforming socialist countries with persistent output decline and inflation, stop/go cycles, declining or inadequate domestic saving/investment rates and foreign direct investment, failure in achieving currency convertibility, continuing monopolistic market structures, failure in privatization and/or governance of medium to large scale enterprises, high budgetary deficits are concrete examples of pessimistic scenario or failing reforms.

The pessimistic scenario is forecast *not because of disappointing actual outcomes* of reform measures, but rather because of (a) *severe problems persistently besetting these economies*, namely budgetary deficits, soft-budgetary constraint and management problems of enterprise sector, BOP problems, acute uncertainty about present and future economic prospects and political stability, unsatisfactory growth of private sector, and persistent (high) inflationary tendencies, and (b) *lack of a clear-cut policy package/approach*, frequent policy reversals, rather chaotic, confusing impression about policies, direction and policy guidance.

6 Need for indicative economic planning

(i) Imperfect markets and growth prospects

Following excerpts from Sloman (1991) explain thoroughly the need for indicative economic planning in any country; and this requirement is most urgent and crucial in the reforming socialist countries.

Keynesians argue that, "the problems of inflation, unemployment and industrial decline are much too deep seated and complex to be rectified by a simple reliance on controlling the money supply and then leaving private enterprise and labor to respond to unregulated market forces"(Sloman, p.557).

Imperfect or monopolistic markets discourage investment and new entry; monopoly profits allow inefficient firms survive; but in a recession they will be driven out of business (*ibid*, p. 844).

> *Free markets are often highly imperfect* and will not lead to an optimum allocation of resources. ... Markets frequently reflect short-term speculative movements of demand and supply, and *do not give a clear indication of long-term costs and benefits.* In particular, *the stock market,* the *money market, and the foreign exchange market can respond quite violently to short-term pressures.* Such fluctuations can be very damaging to investment. For example, violent swings in exchange rates, as experienced in the early 1980s, can dissuade firms from making long-term investment decisions to develop export markets. A sudden rise in exchange rates may make it impossible to compete abroad, even though at a lower exchange rate an exporter could have made a large profit (Sloman, p. 557).
>
> The fluctuations inherent in free markets cause *uncertainty about future demand,* supply and prices. This uncertainty reduces investment and hence reduces growth. Keynesians.... refer to the cases of *Japan, France* and *Germany*, where there is much closer *collaboration between governments and industry* than there is in the UK (Sloman, 1991, p. 557) and in the US.

Firms investing in developing and improving products and in training, provide large external benefits to the economy and their social rate of return on investment will be higher than private rate of return. Firms might be unwilling to invest in projects with high risks, even when national economic benefits outweigh cost of failure (*ibid* pp. 843-44). In the case of failing firms, if a rescue program is not assisted by the government, job losses might constitute a substantial social cost (*ibid*, p.844).

The capital market is imperfect in many countries.

> The banks in the UK... [are] concerned with firms' short-run profitability; unlike banks in France, Germany and Japan, they have been reluctant to lend to firms for long-term investment. [Raising finance through stock market make firms] very dependent on the stock market performance of their shares, which depends on current or expected profitability in near future, not on long-term profitability. ...[All this] leads to the UK disease of 'short-termism': the obsession with short-term profits and the neglect of investment that yields profits [only in the medium or long-term] (Sloman, 1991, p. 844).

(ii) Need for indicative planning

"The government should help coordinate the plans of interdependent sectors of industry, and should channel finance to the more promising industries." Even go beyond this and engage in "indicative planning, whereby the government, along with representatives of industry and probably trade unions, works out a strategy for industrial regeneration and growth." To this end the government should provide infrastructure (transport, communications, energy) and private industry would increase its investments, confident in the growth of its markets (Sloman, 1991, p. 558).

Comprehensive approach to industrial planning is indicative planning, which works alongside the market; uncertainties for individual firms would clear or reduce, when inter-dependence of industries are taken into account; bottlenecks or idle capacities will be noticed and taken care of. In the indicative planning process, the government consults with industrialists about their plans and projects, coordinates the plans of firms, industries and sectors and recommends realistic and mutually consistent targets for output and investment. France had used 'Le Plan' since shortly after the war and planning in France up to the late 1970s has been considered successful; investment and growth were higher than in the UK (Sloman, 1991, pp. 845-46).

Turkey, employing indicative economic planning approach effectively, in a mixed economy, achieved 7% (target) growth rate with price stability (inflation rate less than 5% p.a.) during the 1961-68 period.

(iii) Italian planning: the state holding sector

Italian planning is based on *the state holding sector,* which is composed of 6 state holding groups like IRI, ENI. Each holding group is responsible for implementing directives issued by the Ministry of State Holdings. IRI was composed of over 1000 companies in 1985. The holding company has a direct or an indirect controlling interest over the companies. Italian intervention in the economy is a compromise between partial state ownership and state influence in key parts of the private sector (Sloman, 1991, p. 847).

The holding system in Italy has achieved the following: (*ibid*, p. 847).

(a) rapid growth in sectors involved by encouraging high levels of investment, which led to improved efficiency and increased technological competitiveness;

(b) it has taken a more socially responsible attitude than the private sector; employment and welfare objectives have been given priority over profits;

(c) *"it has injected competition into the Italian economy* by challenging many established monopolies (e.g. fertilizer, cement and car production)" and "has helped to prevent oligopolistic collusion by itself refusing to collude;"

(d) "it has helped the government to pursue its *regional policy;"*

(e) *"it has been used by the government as a means of managing aggregate demand*; by varying the levels of expenditure in the State holding sector, the government has better been able to operate its *counter-cyclical policy"*.

This sector's huge losses caused some concern and "several of IRI's assets have been sold off; nevertheless the state holding sector [still] remains high".

(iv) Industrial policy in Japan

Quoting from Sloman (1991, p. 848) Japan, replaced the UK as the

> work shop of the world [being] now the worlds largest manufacturer of steel, ships, cars and lorries, motor cycles, engines, cameras, calculators, big memory chips, televisions, video tape recorders and photocopiers. ... [During 1975-1982], industrial output in Japan grew by 50%, investment averaged 33% of GDP and the rate of automation outpaced all her economic rivals (Sloman, 1991, p. 848).
>
> [The Japanese government has actively encouraged industry in its endeavors] to develop new products and put new life into old products and processes. ... Industrial policy in Japan is guided by the Ministry of International Trade and Industry (MITI), whose role is to encourage cooperation between private companies and to help stimulate investment in new technology and product development. Using a mixture of state aid and legislative power, MITI wields a considerable amount of influence. [Most Japanese, industry, however], is only too willing to take advantage of the services MITI can offer.(Sloman, 1991, 848).

The extent of MITI's active role was highlighted in 1981 with the announcement of a 10-year project of research into next-generation computer technology ... Long-term industrial policy on this scale is certain to give Japanese computer firms and many other industries a superior market position for a long time to come. Cooperation, organization and state aid have proved a successful recipe for Japanese industry in the past and look set to continue that way in the future.

7 Reform and government: strong versus weak government

All discussions regarding the success or failure of reform and stabilization processes and suggested alternative solutions or schemes during transition to a market economy (from a socialist-state or mixed economy) hinge on the strength or weakness of the government and state institutions (public administration). In other words, a strong an incorruptible government is called for the reform process to succeed.

A strong and incorruptible government is defined as the one that would effectively enforce budgetary and monetary discipline, and the hard budget constraint for the enterprise sector and provide law and order in the country; in the latter context, particularly fight corruption, insiders' trading and speculation, regulate monopolies and prepare a competitive framework in products and labor markets at least; prevent cartels and collusion, shady deals in privatization and cooperative enterprises, asset plundering in the enterprise sector; control state enterprises, which should be autonomous in their decisions (production, pricing, buying, selling, employment, investment, financing, except for some effective wage restraint, in cases required and subsidy payments, if any) against mismanagement and illicit activities and effectively prevent such abuses and waste.

Such a politically strong and administration-wise capable and efficient government would not give in unjustified pressures of labor unions and lobbying interest groups regarding reform measures, their sequencing and timing. On the other hand, a politically and administratively weak government which is also bound to live with the soft budget constraint and be corrupt, if not itself, could not prevent corruption and unfair deals (regarding privatization, leakage of administrative price adjustments and of removal government controls, changes in trade regime, etc.) and failure of enterprise reform (continuation of losses and waste). Timing and extent of reform measures (particularly administrative price adjustments, privatization, and trade regime changes, and their leakage will be fertile fields of corruption, speculation and windfall profits; enterprise managements and workers' councils also will participate in this plunder through disruption of production (quantity and quality), distribution and marketing (even discouraging customers from buying and forcing them to purchase from private competitors) for personal gain. All this, not only undermines and shatters fiscal and monetary stability (increasing enterprise losses), but also the reform effort and its image on the public.

A weak government would do disservice to the country and people, by undertaking radical reforms. Everybody would be better off if the status-quo was maintained (only with essential changes to keep the economy running), awaiting a strong government, and in the meantime strengthening the public institutions and their efficiency and setting up the institutions necessary for a market economy. A weak government should definitely avoid comprehensive, particularly 'big bang' approach reform (because it could not manage and successfully complete it) in order not to cause further crisis or worsen the crisis.

And a corrupt (dishonest) government would first attempt to degrade and erode the effectiveness and efficiency of the public administration and justice mechanism (taking advantage also of now fashionable liberalization winds of change, calling for reduction in the size and role of the government) in order to conduct its corrupt dealings and practices unchecked.

So much widespread corruption in the reforming socialist countries is not a surprising phenomenon, on the contrary, under the prevailing circumstances, it is quite normal. In the medium-to long-run the marketplace and democracy will provide the basic remedy; in the short-run, during transition, however, the solution lies in strong government and its efficient/effective institutions.

Contrary to the present political trends and confusion in the reforming socialist countries and in many developing countries, a good public administration and justice mechanism is essential not only for the reform process to succeed in transition, but even after reaching full-fledged market economy. In the reforming socialist countries there is urgent need to rescind the command/order system of the economy and reduce powers of central institutions; but at the same time the need is urgent for entrusting those institutions new functions geared to efficient operation of a market economy. During transition, with adequate devolution, central/regional/local authorities should have sufficient power to

(i) control the enterprise sector against corruption, asset plundering, mismanagement until privatization;
(ii) regulate monopolies and monopolistic practices and ensure competition in distribution and marketing (fight against enterprise and local mafias);
(iii) prevent abuse, misuse of public office for personal gain (insiders' speculation related to administrative price, trade regime, etc. changes);
(iv) control efficient and orderly functioning of the market institutions (commercial banks, financial institutions, social safety net, etc.);
(v) set up an efficient and effective assessment and collection system for taxes and social security contributions, taking also into account the fact that in most socialist countries *income taxation* of private sector is small and negligible and a great deal of private income would never be reported to the authorities (Hare, 1987);
(vi) make indicative economic plans at least during transition and provide forecasts for possible implications and effects of reform measures.

These new responsibilities of the state organizations (and the services required from them) are geared to the market economy. They would require a major redeployment of civil service and enterprise sector personnel, after re-training, which will create significant gainful employment.

A honest government, if not supported by a good/efficient public administration and state institutions is bound to fail and lead to widespread corruption. Many actual failures from moves to and from market economy, could be explained by factors cited above. The fact that a government which could not be provided with reasonably good estimates of effects of its reform measures as in the previous social democratic or socialist experiments (Chile under Allende, socialism in Angola, Mozambique and Ethiopia; it is doubtful that these governments were furnished with estimates of possible outcomes of their policies, because no sensible government, with some sense of responsibility would have initiated such moves) or as in the recent reform experiences of socialist countries (in particular under the 'big bang' approach in Poland and Russia, even the proponents of it admit impossibility of making realistic projections of its outcome in the short-run) indicates that relevant governments are not backed up by an efficient public service and relevant/required expertise, whose terms of reference should also include provision of reliable estimates of the consequences of suggested/proposed moves and reforms.

One can conclude that a program designed and guided by 'the suggested method' could be prepared and implemented by a strong government; a weak government, however, could level the field, prepare the market infrastructure and strengthen public institutions and improve their efficiency.

Chapter 7

Other forecasting and analysis methods developed for countries in transition

Other forecasting and analysis methods developed for countries in transition

Various models, methods for forecasting or analysis of developments in the reforming socialist countries have been constructed and used. An incomplete overview of these methods is attempted in this chapter. These methods/models are either based on past data or assumptions regarding crucial variables to work out effects of policy changes or changes in exogenous variables. Since every year of transition period in a given country is different from the previous or following years, these methods are of little help. Experiences of other counties are not of much use (Polish and Hungarian experiences differ sharply), even when the same policies are exercised since attitudes, environment and exogenous variables are markedly different. Since the transition period is characterized by structural change (the pace of which also changes from year to year) and in general accompanied by high-inflation (under which money also could not remain neutral, since both relative prices and real magnitudes/variables are influenced then), reliable estimation by these methods becomes an impossible task.

1 Models for a centrally planned economy

Many estimation models basically suit the needs of centrally planned economies (but not those of in transition), e.g. Charemza's method (1987) estimating pairs of demand and supply equations under disequilibrium (excess-demand) conditions (all-excess demand hypothesis and exogenous price changes) or Hare's (1987) multiplier analysis in a centrally planned economy with a private sector, assume centrally planned economy to continue.

2 Analysis of shortages in socialist economies: Hare model

Hare (1987) considers that repressed inflation (firms facing supply constraints in the labor market and households facing supply constraints in the product market) may describe shortage conditions under central planning, with a dominant state sector and a smaller, more flexible private sector. But Nuti observes that

> consumers are indeed quantity-rationed in the state sector but are not subject individually to overall quantity constraint since they can always spend their income in the secondary market. It follows that the *supply multiplier*, i.e. rounds of reduction in labor supply (and therefore consumer good supply) which are alleged as a consequence of quantity constraints, do not necessarily occur and can only be expected to be present in the same circumstances in which labor supply would respond negatively to open inflation. ... [Hare also concludes that] supply multipliers do not always arise, as indicated by Nuti, but that when they do, the link with the open inflation case is precisely as he asserts (Hare, 1987).

In the centrally planned economies, it is observed over a long period that the supply of the state sector is insufficient to meet the forthcoming demand, either because its price is too low in relation to wage level in the state sector or because output allotted by central planners for investment, and exports and government expenditures (termed as the states requirement for final output) is too large in relation to total output. Kornai even argues that such shortage is endemic. Hare (1987) employing a simple model with a production function using only labor input, with a state sector and private sector, and with a supply constraint affecting state sector output, shows that an increase in the state's requirement for final output reduces private consumption of state output, by a multiple of the original change in state's requirement (supply multiplier), hence state output as a whole falls, labor supply to the state sector declines; this outcome, however, does

> not depend at all on the behavior of the private sector. ... The tightening of supply constraints in the state sector (i.e. increasing the state's requirement), [however], does affect private sector production: the equilibrium price and wage in the private sector both rise, and output and employment also increases ..., [and all workers experience a fall in their real income. Hare (1987) notes that] intuitively, since state output has become relatively more scarce, one might have expected its relative price to rise. However to restore equilibrium requires a fall in the real wage and with output price and wage level in the state sector fixed, the only way in which this can happen in the model is via an increase in the output price of the private sector (Hare, 1987).

These predicted effects on the private sector variables of an increase in the state's requirement are based on the very hypothetical assumptions of the model using only labor input in the production function. In reality a decline in the output of the state sector through supply multiplier mechanism would also result in a fall of output and employment in the private sector (as a consequence of decline in the supply of material inputs required by the private sector in production, which normally is provided by the state sector), and a rise in the price of its output. All this shows preoccupation with labor-dominated production functions in former socialist economies, with labor input being the main constraint, with over-ambitious investment targets and with cost minimization by firms subject to soft budget constraint all of which ignored the very source of problem, i.e. extreme shortage of material inputs and consumer goods, and ways of eliminating it through market mechanism and profit maximization; and instead tried to eliminate these shortages employing a socialist framework.

3 Forecasting methods for German unification

Pohl et al., (1990) estimated the macroeconomics effects of German unification. They however, *under-estimated most of the problems* (Horn et al., 1992).

Horn et. al (1992) aimed at *quantifying the macroeconomic effects of German unification* for West Germany and other countries. Several simulations were run on the basis of *assumed values for some exogenous variables (namely exports to East Germany, imports of Germany,* public transfers to East Germany, supply of labor, other budgetary effects). It is estimated that the unification boom will end after one year; thereafter lower growth rates and higher inflation will follow and a slight recovery will happen after four years. "The prospects of Germany's economic future are rather uncertain." The assumed values, fixed for a five-year period, were based on quarterly national accounts data for East and West Germany in 1982; these included: (i) exports to East Germany, (ii) imports, (iii) public transfers to East Germany, (iv) taxes and social security contributions, (v) cuts in government consumption (defense, state subsidies). Ex post five-year simulations (using 1983-87 data) of economic development in West Germany without and with unification were compared. Forecasting exports to East Germany has been found difficult, since exports depend on the magnitude and speed of economic stabilization in East Germany, which is subject to great uncertainty; as a consequence a fixed value for five years, based on export figure of 12 months since July 1990, (the date of unification) was assumed. (Higher exports to East Germany will call for higher imports into West Germany.) Since the size of shocks (exports) will not be constant over 5 years, different scenarios are run. Horn et al (1992) conclude that "the prospects for Germany's economic future are rather uncertain".

4 Large econometric models for Poland

Large econometric models constructed for Poland were used for policy analyses purposes in 1980s; variants aiming at prediction of crisis situations, early warning and explicitly taking account of shortages and resulting disequilibria were tried. The models, however, produced poor forecasts for 1982-83 (the time of martial law, in a depressed economy with deep disequilibria) and for 1988 (the time of enormous change in the political environment both inside and outside Poland; policy change towards the market economy with price reform leading to high, open inflation and adoption of liberal rules regarding wage compensation policies that resulted in the wage-price spiral), as would have been expected. Welfe et al (1992) point out that "a forecaster can hardly be blamed for not predicting shocks in economic policy correctly".

The wage variable is *exogenous* in the said Polish econometric model and *its assumed value turned out to contain grave error,* which reflects *inability to predict radical changes in price-wage reforms (*Welfe et al, 1992).

Welfe et al (1992) maintain that

> in the new economic and political environment, forecasting and simulation models may prove to be particularly useful, after they have been reformulated to reflect the particular properties of economies in a state of transition towards becoming market economies. ... [In new econometric models they suggest a] *shift from supply constrained to demand determined regime, allowing for a high rate of monopoly power in the production sector,* the use of fiscal and monetary instruments as major tools of economic policy, higher frequency of economic adjustments.

The basic problem, however, remains for economies in transition; namely the structural parameters are functions of time or other variables, e.g. parameters describing consumer preferences and technical coefficients of input-output matrix will continue to change over time in transition period, until full transformation into a stable market economy is completed.

For example, if there are constraints on the balance of payments (BOP) and the demand for imports are rationed as a consequence, in the short-run the shortage in supplies of imported materials and energy will lead to under utilization of capacity. Welfe et al (1992) use shortage indicators to adjust capacity output, to solve this problem. Underutilization of capacity will, however, entail changes in the capacity output, changes in employment, product prices, etc. magnitudes of which might be forecast if the size and sectoral distribution (adversely affected sectors) of foreign exchange shortages are predicted in advance, which is an impossible task for economies in transition and disequilibria.

According to Welfe et al (1992) foreign exchange shortage and concomitant rationing of imports of intermediary goods, would in the long-run lead to substitution and changes in technical coefficients of material input-gross output system. This conclusion, however, rests on persistent foreign exchange shortage and BOP disequilibrium, which indicates a persistently unsuccessful transformation, which should be avoided. Moreover coefficients of standard input-output table (based on values of output and inputs, as against material input/gross output ratios) will change in the short-run in line with ongoing absolute and relative price changes, rendering the input-output analysis almost useless, in the short run, as well.

It is likely that recent econometric contributions to the analysis of nonstationary time series, i.e. the analysis of multivariate cointegration, which makes an explicit distinction between stationary and nonstationary and hence provides a natural framework for the joint analysis of long-and short-run behavior, might provide a useful device for econometric models for socialist economies in transition (see, e.g. Juselius, 1992).

5 Input-output analysis for a socialist economy in transition with a dual price system

Xu et al (1992) developed a new input-output model for a centrally planned economy (CPE) in gradual transition like China, where a market economy and a planned economy coexist and a dual price system (planned prices and market prices) exists. *All prices are exogenously given.* This model is used to estimate the structural change and effects of exogenous shocks. In a CPE in transition, "the value of intermediate demand is related not only to the quantity and price of input and output, but also to the relative share of plan-market parts," hence the traditional input-output model becomes useless. The method is of limited use, particularly applicable to the Chinese-type gradual reform process; prices are treated exogenously.

6 Scenario approach

Three new studies by the World Bank for the Baltics adopt scenario approach; they don't make concrete predictions but offer possible scenarios based on current situations.(1) The Rollo and Stern (1992) model for foreign trade flows also adopts the scenario approach. The scenario approach suffers from two severe defects: (i) when the current economic situation is unstable (uncertain) and is in a state of flux, the base period data, on which forecasts are made, are unstable; changing the base year or small changes in the base year figures

(1) *WBN*, April 22,1993

would cause wide variations in predictions or scenarios. (ii) Scenarios are based on various assumptions and hypothetical growth paths and hence are subject to the validity of many different assumptions and their variation.

7 Dinopoulos and Lane model

(i) The model

The Dinopoulos and Lane model of a socialist economy, incorporates bargaining power over wages and employment in the socialized sector and shortages that are reflected in the black market.

> The model is used to analyze the implications of liberalization policies, including trade liberalization, an administered price increase, and provisions allowing for increased direct foreign investment. The results suggest that reforms may have different effects under different trade regimes, that small price reforms may have perverse effects, and that foreign investment in a shortage economy may be immiserizing (Dinopoulos and Lane, 1992).

(ii) Assumptions of the model (Dinopoulos and Lane, 1992).

(1) It is assumed that *black market activity exhausts the rent associated with the controlled price.* Whereas in reality, a significant part of low-priced good is bound to be wasted in some households, in industrial use as input and in distribution (less-careful handling and packaging).

(2) It is assumed that *production process in each sector requires labor and sector-specific capital.* (Because of the absence of well-functioning capital markets in socialist economies and central allocation of capital, capital is not mobile across sectors.) *Absence of material inputs* in the production function, in view of shortages in material inputs and foreign exchange is a serious omission.

(3) The production function employed assumes away technological input or *productivity change,* whereas the main objective of market reform is increasing productivity.

(4) Workers that cannot find a job either in the private sector or in the socialized sector engage in *black market activity* and wage level associated with this activity is termed *reservation wage* (the black market wage) and it is assumed that it is *below the wage in the socialized sector.* The wage in the nonsocialized sector also equals the reservation wage, because "a

worker fired from the socialized sector can enter the black market and earn the reservation wage" (Dinopoulos and Lane, 1992).

The following observations are due for these assumptions:

(a) Even if at present, black market and private sector wages are below the public sector wage level, this structure cannot be maintained for long; in fact the Russian cooperative enterprises paid substantially higher wages than the state enterprise sector (Jones and Moscoff, 1991); and rather as observed in countries with a mixed economy, the wage level in private sector exceeds the public sector wage level.

Dinopoulos and Lane (1992), cite that in an earlier version of this analysis, with private firms paying efficiency wages, they found that wages in private sector could not be lower than those in state enterprises. Even in this case, predicted outcome does not reflect reality. In case of professional middlemen dealing in black market, earning level exceeds either wage level.

(b) The assumption that all queuing and black marketing is done by persons who are otherwise unemployed is not valid. As noted by authors, employed consumers and professional middlemen queue, as well.

(5) The assumption that *all goods produced in the socialized sector are sold through the black market* could not be wholly true.

(6) It is assumed that *"the nonsocialized sector is perfectly competitive and produces an output that is different from that of the socialized sector"*. Perfect competition assumption does not hold true at all, because of the small size of private sector and limited number of firms operating in a given line, (great likelihood of collusion). In high-inflation shortage economies, perfect competition assumption in the private sector is illegitimate. Moreover, as can be observed in countries with long mixed economy experience, *private sector during initial stages mainly engages in final processing of inputs mainly purchased from the state enterprise sector.* The same product in many cases is also produced by a state enterprise and sold at lower prices. The distribution network controlled by private cartels, restrain marketing of lower-priced (sometimes better quality) product of state enterprise, in countries where anti-trust regulations do not exist or are not effectively enforced. In this context, comes into the picture lobbying by private sector to maintain low prices charged for inputs procured from the state sector.

(7) The assumption that *"the economy exports the good produced in the nonsocialized sector and imports the socialized sector good"*, is admitted by authors themselves to be *unrealistic,* since many of the exports of

Eastern European countries are produced by state enterprises. Then authors add that disaggregating the socialized sector into exporting and import-competing subsectors would have made the model intractable.

The following observations could be made in this context:

(a) Mathematical models are useful for analysis, but in inferring conclusions from the too-simplified version of the real world, one has to be very cautious and hence authors' claim that the model "offers the potential of answering many questions concerning the effects of economic policies during this transitional stage" is not justifiable.

(b) In the reforming socialist countries most attractive areas for private sector are (i) production and domestic marketing of deficit goods, and (ii) exporting surplus goods produced by the public sector, purchasing them at bargain/official prices. Casual observations indicate that private initiative take these attractive opportunities adequately. Setting-up processing industries for export, using local raw materials, will come to the fore, only after macroeconomic equilibrium and political stability are ensured (in the medium run).

(8) *The taxation assumption* regarding the state enterprises, (taking away all profit) allows no room for improvement and modernization investments through retained profits, in a period, when these are most crucial.

(9) It is assumed that the current labor-dominated management of the state enterprise tries to *maximize wages* (formally the wage differential between the socialized and the black market sectors) and employment. Experience shows that, the management also aims at retaining and squandering profits and funds, to the extent of *asset plundering.*

(iii) Economic model and reality

(1) Labor shortage of the model. The Dinopoulos and Lane (1992) model is static and centers around labor market equilibrium (bargaining over wages and employment in the public sector). Effects of exogenous changes are transmitted through the labor market equilibrium (which in the model translates into attracting or releasing to or from the black market, by withdrawing or employing from or in productive sectors). Whereas even in Eastern Germany 3 million people lost jobs at the initial phase of transition, which implies that (a) labor market equilibrium is not the main objective, as should be expected under market reform, and (b) that releasing labor from black market activity for employment in productive sectors, could not be significant since labor is not the scarce factor.

In the reforming socialist countries, while introduction of a social safety net with a view to hardening the soft budget constraint and thereby enabling/ compelling public enterprises to discharge redundant labor is being considered (see, Hardy, 1992), this model's adjustment mechanism becomes not quite relevant, at least at present. Moreover urgent need in these countries is not a static, but a dynamic model, showing the process of elimination of shortages of material inputs, basic foodstuff, foreign exchange and technology. This model, however is elaborated here, because it gives estimates of effects of price reform and trade liberalization in reforming countries, which are crucial issues from the view point of 'the suggested methodology.'

(2) *Material input shortages: reality.* Nordhaus observes that in the former Soviet Union if the monetary crisis and hard currency scarcity become worse, the republican currencies become increasingly inconvertible, and inter-republican trade break down, then *shortage of material inputs would become more acute* and there would be *"an exacerbation of the problem of bottleneck production declines"*. In fact, in a recent survey of Moscow firms, 88% reported that *"the lack of raw materials, semi-finished goods and equipment were among the most serious obstacles for the growth of production" at the enterprise level* in the last half of 1991. "Only 2% of firms reported that insufficient demand for production was the most serious obstacle" (Fisher, 1992). In China also raw material shortage has been a major bottleneck (Qun et al, 1992).

(3) *Effects of import quota increase under the model and in reality.* In The Dinopoulos and Lane model, the labor market plays the central role, in an economy where labor is in surplus supply and shortages of technology, foreign exchange and material inputs and entrepreneurship dominate. Importance of the equilibrium in labor market can best be illustrated by *tracing the effects of say trade liberalization.* Liberalization of an import quota reduces the black market price of public sector products (import substitute), which causes the black market wage level and employment in that sector to decline. This allows employment and hence output in both productive sectors (public sector and export good producing nonsocialized sector) to increase; shortages are reduced due to an increase in imports and domestic production; the reduction in reservation (black market) wage lowers the negotiated wage (for the public sector). The wage differential (excess wage in the socialized sector) however, being a decreasing function of the reservation wage, increases. Higher output and a lower negotiated wage yields a higher tax revenue from the state enterprise; since consumption of both goods (produced by socialized and nonsocialized sectors) increases, the reforming economy is better off as a result

of trade liberalization. The effects of trade liberalization under a tariff regime are qualitatively the same as the quota increase.

These predictions regarding the effects of trade liberalization are widely divergent from what actually will materialize. Firstly in a widespread disguised unemployment economy (with labor redundancies at state enterprises) assuming labor input increase to lead to output increase is not simply valid, since real bottlenecks in the short-run are in material supplies, imported inputs and new production technology for deficit goods. Under the existing effective constraints, the real outcome of trade liberalization would be as follows:

In case of partial elimination of excess demand under quota, the decline in black market price of good, will reduce black market activity, but there will be no effect on employment and output levels in other sectors, even though black market releases some labor, because labor is not the critical factor in any sector. Unless the good concerned is an important wage good, and price decline is significant, there is no reason for expecting the negotiated wage level to decline, or output level to increase in any sector because of the wage level decline, if any. In the current high inflation and uncertainty conditions of reforming countries, effects of a partial import quota increase, except own price decline of the good concerned, are bound to be nil. Because of what said above, tax revenue increase in the state sector producing the deficit good would not materialize.

Even the acclaimed release of black market labor may not materialize at all, if total shortages in the economy are not wiped out by comprehensive price and trade reforms. Because in high-inflation countries with price control, some shortages are manipulated, accentuated or artificially created by organized groups/mafia (through hoarding, disrupting distribution, creating local shortages) for speculative purposes; and profiteering is not a part-time or temporary occupation, but a full-time professional job. As a consequence elimination of a few shortages, would only divert the black market activity to other products.

With the partial elimination of scarcity, black market activity in related market itself may not decline, if the imported good is of higher quality (real or assumed) and or its price is higher than the fixed price of local product, which is true in most cases, because then another parallel market will emerge dealing with the imported good. (In the Dinopoulos and Lane model, quota imports are sold at black market prices and quota revenues (difference between local sale and cost at world prices) are automatically collected by the government. Whereas, in a price control country, domestic selling prices of imported goods are also controlled normally to alleviate adverse social effects of shortages; as a consequence emergence of a new black market for imported good is imminent. The volume of black market activity may decline, but its value may increase and its employment level will not decline. Moreover, assumption of perfect competition in the black market does not hold true; in many cases the wholesale suppliers to the black market collude and retailers employ mark-up pricing rule, holding supply (hoarding) when necessary. Because of imperfect competition prevailing in the black market, increase in administrative prices, after a short while, leads to higher black market prices (as expected and indicated by casual observations). This is because, for a small margin, it is not worthwhile to engage in illicit trading for individuals and for organized groups, (also because it does not cover overhead) hence supply to the black market declines and price is pushed up.

(4) Black market rate of foreign exchange. Similar mechanism works in free/black foreign exchange markets, whose size is generally small, depending on the volume of transactions that have to be channeled through it under the prevailing foreign exchange system. A central bank can intervene (as occurred in Turkey in 1980s and 1990s) by selling dollars, when the gap between free and official rates widens, and can control the free rate by relatively small supply shocks. Even the official exchange rate could be maintained at lower levels not commensurate with domestic inflation rate by means of sizeable fresh foreign borrowing or overly generous export rebates (as happened in Turkey in 1990 and 1992, when net increase in foreign indebtedness totaled $8 billion and $6 billion respectively), in order to employ the exchange rate as a nominal anchor to curb inflation (at about 60% in Turkey in 1990 and 1992). The wisdom of such an exchange rate policy in an open economy is an open question, since the very survival of import substituting industries and sectors is threatened as well. On the other hand, when external debt service reaches a peak (in 1988 and 1989 in Turkey) or when foreign donors are reluctant to supply fresh loans because of increased economic risks and/or political reasons (as in 1978 and 1979 in Turkey), then the free and official exchange rates shoot up. All this shows that by manipulating supply and causing relatively small supply shocks, it is possible to control black market prices irrespective of underlying economic reality. In fact in Turkey during the 1980-1990 period while consumer prices (Istanbul index) increased 48-fold, US $ exchange rate increased 34-fold and during the 1980-1992 period as consumer prices increased 104-fold, $ exchange rate increased 62- fold.

This policy, however, has devastating effects on economic development and industrial growth, and external debt. The adverse effect on exporting sectors is alleviated by export incentives, at the cost of increased budgetary deficits. An overvalued currency in an economy with a liberal trade regime and no exchange control threatens the very existence of import substituting industries and infant industries, through competition from artificially low- priced imports. But they encourage the development of assembly/processing type industries with a high imported-input content (and a low value-added component), high imports of goods and services, capital outflow and profit transfers by foreign investment. (In fact, import dependence of the Turkish economy increased 2-fold over the 1973-1985 period, Şenesen, 1990.)

Alternatively, if the government wants to push up the black market rate of dollar in order to raise extra revenue by selling dollars in this market (as the Russian government did in 1992, according to press reports), it can easily achieve it by manipulating the flow of supply to the market.

(5) *Effects of trade liberalization under tariff.* The Dinopoulos and Lane (1992) model predicts similar effects of *trade liberalization under tariff as under quota,* provided the free market price of imports (world price plus the tariff) is above the official fixed price, which might be the case even if zero tariff applied. (E.g. after the 400% increase in coal prices in January 1990 in Poland, the prices were still below world levels; see Dinopoulos and Lane, 1992, p. 481.) In this case, shortage is the result of unduly low prices, and could only be eliminated by raising the administrative price to the level of free market price.

In cases where the world price plus the tariff gives a free market price below the fixed price, then trade liberalization would give rise to decline in output and employment in the public sector (import substitution industries). This should rather be the prevalent case, under trade liberalization with tariff with the start of the reform process, after the administrative prices are set free and provided that the exchange rate does not entail overvaluation of domestic currency; because otherwise it would mean that the reforming countries do not have a real adjustment problem, except for overly low fixed prices. In fact recent experience in Central and Eastern Europe, e.g. in Poland and eastern Germany, as also noted by Dinopoulos and Lane (1992) indicates that trade liberalization resulted in a sharp decline in output of the socialized sector.

(iv) *Effects of price reform*

Dinopoulos and Lane model's estimates for effects of price reform differ with the extent of initial price distortion. If the *initial price distortion is small,* output and employment in both productive sectors (public and private) increase, as a result of fall in the black market wage and employment, and hence an increase in *national income evaluated at world prices* occurs. If, however *the initial price distortion is large,* increased output of public sector increases the volume of black market sales and its profits; and hence black market wage and employment may even increase; and then employment and output in the private sector decline (Dinopoulos and Lane 1992).

Whereas Hare (1987) derives different conclusions regarding the effect of state sector price increases on the private sector output and employment, using a different model structure and making different assumptions, by using another, simple model of a centrally planned economy with a private sector, Hare shows that an increase in the price of state sector output (in order to choke off some of the excess demand for state sector), increases the output of state sector and its consumption, decreases supernumerary incomes, and reduces price and wage level of private sector, but its output can move in either direction; and the effect on real wages is unclear. This result is interpreted as follows: The increase in the price of state sector product, first reduces its consumption and increases the labor supply to the state sector and thereby increases its output; and the economy gets closer to the Walrasian equilibrium by administrative price increase.

From above-cited results, Dinopoulos and Lane (1992) draw the following conclusion:

> Small administered price increases are only appropriate if the initial distortion is small. If the distortions are large as in many of the Eastern European countries before the reforms of 1990, and more recently in the states of the former Soviet Union-a small price adjustment may even draw more labor out of the productive sectors into the black market. This argument strengthens the case for a *'big bang'* price adjustment, which allows prices to adjust immediately to their market-clearing levels and thus immediately eliminates the associated black market activity.

Although the suggested method provides an orderly 'big bang' approach and the conclusion of Dinopoulos and Lane regarding the superiority of a 'big bang' price adjustment, (by clearing all markets, increasing efficiency and output in all sectors), is justified, this author does not agree with the adjustment mechanism cited and with the sign of some effects. When price distortion is large, even a small price increase will both increase output in the public sector and the black market activity; and due to the concomitant increased availability of inputs for the private sector, its output and employment as well, will increase. Because in these countries bottleneck is not in labor supply, but in material input supply. Hence national income evaluated at world prices would increase.

Dinopoulos and Lane (1992, p.489) argue that the experience of Eastern European countries in late 1980s and of the former Soviet Union in the early 1980s confirms the adverse effects of small price increases in view of large initial price distortions, since shortages had grown worse then. This evidence, however, is not sufficient to support the Dinopoulos-Lane hypothesis, because there were many other factors causing increased shortages during the 1980s in the socialist countries: namely, increased poor governance of the enterprise sector, monopolistic markets and increased corruption, shortage of foreign exchange (also due to relative or absolute decline in foreign official and private capital inflow because of increased economic and political instability); the very existence of administrative prices, decline in effectiveness of central planning without replacement of the vacuum thus created by market forces.

Another argument for full adjustment of price distortions, is that "gradual price adjustment may also be vitiated by the effect of expectations, as anticipated price increases may create increased incentives for hoarding and thereby exacerbate the shortages" (Dinopoulos and Lane, 1992).

8 An overview of Osband, Hare and Dinopoulos and Lane models: types of production functions, sectoral interdependence and role of scarce inputs

In the *Osband* (1992/A) model gross output is a linear function of productive effort (labor input), and hence output can only increase with increase in productive labor supply, assuming fixed output coefficients (output per labor hour) or through redirection of state production toward consumption goods, and through expansion of non-state domestic production. Hence increase in state output through increased supply of material inputs and as a result of improvement investments and efficiency (productivity) increase due to market reform (the very essence of the reform measures) is ignored.

Similarly *Hare* (1987) assumes production functions for both private and public sector, in which labor is the only factor of production determining net output and effects of material input and imported input shortages could not be investigated, since equilibrium in labor and final good markets feature in the model, and no interdependence between the two sectors exists, except for drawing on the same labor pool.

The *Dinopoulos and Lane* (1992) model assumes a neoclassical production function of net output, with labor and sector specific capital input; and adjustments under reform are via redeployment of labor; material input constraint and technical change do not feature in, even productivity of direct foreign investment is assumed to be "the same as that of the existing sector-specific capital of reforming socialist country."

This much preoccupation with labor input in the production functions (possibly influenced by economic realities in the socialist countries under the dominance of the Marxist theory of value), possibly could not have provided proper guidance for the 1980 reform measures (in designing and estimating effects of reform packages). Because this type of smooth, continuous production functions loses much of their validity and usefulness in shortage economies with extremely imperfect competition conditions, increased supply of one factor may not lead to output increase. For example, even the increased infusion of Western capital to Poland during 1972-1983 was largely wasted with no increase in productivity (Terrel, 1992).

The input-output analysis, which could have corrected this deficiency, possibly was not very helpful, because of changing prices and economic structure under the reform measures.

9 Calvo and Coricelli model of stagflation for Poland

(i) The model and its conclusions

Calvo and Coricelli (1992) observe that abolition of subsidies could cause serious macroeconomic difficulties in the short-run; employing a mathematical model they claim that the stagflation that followed the 1990 stabilization program in Poland is linked to segmented financial market, i.e. the weak credit channels between households and enterprises, and the existence of large inter-enterprise debt.

Dismantling subsidies on energy and transport, could hamper production in sectors heavily using these inputs, if the firms concerned confront a credit crunch (limited access to credit or high interest rates) simultaneously (e.g. the 1990 Polish Stabilization program). In the presence of serious imperfections in the financial market, (which are the features of the financial markets in reforming socialist economies, namely the weak credit links between households and enterprises, and the existence of large inter- enterprise debt, the latter is related to the chronic soft budget constraint), tight credit/money policy might have contractionary effects (the neo-structuralist approach) and lead to stagflation (Calvo and Coricelli, 1992).

(ii) Criticism of Keynesian view of real wage decline

Calvo and Coricelli (1992) maintain that the Keynesian explanation of the 1990 stagflation in Poland by the sharp fall in real wages is inadequate. Because this "argument relies on the assumption that aggregate demand in Poland depends strongly on real wages and that state enterprises do not lower prices when faced with excess supply" (as a result of fixed markup rule). Calvo and Coricelli maintain that following factors are overlooked:

(a) "The household sector has a sizable stock of liquid savings (e.g. at the end of 1989, the stock of foreign currency deposits in household portfolios amounted to more than 45% of GDP, almost three times the stock of domestic money and in Feb. 1990 it amounted to more than 60% of the M3 money supply) that can be mobilized to cover a transitory fall in income".

(b) Although the fall in real wages was about 30%, this measurement does not account for the widespread shortages in Poland in 1989, implying that the *effective* real wage in 1989 could have been much lower; and in fact if measured in terms of dollars, wages increased from $27 in Sept. 1989 to $105 in March 1990 and to $146 in Nov. 1990.

(c) Since workers are virtually shareholders of state enterprises (directly or through profit bonuses), a fall in workers' incomes should be associated with a rise in enterprises' profits by the same amount, and hence impact of a wage cut should be less pronounced.

(d) The supply shock incited by the Jan 1990 increase in administrative input prices (400% for coal, 300% for electricity and 110% for overall producer price, over the previous month) and the credit crunch faced by the enterprise sector in early 1990, (credit to firms per unit cost fell by about 60% compared with its average in 1989) are overlooked. The withdrawal of central bank from its role as lender of last resort in Jan 1990 had foundered the flourishing interfirm credit market, which had its implicit full backing and as a result the market had been slow in reacting to the credit squeeze.

(iii) *Comments on the Calvo and Coricelli model*

Although these observations are valid, credit squeeze can't explain the 1990 stagflation in Poland because of the following:

(a) The existence of *credit crunch* even in early 1990 is dubious, since the credit ceilings imposed on the entire banking system under the stabilization program turned out to be not binding. Calvo and Coricelli (1992, pp. 82-83) explanation of *considerable* increase in the refinancing rate of the central bank for the validity of credit squeeze could not be acceptable in view of the time path of the refinancing rate (average prime rate on loans) rising from 12% (14%) to 36% (46.5%) in Jan. 1990, declining to 20% (22%) in Feb. 1990, 10% (10.5%) in March 1990, and 2.8% (2.9%) in July 1990 and 4.6% (5.1%) in Dec. 1990 and considering inflation rates of 79% in Jan 1990 and 585% average for 1990; because even prime loan rates are negative in real terms and can't be considered high in such a high inflation environment.

(b) The explanation of stagflation by imperfections of the banking sector, particularly by segmentation between household and enterprise sectors (*households* have perfect access to international capital markets, where they can freely borrow and lend at the international rate of interest; whereas, *firms* can only alleviate the credit squeeze by falling into arrears with other firms, which increases the riskiness of the interfirm credit market and dries up sources of funds for solvent and efficient firms, and they cannot get the required credits from the banking sector) was not confirmed by actual developments in 1990, because as interfirm credit declined in mid 1990, banking credit for working capital increased offsetting the interfirm credit decline (Figure: 3, Calvo and Coricelli, 1992, p. 84). As admitted by Calvo and Coricelli (1992, p. 82), "the assumption of no official bank credit is, of course unrealistic".

(c) Calvo and Coricelli admit that, despite easing of credit tightness in the second half of 1990, output has responded much less to credit expansion than to the credit contraction, in contradiction to the expectations of their model. Their explanation is that firms maximize current wages rather than permanent wages as postulated in their model; thus with easing of credit conditions firms offer higher wages and also repay arrears instead of using the proceeds to relieve the liquidity squeeze and to expand output. And they claim that there was sharp increase in real wages in the second half of 1990 and a contraction of inter- enterprise credit in the third quarter of 1990 (Calvo and Coricelli, 1992). Whereas Gomulka (1992) maintains that a large fall in real wages occurred in 1990.

(d) The model's prediction regarding an output fall leading to a decline in permanent household income and hence to an initial trade balance deficit (since the decline in output, on impact, is larger than the decline in consumption) have not materialized in 1990; on the contrary, a trade balance surplus of $2.7 billion has been achieved as against $0.2 billion surplus in 1989.

(e) Calvo and Coricelli (1992) *assume that,* when input prices increase, firms initially facing liquidity constraint, would reduce output, even if output prices increase in the same (or larger) proportion as input prices. This behavior would be rational only if bank credit for working capital were not available or interest rates are exorbitantly high, or if falling into arrears with other firms is impossible; neither of which were true in the 1990 Polish economy. Interest rates, although increased sharply, were still strongly negative in real terms and enterprises achieved high profit rates despite recession because real wages declined sharply (Gomulka, 1992).

10 Forecasting foreign trade of reforming countries

Rollo and Stern (1992), in estimating growth and trade prospects for Central and Eastern Europe, has "adopted an approach based on the *construction of alternative scenarios*", which are based on simplifications of the real world, focusing on key assumption and issues. In view of "the difficulty of projecting over a long period in which structural changes are likely to be substantial", the approach aims at

> *exploring scenarios* which illuminate *possibilities in circumstances. ... The scenarios are not forecasts;* rather they are an attempt to set out the

implications of outcomes at either end of a probability distribution, the mean of which is not only unknown but inherently unknowable.

The (optimistic) scenario is calibrated using judgmental estimates of what is attainable on the basis of actual performance of the most successful less developed countries or of countries which carried out significant liberalization. ... [like Korea, Taiwan, Thailand or Spain; and] *the pessimistic scenario assumes in essence that the reforms do not work.*

Rollo-Stern method "begins with views on the growth of output, move on to exports" and then derive *imports through assumptions on sustainable trade deficits,* using the balance of payments identity (current account balance equals net capital flow). Under the optimistic scenario the impact of best-performance-rates (estimates) on the demand for gross capital flows is examined (Rollo and Stern, 1992).

The suggested method does not make overall assumptions (optimistic or pessimistic), but rather depicts a picture that depends on estimates, judgments or hunches of enterprise governance, and which might turn out to be more realistic; but it could not be the exact replica of actual outcome.

11 Senik-Leygonie and Hughes method for measurement of the competitiveness of the former socialist industries

Senik-Leygonie and Hughes (1992) measured international competitiveness of industries in the former Soviet Union from the 1987 input-output data. They employed tools of the Little and Mirlees (1977) method for project appraisal. In order to further clarify objections raised to their study and findings, the Little and Mirlees method is also critically evaluated in the next section.

(i) Conversion factors: shadow prices

They basically employed Little and Mirlees (1977) shadow pricing and conversion factor concepts. Conversion factor for traded goods is the ratio of the shadow price (border price or the price at which good is sold or bought on the world market) to the domestic price. These conversion factors computed from the detailed foreign trade data for 1988, were applied to the 1987 input-output flows to get trade flows at world prices; imported intermediate inputs were repriced using the same conversion factors. The input-output tables of the Soviet Union with 104 sectors of which 86 cover manufacturing have been constructed using producer prices defined as the sum of the net price received by the producer, plus turnover taxes, and transport markups. In the case of non-traded goods and services, unit values at world prices were obtained by applying their direct and indirect traded good and factor requirements per unit output, the weighted averages of shadow prices. Separate conversion factors (for each activity/sector) were calculated for non-traded goods and services, inputs of intermediate goods imported, labor and capital costs (Senik-Leygonie and Hughes, 1992). Senik-Leygonie and Hughes (p.382) refer to Little and Mirlees (1974, [1976 and 1977] for the methodology employed.

(ii) Conversion factors for traded goods

(1) Use of world prices. "Conversion factors for traded goods were calculated from information on hard currency trade flows recorded either by enterprises or by the Ministry of Foreign Trade" (Senik-Leygonie and Hughes, 1992, p. 383).

"Imported intermediate inputs have been distinguished from domestically produced ones and repriced using import coefficients" (*ibid*, p. 385). Separate information was available on the ratios of world prices to domestic prices for intermediate goods imported from outside the Soviet Union.(*ibid*, p. 383).

Price distortions in infra-CMEA trade were eliminated by converting these transactions to world prices. In fact, "intra-CMEA trade transactions are included in the foreign export and import vectors" (p. 385).

(2) Criticism

(a) CMEA trade

This price adjustment to the CMEA trade flows is not appropriate, since quality of goods involved is inferior to goods on the world market, hence a bias towards exporting industries (increasing their profitability unduly) and towards domestic industries using inputs imported from the CMEA area (decreasing their profitability unduly) is introduced through this procedure. In fact, no CMEA country wanted to import the CMEA goods at even lower prices (than world prices) in hard currency, and as a consequence the CMEA trade collapsed and this collapse corroborates the remark made.

(b) Export and import prices

Senik-Leygonie and Hughes used actual *export prices* of Soviet products (not world market prices, which reflect the Western quality of products) in their calculations; these export prices were, however, *applied to the entire output,* i.e. to domestic sales, as well, which presumably were of lower quality products; this factor introduced a bias in estimates in favor of exporting industries, as pointed out by Hans-Werner Sinn (*ibid*, p. 381).

In the case of *imports* use of world prices, i.e. construction of conversion factors employed (import efficiency ratios, obtained by dividing the world price to the domestic price) are not meaningful and justified at all as admitted by Senik-Leygonie and Hughes, since "*imported goods often have no domestic substitute*" (*ibid*, p. 384).

(c) Trade and inter-industry flows

Weighted averages of prices of traded goods,

> were constructed to match the industrial classification of the input-output tables. Thus, the price ratios for each sector are as typical as possible of its product mix. ... A complete table of conversion coefficients ... [were used] in the same format as the input-output tables. ... [However], the product mix of foreign trade flows is more changing than that of inter-industrial links (*ibid*, p. 385),

which implies that if conversion factors were derived by repricing foreign trade flows of another year, one will get different sectoral ratios.

Instable product mix of foreign trade flows is most unusual for a market economy (except in years of extreme fluctuations in total foreign exchange receipts and capital flows, or other exceptional situations), annual product mix stability of both competing and non-competing imports is even more likely. Annual variations in product mix could only happen when foreign trade is integrated into the national economy(or vice versa, i.e. when the national economy is not integrated into the world economy, as in the case of the former socialist economies) from both inter-industry and final demand sides, and foreign trade flows are determined by central authorities rather on political and military considerations than by domestic economic conditions (which is the case for closed command economies and the CMEA area which were aiming at self-sufficiency and low import dependence).

Since imported input requirements of industries should be stable, annual variations in product mixture of imports could not be explained by inter-industry demand (which to a large extent met from the CMEA sources and through bilateral arrangements). Although Senik-Leygonie and Hughes note that imported intermediate inputs have been separated in inter-industry flows, they don't mention whether input requirements have been further broken down into categories by source (i.e. CMEA area, hard currency zone and through bilateral arrangements).

From all this it is deduced that the bulk of non-CMEA imports are non-competing imports (as also noted by Senik-Leygonie and Hughes) and are mainly for final demand (for consumption or investment). Also that imported goods under the same trade classification category are of a completely different kind and variety than domestic production and hence the use of their prices in the valuation of domestic production and inter-industry use of tradeables is not legitimate at all.

(d) Small versus large economy issue: exogenous or endogenous world price
Alasdair Smith notes that assumption of given (exogenous) world prices, can be justified if the economy concerned is small and faces exogenous world prices, (Senik-Leygonie and Hughes, 1992); otherwise the country will have market power to affect the world prices as well. In case of endogenous world prices, sector-specific factors, differentiated products and transport costs, Senik-Leygonie and Hughes calculations have to be modified (remarks by Alasdair Smith, Senik-Leygonie and Hughes, 1992).

If change in the quantity of a commodity exported or imported by a country affects world price, then under the Little and Mirlees method, the world price could not be taken as exogenous, then marginal import cost (MC= price[1+1/e_s] where e_s is the elasticity of supply) or marginal export revenue (MR= price[1-1/e_d] where e_d is the price elasticity of demand) should be the border price. The difference between existing world prices and the marginal cost/revenue would not be important in general for imports, but might be important for exports (Little and Mirlees, pp. 157-161).

(e) 'The suggested method' versus the Senik-Leygonie and Hughes study
'The suggested method', although based on the world market prices, would not allow any of this complications and biases to arise, since each enterprise would value its output and inputs on the basis of the quality of its product, the price it will fetch on the relevant world market, market conditions at home and abroad, relevant demand and supply elasticities, etc.

Moreover 'the method' does not value tradeables (output and inputs) at the official exchange rate, as the Little-Mirlees and the Senik-Leygonie and Hughes methods do, but at the equilibrium rate of foreign exchange. This issue, which is of critical importance for the valuation of non-traded goods, is taken up and dealt with in the section on the Little-Mirlees method.

(iii) Treatment of non-traded goods

Alasdair Smith points notes that

> *shadow prices for non-traded goods* can be expressed in terms of direct and indirect inputs of traded goods and non-traded factors (Senik-Leygonie and Hughes, 1992, p. 379). A distinction is made between traded goods and non-traded ones, such as services or construction, for which international price comparisons are not possible. The input-output

tables have been partitioned accordingly. There are 86 traded sectors (not all of them manufacturing activities) and 18 non-traded ones (*ibid*, p. 384).

"The ratios of world to domestic prices used to convert the input-output flows of the tables were computed from detailed foreign trade statistics for 1989" (*ibid*, p. 385), which implies that the foreign prices of only *actually imported or exported (traded)* goods were employed, not those of un-traded but inherently tradeable goods, as suggested by Little and Mirlees (1977). All tradeables have to be valued at border prices as also recommended by 'the suggested method', since with price and trade liberalization, non-traded tradeables, as well would face competition at world prices.

Martin Hellwig argued that "the use of foreign market prices to evaluate output is legitimate only to the extent that the foreign exchange is allocated by proper markets." Senik-Leygonie replied that "the allocation mechanism set up under the planned economy was still more or less active "(Senik-Leygonie and Hughes, p. 381).

Valuation issue of non-traded goods and traded or imported inputs, and factor inputs, is dealt with in depth in the section on the Little-Mirlees method. *Basic objections are :*

(a) Domestic prices of non-traded goods, in the former socialist countries, were fixed at too low prices (as revealed by severe shortages prevalent), which will lead to undervaluation of their output, when profitability calculation is based on producer prices as in the Senik-Leygonie and Hughes study.

(b) The use of the official exchange rate, when the currency is overvalued in the reforming economies, in the valuation of the cost elements of non-traded commodities (i.e. traded inputs, factor payments - particularly wages) will not allow correct valuation of costs.

The negative value-added calculated for food processing industry by Senik-Leygonie and Hughes might be due to the fact that undervaluation of output outweighs any undervaluation of inputs, in this industry.

According to Senik-Leygonie and Hughes, "negative value-added in food processing is caused either by wasteful use of raw materials and other material inputs or by the low quality of output", or inefficient technology or "lack of incentives to minimize the use of material inputs or to concentrate on producing higher quality output". Regarding poor performance of the food processing industry both in Central and Eastern European countries and the former Soviet Union they extend the opinion that it is due to losses of agricultural products in storage and distribution (*ibid*, p.361).

In these countries, food processing and light industry never got priority and were heavily protected; this fact supports the objection raised above. Wastage and inefficiencies that beset this industry, should as well plague other sectors (except for perishable foodstuffs, where wastage should be higher). Moreover, assigning the losses of agricultural products in storage and distribution to the food processing industry is rather arbitrary, they rather belong to the agriculture sector; and it would have been worthwhile to work out implications if the said losses were assigned to agriculture, which has been found profitable at world prices.

(iv) Cost of capital

Senik-Leygonie and Hughes, for the long-run calculations, included investments, using capital-output ratios and interest rates of developed market economies (because of lack of data on capital stock) also *assuming that the use of materials and labor per unit of output* (at world prices) *would not change, even in the long-run.* Wendy Carlin suggested that use of capital-output ratios of Western industries, explains the result that capital-intensive industries systematically come up as the most profitable industries (*ibid*, pp. 362, 381).

(v) Findings: competitiveness of industries

Senik-Leygonie and Hughes have found that the most competitive branches of the former Soviet Union economy are the ones using primary resources and heavy engineering, which are not traditionally protected and not labor-intensive, and are the most developed. The food processing industry with negative value-added is the worst, followed by textile sector in the Central Asian republics. Agriculture is profitable at world prices.

(vi) Aggregation and fixed coefficient problems

Aggregated data of input-output tables will disguise many important elements of real picture.

As pointed out by Alasdair Smith, by assuming fixed input coefficients, (large changes in input coefficients might take place after exposure of enterprises to world prices, as happened in Eastern Europe in energy inputs) not allowing for technological change and X- efficiency improvements, (*ibid*, p. 379) this exercise is bound to result in a pessimistic estimate, because it ignores the beneficial effects of a market reform.

(vii) Conclusion

Alasdair Smith observes that either Hare-Hughes calculations for Polish industry are inappropriate or Polish adjustment has not progressed along rational lines (*ibid.*, p. 381).

As a consequence of all this, profitability estimates by Senik-Leygonie and Hughes (1992) of the former Soviet industries are not reliable, and rather inappropriate, mainly because the scenario they have simulated is very different from the one that would prevail, if these economies really adopted the world prices or liberalized prices and trade.

The Senik-Leygonie and Hughes study is critically evaluated because it has wider connotations, if its results were appropriate and valid; because then liberalization of prices and trade in the reforming economies should rather be slowed down, if not stopped, and 'the suggested method' which also employs the world prices should not even be tried.

(viii) Similarity of Hare-Hughes and Senik-Leygonie-Hughes methods with 'the suggested methodology'

Hare-Hughes and Senik-Leygonie and Hughes (1992) studies of industrial profitability in the former socialist countries (Poland and the former Soviet Union) employ similar concepts used by the suggested method. Similarities are:

(a) They adopt *international prices* (shadow prices, border prices) for traded goods to judge the efficiency and profitability of industries and enterprises.

(b) "Non-traded goods and services are treated as bundles of traded goods and factors." They "use the weighted averages of the shadow prices for non-traded goods and factors where the weights are the total direct and indirect requirements of traded goods and factors per unit of output."

(c) In calculating the short-run profit rate, shadow price for capital (as well for labor) is taken zero.

(d) In calculating the medium-run shadow profit rate, "the shadow price of capital is [again] set at zero", while the shadow price of labor is taken positive and equals to the Soviet consumption bundle repriced at world prices.

(e) They recommend a transitional payments union to prevent collapse of the inter-republican trade.

(f) They recommend "a simplified escalating tariff structure on a temporary basis to allow time for industries to improve their performance before being fully exposed to international competition".

(ix) The advantages of 'the suggested method'

In countries which "are going to be much *more open to external trade* than in the past *it is natural to adopt international prices as a basis for judging the efficiency of industries and enterprises.*" For example "inter-republican trade [in the former Soviet Union] will take place at prices close to world market levels as soon as controls over prices and foreign trade are relaxed" (Senik-Leygonie and Hughes 1992).

The suggested method will help predict how enterprises fare as the country integrates into the world trading system, measure competitiveness of enterprises, determine whether there is a mismatch between existing production pattern (specialization, particularly in the former Soviet republics) and international trading pattern (international competitiveness) and see whether price and trade liberalization will disrupt trade. It will help identify enterprises which are effectively bankrupt and determine (a) the burden of supporting bankrupt or loss-making enterprises, (b) most efficient allocation of resources across enterprises and industries to maximize social objectives, e.g. minimizing the level of open unemployment and (c) will be the starting point for further analysis and investigations to evaluate correctly the prospects of currently loss-making enterprises improve their performance in the medium run.

12 The Little and Mirlees method of project appraisal and accounting prices

The Little and Mirlees (1977) method "singles out the values of foreign exchange, savings and unskilled labor, as crucial sources of a distorted price mechanism", and calculates accounting prices which will correct these distortions; and thus differs from some practitioners of social cost-benefit analysis, who believe that economists do better not to introduce this consideration. They also note that "a French school of thought believes that economists should also abjure accounting prices," (p. 362).

Little and Mirlees (1977) proposed border prices (fob or cif prices) be used as accounting (shadow) prices; accounting prices take account of any shortage of foreign exchange; imperfections of policy like distorted tariff structure does not affect the calculation procedure; *rigid quotas, however, may affect the estimation of accounting prices* (*ibid*, pp. 68, 69). The unit of account for border prices is the equivalent of one dollar (convertible currency) at the official exchange rate (*ibid*, p. 71, 151); i.e. the border price of imported goods equals its world price in dollars times the official exchange rate (*ibid*, p.157). Domestic transport costs must also be accounted for; i.e. price at factory should equal to "price at port plus transport cost to furthest point to which imports penetrate minus transport cost between that point and the factory". *Moreover differences in kind and quality of home-produced good from those of imported good, should be taken into account (ibid*, pp. 208-209).

Ratios of accounting prices to domestic market prices are termed 'conversion factors'; i.e. for traded good conversion factors equal ratios of border prices plus internal transport and trade margins to market prices; in other words conversion factor is the inverse of shadow exchange rate.

(i) Valuation of traded goods at accounting prices

Little and Mirlees (1977) "measure all commodities in terms of uncommitted social income [= numeraire, economic profit] measured in terms of convertible foreign exchange", and use domestic currency equivalent of any convertible currency at official or actual exchange rate (*ibid*, pp. 145,150, 151).

By the price mechanism (the exchange rate or multiple exchange rates, with or without tariff and export taxes or subsidies), the accounting prices of goods and services (i.e. their foreign exchange cost or savings) are estimated (*ibid*, p. 353).

Under the conventional methods a single shadow exchange rate is estimated, and according to Little and Mirlees, to *use a single shadow exchange rate is inappropriate.* They resort to conversion factors (which are inverted shadow exchange rates) and use their averages where appropriate. They employ "direct estimates of foreign exchange use or earnings for all important inputs, whether of domestic or foreign provenance" (p. 354).

(ii) Shadow wage rate

Shadow wage rate can be defined as net increase in consumption per worker employed (net resource use, taking into account, marginal productivity of labor and increase in consumption), or extra consumption caused by extra employment); wage conversion factor equals the ratio of shadow wage rate to market wage rate (*ibid*, pp. 270-74).

After estimating the average wage earner's consumption budget (using family budget surveys), one can then use accounting prices of items concerned to evaluate his expenditure on main categories of consumer goods (*ibid*, p. 281). "Thus the worker's consumption conversion factor is an estimate of the foreign exchange cost of an average unskilled worker's consumption" (*ibid*, p. 354).

If it is estimated that worker's consumption (wage) of 10 rupees costs the economy one dollar and the official exchange rate is 5, the wage conversion factor would be 5/10=1/2; which "could be called a shadow exchange rate of twice the official rate (10 rupees to the dollar instead of 5). Any other shadow rate estimate (employing other methods, including black market rates) would be inappropriate to apply the wage component, if it is different from 10 rupees to dollar (*ibid*, pp. 353-54).

"If a devaluation is anticipated, [as] traded goods are valued directly at their foreign exchange equivalent, devaluation makes no difference [for them, but] a lower shadow wage than otherwise must be employed; [this will also] *reduce the accounting price of all non-traded resources,* [i.e. all] non-traded resources will be devalued" (*ibid*, 355).

(iii) Shadow interest rate

"The accounting rate of interest [is] directly comparable with interest on loans payable in foreign currency, or with lending abroad" (*ibid*, p.147). The proper choice of the accounting rate of interest, depends on investible funds available and investment requirements of promising project, and is a matter of experience (*ibid*, p. 296).

(iv) Accounting price for non-traded goods and services

(1) The procedure

The marginal social cost is the value, in terms of accounting prices, of the resources (inputs, labor) required to produce an extra unit of the commodity. *The marginal social benefit* is, the benefit (market price) evaluated in social terms (*ibid*, pp. 162-166).

Accounting price for non-traded goods and services producible at constant cost is equal to "the cost of production, measured at accounting prices." Accounting price of a non-traded good is equal to its marginal social cost, which is the sum of all inputs valued at shadow prices (Little and Mirlees, pp. 165, 211-12).

The social cost / accounting price of a non-traded good or service (say construction) comprise material inputs, labor costs and value of consumption out of profits, all measured at accounting prices; plus annual depreciation converted to accounting prices (conversion factor equal to the ratio of the accounting-price of the machinery to its actual costs) plus interest cost calculated by charging the accounting rate of interest on the value of the fixed and working capital stock (at accounting prices), (p. 214).

If the right amount of non-traded goods is produced, then the marginal social benefit equals marginal social cost (accounting price); marginal product in domestic currency x conversion factor=price in domestic currency x conversion factor (*ibid*, p. 221). "*Accounting prices for inputs from the private sector must always be based on actual prices*" (*ibid*, p. 233). Use of "direct estimates of foreign exchange use or earnings for all important inputs, whether of domestic or foreign" origin is recommended (*ibid*, p. 354).

Non-traded goods are valued by their local production costs in terms of foreign exchange, employing a conversion factor, which is some *average of conversion factors* for particular goods and services; hence *different conversion factors would be used for different non-traded goods (ibid*, pp. 70-71).

(2) Commodities in fixed supply

When commodities are in fixed supply (imports under quota), *marginal social benefit is not equal to market price.* The benefit (social gain) of an investment project increasing supply of a good under a fixed import quota (unchanged), will be based on the domestic market price, but will take into account also the change in domestic market price; and social gains by consumers, the producer and the government through the change in market price, increased supply and increased tax revenue, should be valued at accounting prices (*ibid*, pp. 167-68, 199-203).

(3) Valuation of output of a private sector project

In case of a *private sector investment project,* output, material inputs, labor, depreciation charges, implicit interest cost on fixed and working capital stock, taxes and profit will be first valued at market prices, and then converted to values in accounting prices. Then *capitalist extra consumption and extra saving* have to be estimated. The calculation procedure is laborious, entails many bold assumptions and intelligent guesses (Little and Mirlees, 1977, pp. 199-203). In this case the method would become quite arbitrary in its practical applications.

(4) Definition of non-traded goods

"Accounting prices take proper account of any shortage of foreign exchange"; import *quota restrictions* may, however, result in *a tradable commodity becoming non-traded; then it will be valued as a non-traded good* (Little and Mirlees, 1977, pp. 69-70). Treating a inherently tradeable good, while its world price is available, and valuing it on the basis of grossly distorted domestic price is a severe defect in the method.

(5) Treatment of sales and excise taxes

Sales tax may be *corrective* (on tobacco, liquor and luxuries) or *distorting*. If tax is corrective, then net-of-tax price is a better measure of the social value of the goods than the market price (p. 224). Unless there is evidence that the tax is a temporary measure, then the tax should be considered corrective. *If there is any doubt, a project evaluator should consult fiscal authorities* (p. 225).

Taxes on producer goods are distorting and should be removed/abolished (p. 225). Taxes on commodities which are

> both consumers' and producers' goods present difficulties if the two markets can not be separated. ... Tax on petrol, cars, furniture or typewrites might be regarded as corrective when sold to households but distorting.... when sold to firms. ... In all these cases taxes should be subtracted; exceptionally when the tax is regarded as temporary, one has to guess what the price will be when the tax is removed.... (p. 226).

As a general rule taxes on final non-traded consumer goods should be subtracted from the price and they should be valued net of taxes (p.361-62).

Determination of corrective, distorting and temporary natures of taxes (and tax rate changes) or commodities and expenditures, and estimation of sales to households and firms separately, call for much discretion and it is possible that different project evaluators might reach different conclusions and estimates regarding these items and evaluate their projects accordingly.

(6) Non-traded consumer goods: rationing

In case of *non-traded consumer goods,* when there is *excess demand,* the social value of the good concerned is higher than the estimated marginal social cost of supplying it.

> The social value becomes the price which equates the existing inadequate supply to the demand. ... [If] *there is a case [justification] for restrictions on use or rationing,* and despite this, there is still excess demand, *then the social value is equal to the marginal social cost at the level of output which meets the rationed demand* (p. 232).

Therefore, on the one hand, the actual prices should be adjusted so that supply equals demand and, on the other, accounting prices should vary (using supply and demand as guides for revision of accounting prices). However,

> if the shortage of [a commodity, say] electricity is merely temporary, it would be wrong to put a scarcity value on electricity when the project will probably be using very little until it is in operation several years hence. ... Similarly it would be wrong to put a low accounting price on electricity just because there is, temporarily, excess capacity (p. 232).

This, however, does not imply that one should always ignore supply and demand.

> Accounting prices for inputs from the private sector must always be based on actual prices. ... *To conclude, no automatic method of adjusting the accounting prices of non-traded goods can be recommended.* (p. 233) One should use caution in changing the forecasts of accounting prices (p. 233).

(7) Discretion and arbitrariness in determining accounting prices of non-traded goods

In determining accounting prices for non-traded goods, there are no clear-cut rules, a lot of discretion is involved. For example if "rental income or excess profit arising out of quota accrued to private traders, then apparent social benefit from the government project", producing the good under fixed import quota would be larger, than otherwise. "But in this case, it is highly questionable whether this added benefit (arising from trader's loss due to reduced domestic price caused by increased supply) should be attributed to the project", since the government could have expropriated this private monopoly profit through a tariff, auctioning import licenses or by multiple exchange rates in lieu of producing the commodity itself, or could "have reduced or eliminated the monopoly profit allowing more imports", (*ibid*, p.168), if it could afford.

> Indeed, the possible complications are almost endless. ... The evaluator has to estimate the gains and losses to various social groups, which occur directly and indirectly as a result of the project, and which could not be assumed to have occurred without the project, and then weight them according to some assessment of the social value... (p. 169).

The social benefit of a non-traded good (such as wheat or maize produced for inland), is through reduction in local prices and increase in consumption, rather than through saving imports or increasing exports (although there is trade), (p. 220).

The value to the consumer is "the price he is willing to pay [and] in the absence of rationing it will be very close to the price he actually pays" (p. 220). If there is no market price (irrigation water supplied free or at a nominal charge), then marginal product of water in the production of rice, etc. or marginal product of electricity in industrial output in general, will be estimated and these domestic values (in rupees) will be translated into border price values (border rupees), (p. 222).

(8) Observations and criticism

All this can be summed up as, *accounting prices of non-traded goods* can be taken equal to its production *cost*, if the demand is fully met. On the other hand, if there is excess demand, because supply is fixed under import quota or ban and / or domestic production capacity constraint, then the accounting price has to be based on the *market price*. In case of an investment project increasing the fixed supply, while UNIDO (1972) guidelines consider market price as an adequate basis for calculating accounting prices, Little-Mirlees method calls for general equilibrium analysis, estimation and accounting for all direct and indirect effects of this quantity and price change. Following observations are due:

(a) When the market price becomes the basis for accounting price calculations, then normal profit and excess profit (rental income), along with all unit cost components have to be evaluated at accounting prices and Little-Mirlees procedure requires clumsy and laborious calculations and is based on some bold or crude assumptions (which will be dealt with in due course); whereas, employing shadow prices obtained from optimization exercises would have solved the problem neatly and without complications.

(b) And under the semi-input-output method, these complications would not have arisen at all, since all tradeables (including those considered non-traded under the Little-Mirlees method), are valued at border prices, not on the basis of their exorbitantly high domestic prices and the real resource use implied by their components.

(c) When the non-traded good subject to import ban or excessive exchange and trade restrictions and/or is domestically produced by an unregulated private monopoly or oligopoly, its domestic market clearing price would be too high, completely out of line with the world market price and it is still considered by Little and Mirlees, as eventually being valued at border price; whereas this hypothesis and the basic premises of the method are not valid at all, and the method has in fact broken down. On the other hand, if the good is produced by public sector, then its domestic price will normally be fixed at artificially low prices (as in the former socialist economies) and the method again breaks down, because the fixed domestic price is neither the market clearing price (in view of prevalent shortages) nor has any relation at all with the world market price, but the method is still applied.

This is a serious flaw in the method, from which the semi-input-output method does not suffer, and even the Little-Mirlees method could have avoided this pitfall, by taking the world price of the commodity even when it is not imported;

but then one needs a correct shadow exchange rate (which the method does not produce). However, still some average of calculated conversion factors for exchange rate could be used, which would yield less erroneous appraisals.

(v) Equilibrium in balance of payment

Another fundamental objection to the Little-Mirlees method arises from the fact that estimated accounting prices for foreign exchange, wages and interest rate might not help promote equilibrium in BOP, labor and capital markets.

Little and Mirlees (1977) maintain that models of *linear programming* type often express trade possibilities in a very crude and arbitrary way, by imposing constraints, many of them pure guesses, which have a large effect on the accounting prices estimated (p.296). However, as already pointed out, their method entails much more arbitrary decisions left to the discretion of individual project evaluators; and as a consequence it is more unlikely that changes into BOP, labor and capital markets, through an investment program or development plan drawn up employing their method would produce an equilibrating effect (in the marginal sense) on BOP, labor and capital markets; it would rather add more disequilibria (marginally) into those markets already in disequilibria or imbalance.

Even shadow interest rate, which could easily achieve equilibrium in the capital market, is not unique and is subject to discretion (*ibid*, p. 296).

Little and Mirlees claims that, by right combination of trade policy and the exchange rate, full use of domestic capacity is possible. By raising the accounting rate of interest, investments could he reduced and then consumption would increase. *The accounting prices for commodities determined under the method,* would promote investments that would *balance use of domestic resources and foreign exchange (ibid*, pp. 350-51).

In particular, there is no mechanism in the method or its operational procedures that will guarantee equilibrium in BOP. The accounting price for exchange rate is not a real shadow exchange rate, which would achieve equilibrium in BOP, but is only a measure of protection· through tariffs, exchange and trade restrictions, as implied by domestic prices. In fact, Little and Mirlees mention the objection that the method results in projects, which do little for the balance of payments (*ibid*, p. 355).

In fact, if government, because of the BOP considerations, is restricting investment growth (by capital budgeting), Little and Mirlees recommend *investment projects which will have little negative impact in the construction phase on the BOP* and realize quick foreign exchange earnings, employing few people directly, but *using inputs from excess capacity capital-intensive industries*. (In fact under this method, a domestic industry with no export potential and some excess capacity, will have a lower accounting price for its output, comprising only the foreign exchange equivalent of the labor, fuel, and materials entering into the product; also accounting rate of interest and shadow wage rate will be high due to deflationary policy exercised and the BOP constraint), (*ibid*, pp. 355-56). However, this change in project appraisal rules would *produce wrong projects,* if the deflationary situation or the BOP problem were temporary (*ibid*, p. 365). Appraisal method for non-traded sectors (e.g. compared with the semi-input-output method) and calculation of the cost of private investments also introduce bias towards domestic industries, the latter will be taken up later.

(vi) Actual outcome of investment programs designed using shadow prices: discrepancies

Little and Mirlees objections to optimization methods could be taken care of by using reliable data and relevant constraint bounds, sensitivity tests and testing with ex post data, because except for high inflation and high disequilibria situations or major changes in economic structure or development policies, shadow exchange and wage rates should not vary much. Shadow exchange rates, however, would vary with time horizon of optimization (investment program)and change over time along with variations of export performance, aid inflow and changes in exchange and trade regimes, income growth, etc.

Estimation of shadow exchange and wage rates and implementing the resulting investment program (forecast to be profitable at shadow rates), without taking corrective measures to make actual rates equal to shadow rates, would introduce further distortions in the economy, because exporting and labor-intensive industries promoted would incur losses at actual prices, which will cause further deterioration in internal and external equilibria.

Little and Mirlees (1977), recommend that tariff system should not be protective and that domestic production should be encouraged mainly by *subsidies, especially on labor (ibid*, p. 80). Since labor is often overpriced in the modern sectors of developing countries, labor should be subsidized. By protection, "consumers pay the subsidy directly in the form of a higher price"; if protection is reduced and domestic production for the home market is taxed as heavily as imports and the resultant increase in revenues is paid back to industry in the form of subsidies, distortion from heavy protection will be corrected, consumers will not be affected, since they pay either way (*ibid*, p. 80). "Sometimes for administrative reasons, domestic production is harder to tax than imports, ..., and, again for administrative reasons, subsidies may be hard to administer without inviting corruption" (*ibid*, p. 78).

Recommended substitution of import duties by new domestic tax revenue and subsidies is easier said than done, because of political and tax-collection considerations; and when implemented, persistent inflationary pressure is introduced through the decline in tax revenue and increase in budgetary expenditures (e.g. the Turkish example in 1980s).

Wage subsidy extensively and generously applied since 1982 in South Africa in line with the decentralization policies, to create more employment opportunities for blacks, although helped establishment of several new growth centers, has rather led to dislocation of industries within the Southern African region and waste of funds; and in 1990 had been generally considered as unsuccessful, too costly and not worth-the-while, and hence was to be discontinued.

Moreover wage subsidy scheme, causes actual wages further diverge from the shadow rate (since part of the subsidy will be passed on to wages under labor union pressure), which will lead to further economic inefficiency, increase inflationary pressure through extra burden on the government budget, and is overly difficult to administer and control effectively, virtually is open to pervasive fraud (a characteristic already admitted by Little and Mirlees, 1977, p. 78).

In many countries employment in the modern sector could better be promoted by reducing withholding taxes (income and payroll taxes) on wages, which rather proves to be an employment tax (penalizing employment) if rates are high, than an outright wage subsidy. This could be done in the context of a reduced income tax progression, starting from the lowest income bracket (in Turkey, e.g., tax rate applicable to lowest bracket is 25%), in the light of Laffer curve, (in countries with pervasive tax evasion and severe collection problems).

(vii) Applying the method to chronic-or high-inflation countries

Little and Mirlees (1977, p. 355) recommend the shadow wage rate and valuation for non-traded goods be reduced, when devaluation is anticipated. If it were a real shadow exchange rate or a good substitute for it (as the domestic resource cost of foreign currency obtained by Bruno method), it would have indicated, the need for and the extent of devaluation.

Indeed, valuation of non-traded goods, through various conversion factors applied (some of them averages) to cost or price components would vary with devaluation, since the rate of domestic price increases would lag behind the rate of devaluation (if the latter were successful) and there will be some under-valuation of domestic goods. But, similarly when imminent devaluation is unduly delayed, price increases of non-traded goods will exceed price increases of tradeables, and there will be over-valuation of non-traded goods; to which danger Little and Mirlees draw our attention. Hence this appraisal method has a permanent bias towards non-traded sectors, when applied in countries with over valued currencies, provided that domestic prices are freely determined by market forces.

Hence, in chronic-or high-inflation countries accounting price estimates for foreign exchange (conversion factors), when applied to domestic cost/price components (wages, profits, etc.) would give unreliable results, because of permanent prospects for devaluations or unduly delayed devaluations. In fact recent applications of the method to the reforming socialist countries by Senik-Leygonie and Hughes (1992) and by Hughes and Hare suffer from omission of the above cited warning by Little and Mirlees (i.e., not taking into account this defect).

(viii) Appraisal of private investment

(1) The methodology

Accounting price for private investment is "the value of a unit of social income (measured in accounting prices) which is devoted to investment by the private sector", and is used "to evaluate the worth of capitalist saving arising out of project profits", as well for costing the initial investment of the project (*ibid*, pp. 196-97). The cost of private investment is valued at "the present social value of the same resources used as they would be if the project were not approved" (*ibid*, p. 195). The main alternative use of the funds is usually other private business ventures not requiring government approval. Other alternative uses would be purchasing government bonds, transfer abroad, lending for private consumption, other private projects requiring government approval (pp. 196-97).

This alternatives list by Little and Mirlees however is not exhaustive and excludes many important alternatives, namely purchase of real estate, land and gold, stockpiling of commodities for speculative purposes, deposit accounts denominated in local and/or convertible currency with resident commercial banks, and lending others for private business purposes.

Then an appropriately weighted average of the cost in the different alternative uses will provide estimate of the *accounting price for private investment,* (APPI) *which is normally less than one (ibid*, p. 197).

This accounting price (APPI) requires laborious calculations, e.g. in converting *extra capitalist consumption and savings*, one needs exactly what this consumption expenditure and saving would be used to purchase and then evaluate these purchases at accounting prices, instead of at market prices for the various goods and services. Since detailed information on these is not available, shortcuts and some intelligent guesswork will be employed. *Conversion of the extra saving into accounting prices is 'trickier'* because the uses to which saving can be put are so diverse, but in many cases "something quite crude will do" the job. If market prices of investment goods are guessed to be 100r% above accounting prices, then dividing the extra saving figure by (1+r) will serve the purpose (*ibid*, pp. 199-203).

(2) Criticism
Discounting extra savings by means of an investment deflator (equal to the conversion factor for investment goods) by Little and Mirlees (1977, p. 201) is quite *arbitrary,* and exemplifies one of the many arbitrary features of the method (procedures /modalities worked out) when applied to practical problems. As against whatever arguments Little and Mirlees can raise in favor of such a modality, one can unequivocally object on grounds that the excess of the accounting price over the market price is largely due to taxation (hence it should not be subtracted since there is no social cost involved) and/or that it is not within the control of private investor, it penalizes saving unduly, and that if extra savings are invested in government bonds no such discount would have been applied.

There is some sense (though still not absolutely) in discounting the cost of private investment project (whose components and inputs are already valued at accounting prices) through multiplying by APPI, *ex ante* and only if the government approval in the licensing sense is required for implementation of the project. Even then, when it turns out that the project would be approved, it is a must/essential to re-evaluate it without multiplying the investment cost by APPI. Because once the project approved there is no alternative use for the funds concerned, hence implied advantage by APPI multiplication is not real, but imaginary; in other words APPI does not represent shadow price/cost but shadow/imaginary advantage.

Secondly, the same investment project, whether under private or public ownership will use the same real resources of the economy during the construction phase *ex post,* hence there is no sense/justification at all to assume a lower real investment cost for the private sector project.

Thirdly, Little and Mirlees, by applying APPI to the full investment cost of the project make another mistake by disregarding financing aspect of the capital cost or they make *most unrealistic assumption,* i.e. 100% own-financing by private investor/capitalist which must be very rare all over the world, any way in developing countries. Proponents of the Little-Mirlees method could still unconvincingly claim that, even outside funds are singularly and exclusively mobilized or pooled for this specific project and hence should be treated like own-funds (this assumption, however, is not valid, because bulk of the funds mobilized/pooled for project, in fact, would materialize only when the government approval is granted) and hence justify use of funds for an unworthy project; but the government by not granting approval to this project, in fact, would rather divert whatever resources pooled to a more worthy private sector project. Lastly, in the case of partial bank financing of the project (which is the normal case), none of these arguments in favor of APPI application) are valid.

Fourthly, the government approval always entails many privileges, not only licensing, but soft, concessionary loans, easy access to local and foreign bank loans, foreign exchange allocation, duty-free importation of capital goods and operating inputs, low-priced material inputs, utilities and transport services, tax and other investment incentives, etc. On top of these, APPI application would result in creation of many unviable, economically and financially unsound industries particularly serving the domestic market, which would be as dependent on government subsidies and funding as many public enterprises. Under the circumstances, the private sector project should be appraised not leniently, but rather as rigorously and strictly as the public sector projects, to make sure that they really make a positive contribution to the national economy.

(ix) Alternative methods

Alternative partial analysis methods of project appraisal (like Bruno method and Tinbergen's semi-input-output method) are superior to the Little and Mirlees method, since they don't have the complications mentioned; and provide reliable and useful estimates of critical variables and help achieve BOP equilibrium.

The *Bruno* method estimates domestic resource cost (in local currency, including capital cost) per unit of foreign exchange saved or earned of investment projects and had been in use in Israel for years. It is used for evaluating projects which "produce fully traded or nearly fully traded, outputs" (Little and Mirlees pp. 363-65). This method when applied to a representative sample of projects producing tradeables would give a good measure of currency overvaluation.

The semi-input-output method bypasses all problems related to valuation of output of tradeables classified under the Little-Mirlees method as non-traded (because of import restrictions), because they are duly treated as traded goods (as output of international sectors) and valued accordingly. Domestic sectors are defined as those whose surplus output or excess demand could not be exported or met by importation; hence the aim of economic planning and project evaluation is prevent any deficit or surplus develop in these sectors and make sure that all domestic non-tradeable input requirements of international sectors are exactly met.

Tinbergen's semi-input output model and its variants (Tinbergen, 1967; Pronk and Schereuel, 1969; Kuyvenhoven, 1978; Kızılyallı, 1990, pp. 108-116.) achieve (i) ranking/selection of investment projects producing traded goods on the basis of their direct and indirect net foreign exchange savings/earnings (valuation at border prices) (ii) equilibrium in BOP, and (iii) as an economic planning tool assures full capacity utilization in domestic (non traded good and service producing) sectors; and thus is superior to the Little-Mirlees method as a project appraisal method and economic planning model.

Chapter 8

High inflation problem

High inflation problem

1 The problem

Of the reforming socialist countries, Poland, former Yugoslavia, the former Soviet Union, Bulgaria and Romania experienced or experiencing high-or hyperinflation, as result of market reform and structural adjustment policies. Dornbusch (1992) notes that *unless both the monetary overhang and the persistent and insistent budgetary deficits are addressed at the outset of any attempt to restructure the economy,* dramatic increase in inflation is bound to occur; *"without fiscal austerity stabilization cannot last"* and *"without incomes policy it cannot start;" and that "there is a steeply rising cost of disinflation."*

The generally accepted operational definition of *hyperinflation* (extreme inflation) is by Cagan and sets the benchmark at an inflation rate of 50% a month. *Countries experiencing inflation rates of 10 or 15% a month for any length of time are moving toward hyperinflation.* In order to solve high-inflation problem, stabilization program had to be radical, as the German authorities said in 1948, *'soft measures do not create hard currencies' (Dornbusch,* 1992).

It should be pointed out that dollarization prevents hyperinflation end up in a barter economy and catastrophe finale.

High inflation in Poland and Yugoslavia was preceded by flight from domestic money; the accelerated dollarization characterizes these cases.

2 Private savings and monetary overhang in the former socialist countries

In socialist economies many relative prices have bean historically fixed below market-clearing levels, which give rise to excess demand (Dinopoulos and Lane, 1992); this led to involuntary savings by households, termed as monetary overhang.

Soviet consumers used to save less compared to those in market economies at the same development stage, because of low variability of life cycle income, large state subsidies to basic consumption items, ability of retirees to obtain goods at low controlled prices by waiting in queues (in lieu of buying in a parallel market) and limited choice of financial instruments. Hence it is not clear that accumulated savings are excessive and constitute a monetary overhang (2-3% interest on saving deposits). On the other hand, the uncertain availability of some goods in state stores leads to higher savings, in the form of cash (Alexeev, 1992).

> When the constraints on the availability of financial instruments *limit the portfolio choices of households* to very liquid or monetary assets, as has been the case in the Soviet Union and in most centrally planned economies, it is likely that practically all the involuntary increases in the stock of wealth would take the form of higher holdings of monetary balances, which are defined as excess liquidity or *monetary overhang*. ... The difference between the nominal stock of wealth actually held and the amount desired in the absence of current and past rationing could be defined as *wealth overhang* (Cottarelli and Blejer, 1992).

> In an economy characterized by chronic shortages, not only is forced saving present, but *voluntary saving tends to be higher* because buyers maintain high reserves of purchasing power in order to be able *to acquire goods that appear in the market in a random and unpredictable fashion.* ... That is, money is held primarily not under transactions motive, but under precautionary motive and for storing value (Cottarelli and Blejer, 1992).

In the early 1960s, The level of household wealth in relation to income or consumption was extremely low, compared with wealth/consumption ratios in Western countries (Cottarelli and Blejer, 1992).

With transition to market economy, consumers increased their voluntary savings (during the last five years) and this trend is expected to continue at an accelerated pace, if the Soviet economy is converted to the market system (Alexeev, 1992).

> Over the second half of the 1980s household consumption in the Soviet Union was below the desired level, and therefore, savings were being involuntarily accumulated, mostly in the form of monetary balances. ... [Chronic excess saving] would result in a permanent increase in the average observed saving rate (Cottarelli and Blejer, 1992).

The 1987-1988 reforms loosened central government control over enterprise wage funds, when liquidity of enterprises increased due to accelerated monetary growth (15%) in 1987. This led to a rapid growth of wages and higher private voluntary savings. Saving rate from disposable income rose from 8% in 1987 to 13% in 1990 (Alexeev, 1992).

Reforms cause uncertainty regarding future real income (prolonged etc.) and give rise to incentives to save (for buying private house and consumer durables) which result in higher private savings (Alexeev, 1992).

Cottarelli and Blejer (1992) estimated the undesired holdings of wealth (monetary overhang) in the Soviet Union at end 1990 at about 170-190 billion rubles, close to 20% of GDP and about one third of existing financial assets; they also estimated that a price increase of 45-50% would be necessary at end 1990 to wipe out the monetary overhang (excessive monetary holdings).

Arguments over monetary overhang and excessive savings are misleading and experience of former East Germany and Poland has demonstrated that price liberalization does not immediately lead to dissaving (Alexeev, 1992).

Empirical relevance of *liquidity overhang* as an explanation of shortages is doubted now. Excess demand (shortages) arise rather from a relative price imbalance (an administratively fixed price below the market-clearing level, not from an aggregate liquidity overhang (Dinopoulos and Lane, 1992).

In fact large jumps in the price level of reforming socialist countries after 1990 eliminated monetary overhang and shortages (Commander, 1992).

Elimination of monetary overhang by means of high inflation, at the very beginning of the reform process was both useless and harmful. It was useless because it did not help least in preventing the emergence of persistent high-or hyper-inflation in these countries. Since monetary holdings constituted main component of private wealth in these countries under the circumstances prevailing then, it meant and entailed renunciation of basic tenet of capitalism, private wealth accumulation, which should rather have been promoted. And monetary overhang could have been absorbed without any adverse effect and for a good cause by privatization, particularly of houses and small shops. This exercise not only wiped out monetary overhang, but also caused destruction of already fragile saving habits in the reforming countries, which should rather have been encouraged and fostered, since private saving is pivotal in stabilization programs and economic growth thereafter. Hence this exercise has become one of the many errors made in the transformation process.

3 Lessons from Brazilian inflation: the inflationary process in reforming countries

Brazil has frequently resorted to direct control over prices and incomes, namely under the Cruzado Plan (1986), Bresser Plan (1987), Plano Verao (1989) and

Collor Plan (1990). In the Collor Plan, a massive reduction in money supply and freezing savings accounts were the dominant elements. Brazil used indexation of wages, prices and interest rates and rents; and indexation alternated with periodic freezes. These had little effect on long-term inflationary trends. Inflation rates were 235% in 1985, 65% in 1986, 416% in 1987, just over 1,000% in 1988 and over 1,500% in 1989. The problem with Latin American inflation is rising oil prices, steep rises in interest rates in early 1980s, costly expenditure programs and an inability to raise taxes (1) (Sloman, 1991, p.830).

Parkin (1991) shows that, in an economy *with mark-up pricing and widespread official or implicit indexation of key prices, like wages and the exchange rate, a once-and-for-all change in relative prices can easily produce continuous inflation.*

Parkin, in his analysis of Brazilian inflation, tests several hypotheses of inflation (monetarist, structuralist, cost-push, demand-pull, etc.) and finds out that from 1964 onward, Brazilian inflation became extremely complex and that none of the inflation theories alone are able to explain the inflationary process. Rather different theories explain inflation and the inflationary process at different points in time; that of pricing behavior in middle income countries with oligopolized markets and limited international competition, and with indexation (of wages, salaries, and exchange rate) differing from that in industrial countries, since demand grows more quickly, shows greater volatility and changes more dramatically in structure over time and that the resultant mark-up pricing rule creates more uncertainty about relative prices (Parkin, 1991).

In such an economy, aggregate demand increase mainly results in price rises, not only because of the market imperfections, but also because of structural bottlenecks arising from supply rigidities and foreign exchange constraint; and as a consequence, growth becomes sporadic, depending on the extent of net increase in foreign borrowing; high annual growth rates are realized following periods of stagnation and decline, when net increase in external indebtedness becomes possible. Because in a semi-industrialized country, if imports cannot increase, inflationary pressure is bound to end up in price level increase with little output response, even when markets are competitive.

This analysis of Brazilian inflation in fact shows that in an economy with an indexation rule applying to wages and exchange rate, pricing behavior naturally

---

(1) This author, never believing in the Phillips curve trade-off, in a report to the Turkish Ministry of Finance (after a short study on the spot following a IMF/IBRD meeting) in 1967, in evaluating the then supposedly growth oriented, pro-inflationary policies of Brazil, had identified the root cause of the whole issue as the virtual absence of a taxation system in Brazil, and thereby the existence of a built-in inflationary mechanism in the economy.

becomes markup pricing, and then any money supply shock arising from the budgetary deficit, particularly persistent deficits, leads to chronic inflation, at times reaching to hyperinflation proportions.

In a high-inflation economy, it is quite normal for households and firms hedge against inflation through mark-up pricing, indexation, dollarization, capital outflow, investing in real estate and gold. Still with these inflationary cost-push mechanisms and distorted allocation of resources, had the budgetary deficits were eliminated for good, there is no doubt inflation would come to an end after a while. On the other hand, if the root cause is not tackled with, and some partial palliatives are applied to control inflation, like wage and exchange rate anchors, temporary price freeze, (to eliminate cost-push elements), along with some monetary restraint and a little fiscal discipline, the outcome would be some temporary relief in price rises and contraction of output, and a permanent loss through reverse- protection (nominal exchange rate anchor), and increase in external debt. Vegh (1992) studies effects of sustained real appreciation of the domestic currency, theoretically and empirically, and corroborates this conclusion.

One draws the following lesson, 'if a country is in the quagmire of macro- and microeconomics instability and chronic high-inflation, palliative, partial/ piecemeal measures, stop-gap stabilization programs, only make economic problem worse and economy sinks in more with every such attempt.'

4 Vegh analysis of chronic inflation and effects of stabilization programs

Vegh (1992) using a mathematical model shows that *"exchange rate stabilizations in chronic-inflation countries* have typically resulted in sluggish adjustment of the inflation rate, *sustained real appreciation of the domestic currency, current account deficits, and an initial expansion in economic activity followed by contraction"*; these findings are also consistent with experiences in chronic-high-inflation countries.

In analyzing effects of successive devaluations in chronic high-inflation countries, Vegh (1992). observes that when the reduction in *the rate of devaluation is not credible,* the public expects a higher rate of devaluation in future and hence perfect capital mobility is viewed as temporary and the temporary fall in the nominal interest rate (which reduces the effective price of consumption in the present relative to the future) causes demand for both traded and nontraded goods to increase, which in turn leads to an *initial expansion* in the nontraded goods sector and a current account deficit.

The slow convergence of inflation to the rate of devaluation results in a *sustained real appreciation of the domestic currency,* which ultimately

> reduces the demand for nontraded goods. As a consequence, output falls and *a recession sets in*. The recession may occur either before or when the program ends. The real effects caused by a noncredible stabilization do not depend on whether the program is eventually abandoned, as the public expected, or not (Vegh, 1992).

This analysis of a noncredible reduction in the rate of devaluation applies to the stabilization programs in *"chronic-inflation countries*, where a history of failed stabilizations, together with the ability of the economy to live with high inflation, makes *any attempt to stop inflation less than fully credible."*

"Contrary to common perceptions, lack of credibility does not necessarily generate high real interest rates", in the aftermath of stabilization programs. On the contrary, if additional nominal anchors (such as target for bank credit in the 1985 Israeli Plan, to be achieved by a combination of higher reserve requirements and a higher discount rate, in order to offset the expansionary effects of a large increase in credit to the private sector and virtually to reduce credit to the private sector in real terms at the initial phase of program) are not included in the stabilization programs and as a result real credit grows strongly (as under the Latin American stabilization programs), then the domestic real interest rate falls on impact (Vegh, 1992).

This analysis of chronic-high inflation by Vegh is very relevant to the reforming socialist economies, since persistent high inflation has been a common feature of these countries and coexistence of high inflation and structural reform in foreseeable future is predicted (see, e.g. Vegh, 1992, p. 669). Fisher (1992, p. 77) considers a stabilization program successful if the inflation rate is reduced to less than 30-40% a year.

5 Treatment of hyperinflation: Vegh analysis

"The evidence suggest that, by using the exchange rate as the nominal anchor, hyperinflations have been stopped almost overnight with relatively minor output costs." When the public views the policy change as permanent, (e.g. a reduction in the rate of devaluation), then it is fully credible, then "inflation falls instantaneously without any output costs." Sticky prices do not prevent an instantaneous adjustment because all-price-setting behavior is forward looking. This is because hyperinflationary processes are characterized by the absence of backward-looking behavior and "programs designed to stop hyperinflation usually command high credibility given the unsustainable state of affairs" (Vegh, 1992).

Predictions of a model developed by Calvo and Vegh, and employed for analysis of high inflation by Vegh (1992) have been born out by the hyperinflation experiences of Austria (1921-22), Germany (1992-23), Hungary

(1923-24), Poland (1923-24), Russia (1921-24), Hungary (1945-46), Taiwan (1945-1952, interestingly hyper-inflation stopped without any fiscal adjustment, with no prospects of any future fiscal adjustment, but with massive aid from the US in mid-1952 to balance the budget), and Bolivia (1984-85). On the basis of these evidences, "a good case can be made that hyperinflation has, in fact, been stopped suddenly with no major costs. The contractionary forces that have come into play seem to result from real distortions brought about by hyperinflation rather than by monetary stabilization itself" (Vegh, 1992).

6 Conclusions

Dornbusch concludes that if inflation is high and variable, then it will be the most important issue; and reducing inflation should take first priority. Governments, however, will be tempted into, "superficial remedies, which help in the short run but set back economic activity because they create uncertainty". "In economies in which price control has been the rule, the recognition of the problem may be the most serious issue". Beyond the initial correction of subsidies, there is the broader issue of the risk of serious inflation, which may "emerge either because of an initial monetary overhang or because the subsidy correction does not go far enough;" "deficits remain and money creation starts to interact with corrective inflation"; the Soviet Union is an obvious example of this practice (Dornbusch, 1992).

Under such conditions "the first priority... must be to reduce inflation"; and to this end "a lastingly balanced budget is required to achieve financial stability". Because "without financial stability, economic reconstruction and growth will simply not occur" (Dornbusch, 1992). All these assertions by Dornbusch are justified, however, as experience in high-inflation countries and the reforming socialist countries shows, it is 'easier said, than done' ; required radical measures could not be taken by weak governments, which can afford only palliative, superficial remedies (also under the pretext that the Philips trade-off exists) and (in reforming countries at the same time) to slow down the structural adjustment process (through ad hoc measures with resultant continuation of general relative price distortions and allocative inefficiencies).

Under the circumstances, the remedy for hyperinflation pointed out by Vegh suits best the needs and 'the suggested method' could provide the framework for such a shock therapy.

Chapter 9

Dollarization

Dollarization

Dollarization has become an important phenomenon in Poland (as well in Turkey), by reducing effectiveness of monetary policy and creating complications in macroeconomic management. The 1990 Polish reform has aimed at reducing dollarization, without much success. Now, dollarization has started in Russia.

Because of the importance of dollarization in the reforming countries, it was considered essential to summarize Latin American experience in dollarization as described and analyzed by Guidotti and Rodriguez (1992).

One dubious advantage of dollarization is its prevention of hyperinflation reaching crisis proportions (i.e., domestic money losing all its functions and the economy reverting to barter transactions) and thus enabling survival through persistent hyperinflation.

1 Latin American experience in dollarization

Since the 1970s, in Latin American countries with high inflation (Argentina, Bolivia, Peru and Uruguay), the currency substitution has been going on under the name of dollarization, "the US. dollar has gradually but persistently been replacing national currencies in the performance of all types of monetary services. Not only have dollars replaced national currencies in local portfolios, but dollars are often being used for settling current transactions and as a unit of account" (Guidotti and Rodriguez, 1992).

Guidotti and Rodriguez (1992) observe that, "dollarization goes to the very core of money and the monetary system". "It may well be that in the future the national monies in some of these Latin American countries will end up being used only to carry out small-change transactions and those that governments want to reserve for themselves", such as tax payments, payments to civil servants, etc. The issue at stake is the survival of national monies, in the face of competitive challenge posed by superior dollar. Several national monies already do not serve the store of value function; since it is hard to justify any holdings of non-interest earning money in these countries, as a store of value. "The minimal holdings of non-interest bearing domestic money are used almost exclusively for transaction purposes, and even then they have to compete with dollars, which are also used for the same purposes in a wide and expanding variety of transactions." Bolivia, Mexico, Peru and Uruguay have a widespread network of foreign exchange houses, as well as street vendors.

Guidotti and Rodriguez (1992) note that dollarization in Latin America has been greatly facilitated by freedom granted to financial and currency markets since 1970s. The elimination of foreign exchange control and allowing residents to hold foreign exchange have enabled dollarization to expand from its traditional role of store of value to unit of account and medium of exchange. In the said Latin American countries, transactions regarding real estate, cars, electric appliances and private school fees are denominated and settled with dollar bills. E.g. in Peru in mid-1991, the highest-denomination domestic bill was equivalent to $7, which clearly shows that most high-value transactions are settled with dollar banknotes.

Guidotti and Rodriguez (1992) observe the persistence of dollarization, despite wide fluctuations in inflation and interest rates. Dollarization measured as the ratio of foreign currency deposits to the sum total of M2 (in domestic and foreign currency) reached 60% in Bolivia (in 1990), 25% in Mexico (1981), 60% in Peru (1984) and 70% in Uruguay (1989). In Bolivia dollarization started with the August 1985 stabilization plan to fight hyperinflation, when dollarization was at a low level following the November 1982 de-dollarization scheme (under which foreign currency deposits held by private sector were effectively confiscated). Dollarization starting in late 1985 from near zero, increased to 50% by early 1987 and continued to increase by 3-4% a quarter, despite a rapid drop in inflation. By the end of 1990, Bolivia had a very high degree of dollarization, with foreign currency deposits accounting for half of the total demand deposits and 80% of the financial system's assets and liabilities denominated in dollar.

Guidotti and Rodriguez (1992) note that, similar experiences occurred in Uruguay, where dollarization increased steadily to 70% by the end 1989, despite falling inflation differential.

> Since 1974 the process has been fueled by a policy of free currency convertibility and a financial system that permits deposits to be made in either domestic or foreign currency at market-determined interest rates. ... [Moreover] in 1976 foreign exchange was granted the status of legal

tender when the government allowed commercial and financial transactions to be denominated and settled using foreign currency.

In fact Guidotti and Rodriguez (1992) conclude that "dollarization in Latin America is the product of the financial liberalization processes implemented during the 1970s and 1980s, which have allowed greater competition in monetary and financial service"; hence it is quite normal "to see the currency that provides the cheapest services gaining a rising market share".

It should be pointed out that Guidotti and Rodriguez (1992) analysis of dollarization is based on amount of dollar bills held within the financial system since the amount of dollar banknotes held outside the financial system are not available. The extent of dollarization in Latin America is larger than the figures used in the study, considering also the capital flight.

Dollarization episodes of Mexico and Peru ended with a *forced de-dollarization*, in August 1982 and July 1985 respectively. De-dollarization took the form of a de facto conversion into domestic currency of foreign currency deposits held by the private sector; effectively implied a confiscation and has accompanied by the imposition of capital and exchange controls. Anticipation of de-dollarization prompted a run from foreign currency deposits in Mexico and Peru (Guidotti and Rodriguez, 1992).

2 Guidotti and Rodriguez analysis of dollarization

Early studies of dollarization were based on an asset view of monetary holdings, treating demand for different monies as a stable function of income, wealth, etc., and their respective opportunity costs, measured by inflation rate differentials or by nominal interest differential corrected by the change in exchange rate; in other words, currency substitution was considered as an optimal portfolio composition problem in a world of capital mobility. Recent studies, however, considered currency substitution in the context of transactions demand for money, abstracting it from the store of value motive and from portfolio composition considerations, assuming that foreign and domestic money are *imperfect substitutes*. Under the standard approach, dollarization is considered as easily *reversible* once the relative rates of return on alternative monies are reversed, since stable money demand functions (in interest or inflation rates) are assumed. This reversal, however, has not been observed in the highly dollarized Latin American economies during the last two decades. Rather there has been a systematic tendency of money demand to fall while inflation has fluctuated widely. In dollarization countries, a significant fall in real cash balances occurred, which cannot be explained by changes in inflation rates or in income. In several instances, dollarization and changes in money demand are not related to changes in inflation or interest rates (Guidotti and Rodriguez, 1992).

Guidotti and Rodriguez (1992) suggest that

> the unexplained fall in real money demand is due to an ongoing dollarization process that depends not on a *rising inflation* rate but on a *high inflation* rate that gradually induces more and more transactions to be transferred to the dollar system. What is observed does not appear to be exclusively the result of a portfolio composition decision, but rather a wider process through which markets are gradually changing the currency in which transactions are *denominated and settled. Contrary to Gresham's Law, it is the good money that displaces the bad money.*

The Guidotti and Rodriguez (1992) model is based on

> a process in which costs are involved in switching the currency denomination of transactions, accounting for also the economies of scale in using a single currency. Once the local currency has been adopted by a particular fraction of the market, the decision to switch to dollar depends on which currency is the cheapest in terms of opportunity cost and the transaction cost involved in switching to a different currency. Some significant inflation differential may be necessary to induce a move from local currency to dollars. Once the switch is made, a fall in local currency inflation rate may not necessarily imply that the national currency will be used again, [which will depend on transaction costs]. ... The transaction costs of dollarization will define a band for the inflation differential within which there will be no incentive to switch between currencies. Transactions made in local currency will continue to be so if the local currency inflation changes but remains within the band. Above the upper value of the band, the local currency gradually disappears as the economy becomes fully dollarized; below the lower value, de-dollarization occurs and all transactions are carried out in local currency, because the local currency is clearly superior to dollar. Within the upper and lower bounds, the local inflation rate may vary without inducing any changes in the degree of dollarization.

Although valid reasons for money demand to be a stable and elastic function of the inflation rate are admitted, the possibility arises that above a certain inflation rate, a dollarization process may start through which all transactions in the economy will gradually be transferred into dollar. Therefore increases in the *velocity of circulation of money* are not only positively associated with *increases in the inflation* rate but also with *the level of the inflation rate,* and hence *high-inflation countries may experience an ever-rising velocity* rather than just a high level of velocity.

An economy may progressively become more dollarized over time in response to a high inflation level, rather than just in response to increasing inflation.

In studying dollarization, as pointed out above, generally imperfect substitution between local currency and dollar is assumed (in order to obtain stable money demands as functions of the relevant opportunity cost), which means that domestic and foreign currency provide basically different types of services. Guidotti and Rodriguez (1992), on the other hand rightly assume simultaneously that, fundamentally domestic and foreign currencies are perfect substitutes, since both are a medium of exchange for the same commodity; and that they are imperfect substitutes, because there are economies of scale in using a single currency and there are transaction costs in switching the medium of exchange of transactions.

3 Conclusion of the Guidotti and Rodriguez study on dollarization

Some policy conclusions of the said study are summarized below, because of their implications to the ongoing dollarization in the former socialist countries:

(i) In the dollarization process, while the foreign currency holdings increase over time, foreign exchange reserves fall, reflecting a reduction in the demand for domestic currency. "With a flexible exchange rate regime and a constant rate of growth of the money supply, dollarization would have a feedback on inflation. In particular, as the real demand for money falls *inflation would be higher, than the rate of monetary expansion* ". Moreover since the dynamic process of dollarization is explosive, dollarization may lead to a period of accelerating inflation (Guidotti and Rodriguez, 1992).

(ii) *Dollarization process is irreversible, i.e. transitory changes in inflation may have permanent effects on the degree of dollarization,* as the Bolivian and Mexican experiences show. When a stabilization plan is implemented and domestic inflation rate is drastically lowered, if the inflation differential does not cover the transaction cost required, the degree of dollarization will not change (Guidotti and Rodriguez, 1992).

(iii) Once dollarization is ongoing, reductions in inflation rates may not achieve any significant increase in the degree of monetization and the money demand may behave in a "perverse" fashion, since reductions in the rate of inflation may be associated with reductions in the demand for money.

(iv) Financial liberalization or lifting of restrictions on financial activities may generate the dollarization process, even without a significant change in the inflation rate, since financial liberalization reduces the marginal cost of adopting a second currency for transaction purposes.

4 Implications on macroeconomic policy-making

Guidotti and Rodriguez (1992) observe that dollarization imposes serious constraints on the nature and objective of stabilization policies, since small reductions in inflation rates may not necessarily imply any significant increase in the degree of monetization; i.e. if objective is to reverse an ongoing dollarization process, the target of livable inflation rate is not sufficient, a domestic inflation rate lower than that of dollar is required for such a reversal (i.e. making the local currency the better alternative). "There is a irreversibility nature of the dollarization process, which contrasts with the observed stationarity of the inflation differential." Under the Guidotti and Rodriguez (1992) model, even if domestic inflation is reduced below the dollar inflation rate, de-dollarization does not occur; for dollarization to be reversed it is necessary to have a domestic inflation rate that is lower than the dollar rate minus the lower bound of the inaction band; and these factors explain why in the referred Latin American countries voluntary de-dollarization has not been observed.

5 Effects on the US economy

Increased dollarization abroad (at zero cost to the US, for dollar banknotes held by the public and with monetary institutions) during late 1980s and early 1990s, have enabled the US to finance part of its budgetary and BOP deficits readily. This phenomenon, however, probably led to higher imports and higher government consumption, which lowered domestic savings and along with investments through Feldstein-Horioka effect. This possibly have been to the advantage of US on balance, in the short run, but in the long run possibly lowered growth potential and competitive edge of the US economy. In fact, the investment/GDP ratio of 15% of the US economy compares unfavorably with the Japanese ratio of over 30% and almost 40% of the 'four dragons', which is the main cause of the virtual stagnation of the US economy since the late 1970s.

Chapter 10

Demise of CMEA and collapse of CMEA trade and inter-republican trade of the former Soviet Union

Demise of CMEA and collapse of CMEA trade and inter-republican trade of the former Soviet Union

1 Optimistic expectations

Optimistic estimates regarding the effects of phasing out the Council for Mutual Economic Assistance (CMEA) have not materialized; it caused substantial output loses almost in every member country. Economic growth problem of Poland was "compounded by the much worse-than-expected disruption of trade with the former Soviet Union."(1)

Geron (1990) has predicted that with phasing out CMEA and switch to hard currency settlements, members' trade with the Soviet Union would change only slightly and that the Soviet Union would still be interested in continuing to supply its East European neighbors.

Fischer (1992) along with others has estimated that Russia would be less affected by the breakdown of inter-republican trade and the ruble area, because of its size and wealth. However, it turned out that, Russia has been hard hit by the collapse of the CMEA and inter-republican trade. Inter-republican trade declined by 50%. Imports into Russia declined from $83 billion in 1990 to $46 billion in 1991.

2 Senik-Leygonie and Hughes estimates of inter-republican trade and out-turn

Senik-Leygonie and Hughes (1992) in their analysis of inter-republican trade, after the dismantlement of the former Soviet Union, conclude that, once the price mechanism is allowed to operate, trade flows between republics will change radically to exploit comparative advantage. Senik-Leygonie and Hughes, however, do not predict which commodity will be exported by which

(1) Interiew with Luca Barbone of World Bank, WBN, Sept. 10, 1992.

republic, but determine each republic's overall trade balance and terms of trade; namely peripheral republics in Central Asia and the Baltic will be large losers on both counts. The *Russian Republic "will be least affected," in fact will be the big winner*, i.e., the break-up of the Soviet Union has relaxed Russia's external constraint, therefore moving to world prices will benefit Russia. Kirgizistan and *Latvia will be hit hard* (Senik-Leygonie and Hughes, 1992).

In 1991 a shift from transactions in non-convertible transferable rubles to dollars transactions led to a contraction of the trade between the countries of the former CMEA by 60% (Senik-Leygonie and Hughes, 1992).

It seems optimistic estimates of Senik-Leygonie and Hughes for Russia, have not materialized yet; it will take more than decade for their assumptions to prevail. However, it is more likely that those assumptions would not prevail at all, unless a quick remedy in the form of a multilateral clearinghouse arrangement is founded, as also suggested by them (*ibid*, p. 377) and supported by Jan Flemming (*ibid*, p. 378). Because, otherwise extremely specialized production sources of the CMEA trade will dry up, unless diverted to world markets. E.g. Central Asian republics will continue to import from Russia as long as they receive favorable treatment, like financial transfer, etc (as also indicated by Fischer, 1992); otherwise they will establish other trading links. So far the former have materialized, i.e. output declined as a consequence of collapse of CMEA trade, implying that if this trend continues, there will be no production surviving for CMEA or inter-republican trade.

In fact, Russia's

> interrepublic trade has collapsed. So have trade arrangements with Eastern European countries. The decline in trade has caused imports into Russia to drop by up to 70% during the past year or two. Exports have also declined by a comparable amount. ... As a consequence production has dropped between 25% and 30% in 1991 and 1992. And production could drop an additional 10% to 15% in 1993. [Inflation rate has been very high- possibly reaching 2,000% for 1992.](2)

Regarding *the Baltics,* Senik-Leygonie and Hughes estimates have materialized. In the Baltics, Lithuania and Latvia have been hit hard from disruption of trade with CMEA countries and had severe shortages of imported inputs for health, energy and agriculture sectors. As a consequence the World Bank stepped in in 1992, with loans totalling about $100 million to enable these countries to buy critically needed imports, such as drugs, medicine, fuel oil for heating and electrical power and critical inputs to sustain agricultural production.(3)

---

(2) Interview with Huang, of World Bank WBN, Aug 7, 92

(3) WBN, Oct. 23, 1992.

3 CMEA and its demise

"Trade outside the former Soviet Union had been largely with Eastern Bloc countries and had been carried out in convertible currencies at artificial prices". Because of disruptions in both demand and supply, exports and imports of the former Soviet Union to the Eastern bloc declined in 1991, as did the intra-regional trade (of the former Soviet Union). Being subject to several uncertainties and difficulties, Fischer believes that inter-republican trade will continue to decline further sharply (Fischer, 1992).

The Council for Mutual Economic Assistance (CMEA or COMECON) was founded in 1949, to boost trade among members through bilateral relations and preferential treatment and it effectively handled a large volume of trade with few breakdowns and had "a great deal of internal logic" according to Martin Schrenk (World Bank, 1992/G). In effect, the Soviet Union provided cheap raw materials in return for Eastern Europe's manufactured goods. Pricing system of CMEA was poor and members had no way of measuring the gains or losses from trade. The inefficiency eventually killed the trade scheme. By 1987 reformers saw the CMEA as a stumbling-block to growth of trade, and after the reforms, frictions among members worsened and trade began to unravel and on Jan 1, 1991 the CMEA was phased out (World Bank, 1992/G).

4 Effects of demise of CMEA

At its peak the CMEA accounted for more than one-half of all trade among member countries. As a consequence of disintegration of CMEA, trade among the former CMEA members is estimated to fall from 60% in 1992 to 20% in the next few years. According to a World Bank report overall *Eastern Europe's trade of manufactured goods, however, is predicted to quadruple over time, as a result of expected jump in trade with the West.* While the CMEA was crumbling many Western countries removed trade barriers to the CMEA members; US and EC have either eliminated or on the way to remove high tariffs on the products of former CMEA countries; the West has substantially improved equal or even favorable treatment (World Bank, 1992/J).

Many former CMEA countries *upgraded their "soft goods" for export to the West or eased import and export licensing;* some members made *barter deals with the former Soviet Union* (World Bank, 1992/H). Under the prevailing circumstances the estimated big jump in trade of manufactures with the West replacing CMEA trade, is overly optimistic, when the output of the region is contracting and the prices are skyrocketing.

5 Effects of association with/accession to the EC

According to a World Bank report, expanding trade and investment links with the West through full membership in the EC, Eastern Europe could speed up its transformation and achieve a new economic miracle in the late 1990s earliest. Relatively skilled labor force accustomed to low wages and proximity to the industrial heartland of Europe could attract EC investors. Eastern Europe's association with EC (already Czechoslovakia, Poland and Hungary are associate EC members) would weaken competitive strength (preferential trade status) of Mediterranean EC associates like Turkey in exportation of manufactures to the EC market (World Bank, 1992/K).

If Eastern Europe limit their imports to balance external payments and save hard currency, then manufacture exports of Yugoslavia, Finland, India and to a lesser extent, Algeria and Egypt, to the former Soviet market would collapse. The developing countries, may, however, benefit from importation of cheaper Eastern European products, and from exportation of consumer goods and new products (like tropical fruits and beverages) to meet the pent-up demand of consumers in Eastern Europe (World Bank, 1992/K).

If the all reforming socialist countries in Central and Eastern Europe and in the former Soviet Union are combined together, this region has huge potential (4) for development of agriculture, energy and metals, and services, considering also the large pool of labor; as a consequence *prices of some primary commodities may decline,* when the region becomes a major exporter of these commodities.(5)

These trade reports are overly optimistic, in view of (i) growth prospects predicted by other economists and studies (covered in the relevant section), and (ii) poor reform performance- from actual outcome and policy package content viewpoints. In fact optimistic estimates by Rollo and Stern (1992) indicate not a miracle by the year 2000, but attainment of 1988 levels of GDP only. Some, possible exceptions, like Hungary, the former Czechoslovakia and the Baltics, also have to compete with Eastern Germany in this respect and would be affected from the adverse macroeconomic effects of the German unification, tight world capital markets forecast and uncertainty in the former Soviet Union.

---

(4) There is no doubt about the potential, but in order for those resources and potential to be tapped, the prerequisite is establishment of economic and political stability and to start with the growth process, which seems to be rather uncertain under the circumstances.

(5) Ron Duncan of the World Bank, WBN, Feb. 20, 1992.

6 The ruble zone, the inter-republican trade within the former Soviet Union and recent developments

In early 1992, the 15 republics of the former Soviet Union continued to use one currency and "have agreed in principle to allow free passage of goods among them". However, the Baltics and Ukraine intend to introduce their own currencies and goods are not flowing freely among republics. Central Asian republics will probably stay in the ruble area as long as they continue to receive transfers from Russia, through budgetary transfers, trade credits or by pricing Russian exports at internal Russian prices (i.e. net of export taxes). For 1992, Russia agreed not to levy export tax on oil shipped to other republics (Fischer, 1992).

Although it is argued that the inter-republican trade would hold up better if the ruble zone were maintained (Fischer notes that, a country with an independent currency, would have one more instrument with which to attain its free trade aim, namely exchange rate changes), Fischer (1992) argues that, under this system it would be difficult to make required wage adjustments (in individual republics), which could easily be done through exchange rate changes.

New currencies can be introduced cooperatively by retiring an equivalent volume of rubles held within the territory of the republic and replacing them with the new currency (Fischer, 1992).

Fischer estimates (1992) that Russia would be less affected by the break-down of inter-republican trade and the ruble area, because of its size and wealth. Success in Russia's macroeconomic stability would also reduce availability of rubles to the other republics to cover their budget deficits.

"The breakup of the ruble zone would speed the decline of inter-republican trade, especially if currencies are not convertible". The economies of the republics of the former Soviet Union were very closely integrated, and highly specialized more than market economies are likely to be. E.g. the ratio of inter-republican exports to net material product was 70% for Belarus and 57% for the other 10 republics (average) in 1988; implying an average inter-republican export/GDP ratio of 40-45% for the smaller republics. "This is about the same as the dependence of the smaller European economies on intra-European trade." However, because of the extreme specialization of production in the former Soviet Union, the republics should be more interdependent for vital production inputs after economic reform (Fischer, 1992).

Drastic change in relative prices as a result of reforms, will disrupt production and trade within the former Soviet Union, and will produce balance of payments shocks on energy importing republics (Russia's agreement to supply oil at prices lower than the world prices in 1992 would only provide a temporary cushion). To avoid the complete collapse of the former intra-Soviet

Union trade, it seems a series of bilateral trade deals would replace the previous multilateral trade scheme. Under these barter deals, Fischer estimates that inter-republican trade would decline to 44% of its previous level (Fischer 1992).

Theoretically one can argue that this decline in trade and hence destruction of inefficient production, would lead to an efficient output pattern, provided that resources and factors released could be readily redeployed and employed efficiently elsewhere. The circumstances prevailing in the former Soviet Union and the recent experience in Eastern Europe rather suggest that the trade related shocks (as also pointed out by Fischer) would lead to a too rapid decline in output, with significant adverse effects on the reform process.

In fact, imports into Russia declined from $82.9 billion in 1990 to $45.6 billion in 1991 and the proposed aid package of $24 billion was not adequate to offset the dramatic decline on imports. Lawrence Summers adds that

> it is unlikely that imports will rise to even two-thirds of their historic level in the next few years, even if the entire scheduled aid package were disbursed. The situation is considerably bleaker in the 14 non-Russian republics; ... import compression in the former Soviet Union, even without taking account of the breakdown of internal trade, is likely to be several times as serious as import compression in Poland and other parts of Eastern Europe (Fischer, 1992).

> [Brainard and Perry (1992) observe that] just as trade has declined sharply between the former ruble zone countries and the former Soviet Union (i.e. COMECON trade), the breakup of the former Soviet Union would speed the decline of inter-republican trade..., [and] in the light of the *great interdependence among the republics, reflecting the specialization in production* that characterized the former Soviet Union, such a decline in trade would almost surely lead to a large decline in total production.

Moreover the extreme specialization observed in the economies of republics and industries, implies that many enterprises and their labor force must have the highest level of technical know-how, skill, and experience accumulation in that production line (Fischer notes this technology advantage and monopoly, and survival possibility of parts of these firms in the new regime). Because of this know-how, skill, experience build-up and easy access to the existing distribution mechanism, one can claim that these enterprises will have comparative advantage over their local competitors, unless locational factors and disadvantages outweigh it or foreign direct investment is involved. These enterprises are most likely to recover from the effects of change in relative prices (as cited unless locational disadvantages overwhelm). Despite zero tariffs, competition from imports, because of long distances/high transport costs, and extreme shortages of foreign exchange/undervalued currency (which will further worsen if these industries sink) might not constitute a severe threat, at least in the medium run.

Furthermore, if these enterprises are destroyed, (implying most of the industry and hence of GDP are wiped out along with), it is unlikely that the foreign direct investment will be attracted at all, unless it is resource-based exporting industry.

On these grounds, one can argue that, allowing these industries sink, due to inter-republican trade-shocks or by not providing them sufficient time to adjust, could not be termed as a sound policy for the medium run, and in the long-run, it would lead to an impasse, if not a disaster.

7 Break-down of the ruble zone and prospects for inter-republican trade

Nordhaus points out that because of the "highly *specialized structure of the former Soviet Union economy", "the collapse of the economies of its trading partners will boomerang upon itself*". "Even a healthy economy like *Finland* has suffered a major downturn because of the collapse of its southeastern trading partners." This adverse development could be averted with the establishment of stable currencies in the republics with external convertibility; this could happen, however, very slowly (Fischer, 1992, p.122).

Nordhaus thinks, in the meantime, because republics refuse to sell their goods for *the abacus rubles* of other republics, *growing trade barriers among republics* will emerge. Monetary trade would then gradually turn to hard currencies, but since dollarization is an expensive operation, this is not a way out. Then *"inter-republican trade might then gradually degenerate into barter"*. "Barter would gradually lead to a breakdown in vital production links", and shortages of "indispensable inputs for nuclear power plants, oil and gas production, railroads and other transportation links, and medical supplies" (Fischer, 1992, p.122).

The quick introduction of independent currencies by the republics (which will enable them to run their own monetary and fiscal policy and to have internal convertibility between currency and deposits), suggested by Nordhaus (Fischer, *ibid*, p.123) is no remedy to the breakdown of inter-republican trade (unless all currencies achieve external convertibility as well shortly). Neither is Nordhaus' other suggestion, i.e. launching an industrial policy in this vacuum and chaos (which is a must, but could only be effective if an orderly transformation, quick or gradual, is achieved).

8 Need for a multilateral payments mechanism for inter-republican trade

With a view to mitigating the inter-republican trade shocks, a payments mechanism like the European Payments union (EPU) is proposed, in order to reap gains of a multilateral, rather than bilateral, clearing system. Against this proposal, it is argued that this will lead to central planning of trade and imposing quantitative restrictions and would delay convertibility. Particularly Russia opposed this idea because of the EPU precedent, which shows the EPU Board playing "a major role in managing trade and payments among its members" (Fischer, 1992).

Summers believes that there is a clear case for multilateral clearing scheme to conserve on scarce hard currency reserves, but a much weaker case for extension of long-term credits between republics or from the West to a inter-republican payments mechanism. Because then "the republics with the least responsible macroeconomic policies will have the largest trade deficits and will therefore, have the greatest access to finance"; and hence the Western finance would be available through this scheme without conditionality (Fischer, 1992).

Fischer proposes a *modest multilateral payments* mechanism (Inter-republican Payments Mechanism), (i) to clear payments, multilaterally, and (ii) to economize on reserves. *The issue is not convertibility versus payments union;* because even with convertibility, *a clearinghouse arrangement is needed* (among central banks of the republics), because *the banking systems in the former Soviet Union are underdeveloped.* Credits extended by the payment mechanism will prevent bilateral balancing of inter-republican trade; onerous settlement provisions will be imposed when imbalances increase and upper limits will be set on imbalances. Moreover *"convertibility is not a full substitute for such arrangements because the republics will be short of reserves."* The mechanism will economize on hard-currency reserves. This payment mechanism should be used to settle current account imbalances, not as a source of long-term financing (Fischer, 1992).

This mechanism would "encourage collaboration in designing banking and payments systems and help prevent potentially harmful trade and currency reforms by the republics" (Fischer, 1992).

A multilateral payments arrangement "could be seen as a mechanism through which external assistance could be funnelled to the republics and conditionality for such assistance could be imposed." The best solution for any payments scheme is full convertibility, with adequate reserves, for all currencies of the republics. "But convertibility with adequate reserves will not happen anytime soon, and trade can be destroyed too rapidly if nothing is developing in its place." *Fischer* (1992) concludes that *"in the area of inter-republican coordination and payments, as in privatization, the best is the enemy of the good,* and the transition has to be managed".

9 Conclusions

It can be concluded that as observed by Summers, there is a clear cut case for a multilateral payments scheme. A simple clearing house type multilateral payments arrangement set up in 1968 for the RCD (Iran, Pakistan and Turkey) area,(6) with modest credit ceilings and quarterly settlement of balances in hard currency, had created some inter-regional trade. In case of the former Soviet Union, trade flows already exist and with 15 members a large volume of inter-republican trade could be financed even with modest credit ceilings, unless Russia becomes the only creditor. Even in this case, with quarterly settlement in hard currency of any remaining balances after multilateral clearing, the burden on creditors is alleviated and for debtors payments in hard currency will entail small amounts. Under such a scheme, a trade flow 4-5 times the credit limits of members could be financed, with insignificant amount of hard-currency payments (reserves).

As observed by Brainard and Perry (1992), "whatever is done about individual currencies, trade among the republics is likely to move toward world prices and away from the fixed and artificial prices at which goods have been exchanged in the past." ; hence there will be no distortion (by diverting trade to artificial channels or by compelling members to buy or sell from or/to other members, since members are free to buy or sell those goods from/ or to other countries). Moreover, provided that full settlement of balances after multilateral clearing in hard currency (so that every quarter full amounts of credit limits are restored), inter-republican trade is virtually conducted in hard currency. Members can also *alleviate any inconveniences* arising from the scheme through agreeing to a *lower credit limit* (extended to the payments scheme), by designating an existing central bank to carry out the clearinghouse function, and in extreme cases by *excluding critical commodities or imposing export quotas on them.*

Since trade flows financed with such mechanism, are shaped under market forces and since creation of such a payments mechanism would avert the worst possible crisis (complete collapse of inter-republican trade with huge output declines and vital shortages of indispensable inputs), international financial organizations, if not bilateral donors, might even be interested in its funding, with a view to increasing the credit limits of the scheme. This is possibly one of the best channels for Western aid during the first phase of transition, since it is for maintaining an existing trade flow and production at world market prices (in

(6) In whose drafting this author was involved.

fact lower prices due to poor quality, but there is a ready market) and also because aid is not wasted by increased government expenditures or subsidized private consumption. Upon successful operation of the scheme, members also might well entrust part of their foreign exchange reserves to the scheme. Even when transformed into a payments union, the scheme could only enhance external viability of members, and thus help with earlier achievement of convertibility of members' currencies, than delay it. It is also up to members to design the payments union (its jurisdiction, powers, etc.), not necessarily copying the European Payments Union; it might well be designed to increase competition and free play of market forces. Had a similar mechanism been established to replace COMECON, large output losses suffered by eastern Germany and Poland, as a consequence of COMECON breakup could have been avoided.

10 Latest developments in internal trade barriers within the former Soviet Union and clearing-house arrangement

In order to avoid soaring unemployment, the 15 republics must maintain enough interstate trade; if these countries cannot export each other over the next few years, they will have a costly drop in sales; the interstate system claimed 61% of Russian trade and 80% of other republics' trade; interstate trade by mid 1992 had dropped by 50%.(7)

Although the aim is less inter-republican trade in the medium run and more trade with the West, the ties cannot be broken overnight (World Bank 1992/D). World Bank is of the opinion that "trade relationsamong the republics, which are currently in disarray, need to be overhauled" (8) and that the internal trade barriers should be removed.(9)

According to the World Bank,

> the former Soviet Union [is] now confronting *an economic crisis much worse than the Great Depression.* Exports have fallen by half over the last two years. Average GDP declined by about a fifth [in 1992]. *Prices are rising at 25% to 30% a month.* In Russia, the drive to establish a market oriented economy is faltering in the face of hyperinflation and political opposition. The major obstacle to progress is the constitutional crisis and the lack of political consensus on the direction of reform. ... *Fifty million Russian people - a third of the population - are now living below the poverty*

---

(7) Interview with D.Tarr and C.Michalopoulos, authors of World Bank 1992/D). WBN, Sept 25, 1992.

(8) Speech by World Bank President Lewis Preston, WBN, June 19, 1992.

(9) Speech by World Bank President Lewis Preston, WBN, Sept. 25, 1992.

line. More that half of all households headed by women have fallen into poverty.[10]

A World Bank report (1992/D) recommends :

(i) Cutting export restrictions applying to inter-republican trade,

(ii) Coordination of monetary policies,

(iii) *Allowing enterprises and companies to deal among themselves in lieu of forcing them to work through the state,*

(iv) *Setting up a temporary "clearing union"* or similar arrangement that would bridge the trade gap among states dealing in inconvertible currencies, which would *also prevent government interference with the inter-republican trade and allow trade to flourish among enterprises,*

(v) Creation of temporary preferential trade areas among the republics to keep vital trade alive.

11 Final words

It is now obvious that the break-down of CMEA and inter-republican trade through enforcement of hard currency settlements by all member countries has turned out to be a fatal mistake and that a temporary multilateral clearinghouse arrangement (with quarterly or monthly settlement of outstanding balances in hard currency and at competitive prices) would have perfectly served the needs and aims of the members and could have salvaged much of the previous trade and output. Because low quality products of the former socialist countries during the transition period could only be marketed in their traditional markets (CMEA and developing countries) and only by means of bilateral trade arrangements (as in the case for Russian and Hungarian barter deal for foodstuff, buses and pharmaceuticals), a multilateral clearing arrangement was and still is a better option.

[10] Preston Wilson, (speech), WBN, April 1, 1993.

Chapter 11

Hardening the soft budget constraint

Hardening the soft budget constraint

1 Soft budget constraint

The soft budget constraint describe a system whereby enterprises receive various forms of subsidies more or less automatically and have any operating profits largely expropriated. If enterprises are required to meet quantitative targets and prices are administered, then it becomes necessary to soften the budget constraint. Under the soft budget constraint a firm anticipating a bailout, when faced with a liquidity constraint not only modifies its production decisions, but also lacks any incentive to do something about the liquidity problem.

In the absence of a hard budget constraint, allowing enterprises more flexibility may encourage rent-seeking behavior;

> half measures that grant managers power without responsibility may drag the economy farther away from an efficient allocation and make it more vulnerable to disturbances.
>
> [Competition can function effectively,] when enterprises have the means and incentives to pursue their individual interests, and when the institutions of financial discipline are in place, such as the absence of systemic subsidies and capricious taxation, the separation of lenders from borrowers, a mechanism to remove unsatisfactory management, and the ultimate threat of bankruptcy (Hardy, 1992).

Managers of public enterprises used to conceal excess, slack capacities, redundant workers and stockpiles of scarce materials (which are referred as hidden reserves), to ward off pressure of higher targets. The central planner, as a counter-measure, relied on a firm's private information and exerted tautness by setting targets higher than permissible (in view of the rationed inputs constraint to utilize idle resources). "Tautness is a strategy to countervail concealment" or vice versa (Zhou, 1992).

"Firms conceal information by under-stating its productivity or capacity, or by exaggerating production cost and requesting more subsidies. Firms conceal its productivity [also] by requesting more inputs" (Zhou, 1992). In a market economy, at least there will be no need to stockpile excessive inputs.

> [All reform proposals] for Eastern Europe have insisted on the hardening of budget constraints, even at the cost of many plant closings and the laying off of many workers. Even in the West during 1980s restructuring of the loss-making enterprises entailed denials of usual subsidies; however, even in the recent past examples of industries salvaged from bankruptcy by a fresh injection of public funds, are not uncommon (Hardy, 1992). [One should also note protection from imports granted to declining industries in the West.]

In Eastern Europe, budgetary subsidies in 1980s were almost 10% of GDP. Budgetary support by European Communities (EC) for the agricultural sector averaged 0.6% of members' GDP during 1980s. Pervasiveness of soft budget constraints, suggest that a policy not to subsidize loss making enterprises might not succeed, because it may lack credibility. The issue is even analyzed as a game theory problem, commitments and incentives to fulfill targets are considered. One means of generating commitment to policies, is to build a reputation for toughness or to imitate the behavior of a genuinely tough player ('tit-for-tat'), and close down a few prominent loss-making enterprises. "The imposition of a hard budget constraint is considered necessary for price signals to be meaningful and for resources to be induced to move toward an efficient allocation" (Hardy, 1992).

As experienced in Poland in 1990, in a *high-inflation economy,* with frequent devaluations, even inefficient enterprises make high profits and need not to undertake any cost-cutting measures and *pace of structural adjustment slows down (*Gomulka, 1992). *Hence high-inflation acts as soft-budget constraint on enterprises.*

2 Agency problem and corporate bureaucracy in capitalism

The soft budget constraint entails (i) *an information or agency problem,* and (ii) *the problem of credible commitment on the part of the State* (Bardhan and Roemer, 1992).

The agency problem arises from the fact that the state "may not have the full information to decide the extent to which a firm's bad performance is due to factors beyond the manager's control" and hence cannot demand efficiency of management. The agency problem does not exist in owner-managed firms under private ownership. Large scale enterprise under corporate capitalism face similar problems with the separation between ownership and management (Bardhan and Roemer, 1992).

This is a well-known problem of corporate management, with large body of share holders not being able to monitor activities of management properly and management satisficing in lieu of maximizing profit. Under the influence of intrafirm politics and corporate bureaucracy (top management, middle management, divisions), corporate firm might rather aim at a satisfactory target (profit, sales) or maximize sales (firm's market share) or act partly according to the interests of the management group (see, e.g. Mansfield, 1990, pp. 15-16).

3 Disciplining managers and credible commitment

Finance theorists claim that "the primary *disciplining of managers comes through the capital market and the managerial labor market*". Continuous assessment of managerial performance through the stock market and "the threat of corporate takeover is supposed to keep managers honest and the firm efficient and thus to resolve the conflict of interest between those who bear risk and those who manage risk. But the financial discipline of corporate takeovers is usually a *delayed and wasteful process*".

In fact in US considerable corporate value is destroyed by managers before they face a serious threat of disturbance. "Takeovers are like buying used firms, and are subject, as such, to Akerlof's lemons principle". Whereas France, Germany and Japan, provide an *alternative model of monitoring by involved parties* (banks, financial institution) without resort to corporate raid; a feature of Anglo-American game (Bardhan and Roemer, 1992).

The discipline of the managerial labor market can be reproduced in socialist economies in transition by relating a *manager's reputation and future wages to the performance of the currently managed firm* (Bardhan and Roemer, 1992).

Bardhan and Roemer (1992) have indicated the importance of lack or existence of credible commitment on the side of the state. Zhou(1992) shows that if there is a *credible commitment to a predetermined reward scheme* over multi-period planning horizon, then firms will reveal their private information (will not conceal them) and inefficiency can be reduced. The coexistence of taut planning and hidden reserves results from bargaining strategies of planner and the firm in dynamic planning. Inefficiency can be reduced if some sort of commitment can be implemented/enforced by a third party. This was not possible in centrally planned economies, where the planners are all-powerful, but it is possible in market democracies (Zhou, 1992).

4 Credibility of bankruptcy threats

A reforming government starts with *low credibility;* it has to shock workers and managers into behaving like profit maximizers and to demonstrate commitment that may welcome *selective bankruptcies* or partial closure, and accept resultant losses in output and employment. Because *rapid growth in unemployment* and output losses increased claims on the budget by firms and unemployed, this *raises doubts about commitment to fiscal correction* (Commander, 1992).

Centralized control over expenditures and access to credit of public enterprises in the transition period per se create management problems. *Hardening the budget constraint* and squeezing access to public funds, may induce enterprises to *reduce their costs, but they as well may reduce the quality and quantity of their output.* And the threat of bankruptcy will not be convincing, while *capital markets are not developed and new entries are not forthcoming* or adequate to compensate for exiting firms. *Moreover if privatized firms are bailed out,* state firms could not be threatened by bankruptcy (Bolton and Roland, 1992).

5 Building credibility/toughness and social safety net

After years of concessions, "a mere announcement of a new policy of toughness without institutional changes may not be granted much credence, and defending a reputation for not subsidizing loss makers relies on a degree of coordination of expectations that is implausible in a complex economy". Hardy (1992) shows that *the introduction of a suitable social safety net* (a cushion against unemployment) will convince enterprises that the government has less motive to cover their losses. The imposition of a hard budget constraint on enterprises, however, will have implications for monetary conditions in a reforming country, namely demand for precautionary balances will increase.

> The traditional argument for a social safety net is based on fairness: since people typically have one job each but are not individually responsible for the fate of their employer, the cost of an adverse shock ought to be spread between those directly affected and the rest of society. ... In utilitarian terminology, aggregate utility is maximized by equalizing marginal utility across individuals, [hence income should be smoothed] (Hardy, 1992).

> Financial markets are likely to remain under-developed in an economy with pervasive softness of budget constraints because they are not needed when income is smoothed through grants and concessionary government loans. The hardening of firms' budget constraints will provide incentives for the introduction of new financial instruments. [Hardy (1992) concludes that] a social safety net must be established if budget constraints

are to be made truly hard, and that the early encouragement of financial markets will be both more successful and more important, once firms can be sure that a government rescue will not be forthcoming.

It should, however, be pointed out that, under semi-soft or hard budget constraints, if inflation and inflationary expectations are not fully eliminated and particularly when high-inflation becomes chronic, then compelling enterprises to borrow from financial markets at commercial rates of interest (which in Turkey runs at 30-50% real rates per annum) puts loss-making enterprises under unbearable debt service burden; and the hard budget constraint loses credibility.

Governments are disproportionately concerned about large closures. If the probability of rescue was proportional to size, *firms would then have further motive to increase employment.* "However a well-funded social safety net would strengthen the government's resistance to demands for special treatment even from large interest groups." If unemployment compensation is too generous, it may discourage mobility and effort on looking for work (Hardy, 1992).

6 Conclusion: hardening budget constraint

Financial discipline and hard budget constraint could be enforced by means of five instruments put down below:

(i) There should be a *mechanism to sack managers* of workers' council administered enterprises by the relevant government department, when financial and economic performance (particularly losses and subsidy requirements) have not lived up to expectations (estimates) because of mismanagement, wage increases, etc.

(ii) Hopelessly failed enterprises should be let *go bankrupt systematically,* but on a *selective basis.*

(iii) *Immediate privatization* (partly or wholly) could be used as a *continuous threat* on failing enterprises. Employment biased workers' councils would act more responsibly under such a threat, because privatization in general would entail large-scale lay-offs and scaling down of activities.

(iv) Setting-up a social safety net.

(v) A credible commitment to a predetermined reward scheme along lines suggested by Zhou (1992).

7 Interfirm credit market and need for banking reform

Calvo and Coricelli (1992) note that

> The financial system of classical centrally planned economies may be simply characterized as being composed of highly *separated monetary circuits: household money and enterprise money.* ... In practice the banking system is monolithic, with the central banking directly administering all the monetary transactions of enterprises.

In a reformed planned economy enterprises have some degree of freedom in determining wages, prices, input demand, and investments. Enterprise money is passive (in the sense that monetary flows in the enterprise sector adjust automatically to planned real flows), if *central bank accommodates all actions of the enterprise. Because bankruptcy is ruled out,* attempts to curtail central-bank credit are quickly followed by a *compensatory expansion of interfirm credit,* which bears little risk, because the central bank is de facto forced lender of last resort, and hence is unable to control the supply of liquidity.

> As a result, stabilization programs tend to fail, and repeated attempts to lower inflation may solidify the interfirm credit market. Thus *stabilization programs launched under these no-bankruptcy conditions may induce a higher inflation plateau* in the future and reduce even further the ability to control the supply of liquidity (Calvo and Coricelli, 1992).

> Reformed planned economies still tend to be characterized by *strongly segmented credit markets and very weakly integrated monetary circuits* of households and enterprise sectors. However, unlike centrally planned economies, development of a *thick interfirm credit market allows state enterprises in reformed planned economies to escape official credit ceilings,* [which result in a loss of monetary control by the monetary authority], (Calvo and Coricelli, 1992).

> Interfirm credit plays an important role in the reformed planned economies of Hungary (since the 1970s), Yugoslavia, Poland and China. In Yugoslavia the stock of interfirm credit was estimated at 43% of gross social product in 1987, in Poland at around 48% of GDP at the end of 1989.

In the policy package of 1989, *the solution to this problem was deemed as one of the main targets by the Chinese government.* In China, in 1990 *arrears in payments of interfirm credit* and arrears in payment of working capital credits from the banking system were 20% each of the working capital of all state enterprises (Calvo and Coricelli, 1992).

Chapter 12

The enterprise reform

The enterprise reform

1 Problems: integration, cost minimization, excess capacity and soft budget constraint

Industrial structure in Eastern Europe with its *high degree of horizontal and vertical integration* is the legacy of centralized planning.

In centrally planned economies profits accruing from the state sector production is paid directly into the state budget. Hence it can be assumed that *state enterprises aim at cost minimization* (Hare, 1987).

What used to be true in developing countries regarding excess capacity, is now applicable to the reforming socialist countries. Little and Mirlees (1977) observed that in developing countries, *under-utilization of installed capacity* is highly prevalent (not the result of any general deficiency of demand) because of: (i) capital is excessively cheap, (ii) labor laws and practices inhibit multi-shift working, (iii) labor troubles, (iv) exchange controls make it difficult to get spares and materials, (v) technical failure or incompetent management. And then increased demand would be satisfied by imports, although apparent excess domestic capacity exists; but machinery is idle a lot of the time.

On top of these, the state enterprises in the reforming countries take advantage of *soft budget constraint* which leads to larger size operations, inefficiency, taking high risks and increased inflation.

If the soft-budget assumption is valid, then a firm anticipating a bailout, when faced with a liquidity constraint, not only modifies its production decisions, but also lacks any incentive to do something about the liquidity problem. "If the government is known not to provide bailouts, risk aversion may lead to an undersupply of entrepreneurship" (Hardy, 1992).

In the anticipation of bailouts under the soft budget constraint, *"firms will tend to become too large* and to undertake projects with too large a risk of being unprofitable". The soft budget constraint *has an inflationary bias.* "The subsidy to keep a firm operating after losses have been incurred may be financed by money creation. With many firms in the economy, some of which are always in difficulties, sustained inflation will result" (Hardy, 1992).

2 Effect of price reform on enterprises and structural adjustment

When profitability of enterprises increase through windfall profits arising from price reform, pressure for improving efficiency lessens, the bankruptcy rate drops and real wages increase instead (as it happened in 1990 in Poland); on the other hand when profit squeeze emerges and the threat of bankruptcy becomes real (as it happened in Poland, in 1991, due to the large appreciation of the domestic currency, the collapse of CMEA trade and terms-of-trade losses, about one-third of all state enterprises becoming loss-makers) then the tempo of structural adaptation quickens (in Poland as a consequence nearly 10% of state enterprises were liquidated for financial reasons in 1991). As a consequence in 1991 in Poland, the international reserves declined and fairly large budget deficit developed (due to collapse of enterprise profits). And "in order to help the enterprise sector real interest rates were reduced" (Gomulka, 1992).

3 Lessons from the East German experience in restructuring and privatization: its applicability on other countries

In former East Germany *privatization* has been marked by *a high rate of restructuring* and has been uniform across different sizes of firms. Operating costs of Treuhand, the government agency in charge of privatization amounted to DM 20 billion in 1991 and estimated at DM 30 billion for 1992. There are difficulties in financing the DM 600 billion asset sale; which caused interest rate to rise and capitalized value of the Treuhand assets' returns to fall, which in turn lowers the bids. On the other hand, East German industrial output is stagnating at one third of its pre-unification level and employment has fallen by 58% and still declining. No other country in Eastern Europe could afford Germany's approach (Carlin and Mayer, 1992).

In view of, *deficiencies of the state* in the form of *the poor finances of the public sector and corrupt bureaucracies* in Eastern Europe, one might be tempted to *opt for "bottom-up" approach, in lieu of the German bureaucratic "top-down" approach.* The bottom-up approach will allow managerial abilities to emerge through initial privatization and incentives will induce far better performance than the top-down approach. Wide social/private divergencies, however, will hinder the natural emergence of a ruling class during transition. Even Treuhand in Eastern Germany had a hard time in preventing western firms from stripping assets and skilled labor from public enterprises and in containing the power of incumbent management and in avoiding default. Moreover in

Eastern Europe, auctions could not achieve the desired results and widely distributed shares could not provide adequate control over corporate activities (Carlin and Mayer, 1992).

4 Legacy of socialism

(i) Concentration of industry and monopolies

Enterprises in the Soviet-type economies are more than 10 times the average size of those in the developed market economies. Industrial concentration in socialist economies is encouraged and preserved by rules regarding entry, finance, hiring labor etc. and hence monopolization is enhanced (Newbery and Kattuman, 1992).

E.g. whereas in Western Germany there are some 2 million firms of which 340,000 are industrial enterprises, in eastern Germany there were some 800 enterprises grouped into some 300 conglomerates (Hillman, 1992).

In Russia there are 25,000 industrial enterprises that employ about 25 million people. "Some enterprises employ as many as 100,000 workers and are the main-if not the only- employer in some cities." "Most of these enterprises are operating at a loss".(1)

(ii) Management problems and need for restructuring

> The managers who run these enterprises have only a limited understanding of the concept of profitability, and *many enterprises have become non-viable in the country's new economic environment.* ... Without enterprise restructuring, there can be no transition to a market economy, ... [these enterprises either have to privatized or restructured so that] they can survive and compete in new open markets.(2)

> Enterprises do not know how to run a company in a market-oriented economy. Enterprises have practically no knowledge of budgeting, accounting or auditing. ... The country lacks a legal system designed to support market activities. ... There are essentially no financially sound commercial banks that can channel funds to viable enterprises.(3)

The restructuring pace had better be quick, because otherwise entrenched interests strengthen and waiting too long in uncertainty "may result in more *spontaneous privatizations,* many of which may be inequitable or mishandled.

(1) Yukon Huang of World Bank (interview), WBN, Aug 7, 1992.
(2) Yukon Huang of World Bank (interview), WBN, Aug 7, 1992.
(3) Yukon Huang of World Bank (interview), WBN, Aug 7, 1992.

If the government moves quickly, it is more likely to establish some order over the process and resume growth earlier."[(4)]

(iii) Enterprise restructuring and regional policies

Some giant firms dominate the economy of a city or region, hence politically it is not possible to close them down and therefore regional and restructuring industrial policies have to be developed for them. Russia can't leave such restructuring to the market forces, because the market for corporate restructuring does not yet exist; i.e. *privatization is not an adequate restructuring policy* in this case, and "pretending that restructuring will take place if left to market only delays doing what has to be done". On these grounds, Fischer (1992) recommends setting up a *Restructuring Agency,* operating with external financial and expert support, to deal with firms that do not go into the privatization pool, to develop restructuring plans and if necessary take phased steps to shut down firms. Summers, however, is not sure of the success of such an agency, assessing the proposed restructuring plans enterprise-by-enterprise, and liaising with the banks to which the enterprise is in debt (Fischer, 1992).

5 Plunder of assets of state firms

(i) Privatization experiences in Poland

In Poland privatization is carried out through (i) leasing (pseudo-privatization), (ii) collective ownership (workers own the majority of stock), or (iii) dispersed private ownership, or (iv) foreign ownership. *Workers oppose the whole privatization program*, when faced with collapse of their enterprises and prefer *"the collective security of employee stock"* (Poznanski, 1992).

Many features observed during communist privatization efforts (e.g. non-state sector developed in the form of political capitalism, under which state assets were transferred to people of political influence at very low prices) *have continued under post-communist rule, namely rent seeking, corruption, parasitic relations with the state sector, tax exemptions, tax evasion and transfer at prices reflecting a fraction of its true value* (Poznanski, 1992).

In Poland, state firms to be privatized have embarked on a *self-destruction course,* given the present legal status of the state enterprises and their short-run economic interests. The three parties involved, the employees' council, managers and trade unions, realize that they will not maintain their present positions once the enterprise is privatized. Therefore, they oppose privatization,

(4) Yukon Huang of World Bank (interview), WEN, Aug 7, 1992.

sell-off or rent the company's assets and thus *endanger the viability even survival of the* firm in the new competitive market environment (Bienkowski, 1992).

Some phony privatization entailed *creation of nomenclature companies,* distributing huge dividends to shareholders. Recently proposed rapid privatization procedures are bound to be rife with abuse and corruption. On the other hand *"the government is slow or reluctant to restore the property to the lawful owners".* There is a deep rooted feelings of suspicion of foreign capital, which "has been associated with double-dealing and turning the Poles into second-class citizens" (Bienkowski, 1992).

(ii) Eastern European and the former Soviet Union experiences

Sachs (1991) claims that, in view of recent experience in Poland, market socialism entailing liberalization without privatization is destructive, because it gives the managers and workers of state enterprises autonomy without responsibility, and this often leads to their joint plunder of firms' assets. This argument could only justify give-away or rather throw-away privatization with immediate effect, because then plunder of assets by management and workers of firms awaiting privatization without restructuring could be stopped. However, what is called for is not immediate give -away privatization, but restructuring in the meantime. Bardhan and Roemer (1992), maintain that addressing "the key incentive and agency problems in the management of a public firm" is a better way of handling those problems, than privatization.

The usual inertia of state enterprises in Poland was compounded by the *prospect of privatization,* which *increases uncertainty* to both managers and workers, which induce them to ignore the long-term. Gomulka (1992, p.370) considers that "the privatization of large enterprises begins with their *commercialization,* a step that has chance to improve the performance somewhat, by clarifying the role of managers as industrial leaders"; and that "structural changes of large enterprises, including their privatization, represent disturbances which may cause further falls in output". And hence a return to the pre-reform level of GDP before 1995 is deemed unlikely by Gomulka (1992).

The World Bank (5) from the experience in Central and Eastern Europe learned that *"massive price changes, essential* though they are, can be *defeated without structural change in the enterprise sector,* [and that] *ownership* issues must be quickly settled to establish *barriers against theft and decapitalization of enterprises".*

---

(5) Speech by World Bank Vice President Wilfried Thalwitz, at a seminar for Ministers of Education from the Commonwealth of Independent States, WBN, March 19, 1992.

(iii) Chinese experience versus Eastern Europe practice

Reforming state firms in China did not give rise to the expectation that they might be privatized in the near future. The mere expectation of privatization may create perverse incentives (e.g. plundering of assets by incumbent managers *as witnessed in Poland and Hungary)* which are difficult to control. In order to counteract these perverse incentives, incumbent managers of the state firms may be provided with a stake in privatization of their firm (e.g. a buy-out option when no alternative buyer appears), (Bolton and Roland, 1992).

Even when the political will for rapid privatization is strong, its implementation will take several years. Hence it is necessary to improve the efficiency of the state sector awaiting privatization. There is no necessarily sharp discontinuity between private and public ownership. *The Chinese reform process was successful in moving state enterprises into semiprivate firms,* without full-blown privatization. This gradual transformation process gave enterprises *greater autonomy over production decisions* and allowed them to *retain a greater fraction of profits.* These reforms increased productivity (Bolton and Roland, 1992).

As against the Chinese experience, *previous partial reforms in Hungary, Poland and Soviet Union,* which allowed *greater autonomy in* decision-making and gave higher *retained profits,* were not as successful in terms of productivity and unleashed inflationary pressures. In contrast, *Chinese reforms were more radical and aimed at creating a significant private sector from below* (Bolton and Roland, 1992).

6 Workers' councils and workers' stake in transition

Calvo and Coricelli (1992) in their analysis assume that firms controlled by workers' councils *maximize the present value of wages* (evaluated at international interest rate) in Poland. Blanchard et al assume that in Poland the state enterprises *do not lower prices* when faced with excess supply (because they follow a *fixed markup rule).* Calvo and Coricelli assume that *firms are price takers but wage makers.*

"In a reforming socialist economy the employees often dominate the enterprises' management through worker-led enterprise councils", i.e. workers implicitly have some property rights over the enterprise that employs them. The vagueness of property rights over the state enterprise and frequent state interference with the decision-making process, together with soft budget constraints (the state taxes exceptional profits and accommodates any losses through subsidies and easy credit), and the substantial domestic market power enjoyed by many state enterprises, may imply that the enterprise's *wage and employment is the outcome of bargaining between the government and the enterprise's employees* over their shares of the enterprise's earnings (Dinopoulos and Lane, 1992).

Bonin (1992), relying on literature on Western producer cooperatives, and employing a shared-decision making model, argues that *workers acquisition of shares in their large state-owned company,* would enhance worker productivity, provided that the *participation of a core investor in company governance is secured.*

"In enterprises threatened with partial or complete closure, the workers may prefer lower real wages to unemployment. There is already evidence to this effect" (Gomulka, 1992).

The argument that *lower real wages* reducing the threat of bankruptcies would *slow down restructuring* (see, e.g. Gomulka, 1992, p.370), but they should be *tolerated* because reducing unemployment and inflation, they enhance the *survival of reform* process, could not be acceptable. On the contrary, at the initial phase, lower real wages is the key instrument of reform and restructuring. Sufficient time should be allowed for the learning process, adaptation to new technology and marketing techniques, and lower real wages provide this essential time. Even in early 1980s of USA, lower real wages enhanced recovery. Because the other alternative is the East German reform process, whose financial, social and political costs could not be undertaken by any other reforming socialist country, which is a view subscribed by Gomulka (1992, p. 370) as well. Hence lower real wages is not *necessary* evil to be tolerated for the survival of reform process, but is the most *useful device of (key to) orderly transformation.*

7 Corporatization

Fischer considers that, corporatization, which is the first step in privatization of large firms, and which entails moving firms out of bureaucratic control and into the control of corporate board, can be achieved within months. Fischer suggests that workers and experts should be represented on these boards, but the nomenklatura should be kept out. As in Hungary, privatization by existing firms, subject to the state approval can go ahead, while other privatization schemes are being developed (Fischer, 1992). Summers observes that corporatization through giving incumbent workers and managers in firms a claim (that will ultimately be sold), provides an incentive to maximize enterprise value, even before privatization.

Nordhause has following observations and reservations in this respect: "The first step to privatization is usually thought to be *corporatization, which involves separating state-owned enterprises from the government in corporate form* with their own management and boards of directors". This step has, however, been postponed in Russia until Sept. 1992, and since "old habits die hard", the privatization minister Anatoli Chubais has given orders to dismiss their leaders if they "fail to meet their targets" (Fischer, 1992).

Fischer suggests a *privatization scheme / strategy,* under which all large firms present a restructuring plan to the privatization agency and those firms, which presented "a plausible restructuring scheme that does not involve large externalities for a given region or city", go into a privatization pool. Ownership rights for the firms in the privatization pool should be distributed to citizens, workers and managers, through a voucher scheme (one that gives individuals ownership in holding companies, rather than in individual firms). In view of the Eastern European evidence, that such schemes can get stuck, Fisher (1992) argues that, there is more reason for urgent action. During the restructuring, Fischer considers that *a widespread write-down or even write-off of enterprise debts,* would be useful. The banks could be compensated by giving them diversified portfolio of firm equity and government bonds. Summers observes that the banks are in difficulty because, their principal assets are bad loans to the state sector. "Without viable banks, enterprise restructuring and liquidation is difficult to arrange." Many new and specialized banks are set up to lend to new enterprises, but in fact more financing goes to state enterprises than to new enterprises. The existing banks have not yet been reformed. Financial sector reforms have lagged in Eastern Europe, except in Hungary (Fischer, 1992).

8 Privatization of monopolies and anti-trust regulations

As a legacy of the past socialist organization of industry, many state enterprises are monopolies. Since there are efficiency gains from privatization of monopolies, *Hillman suggests that privatization should await creation of a competitive market structure (*Hillman, 1992). Privatized natural monopolies have to be *regulated,* even though it will reduce, its sale value.

In Poland and Hungary authorities have power to prevent monopolistic practices and restrain monopoly powers. It is a difficult and important task to establish and *implement a politically independent competition policy* and to undertake restructuring and demonopolization of large enterprises before privatization. There is *need for competition policy* in Eastern Europe and it has to be *institutionalized (*Newbery and Kattuman, 1992).

The existing vertical and horizontal integration, in socialist countries-in transition, increase market power and make entry difficult. Introduction of international competition into product markets, along with some antitrust regulation are prerequisites. The governments of South Korea and Taiwan, using "the carrots of soft loans and other benefits and the stick of international competition" have been able to force firms (many of them in the public sector) to high technology products and competitive prices. These instruments could be employed (Bardhan and Roemer, 1992).

As noted by Bardhan and Roemer (1992), breaking state monopolies, eliminating large-scale subsidies, introducing market mechanism and competition with painful adjustments and dislocations, organizing a viable commercial banking sector, overhauling the legal system etc. are formidable tasks.

Replacing state monopolies by private monopolies could not be justified, possibly except for a high-technology sector, with regulation. *Enforcement of regulation with a weak* government is unlikely. It might be better to keep some public firms in critical sectors for competition purposes. In Turkey, public firms in textile, meat and dairy products sectors, were useful in introducing and maintaining much-needed competition in these sectors.

9 Lessons from the Far-East experience

The success stories of the Far East (Korea and Taiwan) follow a *strategy of industrial concentration,* the governments providing subsidies to picked *conglomerates* to expand and dominate their markets. In Korea the conglomerates were forced (even by threat) to invest in export oriented industries, rather than speculating and transferring their wealth abroad and were lent substantial sums, at subsidized interest rates, and allowed tariff drawback on imported inputs used in export production, provided that they were successful in exporting. These firms were prevented from exercising undesirable market power at home *by price controls. Korean planning theory was based on reaping economies of scale, preventing abuse of monopoly power* and limiting entry to avoid dissipation. The government, following the example of Japan, aimed at creating at least *duopoly competition* in key sectors in the domestic market. In Korea, *export performance was the criterion* for access to resources and provided the government *undistorted information.* Advantage of reward-successful-exporters principle is obvious (Newbery and Kattuman, 1992).

The problem facing the reformers in Eastern Europe is their inability to credibly commit to future actions, which stems from *the lack of objective information. In socialist economies in transition, the government is weak and enterprises are powerful*; many inefficient enterprises are among the largest. Restructuring and deconcentration, by *reversing the original concentration process of amalgamating separate plants into conglomerate enterprises,* is called for. This is happening in Hungary. *Deconcentration* will help decentralize control and incentives, *increase competition in product markets* by replacing inter-enterprise transaction by market transactions and by facilitating entry, enable banks to assess credit-worthiness of enterprises appropriately and reduce political bargaining power of conglomerates in respect of protection and subsidies. *Deconcentration might be disadvantageous,* if it entails the *break-up of vertical integration* or if the conglomerate concerned is *a heavy exporter* (Newbery and Kattuman, 1992).

10 Bardhan and Roemer proposal

(i) The proposal

Drawing upon the Japanese system of monitoring, Bardhan and Roemer (1992) propose two variant of corporate control, under which the state does not own a public firm directly. "The firm will be a joint stock company with some of its shares owned by its workers; but a major part of its shares owned by other public firms in the same financial group, together with the main investment bank." Bardhan and Roemer (1992) maintain that "the proposed bank-centric financial system" is "potentially superior to that of the stock market-centric system," since "the main bank and the group partners have a larger stake in and more inside information about a company than the ordinary shareholders in a stock market-centric system".

Moreover under the stock market system, investors may be too much concerned with *short-run profitability* because of highly imperfect information about the activities of the firm. A firm's planning horizon can be lengthened, if the lending bank, as a delegated monitor is involved. It is empirically confirmed that shareholdings in bank-oriented systems are of longer-term nature than in the stock-market operated systems (Bardhan and Roemer, 1992).

(ii) Evaluation of the proposal

The Bardhan and Roemer proposal could be employed as an *interim measure during transition,* to increase efficiency of the state firms awaiting development of full-fledged capital market or formal privatization (block sale to domestic or foreign capital). Provided also private domestic and foreign capital participation in the so called "main bank" is secured, if not from the beginning, over time. Without eventual sale of a sizeable portion of public assets and development of a strong private sector with private banks of financial institutions, neither market economy nor political democracy could thrive in these countries. If only small entrepreneurs, are allowed to run private firms as stipulated by Bardhan and Roemer or Lange's version of market socialism is considered, the proposed scheme is bound to fail.

Under the original proposal, the main banks are considered as public banks (where the state owns a majority interest), and as such they will act according to government policies and instructions, whatever their legal status is. A politically corrupt government in particular, will dictate their lending policies (the comeback of soft budget constraint), their pricing, employment policies and management recruitment and dismissal decisions of public enterprises through the main bank. This is what happened in Turkey after 1950 with a mixed economy and where exist several state banks to finance and monitor activities of public enterprises in their specialized fields and a supposedly autonomous State Investment Bank to finance working and investment capital requirements of public enterprises on project and profitability basis. The only exception was the 1961-65 period, when a politically incorruptible government was in power and the performance of public enterprises improved in every respect. The basic mechanism of the proposed scheme or its variants work in apparently similar environments, (Japan, France, Nordic countries) because some or all of the following reasons and conditions are valid: There is a strong private sector and market economy, the banks concerned are private, the government is incorruptible.

(iii) Criticism of the proposal

Under the proposal mutual funds, which initially hold the same portfolio of large firms, are set up and adult citizens are distributed vouchers which entitle each to a per capita share of the income of each mutual fund. Citizens could trade their shares in mutual funds for shares in other mutual funds, but could not liquidate their portfolios, i.e. sell them for cash and shares could not be purchased by money. If a firm's performance is not satisfactory, mutual funds would sell its stock and its stock price will fall (Bardhan and Roemer, 1992). If, however, all or most of the public firms are performing poorly, with no profit to distribute, mutual funds would not be able to move in a profitable portfolio and their stock would be worthless paper.

Because as observed by Bardhan and Roemer (1992), under the socialist system (including under their proposed system), bad projects are more likely to be "allowed to continue too long"; whereas under the capitalist system "projects are abandoned too soon", since "lay-offs and bankruptcies politically [are] more tolerable" even though "large bail-outs by the state are not uncommon".

On the other hand it is true that managers of public enterprises with a soft budget constraint does not act boldly and take high risks, despite the fact that the state is the risk-absorber of last resort, due to political accountability, i.e. in order not to rock the boat (Bardhan and Roemer, 1992). But the urgent problem of the reforming socialist countries, is not new investment projects, (which will be taken up by private sector, any way, if profitable), but how to handle the existing firms and plants.

Under the proposed scheme, even when a firm becomes a complete failure and hopeless case, its liquidation could be unduly prolonged, because its stock would be kept by some mutual funds (nobody would be willing to buy them), which along with the financing bank, would lobby for its rescue, just to recover some of their losses; whereas with a touch of market (if all shares could be sold for cash and shares of firms are also kept by individuals) to the scheme, quick liquidation would be possible, because then widely dispersed stock-holders could not wield such a pressure.

11 Conclusions

The state enterprises under socialism was supposed to minimize costs and had a tendency to become too large and increase employment under the soft budget constraint. Capacity utilization, which was low due to input shortages, has now become lower. These enterprises applying the fixed markup pricing rule, with reform process are now maximizing wage bill. Price liberalizing giving rise to higher enterprise profits led to wage increases (unless wages were controlled) and reduced impetus to restructure and increase productivity. Enforcement of the hard budget constraint might change this behavior and force firms and workers to accept lower wages.

The East German example of restructuring and privatization could not be repeated elsewhere. Quick restructuring before privatization is essential and inevitable; because otherwise too many enterprises have to be shut down with huge output and employment losses. (The maxim should be 'best is the enemy of good'). As Huang puts down "without enterprise restructuring, there can be no transition to a market economy". It is impossible to attract private or foreign investors to existing too large state enterprises.

In restructuring, those who have power, should also have responsibility. Managers and workers should have a stake in privatization, so that they don't plunder assets of their firms, in the anticipation of privatization.

Plunder of assets of state firms by their managers and workers, and through privatization for asset-stripping purposes, the communist-type privatization (nomenclature companies), give-away privatization, etc., should be prevented. Without adequate government authority and control, this (prevention of asset stripping) could not be achieved. An efficient and strong government machinery is a must for orderly restructuring and privatization of enterprises, and smooth transition in general. This factor (its existence or absence) possibly explains the difference between the East European and former Soviet Union experiences and the Chinese reform approach and outcome.

The degree of industrial concentration is very high in the reforming countries, with many too large companies and conglomerates; hence de-concentration is useful in principle, for increasing competition in product markets, privatization and reducing the political power of big enterprises vis-a-vis the weak governments of transition period. In countries where it could be successfully employed, however, adoption of the Far-East model of industrial concentration would be a better strategy.

Corporatization is the first step in restructuring and privatization. Writing-down or writing-off enterprise debts outstanding and imposing ceilings on enterprise borrowing from the banking sector and on interfirm credit are called for.

Regional restructuring agencies (a variant of Fischer's proposal) and an improved version of Bardhan and Roemer's mutual funds and main (investment) banks proposal could help enterprises and the relevant government departments with restructuring.

Competition policy has to be institutionalized. In breaking up public monopolies or privatizing them, possible adverse effects on technology accumulation, R&D, and investments should be taken into account and the nature of market structure that would evolve as a consequence and its pricing rule and strategy should be predicted; and each case should be decided accordingly, on its merits. In the breaking-up of horizontal integration of monopolies, creation of a competitive market structure with immediate effect, should be aimed at.

Chapter 13

Privatization

Privatization

1 Experience in Eastern Europe

Analysis of mass privatization in Germany, Czechoslovakia, Hungary and Poland shows their privatization has been much *slower than expected* except for East Germany. There was *success in the privatization of shops and small business only.* Early expectations were that 50% of public assets would be sold within three years (Bolton and Roland, 1992). It is desirable and practical to privatize small-scale retail and service sector firms (Newbery and Kattuman, 1992).

In Hungary the desire to sell large enterprises at a fair price, has slowed down privatization. Poland and Czechoslovakia are more concerned to transfer them rapidly, if necessary by *giving them away through voucher schemes* (Newbery and Kattuman, 1992).

The network of utilities (rail, electricity, gas, water) can be kept in the public sector or could be made quasi-autonomous corporations subject to regulation (Newbery and Kattuman, 1992).

2 Privatization by direct sale

Privatization by direct sale method requires valuation and monitoring against corruption. In Eastern Germany, Treuhandanstalt had privatized some 6,000 large and medium-sized enterprises by mid-1992, with some 5,000 remaining to be sold; some 1,000 enterprises had been privatized through sale to existing management, some 500 had been returned to original owners, and some 1,000 had been closed (Hillman, 1992).

Hungarian privatization is by direct sale, under the monitoring of the State Privatization Agency, and "with an emphasis on foreign joint ventures".

Hungary has been most successful among Eastern and Central European countries in attracting foreign investment (Hillman, 1992).

If privatization entails a substantial debt obligation to the government, it carries the risk of *large-scale endogenous reversals of privatization via bankruptcy*, when there is massive uncertainty about relative prices, wages and the general level of macroeconomic activity (Bolton and Roland, 1992).

According to Bolton and Roland, privatization through sales has been dismissed too soon, on grounds of the *low level of private wealth* and *valuation problems* in the absence of capital markets. They propose auctioning off state assets in exchange for cash and non-cash bids; i.e. buyers issue claims on future revenues (Bolton and Roland, 1992. This scheme, however, place a considerable burden on the evaluation of competing bids, in the form of administrative expertise and time required to process such claims. In reforming socialist countries, the central government is just beginning to regain credibility and hence simple solutions should be preferred; auctions are complicated affairs. The operation of the *Treuhandanstalt* (THA) in the former East Germany, however, is a success story in this respect. THA is the state institution charged with enterprise restructuring. The German approach involves gradual devolution of control from government to the private sector and eventually to management (Carlin and Mayer, 1992).

3 Give-away or rapid privatization

(i) Effects on macroeconomic and political stability

Lipton and Sachs (1990) and *Blanchard et al* (1991) recommend that privatization in Eastern Europe must *proceed by free distribution and before restructuring.* Bolton and Roland (1992) reject the argument that state assets should be given away in order to effect more rapidly the privatization. "In view of the fiscal crisis facing economies in transition, it is crucial for governments to try to maximize the proceeds from the sales of State assets". Moreover considerations of fairness and politics do not favor rapid privatization by give-away; rapid privatization has a trade-off with budgetary and macroeconomic stability; rapid privatization might endanger budgetary and macro-economic stability.

The effects on the government budget of the loss of cash-flows from the previously state-owned firms in Czechoslovakia, Hungary and Poland are dramatic. Moreover, tax authorities are having *increasing difficulties in collecting tax revenues from the remaining state sector.* These difficulties will be compounded once these firms are privatized (Bolton and Roland, 1992).

Decentralization of decision-making by state firms may reduce revenue from these firms, despite a sharp increase in productivity, as experienced in China after the recent reforms in this respect. In China government revenues declined and *budget deficit increased when the economy was in a boom, and the resultant inflation forced the government to interrupt the reform process, which* in turn *triggered a severe recession at the end of the 1980s. A similar scenario awaits Czechoslovakia, Hungary and Poland,* if erosion in State revenues could not be controlled, following the privatization (Bolton and Roland, 1992).

Poznanski (1992) maintains that "privatization must not serve short-term policy objectives, no matter how pressing" (to use it *as a source of revenue* needed for balancing budgets and absorbing the monetary overhang); it "should primarily serve as a way *establishing a viable, effective economic order in the long run"*

The conviction that the gradualism of post-war communist reforms was responsible for their ultimate failure, led to a temptation on the part of many new political leaders to pursue *rapid privatization.* Poznanski (1992), however, points out that "a full-scale privatization *program is potentially far more politically destabilizing than those gradual communist reforms* because everyone will be affected by the wholesale reallocation of wealth and power". Hence privatization should be implemented with prudence. Poznanski favors foreign direct investment.

(ii) Effect on management

Privatization through mass give-away (such as the voucher system of Czechoslovakia) *favors incumbent management, i.e. it leads to the privatization of cash-flow claims, but not the privatization of control*; absence of well-functioning capital markets makes *it impossible to remove inefficient incumbent managers through takeovers;* and since the monopolistic structure of the old state sector will not be broken up, product market competition will not drive out inefficient management. In Poland by creating financial intermediaries (holding companies), supervision and control of incumbent management is proposed; effectiveness of holding companies (or regulatory authorities) in this respect is questionable (Bolton and Roland, 1992).

(iii) Evaluation of give-away scheme

Hillman (1992) considers the transition from socialism requires, *first "abolishing planning and declaring a market economy"* and then effecting accompanying *ownership transfer,* and *delays in privatization "defers the efficiency gains from a private-property-based market economy"*, with the bulk of industrial sector remaining in the state sector, subject to political discretion, which resembles the market socialism experiments of Hungary and Yugoslavia, "albeit by default rather than by design". Hence according to Hillman, efficiency and macroeconomic stabilization considerations (to eliminate soft-budget constraint) outweigh distributional concerns, in favor of *rapid privatization. Hillman favors give-away method* rather than privatization by direct sale, because the latter would require correct valuation (which can be intractable) and monitoring of each sale against possible corruption. Moreover citizens may not agree with the disposal of direct sale proceeds at the discretion of elected representatives; i.e. they may prefer individual wealth increment to provision of a public good through disposal of sale proceeds. Whereas in case of give-away transfer, initial owners can transfer ownership to others at their own discretion and can extract maximum value from the state's assets and become direct beneficiaries (Hillman, 1992).

A counter argument is based on paternalistic considerations, namely, the people do not know how to manage a portfolio of assets, hence will be exploited by the market or will sell shares immediately to speculators. And as a consequence it is proposed that mutual funds should hold the people's assets for them. (e.g. Blanchard and Layard). Hillman asks "but then, who will monitor the managers of the compulsory mutual funds?" and maintains that a compulsory mutual fund system "exclusively designed to hold individuals shares is socialism returning from back door with a new class of social managers" (Hillman, 1992).

Hillman's privatization scheme might be successful in the medium to long run; but in the short run it is of no use. Because under the give-away scheme, until the genuine private sector takes over the management, state enterprises will continue to be under the control of existing management and workers' councils; (this is because with dispersed small shareholdings, any organized minority group could easily take control of the firm and the existing management and workers' council are in the best position to do so); hence the existing poor management and the asset plundering are bound to exacerbate, because government control and supervision also will be lifted. In the absence of effective government control and supervision, this controlling interest (group) would rather maximize their own wealth rather than profits of the firm and will engender a process which will end up with the self-destruction of the firm (see for further evidence, e.g., Poznanski, 1992 and Bolton and Roland, 1992).

And domestic and foreign private capital will be interested in acquiring shares of state enterprises, on a significant scale, only after macroeconomic stability with growth is achieved and the enterprises concerned have survived transition in reasonably good shape.

4 Conclusion

As Poznanski (1992) points out, *"the paradox of privatization is that while its aim is to reduce the role of the state, it could never succeed without the state playing an [active] part, throughout the transition period"*. The state, during transition, should manage and restructure state enterprises and shed excess labor.

5 Direct foreign investment

Direct foreign investment both augments productive resources of these economies and is a vehicle for technology transfer.

(i) Role of large and expanding markets

In Eastern Europe Hungary and former Czechoslovakia witnessed higher levels of private investment.

"Foreign investors tended to sink much.... money into countries boasting large and expanding markets. Between 1985 and 1991, more than one-half of the foreign direct investment in the developing world went to six of the countries with the largest markets-Mexico, *China, Malaysia, Argentina,* Brazil and Thailand." (Pfefermann and Madarassy, 1993.) It is interesting to note the absence of former USSR, Turkey, Poland from this list, for obvious reasons (explained above).

(ii) Role of tight economic policies and good infrastructure

"Tight economic policies proved to be the biggest draw for private investment. Most of the countries showing the biggest jumps in investment reported improved fiscal balances and increased savings. Most countries with the smallest (investment) rises or even declines, reported declining savings" (Pfeffermann and Madarassy, 1993) This is because the former indicators imply and represent existence of economic/fiscal stability and a good infrastructure.

"Investors want continuity" and "want to be sure that 10 years down the line, the business climate is not going to be any worse than it is today." Increase in public investments does not slow down growth, because an economy without a good infrastructure could not be very efficient and would not attract private investment. *Private investors more interested in a good infrastructure than government subsidies.*[1]

Recent reforms in the developing world, particularly *liberalizing trade and capital flows,* achieving economic stability and creating a better business climate contributed to this jump in private investments, provided developing countries offer lower production costs, since a plant set up even in a low-income country today will be "nearly as advanced and state-of-the-art as one built in Germany, Switzerland or the United States-but cheaper to run". One of the reasons for the

---

(1) Interview with by Guy Pfeffermann, World Bank News, Jan. 22, 1993.

so-called *Asian miracle,* besides establishing a first-rate macro management, is creation of an attractive environment for private investors, through building *appropriate infrastructure, efficient transport and communication facilities, good government institutions with minimal red tape and computerized bureaucracy.*(2)

In the *former Soviet Union Fischer* (1992) "emphasizes the need to develop the *infrastructure,* as well as the *legal, financial and educational systems,* that a private sector in a market economy requires".

(iii) Prospects for private capital inflow into reforming socialist countries

Banks having well learnt the lessons of 1970s lending boom in the 1980s, and being "under pressure from poor performing loans to less developed countries, recession in the US and Western Europe, and the Bank [for] International Settlements' rules on capital adequacy", are all very reluctant to lend *except for viable projects.* Firms, hit by recession in OECD markets, similarly are not willing to commit themselves to long term involvements in countries which *politically and economically unstable and "lack any settled legal and commercial framework appropriate for a market economy." "Successful IMF programs* will help establish credibility but are liable to be knocked off course by shocks"; but they are *necessary conditions but not sufficient,* since successful *IMF and IBRD conditionality* does not provide a real long-term commitment to a market economy; what matters for private investors is *"the political and economic substantability of the reform process"* (Rollo and Stern, 1992).

Association with EC is crucially important in this context, since the market will be well-established and along with, if not democracy, at least political stability; this will provide the long-term political anchor, and confidence now required by potential foreign investors. The association agreements with EC, by providing for (i) a program for regulatory reform, anchors the market, (ii) trade access, encourages the supply response, (iii) aid received will get the required infrastructure built and (iv) political commitment to democracy, gives an overall anchor (Rollo and Stern, 1992).

Experience of Spain shows that from mid-1970s on with deregulation and democracy capital inflow started, but only after EC membership direct investment and equity capital inflow became significant. Moreover Spain's timing of economic reforms was also right, because in late 1980s the world capital markets had surplus supply. Still it took a long time for Spain to achieve credibility among foreign investors (Rollo and Stern, 1992).

In the 1980s world capital markets are going to be tight with high real interest rates (Germany is going to be a net importer of capital). A tight capital market will put a premium on political and economic stability. Judging from the

---

(2) Interview with by Guy Pfeffermann, World Bank News, Jan. 22, 1993

Spanish experience, it will take longer for the reforming socialist countries to attract private foreign capital, and the rate of return will need to be much higher, even when reforms are successful. Foreign capital requirements of the reforming socialist countries could be far above the levels experienced world-wide so far; there is no precedent of capital flows of such magnitude; and in order this to materialize, it would be necessary "Western Europe and the US to adjust policy significantly" "to compensate for the shift of Germany from a net creditor to a net borrower", and the required shift would be greater if less-developed countries become again net absorbers of world capital rather than, as now net creditors (Rollo and Stern, 1992).

In view of "the relatively *tight prospective capital markets over the next decade*" Rollo and Stern (1992) rather consider "*reduction of domestic consumption* to make way for investment" as the best alternative under the circumstances, if it were feasible; but point out that excessive restraint on consumption is implausible over the next 20 years. However, as shown in chapters 20 through 22, paradoxically cutting down consumption is the only way out of current unemployment problems of the West, incidentally.

The reforming Central and Eastern European countries, as suggested by Rollo and Stern (1992), if they choose to build up on the advantages regarding the *high level of human capital and proximity to Western European markets* (provided market access to EC is assured), could *enter into factor cost competition* through low wage policy and thus attract substantial foreign direct investment.

When the reform process is not successful (the pessimistic scenario of Rollo and Stern, 1992) i.e. when "the failure of growth in Eastern Europe, the lack of supply response, the low level of consumption, the poor penetration of export markets and the presence of trade barriers against them, the uncertain macro-economic policy environment in the region and probably, political instability" due to failure of economic reform, prevail, *then private investors will be scared off.*

Chapter 14

The Polish reform experience

The Polish reform experience

1 Price reforms of the 1980s

In Poland the price reform of 1982 aimed at changing relative prices and reducing monetary overhang and led to a initial jump of 100% in the price level, which translated into an accelerated inflation rate, which stabilized at 15-20% p.a. before 1987. This result is considered normal for a shift from a fully controlled prices to a mixed system (controlled cum market prices). During 1980s persistent current account deficits and sizeable premium on the black market exchange rate are indicators of *repressed inflation;* the latter could not be reduced despite frequent devaluations (Commander and Coricelli, 1992).

The jump in 1989 in inflation to 250% was caused by fiscal deficit close to 8% of GNP. Frequent devaluations, liberalization of food prices, major shocks to administered prices and introduction of an ex post indexing scheme in 1989 generated a *wage-price spiral* which led to *hyperinflation. Money alone could not anchor the system in the absence of exchange rate and wage stability;* neither the price controls (since administrative prices were increased and price controls were lifted), (Commander and Coricelli, 1992).

2 The 1990 stabilization program and reforms

As a consequence some *anchors (the exchange rate and wages)* had to be *reinstalled,* temporary restraint on adjustment to remaining administered prices were applied and *accommodating role of money was broken* (the independence of central bank, interest rate policy and credit ceilings), after Feb. 1990. Despite these measures, trade liberalization and a major fiscal correction, *inflation rate rose to [585%] in 1990* (Dornbusch, 1992) and expected to fall in 1991. During 1990 (first 8 months), however, industrial output declined by 28% and unemployment rose to 7.5% of the labor force (Commander and Coricelli, 1992).

According to Gomulka (1992), the Polish reform programs were initiated by a severe decline of the internal and external credibility of macroeconomic policies in 1989, with massive subsidies leading to large budget deficits and near hyperinflation, and the rapid rise of external debt. The inflation rate of some 30% a month in the second half of 1989, drastically reduced real money balances and the monetary overhang was eliminated. Toward the end of 1989, price distortions were large (e.g. the price of coal was about 10% of the world price), interest rates, although sharply increased were still strongly negative in real terms, the official exchange rate though was increased sharply was still much below the free market rate, making rationing of the foreign exchange necessary (Gomulka, 1992).

3 Specific measures of the 1990 program

The program was an exchange-rate based, *heterodox program,* with tight fiscal and monetary policies and with three nominal anchors: the exchange rate, nominal wages and credit ceilings. By cutting subsidies and removing income tax relief, improvement in the 1990 budget to the tune of 12% of GDP, was planned as against the 1989 deficit of 7.5% of GDP. Ceilings on domestic assets of the banking system were imposed (allowing 22% growth in the first quarter of 1990 and 50% for the whole year). Ceilings on the lending of each commercial bank were imposed in Sept. 1990 (Calvo and Coricelli, 1992).

On Jan. 1, 1990 the exchange rate was unified at a 31.6% devaluation, and this rate was maintained until May 1991. An active interest rate policy was planned and used to defend the peg (Calvo and Coricelli, 1992).

> The permitted increase in the wage bill was set at 30% of the rate of inflation in January 1990, 20% in Feb., March and April; and 60% for the rest of the year, except in July it was set to unity. Enterprises were subjects to tax penalties of 200-500% on any increase above these ceilings (Calvo and Coricelli, 1992).

In January 1990 most remaining price controls were removed, with no more than 3-5% of retail prices set by the state (Calvo and Coricelli, 1992). Whereas according to Gomulka (1992, p. 366) 17% of retail prices were determined by the government.

Foreign exchange restrictions on current transactions were abolished, but enterprises were required to surrender all foreign exchange receipts to the central bank. *All quantitative restrictions* on imports from the convertible currency area were abolished and *a unified, low customs tariff of around 4% for* commercial and personal imports was introduced (Calvo and Coricelli, 1992).

4 Money and credit, interest rates and dollarization

High interest rates, reserve ratios, administrative credit limits and moral suasion have been used to control demand for credit. Credit limits were not set too tight in order to prevent escalation of interfirm involuntary credit (arrears), but in fact the latter increased sharply in the first half of both 1990 and 1991 (Gomulka, 1992).

High interest rates (20% in Feb. 1990) were used to induce transfer of savings from dollar accounts to zloty accounts. A major policy objective of the stabilization program was to increase the share of zloty-denominated money in total money supply and thus support convertibility of the zloty at the set exchange rate. The credit squeeze in early 1990, prompted enterprises to sell most of their foreign currency deposits to the central bank.

> *The household sector,* which was the major holder of these deposits, has however *continued to keep its foreign exchange, even though its purchasing power was much better protected if moved into zloty-denominated deposits.* This behavior was clearly evidence of the limited confidence of private dollar holders in the success of the stabilization program throughout 1990 (Gomulka, 1992).

The share of zloty-denominated money in total money, however, increased from 41% in Dec 1989, to 59% at end 1990 and to 75% at end 1991 (Gomulka, 1992). The decline in dollarization implied by these figures, does not reflect the true trend in view, of overvaluation of zloty vis-a-vis foreign currencies by a great margin.

5 The aims of 1990 reforms: price liberalization and structural adjustment

Gomulka (1992) expounds the immediate aim of the 1990 reformers as to put into place a *market-based price system.* The transformation was in two steps; first, from a centrally regulated economy to a market-oriented socialist economy and then into a full-fledged market economy. In the initial phases of the reform, the public sector continues to dominate (Gomulka, 1992).

Primary aims of the 1990 stabilization program for the year 1990 were (i) increase in international reserves, (ii) *reduction in the share of dollar holdings* in the total money supply and (iii) *price liberalization and increase in administrative prices; price stability was secondary* to these aims. *Money supply* was the only *nominal anchor in 1990;* in *1991 the exchange rate and incomes policy became nominal anchors.*

The anti-inflationary program did not involve a sharp drop in real wages, but this did occur in 1990, which enabled enterprises to maintain high profitability despite a recession. In 1990 the pace of *structural adjustment was slow, with few bankruptcies* and except for exports, which were promoted by a series of *devaluations,* which in turn also helped with *high profitability of enterprises.* This export promotion policy, however, was inflationary, "by increasing the cost of imports and by contributing to monetary expansion" through the trade surplus. *Resulting inflation and high profitability* environment enabled *inefficient enterprises* to make profit and hence *not to undertake any drastic, cost-cutting measures.*

6 Competitive markets and de-monopolization

In the 1990 Polish reform program, with a view to creating competitive markets and a large, ultimately dominant private sector, "an increase in the number of independent enterprises, by breaking up existing large firms and monopolies, lowering the entry barriers to new firms, and an ownership reform" was given priority. It was, however, observed that proper de-monopolization would take a long time. In order to reduce the impact of the monopolized market structure, currency convertibility was considered essential (Gomulka, 1992).

7 External debt and exchange rate

On 1 January 1990 Poland unilaterally suspended serving the medium and long-term debt to commercial banks; on 5 Feb. 1990 the IMF approved a stand-by arrangement, on 18 April 91, extended the fund facility to the amount of SDR 1.2 billion, on 19 April 1991 the Paris Club reduced the Polish debt of $33.3 billion by 30% or $10 billion (Gomulka 1992). External reserves of Poland increased from $2.3 billion at the end of 1989 to $4.5 billion in Aug. 1992, also due to $10 billion external debt reduction and SDR 1.2 billion IMF stand-by facility.

"The internal convertibility of the zloty and the stability of the exchange rate are two major achievements of the reform so far." The stability of the exchange rate may seem remarkable in view of 585% (Gomulka uses 250%) increase in prices in 1990; the deep recession and the liberalization of exports must have contributed to this stability. The relative (real) exchange rate calculated as the ratio of the official exchange rate to the rate implied by the purchasing power parity, had declined from 4.26 zloty per $ in January 1990 to 2.26 zloty in December 1990 (Gomulka, 1992).

On the other hand, "*Michael Bruno* suggests that Poland set too high an exchange rate at the start of its stabilization", with concomitant inflationary shock. Whereas *"in Israel, a slightly overvalued exchange rate was used* as part of the anti-inflationary strategy" (Fischer, 1992, p. 93).

Although views of Bruno and Gomulka regarding the exchange rate of Poland in 1990 differ, both of those views ignore the fact that this rate should be grossly out of line with the real purchasing power and long-term equilibrium rate of zloty in view of 585% domestic price increase versus 32% devaluation. The problem with the chaotic 'big bang' approach is that, it is impossible to determine (long-term) equilibrium levels of exchange rate, wages and money supply (credit) and set any meaningful (realistic) nominal anchors (as attempted in Poland in 1990). Because even exchange rate anchor could be sustained through massive aid inflow, and wage/ price spiral could not be averted.

After the Jan. 1991 devaluation of 32%, zloty was devalued by 17% in May 1991 and continued to be fixed for most of 1991. On 14 Oct. 1991 a crawling peg (adjusted to a basket of five currencies) was introduced (Gomulka, 1992). The stability of exchange rate in 1990 and 1991, although remarkable, does not indicate that the pegged rate is the long-run equilibrium rate (the sharp worsening of the trade balance towards end 1990 indicates that it was not even short-term equilibrium rate). In fact $10 billion reduction in external debt and the IMF stand-by credit helped with achievement of the short-term equilibrium in BOP. Provided foreign donors agree a substantial increase in net capital inflow, a country could sustain an overvalued currency; but when capital movements are reversed devaluation at a high rate would be required.

Under the 'big bang' reform approach when the existing trade and exchange systems are dismantled, without taking effective measures for orderly transition on that score, with increasing uncertainties, demand of economic agents for foreign exchange will rise beyond bounds; and hence the fate of exchange rate will be determined by the size of official foreign capital inflow; if the inflow is ample as in Poland, currency could be grossly overvalued and as in Russia, if aid inflow trickles only then the market exchange rate shows gross undervaluation of the currency; and then price /wage /devaluation spiral carries on beyond control.

8 Effect on productivity of aid inflow

It is worthwhile to estimate effects of massive aid inflow into Poland (and consequent overvalued currency) on productivity of Polish economy. Terrel (1992) analyzed effects of western capital on the Polish industry, and makes following observations: During 1972-1983, there was a massive infusion of Western capital to Poland, but this did not raise productivity and investment in Western capital (machinery, equipment and technology) was wasted, because of shortages of complementary inputs, because of difficulty in the absorption of Western technology. Specifically failure was due to delays in the construction of factory buildings to house the new machinery, underutilization of imported machinery, delays in supplying complementary parts, shortages of managers and technicians, overcentralization and bureaucracy in planning and management. Estimated efficiency of Western capital in Polish industry during 1961-1983 suggests that, "an infusion of Western capital into an economic system that is not sufficiently market oriented is likely to be ineffective".

"The Polish economy of the 1990s is more decentralized and enterprises face harder budget constraint." However, Terrel (1992) concludes that, "since most enterprises are still state-owned, and financial markets are underdeveloped, a rapid infusion of Western capital could result in a large foreign debt with little improvement in productivity." Along the same lines Koves and Marer (1991) maintain that, it is unwise to allow unreformed state enterprises unrestricted access to foreign exchange and unlimited rights to import goods. Enterprise managers may correctly think (calculate) that enterprise debts will be taken over eventually by the state.

9 Recent developments

Poland is expected to grow by 2-3% in 1993, "making it the first Eastern European country to achieve economic growth in its transformation".(1)

In 1990, Poland had "thousands of inefficient, money-losing state-owned enterprises making shoddy goods". By end 1992, 1,600 enterprises were sold off; but about 8,200 enterprises and 770 companies (comprising 2/3 of the country's enterprises) were still in the public sector. A parliamentary vote in April 1993 will result in the sale of 600 more enterprises.(2)

Restructuring and selling off inefficient enterprises will also help solve the problems of ailing state-owned banks, which currently prop up the money-losing enterprises.(3)

A $450 million enterprise- and financial-reform loan from the World Bank will speed up privatization of Poland's worst money-loosing enterprises, which operate mainly in heavy industry (steel, chemicals and shipbuilding) and the state banks.(4)

With enterprise restructuring, unemployment will increase. Under a moderate success scenario developed by the World Bank, unemployment rate is expected to rise from 14% in 1992 to 15% in 1993, while GDP increase by 3%. Hence, overgenerous pension scheme is to be reformed in 1993.(5)

Private enterprises are growing rapidly. In 1992, while the production of the public sector declined by 5%, private industrial sales rose by 32%, and

(1) WBN, May 6, 1993.
(2) WBN, May 6, 1993.
(3) WBN, May 6, 1993.
(4) WBN, May 6, 1993.
(5) WBN, May 6, 1993.

while output of the state construction firms fell by 38%, private output increased by 32%. Small private firms, processing agricultural products (bakeries, butcheries) are increasing rapidly all over the country.[6]

Even before the 1990 reform program, private farmers owned 75% of the farmland, and the country was self-sufficient in food production. The agricultural marketing and distribution system has still been inefficient in early 1993 and about 85% of agroindustry is controlled by state firms. A $300 million World Bank loan will help privatize and restructure sugar, poultry and potato industries and state-owned farms. "The switch from subsidizing state-run farms and agroindustries will allow the private... farmer to become more competitive..." Prospects for farm exports, however, are not good, since its former buyers (in Eastern Europe and the former Soviet Union) do not have enough foreign exchange and the West is raising barriers to Polish exports.[7]

10 Privatization

Fischer (1992) notes that while in Eastern Europe "the stated preference has been for rapid privatization", in practice *the progress in privatization has been disappointing, especially in Poland.* The privatization of small-scale (primarily retail) firms, whose lease or purchase is often financed by the government agency making the sale or lease, has been considerably successful.

Privatization of medium-and large-scale firms in Eastern Europe has been less successful; although, the former Czechoslovak voucher scheme could bring about privatization of much of the industry (Fischer, 1992). Poland in late 1992 announced plans to privatize 600 state companies.[8] Privatization and the management of state enterprises constitute major problems to be tackled with.

11 Housing shortage

Poland has a severe housing shortage, with an estimated 11 million housing units, about 10% less than the number of households and much of the existing state-owned housing stock is run down. One of the main causes of the housing crunch is that housing has been underpriced for decades. A new housing project of $677 million in 1992, which will be partially financed by the World Bank, provides for an increase of 15,000 in the number of housing units and "promotes a financially sound, market-oriented housing sector", also by setting up a commercial mortgage system to enable about 27,000 households to purchase housing units.[9]

---

(6) WBN, May 6, 1993.

(7) WBN, May 6, 1993.

(8) UBN, Sept. 10, 1992.

(9) G.C. Guarda of World Bank, WBN, July 2, 1992.

12 Behavior of people toward reform

Surveys conducted in the 1980s showed that the majority of Polish people desired a market solution, but without realizing the consequences or (understanding the implications) of market reforms (Gomulka and Polonsky, 1990).

13 Outcome and prospects

Poland embarked on its accelerated transition to capitalism in mid-1989. The Polish stabilization program of 1 Jan 1990 aiming at economic transformation and stabilization caused stagflation immediately (the inflation rate accelerated sharply and industrial output fell). The program was *supposed to lead to initial expansion,* but it *resulted in deep recession. The structural transformation, however, caused fall in output, only if new prices are lower than new average costs, otherwise output should not fall* (Calvo and Coricelli, 1992).

In Poland, consumer prices increased by 251% in 1989, 585% in 1990, 71% in 1991 and were running at an 50-55% annual rates in the first half of 1992.

Fischer (1992) observes that in Poland, two years after the start of the reform, growth is not yet visible, the industrial structure has not changed and early promises have not been fulfilled.

Polish exports to the Soviet Union declined by 90% in 1991 over 1990, whereas a few years earlier the USSR was buying 30-40% of Poland's total exports (Bienkowski, 1992).

Poznanski (1992) considering the lack of experience to set up markets and to operate properly the newly legislated institutions, estimates that it will take more than a generation for the market economy to succeed with own efforts.

Jan Adam, (10) in view of the *present experiences of Poland and Hungary,* does not think a *market reform* "can afford *to drop price and wage controls all at once"*

Under the Polish reform process, "the costly readjustment of foreign trade away from the former CMEA area to, mainly, Western Europe has been completed" and "the quality of the price system has been radically improved and small-scale privatization has been nearly completed". The Polish reform process of 1990s produced following "major negative surprises: (i) deeper and longer recession, (ii) higher unemployment and inflation, (iii) a slower pace of restructuring and (iv) lower foreign investments" (Gomulka, 1992).

According to the official statistics GDP fell by 11.6% in 1990, industrial GDP by 22%, domestic expenditure by 15.4% and total consumption by

---

(10) Book review on Ivan T. Berend, "The Hungarian Economic Reforms. 1953-1988". Cambridge, 1990, Journal of Comparative Economics, 16, 1992, pp. 774-777.

11.7%. Unemployment reached about 12% of the total labor force and 16% of non-agricultural labor force by the end of 1991. In 1992 unemployment is expected to reach 20% of the non-agricultural labor force. This is because "in the short run, higher efficiency is likely to imply more unemployment and more recession". "The second year of the reform (1991) proved to be substantially more difficult than the first one, seriously straining social support for the reform process" (Gomulka, 1992). In 1991 GDP declined by 7%. Although an output growth of 1% was expected for 1992, it turned out that a further 1-2% decline in GDP is to materialize.(11) In Poland GDP is not expected to return to the pre-reform level before 1995 (Gomulka, 1992).

Economic growth record of Poland, in the two years following the shock therapy has not been satisfactory according to the World Bank evaluation. Although queues have disappeared and availability of high quality goods and services has improved, and risk of hyperinflation and a massive default on international obligations and hence disruption of trade and production have been avoided, economic problem was "compounded by the much *worse-than-expected disruption of trade with the former Soviet Union*". Now hopes are on accession to the European Community (EC) in a decade; however, Poland being a producer and exporter of agricultural and food products raises complex issues.(12)

"The reform program has essentially stayed on course, with all its ups and downs". "Real wages have been reduced". Improvements in social safety net and retraining schemes have been introduced.(13) However still there is possibility of a major labor strife. Privatization and the governance of public enterprises are still major remaining issues.

14 Stagflation dilemma

As noted above, output decline in 1990 and 1991 and hyper inflation in 1990 were considered as surprising developments by Gomulka, Fischer, Calvo and Coricelli. Calvo and Coricelli (1992) do not expect output decline, unless new prices are not lower than new average costs.

Whereas both outcomes should be considered normal under the chaotic 'big bang' approach; hyperinflation as experienced in Poland in 1990 and in Russia in 1992 stem from wage/price (in Russia plus devaluation) spiral, 'grand uncertainty' surrounding the economy (loss of direction) and extreme chaos in the enterprise sector; these factors have also contributed to output decline obviously. Poland in 1991 averted hyper-inflation thanks to (i) braking the reform and restructuring process, and (ii) dollarization (as explained in the

(11) WBN, Sept 10, 1992.
(12) Interview with Luca Barbone of World Bank, WBN, Sept. 10,1992.
(13) Interview with Luca Barbone of World Bank, WBN, Sept. 10, 1992.

relevant chapter, in Russia this has not helped because of the extreme shortage of dollar supply in that country). Slowing down the pace of the restructuring and reform process and the resulting stop-go sequence is both costly and self-defeating to the purpose.

Commander and Coricelli (1992 also point out that increased reliance on price adjustments during transition to redress macroeconomic imbalances further destabilized the system and failed to address the sources of imbalance (wage drift and cost increases due to devaluations), because of the absence of conventional equilibrating mechanism and the presence of monopolistic pricing behavior.

In addition to factors cited above, declining output in 1990 and 1991 could also partly be explained by increased competition from imports arising from extreme openness and monopolistic structure of the economy.

(i) *An overvalued currency:* the exchange rate was pegged after 32% devaluation in Jan 1990 until the May 1991 devaluation of 17%, and was virtually fixed for most of 1991 (Gomulka, 1992, p. 365). These devaluations are too moderate as against inflation rates of 586% and 70% in 1990 and 1991 respectively, and around 50-55% in 1992.

(ii) *Elimination of quantitative import restrictions and exchange control,* and introduction of an *extremely low customs tariff* at around 4%.

(iii) *Monopolistic structure* of the socialist and reforming socialist economies are well known; and is further evidenced by decline in Polish imports in 1990 by $500 million, when foreign trade and exchange regime was liberalized and external reserves increased by $2.2 billion. (In 1990 exports of Poland increased by $150 million to $13.6 billion, and imports declined to $9.8 billion).

Gomulka (1992, p. 365) admits that

> the exchange rate began to act as a nominal anchor by the end of 1990, [as evidenced by] the sharp deterioration of the trade balance and some reduction of the profit margins, despite an improvement in the level of economic activity. In view of the continuing high inflation, there was a need to change the exchange rate policy at some point from the fixed peg to a crawling peg. [But the continuation of the fixed rate for most of 1991,] contributed to the collapse of enterprise profits and the consequent crisis of the state budget.

In fact at the end of 1990 the balance of payments worsened (Calvo and Coricelli, 1992, p. 85) and trade balance deteriorated sharply in 1991 (Gomulka, 1992, p. 365). The marked improvement in trade balance in 1990 should be due to decline in consumption and investment expenditures, because consumption per capita (in 1987 US dollars) declined from $1,040 in 1989 to $860 in 1990 and investment from $560 in 1989 to $410 in 1990. In 1991 the trade balance worsened because despite a further fall in per capita investment to $310, consumption rose to $930.

It seems that the Polish economy is bogged down in many dilemmas and disequilibria: Price/subsidy reform versus inflationary/output effects, fixed exchange rate versus worsening external balance/inflation, Dollarization, output/investment decline despite negative real interest rates, pros and cons of high interest rates, high unemployment, continuing inflationary threat and expectations, etc. All this, could have been averted and still could be overcome, if the suggested methodology is employed, which would provide a fresh start with a clean slate.

The present Polish economic and monetary policies are very similar to the Turkish ones (from 1980 on), although the real structure might be different. Judging from the 1980-1992 Turkish experience (see, e.g. Kızılyallı, 1989) the following conclusions can be tentatively suggested; however, limited availability of recent data is a serious constraint. Under the present policies and circumstances, the real income per capita in Poland would continue to stagnate, (particularly due to extreme openness and high rate of dollarization), the inflation rate would flare up when expansionary monetary and fiscal policies are exercised; positive real interest rate would further depress investments and eventually add to inflation through its effects on the budgetary deficit (crowding-out effect). External debt would increase; floating exchange rates would improve external balance, but would have cost-push effects. Alternatively if the export incentives mechanism is employed, the budgetary effect would be expansionary; investment incentives would be called for to stimulate private and foreign direct investments, which would ironically imply creating a private sector heavily dependent on budgetary subsidies, tax rebates and exemptions and hence inefficient - to which danger Kornai (1990) has drawn attention. In lieu of an inefficient state sector; expansionary policies would increase external debt disproportionately, (in Turkey 5% increase in GDP growth rate requires $5 billion increase in net external indebtedness; unless public sector deficit is reduced by increased taxation; efficient operation of state enterprises, privatization, etc., and domestic savings are increased substantially; and inflation is ended; as observed in, Kızılyallı and Çiller, 1987, and Kızılyallı, 1989) and would be constrained by availability of fresh loans. The only *feasible option* for growth would be a *sufficiently low real wage level* to attract private and foreign direct investment, which as observed by Gomulka

(1992, p. 357) "can only be implemented by a strong government", coupled with economic stability and reduced uncertainty regarding future economic and political prospects.

Moreover long-run growth prospects are even more bleak, because of the expected decline in saving propensity (and Feldstein Horioka effect). Even in Eastern Germany, it was observed that households and enterprises do not save (Dornbusch and Wolf, 1992). In the other reforming socialist economies, it is normal to expect the present generation not to save, also because it would be difficult to change the behavior developed under socialism (where there was no need for individuals to save to tide over income fluctuations and for retirement, and monetary overhang was rather forced saving or delayed consumption). Existing enterprises due to restructuring and competition from imports, would face profit squeeze and would not be able to save (retained profits) and invest. Hence the only way out is foreign direct investment, which can flow in substantial amounts only after economic and political stability is attained. In addition, newly developing domestic private sector and privatization of public housing could help overcome the savings constraint. Slow pace of privatization and growth of private sector, coupled with rapid dollarization (in Poland and Russia), however, rather make domestic savings constraint more binding.

15 Dollarization

Another lesson that can be drawn from the Polish experience concerns timing of launching *currency convertibility*. As observed by Guidotti and Rodriguez (1992), "financial liberalization or, generally, the lifting of restrictions on financial activities may generate a process of dollarization even without a significant change in the rate of inflation".

Introduction of convertibility with free capital movements in a high inflation economy, "as a psychological signal to enterprises and the public" and "as an economic instrument to improve the mobility of resources between net exporters and net importers" (Gomulka, 1992, p. 357) is not a sound policy because, it leads to increased dollarization in the long run; the Turkish experience in late 1980s suggests this result. In Bolivia dollarization started with a stabilization plan to fight hyper-inflation in 1985, and increased from near zero to almost 50% in 15 months and continued to increase further, even when inflation rate recorded a sharp decline, and rose to 60% of M2 at end 1990.

Dollarization could only end with a forced de-dollarization (de facto expropriation of foreign currency deposits, by exchanging them for domestic currency deposits at an official rate) as exercised in Mexico in August 1982 and Peru in August 1982 (Guidotti and Rodriguez, 1992).

Chapter 15

The Hungarian reform experience

The Hungarian reform experience

1 Reforming until 1990

"Hungary has experimented with economic reform since 1986, but it was not until mid-1990 that the country began taking major steps to a market economy". The government has an ambitious program to secure economic growth and international competitiveness. "Hungary has been a front-runner in the economic transformation of Central and Eastern Europe".(1)

Hungary adopted the gradualist reform approach. *After the 1968 reform, Berend does not think there was any substantial new development of the Hungarian economic model even in the 1979-87 period.* In 1968 a new model of collective farms was developed; *markets for commodities were permitted but central price controls and wage regulation continued; central planning* of macroeconomic magnitudes, *including sectoral (and by industrial branches) distribution of investment funds and collective ownership remained. In the first half of 1980s private ownership had been expanded.* In the 1980s monetary and fiscal policies were increased; in 1986-87 it was accepted in principle that the market should be extended to capital and labor; in 1984 normative wage regulation was replaced by *wage regulation* by taxes (Berend, 1990). While Hungary had the appearance of a market economy by the late 1980s, it still had not made the decisive break to a decentralized market system-there is visible and invisible regulation of trade. Breaking the behavior patterns of government officials and enterprise managers, described as 'soft budget constraint' by Kornai is crucial, and it takes time to change them (Koves and Marer, 1991).

(1) WBN, April 22, 1993.

2 Persistent inflation: cost-push effects/aggregate supply shock

According to Commander and Coricelli (1992), inflation in Hungary (1960-87) had a marked inertial component, due to the large share of administered prices. *Constant markup rule, inflexible wages and lagged adjustments to administered prices strengthens the persistence of inflation.*

In Hungary "although foreign prices are important in the transmission of inflation, *cost-side factors have greater weight.*" Demand-side pressures rather affect adjustment to administered prices. No relation between output or capacity utilization and prices exists, which shows that despite *the introduction of market-based reforms in Hungary, no underlying mechanism of equilibrium in the economy exists* Commander and Coricelli, 1992).

3 Wage drift: Hungary versus Poland

As there is no effective endogenous mechanism of wage restraint in a socialist economy, wage drift is common. In Hungary centrally imposed wage norms and bargaining rules restricted wage drift. In Poland where wage drift was not restrained, wages and exchange rate changes were the two variables which caused high inflation (Commander and Coricelli, 1992).

4 Privatization

Hungary has avoided grandiose schemes of privatization and encourages current management and workers to pursue the sale of their firms, subject to approval by the State Property Agency, and has made some progress with privatization of larger firms (Fischer, 1992).

5 Reforms of 1990s

Reforms since 1990 in Hungary comprise liberalization of foreign trade and investment flows, introduction of social safety net, the tax and banking systems, and labor market policies.(2) OECD survey concludes that *market-oriented reforms have progressed more rapidly than the restoration of macroeconomic equilibrium.*

6 Maintenance of infrastructure

Hungary started repairing long neglected roads and bridges in 1993, with the help of a World Bank loan of $90 million. Roughly one in every four major

(2) OECD Economic Surveys: Hungary, 1991, Paris, OECD, 1991.

roads and bridges in Hungary urgently needs repair; a large backlog of repairs accumulated because of tight budgets, neglect, inefficiency, etc.[3]

7 Actual outcome: success of gradualism

In Hungary consumer price index increased by 17% in 1989, 29% in 1990, 35% in 1991, 23% in 1992 (annual rate implied by May 1992 figure). Exchange rate was stable in 1990, devalued by 19% in 1991 and was again stable in 1992. Per capita GNP increased from and $2,620 in 1989 to $2,780 in 1990; and in constant (1987) US dollars declined from $2,400 in 1989 to $2,320 in 1990 and $2,110 in 1991 (88% of the 1989 level).

It is observed that with *gradualist reform approach* and wage restraint Hungary achieved, (i) relative price and exchange rate stability (compared with the other reforming socialist countries Hungary is much better off on this score), (ii) attracted highest level of foreign private investment in Eastern Europe (Pfefermann and Madarassy, 1993) and (iii) suffered lowest GNP loss (even Czechoslovakia's per capita GNP in 1991 was 77% of the 1989 level).

8 Comparison of Hungarian and Polish inflationary processes and explanation of inflation

The Hungarian and Polish experience with price reform starting in early 1980s shows a sustained upward shift in the price level. In Hungary inflation has consistently ratcheted upward (30% in 1990, a likely 50% in 1991), in Poland inflation was higher, 100% in 1982 with the price reforms of 1982, 60% in 1988, and burst in 1989 with market reforms to 250%, (Commander, 1992) and to 585% in 1990. In Hungary and Poland price level effects have been followed by *persistent inflation.* In Poland, 18 months after the start of stabilization, the price level was 5 times higher, output and real wages 40% lower and unemployment was at 10%. Commander (1992) argues that inflationary persistence is related to *expectations* and credibility and that autonomous wage-push or price-push are not major explanatory factors behind stubbornly high inflation rates in several of these economies recently. Calvo and Coricelli (1992) maintain that persistent output contraction and inflation are caused by technological *supply side shock* (rise in input prices) and a *credit market shock* (arising from *monetary crunch through segmented financial system* and stock of interenterprise debt, a legacy of soft budget constraint), rather than demand side developments. A monetary crunch raises the cost of working capital and hence causes output contraction and labor redundancies. There is no mechanism for channeling household savings to the enterprise

(3) WBN, Dec. 23,1992.

sector (Commander, 1992). As a consequence *standard macroeconomic policy prescriptions may not be appropriate in a reforming socialist economy* (Commander, 1992).

In these countries a series of price liberalization measures reduced the relative share of administered prices (to 20% in Hungary in 1989 and to 45% in 1989 and 10% in 1990 in Poland); what called free or contract prices in these countries are not wholly free from administrative interference (established markup rates and other guidelines constrain price growth), (Commander and Coriceli, 1992).

Price reforms entailed *greater explicit linking of domestic prices to foreign prices.* In Hungary during 1979-80, *producer* prices (mainly *for exportables)* were explicitly *linked to international prices* through the competitive pricing rule. In Poland the effect of foreign prices on administered prices remained weak. Transaction prices for exporters and importers were equalized to domestic market prices, through subsidies and taxes by the equalization settlements system.

In Hungary import and domestic prices moved closely during the 1980s; after 1986 however, Hungarian inflation exceeded inflation abroad. In Poland, import and domestic prices moved together after 1982 and currency devaluations had a strong imported inflation effect.

"In Hungary and Poland, in the 1980s consumer prices, wages and unit labor costs moved together closely; similar ground rules for reform, however, generated divergent inflationary paths". Commander and Coricelli (1992) explain the Hungarian inflation (1960-87) by an increase in unit labor costs and excess demand; these had more powerful effects than first-round import price effects. Inflation had an inertial component, due to the importance of administered prices. *There was no evidence of structural change in Hungary up to 1987.*

Chapter 16

The East German experience

The East German experience

1 Introduction

The State Treaty which created an economic, monetary and social union, between West and East Germany came into force by July 1991. "Today, Western Germans balk at the vast cost of reconstructing the East and even doubt that the task can be done". In Eastern Germany, which functions as a welfare colony, "the initial support for market economy has been replaced by cynicism, if not outright hostility". There is an increasing public demand for the state to support and sustain Eastern Germany industry (Dornbusch and Wolf, 1992).

2 Nature of transition problem

Akerlof et al consider the German transition problem, as a Keynesian depression and recommend an across-the-board, substantial labor subsidy. Whereas Dornbusch and Wolf, (1992) consider the presence of Western Germany to underwrite the social security system, and thus provide for wage increases ahead of productivity in Eastern Germany, as a disadvantage.

The availability of Western German support provides Eastern Germany favorable conditions for a rapid transition. Because through unification, Eastern Germany inherited, not only a complete set of institutions of the highest standard (legal system, property rights, unemployment compensation and a pension system, a hard currency, system of public finance and banking system with branches opened immediately in the East, accounting system, free trade access throughout Europe, etc.) but also access to enable administrators to run these institutions. Under the monetary union, the Federal Republic guaranteed the liabilities of the banking system of East Germany.

The gains from wholesale importation of legal institutions (wherever politically feasible) outweigh the disadvantages, since it is speedier and adoption of market-proven institutions creates an attractive environment for business and privatization (as against the risk of populism in home-grown institutions) (Dornbusch and Wolf, 1992).

3 Criticism of transition policy

According Dornbusch and Wolf (1992) the transition policy failed on two grounds:

(i) All *debts of enterprises were not written off* at the outset; because "debts mar the balance sheets of firms and banks and complicate the restructuring process and privatization negotiations" Enterprise debt could have been canceled and taken over by the state, the resulting increase in public debt to be retired with sale proceeds of privatized enterprises. Some, however, argue that these debts were not a major obstacle to privatization, since the Treuhand has taken over the debts of enterprises when it was necessary.

(ii) Restitution of property rights to previous owners, hampers swift restructuring and rebuilding, with more than one million claims made and 5-15 claims to the same asset. Outstanding claims on real estate and residential housing prevent current occupants to these buildings, thereby increasing cost to the national economy and making emigration more attractive. It also amounts to de facto expropriation from Eastern Germans and hence reduce the wealth of Eastern German households. On these grounds, Dornbusch and Wolf deem restitution and time-consuming process of settling pending claims as a stumbling-block to rebuilding and restructuring, unless a dramatic move is made, for which time is considered too late now (Dornbusch and Wolf, 1992). There still exists, however, another option to sort out this difficulty by converting restitution claims into pecuniary compensation in lieu of restoration in kind, unless claimants plan to move to Eastern Germany.

4 Wage policy

While wages in the East have moved quickly to reach half the Western German level and are on the way to parity, the Eastern German productivity is only one-third that of Western Germany. (While the Eastern German productivity level is similar to that of Korea or Hungary, the wage level matches that of the US and is ten times greater than that of Czech or Slovak republics.) Rather than the initial currency conversion rate, the behavior of labor unions and geography (proximity) are to blame for rapid wage increases in Eastern Germany according to Dornbusch and Wolf (1992). Lewis Alexander considers the role of government, which initially was the principal shareholder of most eastern firms and firmly committed to rapid increase in income level in the East, was responsible for wage increases in wage negotiations (as representative of management), rather than union intransigence, and *(ii)* the extension of generous social insurance schemes to Eastern Germany has insulated Eastern German incomes from the sharp decline in the demand for Eastern German labor (Dornbusch and Wolf, 1992, Comments and Discussions).

5 Effects of high-wage policy on productivity and unemployment

Overly high wages was found to be an important source of unemployment in Europe during the 1980s (Dornbusch and Wolf, 1992). Views on productivity effects of higher wages and unemployment benefits are divergent:

Charles Murray maintains that "simultaneously paying people higher wages and increasing the generosity of unemployment insurance will have little effect on productivity". Lawrence Katz "suggested that Puerto Rico and the north of England are persistently depressed regions", in line with the Murray view. Then increases in real wages in eastern Germany might lead to persistent unemployment and transfers continuing for a long time. The "Akerlof-Yellen" view, on the other hand suggests that higher wages will call forth greater work effort and result in much rapid increase in productivity (Dornbusch and Wolf, 1992, Comments and Discussion).

6 Transfers from Western Germany and domestic savings

In 1991 transfers from Western Germany to Eastern Germany (income transfers and for financing reconstruction) totaled DM 139 billion and are estimated at DM 180 billion in 1992 (5% of German GNP), one-third of which will support investment. These massive transfers explain why the collapse in production and the sharp increase in unemployment did not translate into a worse cumulative depression (Dornbusch and Wolf, 1992).

Households and firms in Eastern Germany are not saving. "Economic prosperity would happen sooner in the East if a larger fraction of transfers were saved and invested". On the other hand, without a substantially increasing purchasing power in the East, the service sector would not come into existence, which is an important part of the reconstruction program. Savings in the East should, however, increase after the pent-up demand for durables is satisfied (Dornbusch and Wolf, 1992).

After unification in July 1990, West German taxes were gradually introduced in 1991 in East Germany (Horn et al, 1992).

7 Privatization

Eastern German privatization is progressing at an extremely rapid pace, with some 30 companies being privatized a week. The privatization agency, the Treuhand, at the outset had 9,000 industrial enterprises, 45,000 establishments, 20,000 commercial enterprises, 7,500 hotels and restaurants, numerous retail shops, and farms, with 3 million jobs, to privatize. By February 1992, 5,500 industrial firms had been sold or closed. Some 5,000 companies are still to be sold. Most firms were sold to foreigners (resident in Western Germany or elsewhere) who have business in the same or similar lines, which brought about immediate access to capital, technology, management, marketing skills, markets and brand names. Banks have not played a significant role in privatization. Potential buyers are required to submit employment and investment plans with guarantees. By Feb. 1992, employment guarantees for more than 1 million workers and investment commitments totaling DM 140 billion were secured. The eastern German privatization with predominance of foreign investment and management differs sharply from the other reforming economies, with predominance of resident ownership and management (Dornbusch and Wolf, 1992).

8 Output decline

From 1989 to 1991, real GDP in Eastern Germany fell by 42%, with a slight turn-around toward the end of 1991. Upward shift of the import demand function induced by free access to Western goods, coupled with generous income transfers (complete and radical import liberalization and marketing skills of Western German distributors), increased unit costs and disorganization on the supply side, along with the decline in demand for eastern goods, all contributed to the sharp decline in output, especially in industry. Imports have exceeded GDP in absolute amount, because of massive transfers from Western Germany. In the East households and firms are not saving (Dornbusch and Wolf, 1992).

According to Horn et al (1992), after German unification, revaluation of the East German mark by 300% and poor quality of products reduced competitiveness of East German firms due to high production costs. Domestic demand for East German products fell because of price effects and consumers' preference for Western products. East European markets were lost due to the dismantling of COMECON (because of the requirement for payment in convertible currency). Nominal value of industrial production declined by 50%

in the second half of 1990, and real GNP declined by 25% in the second half of 1990. Real consumer demand, on the other hand increased, and was financed by financial transfers by the Federal government, and by the reduction of accumulated savings. Employment declined by 1.3 million; unemployment rose to 840,000 (9.5%) in May 1992. Adjusted for part-time workers, unemployment rate was 22% in May 1991 (Horn, et al., 1992).

9 Investments

Tentative estimates of the investment required in eastern Germany to achieve 80% productivity equalization over the next decade is DM 1 trillion. Investments, in eastern Germany has increased from 24.8% of GNP in 1990 to 37.4% in 1991, worth some DM 72 billion. Real gross fixed investments have increased by 18% in 1991 and is expected to increase by 26% in 1992. In the near future, investment growth is expected to keep pace with GNP growth with record investment rates (Dornbusch and Wolf, 1992).

10 Unemployment

Since the fall of 1989 till January 1992, some 3 million people have lost their jobs in eastern Germany. Employment declined in every sector, with largest decline in the industrial sector. Public work programs and continued short-time work (disguised unemployment) accounted for almost 1 million jobs, by January 1992. Labor force declined by more than 1 million, as workers migrated, commuted or chose early retirement. Moreover the participation rate of females in the labor force declined significantly (Dornbusch and Wolf, 1992). Nearly 30% of the labor force is unemployed, when short-time work and job programs are factored in.

11 Commuting and migration

Migration or commuting is considered an obvious solution to unemployment in eastern Germany. Nearly one-half million eastern Germany residents work in the West, with a reasonable commuting time. Commuting may strike the best balance between earnings and the cost of living in eastern Germany. Commuting doubles earnings without the large extra cost of housing in the West. With an average commuting time only 40 minutes, number of commuters could double or triple. On these considerations, migration and commuting should be encouraged with a view to equalizing incomes more rapidly and with less unemployment. If another 1 to 2 million workers move to the West, the bleak unemployment outlook in the East would be solved. In the past 2 years, the West created almost that many jobs by running *a high-pressure economy* (pushing capacity utilization to a peak for the decade, the unemployment rate fell to its lowest level in a decade despite large immigration, wages increased in excess of productivity growth, Bundesbank raised the interest rate and pursued tight monetary policy to check inflationary pressure), (Dornbusch and Wolf, 1992).

Akerlof et al consider unemployment is the main reason for migration. Home ownership reduces migration; "among homeowners, only one-third are willing to migrate in the medium run." (Dornbusch and Wolf, 1992) Hence restitution of property right in kind, in lieu of in financial terms, speeds up migration, which entails a net increase in cost to the national economy, through extra cost of housing, utilities and infrastructure in Western Germany.

12 Burden of unification on Germany

Unification moved the Western German Economy into overheating and inflation, increasing demand for Western German goods, pushing capacity utilization to a peak, decreasing unemployment, increasing wages and interest rate, and the onset of a solidarity tax (6.5% income surtax schedule to expire in 1992). The cost of unification was largely financed by borrowing; the German public debt grows at rates similar to the growth of US public debt in the 1980s. The German capital market came under pressure from budget deficits resulting from transfer payments and through investment outlays related to improving infrastructure and business formation in the East, with "high long-term real interest rates implicit in nominal yields of 8% and a declining inflation rate". These high long-term rates, have not yet slowed down investments particularly in the East, because of pervasive subsidization of investment. "Investments in Western Germany will fall unless major budget efforts are forthcoming or Feldstein- Horioka effects are not present at all". The decline in investment would make it difficult to sustain high and rising real wages. So far a current account deficit has financed the cost of unification (Dornbusch and Wolf, 1992).

Dornbusch and Wolf, consider rebuilding Eastern Germany as an investment project, including part of the consumption smoothing in the East financed by transfers, and hence accept increasing taxes moderately and predominantly using debt finance, as the correct approach. Transfer payments is "interpreted as part of an investment in political transition that avoids divisive politics and fosters a stable business environment". There is, however, no prospects for a reduction of transfers to Eastern Germany. In the Western Germany private savings have not declined and capital formation have not suffered much (Dornbusch and Wolf, 1992).

Running a high-pressure economy in Western Germany, (i.e. high capacity utilization), would both attract migrants and immigrants from the East and would provide an incentive for new capacity creation, which would largely locate in the East. A major scaling down of military expenditures and replacement of the draft by volunteer army, in line with reduced need for a strong defense posture in the post- communism and unification era, would release resources for reconstruction and ease of budgetary pressure (Dornbusch and Wolf, 1992).

Employing econometric models Pohl et al and Horn et al aimed at quantifying the macroecenomic effects of German unification. Pohl et al (1990) underestimated most of the macroeconomic problems of unification. Horn et al (1992) estimate that the unification boom will end after one year ; thereafter lower growth rates and higher inflation will follow; and a slight recovery will happen after 4 years. Horn et al conclude that "the prospects of Germany's economic future are rather uncertain".

13 The German catch-up issue: growth and convergence

(i) Views of Barro and Sala-i Martin versus Dornbusch and Wolf: minimum 30 years versus maximum 15 years

The Eastern German productivity level, being one-third of the Western German one, estimates differ regarding the catching-up time. Barro and Sala-i Martin estimated that "it would take 35 years for half of the initial East-West gap to be eliminated".Growth advantages become small and diminish as productivity differences narrow, because the growth rate differential is negatively related to the gap between productivity levels of two regions. Barro considers, the eastern German productivity catch-up is similar to that of the Southern US catching up with the North and Italy's South catching up with its North, where the catch-up was desperately slow. Dornbusch and Wolf (1992), however, deem that the US precedent is not relevant, because of small size of Eastern Germany, proximity and advanced communications and transport facilities (Dornbusch and Wolf, 1992).

According to Barro and Sala-i Martin "the Eastern German growth would start off around 3.4 to 3.8% a year and then gradually fall off to the western German growth rate of 2% a year"; and it would take more than a century to catch up. This analysis does not take into account the special factors of the eastern German transition, even the expected investment boom.

In the Eastern German case high skill/ education levels, geographic proximity, reduced risk factors and information costs through political union, and massive subsidization of firms are the special factors that would contribute to a fast productivity growth. Using an alternative Barro model and an average of the coefficients obtained by Barro, Dornbusch and Wolf estimate that *"an extra 20 percentage points of GDP in investment yields only an additional 1.3 percentage growth a year in productivity"* (Dornbusch and Wolf, 1992).

If it is assumed that Eastern Germany will repeat the high-growth performance of Japan, Taiwan, South Korea, Hong-Kong and Singapore, with very high investment rates, it would take three decades Eastern Germany to achieve 80% of Western German productivity (starting from an initial gap of 70%).

It is, however, considered that Eastern Germany could achieve *80% convergence to western German productivity level in the next 15 years thanks to special factors and unusually rapid rate of capital formation.* "The extent of the adoption of new technology will far exceed the levels in the other post-socialist economies"; "The Treuhand strategy of selling enterprises to firms that operate in the same or a similar field" will greatly count on this score. Moreover eastern Germany will attract a disproportionate share of investment in Eastern Europe, because of the absence of political risk, the massive investment in infrastructure undertaken by the public sector, the market experience of the administration, availability of inputs from Western markets, free access to the European Community (EC), the fact that the Feldstein-Horioka effect [that national investment rates are determined/constrained by national rates of saving] will not affect eastern Germany separately, extensive subsidies to capital formation in the East (as high as 50%), the less 'green' attitudes of population and administration, and the fact that Eastern Germany is a natural location for expanding Western German firms (Dornbusch and Wolf, 1992, pp. 250-51).

Considering that the extra 20 percentage point increase in investment can yield only 1.3% increase in growth rate (Dornbusch and Wolf, 1992), (in Far Eastern countries investment rate is also 40% of GDP); that the unification boom will end in a year and thereafter lower growth and higher inflation rates will follow with a slight recovery after 4 years, and that the prospects of German economy are rather uncertain according to Horn et al (1992) and that the Eastern German wage increases far exceed productivity growth, one could conclude that the 15 year catching-up estimate by Dornbusch and Wolf is overly optimistic.

(ii) Validity of the precedent of the 1947- 1950 German recovery

Lewis Alexander claims that the productivity gain observed in West Germany between 1947 and 1950 or 1951 (roughly 50% in the industrial sector) could serve a precedent for rapid convergence now and the postwar economic 'miracle' could repeat itself. During the first phase of that reconstruction period, by elimination of economic controls, uncertainty over basic property rights and the economic system and releasing repressed inflation, prewar output levels were achieved rapidly, without changing "the utilization of inputs", implying a dramatic increase in productivity (Dornbusch and Wolf, 1992, Comments and Discussion).

The postwar reconstruction period could not serve as a precedent for the current Eastern German recovery. Restoring output to prewar levels, following destruction of fixed assets and interrupted factor/input supplies during the war, is a completely different proposition. Firstly technological and economic obsolescence of fixed assets was of minor importance. With little investment and required repairs, the existing production facilities could be restored to full capacity and full capacity utilization of this facilities could be achieved by means of orderly flow of inputs and elimination of critical bottlenecks and shortages of factor and input supplies; all this might entail little increase in the total use of inputs and factors; but more important and critical is the change in composition, distribution and regular flow of inputs. In view of the fact that, "war damage to production facilities was relatively minor" and "wartime additions to the capital stock far outweighed war damage and allies' dismantling", it is obvious that required repair of fixed assets would have cost little, hence its marginal product would be very high. As the Italian and French achievements of prewar industrial production levels in 1947 and 1948 respectively are not shown as precedents, the overdelayed (due to allied occupation) but normal West German recovery/ restoration in 1950 either could not be taken as a precedent in this context.

Stanley Fisher indicated that initially convergence was rapid in the Israeli-occupied-territories after the 1967 war, mainly due to migration, per capita income nearly doubling in five years. But "then convergence essentially stopped" (Dornbusch and Wolf, 1992 Comments and Discussion). This is much more recent and relevant precedents than post-war German growth or post bellum growth of Southern US.

Lewis Alexander estimates that if investment per employee in eastern and western Germany remains the same for ten years, eastern German productivity will be 84% of the Western German level at the end of the period, not counting productivity increase due to the transition to market system, the newer vintage of eastern German capital stock (due to rapid capital accumulation in eastern Germany) and the technological change/improvements embodied in the capital stock, entailed. In fact, using a medium sized macro-economic model, Alexander et al, estimate that "output per worker in Eastern Germany converges to the Western German level at an average rate of 14% over the first 15 years" driven by increased investment (Dornbusch and Wolf, 1992, Comments and Discussion). This view is based on the rapid growth of capital stock in Eastern Germany, which might not materialize, because the rate of return to capital is likely to fall with rising wages.

(iii) Conclusion on the catch-up issue

More important in the near future is the fact that when wage parity with the West is attained, profitability of investments in Eastern Germany would decline and a big investment push foreseen as the main factor for the catch-up will slow down, even if overly generous subsidies are sustained indefinitely. On the other hand, the rationality of setting up overly subsidized industries, replacing inefficient socialist enterprises, could be questioned. Kornai (1990), has warned about the danger of this pitfall. Under the present policies it is doubtful that productivity catch-up will ever be attained, unless the said dilemma is resolved. It is a chicken-and-egg problem, since productivity can't increase because it is too low to justify unsubsidized private investments.

The eastern German catch-up issue, in a few years will evolve into (and determined by) polarization (effects), depending on comparative advantages or disadvantages (pull/push effects) of localities and cities in the region, vis-a-vis changing internal and external conditions, which could not be predicted precisely now. Also one should note a remark by Martin Baily (Dornbusch and Wolf, 1992, Comments and Discussion), that the presently high rate of investment in eastern Germany does not indicate that the return to capital is high, because "most of the investment is flowing into residential construction, rather than into industrial capital".

14 Present unification policies versus 'the suggested approach'

If the suggested approach of immediate political union, but a gradual economic union were adopted; then a gradually declining internal tariff (say in 5 years vanishing, and at moderate rates, to protect the Eastern German economy against Western German products), would have saved some jobs and output and finance part of the reconstruction cost; industries serving ex-Comecon markets could have survived at least in the medium-run; with DM legal tender, free capital movements, privatization and increased or free access to markets, technology, critical inputs and factors, etc., productivity of eastern Germany would have increased, with less decline in output and employment; migration and commuting possibly would have been at the same level, except for migration component if pecuniary compensation replaced restitution of property rights; investments in Eastern Germany would not be less, if same incentives were offered.

Adoption of this approach however, would have resulted in a sharply contrasting outcome from the present picture, in following respects:

(i) Consumption shock (on Western Germany and zero or negative saving rates for Eastern households and firms) would have been averted, because a gradually declining internal tariff would have induced postponement of demand for durables and hence even have increased private savings in Eastern Germany. This would have made possible to avoid the current overheating of Western German economy, with its concomitant adverse national and international effects.

(ii) Transfer payments to Eastern Germany, would have been lower, due to revenue from internal tariff and because of less need for public work programs and continued short-time work (disguised unemployment), currently employing 1 million workers.

(iii) Wages in Eastern Germany could have kept pace with productivity increase, because of predominance of the threat of unemployment otherwise. This would have averted the dilemma awaiting Eastern Germany, in a couple of years, when wage parity with the West is reached. Overly generous subsidies on investments in the East and the wage differential, so far have by-passed this dilemma. High wage level not commensurate with productivity level, will eventually slow down the present investment drive in Eastern Germany despite generous subsidies under the present policies.

It is argued that the small geographic size of Eastern Germany, short distances to commute to work in the West, would not have allowed a *low-wage strategy* anyway (Dornbusch and Wolf, 1992). Maintaining economic entity of Eastern Germany at the initial phase, would have made possible to keep wages lower in the East longer, since migration and commuting now despite full union, provided jobs only to 1 million persons, out of 3 million unemployed after unification.

(iv) Productivity increased in Eastern Germany in 1991, due to decline in hours worked in a delayed response to the sharp drop in Eastern German industrial production. The extreme openness of the Eastern German economy and the rapid increase in wages, were partly responsible for stagnating output, despite productivity increase. Lewis Alexander concludes that (Dornbusch and Wolf, 1992 Comments and Discussion) "had wages not increased so much, and or had *some mechanism* such as an exchange rate depreciation *or tariff* been available to divert eastern German demand away from foreign products, surely this increase in productivity would have resulted in an increase in output". The suggested approach would have provided that tariff mechanism and a restraint on wage increases.

(v) The burden of unification on the Western German economy would have been much less, as a result of internal tariff revenue, domestic savings in Eastern Germany, partly surviving COMECON trade, and through avoiding over-heating and interest-rate hike.

(vi) Because of the partial survival of COMECON trade through a multilateral payments scheme, output in the Eastern Europe and in the former Soviet Union would have declined less and consequently the German aid to the reforming socialist countries could have been kept at a lower level.

15 Most recent developments and final conclusion

According to recent press reports, developments in the early 1993 rather confirm pessimistic views regarding the German unification. The German economy is now beleaguered by rising taxes and national debt, strikes and stagnation. In 1992, the West German economic growth was less than 2% and in 1993, a 7% fall in industrial output is expected. The cost of East German recovery is now estimated at $1 trillion, i.e. $100 billion a year for a decade. Privatization by Treuhand has also bogged down in bureaucracy and property rights issues; e.g. "$125 billion in potential investment is stuck in the pipeline because of uncertainty over property ownership".(1)

The German economic union approach generated three processes which are both damaging and irreversible:

(i) The wage level in Eastern Germany rose well above its productivity and as a result of the May 1993 strike, it will further rise and be equal to the western level by 1996, with its concomitant adverse effects on investment and consumption.

(ii) Eastern Germany, once ranked as the 12th industrial economy in the world, is now rapidly becoming deindustrialized; whereas, in the interim period, the eastern industry could have served its markets in the former socialist countries and in developing countries, through a temporary multilateral clearing arrangement replacing the CMEA trade, and possibly part of it might have survived ever thereafter.

(iii) Consumption has been preferred to investment through one-to-one exchange of the ostmark with the Deutsche mark, wage policy and generous transfer payments to Eastern Germany. A process to convert loanable funds into consumption by means of taxation was created at a

---

(1) Time Magazine, May 24, 1993, p. 35.

time when even West Germany needed a reverse mechanism to convert consumption into loanable funds through taxation, to solve the chronic structural (virtually permanent) unemployment problem. (E.g. German, failed to invest in the new steel technology of continuous casting developed by a German firm.)

The consumption-oriented policies of unification also led to the Western German economy's overheating, caused by overspending of dissaving Eastern Germans, which in turn induced initial optimistic expectations, and a short-lived boom, which caused further entrenchment of inefficiencies inherent in the Western German economy and high wage costs. In contrast, under 'the suggested approach', investment expenditure both in Eastern and Western German economies would have been boosted. In fact, 'the method', that basically employs the 'big-bang' approach with indicative planning, and recommending phased economic union and continuation of the CMEA trade in a modified fashion in the new setting, as compared with the 'big-bang' with market only approach adopted during unification, would have averted all these harmful consequences.

Chapter 17

Recent developments in the other reforming socialist countries

Recent developments in the other reforming socialist countries

Depending on the data and information availability, recent developments in the other reforming socialist economies are described below.

Appended tables (No.17.1-17.4) include per capita GDP, GNP, consumption and domestic investment data and GNP/GDP growth rates in recent years, compared with developing economies.

1 Albania

In Albania, for 45 years central planning had decided, allocated and distributed everything in all sectors of the economy. *"when the political system crumbled in 1991, the economy collapsed," because no alternative system was in place to replace the abolished one. "The result was economic and social chaos".*(1)

"The country's economy had screeched to a halt", in 1991 and 1992. "Agricultural production dropped by more than 30% as the government began privatizing cooperatives. Wheat production dropped from 600,000 tons in 1989 to 354,000 tons in [1991]". "Agriculture employs one-half of the population and yields more than one-third of the country's income". Production in the mining and industrial sectors has also plummeted. The country in 1992 faced an acute shortage of spare parts, fertilizers, vehicles and equipment needed to revive or expand production of agricultural and industrial goods, minerals and electricity. They obtained (2) an IDA loan of $41 million to finance imports of goods desperately "needed to keep the economy afloat and prevent further deterioration while a new market-oriented system is being put in place".(3)

---

(1) Dethier of World Bank, WBN, July 2, 1992.
(2) Dethier of World Bank, WBN, July 2, 1992.
(3) Dethier of World Bank, WBN, July 2, 1992.

In 1991, the government launched a land-reform program, which parceled out the land held by cooperatives (which covered 3/4 of Albania's arable land) into 380,000 farms, averaging 1.5 hectares each. On these small holdings many farmers could not even produce enough food to feed their own families, also because the reform program did not envisage giving capital to farmers, which caused farmers to work without many agricultural inputs, in 1991 about 90% of farmers had no fertilizer for their fields. Hence agriculture has returned to subsistence farming. Average rural earnings (income) is $20 per month.(4)

The land reform led to widespread scavenging of infrastructure materials; telephone wires were used to fence fields and as a consequence 1,000 villages were left without telephone lines; a third of the water systems and one-quarter of the electricity network and some 1,000 village schools were ruined during civil unrest in 1990. Albania's rural infrastructure (roads, schools, health centers) are in worse shape. Under the old regime, infrastructure could not be maintained because of lack of funds and inefficiency; after breaking up the cooperatives, no authority is in charge of maintaining and repairing rural infrastructure ("under the old system, the cooperatives carried out one-third of the national investment in rural construction and one-half of investment in land projects".) An IDA loan of $36 million obtained in 1993, will help Albania to tackle rural poverty, by enabling farmers to buy agricultural inputs and other essentials and rural workers to set up new small-scale businesses or buy livestock, and get rural works projects going.(5)

In Albania GDP per capita is below $400, annual population growth rate 2% and literacy rate is 88%.

Albania has fertile land and ample rainfall, which makes possible a rapid rise in agricultural output, and the country's hydropower, mineral and oil resources could bring substantial foreign exchange earnings.(6)

2 Armenia

Armenia suffered heavily from the dissolution of the USSR and crumbling of the tightly woven interrepublican trade network along with it, being "long dependent on cheap Soviet imports and vast Soviet export markets". Moreover, the war over Nagarno-Karabakh and the aftermath of the 1988 earthquake also hit hard. The 1988 earthquake destroyed enterprises, workplaces and buildings which produce 40% of Armenia's manufacturing industry. "Roughly 10% of the population still lives in temporary housing".(7)

---

(4) Rory O'Sullivan of World Bank, WBN, Feb 25, 1993.

(5) Sullivan, WBN- Feb, 25, 1993.

(6) Dethier, WBN, July 2, 1992.

(7) Interview with Chris Hall of World Bank, WBN, April 1, 1993.

Armenia has started reforming the economy after independence. "In 1991 it became the first former Soviet republic *to privatize agricultural land"* (agriculture is a minor sector, however, due to lack of arable land). It *"freed prices on many goods, eliminated export taxes and import restrictions,* equalized direct tax rates, enacted *banking-reform law* and *enterprise legislation* and started *privatization of small shops.*(8)"

"A privatization commission has been set up to sell off some 10,000 small firms and 700 large firms and 4,000 unfinished construction sites. *By 1995, the government hopes to privatize all small-scale enterprises and about 25% of the large manufacturing concerns"* Domestic revenues of the government have plummeted, because Armenia imposed *a value-added tax* without preparation and lacked the staff and administration to collect taxes; and as a consequence large cuts in expenditures and services have to be carried out.(9)

Priority reform and restructuring *issues* are *increasing economic management capacity, raising domestic revenues,*(via devising a new tax policy and setting up a customs administration), *privatization* and implementing the *banking reform.* "Despite help from the Armenian diaspora", "the country still lacks the staff who know how to shape reforms and guide a market economy". New financial skills for a market economy, such as commercial banking, accounting and auditing have to be developed.(10)

Performance of commercial banks are unsatisfactory; "many banks are currently insolvent and make too many risky loans". "The sharp drop in tax revenue, combined with a falling economic activity, have produced a large fiscal deficit." (11)

Despite economic reforms, "much of Armenia's economy still follows *a centrally planned pattern of production and trade* and is dependent on the production of goods at aging factories with obsolete equipment." Stabilization has not been achieved, because of lack of a stable currency, war and policy inexperience.(12)

The ongoing war with Azerbaijan, has cut off Armenia's main energy supplies and its primary rail and road links to the rest of the former Soviet economy. "During the [1992/93] winter Armenia could only import 10% of its fuel needs."(13)

Armenia's economic output has steadily declined since 1987 when the Soviet trade network began to unravel; for years, it

---

(8) Interview with Chiris Hall of World Bank, WBN, April 1, 1993.

(9) Hall, WBN, April 1, 1993.

(10) Hall, WBN, April 1, 1993.

(11) Hall, WBN, April 1, 1993.

(12) Hall, WBN, April 1, 1993.

(13) Hall, WBN, April 1, 1993.

depended on cheap, subsidized oil, gas, and raw materials from the other republics and relied on Soviet consumers to buy its exports. Russia consumed 60% of Armenia's exports alone and the Ukraine bought another 20%. The loss of Soviet markets, combined with a total trade and energy blockade on Armenia, caused the country's output to fall by 45% in 1992. [Over the 1987-92 period per capita GDP fell by 13.4% p.a., from $2,150 in 1987 to $1,200 in 1992.] The Armenian economy is very badly off at the moment, with activity at a virtual standstill.(14)

Here one observes (i) a reform effort without any meaningful direction (groping its way) (ii) idiosyncrasy of starting a war (unless there are ulterior motives) leading to complete cut-off of energy, transport and trading links with actual and potential trading partners and ending up with complete isolation of a land-locked country, which can never be self-sufficient and can only survive with specialization and substantial foreign trade; (iii) that dismantling of CMEA and inter-republican trade and bilateral payments mechanism caused severe output and foreign trade declines for Armenia; (iv) that under existing policies, Armenia could never achieve economic stabilization and growth, unless it receives substantial external aid permanently.

3 The Baltics

(i) Estonia

After independence in August 1991, output declined by 10% in 1991; per capita GDP in 1991 was $3,830; over the 1980-91 period per capita GDP growth rate was 2.1%.(15)

In 1988, Estonia's purchases of 'soft currency' imports from the former Soviet Union amounted to 54% of GDP, by 1991 this percentage fell to 26%, "because of payment problems, sharp drops in production and political turmoil in the region". "Estonia made up for this drop in Soviet imports by increasing 'hard currency' imports from non-Soviet countries", which jumped from $112 million in 1990 to $200 million in 1991.(16)

"But [the current] shortage of foreign exchange is likely to force Estonia to cut these imports by 15-30% in 1992. The cutback is slowing the Estonian economy by causing widespread shortages of spare parts, chemicals and other goods"."In early 1992, Estonia's electricity and residential heating suffered from low fuel-oil supplies", and shortages of spare parts and chemicals. Crop and livestock production had fallen in 1992, because of input shortages and

(14) Hall, WBN, April 1, 1993.
(15) WBN, April 22, 1993.
(16) WBN, Oct 1, 1992.

drought; transport suffered from spare part shortages and the health sector from shortages of medical supplies.(17)

As a consequence of all this, a sharp decline in output and import availability occurred and a foreign exchange shortage has arisen. In late 1992, the World Bank provided a rehabilitation loan of $30 million, to help maintain output in key sectors in 1993 by *financing critically needed imports for "power, heat, transport, agriculture and health services, while the government shifts to a free market system,"* and "continues to implement its [ambitious] economic reforms." The reform program includes stimulating the private sector, making enterprises and the banking system more efficient, legal reform, privatization and setting up new auditing and procurement systems.(18)

Despite further decline of output in 1992, downward movement has slowed during recent months and industrial output has stayed level in December 1992 and January 1993; it is possible that the economy is already bottoming out. Recovery will be achieved by sound policies, such as a stabilization program, put in place, structural reforms and a currency board to control monetary expansion and keep inflation down. Since 1991 exports to the West, mainly wood products, garments, textiles and fish to Scandinavia have quadrupled. Previously Russia bought the bulk of Estonia's exports; now, Finland is the number one buyer.(19)

New World Bank studies for the Baltics, estimate that Estonia, might achieve economic growth in 1993, buoyed by sound policies and strong exports to the West. The studies do not make concrete predictions but offer possible scenarios for the Baltics based on current situations.(20)

Despite its rebound in early 1993, "Estonia's current economic output totals only 60% of the 1989 level"; and to climb back to a full recovery, privatization must be accelerated. So far only 7 of 300 large state enterprises have been sold and the sale of 20-30 more is expected soon. Estonia's economy has the highest degree of concentration on industry among the former Soviet Union republics. Many enterprises, however, suffer from overstaffing, poor technology and management,and poor quality of products. As a consequence of ongoing economic adjustment, the unemployment rate was expected to climb from 0.5% to 10% by the end of 1993.(21)

---

(17) WBN, Oct 1, 1992.

(18) Lewis President, World Bank President, WBN, Oct 1, 1992.

(19) WBN, April 22, 1993.

(20) WBN, April 22, 1993.

(21) WBN, April 22, 1993.

(ii) Latvia

"Latvia's economic output fell substantially from 1990 to 1992, mainly from the collapse in trade links" with the former Soviet Union; in 1992 GDP dropped by 33% and fell to only 40% of the 1990 level by the end of 1992. Per capita GDP was $3410 in 1991 and had grown by 2.8% p.a. over 1980-1991.[22]

"*Latvia freed most price controls in 1991,* about one year earlier than in other former Soviet Union countries." *Latvia was also "the first former Soviet Union country to establish a foreign exchange market free of government control.";* it "has *successfully introduced a new currency,* the lats, free from the ruble"; it has *reduced the inflation rate to around 2-3% a month from nearly 50% a month* in early 1992. "The Latvian economy has not yet bottomed out"; "the economy could bounce back by late 1994 if reforms go ahead as planned and scarce imports keep up with demand."[23]

Progress on other reforms has been mixed, with privatization of enterprises and banks falling behind. Without state banks and large and inefficient firms being restructured or privatized, Latvia can not expect increased investment and economic recovery. Shipping is the biggest export earner; exports of wood, wood products and fish have to be boosted for recovery.[24]

(iii) Lithuania

"The Lithuanian economy suffered the most of the three Baltic nations when it broke from the former Soviet Union in 1991." About 85% of Lithuania's trade was with the former Soviet Union; almost all energy imports came from those countries; "after independence, those trade ties all but collapsed, claiming one-half of Lithuania's output".[25]

"Lithuania was... somewhat slower in launching economic reforms..."; it introduced a *temporary* national currency in October 1992; it is still dependent on the former Soviet Union for 3/4 of its trade and trade with the West is picking up slowly. Macroeconomic stability is still a problem. "Lithuania moved quickly into privatization,... faster than all other reforming socialist economies." The country has to import crude oil from Russia for its refinery, the only one in the Baltics, at least in the short-term. It has to continue its energy price reforms and take energy conservation measures to stop inefficient and wasteful use.[26]

---

(22) WBN, April 22, 1993.
(23) WBN, April 22, 1993.
(24) WBN, April 22, 1993.
(25) WBN, April 22, 1993.
(26) WBN, April 15, 1993.

A recent agreement with EC granting preference for textile exports of the three Baltic countries may help its exports.[(27)]

Lithuania's per capita GDP was $2,710 in 1991 and had grown by 2.5% over 1980-1991.[(28)]

Lithuania's turnaround "may not arrive before early 1995, if the country does not revive its traditionally heavy trade with the other former Soviet Union countries."[(29)]

4 Bulgaria

"Bulgaria had a much worse starting point than the other Eastern European countries", because (i) it was more heavily dependent on CMEA trade than any other country in the region; up to 80% of its external trade was with CMEA area. The official unemployment rate at the end of-1992 was 15%, one of highest in the region; (ii) its private sector was very underdeveloped (contributing only 2% of economic activity), when the communist system collapsed.[(30)]

"In 1990, Bulgaria declared a moratorium on its debt, now totalling $12 billion". "In late 1990 and 1991, there were food shortages"; these have been eliminated when food production increased.[(31)]

"Acute energy shortages arose in Bulgaria about two years ago, when low-cost oil imports from the Soviet Union dropped off." Prices of coal and energy had been artificially low until the government launched reforms in 1990.[(32)]

Bulgaria has suffered heavy output losses since 1989, when CMEA trade collapsed, which would eventually claim one-third of the country's economic output. Output fell by 11.8% in 1990, 23% in 1991 and 8% in 1992; and GDP will probably decline by another 4-5% in 1993, before it resumes growing in 1994.[(33)]

Bulgaria launched a comprehensive reform program in early 1991, "targeting the financial system, state-owned enterprises, trade, prices, the agricultural sector and social services." The reforms paid off and helped slow down economic losses, but when a turnaround was in sight, the reforms lost their momentum, because of political difficulties; and this led to a slowing of stabilization and structural reforms. This slow-down may delay recovery by one

---

(27) WBN, 11 March 1993.
(28) WBN, April 22, 1993.
(29) WBN, April 22, 1993.
(30) WBN, April 15, 1993.
(31) WBN, 11 March 1993
(32) WBN, April 15, 1993
(33) WBN, April 15, 1993.

year. The reform program has had its stops and starts, and has not stopped the decline in GDP.[34]

"The first signs of the turnaround came in 1992 when both exports and imports increased", and the trade account recorded a small surplus in the first half (of 1992).[35]

Bulgaria has put in place the legal and institutional framework for privatization and financial sector reform; but these have to be implemented. They still have to start privatization of small firms through auctions.[36]

"Small business and private sector activity has increased both retail and wholesale trade." "Now, all of the major metropolitan areas are full of shops where goods are freely available." A very healthy orientation of trade toward Western European markets has started. The external debt moratorium has constrained private capital flows, including trade credits and direct foreign investment; a debt-reduction agreement is being negotiated.[37]

A recent reform agenda for Bulgaria includes enterprise restructuring and privatization, financial sector reform and agriculture. Privatization of even small firms has not started; banking reform is awaited. Through agricultural reform (privatization of assets), Bulgaria could become a big exporter of agricultural products and also has great tourism potential. Recent trade agreements with EC and EFTA might help its export trade, but Bulgaria's main export items like agricultural products and iron and steel fall outside the scope of these agreements and are subject to protective clauses.[38]

5 Former Czechoslovakia

In Czechoslovakia the consumer price index was stable in 1989, increased by 10% in 1990, 58% in 1991,(wholesale prices by 70%),and 9% in the first half of 1992.

Per capita GNP declined from $3,450 in 1989 to $3,140 in 1990; and in constant (1987) US dollars from $3,500 in 1989 to $3,430 in 1990 and $2,690 in 1991 (23% decline from the 1989 level).

(i) Pollution and energy use

> On a per capita basis, pollution in Czechoslovakia is the highest in Europe, and pollution in Northern Bohemia is 10 times the average in the country. ... Nearly one-third of the population is exposed to dangerous levels of air and water pollution. ... Drinking water in many cities does

(34) WBN, April 15, 1993.
(35) WBN, April 15, 1993.
(36) WBN, April 15, 1993.
(37) WBN, April 15, 1993.
(38) WBN, May 28, 1992.

> not comply with international standards. Food is contaminated with heavy metals and organic chemicals... It will be decades before the country's main environmental problems are resolved. ... According to World Bank estimates, the total investment needed to achieve acceptable environmental standards in Czechoslovakia is more than $50 billion.[39]

"Prices for energy and raw materials were low, leading to overuse, waste and high levels of pollution. The average person in Czechoslovakia consumed up to 500% more energy than the average person in most Western industrialized countries". Concentration of heavy industries, which used large amounts of low-quality coal, also contributed to increased pollution. The introduction of market pricing for energy and other raw materials has led to higher prices, which should encourage conservation; also petroleum consumption is declining, because petroleum products are now being allocated almost exclusively to the transportation and chemicals sector.[40]

(ii) Privatization

An Indian hotel group will upgrade the country's premier tourist hotel on a long-term lease basis (the Czechoslovakian company that currently owns the hotel will retain ownership, but it will be privatized), investing $25 million.[41]

The oldest bank of the Czech and Slovak Federal Republic (Zivnotenska Banka) was privatized with assistance from a German merchant Bank, BHF and the World Bank affiliate, IFC. This was the first privatization of a financial institution, by which a state-owned bank was transformed into a joint-stock company (IFC purchased 12% of the stock and BHF 40%), the remaining 48% will be transferred to the public, mostly through a voucher system.[42]

6 North Korean reforms

"The North Korean reform effort since the mid-1980s has been motivated by the increasing seriousness of the problems typical of centrally planned socialist economies". The enterprise system of North Korea, can be considered as a "variant of the centrally planned socialist economy with some incentive schemes such as profit retention and worker bonuses". In North Korea, "the soft budget constraint, runaway input demand and hoarding, overcentralization, and related disequilibrium (shortages), ineffective worker incentive provisions and related collusive and opportunistic behavior" are prevalent (Kang and Lee, 1992).

---

(39) WBN, May 28, 1992.
(40) WBN, May 28, 1992.
(41) WBN, May 28, 1992.
(42) WBN, Feb 20, 1992.

The mid-1980s reform program emphasized the financial independence of enterprise (hardening budget constraint), material incentives and the payment-by-result principle, vertical or horizontal integration and increased enterprise autonomy (Kang and Lee, 1992).

Judging from the fact that no significant improvement of performance of Chinese state enterprises has occurred exercising a decade of reform efforts along similar reform measures, Kang and Lee (1992) conclude that the North Korean economic reform will not be successful. "The Chinese lesson was that without radical changes in property rights relations and the emergence of a more competitive economic environment, any attempt to vitalize the state sector is likely to fail."

The August Third program in 1984 which encouraged the nonstate sector to rely on market mechanism and promulgation of the joint venture law in 1984 will not achieve the declared objectives, because the Chinese experience shows that "such a dualistic approach will eventually bring about competition problems between the state and nonstate sector and between plans and markets" (Kang and Lee, 1992).

The inference by Kang and Lee, based on the Chinese experience is premature, inappropriate and arbitrary (because, the basis of comparison, the Chinese experience is evaluated wrongly). It is inappropriate, because supposedly the same policy exercised in two countries may differ considerably in implementation (e.g., Turkey in 1980s supposedly pursued export promotion and capital accumulation policies, focused on big conglomerates, similar to those of South Korea, but these resulted in fraud through fictitious exports to take advantage of an export-tax rebate and a huge increase in the external debt, rather than in an output/investment response, in sharp contrast with the Korean economic miracle. The Chinese gradualist, double-track reform is now acclaimed as a major success, with 8-9% real GDP increase p.a. over a decade and a sizeable reduction in poverty.

7 Romania

In Romania the consumer price index rose by 10% per month in the last two months of 1990, 2.3 times in 1991 and some 100% in the first half of 1992.

Per capita GNP declined from $1720 in 1989 to $1,620 in 1990; and in constant (1987) US dollars declined from $1,960 in 1989 to $1,650 in 1990 and $1,420 in 1991 (28% decline from the 1989 level).

In 1992, Romania started to transfer 8 million hectares of state-held farms to individuals or private farmer associations (before the 1989 revolution, the government controlled 10 million hectares of arable land). The shortage of investment credit has been an obstacle to the growth of a private agricultural sector; "masses of small farmers are in need of capital and technical assistance."

"A World Bank loan of $100 million will be provided to two major banks, which will lend money to farmers, private farmer associations and agricultural businesses to finance investments in lei or in dollars" to step up production, processing and marketing activities.[43]

8 Moldava

Moldava became independent in August 1991. Moldava's GDP had fallen by more than a third in 1991 and 1992,

> a civil war was fought in 1992, and the country's traditional trade relations all but collapsed with the disintegration of the Soviet Union. Moldava is a highly agricultural country; agriculture employs 30% of labor force and yields about 40% of the country's output, and together with food processing, supports more than 50% of the country's 4.4 million people.[44]

While Moldava was suffering from its break with the close-knit interrepublic trade scheme of the former Soviet Union, a drought hit hard agricultural production. Moldava had almost totally relied on Russia for energy supplies, but after independence, oil and gas prices rose toward world levels, which Moldava could hardly afford. The higher prices restricted supplies and stalled the economy. By the end of 1992, output had declined by about 40% since 1990, and inflation reached 1,500% annually. Had the drought not hit, the trade shocks might have caused about 15% decline in output in 1992, but the drought added another 16% drop. Reforms have been slow because of political factors and other constraints; although a number of key laws have been adopted which reduce the government's role in the economy.[45]

9 Former Yugoslavia

In Yugoslavia consumer prices increased by 90% in 1986, 120% in 1987, 194% in 1988, 12,500% in 1989, 5,800% in 1990 and 117% in 1991.

---

(43) WBN, June 19, 1992.
(44) WBN, 18 March 1993.
(45) WBN, 18 March 1993.

Table 17.1
GNP per capita of the former socialist countries and several developing countries (in current US dollars) 1988-1990

	1988	1989	1990
Bulgaria	2760	2710	2250
Czechoslovakia	3350	3450	3140
Hungary	2480	2620	2780
Poland	1850	1890	1690
Romania	..	1720	1620
Turkey	1280	1370	1640
Yugoslavia	2710	2940	3060
Korea	3600	4400	5400
Thailand	1030	1220	1420
Malaysia	1930	2120	2320

Source: World Tables-1992, IBRD

Table 17.2
GNP per capita of the former socialist countries and several developing countries (in 1987 US dollars) 1988-1991

	1988	1989	1990	1991
Bulgaria	3170	3170	2850	2050
Czechoslovakia	3440	3500	3430	2690
Hungary	2390	2400	2320	2110
Poland	1680	1740	1470	1370
Romania	1950	1960	1650	1420
Turkey	1280	1240	1340	1340
Yugoslavia	2700	2710	2510	..
Korea	3450	3730	4030	
Malaysia	1950	2060	2230	2350
Thailand	990	1090	1200	..

Source: World Tables-1992, IBRD

Table 17.3
Per capita consumption and domestic investment of the former socialist countries and selected developing countries 1988-1991
A. Consumption per capita (1987 US dollars)

	1988	1989	1990	1991
Korea	1810	1970	2130	..
Malaysia	1020	1140	1260	1350
Thailand	620	690	740	..
Bulgaria	1550	1580	1590	1440
Czechoslovakia	1660	1690	1750	1700
Hungary	1500	1530	1460	1370
Poland	1030	1040	860	930
Turkey	870	890	1000	930
Yugoslavia	1160	1130	1430	..

Table 17.3 (continued)
B. Domestic investment per capita: (1987 US dollars)

	1988	1989	1990	1991
Korea	1030	1310	1540	1700
Malaysia	530	620	750	870
Thailand	290	330	400	410
Turkey	300	280	320	250
Bulgaria	1120	1070	800	460
Czechoslovakia	940	990	1040	550
Hungary	640	630	570	530
Poland	530	560	410	310
Romania	480	460	450	280
Yugoslavia	570	620	280	..

Source: World Tables-1992, IBRD

Table 17.4

Growth rates of GNP and GDP of the former socialist countries and selected developing countries: 1986-1991

A. Gross national income average annual growth rate (%)

	1986	1987	1988	1989	1990	1991
Korea	15.3	13.7	12.8	9.3	9.0	..
Malaysia	-7.0	11.0	11.4	8.1	11.6	7.9
Thailand	7.0	9.4	12.7	11.7	11.4	..
Bulgaria	5.1	6.8	1.4	-0.1	-11.6	-28.3
Czechoslovakia	1.7	1.5	3.5	2.0	-1.9	-21.3
Hungary	0.1	4.9	0.8	0.3	-3.3	-9.4
Poland	4.6	2.5	4.3	3.7	-15.0	-6.4
Romania	0.2	1.1	18.6	1.0	-15.7	-13.7
Turkey	10.0	7.5	3.8	-0.8	10.1	1.9
Yugoslavia	7.0	-3.3	-2.0	0.9	-7.0	..

Table 17.4 (continued)

B: GDP average annual growth rate (%)

	1986	1987	1988	1989	1990	1991
Korea	12.3	11.6	11.3	6.4	9.3	8.7
Malaysia	1.2	5.4	8.9	8.7	9.8	8.6
Thailand	5.1	9.6	13.4	12.2	10.3	8.2
Bulgaria	4.2	6.0	2.6	-0.6	-11.6	-25.9
Czechoslovakia	1.8	0.7	2.6	1.3	-3.5	-14.7
Hungary	1.5	4.5	-0.5	0.1	-3.9	-7.7
Poland	4.2	2.1	4.0	0.3	-12.0	-8.0
Romania	2.1	0.5	-0.3	-5.8	-8.1	-9.0
Turkey	8.3	7.5	3.7	1.3	9.1	2.4
Yugoslavia	3.6	-2.0	-1.6	o.6	-7.6	..

Source: World Tables- 1992, IBRD

Chapter 18

Chinese reform experience

Chinese reform experience

1 Self-reliance and open door policies, and role of comparative advantage: 1953-1978

During 1953-1978 China pursued a radical import substitution strategy, under *Mao Zedong's self-reliance policy* (self-reliance for the nation relative to the world economy and for provinces relative to the national economy) which was substituted in 1979 by outward-looking strategies (open door policy with market liberalization). Because of the size and economic diversity of China, regional policies also become important (Prime, 1992).

The rule of comparative advantage was not adhered to in China, in respect of location decisions; even after the reforms, the notion of *comparative advantage* plays a role regarding international trade rather than domestic trade. Now "China accepts and encourages different rates of development across regions", opens coastal cities and regions to foreign investment and trade, and pursues "a *coastal-led development strategy* which contrasts sharply with self-reliance" (Prime, 1992).

Protection of local enterprises by local officials still continues and "cases of localities processing their own materials rather than selling them to other areas with more modern plants" are not uncommon. Hence self-reliant trends still continue in provinces and "reliance on other areas for supplies continues to be problematic" (Prime, 1992).

(i) Response to policies

Prime (1992) has found that *the production pattern in Jiangsu province has conformed to the official policies* (the self-reliance policies of the Maoist period, as well as market reform policy later) and that during 1957-1978, specialization did not increase, whereas *between 1978 and 1988 specialization increased.* Over the 1978-1988 period, geographical specialization was important in village industry, indicating that *small, collective enterprises were more responsive to market pressures than state enterprises.*

(ii) Actual outcome of policies

Under the previous system in China state enterprises had no autonomy in production and operation and faced *no competition from market mechanism.* Enterprises lacked enthusiasm for improving management and economic performance.

As a consequence *from 1953 to 1980,* while China's *fixed assets increased 21 times, total industrial and agricultural output increased 3-fold, and the people's living standards rose 1-fold.* Fixed assets per worker in China in 1980 was close to that of a middle-income country and 4 times that of a typical low-income country; yet the net product per worker was only 50% more than that of a low-income country and less than half that of a middle-income country. In the fast growing processing industry 55% of equipment is very old, only 20% of equipment is relatively advanced (Qun, et. al, 1992).

2 Chinese price reforms

(i) Dual tract price system

The Chinese price reform aimed at breaking up the highly centralized price control system, adjusting and freeing prices, and introduced the *'dual-track' price system* for means of production. Price adjustments comprised, *raising prices of agricultural products, some raw materials and fuels,* and aimed at *reducing the 'scissors gap' between industrial and agricultural products,* promoting agricultural development and *improving the proportion between raw materials and processing capacity* through changing the price structure of industrial products, which in turn brought about *better products structure, diversification* and more reasonable development of industry (Qun et al, 1992).

Reducing the proportion of agricultural and sideline materials and raw materials sold at planned prices and increasing those sold at negotiated or market prices (of the total amount of farm products sold by peasants, 92% were at fixed prices in 1978 and only 37% in 1986; of the total amount of retail consumer goods, 97% were sold at fixed prices in 1978 and 47% in 1986; the balance in both cases being sold at state guidance and market prices) and state adjustment of planned prices were the two important channels of price adjustments (Qun et al, 1992).

Qun et al.(1992) conclude that *price reforms* have to be *coordinated with other reforms, before* it can be *perfected.* Large rises in the prices of farm and subsidiary products and of raw materials put tremendous pressure on industrial development and became the main cause of increased losses in state-owned industrial enterprises.

In China, *the range and time of price adjustment in means of production are controlled, in order to enable user enterprises to adjust to price changes* through improving their product structures and production procedures (IGEL, 1992).

(ii) Evaluation of dual tract

In China during the transition, *to combine the impact of both planning and the market on enterprises,* the *'dual-track' price system* for means of production (raw materials, fuels, power, labor) was introduced. The system brought about an *abnormal difference between planned and extra-plan prices* (market), which led also to *illegal trading.* It is now admitted that *the system's defects outweigh its merits.* Although it is proposed that the *system should not continue for too long, it should not be abolished either too quickly.* Many enterprises are unable to pay for the rising prices of extra-plan raw materials. *Stabilization of the prices of the means of production is a major goal* of present Chinese economic planning, which would improve enterprise estimates, plans and their implementation (IGEL, 1992).

The 'Dual-track' price system is open to all kinds of misuses and abuses (speculation), inefficiency and waste in producer and user industries; however, once launched, as evidenced by the Chinese experience, could not be rescinded or reformed quickly.

In implementing price reforms, maintenance of a relatively stable general price level is a major goal of Chinese economic planning (IGEL, 1992). Under such a constraint (general price stability), price reforms are bound to take an overly long time, with concomitant waste, inefficiency, speculation (and need for a strict control mechanism) generated by the dual price system.

3 Foreign exchange regime and rates

Before the economic reform, the Chinese economy was a closed economy with a few ties with the world economy. After the reform, the economy has opened up to the world economy, and the foreign exchange rate was used to make necessary adjustments between domestic and world market prices (Qun et al, 1992).

But because the Chinese economy has been isolated from the world market for such a long time, it has little ability to adjust to world market changes. Moreover because of inferior equipment, production processes and management, despite improved competitive strength due to exchange rate adjustments, costs are still high and product quality is low and export industries suffer losses, due to low export prices realized. Foreign exchange earned is not retained by export manufacturers and its retention rate is disparate with their foreign exchange requirements, tax rebates to enterprises on foreign exchange earnings are not remitted in good time and as a consequence of all this, actual export proceeds do not compensate production costs (Qun et al, 1992).

Qun et al (1992) recommend that export receipts, to which enterprises are entitled, should be retained by them and tax rebates due on these receipts should be promptly paid to enterprises.

Because of foreign exchange shortage the *'dual track"* price system has developed in this field as well; with the *free market rate more than double the fixed rate.* As a consequence production costs of industrial enterprises using imported inputs and which are short of foreign exchange (hence have to resort to the free exchange market) have skyrocketed and these enterprises incurred losses (Qun et al, 1992).

Export manufacturers do not monitor world market demand developments and 'fall into blind production'. Because, under the current foreign trade system (the purchasing system), industry and foreign trade are isolated, they do not coordinate with each other. Qun et al (1992) recommend that the foreign trade system should be changed from the 'purchasing system' to 'agent' system, under which a coordinated relationship is created so that manufacturers will be well informed of world market developments and set targets accordingly.

4 Bottlenecks and shortages

Lopsided industrial structure with the power supply being inadequate to meet requirements of industrial production, and the slow growth rate of raw material-producing sectors, compared to the fast-growing processing industry, have created major bottlenecks in power and raw material supply, and idle capacities in industries using these inputs. Outdated processing equipment is the feature of processing industry, which also faces severe raw material shortage. (Qun, et al, 1992).

"The shortage of raw materials has always been an acute problem in China because its raw materials industry lags behind the development of processing." On top of this the *dual track pricing* of means of production and an *imperfect market mechanism leads to resale of raw materials in short-supply* (Qun et al, 1992).

30% of Chinese industry relies on farm produce as raw materials. After reform, agriculture has developed rapidly and supplied industry adequately, so that in 1984 a surplus was realized in grain and cotton output. This led to an erroneous reduction of acreage under grain and cotton in 1985, which resulted in cotton and grain supply becoming tight in the subsequent 3 years.

In China, in order to alleviate the shortage of power, transportation and raw materials (in relation to processing capacity), (Qun et al (1992) recommend that the state should give priority to the development of these sectors. As an incentive measure for promoting basic industries and industries processing commodities in short supply, reduction of income tax rates and increasing retention rates are proposed (IGEL, 1992).

5 Enterprise losses, remedies and subsidy policy

(i) Causes of enterprise losses

(a) Problems of enterprise governance

"Among the state-owned enterprises, local enterprises took first place both in the number of deficit enterprises and in the amount of loss." Similarly small enterprises which are of duplicative nature and operate at inefficient scales, suffer more serious losses compared to large enterprises. Of the state–owned enterprises reporting deficit in 1986, 50% were due to poor management. Any real improvement in management will take time because of the long-standing restrictions of the former socialist structure system (Qun et al, 1992).

Poor quality of managerial personnel, unwise business decisions, disunity in management and frequent changes in management were manifestations of problematic enterprise leadership (Qun et al, 1992).

Lack of scientific management methods in production and operation, as indicated by absence of work quotas, bookkeeping of materials, regulations for quality check, a clear-cut reward and penalty system, led to low productivity and waste. Low technological level, obsolete equipment, poor quality of personnel, outdated and poor quality products and poor marketing were the third group of factors causing low productivity and losses. All these problems were widespread in China (Qun et al, 1992).

(b) Uneconomical scale of operations and lack of specialization

Industries are losing money because of *the small scale of specialized production.* Increasing the size or scale of operation would improve economic profitability (IGEL, 1992).

Many enterprises manufacture the whole range of parts needed for their products; inter-enterprise cooperation and level of specialization are very low, resulting in uneconomic size/scale of activities and enterprises, and waste from duplicative and 'blind' investments. In order to distribute small enterprises evenly among different departments and areas, substantial wastage of investment funds was incurred. As a consequence productivity in small enterprises increased only as fast as that of large enterprises and small enterprises suffered more serious losses (Qun et al, 1992).

(c) Lack of market information and response to market
In China an important cause of losses were *lack of access to the latest market information* regarding supply and demand, insensitivity to market signals and ignorance of productive capacity and scale of industry and product trends. It is admitted that in transition, with undergoing reforms, external environment of enterprises would be volatile and more difficult to monitor and respond correctly (IGEL, 1992).

(d) Macroeconomic policy aspect: high-speed growth, imbalance in industrial structure, excess capacity in processing industries, shortage of raw materials and protection policy

> Development of the operational mechanism in enterprises and *elimination of internal factors of loss* should be combined with *improvement of the larger macroeconomic environment.* ... There must be determination to eliminate quickly those enterprises that have long had deficits so as to create a better macroeconomic environment and pave the way for deepening reforms (IGEL, 1992).

In reversing losses, focus should be "on both deficit enterprises and unprofitable products in profitable enterprises." It is a fact that *"profitable enterprises are now losing more money on unprofitable products than the total losses of deficit enterprises"* (IGEL, 1992).

In China in 1984 and 1985, during the period of fast growth, *duplicative processing industries* were set up, relying on limited local/regional raw material sources. This process ended up with creating processing industries which were forced to operate under capacity or close down due to lack of necessary raw materials (IGEL, 1992).

Deficit enterprises increased as a result of fast growth of processing industries and sluggish growth of basic industries. "This *imbalance in industrial structure* was caused by blind pursuit of *high-speed growth* over a long period of time without regard to economic results" (IGEL, 1992).

"At present to realize a long-term, stable, and appropriate rate of industrial growth is quite difficult". Because productive capacity is now restrained by structural imbalance and economic tightening, any relaxation of restraint, will again lead to industrial overheating. The urgent task, now is to stop the *overly fast growth of ordinary processing industries*, which produce oversupplied popular goods, and eliminate losses through adjusting the industrial structure and stabilizing speed. In this context, credit for fixed asset investments in processing industries should be put under strict control. It is recommended that local enterprises and regional *enterprises should invest their surplus funds in basic industries,* or leasing, contracting or merging with deficit enterprises (IGEL, 1992).

In China *mistakes in import and export policies a*re blamed for hampering the development of some industries and high tariff protection of electrical and machinery products and high-grade consumer durables is proposed (IGEL, 1992).

In China all *deficit* enterprises do not fall into the category of declining/shrinking industries with poor technology and management, but include also some developing industries, such as *automotive, electronics and petrochemicals*, with good management and technology (Zhao, et al, 1992; Qun et al, 1992).

Qun et al (1992) recommend that infant industries namely, "deficit enterprises in the emerging industries should be nurtured and helped to improve their management, to update technical equipment and to enhance competitiveness", while deficit enterprises in declining industries should either be transferred to other enterprises or go bankrupt.

(ii) Subsidization of industry

(a) Eating from the same pot

Under the former socialist system in China, all profits of enterprises were handed to the State and allocated by it. After the partial market reforms, with large price increases in raw materials, agricultural products and wage increases, processing industries faced acute shortage of funds for development (to update equipment and technology) and in the end many enterprises lost heavily because they could not keep up with market changes (Qun et al, 1992).

At present China is a planned economy, where *the state determines industrial structure, resource allocation* and market according to plan, and *the market mechanism determines the fittest to survive;* i.e. *both planned adjustment and the market mechanism coexist.*(Qun et al,1992).

The problem of "eating from the same pot" (another version of soft budget constraint) has not been fundamentally resolved, between the state and enterprises, which caused enterprises to take no responsibility for losses and lacked enthusiasm for improvement. In China, still the problem is the state "collecting too much" or "collecting too little" from enterprises and transferring resources indiscriminately (Qun et al, 1992).

China with the 1980 partial market reforms introduced the system of *'eating in separate kitchens'* for enterprises, which replaced the system of *'eating in one kitchen'* (ton zao chifan). The recent reforms do not aim at restoring the 'single kitchen system', rather to *redefine the roles and functions of state, enterprise and local administrations with respect to investments and funds*, and allow the three parties to have their own funds, projects, and duties (IGEL, 1992).

(b) Subsidy policy

For a long time in China deficit enterprises were *indiscriminately subsidized* by the state *under a uniform policy.* This system has more disadvantages than it has merits. Since the basis of this policy is *the lack of detailed investigation results and findings of deficit enterprises,* it fails to identify the root causes of losses. Moreover, subsidies enabling deficit enterprises to carry on for a long time despite losses, induce no incentive to reverse losses. Furthermore, subsidies add a heavy burden on the state budget and cut down development effort (Qun et al, 1992).

Qun et al (1992) recommend a discriminating, *flexible subsidy policy,* with a view to eliminating enterprise losses. Enterprises developed without foresight (blindly) or using depleted resources (coal mines) should be allowed to wither away (shut down or go bankrupt), by the 'law of development'.

For enterprises with *good technical equipment, but poor management,* Qun et al (1992) suggest a *contracting system.* For enterprises with old-fashioned equipment, insufficient funds and outdated product structure, loans or subsidies, and technical assistance to make good these defects are recommended.

Qun et al (1992) recommend for *small enterprises* with low technology level, poor management, outmoded products and high materials consumption, *horizontal cooperation,* auction, leasing or close-down, with a view to transforming them into specialized units.

For enterprises suffering losses *because of state policies* on prices, taxes and exchange rates, Qun et al (1992), recommend that the state should suitably reduce taxes, increase profit retention rates or give compensation to these enterprises.

Qun et al (1992) observe that *during transition,* "when the internal operational mechanism needs improvement and when the external environment including the market, price, industrial and product structures are not yet well adjusted, it is too difficult for deficit enterprises to improve operations on their own." *The state "must not let them sink or swim on their own",* but must strengthen their leadership and internal operational mechanisms, pressurize enterprises to improve management and product quality and to lower costs, and provide them with a better external environment.

(c) Subsidy targets and norms

For deficit enterprises, which are unable to reverse their losses, *a subsidy target* could be given; losses beyond the target amount would not be compensated at all and those less than the target balance of the subsidy would be retained by the enterprises. Enterprises potentially capable of reversing losses, could be given *subsidy norms*, while losses beyond the norm would not be compensated, losses less than the norm or profits made could be shared with the state according to contract. Enterprises that should be able to reverse losses, would not be subsidized for actual losses incurred and would keep all profits made (IGEL, 1992).

(d) Task force for reversing losses

Qun et al (1992) suggest following broad modus operandi regarding reversing losses, modalities of which could be further worked out:

Departmental or regional heads and chief executives of enterprises should be made responsible for the task of reversing losses and a *special task force* with organizational backup should be set up to this end. "Positive and feasible plans should be made to set clear targets to reverse losses." "The leadership should monitor and make monthly checkups on the goals and measures of every deficit enterprise." Leadership should frequently visit the grassroots or send senior people from departments to the deficit enterprises to find out the true situation. Enterprises should be assisted with improving management, reducing material consumption, and improving product quality. Options of stopping production, shutting down plants, merging, etc. should be actively investigated.

(e) Rules for rescuing enterprises and bankruptcy regulations

The state should adopt a policy of not supporting indiscriminately all deficit enterprises. *Bankruptcy regulations should be coupled with measures for rectification and rescuing/salvaging potentially viable enterprises.* This becomes a more urgent task nowadays, since recent changes in macroeconomic environment and many abnormal factors threaten almost all enterprises. Banks should grant *low-interest loans* to enterprises that incur losses due to abnormal factors, and that are capable of reversing losses but lack the funds to undergo technological upgrading (IGEL, 1992).

Enterprises located at inappropriate sites or which have exhausted their local material supply sources, or are producing oversupplied or poor quality, high-priced goods and have no prospect of reversing losses, should go bankrupt. Assets of bankrupt enterprises could be transferred through leasing, contract bidding or auction. A special fund for loss reversals should be set up (IGEL, 1992).

(f) Investment companies

In China the Investigative Group (IGEL, 1992) recommended setting up a number of investment companies with a view to *introducing competition into the selection, design, construction and equipment supply of investment projects through bidding.*

6 Enterprise reform

(i) More autonomy and strengthening management

The operational system in enterprises is defective; enterprises do not take responsibility for their own profits and losses, *they do not have enough autonomy to use their funds,* other hands dip into the enterprise pot; although they bear certain responsibilities in production, they do not bear the responsibility and *threat of bankruptcy* for risks. Enterprises should be able to *self-accumulate, self-develop, self-operate and bear responsibility for profits and losses.* The property relationship between the state and enterprises should be straightened out, contracting, leasing, and transfer should be promoted and the shareholding system should be tried out (Qun et al, 1992).

The crux of improving enterprise management and of *making enterprises autonomous* and responsible for their profits and losses, "lies in establishing an operating mechanism that will exert pressure, has motivating force and is a force for self-restraint". This calls for *strengthening enterprise management,* tapping internal potential, stimulating employee initiative and improving operational mechanism. *Contracting and leasing* could be adopted to reverse losses (IGEL, 1992).

The internal operational mechanism of enterprises should be reformed to cater for better management and improved regulations for personnel, funds, materials, production, supply and sales; and "to reinforce control over materials consumption, supervise and test quality, manage finances and strengthen cost-accounting" (Qun et al, 1992)

(ii) Rewards and penalties

Existing norms for material consumption and labor in all industries should be revised and *rewards* and *penalties should be imposed* in accordance with systems and norms (IGEL, 1992).

(iii) Recruitment and think tanks

The long-standing practice of direct appointment of all directors and managers of enterprises by government departments and frequent changes in enterprise management must be changed. The management stratum of enterprises should remain relatively stable, and enterprise should have 'think tanks' or expert groups, technical and financial specialists, to help the management and supply it with reliable information and analysis for decision-making. The enterprise managers and directors should be recruited through a competitive bidding system, so that experts, professionals and talented people can form the management (IGEL, 1992).

(iv) Cost accounting

Quality control, cost management and accounting, auditing and cost monitoring systems should be established to deal with problems of poor quality, high material consumption and rising costs. Fraudulent or misinforming accounting practices and statements should be made legally liable under a *'Cost Law'* (IGEL, 1992).

Reporting of loss, verification and auditing should be governed by clear-cut regulations in accordance with the *Bankruptcy Law.* Strict auditing should be done to protect state interests, while calculating accurately economic performance of the enterprise and providing motivation and pressure to reduce and reverse losses. Policy and operational losses should be clearly defined (IGEL, 1992).

7 New forms of enterprise restructuring: contracting leasing and mergers

Recent reforms should encourage interenterprise contracting, leasing or merging in order to bring about transfer of operational rights and ownership (IGEL, 1992).

In China enterprises, without changing ownership and legal status, were leased, contracted to employees individually or collectively in the early 1980s. This measure was not successful in enterprises where the products had no direction, were of bad quality and highly priced. But in cases where the products direction was correct and market was assured, but losses were incurred because of inferior management or changes in external environment, contracting or leasing of deficit enterprises to employees was very successful and has become widespread in all regions and economic sectors. Contracting, leasing or merging could either transfer ownership or operational rights (IGEL, 1992).

(i) Joint-operation and contracting

Increasing *horizontal economic ties* between deficit enterprises and enterprises that are strong technically and financially, through *joint operation agreements* also proved quite successful. Under this method technology transfer, better specialization, consulting and full utilization of funds are achieved. The stronger enterprise helps out the other with technology and finance (Qun et al, 1992).

Contract responsibility system for reversing losses, adopted by many deficit enterprises, has *proved to be quite helpful.* "The system works through changes in the internal operational mechanism, strengthening management and suitably increasing external pressures to generate internal motivation for improving operation and product quality." Under this method "deficit enterprises and their superior departments sign contracts to reverse losses within a given period. No subsidies are given for losses exceeding contracted terms and reduction of losses beyond contracted terms are either shared or kept fully by the enterprise" (Qun et al, 1992).

(ii) Leasing

Leasing is suitable for small-scale state enterprises, which have no market for their products and could not transform to other industries or trades, and have long sustained deficits. It represents the reform to 'separate the two rights', i.e. the right of ownership and the right of management, in order to strengthen the internal operational mechanism. Under this method, deficit enterprises are leased to collectives or individuals for a given period of time and for a given rent. Profits over and above the rent sum are divided and used according to the contracted terms, which are designed to give incentive to the contractor. Leasing proved to be very useful; it enabled leasing out the work force and led to development of new products (Qun et al, 1992).

(iii) Merging

In cases where profitable enterprises were constrained in their development by limitation in production factors, allowing them to contract, lease or merge with deficit enterprises helped them in overcoming the shortage of production factors (IGEL, 1992).

Merging is effected either by the buying-out of a deficit enterprise or by taking over the debts of the deficit enterprise by another enterprise. Merging is conducive to efficient allocation of factors of production, development of better product structures and efficient utilization and employment of funds (Qun et al, 1992).

8 New role of government in industrial development

In China *governments, under mandatory planning, directly interfered in enterprise production and operation decisions.* Now *with reforms the government's function* is to affirm *industry's strategic goals,* stipulate *industry policies* and plans and undertake *inter-industry coordination.*

Under the new approach, the central government would invest in basic industries and a national network of *infrastructure,* such as post and telecommunications, transportation, major power projects, *high-technology and new defense projects. The local governments* would handle *local* transportation, post and telecommunication facilities, tertiary industries, public utilities and agriculture. *The aim of recent reforms is to separate government's investment and control functions and make enterprises the primary agent in investments* (IGEL, 1992).

9 High-speed versus stable growth: Turkish and Chinese experiences

An economy under inflationary threat, contradicting false premises of the Phillips curve trade-off between growth/employment and inflation, grows at much lower rate on the average in the medium and long run, compared with a stable economy, and growth becomes sporadic, unpredictable with substantial wasteful/ duplicative investments, many of which fail disastrously with disruptive economic, fiscal and social consequences, in the following low-or no-growth years and entails a big jump in external debt, as evidenced by the Turkish economic experience (the stability years of 1960's versus the high-inflation period of the 1980s).

Similar phenomenon (albeit not in the same degree) is observed by Qun et al (1992) in China during the 1980s; the 1981-82 structural adjustment process brought about a slump in 1981 and the 1984-85 high-speed growth period was halted by tight credit measures. The unavoidable 1981-82 structural adjustment program, aiming at reducing imbalance between heavy and light industry, increasing production of goods in short supply while reducing production of oversupplied goods and curtailing fixed capital investments, caused the industrial growth rate to plummet, enterprise losses to skyrocket (there were 22% more deficit enterprises and 33% rise in the amount of losses in 1981 over 1980) and resulted in the first debit peak since 1979.

According to Qun et al (1992), the 1985 growth peak, the first since 1979, with industrial output increasing by 14% and 18% in 1984 and 1985 respectively was halted by tightening credit. Reducing loans for working capital across the board, paralyzed many enterprises, brought about a surge of losses (the amount of loss rose by 74% in 1986 over 1985), and led to the second debit peak since 1979. A large increase in imports of chemical fertilizers, cars and electronic manufactures in 1985 which accompanied the growth peak, hit hard domestic fertilizer, automotive and electronic industries, skyrocketing their losses.

Qun et al (1992) attribute the surge in "the numbers of deficit enterprises in low industrial growth years to blind development of enterprises in the period of high growth". When aggregate demand exceeds aggregate supply, many small and medium-sized enterprises are formed, which appear profitable despite their poor quality products. High speed growth, however, could not be sustained too long, because macroeconomic imbalances lead to "shortage of funds and foreign exchange, and bottlenecks in the supply of raw materials, energy and transportation". And when the growth rate eventually drops, many enterprises become deficit enterprises and a new debit peak is formed.

As observed by Qun et al (1992), in high-growth years, with aggregate demand outstripping aggregate supply, money supply increase also was excessive, with money in circulation increasing by 43% in 1985, 23% in 1986 and 19% in 1987 far exceeding the real growth rates of the national economy and leading to rising prices.

Inflationary pressure, coupled with excessive money supply and the "dual track" pricing of means of production and imperfect markets in China, led to large price increases of raw materials, farm and subsidiary products in 1986; which in turn caused manufacturing cost increases for state-owned industrial enterprises and increased losses. Qun et al (1992) conclude that price rises arising from high speed growth in 1985 in China, led to increased enterprise losses in the two subsequent years, when growth slowed down, but raw material prices continued to rise (low growth rate and rising prices will jointly push deficits higher).

Qun et al (1992) rightly conclude that although low growth rates are apparently to be blamed for big losses of enterprises, high speed growth sows the seeds of future trouble and losses by exacerbating structural imbalances and inconsistencies, and therefore a stable growth rate is the correct strategy.

10 Achievements of the 1979 market reforms

(i) Productivity increases

The measurement of *productivity effects of market reforms of 1979* resulted in mixed results. While, Gene Tidrick estimated that productivity in state industry decreased by 0.1.-1.2% from 1979 to 1983, and Nicholas Lardy's estimates for state industry indicate an average 0.3% annual fall in productivity during 1979-85; Kuan Chen et al, using revised capital stock figures (adjusted for price increases and nonproductive investment) estimated 4.8-5.2% productivity increase during 1979-1985. The former two studies used unrevised data (Prime, 1992).

Prime (1992) using revised (deflated) capital stock figures and employing Cobb-Douglas type production function, estimated that the industrial productivity in Jiangsu province fell by 1.7% p.a. on average during 1953-57, by 8.4% p.a. during 1958-1965, and increased by 5.1% p.a. during 1966-70 and by 0.2% p.a. during 1971-75 (the cultural revolution period: 1966-75), and increased by 5.3% p.a. during 1981-85 and 3.3% during 1986-1988. *From 1953 to 1978, while productivity fell an average of 2.1% annually, during the reform period from 1979 to 1988 productivity increased an average of 4.4% annually.* Prime concludes that *"reforms have had a positive effect on productivity"*.

(ii) Productivity gains in the state industry versus in collective industry

Observing that the *higher than average industrial growth* in Jiangsu province during the reform period was largely due to *relatively faster growth in collective industry, compared with state industry,* Prime (1992) examined "whether the collective sector exhibited higher growth in productivity when compared with the state sector", using adjusted capital figures for inflation and housing. Using *gross output*, Prime estimated that while *productivity in the state sector increased 4.1% p.a. during 1981-88, in collective industry it increased by 6.2% p.a.* over the same period. If *net output* figures are used, *the results reverse*. In this case productivity increase was 2.3% in state industry versus 1.7% in collective industry (Prime, 1992). This might be explained by (i) inefficient, wasteful use of means of production in the state industry, (as might be expected, since they were lower-priced), despite shortages of raw materials and utilities, and (ii) by the exclusion of intermediate inputs in the conventional production function specified; i.e. if intermediary inputs were included in the explanatory variables, then even productivity increase measured in the state sector, even using gross output figures, might have been less than that of the collective sector.

(iii) Recent developments and overall performance

China's *annual average economic growth rate was about 8% over the last decade* because of increasingly open and market oriented policies, and increased public investment in education and health.(1)

China *recently increased the pace of reform*, particularly in the areas of prices and public enterprises. During the last few years, including 1991, GDP has grown by 9% p.a.; 7-9% growth is expected in the next few years. China's growth path was not smooth during the reform period; rapid growth periods were followed by periods of contraction, because *fine-tuning of the economy was not possible* as *instruments of demand management* (interest rates, reserve requirements for banks) still remain *under developed.* As a consequence blunt measures (like *administrative control over investment, consumption and trade*)

---

(1) Speech by Attila Karaosmanoğlu, Managing Director of the World Bank, before the World Economic Forum, in Davos, Switzerland, Bank's World, March 1993.

have to be employed, to check overheating of the economy, which led to sharp downturns.(2)

A better explanation of this irregular growth path, which can also explain the sporadic/intermittent/interrupted growth path of Turkey during the last two decades, is as follows: In developing countries the potential output is based not only on productive capacity, but also on the availability of intermediate goods, foreign exchange and external financing. A high-rate growth period implies overutilization of capacity and exceeding the potential output in this sense; as a consequence, in the subsequent period the actual output is bound to revert to its normal (potential) level, whether monetary/fiscal tuning is fine or blunt.

China's reform policies aim at *"transition from a socialist economy into a mixed economy"*. Reforms aim at "opening up the economy and providing for growth, particularly in the non-state sector." China faces *transport and energy bottlenecks* presently, because of rapid growth rates achieved.(3)

Per capita income in China rose from $130 in 1970, to $370 in 1990; *reduction in poverty* was also remarkable over this period, *in the late 1970s one-fourth of the population was living in absolute poverty, now only 8-9% of the population* is absolutely poor. China exercises influx control, i.e. restricts migration from rural areas to large cities.(4) The absence of shanty towns is a striking feature of China's great cities; however, in order further to reduce poverty, China is urged by the World Bank to ease up on its migration restrictions within the country.(5)

China is expected to achieve a *$12 billion trade surplus in 1992*. China is the second-largest exporter of food and the third-largest exporter of manufactured goods among developing countries; Chinese exports concentrate on clothing, toys, games, sporting goods, textiles, fabrics and telecommunications equipment. Chinese exports of textiles, clothing and processed agricultural products *face trade barriers* in US, EC and Japan.(6)

11 The theory of Chinese gradualist reform approach: Byrd's conclusions versus reality and 'the suggested method'

During the entire reform period (1978-1990), real GNP in China grew by 8.8% p.a. and per capita GNP by 7.2%. Unlike Hungary in 1968, China did not

---

(2) Interview with Shahid Javed Burki, of the World Bank (Director of China and Mongolia Dept.), WBN Sept. 3, 1992.

(3) op. cit.

(4) op. cit.

(5) NBN, Oct 29, 1992.

(6) Interview with Shahid Javed Burki, of the World Bank (Director of China and Mongolia Dept.), WBN Sept. 3, 1992.

abandon central planning (whose core is material balances), instead *gradually reduced the scope of planning* and *increased the share of goods allocated through the market mechanism* from the early 1980s on. Byrd has found that the share of market is relatively high and has grown over a wide range of producer and consumer goods and that *long-run market integration* across different regions of China is taking place in many goods (Byrd, 1991).

According to Byrd, Chinese gradual reforms, has *shifted planning from direct resource allocation to redistribution of rents* (embodied in goods subjects to plan allocation at low state-set prices). In China, however, *capital and labor markets are much less developed than the goods market,* and central or local *governments* still have *control on employment and investments,* directly or indirectly (Byrd, 1991).

The Chinese reform strategy centers around the *two-tier system*, which means *dual price system* in the goods market (a lower plan price and a higher market price), in the narrow sense, and *plan and market coexist* and *the market grows out of plan,* in the broader sense. Under this system, *enterprises are imposed input quotas and output targets* both in plan prices by central plan, which must be fulfilled. *Outside the plan, the enterprise is free to buy inputs and sell outputs in the market* at the market price (Byrd, 1991).

Byrd, employing a general equilibrium model incorporating features of the dual price system, has shown that, if all agents in the economy are not constrained by planning quotas, then equilibrium under the dual price system replicates market equilibrium without plan, and hence Pareto optimum is attained; this finding confirms the view held by young Chinese reformers supporting the dual price system, i.e. "only the marginal matters" (Byrd, 1991).

Since its introduction in the mid-1980s, *the dual price system* had been a controversial issue in China; i.e. the choice between the *two second-best solutions for price reform:* (i) *rationalization of administrative prices before price decontrol,* versus (ii) *use of the dual price system to reduce the share of output allocated at plan prices* without attempting to rationalize the administrative prices. *Byrd's* equilibrium model suggests that *the second choice is preferable* (Byrd, 1991 and Yingi Qian).(7)

There is, however, one obvious drawback of the dual price system, also noted by Qian, namely it is *open to corruption.* The second disadvantage, not revealed in the interpretation of Byrd's general equilibrium model, because of its assumption, namely *'none of economic agents in the economy is constrained by planning quotas' hinges on the speed of reform,* i.e. rate of increase in the share of goods allocated by the market mechanism.

In other words, if the *potential growth rate of the market sector exceeds the actual rate of decline in the planned output, then resources (capital, material*

---

(7) Book Review on Byrd (1991), Journal of Comparative Economics, 16, 1992, pp. 778-780.

input, labor) left for use by the market sector after the state apportionment would be less than what they require, which implies a lower total output level than possible. In the absence of competitive capital and labor markets and a goods market though better functioning but subject to limited competition from imports, it is *difficult to judge at a point in time, whether economic agents are constrained or not by planned quotas.* Hence welfare conclusions derived from Byrd's model are bound to remain hypothetical; in fact they are, because the Chinese economy is beset by shortages of raw materials and utilities and retarded growth of basic industries as against rapid growth of processing and light industries (see, e.g. Qun et al, 1992; IGEL, 1992).

In fact this view, is also corroborated by a recent World Bank (1992) study which concludes that *many of China's previous economic problems are the result of 'incomplete' reforms,* and observes in China "a renewed recognition that *only further economic reform can solve the fundamental issues facing the economy."*

Under 'the suggested method', Pareto optimum is achieved through freeing all prices and opening up the economy for foreign competition; hence 'the method' is superior to the Chinese gradualist reform process. The Chinese gradualist reform approach, however, is far better than the chaotic and/or sporadic reform approach adopted by Eastern Europe and the former Soviet Union, both in theory (theoretical foundations) and practice (actual outcome).

12 Macroeconomic instruments

(i) Need for forecasting implications of reform measures

In order to ensure implementation of reform and adjustment measures properly, *Qun et al (1992), stress the importance of predicting repercussions of reform and adjustment measures* with a view to devising and designing corresponding complementary and coordinating measures against the aftermath of reform. Therefore they suggest that "the state, before announcing new reform policies particularly in the areas of prices and taxes, take into account *their potential impact on different industries* and enterprises and announce corresponding measures for adjusting interest distribution and structure." They observe that "the *current price and tax reforms in China do suffer from insufficient preparation, overly large strides* and inefficient control", which have created pressures beyond the bearing capabilities of enterprises. And they suggest that "the state should focus on the *feasibility of various new reforms*" during the preparatory stage in order to ensure success in implementation. Enterprises should be able to foresee their future in the aftermath of reform and should not be left to sink or swim on their own (Qun et al, 1992). 'The suggested method' definitely could make a contribution in this respect.

(ii) Reforming macroeconomic management and imperfect market mechanism and enterprise deficits

"Modernizing macroeconomic management and avoiding erroneous decisions and large fluctuations in economic development are crucial to *stable economic development and reducing enterprise deficits." The reform of the macroeconomic management system* should be improved on two grounds: (i) further straightening out the *distribution relationship between the state and enterprises*(resource allocation: retention or taxation of enterprise profits and foreign exchange earnings, allocation/ transfer of funds and resources to enterprises), (ii) *improving the market mechanism* (Qun et al, 1992).

The *Imperfect market mechanism* in China left some gaps/ voids in the macroeconomic management system, after "the unitary state control of materials distribution was changed and *a large proportion of materials turned from direct state allocation to market adjustment*". "But because of *supply shortage* and the fact that *only the price raising mechanism but not the adjustment mechanism [to increase supply] was functioning,....* industrial enterprises were brought under unbearable pressure and fell into losses. Thus the defective market mechanism left macroeconomic management in a dilemma and resulted in enterprises being unable to compete fairly" (Qun et al, 1992).

Qun et al (1992), to remedy this defect, recommend that *priority items in short supply* to be put under *unified state allocation* and *stricter control* be imposed over the portion under the market adjustment, for which the state should set *ceiling prices* and prohibit markups (materials should go through direct channel from producer to users). Under 'the suggested methodology' all prices would be freely determined and there would be no shortages.

(iii) Need for indicative planning

Indicative planning will be helpful in preventing oversupply of popular goods by processing industries, after lifting of central control and command economy rule. This is what has happened in China after partial market reforms. It is now urged that credit controls should be installed to limit strictly credit for fixed investments of processing industries and guide them to manufacture products in "short supply on the domestic market and have competitive power on international market" (IGEL, 1992). If 'the suggested method' was employed, there would not be the need for such direct credit controls.

Chapter 19

The experience of the former Soviet Union

The experience of the former Soviet Union

One permanent feature of Perestroika was its "never ending state of flux" (Jones and Moskoff, 1991).

1 Development of the 1990 reforms

(i) Reform episode

The results of reforms have not been uniformly successful; often leading to worsening shortages, increasing income inequality, corruption and an absolute decline in output, occasionally in crisis proportions as in Poland in 1981, former Soviet Union and Bulgaria in 1990 (Osband, 1992/A) and Russia in 1992/93.

> The economic cornerstone of perestroika, or 'restructuring' was intended to be the *devolution* of authority from central planners to firms. *In practice enterprises gained much more influence over wages than over product lines or prices* charged to customers. From January 1988 through December 1990, official real wages rose 24%, about as much as they had in the previous 12 years. ... For an economy already in precarious condition, the surge in nominal demand was a serious blow.

By late 1989, the economy was in crisis with black market prices soaring, output falling, corruption spreading, inequality growing, labor discipline eroding and workers' living standards declining (Osband, 1992/A).

The retail price index in the Soviet Union remained basically unchanged during the period 1960-80; in "the 1980s it increased by slightly more than 1% a year." Limited availability of consumption goods in the official market and pervasive price controls, which became more pervasive in the second half of the 1980s, resulted in a repressed inflation (Cottarelli and Blejer, 1992).

"*Forced saving and repressed inflation* have been a permanent characteristic of all centrally planned economies"; mild but "chronic macroeconomic *rationing is an essential component of macroeconomic management* in centrally planned economies" (Cottarelli and Blejer, 1992).

All this made price reform imperative, with official retail food prices unchanged since 1962, despite procurement prices (paid to farmers) had risen substantially and direct subsidies for meat and milk alone amounting to 5% of Soviet GDP. Price reform proposals, however, even with attendant compensation to make them more palatable, did not go through. And

> the announcement in May 1990 of retail price increases contributed directly to the downfall of the Ryzhkov government, although the pricing decision itself was quickly retracted. ... By mid 1990, the normal retail distribution network had virtually collapsed. Sales were increasingly conducted by invitation only, often through work places that used them for payment in kind. The proliferation of barter and barter-like transactions disrupted established economic links and exacerbated tensions between republics. On 2 April 1991, prices of consumer staples were almost doubled and prices of some consumer durables were decontrolled, with some cash compensation to households. Black market prices fell and shortages eased, but a surge in wage increases and the further erosion of fiscal discipline nullified much of the gains.

After the break up of the Soviet Union, Russia decided to free most prices at the beginning of 1992, which forced most of the other ex-Soviet republics to follow suit; but attempts to compensate the public for higher prices led to a very high inflation (Osband, 1992/A).

Following description of the former Soviet Union economy on 16 October 1990, in the *U.S.S.R. Presidential Guidelines for the Stabilization of the Economy and Transition to a Market Economy,* is much more valid in March 1993, according to press news:

> The position of the economy continues to deteriorate. The volume of production is declining. Economic links are being broken. Separatism is on the increase. The consumer market is in dire straits. The budget deficit and the solvency of the government are now at critical levels. Antisocial behavior and crime are increasing. People are finding life more and more difficult and are losing their interest in work and their belief in the future (Osband, 1992/A).

(ii) Recent reforms

"The January 2, 1992 Price reform in the Russian state sector did not fully liberalize the retail prices of goods" (Leitzel, 1992). However, price liberalization has been implemented in Russia by mid-1992.(1)

> In Russia in early 1992 most prices were freed, except those for a few staple foods, energy and housing. ... But, *unless price liberalization is accompanied quickly by further macroeconomic stabilization* and systemic reform including privatization and *enterprise reform, the risk of hyperinflation and continued deterioration in economic prospects is very real.*(2)

"The reform agenda is in many ways similar to that in other reforming countries in Central and Eastern Europe". But it is far more difficult and complex, because of the unprecedented scale of reform, (e.g. privatization in Russia alone involves 18 000 large enterprises) and of the fact that central planning was more deeply rooted in the former USSR than in much of Eastern Europe.(3)

The recent reform program in Russia includes(4) "*privatization and restructuring of state- owned enterprises,* promotion of foreign direct investment, pro-competition and *anti- monopoly policies,* reform of financial institutions and *the commercial banking sector* and *establishment of a social safety net.*"

Russia has liberalized prices, *encouraged small-scale privatization* and put into effect bankruptcy legislation.(5)

Because of the dissolution of the Soviet Union, *output declined by 25% in 1992, inter-republican trade declined by 50%* and external trade is constrained by *a shortage of hard currency.* The former Soviet Union suffers from *large budget deficits, rising inflation rates* and *erosion of living standards. The productive sectors are under state or collective management,* with *uncompetitive prices and subsidies.* "Infrastructure is aging and run-down."(6)

---

(1) Speech by Lewis Preston, World Bank President, WBN, June 19,1992.

(2) WBN, June 19, 1992.

(3) as (2).

(4) As stated in the rehabilitaiton loan document of $ 600 million by the World Bank (WBN, Aug 7, 1992).

(5) Iterview with Y.Huang of World Bank, WBN, Aug. 7, 1992.

(6) Speech by Lewis Preston, World Bank President, WBN, June 19, 1992.

(iii) Outcome

Inflation and unemployment are the feared economic problems, that will stem from conversion into a market economy-free prices and privatization. Inflation could be fueled by the *monetization of budget deficits,* during transition from socialist economy. The budget deficit, in turn, could arise from *a failure to replace the implicit tax collection methods characteristic of socialist economies with explicit procedures* and from failures to reduce state subsidies sufficiently. Irresponsible monetary and credit policies, as well, will lead to inflation (Leitzel, 1992).

Because of the extreme shortage of convertible currencies, the black market rate of dollar skyrocketed, and as a consequence,

> Russian per capita GDP, on a purchasing power basis, is about equal to Mexico's, using the early 1992 *black market exchange rate yields an unrealistic estimate less than one-tenth as large,* reflecting the current shortage of tradable goods and foreign exchange. Output has declined about 20% during 1990 and 1991.

Because of the decline in inter-republican trade and other problems, *Fischer expects further deep declines in output,* which means that *the former Soviet Union would suffer far larger and deeper recessions than the countries of Eastern Europe have been experiencing* (Fischer, 1992).

The Russian inflation has been running at a monthly rate of 55-60%, at the beginning of 1993 and is on way to hyperinflation, save a miracle. From August 1992 to January 1993, the ruble has lost value against US dollar by about 300% and according to Vasili Soldatov, Chairman of the Board of the Russian Stock Exchange Bank, "the government simply does not have any mechanism to stop the fall of the ruble." At current exchange rates the average monthly wage of 13,000 rubles amounts to $22 only.(7)

The most recent evaluation by the World Bank (8) is as follows: In the former Soviet Union, exports have fallen by half during 1991 and 1992; *average GDP declined by about 20% in 1992.* Prices are rising at 25 to 30% a month.

> Fifty million Russian people - a third of population - are now living below the poverty line. ... *In Russia, the drive to establish a market-oriented economy is faltering in the face of hyperinflation and political opposition.*

---

(7) Time magazine, Feb 8, 1993

(8) Speech by Lewis Preston, World Bank President, before the Foreign Policy Association, WBN, April 1, 1993.

The major obstacle to progress is the constitutional crisis and the *lack of political consensus on the direction of reform.*

(iv) Recent reform agenda

The current Policy objectives in the former Soviet Union are put down as follows by the World Bank: [9] "Macroeconomic stabilization, free markets, a functioning infrastructure and a market-based legal framework", are all necessary for supporting "a growing private sector, the efficient allocation of resources and the restoration of growth".[10]

Macroeconomic stabilization and rampant inflation is the foremost issue; the central bank must stop the reckless issuance of credit, whose main recipients are the large-scale enterprises. Oil production in Russia is rapidly declining (at the rate of a million barrels per day over 1990-1992). Substantial public and private investment is needed to rehabilitate key sectors (oil and gas).[11]

Controls on entrepreneurs still are excessive and a modern *banking sector does not yet exist.* There exist *export controls* and tendency to create *artificial trade barriers* among the independent states of the former Soviet Union.[12]

Stern[13] identifies *six areas of reform,* which are fundamental to all the adjustment programs, on which the World Bank has been working with the governments of the 15 republics and in close collaboration with the IMF.

(a) *Price decontrol:* Significant progress in freeing prices and adjusting upward those remaining under control has been achieved.[14]

(b) *Legal reform* is underway, adapting legislation to the needs of a market economy, and is vital for commercial activity and private investment; some progress is made. The objective is to adopt "a commercial code that recognizes private property, deregulates entry and exit, defines bankruptcy procedures" and provides a legal remedy against breach of contract; a banking law that authorizes the central bank to supervise and regulate lending activities of commercial banks; and "a foreign investment law that clarifies the regulation of foreign capital and profit remittances."[15]

---

(9) Speech by Lewis Preston, World Bank President, before the Foreign Policy Association, WBN, April 1, 1993.

(10) Speech by Ernest Stern, World Bank Managing Director, at Tokyo Conference on Assistance to the Newly Independent States, WBN, Nov. 5, 1992.

(11) Speech by Lewis Preston, World Bank President, World Bank News, Jan 22, 1993.

(12) Speech by Lewis Preston, World Bank President, World Bank News, Jan 22, 1993.

(13) Speech by Ernest Stern, World Bank Managing Director, at Tokyo Conference on Assistance to the Newly Independent States, WBN, Nov. 5, 1992.

(14) op. cit.

(15) op. cit.

(c) *Enterprise reform:* The large-scale enterprises, which are *the main recipients of credit explosion,* must be reformed. *Subsidies and credit directed to this sector, including agriculture,* amount *to nearly half of GDP.* These subsidies are the root cause of the economic crisis and must be substantially reduced immediately.[16]

In this context, it is important, "to define a framework for corporate governance, to allow orderly entry and exit and to promote competition and efficiency." The dilemma is enforcing financial discipline (hardening budget constraint) and ending up with mass unemployment or to continue with soft budget constraint in order to keep enterprises open, in view of the facts that social safety nets are not yet in place and in already contracting economies, redeployment possibilities of labor are limited (due to limited labor mobility and employment opportunities).[17]

(d) *Privatization:* "In the final analysis, only the private sector can deliver incomes and employment on the scale required." Of about 200,000 small firms, "a significant number have already been privatized." The process must be accelerated to create jobs and entrepreneurs.[18]

Without *privatization*

> the effects of price liberalization will be lost to the public monopolies, demand will not determine production and incentives for productivity increases or innovation will remain inadequate. ... The privatization of medium-to-large scale enterprises has barely started, however, although vouchers now are being distributed. There has been only limited land privatization.

The pace of privatization in other republics varies; in Ukraine, the legal framework and a privatization program have been approved, but implementation has been slow; 3 million hectares of land privatized in 1992; a small but dynamic private sector is growing rapidly. In Armenia, Kyrghyztan and to some extent in Georgia, implementation of privatization programs has been impressive.[19]

With the help of a $90 million World Bank loan, Russia is going to set up a *Privatization center* to be in charge of planning and carrying out enterprise reforms and the privatization of up to 25,000 medium-and large-scale

---

(16) Speech by Lewis Preston, World Bank President, before the Foreign Policy Association, WBN, April 1, 1993.

(17) Speech by Ernest Stern, World Bank Managing Director, at Tokyo Conference on Assistance to the Newly Independent States, WBN, Nov. 5, 1992.

(18) Speech by Lewis Preston, World Bank President, before the Foreign Policy Association, WBN, April 1, 1993.

(19) Stern, op. cit.

enterprises and 200,000 small manufacturing, retail and other businesses under municipal or regional ownership.[20]

(e) *Financial sector reform* complements privatization and enterprise reform, by mobilizing resources and channeling them into productive activities.[21] As noted above a modern banking sector does not yet exist.[22]

(f) *The social safety nets* The current safety net or *welfare system is largely hidden* (full employment policies and low-priced subsidized basic goods). *With reform, an explicit welfare system* (an explicit unemployment compensation, and ration coupons distributed to the poor) will be installed; *net cost of this change will be zero, since subsidies are eliminated, and this change will not lower average living standards* (Leitzel, 1992). In fact, living standards have significantly declined and "a third of the population are now living below the poverty line."[23]

The Social safety nets used to consume 40% of national budgets, which is no longer affordable. For inflation contained, "social benefits need to be targeted to the most needy."[24]

In a World Bank Report (1992/F), Nicholas Barr recommends that the Russian Federation scrap the old Soviet social benefits system, in which 10% of GDP was doled out. Barr proposes changes in benefits payments, retirement rules and worker-employer contributions, and streamlining the unemployment benefits, which must be brought down to subsistence-level payments (under the current system the benefit package for unemployed is close to the average national income).

According to Leitzel (1992), *"unemployment may rise during a transition if significant distortions (like fixed prices) are not corrected as enterprise budget constraints are hardened."* In fact, unemployment has risen, when distortions were removed and even when the soft budget constraint were further relaxed. This only shows, *difficulty of forecasting when the economy is in a state of flux.* Moreover, it could *a priori* been maintained that *replacement of bilateral trade links* (CMEA and inter-republican trade) by liberal trade and exchange regime on paper (zero tariffs, payments in convertible currencies, convertible ruble) along with almost complete price liberalization, *on impact would have led to substantial output declines and unemployment.*

"Bloated state-owned factories in Russia often employed too many workers in relatively few jobs." Based on the experience of Eastern Europe, it was

---

(20) WBN, Dec. 23, 1992.

(21) Speech by Ernest Stern, World Bank Managing Director, at Tokyo Conference on Assistance to the Newly Independent States, WBN, Nov. 5, 1992.

(22) Preston, WBN, Jan 22, 1993.

(23) Preston, April 1, 1993.

(24) Stern, WBN, Nov. 5, 1992; Preston, WBN, June 19, 1992.

estimated that unemployment in Russia could rise to 2-4 million in mid-1993 and 10 million during 1994. With the sudden, anticipated rise in unemployment, Russia would need to build up its employment services, put in place a social safety net (to protect the welfare of its citizens during transition) and deploy labor more efficiently.(25)

In concluding it should be pointed out that, the creation of a social safety net is critically important, in order to buffer the impact of transition and reduce social and political tensions.(26)

2 The Shatalin plan

(i) The plan

The Shatalin 500-Day Plan would have transformed the Soviet Economy into a market economy within 500 days, starting on Oct. 1, 1990.

> The sequencing of the Shatalin Plan differs from the sequencing of plans now being implemented in Russia and Eastern Europe. The first 100 days would have been devoted to privatization and stabilization. Small businesses, housing, and vehicles would have been privatized and large companies corporatized.

Revenues from privatization would have helped the budgetary balance substantially.

> A market structure was to be put in place. ... Wages were to be indexed. The multiple exchange rate system was to be replaced by a single rate. Imports of consumer goods were to be increased. The Soviet Union was to have cut back foreign aid. Prices were going to have been liberalized only after macroeconomic stabilization had been assured and the market structure-including privatization - had been put in place. Between days 100 and 250, prices would have been liberalized, larger firms would have been privatized, and the first stage of agrarian reform would have been completed. During the next phase, lasting to day 400, privatization would have continued, antimonopoly activity would have been strengthened, and prices would have been fully liberalized. Internal ruble convertibility was to have been achieved. The plan envisaged widespread bankruptcies and saw the need for measures to support the unemployed. The last 100 days were envisaged as the beginning of the upswing (Fischer, 1992).

---

(25) Press speech by Timothy King of World Bank, WBN, Nov. 25 1992.
(26) Lewis Preston, World Bank President, WBN, April 1, 1993.

"The Shatalin group believed that a price jump at the start of a reform plan could be politically unacceptable", and that privatization (asset sales) could help remove the monetary overhang. The plan placed much less weight on early convertibility than most Western plans. "The plan also did not emphasize external assistance, believing that the Soviet Union could manage largely on its own." "The plan recognized the need for greater republican autonomy," hence did not foresee the imminent collapse of the Soviet Union (Fischer, 1992).

(ii) Evaluation

Fischer (1992) considers the 500-day target was *unrealistically ambitious* and that *a sequenced program is sensible; that putting "the elements of market system in place before liberalizing prices was based on the fear of perverse supply responses by managers* of state-owned enterprises." Fisher also rightly maintains that privatization before liberalizing prices is problematic, because it is impossible to value firms for sale when current prices and profits provide little guidance to future performance (*ibid*, p. 88).

This last argument by Fischer is a valid, general principle which should be complied with the privatization of large enterprises. Under the Shatalin plan, however, privatization of small businesses and housing during the first 100 days, would have created greater advantages by eliminating monetary overhang, creating a much-needed dynamic retail trade/ service sectors (improving competition in retail trade and distribution) and by delivering some goodies to the populace (home-ownership, improved service), than the valuation disadvantage. Moreover the size of valuation-error could have been minimized by (i) privatizing small business on lease basis (with the understanding that in the future sale, incumbent tenants would be given privileged treatment, so that they can start with modernization, improvement investments) and (ii) selling houses to citizens and estimating the real value (valuing the construction cost at world prices, increasing down-payment, indexing installments, etc. or choosing the best bargain on auctions (since, "lack of information concerning prices leads to search for the best bargain" (Hahn, 1981). Under 'the suggested method,' privatization along these lines, during the preparatory phase is recommended. (Also note that Fischer is for leasing in small-scale privatization, because then financing would come from the state sector, and points out the urgency of improving the distribution sector, which is vastly underdeveloped in Russia, *ibid.* pp. 100, 96.)

As for the privatization scheme of Shatalin plan for larger firms between days 100 and 250, when prices also would have been liberalized, one can maintain that, both targets were unrealistic, because neither prices would have stabilized by day 250, nor privatization of large firms could have materialized on a significant scale even by day 400. Moreover, indexation of wages under the Shatalin plan, would easily have led to a wage/price spiral, and rampant inflation.

On the other hand the Shatalin group is right to be concerned about putting the elements of a market system in place before price liberalization, because of the possible perverse supply responses by state enterprises. Under 'the suggested methodology', during the preparatory stage, all required legal, institutional, framework for a market mechanism could and should be put in place.

However, basic weakness of the plan is liberalizing prices, with wage indexation; because even if macroeconomic stabilization (budget balance, price and unified exchange rate stability) is achieved during the first 100-250 days (which would be a remarkable achievement), stability would have been drastically disturbed with price liberalization and subsequent currency devaluations and wage increases. Whereas, under 'the suggested method', prices, exchange rate and wages will be adjusted simultaneously on the first day of the new program (these increases could not even be counted as inflation), and then maintaining wage and exchange rate anchors will be possible, at least for a year, provided actual out-turn matches estimates.

3 Money and credit policy

(i) Functions of money in socialist economies and present picture in the former Soviet Union

In the centrally planned economies, money holdings were not kept primarily for transactions purposes; money was held for precautionary purposes and for storing value.

"Money is primarily a *store of value* in the Soviet Union"; hence *"the money-to-income ratio should be interpreted as a wealth-to-income ratio."* As money is not primarily held for transaction purposes, standard indicators of monetary disequilibrium, like a decline in *money velocity* may be misleading (Cottarelli and Blejer, 1992). Money is also held for *precautionary purposes,* which, however, is related to income.

Nordhaus notes that *economic reforms in the former Soviet Union must simultaneously "manage the monetary and fiscal system, as well as the external indebtedness of a crumbling empire", and hence the standard stabilization programs are not applicable,* in view of the breakdown of inter-republican trade and of the monetary system (the ruble zone). Even before the break-up of the Soviet Union in August 1991, the government could not conduct monetary policy with respect to household spending (in principle it could use credit controls for enterprises). "The breakup of the Soviet Union has led to a proliferation of monies in the ruble zone". Today internal inconvertibility of the ruble is increasing, because de facto there are 19 different forms of money: (1) The paper ruble (cash money) circulates everywhere in the former Soviet Union, (2) the ruble accounts (noncash money) of enterprises in the banking systems of each of the 15 republics. These ruble accounts, which Nordhaus terms as '*abacus rubles*' "do not appear to be convertible into abacus rubles across republican boundaries and have different values on exchanges". "The abacus ruble appears to be selling at a discount of 40% relative to the paper ruble." (3) The 17 the money is the Ukrainian coupon, which seems at par with the paper ruble. (4) Hard currencies like dollar and (5) hard currency accounts of the Vneshekonombank (the Bank of Foreign Economic Relations) which were frozen in Dec. 1991, when Russia ran out of hard currencies. In addition Belarus is going to introduce a coupon and Estonia an Estonian crown (Fischer, 1992).

(ii) Monetary and credit policy in the 1990s in the former Soviet Union

The issue of monetary and credit policy in Russia is mired in a dispute between the Central Bank and the Ministry of Finance; the central bank, with the support of parliament arguing that tightening credit now (in 1992) will lead to unemployment and bankruptcies and the Finance Ministry willing to tighten credit as part of the stabilization program. "Budget stabilization alone cannot stop inflation if the central bank continues to expand the stock of credit by lending to the private sector. Both the quantity and cost of central bank credit matter," since the *real lending rate of the central bank is very negative* (Fischer, 1992).

The central bank does not want to starve existing firms of finance, since the credit policy at this stage cannot be divorced from issues of enterprise reform and regional policy. *"Enforcement of tight credit constraints* could lead to closing of enterprises. *In the current distorted price and financial systems, the wrong firms might close."* Moreover, "given the geographical concentration of industry, such closing-even if they were justified on economic grounds- could *devastate the economies of entire regions,"* as happened, in the shipbuilding regions of the former East Germany. Since formulation of a regional policy and its financing through the budget is unrealistic, given the budgetary constraint, *the provision of cheap credit is a substitute for regional policy* (Fischer, 1992).

Fischer (1992), however, argues that Russia should tighten credit policy now and move quickly ahead on economic restructuring (primarily privatization) and the formulation of regional policies, despite *the fact that the central bank's concerns and arguments are not in principle incorrect.* And adds that, *since prices have been liberalized, which would "encourage normal supply response,* including disgorging of inventories (a process which *would help reverse expectations of rising prices* and move goods into distribution channels"; *tight credit policies might lead to massive unemployment, if at all, "within a year if no industrial restructuring takes place."* In fact, in the reforming Eastern Europe, few firms have been closed and unemployment has increased only slowly (Fischer, 1992).

However destocking cannot take place if prices are continuing to rise, which will lead to shortages for both consumers and user industries. And user industries could not make the 'normal supply response' due to material input bottlenecks. Rising price trend in Russia in 1991 and 1992 reaching hyperinflation proportions recently, makes this argument more valid than Fischer's hypothesis about destocking and expectations. Outcome of reform process in Poland also contradicts, Fischer's estimations regarding the size of unemployment and enterprise closures. In Poland, where the reform process is very similar to that of Russia, with price and trade liberalization, and with a very low tariff rate (4%), frequent policy reversals have taken place to lessen the effects of severe hardships which have emerged. (In Poland unemployment reaching 20% of the non-agricultural labor force or more and increasing bankruptcies are estimated for 1992 by Gomulka, 1992).

In order the stabilization effort to succeed and attract Western financial assistance, Fisher suggests that the monetary policy has to be tightened, by means of a limit on domestic credit creation or maintenance of a fixed exchange rate and a positive real interest rate (Fischer, 1992). It should be noted that even in Poland, with a lower inflation rate in 1991, positive real interest rates have not materialized; for Russia it is a more unrealistic target. Also with the current inflation running above 2,000%, maintenance of a fixed exchange rate is out of question.

4 Foreign trade and convertibility

Foreign trade and convertibility issues in the former Soviet Union are dealt with in various other parts of the book, herein some other aspects and views are presented.

The main achievements of *'perestroika'* in *foreign trade* have been legislative; the share of the Soviet Union in world trade continued to remain small, concentrating on export of energy and raw materials. Geron does not expect the existing trade patterns to change for at least a decade; these are marred by excessive bureaucracy and the present economic chaos (Geron, 1990).

There exist export controls and tendency to create artificial trade barriers among independent states of the former Soviet Union.[27]

---

[27] Lewis Preston (Speech), World Bank President, WBN, Jan 22, 1993.

Ruble convertibility necessitates internal price decontrol. If prices remain fixed when trade is freed, arbitrageurs would purchase Soviet goods that are relatively underpriced, and export them at higher world price. Such arbitrage activity would result in a huge wealth giveaway by the Soviet government. To avoid this outcome in a regime with ruble convertibility and free foreign trade, the Soviets would have to have free prices internally. Adopting a policy of ruble convertibility therefore commits the Soviets to price liberalization (Leitzel, 1992).

There is already a degree of ruble convertibility in the Soviet economy. ... Decrees have been issued in Russia calling for a near complete liberalization of foreign trade and currency transactions; restrictions, however, still remain (Leitzel, 1992).

Balance of payments assistance and a ruble stabilization fund have been requested by Russia and supported by Jeffrey Sachs and the Grand Bargain Program (Leitzel, 1992). The Soviets owe some $60-85 billion to the West. If Soviet gold reserves are at $3 billion, *the former Soviet Union will be faced with debt servicing problem in the near term (*Leitzel, 1992).

5 Priorities and key sectors and long-term prospects

(i) Priorities

According to the World Bank[28], *unlocking the productive potential of key sectors* such as *energy and agriculture,* and removal of internal trade barriers through fundamental structural reforms are of vital importance in the former USSR.

Fischer believes that in Russia, "*the reform program will face severe political difficulties in a few years if structural policies are not addressed* as intensively now as stabilization and financial assistance." In the longer term Fischer believes that *the most important areas of restructuring are developing the distribution sector, restructuring industry; and expanding the energy, agricultural, and financial sectors,* in all of which privatization is essential; in other areas, the government will continue to play an important role, including improving infrastructure (Fischer, 1992).

Summers considers that Fischer's emphasis on infrastructure investments in the former Soviet Union is not justifiable, because (i) the infrastructure, although not good, is not too bad, (ii) "the available aid flows are trivial relative to the cost of modernizing the infra-structure", and (iii) *support for*

(28) Speech by Lewis Preston, World Bank President, WBN , Sept. 25, 1992.

consumption have a higher priority than support for new infrastructure investment (Fischer, 1992).

"The current state of *the transport system is likely to be a major constraint* to Russia's economic recovery." "The country's vastness poses a challenge to the creation and maintenance of a viable transportation system. The break up of the former Soviet Union has exacerbated the problem."[29]

"Because of inadequate maintenance, roughly 60% of *Russia's road network needs to be rehabilitated or upgraded" at a cost of $22 billion* (conservative estimate) over the next 5-7 years. Also there is a shortage of vehicles and spare parts due to disruption of supply from the CMEA area and Russia's lack of foreign exchange.[30]

The rail system dominates the Russian transportation system and handles 90% of freight traffic, and "rail will remain the prime mode of freight transport for the foreseeable future." Ports also have suffered from lack of investment.[31]

(ii) Energy sector: prospects

Summers considers that the energy sector should be a crucial locus of reform.

> *The potential gain in export revenues* from increasing the efficiency of petroleum production and increasing efficiency in energy use probably *exceeds $100 billion by the end of 1990s. Right now energy intensity per unit of GNP is more than 5 times the corresponding figure in Europe,* and easy repairs could raise drilling and shipping productivity substantially.

Investment in the energy sector, could also provide much-needed hard currency (Fischer, 1992).

Russia has been *giving large subsidies* to the other republics by selling commodities, principally *oil, at very low prices.* This problem, however, have been largely redressed by raising the prices to the world price level (Fischer, 1992).

It is proposed that by selling oil leases and other assets, Russia could acquire much needed foreign exchange. However, some Russians are concerned about foreigners buying much of the productive sector and natural resources at the currently under-valued exchange rates (Fischer, 1992).

"Increasing production of gas, halting the decline in oil production and the maintenance of existing coal production facilities in working condition are *priorities for the Russian government."* Crude oil output has fallen from 570

---

(29) WBN, Aug 7, 1992.
(30) WBN, Aug 7, 1992.
(31) op. cit.

million tons in 1987 (peak) to 455 million tons in 1991, a greater fall was expected in 1992. This decline was due to rapidly depleting reserves, under-investment and poor incentives (low domestic energy prices, in mid-1992 these were 20% of world prices and there was an unrealistic exchange rate).[(32)] In fact, by mid 1992, oil output and exports did decline.[(33)] Gas production increased for two decades and stabilized in 1991; a decline in 1992 is estimated. Because of inadequate equipment investment and maintenance, coal output has severely declined in recent years. Many conventional power plants, transmission and distribution lines are in poor shape.[(34)] In fact, oil production had fallen by one million barrels a day in the last 3 years and exports had declined by 50% from the 1990 level over 1991 and 1992.[(35)]

Growth of oil sector, by encouraging both foreign and domestic investment, is crucial for oil-exporting republics from viewpoint of economic stabilization through export and budgetary revenue effects. In fact, the future of public services in many republics hinges on resources raised from the petroleum industry. E.g. in Kazakhstan, economic recovery over the next 10 years depends mainly on the development of oil and gas resources.[(36)]

Without an infusion of increased local and foreign capital, and new technology, the decline in oil output will continue. In order to stabilize oil production at the 1993 level (about 350 million tons), an investment total of $50 billion, between now and the year 2000 will be required. Otherwise, Russia will be an oil importer by the end of the decade, with disastrous consequences.[(37)]

(iii) Agriculture

"The former Soviet Union has a basically *free and legal market in food, the kolkhoz markets." Unless price controls are imposed no food shortage will emerge*. "Incentives to divert state crops to these free markets are so large that *the official government harvest statistics cannot be trusted*" (Leitzel, 1992).

The ability of the Soviet *food distribution system* to harvest and market the grain is, a matter of concern. "But burgeoning private activity is ameliorating the distribution difficulty." In fact, "reports of *massive Soviet food wastage due to inefficient harvesting and distribution long precede Perestroika*" (Leitzel, 1992).

---

(32) WBN, Nov. 5, 1992.
(33) WBN, Aug. 7, 1992.
(34) WBN, Aug. 7, 1992.
(35) Lewis Preston, (speech), WBN, june 19, 1992 and April 1, 1993.
(36) Speech by Michael Levitsky, of the World Bank, WBN, Nov. 5, 1992.
(37) Speech by Preston, WBN, June 19, 1992 and April 1, 1993.

> With the *breakdown of the state system and the tolerance of spontaneous privatization,* the same incentives that used to exist for food from private plots now exist for a much larger percentage of the crop. *Nominally state-owned crops can now be sold for private gain at free prices* [reference is made to activities of Moscow commodity exchange]. [If] the state does not clamp down on such private activity, the difficulty in food distribution should be reduced, (Leitzel, 1992).

Agricultural output fell by about 10% in 1991 in the former Soviet Union, declining trend can continue into 1993, unless extraordinary measures are taken to increase the availability of critical inputs (improved seeds, farm equipment, spare parts for machinery used in producing, harvesting, transporting and processing crops). "A quarter of total crop production is lost to pests," and in addition, 25-30% of harvested crop is wasted in storage, transportation and distribution. Storage facilities can handle only about 60% of present requirements; cold storage, and transportation systems and food-processing industries are inadequate and / or inefficient. Economic incentives to boost production don't exist.(38)

Waste and inefficiency plagued agriculture in the former Soviet Union in the past, more than any other sector. Agriculture offers large potential; and success or failure in agriculture, will strongly influence transition. The sector accounts for roughly one-third of investment and employment in the former Soviet Union (World Bank, 1992/ B).

Agricultural reform should address price, subsidy, credit and trade policy issues; freeing up prices, revision and control of subsidies for producers and consumers, diversification of the rural commercial banking system, and facilitating domestic and foreign investment in the sector, are all called for. Enterprises that produce and distribute agricultural inputs and that process agricultural produce have to be privatized; substantial change in the system will take 3 to 5 years. Success in the reform, however, will lead to more efficient agricultural production, a greater variety and quality of foodstuff and reduced imports of agricultural products (World Bank, 1992/B).

6 Foreign investment

The foreign direct investment which along with brings not only finance but also management expertise and technology, *would not flow on a substantial scale to Russia* (e.g. it is flowing now to *Hungary* at a scale more than 3% of GNP) *until some stability returns* (Fischer, 1992).

---

(38) WBN, Aug. 7, 1992.

Russia's external financing requirement (fresh loans) might be about $15 billion per annum in the next few years, most of which should come from official sources. *Substantial flows of private capital* (in particular foreign direct investment in the energy sector) *are not to materialize until economic reforms take root.*(39)

Vague and confusing laws hamper foreign investment in the 15 states of the former Soviet Union. Frequent changes in laws concerning business and investment increase confusion and uncertainty for foreign investors. Western capital mostly flows into joint ventures and total direct foreign investment was close to $1.6 billion in mid 1992; however, *inflows have slowed down in recent years* with $640 million in 1989, $480 million in 1990 and $240 million in 1991 (World Bank, 1992/C).

Investors remain uncertain about vague laws regarding repatriation of profits and foreign exchange regime, and are constrained by weak banking, financial and business services. "Western companies are very concerned about the political stability of the republics and if a country is considered politically unstable, investors become skeptical that existing legislation and economic policies, no matter how attractive, will last" long (World Bank, 1992/C).

Joint ventures are mostly in services and light industries (Geron, 1990). Hill (1991) suggests joint ventures in manufacturing of machines. (although in some sub-sectors of this sector, the former Soviet Union have expertise and high standards) in order to improve Soviet expertise in lines standards are not high.

Most of the foreign investment flows into joint ventures, also because under the former USSR, *joint ventures* were the only channel foreign nationals could invest in the country. Now some republics allow wholly-owned foreign subsidiaries and equity investment in domestic firms. Joint ventures are concentrated in *manufacturing;* but in the Baltics in retail trade (World Bank, 1992/C).

Most of the foreign investment flows into Russia, followed by the Baltics, and the Central Asian republics are least successful in luring foreign capital. Largest investor in the republics is Russia, followed by US, Germany, Finland, Ukraine, Poland, Italy and UK (World Bank, 1992/C).

7 Development of private sector and privatization

In the former Soviet Union there is a widespread *informal, second economic sector,* whose activities are not recorded in official statistics (Leitzel, 1992). *Privatization of small firms by auctioning* started in April 1992, but *local authorities are not enthusiastic about sales.* Small-scale privatization is both urgent, as a precedent and signal, and important, because *the distribution sector*

(39) Interview with Huang, WBN, Aug 7 , 1992.

in Russia is very much under-developed. "Growth in this area is likely eventually to come from new firms, but opening up the sector requires the privatization of existing firms owned by local authorities." In this respect, existing stakeholders should be given incentives in order to obtain their support for privatization (Fischer, 1992).

Nordhaus observes that while output has fallen 10-20%, "there is *no sign of private production* of goods." "Aside from the simplest economic activities, *it will take much longer for private initiative to spring up to replace the state sector;"* and hence there is an urgent need for "an *industrial policy* to cope with the collapse of production in key industries like food, energy, transportation, and exports" (Fischer, 1992).

Despite seven years of partial reforms and *significant private activity, "the government probably still directs production and distribution of the bulk of both public and private goods* in the former Soviet economy" (Leitzel, 1992). *A small but dynamic business sector is emerging in Ukraine; in all the Baltic states* small businesses are growing. About 20% of Lithuania's work force is now estimated to be in the private sector.[40]

A significant number have been privatized out of about 200,000 small firms.[41] A Privatization Center is going to be established with a World Bank Loan.[42] A modern banking sector, to support economic activities and essential for the private sector development, does not yet exist.[43]

Compared with Western economies, a far smaller fraction of total employment is in wholesale and retail trade and finance, all of which must expand in the future (Fischer, 1992).

Nordhaus states that Russia urgently "needs an *industrial policy to cope with the collapse of production in key industries like food, energy, transportation, and exports." It will take too long for private sector to spring up to replace the state sector.* The key issues to be addressed are *"how to reinvigorate production when the state has withdrawn,* how to *prevent pauperization* when the hoards run down, *how to introduce a spirit of enterprise* where it has been rooted out, or how to extract money from the West when it gets bored and the stabilization fund is used up" (Fischer, 1992, p.123).

Market infrastructure in the former Soviet Union is inadequate as reflected "in the difficulty in enforcing contracts, sparse credit markets, problematic communications and transportation systems, and uncertain property rights." Provision of the public goods necessary for a market economy (the legal system, banking, accounting, market infrastructure, transportation infrastructure, communications networks, training and research in social sciences, financial

---

(40) Speech by L.Preston, World Bank President, World Bank News, Jan 22, 1993.

(41) Lewis Preston, World Bank President, WBN, April 1, 1993.

(42) WBN, Dec. 23, 1992.

(43) Lewis Preston, WBN, January 22, 1993.

incentives for the Soviet Academy of Sciences, social welfare programs, etc.) would promote private economic activity in the former Soviet economy (Leitzel, 1992).

8 Privatization and monopolies: substitution of private monopolies for public monopolies

In view of disappointing outcome of reforms and of the economic and political instability and uncertainty prevailing in many of the former socialist countries, it is unlikely that domestic and foreign capital will be interested on a large scale, in medium-to - large scale privatization. It seems that, taking into account this constraint, give-away privatization through voucher scheme is being planned in the former Soviet Union. This could not be a real solution, (this has been dealt with elsewhere).

Regarding the argument that replacement of public monopoly by private monopoly or competitive market would increase productivity and innovation, the following observations are made. If a competitive market replaces an unregulated monopoly, consumers would be better off for sure, but productivity might decline due to smaller scale of production (if there are economies of scale), Research and Development (R&D) expenditure would decline as observed with the break up of monopolies even in US, and technology would improve only if foreign direct investment is involved. Replacement of public monopoly by duopoly or oligopoly will have similar effects.

If private monopoly substitutes for public monopoly, at the onset a once-for-all technological and organizational improvements might increase efficiency and productivity, but in the long run there is no reason for assuming that a private monopoly would spend more on R&D and innovation than a public monopoly (even a case can be made for the opposite view). Only if the new monopoly is a foreign direct investment or a joint venture, then technological and organizational efficiency and innovation will rise(either imported technology or locally developed, due to ample supply of engineers, scientists, technicians, in the former socialist countries).

Due to the latter effect (i.e. lower cost of R&D in these countries), it can be argued that, in order to develop advanced technologies and achieve international competitive power, state monopolies (in sectors where technological advance still continuing) should rather be converted to joint-ventures with high-technology foreign companies.

9 Education and technology and high-technology industries: potential and problems

The former Soviet Union produces a third of all the world's doctorates in science and engineering and has a highly educated workforce. It is also well-endowed with natural resources, which indicate a 'great potential' for growth.[44]

The technological performance of industry in the former Soviet Union and CMEA Countries is not uniform across manufacturing sector. In certain areas, the former Soviet Union has advanced manufacturing technology, particularly in the manufacture of machines of precision and robotics, they have very high standards and expertise (Hill, 1991).

The Soviet Union was able to import machines manufactured in Easter Germany and in Hungary at half price of Western machines (Hill, 1991).

Higher education and science should be refocused toward the needs of a market economy, namely skill base in modern business management, economics, engineering and agricultural knowledge should be developed. Retraining of adults unemployed by the restructuring process should be addressed.[45]

10 Military conversion

Under the Soviet Defense Conversion Plan approved in December 1990, main task is not physical conversion of production facilities from military to civilian production, but rather an increase in the production of civilian goods that are already made in the defense complex. The conversion plan involves a centralized approach, i.e. defense enterprises are to be told by central planners the kind and quantity of consumer goods to be produced (Leitzel, 1992).

This implies that the idle capacity will be utilized for civilian production. Decline in defense expenditures should increase civilian production of the defense complex. This civilian production should, however, be a viable operation by itself and be sold at free prices (Leitzel, 1992).

Defense production could also be converted to the provision and maintenance of infrastructure. This type of conversion will both decrease open unemployment and "supply public good that appears to be currently under-supplied". Improvements in infrastructure complement market reform since the current short-comings of the transportation and communication systems constitute a major bottleneck to conducting business (Leitzel, 1992).

It should be noted that Western experience with decentralized military conversion has been dismal. "Conversion schemes aiming at physical conversion of productive assets from defense production to consumer goods production are not promising, whether undertaken in a centralized or decentralized fashion" (Leitzel 1992).

---

(44) Speech by Lewis Preston, World Bank President, at the World Bank Annual Meetings, WBN, Sept. 25, 1992.

(45) Speech by Wilfried Thalwitz, World Bank Vice President, WBN, March 19, 1992.

11 The health sector

In the former Soviet Union, because of chronic underfunding (only 3% of GDP is allocated to the health-care system) and problems related to central planning, health services were barely adequate, and now are in a state of near collapse. "The disruption of supply arrangements within the Council for Mutual Economic Assistance (CMEA) and former Soviet Union, has left Russia dependent on imports for approximately 60% of pharmaceuticals and other medical supplies."(46)

12 Developments in other republics

Output structures and exports of other republics than Russia were much more *specialized* (Senik-Leygonie and Hughes, 1992).

Economic output declined by 15% in 1991 in the former Soviet Union, and declines of 15-25% are expected in 1992. A turnaround is not yet clearly in sight, particularly in republics which are most affected by disruptions in interrepublican trade and price increases for oil and other raw materials imported from Russia. Shortages of food, medicine, and fuel for heating and transport have become acute in many places.(47)

Economic reform of the Russian Federation, Belarus, Kazakhstan and Kyrgyzstan focuses on price and trade reform, privatization and enterprise reform, and financial sector and legal reforms, reforms in the key sectors of agriculture, energy, infrastructure and housing and development of an improved social safety net for the transitional period, and training programs and institutional reforms.(48)

Evaluation of aid-donor nations and international organizations in Dec. 1992, regarding the other former Soviet republics are summarized below:(49)

Economic transition in *Kazakhstan* may be difficult, but *"medium-term prospects are favorable,* if the right policies could be put in place and the necessary external support is forthcoming." Kazakhstan's strong agricultural economy and its oil and other natural resources could finance a rapid economic growth.

In *Kyrgyzstan,* "output and consumption have dropped considerably since the break-up of the Soviet Union". "The country was firmly placed *on the path to economic reform"* and its "financing needs for 1993 could be met particularly if traditional financing flows within the former Soviet Union were to continue."(50)

(46) WBN. Aug. 7, 1992.
(47) WBN, June 19, 1992.
(48) WBN, June 19, 1992.
(49) WBN, Dec. 23, 1992.
(50) op. cit.

Kyrgyzstan launched reforms in 1990, ahead of many other republics to transform its command economy into a market-led economy. The reform program aimed at "reducing the state's role in the economy", and included a new taxation system, an autonomous central bank, price liberalization and reforming family allowances. In 1992, privatization have started (by January 1993, 12% of state assets, mostly small trade and service enterprises were sold off) and barriers to private sector activity in trade and distribution were removed by the end of 1992.(51)

Kyrgyzstan has "a well educated population, a strong industrial base and a good infrastructure", but some of the industry is specialized to supply goods to the former Soviet Union. The breakup of the Soviet Union have had adverse effects on exports, imports (which used to be at subsidized prices) and incoming cash transfers; and many industries have stopped production completely. While cost of imports is rising, export proceeds have been declining. In 1992, economic output fell by about a quarter; and it is estimated that about one-third of population now lives below the poverty line. In 1993, it is expected that economic output to be 40% lower than in 1990. "Real wages fell by 37% between early 1991 and late 1992, and pensions and minimum wages have dropped to only a few dollars a month." By the end of 1992, inflation has accelerated to 2,000% for 1992.(52)

An IDA credit and accompanying co-financing arranged in 1993 will fund imports of urgently needed inputs, raw materials and spare parts to keep the economy running, and will support currency stabilization operations (domestic currency, the som introduced in May 1993) and loans to private enterprises; and will enable the country make full use of 1 million hectares of irrigated land and diversify agricultural product mix (reducing concentration on livestock).(53) Kyrgyzstan is expected to start economic growth by 1997, earliest.(54)

As proclaimed by the government, *Azerbaijan,* which is "building a democratic secular state, based on universal human values, and guaranteeing the rights and *freedom of the individual and entrepreneurial initiative,"* had accelerated reforms, that include a *stabilization program,* basic *structural reforms* and other actions in energy, agriculture, industry and infrastructure sectors.(55)

As declared by the government, *Uzbekistan* "is firmly committed to a *comprehensive reform program,* which includes a *virtual elimination of the state-order system, price liberalization, reduction and elimination of most*

---

(51) Kutlu Somel of World Bank, WBN, May 20, 1993.

(52) op. cit.

(53) op. cit.

(54) op. cit.

(55) WBN, Dec 23, 1992.

subsidies, promoting private entrepreneurship and *reform of the financial sector."*[56]

13 External assistance requirement

For economic and political stability, the reforming republics need humanitarian, technical, general financial assistance and access to Western markets. In view of past experience, *Fischer* (1992) observes that *"aid has been helpful when it has been used to support programs chosen by recipient governments to which they have been fully committed."*

The balance of payments support for Russia, calculated on a need basis, will be rather temporary, because BOP position of Russia is inherently strong. Fischer (1992) maintains that *conditionality* that accompanies the IMF and World Bank assistance *"urges gradualism when shock treatment is needed."*

Massive *food aid* might postpone remedies for the current deficiencies in the Soviet food system, (slowing down the process of removing state controls over Soviet agriculture and "farmers may reduce their planting next year if food aid lowers prices on the free markets" (Leitzel, 1992). In the short run, however, there is a need for maintaining the relation between food prices and minimum wage at a satisfactory level.

Conservative estimates place the external aid requirement of Russia at $20-25 billion for 1992 and $20 billion for other 14 republics. "The focus on Russia is justified because of its multiple linkages with the other 14 states", but the total financing requirements of the other states, which is roughly the same as Russia's, should not be forgotten.[57] "Official agencies alone cannot possibly meet the huge financing requirements of the former Soviet Union. Foreign private investors will have to play a major role. Even more importantly, *domestic investment must be mobilized."* The former Soviet Union is "rich in human capital, technology and natural resources"; hence, "provided a political consensus can be attained, the long-term outlook is good", and external aid and IBRD can play a catalytic role in this respect.[58]

14 The need for a new Marshall plan

There is no doubt that history will give due credit and recognition to the former USSR president Mikhail Gorbachev for 'glasnost' and 'perestroika' policies and for starting the disarmament process, all of which led to hopes of world peace and the onset of an economic and political transformation process in all of the socialist countries. The whole of mankind should appreciate the importance

(56) WBN, Dec 23, 1992.
(57) Speeches by World Bank President Preston, WBN, June 19,1992 and April 1, 1993.
(58) op. cit.

of this dramatic change to (eventual) world peace (hopefully) and to freedom, and assist the reforming countries by means of a new Marshall Plan, which would also increase aggregate welfare of the world through reduced armament expenditures and expanded trade between the former blocs.

So far the rest of the world has failed in fulfilling its expected responsibilities, by unduly delaying its response on grounds of awaiting the irrevocable reform process or a sound transformation program to be launched. Gorbcahev's gradualist reform approach was justifiable considering the circumstances surrounding the enterprise sector and breakdown of the government authority.

Although Shatalin plan could be criticized, it was far better than the 'big bang' approach which followed it, and also because Shatalin plan could have been adjusted and corrected during implementation, whereas under the 'big bang' approach no such corrective mechanism (revising the course) exists, since chaos could only create more chaos.

If failures in the reforming economies persist and poverty of the masses increases, there is the danger (signs are already visible: internal strife, wars in the former Yugoslavia and Caucasus are first indications) that the next phase will be despotic regimes with arms trade and external wars. It is high time to assist the reforming countries in every way possible.

It should be kept in mind that the socialist economies collapsed from within; although capitalism proved its superiority, pure capitalist system ('marketplace only' approach) is presently beset by major problems. In fact the West with high equilibrium unemployment levels and regular cycles of recession and inflation, is itself in a big economic crisis. The successful economies of Far East are not exercising the pure capitalist system; their economic model also include indicative economic planning and the state guidance and regulation of the economy. It is now obvious that the equilibrium unemployment (structural unemployment) level has risen significantly since the late 1970s and presently is at 10% in some countries and is accompanied by economic stagnation or stagflation (reduced production and investment, and immediate emergence of inflationary tendencies when reflation policies are exercised). The current *stagflation* in the West is explained under the Keynesian view by the following factors (see, e.g. Sloman, 1991, pp. 555-56):

(i) Cost-push pressures created by the oil price shocks of 1973/74 and 1978/79. (ii) Confinement of excess demand to certain sectors. (iii) The increased concentration of economic power in large multinationals and labor unions. (iv) Reduced production, investment and employment creation by firms influenced by pessimistic expectations of declining demand and sales (v) Downward stickiness of wages and prices. Keynesians point out that these factors and problems are not of a short-term nature that markets will soon correct and hence a deliberate policy of reflation is needed.

The problem of *stagflation and industrial decline* in the West is attempted to be explained by short-term factors and cyclical remedies are applied; whereas all these problems are of long-term nature. It is now acknowledged, at least by Keynesians, that the structural problems, such as the long-term declining trend in certain industries, replacement of labor-intensive processes by computerized production processes in manufacturing and increased use of robots in the economy, which are blamed for high unemployment, are not of temporary nature (see, e.g. Sloman, 1991, p. 556).

All this can be summed up as that the productive capacity in the West is inadequate to offer sufficient gainful employment to reduce unemployment permanently and reflation policies, through monetary expansion or increased budgetary deficit, in general end up with inflation, because they lead to both financial and resource crowding- out of private investment. Because the economy is at the new, possibly lower, potential output level (revised downward to take care of declining or presently inefficient industries confronting foreign competition; this reduction, however, possibly is not or could not be fully taken into account in calculating the potential output), otherwise, if reflation is exercised on the basis of new/reduced potential output levels, stagflation should not follow.

The reforming socialist countries present a challenge and opportunity to the West; these countries need all the goods that could readily be supplied by the West; if productive capacity is expanded in the West to accommodate this need, present high-structural unemployment and stagnation problem in the West could be resolved; and if ensuing trade is financed under a new Marshall plan, which could be designed in such a manner that orderly transformation could be speeded up and shortage of critical inputs and consumer goods could be overcome.

> [As observed by Lewis Preston], In the US over 7 million jobs in the export sector and trade with developing nations is the fastest growing segment of the economy. Helping poor countries to become richer is one of the most effective ways to create jobs and wealth... in the US. Conversely, not helping the poorer countries carries negative consequences: increasing number of refugees will crowd across borders, compounding unemployment problems; drugs and disease will spread further; and the environment will be irreversibly damaged. The US.-and every other nation-also has a vital interest in wrenching transitions that are taking place in Eastern Europe and the former Soviet Union. An entire region has embarked on a political, social and economic transformation which has few parallels in history.(59) [One should also take into account

(59) Speech by World Bank President Preston, WBN, April 1, 1993.

that] the former Soviet Union is facing an economic crisis much worse than the Great Depression.[60]

This new Marshall plan could not be financed by borrowing, because all over the world capital markets are already tight and crowding-out effect of additional borrowing for this purpose will only lead to reduced private investment. Hence the only viable option is through appropriate taxation measures, which will increase total savings by reducing consumption. The US definitely needs such a measure (like introducing VAT, etc.) in view of the long-term increasing trends in private and total consumption over the 1973-1992 period and the long-term declining trends in both gross domestic saving and capital formation which can be discerned from Table 19.1. This topic will be taken up later.

Table 19.1
The US: Some macroeconomic parameters (as percentage of GDP)

	1973	1981	1986	1992
Private Consumption	62	64	67	69
Total Consumption	80	82	84	85
Gross Domestic Saving	20	18	16	15
Gross Domestic Investment (gross capital formation)	20	19	19	15

Source: World Tables, IBRD; IFS, IMF, March 1993

15 Modalities of external aid

This plan would promote orderly transformation and speed up market reforms if used for following purposes:

(i) To overcome shortages of critical inputs and consumer goods on an ad hoc basis. (Systematic aid might discourage output response from domestic sectors.)

(ii) Technical assistance for enterprise reform, market reform and for the establishment of market institutions.

---

(60) Speech by World Bank President Preston, WBN, April 1, 1993.

(iii) Co-financing or participation in loan-financing of direct foreign investments and joint ventures.

(iv) Establishing a joint scheme for export insurance and a guarantee scheme for compensation of losses related to investment disputes, justified under the standard international law: Absence of market infrastructure and legal framework in the reforming socialist countries inhibit businessmen and private investors from involvement in these countries. If compensation approved by appropriate international institutions under international law, is paid out by such a mechanism, a major obstacle to trade with and investment in these countries would be removed.

(v) To establish a stabilization fund for current account convertibility of local currencies.

(vi) To fund infrastructure investments which cause a severe bottleneck.

(vii) To finance establishment of a commercial and investment banking sector with foreign or joint ownership.

(viii) Establishment of a modern distribution mechanism (wholesale and retail).

(ix) To finance investments in key sectors (taking advantage of ample natural resources and human capital stock), such as exporting industries (oil, gas, agriculture) with a high potential and joint ventures in skill-intensive or high-technology industries.

Chapter 20

The theoretical foundations of reform programs

The theoretical foundations of reform programs

1 Structuralism versus Keynesian views on the 1990 Polish reform program and actual outcome

According to the *structuralist view,* large changes in the microeconomic environment of enterprises would cause a recession in the particular circumstances prevailing in post-communist countries during transition. "In particular, *sharply raising some input prices has made the production of specific goods unprofitable and sharply raising some output prices had reduced specific demands"*. The new relative prices required a corresponding change in the whole production pattern, but because of the prevailing rigidities, some resources had to become unemployed before they could be redeployed to produce goods that are in demand and profitable with new prices. The output loss of this micro-adjustment of the supply side was augmented by phasing out the forced buying of goods (forced substitution). The collapse of trade with CMEA area was another factor. "Since all these adjustments are large and necessary, structuralists expected the East European recession to be deep, long and inevitable ", "similar to the *Western recession of the early 1980s, following the oil shock of 1979"* (Gomulka, 1992).

On the other hand, Calvo and Coriceeli (1992) maintain that the structural transformation would cause a fall in output, only if new prices are lower than new average costs, otherwise output should not fall.

Keynesians emphasized the negative impact on economic activity of policies which were reducing aggregate demand, assuming implicitly that *"the full employment output has remained unchanged, despite the dramatic change of the microeconomics environment"*. The main thrust of the Polish reform policy implied that the structuralist doctrine has been dominant. However, given the monopolistic market structure and limited price flexibility, the choice of government policies would have a major impact on aggregate demand and hence it was decided not to deflate more than necessary. "In practice, given the large uncertainties about the potential impact of the reform measures on activity, the tendency was to be more rather than less restrictive in the first few months following the big bang, which in turn led to an excessively expansionary policy in the second half of 1990" (Gomulka, 1992).

One can not accept the view that the full employment output would not change during transformation. Because some plants would lose markets at home and abroad, because of low quality of products and high unit costs in real terms. External sales would decline due to phasing out CMEA. Even if the aggregate effective demand in real terms is maintained at pre-reform level through inflation-indexed wage, government and investment expenditures increases, foreign competitors' penetration into the domestic market would reduce demand for domestic production. Closure or reduced output of un-competitive plants would also reduce inter-industry demand for locally produced intermediary goods. Increase in exports, to what extent would compensate, above-mentioned declines is an open question, this increment, however, has to be estimated, for the final analysis. However, in all countries, output, in fact, has declined, also because of wrong policies, such as (i) immediate abandonment of CMEA, without a temporary multilateral clearing-arrangement during transition, (ii) very high estimation errors in predicted effects of reform measures and resulting inconsistency between policies and economic reality, etc.

It is obvious that a new production pattern matching new demand pattern, in line with new relative prices and other structural changes stemming from new trade and exchange regime, introduction of monetary instruments and policies, new taxation and subsidy policy, dollarization, etc., has to develop during transformation.

2 An appraisal of the Keynesian theory on stagflation and unemployment

(i) Views on free markets

Neo Keynesians argue that free market work inefficiently, invisible hand of free markets will not lead to an efficient allocation of resources when externalities and public goods exist; moreover, price signals are distorted by economic power; most wages and many prices are sticky; free markets frequently do not clear and settle below full employment and government intervention is a must. Moderate Keynesians accept that, when unions are faced with growing unemployment, wage increases will be limited.

Keynesian micro foundations of macro models, emphasize *the non-competitive nature* of the economy. Most firms are setting their own prices rather than accepting those set in markets. Their unit costs being fairly constant, they add a fixed markup to their costs in price formation, which is still formulated under profit maximization in a non-competitive market. Firms do not adjust prices frequently because to alter prices is costly, unless cost increases (due to wage, tax changes or ongoing inflation) are sizeable. Hence they normally do not change price but quantity of output/sales when aggregate demand changes; i.e. cyclical fluctuations lead to cyclical variations in output and in employment rather than in price. Similarly wages respond to price and productivity changes, but are insensitive to short-term cyclical fluctuations in demand.

As a consequence Keynesians claim that the main impact of fluctuations in the aggregate demand is on output and employment; in contrast, monetarists argue that the main impact of shifts in the aggregate demand is on prices. Keynesians also maintain that recessionary gaps can persist for long periods, unless eliminated by stabilization policy.

(ii) Sticky wages and prices, and entrenched unemployment

"Extreme Keynesians argue that there is no automatic mechanism to eliminate demand-deficient unemployment even in the long-run", because wages are sticky downwards and any reduction in wages will further reduce consumer demand, and "expectations are likely to remain pessimistic". And even after the economy has pulled out of recession, a high level of demand should be maintained to encourage R&D, innovations and investment generally and thus to achieve more rapid growth of potential income. Moderate Keynesians advocate use of anti-cyclical demand management policy, once the economy is back to near full employment (Sloman, 1991, p. 559). One observes that, in lieu of encouraging R&D and innovations by means of an unnecessarily expansionary policy and risk inflation, it is more effective and less costly to subsidize these expenditures directly.

Keynesians argue that as a consequence of greater downward rigidity of prices and wages and with the short-run Phillips curve being kinked at the current level of real aggregate demand, reduction in real aggregate demand will only have a marginal effect on inflation. Labor unions would prefer lower employment by natural wastage to reduction in real wages.

As the number of long-term unemployed workers grows, *many unemployed will be deskilled* and number of effectively employable (the effective labor supply) will decline despite high unemployment; then *unemployment becomes deeply entrenched.*

If people believe that a contractionary policy will lead to a recession, then firms will stop investing and will cut their workforce; whereas if they believe that it will stop inflation and increase firms' competitive power, business investments may increase.

(iii) Stagflation

Keynesians argue that stagflation can occur because of two reasons:

(a) Cost-push and expectations-generated inflation and structural unemployment might lead to stagflation.

(b) Slacks of firms might vary because of different levels of spare capacities and inventories carried; hence response to rising demand will be either raising prices or output, or a mixture of both (Sloman, 1991, pp. 608-609).

(iv) Expansionary policies and their effects

Unless the economy is at full employment, Keynesians argue that expansionary policies would increase output and employment, since there is plenty of slack in the economy. Moreover, the natural level of output and employment is not fixed, because with increased investment productive capacity, output and employment will expand (a gradual but sustained expansion of aggregate demand might play the trick; firms observing the economy expanding and their orders growing, will increase investments under optimistic expectations). New more efficient technologies embodied in new capital goods and on-the-job training of the newly employed, will cause productivity gradually to rise as investment and employment increase.

Against these neo-Keynesian views, one can argue that, the economy would rather be at the potential output level, if expansionary/contractionary policy cycles do not disturb macroeconomic equilibrium. By means of cyclical policies and frequent policy reversals, a steady growth of output and investment and optimistic expectations could not be achieved, there is ample evidence corroborating this view; the prerequisite for steady growth is price stability and a higher level of saving, than achieved in the West.

(v) An appraisal

Keynesian analysis of free markets, sticky wages and prices, and stagflation is valid for many economies, but their policy recommendations would rather lead to inflation (increased expenditures on public works, some form of reflationary prices and incomes policy), international inflation (through international reflation) and inefficiencies (control of exchange and interest rates and more protection through import controls); except for greater cooperation between government and industry (indicative planning) and structural policies (regional development policies for high-unemployment areas and retraining policies) which might help.

In fact some Keynesians rightly worry that, once the government is committed to maintaining full employment, much of the discipline would be removed from wage bargains; and then the commitment to full employment would lead to accommodating increases in the money supply.

Some economists maintain that both price stability and full employment objectives could be attained most of the time if the government gives priority to price stability over full employment, whenever the two objectives come into short-run conflict, then wage-cost inflation may not occur even at full employment and inflationary effects of the supply or the demand shocks would be easily quelled with minor recession, because inflationary expectations and inertia would never have a chance to become strongly entrenched. (See e.g. Lipsey, et al, 1990, p. 734). It should be pointed out that by means of this strategy, price stability could be achieved, but not full employment of labor; the latter objective calls for increased saving and growth-oriented policies; anti-cyclical expansionary policies could not achieve it, as ample evidence, in the West and developing countries, indicates.

3 An appraisal of neo-classical and monetarist theories and their policy recommendations

(i) Monetarist views and comments

According to the monetarists or new classicists, there is no long-term trade-off between wage inflation and economic growth (national income). Keynesians and monetarists agree on the automatic adjustment mechanism, i.e. deviations of national income from its capacity level (full-employment income) would give rise to changes in wages and prices, which would eventually restore full employment.

Keynesians also agree that demand-shock inflations generated by increases in private-or public-sector expenditures, unless validated by monetary expansion, would be brought to a halt by the automatic adjustment mechanism; and that supply-shock inflations cannot continue indefinitely unless accommodated by monetary expansion.

Sticky wages, as well as downward inflexibility of the price level, however, are observed facts, as pointed out by Keynesians. Moreover, saucer-shaped cost curves, typically found in manufacturing, make sticky pricing policies profitable. As a consequence, the automatic adjustment mechanism is in fact slow and painful.

> Moderate monetarists maintain that - markets adjust fairly quickly - perhaps within one or two years, ... the short-run Phillips curve is downward sloping ... ([i.e.], a rise in money supply and hence aggregate demand will lead to temporary reduction in unemployment), ... but the long-run curve is vertical (Sloman, 1991, p. 559).

The view on the short-run Phillips curve is acceptable only under the Lucas supply curve hypothesis. The Lucas aggregate supply curve or surprises-only supply curve postulates that only unexpected price changes (surprises) will lead to output response; expected price changes will not cause variations in economic output. And under the theory of rational expectations, people do not make persistent, systematic errors in predicting the overall inflation rate, they may only make unsystematic errors. Rational expectations theory, combined with the Lucas aggregate supply curve maintains that systematic attempts to use monetary policy to stabilize the economy will lead to systematic changes in the price level, but will not influence output (neutrality/policy invariance postulate).

"The new classical/rational expectations school maintains that markets clear very quickly and expectations adjust virtually instantaneously to new situations"; that "the short-run Philips curve is vertical, as well as the long-run"; that tight monetary policy will reduce inflation, it does not increase unemployment and that *rising unemployment is entirely due to a rise in the natural level of unemployment* (Sloman, 1991, p. 558).

Monetarists maintain that unemployment may be temporally reduced by raising aggregate demand above the potential output or increased by lowering aggregate demand; but the long-run Phillips curve is vertical; and inflation is entirely dependent on aggregate demand, which is turn is determined by money supply.

According to monetarists, natural (equilibrium) level of unemployment had increased over time because of increase in frictional and structural unemployment as a consequence of increased labor union power and generous unemployment benefits in the West; e.g. in the UK natural unemployment had increased from 1.5% in the 1960s to 6-8% in the 1980s; and as a consequence the Phillips curve has moved to the right (Sloman, pp. 554-55).

As a remedy, monetarist recommend improved factor mobility and structural policies, like supply-side policies, which in general turned out to be inflationary and ineffective as the US and Turkish experiences in 1980s show . This school also favors laissez-faire policies (Sloman, 1991, p.558). The monetarist analysis is basically right, only prescribed remedy will prolong unemployment, and slow down growth, because through laissez-faire policies equilibrium unemployment cannot be reduced. Monetarists believe that "all inflations are caused by excessive monetary expansion and would not occur without it" and that "the economy is inherently stable, because private sector expenditure functions are relatively stable" (Lipsey, et al, 1990, pp. 806, 807). The former statement, although always true ex post, is a tautology.

The difficulties encountered in and impossibility of maintaining monetary growth on targets (considering also the validity of Goodhart law), e.g. in the UK under Thatcherism, reveal that focusing on monetary growth only may not even solve the inflation problem satisfactorily, nor growth. Even when tight monetary conditions are enforced, commercial banks, unless credit is quantitatively restricted, may expand their lending in various forms, in response to increased credit demand arising from aggregate supply or demand shocks, rising prices, etc. Moreover, if the government budget is not balanced, authorities will find all sort of means of financing the deficit.

Regarding the second statement, in view of the rising trend of private consumption and declining trend of saving in the industrialized countries, as percentage of GDP, it might be worthwhile to check whether the private consumption propensities has been rising as well.

Monetarists believe that forces of competition are strong enough that macro economic models based on perfect competition in all markets is realistic. Hence departures from full-employment equilibrium, would be quickly rectified, because in competitive markets, prices and wages are flexible, and the automatic adjustment mechanism works quite efficiently.

Although monetarist assumption of perfect competition is not valid, since it is a fact that most of the markets are under imperfect competition, all markets, except for labor market, are normally in equilibrium (competitive, monopolistic or oligopolistic equilibrium, in the sense supply equals demand at the market price), except at times of extreme supply or demand shocks and volatile high inflation. And it is not possible to change equilibrium level output and employment by anticipated monetary expansion, even in the short run, in markets where imperfect competition prevails. Hence micro underpinnings of macro models and policy packages could realistically be equilibrium at the potential (redefined as realistic maximum) output level in all markets, except the labor market.

The realistic potential output is less than the full-employment output under perfect competition, and is determined by the existing relative prices, productive capacity and technology (including available skilled labor pool) and prevailing market conditions; and since the variables determining the maximum level could not be changed by monetary and fiscal expansion, particularly in the short run, it is considered fixed in the short-term. This potential level decreases and increases in line with declining industries, economic growth and increased import penetration, hence fluctuates over time.

In the UK Keynesians argue that equilibrium unemployment increased because of several factors which include increased competition from abroad and the decline of many older industries (Sloman, 1991, p. 805).

In an economy with sustained inflation (low or high), where imperfect competition prevails in the majority of markets, all monetary and fiscal expansion signals (monetary growth, government budget and BOP deficits, and price indices) will be closely monitored. Any expansion signal would lead to price increases in imperfect competition sectors, and even competitive sectors facing immediate input cost increases would not be able to respond to demand increase by output expansion, rather their prices only will rise. The role of speculation also should be taken into account. Even in most competitive markets (agricultural produce), farmers withhold their output when they expect price increases, and speculators start hoarding stocks.

Perfectly competitive markets assumed by all monetarist theories are widely at variance with the facts as observed by Keynesians; the theories should be based on empirical observations and empirical relevance should be the ultimate arbiter of the value of a theory. In imperfectly competitive markets, where firms have some market power and are price setters, prices are changed infrequently and small changes in demand are accommodated by changes in output rather than price. However, a profit maximizing firm with some market power, operating in a imperfectly competitive market, will increase prices, when expansionary policies lead to an aggregate demand shock, without any output response, unless the economy is in a deep recession. This is because, the firm is in a position to evaluate the demand increase correctly (not like price takers), and will consider the aggregate demand shock as a good occasion to pass on the past cost increases and put in force the new price list, taking into account also imminent cost increases.

(ii) Fixed monetary growth rule

The K-percent rule of monetarism, cited even in the standard textbooks, is most inappropriate, since it will have a destabilizing effect when confronted any major disturbance (like the oil price shock), whereas a monetary policy geared to price stability would rather have a stabilizing effect in most of these cases. In case of cyclical output decline arising from a major crop failure, or decline in export proceeds, predetermined monetary growth would lead to additional rise in domestic prices, and also increase in imports. If shortage due to crop failure is offset by extra imports, there would have been no significant change in the price level. (Although, otherwise higher producer prices due to poor crop, would partly compensate lower farm incomes; however, stabilization of farm incomes would require additional measures, anyway. And employing only one instrument-monetary growth, one cannot achieve all objectives: price stability, BOP equilibrium, incomes policy and economic growth). In the case of cyclical or secular decline in export earnings, the case against fixed monetary growth is clear-cut. As monetary expansion will continue in the face of declining output,

BOP will further deteriorate because of the rising domestic price level (relative price effect, further decline in international competitive edge) and excess demand (income effect) and as a consequence of increased domestic absorption of tradables, all of which could be quantified in a macroeconomic model.

In case of a significant change in prices of imported inputs (similar to the oil price shocks or a major change in prices of imported industrial inputs), fixed monetary growth will result in either too tight or too lax monetary position. In case of a substantial external price increase, the approach implied by the K-percent rule would be similar to the neoclassical approach regarding the oil price shock: That is, adjustment without changing the general price level, through decline in prices of other goods and services (not related to oil), which proved to be a painful and long process, with significant output decline, two-digit inflation and high unemployment levels. Whereas the correct approach, then was to let the whole economy and all prices adjust to the major price shock quickly, through a once- and-for-all inflation, change in income distribution and a temporary fall in output.

The experience of the US during the 1980s also supports the views expressed herein; Dornbusch and Fischer (1990, pp. 685-86) note that "the sustained low-inflation growth" during this period (when fiscal policy was not actively used for stabilization purposes) was largely due to the "skill in conducting discretionary monetary policy".

(iii) Monetarism experience in the UK under Thatcher

During 1979-81, in the UK supply-side measures to free up the market were taken. Monetarism under Thatcher in the UK adopted targets for money supply, abandoned discretionary demand management (fine tuning), prices and incomes policy, foreign exchange controls (in 1979), credit rationing and statutory reserve requirements for commercial banks (in 1981); however during 1979-81, the UK experienced its deepest recession since the 1930s (with unemployment rising from 4.7% in 1979 to nearly 10% in 1981), accompanied by high inflation (inflation rose from 8% in 1978 to 18% in 1980) and highly deflationary fiscal and monetary policies (which led to high interest rates (17% in 1979) and appreciation of currency also due to the North Sea oil). During 1982-85, tight monetary policy continued, discretionary policies again exercised, and recovery started in 1982 also due to a fall in exchange rate, inflation fell back to about 5% in 1983 and unemployment continued to rise (Sloman, 1990, pp. 759-60).

From 1979 on, growth of M3 along with other measures of money supply were targeted and during 1983-85, M3 target was achieved, but other measures of money supply continued to grow under Goodhart's law, which states that "to control is to distort" and "if one particular measure of money supply is targeted and measures are adopted to control it, it will cease to be a good indicator of monetary conditions; other measures are still likely to go on expanding". Monetary and fiscal expansion during 1983-1985 increased because of following two factors: (a) while the government sold large quantities of bonds to the public, "the Bank of England purchased huge quantities of commercial bills" (e.g. in the 1983/84 financial year over £ 80 billion worth) to finance industry directly (without firms borrowing from the commercial banks). Despite this injection of liquidity into the economy, M3 figures did not include the bills accumulated by the Bank of England. (b) "From 1983 onwards the record level of the public sector borrowing requirement was artificially reduced by the sale of public-sector assets (British Telecom, British Gas, etc.)". It allowed the government to pursue a more expansionary fiscal policy whilst *appearing* to maintain a tight monetary policy, (Sloman, 1990, pp. 760-61).

During 1985-88, while monetary policy was expansionary to promote growth of private sector activity, "without causing a resurgence of inflation or a run on the pound", fiscal policy remained relatively tight with fiscal drag, which resulted in increased tax revenue, and "a public-sector borrowing requirement of over £11 billion in 1983 turned into a public-sector debt prepayment of over £11 billion by 1988." "The extra money was spent largely on property, consumer durables (a large proportion of which were imported)" and stocks and shares. House prices soared, car sales boomed and sales of electrical goods, furniture and foreign holidays increased dramatically; share prices increased faster than profits and dividends, which resulted in the October 1987 stock market crash. In 1988, reduction in interest rates led to output growth, decline in unemployment, rise in inflation and the current BOP deficit and as a consequence interest rate was increased in late 1988. During 1988-90 period a stop-go monetary policy was pursued depending on inflation, the BOP and exchange rate situation; fiscal policy though influenced by supply-side economics, in 1989 and 1990 no tax cut was made despite large public-sector surpluses, because of rising inflation and BOP deficits (Sloman, 1990, pp. 763-65).

A simple analysis of effects of Thatcherism (monetarist, neoclassical) on economic growth performance and potential of the UK indicates slight improvement in actual growth, but decline in growth prospects. Annual average GDP growth rate increased from 1.7% during 1970-81, to 2.6% over 1980-90, which compares with 2.5% of the 1965-73 period. Inflation rate declined from 14.3% for 1970-81 to 6.6% for 1980-90. Private and total consumption, as percentage of GDP, however increased 2 percentage points, from 60% and 81% respectively during 1970-81 to 62% and 83% respectively over 1981-90. (Private consumption in 1990 was 63% of GDP.) Gross domestic saving declined from 19% during 1970-81 to 17% during 1981-90 and gross domestic investment from 18.5% to 17.7% over the respective periods. Declines in saving and investment indicate that monetarism and privatization have not achieved the ultimate goal, improved economic growth prospects. One also notes that, if the budgetary surplus in late 1980s were used to finance public and private investment (on loan basis), in lieu of public debt repayment, instead of consumption, much needed investment could have been boosted.

(iv) Monetarism : conclusion

Monetarists claim that for stable and high growth, predetermined rules for monetary and budget policy are called for; excessive fluctuations in interest rates cause uncertainty, make long-term planning by firms and household impossible and discourage investment. However, under inflationary conditions to prevent interest rate rise, would require further monetary expansion which would fuel the inflation and eventually would lead to higher real interest rates. Moreover when economic circumstances change, like increase in exports, faster growth of real income and/or productivity, or vice versa, a faster or lower growth in money supply would be required.

Another problem with fixed rules of monetarism is 'which target to aim at?'. Even in case of money supply targets, measures to be chosen are too many, and they don't grow at the same rate. While interest rates are stabilized, inflation/recession, BOP, exchange rate and the government budget deficit problems might emerge or get worse. If exchange rate is the target, then interest rate would be de stabilized; a rise in the world interest rates would warrant a rise in domestic interest rates to maintain exchange rate stability, while domestic recession might require a decline. Rules regarding the public-sector budget (borrowing requirement or debt repayment, surplus or balance) might not guarantee desired monetary growth. E.g. in the UK during 1987-90 money supply grew rapidly, when there was a growing public-sector surplus. And setting a target for the public-sector budget, would deprive the budget of its built-in (automatic) stabilizing property (Sloman, 1990, pp. 767-69).

Moreover ultimate goals of economic policy are economic growth(or employment) and price stability, and it might be better to aim at these final targets, than the intermediate targets, such as money supply, interest and exchange rates and the public-sector budget balance. At this juncture, it should be pointed out that, in theory and practice, without price stability, achievement of all other targets becomes more difficult. Under high or sustained inflation conditions, interest and exchange rates, public-sector budget deficit and money supply increase above targets in most of the instances. Moreover total consumption increases, domestic saving declines (also because public saving becomes negative), and domestic investment declines because of high interest rates. The crowding-out effect of public borrowing increased uncertainty about future economic conditions and variables, expectations of imminent monetary and fiscal contraction, policy reversals and mistakes, etc. - all this will be taken up elsewhere. Hence achievement of price stability deserves the top priority, for ultimate goal (economic growth and reduction in unemployment), considering also that the Phillips curve trade- off is a false presumption, even in the short-run in chronic inflation situations.

4 Supply-side economics

(i) Introduction

Supply-side policies aim at reducing the rate of cost increases. Supply-side economics recommends concentrating on supply by encouraging enterprise and competition to get more rapid economic growth. Tax cuts, increasing incentives, may stimulate output, investment and growth, if tax rates are too high or the taxation system is hindering efficient allocation of resources, effectively discouraging risk-taking, investment and employment.

Tax cuts, however, both increased budgetary deficit and caused deterioration in BOP. Optimistic supply-siders claim, that the output gains resulting from tax cuts will be so large that tax revenue will not fall (also through the Laffer curve effect; i.e. lower tax rates reducing tax evasion and avoidance), has not materialized, on the contrary budgetary deficit and inflationary pressure increased.

(ii) Supply-side views

Supply-side economists argue that, output is determined by real variables on the supply side-growth of factor supplies and changes in technology; classical saving-investment process, with interest rate playing crucial role is important; rate of return as incentive to saving and investment is important.

Feldstein and Summers argue that, combination of inflation and the US tax system has weakened these incentives, because the inflation rate raised the effective rate on corporate income and lowered the after-tax rate of return on investment and reduced incentives to save during the 1970s. They argue that taxing of nominal capital gains and interest earnings during inflationary periods result in increased effective rate on real returns and this in turn will retard saving (Froyen, 1986, pp. 488-89).

"There is abundant evidence that extreme financial instability with large and negative real interest rates interferes with saving." When the return on saving becomes negative, as observed by Mark Gersovitz, households sharply reduce their saving, or shift their saving abroad or accumulate their saving in unproductive assets (Dornbusch and Fischer, 1990, p. 740).

Overly expansionary government spending and resulting budgetary deficits financed by borrowing in the capital market in the 1970s in the US, discouraged capital formation through crowding-out effect, increasing demand for loanable funds and driving up interest rate. If deficit was financed by new money creation, this would also lead to increased inflation, which in turn, would discourage investment and saving (Froyen, 1986, pp. 490-91).

Moreover, under progressive income taxation, as nominal incomes go up as a result of inflation, marginal tax rate on wages increases and causes the labor supply curve shift to the left, giving rise to lower employment (*ibid*, pp. 492-93).

Increased government regulation of business starting in the late 1960s in the US (like pollution control, protection of worker safety) has slowed down economic growth. Because (i) complying with such regulations increased the cost of production, like a supply shock, and caused decline in the labor productivity; (ii) increased regulation has retarded capital formation (hence productive capacity creation), because investment cost of complying with regulations was heavy (Lawrence Summers estimated that in 1970, about 20% of net investment was spent on pollution control). "Moreover, proliferation of regulations discouraged investments by increasing the uncertainty about future profitability of investment projects" (*ibid*, p. 493).

(iii) Supply-side policy recommendations

In order to increase work effort, reduction in marginal income tax rates to decrease the size of 'wedge' between the real wage payment by the employer and the after-tax real wage received by the worker, and moving to a flat income tax and the substitution of consumption taxes for the personal income tax are recommended. Reduction in corporate income taxes by reversing inflation-induced increase in effective tax rate on corporate income (such as depreciation allowance at replacement cost rather than historic cost or accelerated depreciation allowances) and thus stimulating capital formation is recommended. In order to encourage saving, and avoid 'double-taxation' of saving, real not nominal capital gains, interest payments, dividends should be taxed and the inflation- induced increase in effective tax rate on the return to saving should be eliminated (Froyen, 1986, p.494).

Supply-side economist Paul Roberts claimed that the 1964 tax cut in the US, stimulated saving and investment and increased the incentives for labor supply (Froyen, 1986, p. 495). This exercise, however, can not be a legitimate evidence for the supply-side economics, because it simply redressed fiscal drag. The 1964 US tax cut had eliminated the fiscal drag, i.e. restored demand deficiency arising from the built-in stabilizing effect of the government budget in a sustained-growth era (government spending lagging behind rising tax revenue).

It eliminated the depressing effect on national income of falling government budgetary deficit, by increasing disposable incomes, which led to higher consumption expenditures, which in turn, caused national income to rise (Lipsey et al, 1990, p. 633). It rather shows effectiveness of demand-side measures, than supply-side measures; hence the 1964 US tax cut exercise substantiates Keynesian theory, not supply-side economics.

Supply-side economists argue for non-inflationary aggregate demand management, since inflation has perverse effects on capital formation, also through the crowding-out effect of budgetary deficits. Moderate supply-siders recommend avoidance of excessive stimulus through tax cuts and matching of tax cuts by cuts in government spending (Froyen, 1986, p. 495). Non-inflationary demand management is a good proposition, but the supply-side theory has, in fact, an inflationary bias as also shown by practice. Experience also shows that persistent high inflation retards private saving and investment (Turkish experience in 1980s and 1990s), but the supply-side measures have not addressed to and redressed the problem as evidence in the US (1980s) and Turkey (1980s and 1990s) shows.

(iv) Supply-side theory in practice

In the US, Reagan administration indexed tax brackets to inflation to prevent 'bracket creep', and reduced the maximum tax bracket from 70% to 50%, which aimed at increasing saving (Froyen, 1986, p. 504), but saving has not increased at all.

Reagan administration introduced accelerated depreciation allowance for business plant and equipment, increased the investment tax credit for certain types of equipment, introduced the leasing system whereby firms without taxable income could transfer their tax deduction entitlements to profitable firms, reduced non-defense government spending and government regulation in order to realize higher non-inflationary economic growth. Net effect of tax cuts turned out to be greater than expenditure cuts, even though monetary policy was restrictive; Tobin estimated the result as continued stagflation (*ibid*, pp. 505, 508).

The actual outcome in the US was not up to the expectations of the supply-siders. Output grew (-0.3% in 1980 versus 6.8% in 1984), ratios of saving and investment to national income did not change, budgetary deficit and interest rate increased, ex post real interest rate rose from 2.7% in 1980 to 9% in 1984, dollar exchange rate appreciated strongly over 1981-84, because of high interest rates net capital inflow increased, restrictive monetary policy and lower inflation rate reduced imports and encouraged exports (Froyen, 1986, p.508). Lipsey et al (1990, p. 589) conclude that "the aggregate demand effects of the policy were stronger than its supply-side effects in the short-term" "The US enjoyed a rapid recovery from the deep recession of the early 1980s, while many other industrial countries took most of the decade to recover from the recession." The government budget deficit remained unchecked by the end of the decade Effects on business investment, if any, was too little and too late However, the possibility that the supply-side reforms had major effects in improving the functioning of the economy cannot be dismissed lightly.

However any improvement in efficiency in the US economy in 1980s should rather be due to ending the two- digit persistent inflation (thanks to the monetary restraint exercised), increased foreign competition and partly to certain deregulation measures, rather than supply-side effects of incentives, since there has been no increase in saving, investments and growth. Sloman (1991, p. 815) notes that "the massive tax cuts [made under Reaganomics] were not matched by an equivalent cut in public expenditure"; nor did they produce a high rate of economic growth, the huge budget deficits plagued both the Reagan and Bush administrations.

In the UK during the 1979-82 period although a number of supply-side measures were taken, industrial output fell and unemployment rose dramatically. The 1979-82 UK recession, deepest since 1930s, was caused by restrictive monetary policy and a high exchange rate. As a consequence of this recession "much of UK industrial capacity was lost for ever". Many redundant workers became long-term unemployed and de-skilled. Surviving companies increased efficiency and introduced new technology. "The rate of increase in productivity was higher in the 1980s than in the 1960s. But to what extent this is attributable to the government's supply-side measures rather than to other factors, such as international competition and a more rapid rate of technological advance is not clear" (Sloman, 1991, pp. 823-24).

(v) Keynesian views on supply-side economics

According to Sloman (1991, pp. 812-13), "Keynesians advocate supply-side policies to improve the inflation-unemployment trade-off; to shift the Philips curve to the left. If successful, such policies could lead simultaneously to both lower unemployment and lower inflation".

James Tobin argues that lower growth rates in 1970s in the US were the result of the oil shock and restrictive monetary policy actions (mistimed monetary actions, monetary policy 'overkill'). The neo-Keynesians claim that persistent inflation (inflationary growth in aggregate demand) could not play an important role in reducing the real output growth rate; that slower capital formation can explain relatively little of the slow-down in output growth; and that slowdown in net capital formation in the 1970s is primarily explained by the low growth rate of output during that period, which caused investment demand to lag, because causation runs from output to low investment rather than in the reverse direction. And if output growth is the primary variable explaining investment, then the best way to stimulate investment is to keep economy operating at a high growth rate, because investment would be at a low level if the economy is below full capacity. Tobin states that the slowdown in business capital formation in the 1970s is the result of weak investment demand than low level of saving supply (Froyen, 1986, pp. 498, 393).

It is a fact that causation runs from output to investment; high *real aggregate demand* and demand for the products to be produced are crucial in investment decisions; high profit rates on current production or potential investment projects, even though might lead to higher retained profits, would not result in investment decisions, unless a *real permanent* growth in demand for output is estimated. However, a nominal demand increase resulting from anticyclical expansionary policies, which would likely to be temporary, would not affect even production decisions, not investment decisions.

It is well-known that, in expansionary aggregate demand policies, overshooting and inflationary bias are commonplace and as a result long-term real interest rates rise, reflecting inflationary pressure and expectations, increased uncertainty (due to expected credit squeeze in near future and downturn), and investment growth retards in response to rising long-term lending rates, uncertain or bleak business and macroeconomic prospects. Hence noninflationary aggregate demand management is a prerequisite for steady economic growth.

Sharp rise in real interest rate in 1984 indicates saving shortage and large budgetary deficits during 1980s indicate significant crowding out of private investment had occurred. Despite the direction of causation, high saving and investment rates go together (if financing at reasonable terms is not available, a viable and sound investment project is bound to be postponed), shortfall in either one causes repercussions and backlashes, which may lead to a vicious circle. (A process, starting with saving shortage as in the 1980s in the US, might end up in retarded investment growth, owing to decline in competitive edge and application of advanced technology, due to investment shortfalls in the meantime, pessimistic business and macroeconomic prospects, despite very low interest rates as in the 1990s.) In other words, high steady growth rates of income, saving and investment (also through industrial and intersectoral interdependence) prepare ground for more growth and low intermittent growth rates invite pessimism and lower growth. Moreover in the Far Eastern countries, very high growth rates coincide with sharp decline in private consumption, increase in domestic saving and investment. It is the chicken-egg problem, but there is no likelihood for fast economic output growth, when consumption is on the rise as in the US from the late 1980s onwards and in Turkey from the 1980s onwards.

(vi) Criticism of the supply-side economics

There is no conclusive evidence that high income tax rates reduce work effort, unless the tax rates are absurdly progressive.

James Tobin argues that marginal income tax rates are higher in Western Europe. Marginal tax rate in the US was stable at 18-18.8% during 1960-1975 and increase to 21.5% during 1975-80 has not reduced labor supply or labor force participation rate. Supply-side effects of income tax cuts are secondary and the demand-side (inflationary) effects dominate, and the price level increases unless there is a deep recession. Moreover tax schedules could be periodically revised to offset the effects of inflation (Froyen, 1986, p.499).

Reduction in income and company tax rates on profits and other incentives on investment lead to higher capital intensity or investments with lower rate of return. The former factor increases capital-output ratio and reduces employment effect of investment; and the latter leads to creation of financially and economically unviable private sector, heavily dependent on government subsidies, incentives, tax exemptions, low-interest-rate loans or grants, etc. for survival; one should not also neglect the fraud and corruption element in all these dealings. In Turkey, many of these enterprises are as dependent on the government budget as the state enterprises.

It is essential that the taxation system should not hinder efficient allocation of resources and competition, should not discourage saving, investment, risk-taking and employment. It is not a matter of tax cuts and tax incentives; it is overhauling the taxation system of a country from this angle.(1) Moreover a tax cut, increasing the budgetary deficit would increase inflationary pressure and crowding-out, hence will defeat the very aim of supply-siders; because it is obvious that, whereas the demand-side effects of tax cut and incentives are certain and immediate, the supply-side effects are dubious and long-term, in theory and practice.

However, it is true that high rates of payroll taxes (social security premiums) as in Turkey (34%) and in the US (15%) constitute an employment tax and effectively slow down job creation and induce introduction of labor-saving technology.

The 'double taxation' of saving argument and the view against income tax progression are not new, and the fact that in the 1950s and 1960s the West recorded high rates of growth despite these, indicates that unless coupled with two-digit inflation and fixed tax brackets, they do not impede the growth of saving, investment and the economy.

---

(1) E.g. such an analysis was conducted in my "Turk Vergi Sisteminin Ekonomik Analizi, (Economic Analysis of the Turkish Taxation System)" Ankara, 1969; and my "Katma Değer Vergisinin Ekonomik Etkileri, (Economic Effects of Value-Added Tax)". Ankara, 1973, the latter estimating possible outcome if VAT were introduced then in Turkey.

The supply-side theory brings about a very unfair and non-neutral income taxation system, which virtually exempts or taxes at very low rates all kinds of capital income and capital gains, and taxes heavily wage, rental and farm income, and profits of small- and medium-scale business (which are not literally or virtually entitled to any tax incentive or exemption). As a consequence this distorts both the income distribution and resource allocation, and leads to widespread tax evasion and avoidance; this is what has occurred in Turkey at least.

There is no doubt that increased incentives particularly to big business would lead to higher profits, but there is no automatic mechanism to transfer them into business investments, unless there exists, a lasting real growth of demand for output. In developing countries, e.g. in Turkey, profit increment is largely invested in real estate and finances capital flight, since capital grants and concessionary loans for investments reduce self-financed portion of investments, many of which would have been implemented any way (without incentives).

The supply-side incentives aiming at increasing saving directly could not be effective (e.g. slight increase in interest rate through reduction in income tax on interest income could not increase private savings or higher profits would not automatically lead to higher retained profits, etc.); and the best approach for an increased saving rate is to reduce consumption. In order to reduce private consumption, tax revenue has to be increased to cut down private disposable income, provided that revenue increment is invested and not spent on current expenditures. Assuming the effects of income and expenditures taxes, yielding the same revenue (reducing the private disposable income by the same amount), on consumption and saving are about the same, except for the interest-rate effect (2) and depending on, whether dissaving or saving households dominate (3) (Bent Hansen, 1958); theoretically one can choose either tax to get about the same effect, taking also into account the fact that for equal yield, the rate of expenditure tax must be higher than the income tax, if savings are positive. However, there are practical limits on the optimum average and maximum tax rates, from enforcement and tax evasion viewpoints (Laffer curve argument); whereas the income tax rate can safely be 25-35% on the average with a maximum marginal rate of 50-60%, the expenditure tax rate could not exceed 10-15%, particularly in developing and the reforming socialist countries. As a consequence, the scope for substitution of expenditure taxes for income taxes,

---

(2) Reduction in interest rate brought about by income tax and the effect of interest rate decline on real consumption and saving.

(3) Prest shows that expenditure tax increases saving more than income tax (A.R. Prest, "The Expenditure Tax and Economic Development", in Public *Sector and Economic Development,* Madrid, 1963, pp. 120-33; and A.R.Prest, "The Expenditure Tax and Saving", The Economic Journal, Sept. 1959.

as suggested by supply-siders, is practically limited; a modern economy needs both kinds of taxation.

There is no doubt that too many regulations and unnecessary intervention in business activities create complications for production and investment decisions; however, workers' safety regulations and pollution control are essential, and both have their pay-offs, to the firms concerned as well. The pollution control, if exercised worldwide (which should), should not affect relative profitability of firms and investment projects across countries. Until a worldwide agreement on pollution control is reached, anti-pollution measures could be partly funded by general tax revenue or a very general pollution tax on all pollutants and beneficiaries, with high rates applying to heavy pollutants).

Unnecessary regulations and red tape should be weeded out, but not only for business, but for individuals as well, which causes loss of many work-hours for employees and employers(e.g., in Turkey). Deregulation of industry is taken up elsewhere.

It seems that the basis of supply-side theory is persistent high-inflation and the supply-side measures are largely reactions to this phenomenon. Hence the best solution to these complaints lies in eliminating inflation, not in the supply-side incentives recommended, which make two-digit inflation permanent, if fully exercised as in Turkey in 1980s and 1990s, or cause inflationary pressure, as they did in the US where a moderate dose of them being applied during 1980s.

Moreover, there is no supply-side remedy to many of the problems created by high-inflation. In high inflationary conditions, it is not practically possible to calculate income and profits correctly, this subject is well-treated in the accounting theory, long before the supply-siders raised it. The problem for a firm could not be solved by revaluation of fixed assets only, inventories also have to be revalued; in fact, all assets and liabilities have to be revalued using appropriate price indices; it is similar, but more complicated than the deflator problem of national accounts. Hence the issue is intractable even for large firms, and small-and medium-scale firms and households could not handle this problem at all and always overestimate income, hence consumption is encouraged at the expense of saving, in general. Hence the solution lies not in revaluation but ending inflation.

(vii) Conclusion

The main justification for the supply-side economics, except for the deregulation cause and provided that the taxation system does not distort efficient allocation of resources, lies in persistent inflation and it aims at remedying damages of inflation by incentives. However, the supply-side incentives, if significant, perpetuate inflation and this provides justification for generous incentives to the business.

In practice (e.g. in Turkey), the supply-siders and proponents of the Phillips curve trade-off join forces in the cause of inflation and bolster the inflation lobby. While the latter oppose fighting inflation by restricting the aggregate demand growth, the supply-siders oppose income tax reform (aiming at an enlarged tax base, removal of numerous exemptions, and a lower average tax rate applicable to all kinds of income) and anti-inflationary policies, since reduction in the inflation rate would both lower the size of incentives (particularly of interest subsidy) and remove the main justification for the supple-side cause and incentives.

In Turkey during 1980s and 1990s, supply-side policy recommendations have been fully and consistently implemented; VAT has been introduced and income taxes on profits, dividend and interest income have been virtually reduced to 7-10% on the average, generous cash investment incentives on grant and loan basis (comprising 70% of investment expenditure) have been paid [4] and numerous incentives for exports are granted. The result of this campaign has been not steady growth, but steady, *sustained inflation at 70-80% p.a.*

There is no easy solution to the modern economic problems like stagflation and increased level of equilibrium unemployment, attempting non-economic solutions like supply-side incentives (which were rightly called by former US president Bush as voodoo economics) to shift the long-run aggregate supply curve free of charge, are rather damaging and ineffective.

The government could play a pivotal role in boosting private investments and achieving a high secular economic growth rate, not by offering generous incentives to industry (writing virtually a blank check), effectiveness and efficiency of which could not be controlled and determined, but by investing more, directly or indirectly, in human capital formation, R&D and infrastructure, and in high-technology and key industries, on a joint-venture basis, where ideology allows.

5 Incomes policy

(i) Experience of the UK

In the 1950s and 1960s, the UK tried incomes policies to control inflation without any success, and empirical studies verified that these policies had been

---

(4) In fact the capital grant element, excluding the land allocated also virtually free of charge amounts to 60-64% of the investment cost. Because, in persistent inflation at the rate of 70% p.a., a 5-year-term loan, with 1 year grace period, contains a subsidy component equal to 71% of the original loan amount, if the interest rate is 30% and 82% if the interest rate is 10%. (These are the actual terms and conditions of such loans in Turkey.)

ineffective. During the 1972-76 period, increased budgetary deficits and excessive monetary growth led to entrenched high inflation, which was attempted to be treated by incomes policies (direct controls on wages and prices), under the wage-cost push theory. The inflation rate fell only when monetary restraint was enforced toward 1977 (Lipsey et al, 1984, p.710).

(ii) The US experiences

The US experiment with mandatory price and wage controls during 1971-74 aimed at controlling inflation (which was 5% then) as an anti-inflationary device, while monetary and fiscal policy became expansionary to lower the unemployment rate, which was 6% then. Empirical research showed that, the policy was ineffective on wages, but price inflation was restrained by about 2 percentage points, through reduction of profit margins. However, when the controls were lifted in early 1974, profit margins were restored; hence price controls only delayed the required adjustment, the post-control 'price bubble' erased this gain, and by mid-1975, "the price level was about where it would have been with no controls". Hence the wage-price control program did not have a lasting effect on the inflation rate. Moreover the "post-controls price bubble", coinciding with the OPEC oil price shock and the 1974 recession contributed to "the Great Stagflation of 1974-1975" (Lipsey et al, 1984, p.710; Froyen, 1986, p. 606).

In the late 1970s use of incomes policies, as part of a disinflation program was proposed, when both the inflation and unemployment rates were high. A disinflation program based solely on restrictive aggregate demand policy, would be costly in terms of foregone output and higher unemployment. If income policy were used, in concert with restrictive aggregate demand policy in such circumstances, output and employment loss would be lower. It is argued that had income policies in concert with restrictive aggregate demand policies been used in the disinflation program in the US in the early 1980s, the cost in terms of high unemployment would have been less (Froyen, 1986, pp. 602-603, 606).

(iii) Conclusion

Incomes policies are not substitute for restrictive aggregate demand policies in curing inflation. Particularly incomes policies cannot be used to control inflation while expansionary policies are used to increase employment. The early 1970s experience in the US provides adequate evidence to this effect.

Turkish experiences during 1954-60 and 1975-79 with price controls, exchange rate and interest rate (overly negative in real terms) anchors to control inflation, while expansionary policies were pursued to stimulate the economy, ended up with catastrophic results including high inflation (in 1980 over 100%), extreme shortage of goods and critical inputs, declining GDP and a severe BOP crisis.

Prices and incomes policy should supplement demand management policies, not replace them. The government may convince workers to accept lower wages if it reduces taxes or increases benefits; but then aggregate demand will not change. If incomes policy continued beyond 6-12 months, sufficient flexibility should be built in the system to allow for productivity increases.

6 Structural unemployment, potential output and cyclical policies

(i) Rising equilibrium unemployment in industrialized countries

In the early 1980s unemployment in the industrial world rose to record levels and in the early 1990s unemployment has been still high in the US, the UK, Germany, France and Italy. These high unemployment levels are explained by structural unemployment, defined as a mismatch between the structure of the labor force and the structure of the demand for labor.

Some of the current unemployment in Western Europe may be due to overly high real wage levels attained by powerful labor unions (Lipsey et al, 1990, p. 750). Declining industries also cause structural unemployment.

There has been a steady increase in the structural unemployment, also termed as the equilibrium unemployment in the industrialized countries. In the US, the average unemployment rate was 4,5% in 1950s, 4.8% in 1960s, 6.2% in 1970s and 7.5% during 1980-1988. During the 1970-88 period, unemployment showed a rising trend and cyclical fluctuations as well, the lowest rate was 4.9% during 1972-73 and the highest 9.7% in 1982. In France, the average unemployment rate was 1.7% in 1960s and 9.1% during 1980-87 (in 1987, 10.8%); In West Germany 0.65% in 1960s and 6.1% during 1980-87; in the UK 2.7% in 1960s and 10.6% during 1980-87 (Lipsey, et al, 1990, p. 754).

In the UK, Keynesians argue that *equilibrium unemployment increased* because of following factors (Sloman, 1991, pp. 805-806): (a) Competition from abroad, introducing new products often of superior quality and produced at lower cost (e.g. textile) had led to the decline of many older industries. (b) "Shifts in demand away from products of older labor-intensive industries to new capital-intensive products". These changes led to a large rise in structural/technological unemployment, since labor is not, geographically and occupationally, sufficiently mobile, and whose manifestations are regional decline and unemployment.

Hysteresis models (lagged effects of the actual unemployment, insider-outsider models, existence or lack of work experience and on-the-job training) may explain part of the unemployment in Western Europe, through the actual high rate of unemployment and powerful labor unions. In the US, technological changes (increased use of robots and computer-based processes) and increased openness of the economy (increasing integration with the world) have reduced employment, the former by eliminating many assembly line and clerical jobs (Lipsey, et al, 1990, pp. 756, 758). It seems that, the West, when confronted with harsh realities of increasing unemployment and slow economic growth, even in textbooks, now do not accept optimistic maxims or sweeping conclusions such as 'every technological change creates as many jobs as it destroys' and 'division of labor, comparative advantage and free trade lead to the best of the worlds possible and maximizes outputs, incomes and jobs worldwide or in all participant countries'. If the US faces severe problems in redeployment of its labor force, resources and factors of production, after major technological changes and increased import penetration, then it is obvious that the developing countries and the reforming socialist countries will face much severe problems in these respects. This is not a position against neither free trade (open economy),nor technological change, but only to take cognizance of problems that may arise with the full-fledged application of these rules without any reservation and without estimating effects of changes realistically, as happened in Turkey in the 1980s and 1990s.

Certain industries are on decline in the West because of economic and technological changes, and increased competition from within and without; ad hoc government support programs to salvage them are costly losing battles, because the West could not compete in its own market, in labor-intensive and mature industries, with the fast-growing developing countries of Far East, which produce better quality products at lower cost.

The nature of the problem is not temporary, it is structural; it is long-term decline of these industries and continuing shift away from labor-intensive processes in manufacturing; hence cyclical policies could not help. Observing the structural nature of the problem, some economists recommend regional development policies (see, e.g. Sloman, 1991, p. 556) or supply-side incentives. This is curing symptoms, because increasing unemployment, industrial and regional decline are all consequences of slow economic growth and fluctuations. Even in the case of declining industries, problem arises because resources released by these industries are not attracted and employed by growth sectors, because there is no dominant growth sector. Continuous economic stagnation (slow growth and frequent business cycles) hinder innovation and technological breakthrough, and quick expansion of growth sectors. The real remedy to the problem lies in ending the economic stagnation and moving to sustained growth.

In lieu of wasting time and resources in cyclical policies and salvaging industries which should be phased out, the West could instead improve its economic performance by promoting skill-intensive and high-technology industries and sectors, and increasing its overall economic growth rate. The West, however, could give a respite to its declining industries by means of a new Marshall plan, directing these industries to exporting or moving to the reforming socialist countries and other developing countries.

Another promising sector for economic transformation of both reforming socialist countries and of the West (to the post-industrial age) is development of services sector, whose steady growth and employment creation could only be achieved by sustained growth of the economy.

In the US, "the increase in employment in service industries during the past two decades exceeded the total employment in the manufacture of durable goods". Over the past two decades employment in services and retail trade (transportation, communication, eating and drinking, health care, education, hotels and entertainment) grew dramatically in all industrialized countries (Lipsey, et al, 1990, p. 350).

(ii) Nature of the problem: labor surplus

It has to be recognized that the problem confronted is not structural unemployment, defined as mismatch between the skill-content of labor demand and labor supply, but permanent unemployment defined as excess of labor supply over available gainful employment opportunities (determined by the productive capacity of the economy); i.e. it is mismatch between labor supply and the productive capacity.

On the basis of casual observations, it can be claimed that in labor surplus economies, unskilled and semi-skilled labor supply curve is a flat horizontal line (with infinite elasticity) with intercept at minimum wage level (if it could be enforced) or at bare subsistence cost/minimum cost of living. Hence increase in nominal average wage or minimum wage rates if not coupled with increase in marginal product of labor would rather reduce gainful employment on impact, as against the Phillips curve supposition, unless wage inflation immediately led to compensating price increase and matching increase in marginal value-product of labor (and then no change in unemployment). Employment can increase only when expansion in the productive capacity or abnormal (temporary) increase in construction sector output (which seems always have spare capacity or can readily expand its capacity) materialize, which causes the labor demand curve shift to the right.

The solution to 'permanent unemployment' lies not in Phillips curve trade-offs, but in increasing saving and investment rates in the countries suffering from it. It is interesting to note (according to the World Bank data) as a percentage of GDP, gross domestic investment was 33% in Japan, 32% in Malaysia, 37% in Thailand, 37% in Korea in 1990, as against 16% in USA in 1990, 22.8% in Turkey (1980-89). GNP growth rate in 1990 was 5.6% in Japan, 9% in Korea, 11.6% in Malaysia, 11.3% in Thailand, 0.9% in USA and 1.9% in Turkey (1991, the 1986-91 average 5.4.%).

When vicious circle emerges, it is difficult to break it, as the vicious circle of poor countries (low incomes and low savings perpetuate); now in some industrialized countries, low growth rates of income lead to lower investment rates, vice versa; since one can build on strength, this vicious circle can only be broken by increasing investment rate.

(iii) Potential output issue

It is claimed that the neoclassical assumption that capital remains fully employed always is not correct, since average capacity utilization rate varies over business cycles; plants may run on three shifts during booms, but only one shift during recessions. However there is a normal capacity operation (1,2 or 3 shifts) of any plant which defines the potential output. Marginal plants (from viewpoints of technology, marketing, etc.) might work less shifts than profitable ones, always.

With advances in transportation and communications, globalization in capital and product markets, it is now more certain that national, if not regional markets are in equilibrium and if certain industries do have idle capacity, that is because they are not competitive, given exchange and interest rates and the level of protection; in order to rescue these inefficient industries to change monetary and fiscal policy and disrupt macroeconomic balances, and create uncertainties, is a very costly exercise, frequently employed in the last two decades with long-lasting harmful effects and also without achieving their very aim, i.e., reducing unemployment.

A stagflation, even following a supply shock, is an indication that the economy is at its new, declined potential output level. The problem is structural; monetary expansion will only lead to more inflation.

When the economy is at the potential output level, any temporary demand shock is bound to end up largely in price increase, than output increase. In competitive sectors, any demand increase (shift of demand curve) is bound to increase supply, but output price as well rise, as the industry moves up along the supply curve, unless all costs increase simultaneously (which is unlikely) and shifting the supply curve immediately. Over time, however, the supply curve will shift up (and then it will be realized that the relative price of the product has not changed) and output will decline to its original level.

In monopolistic or oligopolistic markets, industry's response to a temporary demand shock would be increased prices, without any change in output. An oligopolistic industry with a saucer-shaped supply curve (prevalent in modern manufacturing industry), adjusting prices infrequently, will consider the time opportune for making pending price revision, taking into account also cost increases to follow the demand shock in the planning horizon. Output or productive capacity will be expanded when the demand increase is considered real and permanent.

All this can be summed up as follows: A post-war market economy is normally at its potential (full-capacity) output level, because of profit maximizing behavior and preoccupation of governments, fiscal and monetary authorities with full employment, except for imperfectly competitive markets (where profit maximization might result in some idle capacity). There is *always excess demand as evidenced by strongly positive inflation rates which are always prevalent.*

Any stagflation claim has to be carefully checked, because output declines in most cases can be explained by:

(a) Plants made redundant or obsolete, because of competition coming from domestic firms employing advanced technology or producing better and cheaper substitutes.

(b) Competition from abroad: "Many economists believe that increased international competition over the past two decades has contributed to increased structural unemployment in the US" (Lipsey, et al, 1990, p. 748).

More open economies of 1980's and flexible exchange rates, increased uncertainty and foreign competition in national economies. Appreciation of currency in the developed world, (as US and UK experienced in 1980s) related to capital movements and interest rate changes (not related to international competitive power, BOP performance or domestic/international inflation differential) and exchange rate anchor employed in developing countries (e.g. in Turkey in 1990) to reduce inflation rate (which resulted in an overvalued currency), caused national sectors confront unfair foreign competition, leading to output and employment losses. In this case remedy is simple, maintaining appropriate, competitive exchange rate will solve the problem.

(c) Firms reverting to their normal full capacity level operations, after the expansionary phase is over and when demand has abated a bit, as a consequence of the shift of the aggregate supply curve due to cost increases.

(d) Real wage unemployment and consequent decline in output: e.g., Lipsey et al (1990, p. 750) note that some current unemployment in Western Europe may be due to excessively high real wage levels realized by powerful labor unions. According to the UK government, the main cause of unemployment in Britain and in the rest of Europe in 1990 was excessively high wages demanded by the monopolistic trade unions (Sloman, 1991, p. 492).

(e) Close-down of unviable new firms or plants set up, under optimistic expectations and forecasts during expansionary phase, when pessimistic expectations set in and monetary policy is tightened.

In all these cases standard anti-stagflation policies (more expansion or supply-side measures) are not only useless, but harmful as well. Continuation of price rises, along with declining output also indicates that excess demand still exists.

Under these circumstances, the government policy should rather be neutral, if not favoring long-term growth through indicative economic planning and/or expenditure and promotion programs for infrastructure, human capital formation, technological development, industrial development on a competitive basis, and regional development all funded by sound financial means, i.e. without increasing monetary growth or budgetary deficit.

The short-term aim of the government policy should be achieving price stability, not reducing unemployment or achieving potential output, (any way, experiences of many countries show that they have not achieved these aims), by appropriate monetary policy and maintaining fiscal discipline (budgetary deficit, if any, should be reasonable, definitely not having any crowding-out effect). The size of government, share of public consumption in GDP, does matter; but more important is its means of financing.

All the points raised herein before become more relevant when one considers the method of calculation of the potential output in the US: The potential output being calculated using a fixed natural rate of unemployment, which was 4-4.5% in 1960s, 5-6% in 1980s (Dornbusch and Fischer, 1990, pp. 17, 441) only takes care of labor market conditions, not existing productive capacity, its utilization and changes in these due to declining industries, technological changes, changes in demand pattern and increased import penetration.

(iv) Night-shift operations

Although studies on capacity utilization in manufacturing industry and night shift operations (salient features of which are summarized below), indicate cyclical variations, the extent and magnitude of these variations in context of overall economy (i.e in terms of effects on total output and employment) could not be measured, but only estimated, due to data problem. "Paucity of suitable time-series data" on a national basis inhibit research on cyclical behavior of shift work, even in the US, because shift-employment data pertain to full-time production workers in establishments with at least 50 or 100 employees in selected metropolitan areas (Mayshar and Solon, 1993).

Rates of capacity utilization in manufacturing vary among industries and countries, and over business cycle. While in industrialized countries average sectoral utilization rates reach or exceed 90%, in developing countries 70% capacity utilization is normal (because of managerial and organizational inefficiencies, technical, marketing, procurement, financing, etc. problems, and constraints). During periods of foreign exchange shortages, capacity utilization further declines; infant industries, new, inefficient or inefficiently-run plants may have low rates of utilization. In developing and reforming socialist countries, many plants are inherently bound to underutilized their capacities because of the said problems, which are due to non-demand factors, hence capacity utilization rates can not be lifted by aggregate demand increase.

There is no unique measure of capacity utilization by industries. Capacity utilization is measured from capital hours, production-worker hours, energy consumption or output (Shapiro, 1993).

In the short run, although the stock of physical capital is quasi-fixed, "the effective stock of capital should not be regarded as fixed if, when labor increases, it goes onto a previously inoperative shift. Labor that works the late shift will have at least as much capital as labor working days" and the workweek of capital increases as a consequence; and "much of the apparent cyclicality of total factor productivity is accounted for by variation in the workweek of capital". Day shifts, however, tend to be larger than night shifts. "The workweek of capital is highly procyclical". "In cyclical industries, such as motor vehicles, the swing in capital hours is as much as 50%" (Shapiro, 1993).

"When a downturn occurs, the second shift is the first to be closed, and the proportional decline in output is greater than in employment". Because of late-shift pay premium, fewer workers are employed on the late shifts. Moreover the daytime employment of overhead production workers, provide essential support services for the night shift. Empirical evidence indicates that variation in night-(late-) shift employment is greater than cyclical employment variation; more specifically, "the late-shift of cyclical employment variation is about twice its share of the level of employment. When full-time employment declines during a recession, about one- half of the decline for manufacturing production workers and one-third of the economy wide decline occur on late shifts". In an upturn, the newly initiated night shifts operate at a lower employment level than the day shifts and total output increases in greater proportion than total employment. The fact that, the discrete changes in the number of operating shifts are an important means of varying output, is well documented for several industries in the US (Mayshar and Solon, 1993). These discrete changes in shift operation obviously affect capacity and capital utilization.

This evidence and modelling by Mayshar and Solon indicate that in a cyclical recovery "total output increases in greater proportion than total employment". This result indicates that expansionary or contractionary policies policies rather work out their effects through night shift operations and their impact on output is greater than on employment, which implies decline in the capital/labor ratio, and which in conventional studies interpreted as short-run increasing returns to labor or inputs. (Robert Hall showed that short-run increasing returns imply that output price exceeds its marginal cost and there are possibly increasing returns to scale and hence the firm has market power- Shapiro, 1993).

Shapiro (1993) taking into account proper measure of capital services by incorporating the workweek of capital into analysis (through capital by its workweek) and employing a Solow production function for gross output, whose inputs comprise net capital, energy, materials, production-worker hours and non-production-worker employment, found that there are no short-run increasing returns to total inputs. Shapiro, however, does not interpret this result as evidence against Hall's inference, cited above. The existence of increasing returns (excess of price over marginal cost) depends on the magnitude of shadow cost of increasing capital utilization, i.e. incremental cost of using capital at night (night shift premium paid to labor and depreciation of capital in use due to increased wear and tear, and inadequacy of maintenance and repair with night-shift operation).

In a nutshell, expansionary demand policies, if effective, will rather increase output than employment; incremental cost of using capital at night based on average shift premia is quite low (Shapiro, 1993); fewer workers are employed on night shifts than on day shifts (Mayshar and Solon, 1993), hence additional labor cost of night shifts is low. All these findings founder the basic premises of the Phillips curve, which is based on significant profitability increase arising from lagged adjustment of real wages to price inflation, which induces firms to hire extra labor and expand output. Because the actual operational mechanism of increasing (or decreasing) capacity utilization and expanding output is completely different from what described under the Phillips curve analysis:

(a) Marginal cost of extra labor hired for night shift is high, because of night shift premium, which will further be increased by wage inflation. The fact that wages never lag behind prices, even when price and wage controls are strictly enforced, as the early 1970s US experience shows, exacerbates the employment picture, furthermore. And as a consequence fewer workers are employed on night shifts.

(b) The most important consideration in deciding night-shift operation is increasing the utilization of existing capital stock and the possibility of achieving increasing returns to scale, not any wage cost advantage (which is negative in fact).

(c) The possibility that these firms might have market power with cyclical increasing returns, implies that imperfect competition is involved; hence response to aggregate demand change will not be automatic, but discretionary and the response might well turn out to be more price increase than output increment.

On the other hand, if there are no increasing returns to inputs due to night shift operation, the firms concerned will consider night-shifts as a temporary arrangement and inconvenience, which will be opted for when it is absolutely necessary (e.g. for maintaining the market share, for accelerated utilization and depreciation of obsolete plants, etc.).

(v) Stagflation and cyclical policies

It is a fact that business cycles do occur because of acceleration principle, sectoral shifts (arising from supply shocks like oil-price shocks, rapidly moving exchange rates, defense conversion, shifts in government spending, technological breakthrough, etc.) and monetary and fiscal policy reversals. Allowing, not blocking (as in the case of the oil-price shocks of the 1970s) adjustment to these shocks and extraneous events and pursuing policies conducive to rapid adjustment process are pivotal in overcoming or ironing out business fluctuations therefrom. On the contrary, monetary and fiscal policy geared to stability of exchange and interest rates, or promotion of social welfare in the abstract or in a vacuum, or increasing ungainful employment, might rather accentuate fluctuations and worsen eventual outcome. Reverting from the peak of business cycle (overheated economy) to normal output and economic conditions, implying decline to the potential output level (from overutilization of capacity [5] to full capacity utilization), which might also entail lagged cost-push price increases in imperfect competition markets, might well be interpreted as a puzzling stagflation.

If coincidence of inflation and unemployment were solely due to excess or deficient demand, then by adjusting aggregate demand to the potential output level, the economy would have operated without inflation and unemployment. However, particularly in modern economies inflation and unemployment frequently coincide and there is some underlying non-demand inflation, and some equilibrium (frictional, structural, regional, sectoral) unemployment, which cannot be tackled by policies which include supply-side measures, as well and whose dominant effects are on the demand side. In this sense, all anti-

---

(5) E.g. Bresnahan and Ramey (1993, p. 215) define capacity overtutilization in the US automobile industry as the period when overtime hours are involved.

cyclical policies fall under this category and are simply palliatives which do not address the core of what is termed as stagflation issue, and only deal with symptoms and side issues.

Under the circumstances, expansionary policies in general fail to generate a sustained recovery, unless by coincidence are accompanied by some favorable extraneous technological, external, etc. developments and end up either in recession with its attendant costs, lost output, unemployment, business bankruptcies and foreclosed mortgages, or in tight monetary position which entail the latter two outcome.

Discretionary anticyclical policies cause more harm than good. They may cause or accentuate fluctuations; they may even create artificial booms which are bound to go bust eventually. In these cases, more important are lasting damages arising from waste of resources, increased consumption and repetition of unfulfilled expectations. Under expansionary policies, many unviable firms are set up, unfeasible investments are made and consumption is boosted through incentives, superficial buoyancy and increased availability of financial resources. Because of repeated failures and busted booms, enterprises might even be hesitant to respond to genuine signals for increased output (risk aversion); this situation is further exacerbated by unpredictable exchange rate fluctuations and in high-inflation countries, by uncertainties about future and impossibility of forecasting basic economic variables and main macroeconomic indicators, on top of these.

Hence, anticyclical policy is a wasteful exercise; fluctuations of actual income during post-war era mostly indicate variations of potential income because of external shocks, technological improvements and changes in demand pattern due to changing tastes, government expenditures, etc. Hence stagflation, in most instances reflect inflationary gap. Best policy to deal with cyclical variation of income is concentration on growth policies (increasing saving and investment), in price stability.

7 Oil price shocks

(i) Views and policies exercised

Views and policies regarding the oil price increases in 1974/75 and 1979/80 differed. For some countries it took a long time to adjust to high energy prices. Some economists argued that oil price increase in 1974 would not change the average price level, since increase in oil-related prices would cause other prices to fall, provided monetary policy is not accommodating.

An inflationary recession (stagflation) affected all industrialized and oil-importing developing countries after the 1974 oil price shock.

Some countries like the US and Italy chose to accommodate the supply shock arising from the 1974/75 oil price increase, by expanding aggregate demand during 1975-80 period to offset the decline in output and employment. This policy resulted in higher inflation (annual average was 8.9% in the US and 16.3% in Italy during 1975-80) and depreciated currencies compared to the countries which chose to have little or no monetary accommodation, like Switzerland and West Germany, with average inflation rates of 2.3% and 4.1% respectively during 1975-80 (Froyen, 1986, pp. 539, 541).

As a consequence of oil price increase (4-fold) over the 1973-75 period, in the US real GNP fell by 1.8%, price level rose by 18.9% and unemployment increased from 4.9% in 1973 to 8.5% in 1975 (Froyen, 1986, p. 248).

The stagflation resulting from the 1973/74 oil price shock is explained by the upward shift of the aggregate supply curve due to increased energy and other input prices. Keynesians argued that if expansionary monetary and fiscal policies, to shift the aggregate demand curve were not exercised, output decline and price increase would have been greater.

Inflation over the 1973-75 period in the industrialized and oil-importing countries could partly be explained by these corrective expansionary policies.

Oil price increases in 1973-74 and 1978/79, accompanied by other commodity price increases, caused both cost-push inflation and recessions in 1975 and 1979-81, all over the world, as governments followed restrictive monetary and fiscal policies to fight against inflation and the BOP crises.

(ii) Stockman's theory: shortage of critical inputs

Alan Stockman's (1988) real business cycle theory rightly posits that shocks to technology and changes in the availability of key products, such as oil or critical intermediary inputs, would cause the vertical long-run aggregate supply curve to shift back and forth causing identical fluctuations in national income; and if the aggregate demand were then stable, price level would also change when output fluctuates. Stockman model has explained the recent behavior of the American economy very well and has been able to analyze spreading of shocks to the different sectors of economy over time.

Three observations can be made in this respect:

(a) Because of preoccupation with the short-term/cyclical policies (monetary or incentive nature of quick-fix solutions), authorities and academics lose sight of longer term/growth (investment versus consumption) aspect of economic policies.

(b) Stockman's empirically verified theory shows the importance of critical inputs (foreign exchange shortage, as well, works in the same manner) in the explanation of stagflation phenomenon, and suggests that monetary and fiscal expansion could not be a remedy for stagflation and that specific policies designed to redress the critical shortages (focusing on the shortage issue directly) would be helpful instead.

(c) What seems to be a novel experience in the industrial economies (shortage of critical inputs experienced during the oil crisis) is commonplace in developing countries and in the socialist and now reforming countries. The shortage of critical intermediary inputs due to BOP difficulties (occasional or due to inflationary policies) leading to a decline in national income and economic output restoring to the potential level when shortages are removed, are frequently experienced in these countries.

(iii) Explanation of oil shocks by Keynesian and neo-classical theories

Keynesian aggregate demand management policies aim at stabilizing output and employment. Whereas, the new classical economics, incorporating the rational expectations concept, claim that anticipated changes in aggregate demand can not affect output and employment; hence they recommend a noninterventionist government policy.

Keynesian criticize the new classical theory on grounds that (a) it cannot explain the prolonged and severe unemployment experienced in the industrialized countries after 1974; (b) the contractual nature of labor market leads to wage rigidities and resultant involuntary unemployment.

The Keynesian theory failed to achieve proclaimed goal (reducing unemployment by increased monetary growth and government budget deficit) during 1973-1984 in the US (see, e.g. Froyen, 1986, p. 350-51).

The Keynesian view on this episode of high unemployment and inflation is that the supply shock caused by the large increases in the world price of oil and other basic commodities, led to higher prices and reduced output and employment (see, e.g. Froyen, 1986, p. 351). This supply shock explanation of stagflation would have been appropriate, if monetary and fiscal expansion had not taken place or had not led to a demand shock (which should have restored the potential levels of output and employment). In fact, in the US. over the 1973-84 period, average annual growth rates of inflation and monetary growth were 7.9% and 6.8% respectively and accumulated government budgetary deficit amounted to $860 billion in current prices (with an average annual deficit of $96 billion), while average annual unemployment rate was 7.25%.

Contradicting the neo-Keynesian (Phillips curve trade-off) view, growth in the US was higher during 1980-89, when there was relative price stability, than in the 1970-81 period with an average 8% inflation. Similarly Japan, reducing its inflation rate from 9% to about 1% over the same periods, was able to raise its growth rate to 4%. Among the industrialized countries, the UK, with the highest (two-digit) inflation, fared worst in the 1970s and managed to increase its average growth rate from 1.7% to 2.6% over these periods by lowering its inflation rate (Table 20.1).

Table 20.1
Inflation and GDP growth rates: 1970-1989 (percentages)

	1970 Inflation Rate	1981 GDP Growth Rate	1980 Inflation Rate	1989 GDP Growth Rate
UK	14.3	1.7	6.6 (1)	2.6 (2)
US	8.1	2.9	4.0	3.3
Japan	9.3	2.6	1.3	4.0
W. Germany	5.0	2.6	2.7	1.9
Korea	16.6	9.0	5.0	9.7

(1) 1981-90.
(2) 1981-90.

Source: World Development Report, IBRD, 1991

The Monetary-policy induced disinflation of 1981-82 in the US ("a well-publicized restrictive monetary policy", "probably as well anticipated as such a policy is ever likely to be") although reduced inflation from its double-digit levels at the start of 1980s to 4-5%, resulted in the most severe recessions since the Great Depression, with unemployment rate reaching 10.8% in November 1982 and GDP declining 2.6% in 1982. Hence it did not turn out as costless in terms of output and employment effects, as claimed by new classical economics, since its analysis of anticipated monetary policy is most relevant in this case. As Robert Gordon observed, the 1981-82 recession should have been as fatal to the Lucas-Sargent-Wallace rational expectations-market clearing models (the new classical macroeconomics) as the Great Depression to pre-Keynesian classical macro-economics (Froyen, 1986, p. 352). Costless disinflation, is not possible, because existence of inflation and inflationary gap implies that GDP is beyond its potential level, and removal of inflationary gap by whatever means, calls for, returning to lower potential level, more definitely so after a major supply shock, when the level of potential output has virtually declined.

Thomas Sargent however, still claimed that "in the new classical framework, ...under very stringent conditions", with a policy "unlikely to be reversed", i.e. with a disinflation policy *credible* to the public, costless disinflation was possible. One requirement for a credible disinflation policy is that along with monetary restraint, fiscal discipline (budgetary balance) must be maintained at present and in the future. When rational economic agents predict growing fiscal deficits, as was projected in the 1980s, then they expect monetary authority to reverse course in the future and increase monetary growth to help finance the budgetary deficits, and as a consequence the disinflation policy would not be credible and hence not costless (Froyen. *ibid*, pp. 352-53). It should be pointed out that for economic growth, monetary restraint (which guarantees price stability) and fiscal discipline (eliminating crowding-out, increases savings and investment) are essential; i.e. the public sector budget balance is also very important, but not on expectational grounds as maintained by Sargent.

In fact, although budgetary deficits increased rapidly in 1980s, as predicted by rational economic agents (accumulated government current budget deficit totaled $1,675 billion-annual average of $167.5 billion-over 1981-90 and accumulated net government borrowing totaled $1,179 billion over 1986-92-annual average of $168.4 billion), price stability and slightly higher average growth were achieved in the US, over the 1980-89 period, contradicting expectations of monetarists.

However, growth rate declined from 2.9%, the average for 1970-81 and 1981-90 periods, to 2.2% during 1981-92 and to 2% in the 1986-92 period, as consequence of declining trends of saving and investment and increasing trend of consumption. In fact total consumption, as a percentage of GDP, in the 1981-90 period increased on the average 2 percentage points compared with the 1970-81 average, gross domestic saving declined 2.5 percentage points and gross domestic investment 2 percentage points. During the 1986-92 period, as a percentage of GDP, private consumption increased 6 percentage points on the average, over the 1965-73 period, while general government consumption declined 4 percentage points, domestic saving 2 percentage points, and investment 1 percentage point. As a consequence in 1992, total consumption was (85% of GDP) 5 percentage points above the 1950-60 average, domestic saving and investment each were 5 percentage points below, at 15% of GDP, (as against the Japanese rates of 33% for each in 1990).

Hence one concludes that, monetarism, by itself, through price stability, did not and could not create the economic environment conducive to saving, investment, dynamic private entrepreneurship and economic growth as stipulated by the neoclassical theory.

(iv) Supply shock, stagflation, consequences of alternative policies

The *real* effects of macroeconomic policies will occur and emerge at firm and household level. Hence, effects of a major supply shock can be derived from an analysis at enterprise level, by studying the effects of a substantial rise in relative prices of raw materials and transport charges on the processing industry and plants spread all over the world. As a consequence of the substantial rise in their unit costs, some of these plants will be unprofitable and close down for good, and even the total output of the industry could decline, if total demand falls in response to rising relative prices of products. This fact means that the potential income has virtually declined overnight, due to the shock. By redeployment of resources left idle, (which is not free of charge, requires extra investment), part of the lost output and employment could be recovered in other plants and industries. The oil price shocks affected in the same manner, only their effects were much more widespread and severe, many industries hit hard. And *redeployment of idle resources required extra investment effort, a big jump in investment* (as a percentage of GDP), *which materialized nowhere; and hence* there occurred a big jump in unemployment instead.

A recent empirical study by Bresnahan and Ramey (1993) on the US automobile industry, basically verifies these views: As maintained by David Lilien, Fischer Black, Steven Davis, and Bresnahan and Ramey, sectoral shifts are major are cause of business fluctuations. Sectoral shift is defined as "any event that raises desired output and employment in some sectors and lowers them in others". "Events such as the oil shocks of the 1970s, exchange-rate fluctuations, [defense conversion] and shifts in government spending", not only affect directly the composition of economic activity, but "affect the level and the dynamics of output and employment as well". In a slowly functioning labor market, after a sectoral shock, the reallocation of workers across sectors takes time. Moreover, "not only sector-specific human capital, but also complementary physical and managerial ... capital must be reallocated or recreated" to create new jobs elsewhere; and "the sluggishness in the adjustment of capital", may slow adjustment of labor. "The sunkness of capital and the shortage of engineering knowledge are the determinants of the macroeconomic response to sectoral shocks". Oil-price-induced shock to the composition of demand would limit industry-wide capacity utilization due to short-run rigidities in supply (hence changing composition of demand would lower aggregate output level in the short run); and in intermediate run, capital and labor would be reallocated to new demand conditions. E.g. the oil shocks of the 1970s, by changing composition of desired sales rapidly led to substantially lowered capacity utilization in the US automobile industry, due to "short-run rigidities in physical and engineering capital". In the intermediate-run, capacity misallocation was redressed by shifting capacity among size classes, however, adjustment of vehicle designs took longer (Bresnahan and Ramey, 1993).

An initial accommodating monetary expansion is required, because otherwise, due to sticky wages and prices, other industries (not hit hard) also would be forced to reduce output and employment. At this point, the Keynesian approach is appropriate, as the neo-classical view would cause a more severe recession than necessary as observed in the US and the UK in the early 1980s. Effects of alternative policies would be as follows:

(a) Continuous monetary expansion (sustained inflation) along the neo-Keynesian theory and as exercised after the 1974-75 oil price shock, would exacerbate and delay the required structural adjustment process and redeployment of idle resources by causing high inflation, increasing uncertainty, and leading to the BOP crisis in some countries as observed in 1970s.

Compared with the 1965-73 period, during 1970-81 period, gross domestic investment as a percentage of GDP (annual average) increased by only one percentage point (to 19%) in the US, did not change in the UK, declined both in West Germany and Japan, which seems to be a secular decline (domestic saving, as well, declined).

(b) Under non-interventionist, neo-classical monetarist policies, although price stability and higher economic growth (should be considered short-term) is achieved (except for West Germany), domestic saving and investment will decline, as observed in the 1980s.

Compared with the 1970-81 period, in the 1981-90 period, domestic investment as a percentage of GDP (annual average) declined in Japan (from 33% to 30%), in West Germany (from 23.5% to 20%), in the UK (from 18.5% to 17. 7%) and in the US (from 19% to 17.8%); in the UK and the US, domestic saving decline was greater (2 and 3 percentage points respectively). In view of these figures, the rising or persistent unemployment in the West, and the recession of early 1980s are not surprising.

(c) Any palliative like delaying the required price adjustment through sustained inflation, subsidized oil prices, subsidies to troubled sectors without estimating correctly long term prospects, as exercised in Turkey, would further increase consumption and waste, worsen the BOP and delay the structural adjustment as experienced in Turkey, during these periods.

(d) In the light of these, the correct policy for a severe supply shock would be, after the initial accommodating monetary expansion, monetary restraint, fiscal effort and other measures to raise domestic saving and investment, industrial and regional policies to address the sector and regions hit hard in an unwasteful and realistic manner (making benefit/cost analyses, aiming at creation of viable enterprises), retraining schemes, promotion of growth and employment creating sectors on a selective and viable basis, and some indicative economic planning.

Comparison of the experience in the 1980s with those of the 1970s, shows that the governments have acquired some experience in dealing with a major supply shock, at least by allowing the necessary price adjustments to take place quickly. The reforming socialist countries should follow suit in this respect. In particular, the reforming countries should prefer the once-and-for-all rise in price levels, suggested under 'the method', which cannot be termed even as a temporary inflation, to continuing high inflation.

(v) Precedent of oil-shock stagflation and lessons from this experience

It should be pointed out that a few countries had overcome oil price shock quickly by making required adjustment quickly, while many others pursued wrong policies and suffered heavily. Similar outcome awaits the reforming socialist countries.

After the oil price shock of 1970s, countries which resisted the required structural adjustment by not allowing market mechanism to work out effects of oil price increase and endure a once-for-all additional increase in the rate of inflation by some 5% at most (the share of oil input in sectoral outputs on the average was 1-2% then in many countries, according to the input-output tables; and allowing for extra percentage points for feed-backs through sectoral interdependence and from transport/freight sector, one gets at most 5%) (6) suffered the longest and severest stagflation (it was not a coincidence that these countries were also in a weak economic position and were also bogged down in stagflation, supply-side economics and the Phillips curve trade-off arguments and their practice); whereas the heavily oil-importing countries of Far East and a few European countries successfully managed the oil crisis (which were, again not by coincidence, on a strong growth path by making the required *adjustment quickly*; e. g. in Korea real GDP grew by 9% in 1974 and 8% in 1975 after 15.2% rise in 1973; in Ireland real GDP grew at 4% in 1974 and 6% in 1975, after 12% rise in 1973 and continued to grow until 0.2% decline in 1983. But, Turkey subsidized oil price for a long period, financed oil imports by borrowing petro-dollars on short-term, kept over-valued exchange rate pegged to reduce open inflation, increased budgetary deficit (subsidy on oil) and monetary growth, in order to maintain economic activity, government and development expenditures at higher levels and GDP growth rate increased to 8.5% in 1974 (from 4.2% in 1973), 8.9% in 1975 and 8.8% in 1976; this process ended up with the collapse of the foreign exchange system in mid-1977 on and of the economy in 1979 and 1980,with declines in GDP.

The difference between the Korean and Turkish experiences after the oil price shock lies in the fact that while Korea achieved high growth rates by increasing domestic saving, Turkey achieved them by supply-side incentives, subsidies and expansionary policies without additional saving effort.

---

(6) In fact, increase in the inflation rate in 1974 over 1973 (consumer price index) was 2 percentage points in Austria, 3 points in Luxembourg, 5 points in the US, Ireland and Belgium, 6 points in France, 7 points in Italy, 11 points in Japan and 22 points in Korea.

Karaosmanoğlu (7) observes that "if economies are not competitive and do not adjust to changing circumstances", jobs will be lost and living standards will decline. If adjustment is delayed, domestic financial discipline will be lost, competitiveness will further decline and external debt increases. Adjustment policies and programs that aim at only increasing efficiency and productivity are not sufficient, they should "include investment in human resources, infrastructure and institutions". Moreover, "many of the problems sometimes attributed to adjustment were present long before economic reforms began", namely food shortage, increasing unemployment, rising inflation and per capita income decline.

(vi) Preoccupation with cyclical policies and standardized prescriptions

"In the 1970s economists turned their attention more to the problems of inflation and the business cycle that were besetting the economy" (Dornbusch and Fischer, 1990, p. 736). This much preoccupation with cyclical problems and policies precluded attention to growth policies and has virtually retarded economic growth worldwide.

When the first oil price shock hit the world in 1973-74, economists and policy makers knew nothing how to tackle with it, since supply shocks were a new phenomenon. In the US the unemployment rate went above 8% at end 1974; in 1975-76 by expansionary (accommodating) monetary and fiscal policy recovery from recession was achieved (Dornbusch and Fischer, 1990, p. 498).

This view reflects the main issue with the applied economics: In case of an apparently new problem (like the oil price shock), new theories are developed and standardized prescriptions are applied all over the world. Whereas a major devaluation of currency introduces much severe and general supply shocks into an economy, and if successful a demand shock thereafter. In the past many countries had successfully resolved severe BOP and over-valued currency problems by devaluation at high rates. Hence the oil price shock could have easily been dealt with if (a) relative prices were allowed to adjust, also with the help of accommodating (limited expansion) monetary policy initially, so that the substitution effects of oil price increase on consumption and production could work out themselves, (b) required devaluations, in countries facing BOP difficulty as a consequence were carried out quickly, and (c) monetary and fiscal discipline were exercised thereafter to achieve macroeconomic equilibrium even sacrificing some output and employment, in the short run.

Many oil-importing countries, however, because of deliberate policy choice under the influence of the then fashionable Phillips curve trade-off and the availability of petro-dollars on a short-term basis, pursued expansionary

(7) World Bank Managing Director, Speech at a seminar, WBN, Nov 5, 1992.

policies on the pretext of avoiding a stagflation, subsidized oil consumption and use, and borrowed heavily from without or within on short term. And as a consequence, many countries faced severe BOP crises and stagflation deepened.

All this is because of the same wrong prescription shaped under the illusive Phillips curve trade-off was being applied in all these countries. Economics can be considered a science, within its models with certain assumptions; there is, however, no standard prescription for practical problems of applied economics applicable everywhere with differing circumstances. In chapter 22, where practical experiences of several countries are broadly reviewed, this aspect is well observed. After the oil-price shocks of 1970s, some countries succeeded brilliantly on economic growth, unemployment and price stability fronts, employing suitable methods tailored to their needs, while others failed disastrously by blindly subscribing to the then fashionable theory.

Similar experience is now emerging in the transformation of the former socialist economies, on the pretext that economics of transformation has not advanced far enough to deal with present problems. Under the circumstances, the rational approach should have been not to implement policy decisions until their consequences were estimated albeit roughly.

8 Crowding-out effect

Increased government expenditures or tax cuts financed by borrowing would raise interest rate and increase user cost of capital, and as a consequence crowding out of private investment expenditures would occur. An investment tax credit, however, might offset crowding out effect of personal income tax.

Financial crowding-out occurs when extra government spending is financed by borrowing and thus investible funds are diverted from private sector and deprives the private sector of the finance necessary for investment. As a consequence interest rates will go up. Although Keynesians argue that interest rate will not increase, if money supply is increased simultaneously; and this will not be inflationary provided that there are idle resources (and then resource crowding-out does not take place). In practice budgetary deficits are commonplace and regular in many countries, and deficit financing is exercised even when the economy is at the natural unemployment level, which implies that both resource and financial crowding-out occurs, along with interest rate increase. When crowding-out occurs, fiscal expansion becomes ineffective, because increases in government expenditure will lead to corresponding decreases in private expenditure; and as a consequence national income would not change, if not decline.

Keynesians argue that even when money supply is fixed, the crowding-out effect on private investments would not be significant because any rise in interest rates or decline in private investments would be small (because businessmen are more affected by the market prospects for their products than interest rates and would invest when demand is expanding, even if interest rates are rising). Whereas monetarists claim that interest rates will rise significantly and sizeable crowding-out will occur.

In an open economy with floating exchange rates crowding-out effect would be greater: Higher interest rates will attract more funds from abroad, which will lead to an appreciation of the exchange rate, which in turn will reduce exports and increase imports; and national income would decline by an amount equal to the increase in trade deficit; i.e. crowding-out in an open economy, will not only cause higher interest rates, but will also lead to an appreciation of the exchange rate through increased capital inflow, which will in turn worsen the trade balance (Sloman, 1991, p. 740). This analysis, however, neglects the inflow of foreign capital, which would add to the investible funds and allow for a greater level of investments, also by stabilizing interest rates (at least limiting further increase), in the short-run. In the long-run, unless expansionary fiscal policy and hence inflow of capital continue, interest and exchange rate, will revert to their initial levels, but increase in external debt remains.

In countries which suffer from chronic shortage of domestic savings and investments (as revealed by very low saving-to-income and investment to-income ratios, like Turkey, UK and the US), financing of public investments and even government expenditures by resorting to internal and external borrowing, is one of the main causes of economic stagnation and sizeable unemployment termed as structural. And these are the same countries which increasingly have recourse to *inflationary or consumption-oriented expansionary policies,* although they are dubbed differently (supply-side economics, Philips trade-off, non-discretionary and non-interventionist pure monetarism, Reaganomics or Thatcherism.(8) They all boil down to inflationary measures, such as tax cuts, ineffective incentives to industry, inadequate expenditure cuts, stop-go nature monetary and fiscal policy, and futile attempts of international trade wars (to export inflation and/or unemployment), all of which have the common feature of frustrating long-term growth prospects, while trying to solve short-term disequilibria, also through crowding-out effects of budgetary deficit financing.

The experience in the 1980s in the US showed that the inflationary impact of the supply-side economic policies are for sure, whereas their supply-side effects are dubious and long-term, if any (see, e.g. Lipsey et al, 1990, pp. 587-89). Despite these facts, the supply-side of economics is very much on the economic policy agenda, as well as the Philips curve trade-offs. While under the expectations-augmented short-run Philips curve analysis, a sustained

(8) In late 1980s, the UK while eliminating budgetary deficit, even reduced the public debt; debt repayments, however, to a great extent boosted private consumption (Sloman, 1991, p. 764).

inflationary gap only leads to accelerated inflation and the long-run Philips curve is vertical, i.e. there is no trade-off between inflation and unemployment.

Common feature of these new schools of economic theory is that they are based on facts, sound observations and plausible analysis, but the causal link between the analysis and policy recommendations is not strong or sound, even sometimes conflicting with the analysis.

An example is moderate monetarists policy recommendations: *Moderate Monetarists* claim that a sudden tight monetary policy in *high inflation situations,* may temporarily lead to a recession; hence "sudden extreme policies should be avoided;" a gradual reduction in the growth rate of money supply is recommended; supply-side policies should be employed to reduce natural unemployment and increase labor mobility. Supply-side policies aim at reducing the rate of cost increases, through restraining monopoly influence on prices and incomes (wage control and regulated prices) and by giving tax incentives, grants for R&D, training of labor and investments in up-to-date equipment (Sloman, 1991, pp. 559, 507).

The recommended supply-side measures would increase the budgetary deficit by reducing tax revenue and increasing expenditures, and since the money supply would also be in creasing, albeit at a lower rate, and as a consequence, (a) inflationary gap will increase, (b) relatively tighter monetary policy and crowding-out effect of the increased budgetary deficit would push interest rates to higher levels, which in turn would reduce private investments, except those directly are benefiting from incentives offered. Hence, economic growth rate will slow down and inflation rate will not be lowered. This is, in fact, what has happened in Turkey during 1975-1993.

Whereas the root cause of chronic high- inflation is generally persistent large public sector deficits (also since monetarists assume that the economy is inherently stable, because private sector expenditure functions are relatively stable and all inflations are caused by excessive monetary expansion and would not occur without it and even supply-shock inflations can not go on indefinitely unless they are accommodated by monetary expansion-as acknowledged by Keynesians as well), the right policy would have been decreasing the budgetary deficit under a credible stabilization package (which will also help redress inflationary expectations) which would directly reduce monetary growth and reduce inflation. Moreover, Latin American experience with high inflation suggest that only quick, drastic solutions are feasible and effective and that gradual methods fail and prolong high inflation (Vegh, 1992).

Since Kuznets data and later estimates suggest that the average propensity to consume (APC) measured in relation to real disposable income is relatively constant (e.g. in the US, APC was 0.92 in 1960, 0.89 in 1970 and 0.92 in 1980; Froyen, 1986, p. 370), in order to reduce consumption and increase domestic saving, tax revenue has to be increased, provided that increased revenue is earmarked for financing investments and expenditure on human capital formation.

Financing current account deficit of the government budget by borrowing leads to increase in consumption at the expense of investment. Assuming average consumption propensity is 0.9, $1 deficit on current account, would lead to transferring $1 of private saving to public consumption, reducing investment by $1 on impact. Whereas financing this deficit by taxation would reduce private saving and investment by 10 cents; hence investment increases by 90 cents compared with deficit financing.

It can be argued that gains in these cases (increased investment) are obtained at the expense of consumption, which is the ultimate aim of economic activities. One can, however, put forward the counter argument that, by allocating part of the tax revenue to increased education and health expenditures, both consumption, albeit public, and expenditures of developmental nature, i.e. investment in human capital (which is and empirically turned out to be pivotal to future economic and employment growth) will be boosted, as against inessential private consumption. (Moreover, the taxation system will be reformed in the process with a view to creating a just and fair system, which is a dire need, in many developing countries, particularly in Turkey).

Suppose that APC is 0.8 in an economy and general government consumption amounts to 20% of GNP and the government capital budget constituting 4% of GNP is financed by borrowing (of which 1 percentage point is foreign borrowing and equal to current BOP deficit). These data imply a private consumption of 64% of GNP and total investment of 17 of GNP (of which 13 percentage points are private investment). If the government budget deficit is financed by additional taxation (amounting to 4% of GNP, implying a 20% additional tax effort), then private consumption reduces to 60.8% of GNP (declining by 5%), BOP deficit vanishes and investment rises by 13% to 19.2% of GNP (of which 15.2 percentage points are private investments, which have risen by 17%) and with a capital-output ratio of 5, GNP growth rate increases from 3.2% to 4.3% as a consequence, assuming a Harrod-Domar type growth model.

In this context, the Keynesian argument that crowding-out will not affect business investments (because businessmen will invest when market prospects are good even if interest rates are rising) should be evaluated. Availability of investible funds will determine ex post investments; with crowding-out private investments can not exceed 13% of GNP, whereas without crowding-out effect they can reach 15.2%. In fact, market prospects will look good when the economy is in a boom, i.e. when financial and resource crowding-out and demand pressures have already emerged. As a consequence some investments will not materialize or be completed because of the ensuing credit crunch (in high-inflation countries credit control might follow), too high interest rates (in high-inflation countries, prohibitive in real terms due to rising risk premium, etc.) or expected economic downturn. Evidence in developed economies does not show that supply-side measures or anticyclical expansionary policies have led to a long-term increase in domestic savings or investments. In a high-pressure economy, supplementing domestic saving shortage by foreign borrowing has limits as experienced in the most developed economy (the US), and increased foreign borrowing does not bring about an increase in domestic investment. In developing high-inflation economies, outcome has been even worse; high inflation, high lending rates of interest and overgenerous supply-side incentives have resulted in increased dollarization, capital flight and real estate investments, substantial default on concessionary loans funded by the government, decline in own-financed portion of private investments, decline in small-and medium-scale business investments, unbearable interest burden of public debt on the government budget and all this has not led to any increase in domestic saving and investment, as percentage of GDP (the Turkish economy in 1980s and 1990s).

Another side effect of crowding-out is increase in the overall capital-output (C/O) ratio, as a result of replacement of private investment by public investment. Taking a C/0 ratio of 3 for private sector and 10 for public sector, which are in line with reality, and employing the figures of the hypothetical example, the overall C/0 becomes 4.7 with crowding-out and 4.5 with extra-taxation. Effects of excessive government borrowing on domestic saving and economic growth in several countries are looked into in Chapter 22.

The West could have mobilized resources through reducing private consumption and government expenditures and increasing taxation, both to solve its unemployment problem (called structural but virtually permanent) and always precarious macroeconomic stability, swinging between recession and inflation. The equilibrium unemployment level which used to be at 1-2% rose dramatically after the oil price shock in the West and approaches 10% from time to time. Apparent cause of this phenomenon is the oil price shocks, the real cause, however, is the saving shortage and prevalence of consumption-induced growth over investment-induced growth; the oil price shock only became instrumental in revealing the real problem and weakness, i.e. inadequate economic growth, and by leading to higher capital/labor ratio made it intractable.

In lieu of taking palliative measures like monetary and fiscal policy shifts and reversals, tax cuts and incentives financed by government borrowing, interest rate adjustments (which move hot money across borders), and indulging in supply-side and Phillips trade-offs theories, the West could solve its problems and help with the rehabilitation of the reforming socialist economies and their integration into the world economy (and thus ensure world peace and welfare) by launching a major saving/investment drive and a new Marshall plan.

9 Gradual versus fast reduction of inflation

Dornbusch and Fischer (1990, pp. 534-38, 580-82), assuming straight line aggregate supply (AS) an aggregate demand (AD) curves and parallel shifts of these curves, show that, under a gradual disinflation strategy (in which monetary growth gradually declines), although inflation declines slowly, the cost in terms of output and employment losses is less than in the strategy aiming at a quick reduction of the inflation rate (which they dub as the cold turkey strategy).

However, by changing slope and curvature of AD and AS curves (say by making AD less steep and AS more steep) and allowing for unparallel shifts of them, one can get insignificant difference in output and employment loss between the two strategies. In fact, the linearity assumption would be valid only if linear functions are obtained empirically or small changes are analyzed (because only then linearization is justifiable), of which neither is the case; and since the analysis starts from a high-inflation-potential-output position, the aggregate supply curve could not be flat in the neighborhood.

Moreover, duration of adjustment and stabilization have to be taken into account in such comparisons of costs. The gradual approach takes 3-5 years on paper, but is of indefinite period in practice. Under the fast strategy, let output decline reach 8% in the first year (which is on the high side), output is restored to its potential level in the second year and normal growth resumes in the third year (which are quite realistic assumptions); and in the gradual strategy output decline averages 2% p.a. over the stabilization period (which can be realistically taken as 5 years), hence output loss amounts to 10%, excluding sacrificed normal economic growth attainable, if stability achieved, over this period.

In practice, Turkey solved high inflation and BOP problems in 1946 and in 1960 employing the fast strategy quickly and successfully; whereas during the 1977-1993 period, several gradual programs were put into effect without any success (only leading to output and employment losses in years of implementation). Following 1946 and 1960 devaluations and stabilization programs, price stability was achieved immediately. The consumer price index (CPI) increased by 4.3% in 1946 and declined by 6.6% in 1947 (against 24.2% average annual increase during 1940-45) and GNP growth rate was 31.9% in 1946 and 4.2% in 1947 (against 6.6% average annual decline during 1940-45, GNP rose by 10.9% p.a. during 1946-53 and CPI increased by only 2.0% p.a.). After the 1960-61 stabilization program, CPI increased by 2.3% in 1960 and declined by 0.7% in 1961 (against 15.2% annual increase over 1954-59) and GNP growth rate was 3.4% in 1960, 2.0% in 1961 and 5.7% on the average p.a. during 1961-69, as against 4.0% annual average during 1954-60.

Dornbusch and Fischer (1990, p.582) claim that "there is a choice to be made between a high-growth recovery that rapidly reduces unemployment and a slow-growth recovery that cuts into inflation, but at the cost of sustained unemployment", This view neglects the growth effect of successful stabilization programs. In theory short-term and long-term effects can be separated, but in practice economic growth (increase in potential output) is realized as the stabilization program proceeds and then rapid disinflation does not entail more unemployment or rapid reduction in unemployment (by means of economic growth) does not increase the inflation rate. This would be the actual outcome of successful fast stabilization programs, as experienced in the Turkish cases cited above.

The credibility aspect of the gradualist strategy (program may be abandoned if a change in political authority takes place or produces more unemployment than expected) is generally underestimated (see, e.g. Dornbusch and Fischer, 1990, pp. 536-37). As a matter of fact, the gradual approach is opted for when the political authority is weak and particularly incapable of taking and implementing the complete set of required stabilization measures, e.g. tax reform and eliminating the budgetary deficit quickly, as the US, Argentinian and Brazilian experiences in 1980s (*ibid*, pp. 539-42) and the Turkish experience during 1976-1993 indicate, and the public is fully aware of this shortcoming, hence the credibility of such a program is nil even at the very beginning. Moreover, the probability of policy reversals in the gradual strategy is very high and this fact is also known by the public at the onset of the program.

Furthermore, more important than the pace of stabilization, is its contents and effectiveness, and the gradual strategy allows the government to disguise basic weaknesses and virtual ineffectiveness of the program by phasing it, i.e. by scheduling easier parts in earlier phases (like sale of profitable public enterprises) and more difficult measures on later stages (tax reform, reorganization of the civil service, restructuring the public enterprises); and these weaknesses, however, do not go unnoticed by the public. Nowadays fashionable phased stabilization programs focus on privatization and play down genuine reforms, like tax reform and streamlining the public sector.

On top of these the long-term contracts issue makes a phased program incredible. Because, even when the stabilization program is credible, the inflation rate will not be reduced, if the changed expectations are not incorporated into wage and other long-term contracts, and if the economy has an overhang of past contracts containing past expectations. Hence it is theoretically easier to lower the inflation rate, when there are no long-term contracts in the economy. In a hyperinflation, long-term contracts disappear and as a consequence a credible policy will have rapid effects (Dornbusch and Fischer, 1990, p.538). However, with the phased program long-term contracts with price escalation clause will re-emerge, and they will not necessarily be mutually consistent and geared to the official inflation estimate. Hence, as Dornbusch and Fischer assert, even if the stabilization program itself (its contents, etc.) is credible, inflation will not end.

Dornbusch and Fischer (1990, p. 694) do not accept Thomas Sergeant's evidence that the four hyperinflations of the 1920s (German, Polish, Austrian and Czechoslovakian) "ended quickly and at a relatively low unemployment cost because government policies were credible", as conclusive, particularly since "it does not clearly show that the hyperinflations did end with relatively little unemployment". In evaluating costs of ending hyperinflation, focusing on short-term costs of disinflation only, is misleading. One should rather compare overall economic performance of the country with and without hyperinflation in medium to long run. There is no doubt that hyperinflation in these countries ended quickly. In the medium to long run, benefits of ending hyper inflation far outweigh any short-term costs, judging from the economic performance of these countries thereafter and comparing them with those of Latin American countries where high-or hyper-inflation persist indefinitely with declining per capita incomes, capital flight, permanent external debt crisis, etc. The crux of the hyperinflation issue is that, only countries which could make a fiscal reform and enforce fiscal discipline (successful privatization like in Argentine presently can only provide a temporary palliative) could end hyperinflation.

Inflation in many countries like Turkey, Latin America continues because the public or the authorities still accept advantages of inflationary financing on faith and exaggerate the costs of disinflation; and modern economic theory has not nullified these convictions. The Phillips curve trade-off was in use in theory and practice in Brazil long before its discovery, in the form of fostering economic development and job creation through inflationary financing of budgetary deficits. In mid-1960s a new justification for this theory was found on grounds that Brazil had exhausted possibilities of import substitution and export expansion, and as a consequence a new era of inflationary financing started for inward industrialization purposes; whereas the basic economic/financial problem of Brazil then and now is the absence of an adequate taxation system. The Republic of South Africa followed suit in the mid 1980s launching an inward industrialization program, along with generous export and investment incentives. The aim was to create new growth centers and generate new demand in the Black population for goods which could be produced by the existing industry (which claimed to have idle capacity, neglecting imported input requirements of that output) through expansionary fiscal and monetary policy, while at the same time facing a severe BOP constraint (because of economic and financial embargo imposed which was restricting its exports and capital inflow). Despite an average annual inflation rate of about 16%, GNP stagnated during the 1980s in this country.

10 Conclusion

Gradual stabilization programs have, in fact, failed worldwide and are bound to fail because of two reasons:

(i) Inflationary expectations could not be broken under gradual approach; moreover expected reduction in the rate of inflation could not be synchronized among economic agents or made consistent.

(ii) Governments unable to take or implement full measures required to end inflation (like achieving the budgetary balance, reducing short-term external borrowing, e.g. like Turkey in the 1980s and 1990s) opt for gradual approach, and all economic agents are fully aware of this fact from the very beginning and the required measures could never be implemented in the course of phased program as anticipated; in fact, in many instances the *real* purpose of the program is not to end inflation as declared, but rather prevent high-inflation to transform into hyper-inflation and domestic currency wholly replaced by dollar (complete dollarization).

11 Balancing the government budget: taxation, incentives policy and privatization

After the oil shocks of 1973/74 and 1978/79 except for the Far East and some Western European countries, the world economy suffered heavily, especially in countries, that had not allowed their economies to make full adjustment to the external shocks quickly in the marketplace and instead have tried and are still trying some 'quick-fix,' type solutions through Phillips curve trade-offs, supply-side economics, pure monetarist approach, consumption-oriented anti-cyclical policies disregarding or overlooking long-term economic growth aspect, privatization of profitable public monopolies, increasing public debt and external borrowing heavily, frequent devaluations without exercising monetary and fiscal discipline, excessive tax and investment incentives, etc. In these countries macroeconomic equilibrium were distorted significantly with every attempt of the governments to redress the problem.

Obvious examples are the non-growing developing countries, the reforming socialist countries and in the developed world, the US and the UK.

Turkey is one example, which could have been another Taiwan or Korea now, if sound economic, financial and monetary policies were pursued in the last two decades. Instead, however, every new American economic policy invention and recipe, before being tested, has been readily applied for two decades and adjustments to open free market economies still have not been completed, and in this process virtual abandonment of income and corporate income taxation on the pretext of supply-side economics and heavy external borrowing have occurred with resultant high-inflation and low economic growth. Turkey could have quickly solved the high-inflation problem of the last two decades by a tax reform and replacing lax and spendthrift fiscal and monetary policies by exerting fiscal and monetary discipline. Even now, macroeconomic balances would quickly stabilize, if ineffective and wasteful supply-side incentives and subsides (innumerable tax incentives and rebates, tax holidays, in real terms strongly negative low-interest-rate loans almost to all investments and to many economic activities, capital grants offered only to large-scale investment projects) were rescinded and the income tax on an enlarged base and at lower rates could have been enforced effectively, as was done in late 1940s,1950s and 1960s.

Aside from the adverse effects on the government budgets, these measures have created a private sector which is as heavily dependent on the Treasury for survival as the public enterprise sector, a pitfall that Kornai (1990) has drawn attention.

The worldwide experience shows that removing a tax is politically much easier than repealing a tax privilege or exemption and levying a new tax is an impossible task. These irreparably damaged taxation systems are the lasting effects of the supply-side theory (or voodoo economics). Turkey in mid- 1980s introduced the value-added tax (VAT) replacing the sales tax, it was rather welcome by businessmen, since it gives the opportunity to retain part of the tax collections, automatically included in retail prices (casual observations suggest about one third is retained by traders and not paid up to the Treasury).

Latin American countries and Turkey, unable to cope with the high-inflation problem, by appropriate means (namely an effective tax reform and fiscal and monetary discipline), in 1980s considered privatization as panacea, attempting also to balance budgets by sales proceeds; but except for Argentina in the 1990s under President Mennem, privatization has not been successful for obvious reasons. Even successful, privatization offers only a temporary relief to ailing government budgets and without an effective taxation system, budget deficits will emerge again after the profitable state enterprises are sold off.

For loss-making state enterprises, privatization seems apparently as the only solution; however no genuine private enterprise will be interested in buying them except for asset-stripping. Hence enterprise reform and restructuring, which first of all should make enterprises immune from government interference with employment, pricing, production and investment decisions have top priority, and then looking into possibilities of making them viable operations through merger, joint-operations, management and technology back-up or renting should follow. (This practice is widely exercised in China.)

The governments which proclaimed privatization as the top priority, have not abrogated the privilege of interference and nationalized more industries and banks (through rescue operations) than privatized (e.g. the 1980-1992 period in Turkey). The state banking sector is another field ripe for corruption (mounting bad debts), where privatization seems politically unfeasible.

Regarding privatization, one should be realistic and pragmatic, quick privatization is practically impossible and also politicians do not want to part with privileges and opportunities for personal or political gain offered by state enterprises; and hence enterprise reform and restructuring, along with gradual privatization, seems to be the only option or the second best solution.

12 Monopoly and oligopoly, regulation and deregulation

(i) Oligopoly, monopoly and deregulation

Oligopolistic firm administers its price; when costs of inputs increase, the cost curve of the firm will shift up, and the firm will raise its prices and lower outputs. When demand changes, it will first change sales at administered prices; change in prices will be decided later, depending on whether the demand increase is temporary or not. So far it is assumed that the demand increase is real; because if the demand increase is only nominal, arising from expansionary monetary policies, not sales and output, but administered prices will be adjusted.

Oligopolistic firms, along with monopolistic competitors and monopolies, in general have flat (saucer-shaped) cost curves, (Lipsey et al, 1990, p.280) with installed capacity based on the normal demand. With flat cost curves, firms adjust output rather than price as demand fluctuates cyclically. Inflationary cost increases are passed on through periodic price increases.

Oligopolistic prices are sticky in the short term, because of saucer-shaped cost curves and because it is costly for multi-product firm to change its list prices. If mark-up is frequently revised and equals the profit maximizing one for normal capacity output, then profit maximization is achieved.

For oligopolistic firms operating in highly or perfectly contestable markets (i.e. where sunk cost of entry is not large as to constitute a barrier to entry), the threat of potential entry works as actual entry and compels existing firms to compete intensely among themselves and prices and output come close to competitive equilibrium levels.

Vertically integrated firm, which controls the supply of an input, could charge competitors such a high price for the input so that they cannot compete with it in selling the finished product.

Many large firms which have potential market power, do not exercise or abuse it. Moreover, if entry and exit costs are low, monopolistic and oligopolistic firms have to consider potential competition. Furthermore in the long run consumers benefit from improved products at lower costs and eventually lower prices.

Since explicit agreement (collusion) is prohibited in many countries, oligopolistic firms maximize joint profits by tacit cooperation and do not engage in price competition. As empirically verified by Jo Bain and Herbert Simon, tacit cooperation or implicit collusion will be higher, when there is a small number of sellers, the market is growing (not contracting), there is a dominant firm, the entry barrier is high, product differentiation is not exercised or nonprice competition (advertising, product differentiation, etc.) is absent or limited (Lipsey, et al, 1990, pp. 276-77). It is interesting to note that, even when tacit collusion is not involved, consumer welfare will be increased only when there is a great number of actual or potential sellers (low entry barrier), otherwise there will be no price competition and the market will not approach competitive equilibrium. Because in case of contracting industries, price competition will be short-lived and will end when main competitors are wiped out; in case of product differentiation consumer will pay higher prices (including high advertising costs) largely for not real but advertised quality and product differences and in case of nonprice competition joint profits are not maximized but costs (largely advertising and product differentiation) are increased and prices are left unchanged (hence neither profits nor consumer welfare is maximized).

Empirical evidence shows that, differentiated products are produced by a few very large firms, more or less competing, and they earn large profits without attracting new entry (Lipsey, et al, 1990, p. 271). And when profits of satisficing firms are not threatened, it is less likely that they will invest in innovation.

The point made here is not for replacing a genuinely oligopolistic markets by monopoly; because this is neither possible, nor efficient. (Aim should rather be to increase competition by lowering entry barrier, and get oligopolistic market approach competitive structure.) In fact, mergers, which is a move in that direction, have not materialized their proclaimed benefits.

In the UK empirical evidence show that mergers have not realized claimed advantages, namely reduction in costs and increased research and development budgets, and they have generally not been in the public interest (Sloman, 1991, p. 444).

The aim is to show disadvantages of replacing a monopoly by a duopoly or oligopoly with limited number of sellers, through deregulation; because then there will be neither price competition, nor greater innovation; on the contrary the latter would decline, unless the firms really compete.

In the 1980s as a result of an increased role in the marketplace, the rate of economic deregulation and privatization has increased. Moreover, it was claimed that regulated utility companies might not be interested in innovation and unregulated firms may introduce innovation. In the US, economic deregulation included financial institutions, natural gas producers, long-distance telephone companies, airlines, trucking and some other industries. Economic regulation (prescribing entry requirements, rules of operation and determining prices) is exercised only in cases of natural monopolies, such as electric power company, where effective competition is not possible and economic regulation becomes a substitute for competition.

With deregulation of prices and entry, many companies, which were protected from competition under regulation, have gone out of business in the US, which is interpreted as an indication that regulation, had encouraged inefficiency. Another similar evidence was the fact that, in the late 1960s, unregulated airlines charged on the average 45% less than did regulated interstate airlines. Airline deregulation in the US has been considered successful since (average load factor) has increased, travelers have saved considerably through lower fares (estimated at $10 billion in 1985) ; but mergers have also increased which created some monopoly power (Lipsey et al 1990, pp. 310-313) . The long-run effect of deregulation, however, remains to be seen.

In 1982, one of the largest monopolies in the US, AT and T was broken up and it divested itself of all local telephone companies. It is claimed that wire telephone communications are no longer a monopoly, given radio and satellite communications and that regulation, as applied to telephone services, penalizes efficiency and innovation (growth). However, in many countries, natural monopolies like telephone, electricity, gas, pipelines and railway services are run by a state enterprise because of major economies of large-scale production (that characterize natural monopolies) and resulting efficiency. In the US vertical mergers are not opposed under the antitrust policy, however, breaking of AT and T entailed cutting of vertical integration. Although it is not likely that this unique move would lead to competition and more innovation, it would be interesting to investigate its effects empirically, which would have a great bearing on breaking up of numerous monopolies in the reforming countries.

When a natural monopoly is privatized along with deregulation, then competition is bound to be ineffective and through profit maximization by monopolists, consumers will be exploited. For example, in the UK, privatized British Telecom (BT) and British Gas have virtually no competitors. Hence critics of privatization have claimed that consumers will be exploited; e.g. in the BT case, despite price formation rule of 4% below the inflation rate, because rapid progress in technology will allow greater cost saving (Sloman, 1991, pp. 463-64).

In Turkey privatization of the Anatolian part of the Istanbul distribution branch of the electricity power monopoly, TEK, has led to higher prices and other charges, to the dismay of consumers, but there has been no improvement in service or any increase in investment.

(ii) Monopoly versus oligopoly cum collusion

The theory and policy against monopoly is presented as *unregulated monopoly versus perfect competition* or oligopoly with fierce competition, whereas the real choice is between *regulated monopoly versus unregulated duopoly or oligopoly* with a few firms, hence comparison should rather be made between the later two. Although antitrust policies also aim at preventing collusion and while regulation of monopolies have been quite successful, performance in anti-collusion policies have been very poor, and *collusion always exist in duopolistic and oligopolistic markets, as indicated* by *prevalence of non-price competition* (advertisement, product differentiation, etc.).

In the EC legislation, collusive behavior and anti-competitive practices, such as jointly fixing prices, limiting output, discriminatory pricing and sharing out markets are banned and fined heavily. However, even in most obvious cases collusion could not be proven in practice. In the UK and in Turkey collusion even in tendering to the public sector (for auctions and contracting services) and tacit collusion in general could not be prevented. In the UK collusive tendering is a widespread practice and unless firms tender at exactly the same price, colluding firms can get away with it. Moreover penalty for such collusion is minimal, namely a court injunction to prevent further price fixing (Sloman, 1991, p. 442).

Even in the most competitive economy, the US, about 35% of GNP is produced by industries that are dominated by either a single firm or a few large ones. Monopolistic, oligopolistic and monopolistic competition firms generally have saucer shaped flat cost (average variable cost) curves and installed capacity based on normal demand (Lipsey at al, pp. 265,280).

In the US, as a result of antitrust policy, concentration or the structure of the economy did not change, but anti-trust laws were effective in preventing price fixing (collusion), (Lipsey, et al, 1990, p.305). Price formation in oligopolistic firms (through collusion) is not different from that of monopolistic firms; differences, however, are in innovation and growth aspect.

(iii) Behavior of large firms: satisficing

Large corporations, will aim at saticficing, cost minimization and will use relatively rigid pricing rules and respond slowly to change. According to the theory of satisficing, developed by Herbert Simon, the modern corporation does not maximize profits, but rather maximizes sales (to hold a certain market share) subject to a profit constraint (satisficing), on the assumption that production cost of output is minimized, and even assumed cost minimization is not realized, because of poor management or because moving to a less costly routine may itself be costly.

Many manufacturing firms and large corporations set their own prices, employing the full-cost pricing rule; and then they do not change prices when demand changes, but the quantity sold. Prices are changed infrequently, except during periods of rapid inflation, then they raise prices when costs and demand increase. Under full- cost pricing, instead of equating marginal revenue with marginal cost, price is set equal to average cost at normal capacity output plus a fixed markup; prices are changed when average cost changes substantially (labor cost or prices of key raw materials) and markups are changed occasionally.

In evolutionary theories developed by Richard Nelson and Sidney Winter, firms carry on established routines, rather satisfice than maximize profits, maintain established markets and market shares. Decision behavior, including pricing and strategic decisions, is routinized. The flexibility and responsiveness to changes in market conditions and incentives are limited. Innovations (new products, new production techniques, new rules or procedures of behavior) are made not to make more profit, but when their profits are threatened. Wasteful practices of 1960s in oligopolistic or monopolistic markets, were shed in 1970s and 1980s because of competition or corporate take over. In the long term, however, only the profit maximizing firm will survive in the marketplace, in line with the principle of 'survival of the fittest', as suggested by Armen Alchian (Lipsey, et al, 1991, pp. 320-21).

Non-maximizing theories imply that firm will not respond quickly or at all to changes in market signals or government policy; however, they will still increase output when demand increases, change product prices and input mix when input prices change significantly; empirical evidence suggests that firms do not exactly maximize profit, but they cannot diverge too far from it (Lipsey, et al, 1991, pp. 328-29).

(iv) The case for public companies or monopolies

If the amount of capital required for setting up an industry is so large that, it could not be raised from financial markets, and/or the investment is risky, and R&D expenditure is too high, then the likelihood of this industry being set up by private sector is almost nil.

A commercially unviable sector might create substantial external benefits, which could be observed when appraised from a national economic viewpoint. Such an industry would not be undertaken by the private sector.

If key industries are in the public sector, then the government may manage the economy better, e.g. regional development policies could be pursued and new industries could be set up with the help of existing public enterprises.

A public or regulated monopoly is a useful instrument (a) for revenue collection (sales and excise taxes), (b) as a source of taxation (payroll, company and excess profit taxes), and (c) for raising saving and investment levels, considering the importance of taxation and saving/investment constraints to the growth and employment creation of modern economies, provided that strict measures are taken to compel the public monopolies to comply with the taxation procedures and make prompt payments for taxes due, and not to cumulate tax arrears.

(v) R&D expenditure and growth aspect

The issue is whether regulated monopoly or deregulated oligopoly would lead to greater innovation and growth. In case of regulated monopoly or larger oligopolists, too low administrative prices fixed would lead to lower R&D expenditure and investment, and as a consequence consumers would lose in the long run.

In the US during the late 1970s, when interest rates rose to double-digit levels, regulated monopolies were still permitted the traditional 6-9% rate of returns, which reduced incentive for new investments (Lipsey, at al, 1990, p. 309). In this manner, the role of big business promoting dynamic advances is curtailed.

Herein, it is argued that a regulated monopoly is preferable to a deregulated colluding duopoly or oligopolistic firms with inadequate R&D budgets and investments.

Lipsey et al (1990, p. 295) claim that oligopoly produce more satisfactory results than monopoly, by introducing new products and cost-reducing technology, in cases where firms are competitive. Oligopoly is the best option when minimum efficient scale is too large, which holds true in many of the modern industries. Some economists theorize that oligopoly would lead to more innovation than would occur in perfectly competitive or monopolistic industries. On the basis of empirical findings, Jesse Markham concludes that technological change and innovation are brought about by large firms operating in oligopolistic markets (*ibid*, p. 286).

As Joseph Schumpeter maintained, monopoly profits provide the greatest incentive for financing innovations and investing in new products and technologies and hence monopoly profits promote economic growth.

Many monopolies in the US over time have been broken by technological developments (creative destruction, one monopoly replacing another through the introduction of new products or new production techniques) as foreseen by

Schumpeter. This is the normal procedure for ending a monopoly not investing in R&D and stagnating, in a constructive manner through market forces, replacing it by a better alternative. Forced breaking up of a utility monopoly, by dissecting its vertically integrated parts, is not creative destruction of a monopoly, but its replacement by a tacitly colluding duopoly.

In oligopolistic market structure only dominant firm will have resources to fund R&D and innovation, and take risks involved to this end; and even these may not have adequate incentive and funds like a monopoly to develop new technology, since significant sums will always be spent on nonprice competition and market share is not assured as for a monopolist, moreover new technology and products developed at huge cost are bound to be applied and produced by competitors as well, hence the best strategy, as in pricing, might well be not 'rock the boat' even in technology. A safisficing firm resorts to innovation when profits are threatened. Moreover, there is a minimum scale of technological research and development, and economies of scale also might be involved.

The finding by Bronwyn Hall (1993) that "the stock market's valuation of the intangible capital created by R&D investment in the [US] manufacturing sector has fallen precipitously" during the 1980s, further exacerbates the issue.

The intangible assets of a firm originate from R&D and advertising, which are sometimes treated as rent-creating activities, and reflect capitalized value of monopoly rents; and are equal to the difference between the market value of a firm and the book value of its assets (Tobin's q is a measure of it). The intangible R&D assets and patents are the most important intangible asset. Patents, which are marketable commodities, although are "the output of a process in which R&D is the input" "current and past patents are unlikely to be the output of current and future R&D" (Megna and Klock, 1993). The other important intangible asset is "the value of the brand names, product differentiation, and goodwill arising from product reputation," which "is typically a product of advertising expenditures and investment in sales and service." (Bronwyn Hall, 1993).

Bronwyn Hall (1993) has found that,

> although intangible R&D assets from 1973 through about 1983-84 were about equally valued with tangible capital, [in the US manufacturing sector], this relationship broke down completely during the mid-1980s, with the R&D stock coefficient falling by a factor of 3 or 4. During the 1970s, advertising expenditures were worth roughly one-tenth of R&D expenditures, but by 1988-1990, the two expenditure streams were worth about the same.

The studies using data before 1985, "typically have found valuation for R&D spending or stock which are consistent with a depreciation rate of about 15-20% per year and valuation at par with ordinary assets". Findings by Hall "are consistent with these earlier results for the pre-1985 period but differ dramatically after 1985". Hall has estimated that "the value of R&D capital relative to ordinary capital was somewhere between 0.6 and 1.0 until about 1983 or 1984," but then it "declined precipitously, reaching a level of almost 0.2 by 1989-1990."; i.e. "the stock market valuation of R&D capital in the US manufacturing firms collapsed rather quickly from a high of 0.8-1.0 during 1979-1983 to a low of 0.2-0.3 during 1986-1991."

Bronwyn Hall (1993) identifies the possible causes of this fall as (i) "a fall in the private rate of return to R&D, (ii) a rise in the depreciation rate of R&D capital, (iii) market irrationality or a change in risk aversion, and (iv) restructuring wave of the 1980s." The estimated R&D capital coefficient (0.25) implies that the expected rate of return on R&D investment is one quarter that of ordinary investment if R&D capital depreciates at the same rate (0.15) it always has; or that the R&D capital depreciation rate has jumped from 0.15 to 0.67 to account for the fall in the R&D capital coefficient from 0.9 to 0.25, if R&D expenditures were growing 5% p.a. (i.e. two-thirds of the R&D capital becomes nonproductive in one year). Of these possible explanations for the decline in the market value of R&D capital, Hall dismisses first three, although admitting some truth in them and singles out the 4 th one, i.e. "the wave of mergers and leveraged buyouts during the 1980s," as the most likely candidate, worthwhile for further investigation.

Herein some views are aired regarding the fall in the market value of R&D stock. Along with the declining trend of total investment in the US during the 1980s (particularly in late 1980s), it is guessed that the R&D investment had also declined. Since economies of scale feature in the R&D expenditure, the output of R&D process and hence its market value had also declined, as a consequence. Moreover, deregulation wave had reduced monopoly power and hence R&D investment in some fields. Furthermore, the US has lost its pioneering role in developing or applying new technology in certain fields. Similarly, increased import penetration and greater uncertainty about future economic prospects and policies had also played a role in this respect.

As important as identifying the causes of this finding by B.Hall (1993), is its consequences. Lower values now assigned to the R&D investment would definitely lead to and so far must have led to lower R&D expenditure. Since R&D and advertising expenditures are worth about the same, firms would be indifferent between spending on R&D and advertising and would prefer product differentiation (being a mixture of both expenditures and less risky) to investing in real technological innovation.

(vi) The breaking up of AT&T

The findings of recent empirical studies on the break up of AT&T are summarized below.

> The divestiture of AT&T's operating telephone companies [in 1984] split the industry vertically into separate local and long-distance companies. Regulators actively encouraged entry and competition in the long-distance market. ... [Since 1984], capacity in the [interstate long-distance] market has roughly tripled; where once there was one nationwide long-distance network, there are now nearly four backbone long-distance networks and roughly 500 providers. AT&T's share of interstate switched-services long-distance usage has fallen precipitously from 84% in 1984 to 63% at the end of 1991. Over the same period, real interstate long-distance prices fell by about 50%, and long-distance demand approximately doubled (Taylor and Taylor, 1993).

The increasing competition and the rapid changes in technology in telephone markets that have swept the telecommunication industry in the last few decades, have accelerated since the break up of the Bell system in 1984. The US Federal Telecommunications Commission (FFC), claimed that

> technological advances in computers, fiber optics, microelectronics, and many other areas transformed the capabilities of 'plain old telephone service' while expanding the range and quality of new services. In place of the monolithic Bell system, customers may now select their telecommunications equipment and services from hundreds of suppliers offering an ever-expanding menu of choices (Braeutigam and Panzar, 1993).

Moreover "new methods of regulating AT&T and the local telephone companies were implemented, including deregulation in some jurisdictions and price-cap regulation for interstate long-distance and carrier access services" (Taylor and Taylor, 1993) . The price-cap regulation (incentive regulation), an innovation of the UK, has replaced the traditional cost-based rate-of-return regulation in over 30 states in the US, with a view to providing incentives for increasingly efficient production and allowing firms to share in the social gains from efficiency with increased profits. The price-cap regulation

> typically allows the firm to choose a set of prices for designated services so that an index of prices does not exceed some level. ... In 1984 the British Government chose to regulate [British Telecom's] prices directly

> through a formula relating price increases for telephone services to the annual change in the British retail price index, minus a specified productivity factor, initially 3%. ... In some jurisdictions (e.g. federal regulation of AT&T's long-distance service), price-cap regulation has been implemented without any limit on the rate of return being earned. In many jurisdictions, price-caps are being implemented along with limits on the rate of return which the firm may keep; these limits are often imposed through 'sliding scale' rate-of-return regulation, which typically allows the firm to keep all profits if the rate of return on investment is below a specified level and then allows the firm to share in profits for at least some levels of the rate of return in excess of that level (Braeutigam and Panzar, 1993).

The traditional rate-of-return regulation is bound to lead to inefficiencies; "the profit-maximizing firm under rate-of-return regulation fails to minimize the cost of producing any observed level of output." In the US, the increasing degree of competition and the rapid changes in technology in telephone markets precipitated the adoption of price-cap regulation for AT&T. Traditional 'cost-plus' rate of return regulation provides distorted incentives in capital investment and little incentive for introducing new and innovative services, and does not encourage optimal efficiency; according to FCC, under this regulation, "to maximize profits, the company has an incentive to manipulate its inputs of capital and labor, without regard to efficiency, and to adopt strategies for investment and pricing based on what it expects the regulatory agency might wish, not necessarily what best serves its customers and society." In a regime of pure price-caps, the regulated firm would be induced to minimize its production costs and pursue economically efficient (cost-reducing) innovation. Pure price-cap regulation would set maximum prices according to a formula that depends on prices or regional incomes. "A regulator might set a ceiling in noncompetitive markets" and allow the firm compete freely in competitive markets. However, "if price-caps are chosen incorrectly, large inefficiencies may result even if inputs are chosen correctly for the level of output actually produced". "While pure price-caps have a number of desirable properties, they are not likely to be observed in the real world", e.g. in a multi-product setting (Braeutigam and Panzar 1993).

Braeutigam and Panzar conclude that

> price-cap regulation is an effective means of controlling the prices of dominant firms when the control of their profits is left to the competitive marketplace; [and that] price-cap regulation is probably most effective as a transitory step on the path toward total deregulation and full competition; [however] the value of price-caps as a policy innovation for the control of

> natural monopoly remains an open question; ... there are no 'welfare theorems' to appeal to, nor is it obvious that overwhelming procedural efficiencies will emerge in the application of the price-cap sliding scale rate of return regulation hybrids now in place or contemplated; [and] from the public-policy perspective, the choice between price-cap style incentive regulation and rate-of-return regulation remains very much an empirical question (Braeutigam and Panzar, 1993).

Moreover, in case of natural monopolies, with dominant firm, market structure would at most evolve into oligopoly, if not remain monopolistic; and although consumers might benefit from efficiency gains, investment in general and in R&D and application of advanced technologies would suffer a setback.

Moreover the price-cap regulation, although is more efficient in the short run, since it enables better utilization of capital sunk, economizing on input use and improving the services offered to customers; in the long run, R&D *and investments will suffer a setback, because of cost-minimization rule entailed and also because the regulating agency would not have a say in these matters,* any more.

According to Hausman et al (1993),

> the break up of AT&T in 1984 into a long distance (and manufacturing) component and seven local-service companies ..... created the opportunity for billions of dollars of annual economic efficiency gains for the US economy. These potential annual efficiency gains arise in part from the establishment of a rational price system for telephone services.

"The price of basic access was well below its incremental (or marginal) cost", and the prices of long-distance services were well in excess of their incremental cost. Raising basic access price, when long-distance prices are decreasing, has not led to decreased penetration; on the contrary an increase of about 4.1 million subscribers realized during 1984-1986, as against an estimated decline of 6 million subscribers during this period. During the period 1984-1990, telephone penetration increased from 91.4% to 93.3%, 10 million additional households subscribed to telephone service, and households without telephone service decreased by 1.1 million. Hence increased economic efficiency due to more cost-based telephone prices has not led to decreased penetration. Hausman et al (1993) conclude that further efficiency gains could materialize if the cross subsidy received by basic exchange access and long-distance prices are lowered (Hausman, et al, 1993).

Several observers have attributed the favorable outcome of postdivestiture US telecommunication service to the pressures of competition. According to Canada Unitel,

> by any standard, the American policy has been a success. Rates have fallen, innovation has increased and usage has grown. ... The US Federal Communications Commission (FCC...) asserted that.... competition in the provision of interstate long-distance service has led to sharply reduced rates, a larger variety of service options, and more rapid deployment of new technologies.... (Taylor and Taylor, 1993).

Whereas Taylor and Taylor (1993) rightly assert that "while it is tempting to ascribe lower prices and increased demand to the pressures of competition, careful analysis shows that this is not the case." They show that "the overall reduction in interstate long-distance prices and expansion of interstate demand is more than explained by the reduction in the carrier access charges paid by the long-distance carriers to the local telephone companies." ("Long-distance companies pay... carrier access charges per minute of use to local telephone companies ... for originating and terminating traffic on their networks. These charges constitute a marginal cost to the long-distance companies"). *The carrier access charges were lowered not under the pressures of demand, but by the decisions of the FCC.* The FCC (i) "shifted recovery of local-telephone-company fixed costs that had previously been recovered from long-distance companies (through carrier access charges) to final consumers (through monthly subscriber line charges)", which lowered carrier access charges paid by interexchange carriers by $6.1 billion annually during 1990-1991, and (ii) "instituted a series of accounting changes which effectively reduced interstate costs while increasing intrastate costs," which in fact reduced carrier access charges by an additional $4.5 billion p.a. by 1990-1991.

> *Net of these payments [i.e. carrier access charges], real interstate long-distance prices fell at about half the rate after 1984 than before. Moreover, regulated competition in the interstate toll market has not led to an expansion of demand.* Despite the introduction of new services and massive advertising and marketing efforts, *toll demand grew no more than would be expected based on changes in price, population, and consumer income. Thus, although the FCC'S decision to reduce carrier access charges has resulted in enormous welfare gains for consumers, competition-or at least regulated competition- is not responsible for these benefits. The substantial price reductions and outward shifting of the toll demand curve that would be expected to arise from vigorous toll competition have yet to materialize* (Taylor and Taylor, 1993).

Taylor and Taylor (1993) conclude:

> Competitive entry into interstate long-distance service has undoubtedly resulted in vigorous competition in the large business market. In the

aggregate interstate toll market, AT&T's market share has fallen and its (firm) demand curve has accordingly become more elastic. Nonetheless, *competition since 1984 has not led to lower prices in the aggregate market or to lower prices for residential and small business customers. In addition, despite massive increases in marketing efforts and a flurry of new service offerings, aggregate interstate toll demand has not shifted outward. Changes in prices (and income and population) fully explain the growth in demand in the postdivestiture period.* In sum, regulated competition and asymmetric regulation of AT&T have yet to bring the benefits of lower prices and expanded demand to all interstate telephone customers.

One concludes that unless market structure becomes fully competitive (which is unlikely by the nature of this market), one does not expect vigorous price competition in this market, competition would rather result in product differentiation. Moreover the declining market share of the dominant firm would probably lead to lower sectoral R&D expenditure .

(vii) Conclusions

Although in the long-run, because of competition or corporate takeovers (in oligopolistic or monopolistic markets), only the profit maximizing firms will survive in the market place, in accordance with the principle of 'survival of the fittest', as suggested by Armen Alchian; in the short and medium-run non-maximizing behavior prevails in large corporations, which implies that firms will not respond quickly or at all to changes in market signals or government policies; although, by and large, firms increase output when demand increases or change product prices and input mix when input prices change significantly, as evidenced by response of the US firms to the oil price shock and abandonment of wasteful practices of 1960s in 1970s and 1980s when their profits were threatened, also through increased foreign competition.

It is maintained that firms do not exactly maximize profit, but they can not diverge too far from it. However there exists a wealth of evidence for non-maximizing behavior and consequences of this behavior in an open economy are devastating from viewpoints of output and employment losses, discouragement of investments and decline in innovation and technological improvement. Because a profit-maximizing firm will quickly respond to changes in markets, technology, government policy and foreign competition, and will have enough own-resources and asset value to raise additional capital, and funds to finance new investments and the introduction of new products and new production techniques, a non-maximizing firm, also facing a profit squeeze, will barely survive in the face of increased foreign competition.

The difficulties of non-maximizing firms operating in genuinely open free markets, have been compounded by uncertainties created by flexible exchange rates, increased foreign competition and some deregulation (which introduced artificial rivals to natural monopolies, reducing R&D expenditure, innovation and new investments). Because a firm's efficiency and competitive power could not be evaluated in isolation from its external competitors. It seems competitors of US firms in Japan, Taiwan and Korea and Western Europe were protected by higher tariffs, restrictive business practices and open or hidden government incentives and subsidies and/or absence of rigid anti-trust laws and hence enjoyed a relatively safe domestic market, which encouraged firms to invest in new capacity, new products and technology. Whereas in the US, it seems firms facing profit squeeze, greater uncertainty, more foreign competition(although under anti-trust regulation some protections is afforded in certain instances) and survival problems have rather engaged in reducing cost and employment, streamlining activities and cutting down size and R&D budgets, than expansion or investment in new technologies.

Although threatened profits, compel firms to innovation, extreme profit squeeze, is more likely to lead to utter failure and rarely to an economic miracle. This policy obviously maximizes consumer welfare, but increases unemployment in the short-run and reduces growth potential in the long run.

In view of developments in Far East and the US during the last decade, one rather subscribes to Schumpeter's view on monopolies. During the last decade, although the US still has pioneered in advanced research and development of new technologies, in economic application of new technologies (except for the defense industries, understandably), Far East has become the leader. Possibly the difference and explanation lies in specific policies (antitrust, deregulation in some areas) and economic environment, growth economy (saving-investment oriented with some protection) versus stagnating, extremely open, consumption-oriented, laissez-faire economy.

As integrating the former socialist economies to the world economy is crucially important and would be beneficial to the whole world, a declining US economy is not in the interest of the rest of the world, since the US economy still provides the largest import market, capital and technological resources and productive capacity; and a recession or a boom in the US still affects the world economy at large significantly. In fact, this phenomenon explains the following controversy, During the Great Depression 1929-1933, although the Federal Reserve failed to address the crisis by monetary expansion and caused chain bankruptcies of the commercial banks in the US, central banks in Canada and the UK reacted to the crisis correctly and came to the rescue of commercial banks and as a consequence bank failures were insignificant in these countries, but still Canada and the UK suffered as severe depression as in the US. On these grounds Keynesians claim that monetary factors were not important and that the major cause of the Great depression was cyclical behavior of investment and consumption expenditure, not the perverse reaction of the Federal Reserve as claimed by monetarists, despite the fact that the 1932 money supply was 35% below the 1929 level in the US (Lipsey, et al, 1990, p. 686). The explanation possibly lies in the fact that if the US economy is in a severe depression, the rest of the world economy even today stagnates as a consequence; and in the 1930s, Canada and the UK could not recover from depression, when the US was in a deep depression even if they had pursued correct monetary and fiscal policies. Because the cyclical problem in the UK and Canada had evolved into a long-term structural problem (loss of a major export market), hence anti-cyclical policies could not have been a remedy; growth-oriented structural adjustment policies (finding new markets abroad and creating effective demand at home) were called for. In other words, while in the US correct monetary policy could have achieved something (if the Federal Reserve had responded correctly to the stock market crash and its aftermath, depression might not have been that severe); in the UK and Canada, the monetary policy was found to be ineffective, because of the change in the nature of depression faced by these countries. A similar situation a rose for Turkey, in the postwar era. With the establishment of the Communist bloc, Turkey lost Eastern Europe as a trading partner, and this is one of the major factors which explains the severe BOP problem of Turkey in the 1950s.

While the monopoly versus oligopoly issue in the industrialized countries is rather complex as explained above, in developing countries and the reforming socialist countries the issue is much more simpler. In developing countries, also because of the lack of effective anti-trust regulation, oligopolists explicitly or tacitly, definitely collude, satisficing and corporate waste are commonplace, effective regulation of monopolies is an impossible task, innovation is not even a factor to be considered, and hence privatization of natural public monopolies could only end up with exploitation of consumers, and not necessarily to higher business savings and investment. In case of breaking up of horizontal public monopolies, at least one viable part should remain under public ownership or control, with a view to creating an oligopolistic market with some price competition. In the reforming socialist countries, except for the innovation aspect (which applies possibly only to Russia) same conclusions hold true.

13 Tariff protection

During the postwar era, there has been a move towards free trade with customs tariffs approaching zero. However, non-tariff barriers in industrialized countries possibly increased in terms of their effect, also with the establishment of trading blocs. Russia has recently removed tariffs completely. The extreme shortage of foreign exchange and the level of the exchange rate make imports virtually imposible.

In the US the average tariff rate started to decline in 1970s, from some 15% in 1950s and 1960s, to below to 10% in 1971 and 3% in 1980s. The average tariff rate (all commodities, trade weighted) in mid 1980s was 3.2% in the US, 3.7% in the EC and 5.4% in Japan (Lipsey, et al, 1990, pp. 858, 855).

Average tariff rates (all goods) showed a declining trend for North America and an increasing trend for Japan over 1950-1987 period; as shown in Table 20.2.

Table 20.2
Tariff rates in some industrialized countries (all goods, percentages)

	1950	1987
Canada	9	6
Japan	4	8
US	13	6

Source: World Development Report, IBRD, 1991, p. 97

It seems that the move to lower tariff rates have led to proliferation of trading blocs, import quotas, voluntary export restrictions and nontariff barriers, price discrimination, hidden export subsidies and antidumping countervailing duties, which are applied somewhat arbitrarily depending on the lobbying power of vested interest groups and all of which are more or as inefficient as moderate tariff protection. This is hypocrisy. Moreover, most of these measures entail loss of customs tariff revenue to foreign producers.

For North America in mid 1980s, it was estimated that consumers pay $150 thousand per year per job saved in the car industry, most of which accrued to Japanese manufacturers because of voluntary export restrictions (Lipsey, et al, 1990, p. 849).

With a view to creating a 'level playing field' really, switch to moderate tariff protection, and absolute removal of all other barriers to free trade would be both a more realistic target and beneficial to all parties concerned.

Such a scheme would provide adequate cushion to domestic industry against external shocks and would introduce international competition at uniform level to all domestic markets, i.e. create a 'level playing field'. A case can be made for moderate tariff protection, aside from the infant industry argument, on the following grounds:

(i) Gains from free trade (economies of scale, competition, innovation, dynamic comparative advantage) could be exploited in countries with a large domestic market or in trading blocs.

(ii) If key industries of a country migrated to other countries, other industries will follow suit, as a result of reverse spillover effects, and de-industrialization will set in.

(iii) Customs revenue if not consumed in current government expenditures, would increase domestic saving and investment, which are crucial for economic growth.

(iv) Under completely free or almost free trade, domestic industries would not have a safe haven for even break-even level production and survival, in case of any onslaught of foreign competition arising from innovation, lower wages, subsidies or new entrants. This phenomenon when occurred will not only cause eclipse of existing industries, but future likelihood of such a threat would impede investment in certain industries because of risks (real or assumed) involved. Whereas under moderate tariff protection, domestic industry, would have time and resources (minimum sales) to adjust and tackle with such a threat.

14 Adjustment process of prices: views of Arrow

(i) Market clearance

In the law of supply and demand models by Walras, Marshall, Hicks and Samuelson, "it is postulated that disequilibrium alters a price in such a way to reduce a market imbalance" However, the model does not supply any mechanism by which prices are changed; who or what changes them? The model implies that the rate of change of any one price depends on the current values of all prices. But the model "recognizes the possibility of disequilibrium, of differences between supply and demand on any one market", and hence is superior to the general equilibrium models which "postulate a permanent equality between supply and demand, for which the mechanisms are even more mysterious." Because, "there is no general theorem that price adjustment according to supply and demand leads to the wiping-out of market imbalances on all markets" (Arrow, 1981, pp. 140-42).

However there seems no consistent way of setting up a *disequilibrium dynamics* which can operate exclusively in terms of *relative prices* (Arrow, *ibid*, p. 148).

(ii) Effectiveness of monetary policy in recession

The only convincing case of monetary magnitudes affecting real variables, is the one in which there are excess supplies on most markets and an increase in the money supply leading to an immediate increase in the real stock of money, with little and slow change in prices, and hence to a higher real national income. Then "the monetary policy could be effective, at least in the short-run." However, "the closer the system moved to full employment and market clearing in general, the less the increase in money stock could translate itself into an increase in outputs and the more it would affect prices." (Arrow, 1981, pp. 147, 149-50)

(iii) Price uncertainty in future and investment decisions

There is "a complete absence of forward markets" (Arrow, 1981.p.143), because even in case of long-term purchasing agreements for agricultural commodities, long-term leases of real estate and long-term credit contracts, there are escape clauses for price, rental or interest-rate increases.

"In the absence of forward markets, the prices at which future consumption will take place are uncertain and this uncertainty will affect not only the goods consumed but also the timing of the consumption." If it is anticipated that markets may be in disequilibrium in the future, a saver who is willing to give up some of his present consumption in return for commodities in the future, will not be able to purchase the required goods either because their prices have gone up (excess supply of numeraire) or because saving bond prices have declined (due to excess supply of bonds or shortage in the supply of numeraire). This uncertainty prospect would affect saving decisions of households (Arrow, *ibid*, p. 144). In reforming high inflation socialist countries anticipated disequilibrium in future markets, is likely to increase present consumption at the expense of future consumption.

Future disequilibrium is a severe problem for investment. "If the markets are sure to clear in the future, then the amount of investment is completely determined by the anticipation of future relative prices (which may well be uncertain)." However, if one supposes that there may be excess supply in the market for the product of investment process,

> then the investment will be geared to the anticipated volume of sales and be much less affected by prices; for if there is excess supply, the amount sold is no longer determined by the firm alone but is also affected by the level of demand. [Because], if market do not necessarily clear, then on those markets where there is excess supply, the general conditions of demand determine sales. Therefore, if excess supply is anticipated, investment will be restricted accordingly as compared with a situation in which markets are anticipated to clear at all times. In the latter case,

> investment will be determined solely by prices, since the firm anticipates selling whatever it chooses to produce (Arrow, 1981, p. 144). This, however, assumes perfectly competitive markets.

"Businessmen in their calculations consider their future sales as limited by demand; and most empirical work on investment has taken the anticipated output as one of the main determining variables;" which suggests that "investment decisions do not depend on anticipation of relative prices and that firms do not anticipate automatic market clearing" (Arrow, *ibid*, 144). In fact in business investment planning if no excess demand (shortage) is anticipated, no investment is programmed.

(iv) The numeraire issue

Kenneth Arrow (1981, p. 142) maintains that "the price adjustment mechanism is not independent of the choice of numeraire" and that "the movements of relative prices can be different with different numeraires". To illustrate and prove this point, Arrow proceeds as follows:

> Suppose that both gold and silver have excess demand -that is, demand exceed supplies for both. If gold is the numeraire, then its price is fixed. If the price of silver responds only to the difference between supply and demand on the silver market, then its price will rise. Hence the price of gold relative to that of silver falls. But if silver were the numeraire, then exactly the same reasoning shows that the price of silver falls relative to that of gold. Equivalently, the price of gold is now rising to that of silver. To be sure if the prices in fact do move toward equilibrium levels then eventually the choice of numeraire will be immaterial. But in the process of adjustment, which may after all, be lengthy, the choice even of the unit in which accounts are reckoned may not be irrelevant.

Some of these statements are not valid. Excess demand can be defined at a price; if gold becomes legal tender in lieu of banknotes, then at the existing silver/gold relative price, excess demand for silver also will vanish, depending on the degree (strength) of excess demand and speed of adjustment of silver price, unless the gold price is pegged in terms of say banknotes units (and internal and external convertibility of banknotes are guaranteed). In the latter case, excess demand for gold also will persist, until the pegged gold price is raised to the equilibrium level or freed; hence except for this case, when gold is the numeraire, its nominal price being fixed, there can't be excess demand for it, because as Arrow asserts (*ibid*,p.146), "money is always acceptable", "there really can't be any excess demand or excess supply of money". However, the real price of gold (its relative price vis-a vis prices of the rest of the commodities) is not fixed. And it should be noted that the relative prices, not nominal prices, affect real magnitudes. Supposing that the excess demands for gold and silver imply 20% and 10% nominal price increases respectively, to achieve the equilibrium levels in term of the previous numeraire, and that as a consequence of gold being made legal tender, an additional 10% increase in its price is called for to meet rise in its demand for monetary purposes, then the nominal prices of all goods have to decline by 30%, as a result of the move to gold money, and the silver price has to fall by 20%, implying an excess supply. Hence the gold price will rise in relation to silver and the choice of numeraire will not affect the result. The speed of adjustment of all prices will determine the time path of price movements.

The excess demand for gold will vanish as a consequence (gold being the numeraire), existing silver/gold relative price reflecting the relative shortages (supply and demand conditions) of the two commodities, may not change thereafter, except for monetary demand component. Because, gold being in short-supply, before becoming the numeraire, its nominal price in terms of the previous numeraire and real price (relative price) will rise, either before or after being the numeraire. And its ultimate relative price to silver, will not be influenced by the choice of numeraire. If the gold price only becomes the unit of account (not the numeraire), the outcome will not change; except for the absence of monetary demand factor, which will lower the size of price movements.

In a multi-commodity world, if the supply of numeraire declines or demand for it increases (e.g. as in late 1980s and early 1990s when due to dollarization in Latin America, Eastern Europe, Turkey, etc. demand for dollar increased) prices of other commodities declines (exchange rates of domestic currencies in the cited countries). Hence overall price index falls, when the supply of numeraire commodity contracts; in such a framework relative price of silver would still reflect, the relative strength of excess demand on the silver market vis-a-vis contraction in the supply of numeraire, it may fall or rise, whether the numeraire is gold or dollar banknote. The outcome in relative prices would not change if silver were numeraire, instead.

(v) Labor market equilibrium

Arrow (1981, pp. 139-40) maintains that the existence of involuntary unemployment, shows that the labor and all other markets do not always clear; and hence money matters in "the analysis of and policy toward short-term economic fluctuations."

One can maintain regarding the labor-market that disequilibrium is almost a built-in feature of modern economies, because after the petroleum shock, unemployment in the industrial countries, except for Japan, Taiwan and a few other countries, was never eliminated, and is on the rise on average. Future prospects are not better and even the better performance of the countries cited could be explained by removing their unemployment through exportation. In this sense it is similar to the unemployment in labor surplus developing countries, i.e. it can't be explained on grounds of cyclical or structural (mismatch between demand for and supply of skills), because it is permanent, unless productive capacity is expanded to provide gainful employment for all. In such a framework, expansionary policies, leading rather to increased private and public consumption (average and marginal propensities), price and wage inflation, reducing saving/investment tendencies, enlarging saving gap and increasing the public and external debt in the long run, as empirical evidence indicates, in countries with chronic inflation (or continuos inflationary gap/pressure, even not reflected in the price level through extremely open economy and virtually unlimited availability of external financing) and high inflation. And due to the Feldstein-Horoika effect, these inflation-prone countries exacerbate the long-run unemployment problem by hindering the growth of productive capacity, while trying to salvage the short-term problem.

(vi) Disequilibrium models

"Disequilibrium theorists, such as Robert Clower, Axel Leijonhufvud and Edmond Malinvaud, stemming from Keynes, argue that the anticipation of future disequilibria can explain why random fluctuations such as occur all the time are amplified (the multiplier effect)". If workers anticipate unemployment, their demand for consumer goods is reduced from its normal relation, with the amount of labor they wish to supply and if at the same time firms anticipate, that "there will be excess supply on their product markets, so they cannot sell as much as they wish at current wages and prices", and then their demand for labor will be reduced below the level corresponding to what they wish to sell. "Clearly the two anticipations can be consistent with each other, producing the situation observable in most recessions where idle men and idle capacity coincide." "In this situation, an increase in the money supply leads to increased demand, which in turn changes anticipations", and so on. However if money prices are decreasing in response to the excess supplies of both labor and goods, then the real stock of money rises, which in turn causes demand to increase without any policy change.(Arrow, 1981, pp. 149-150).

According to Arrow (1981, p. 150)."the key question, in determining whether changes in monetary magnitudes can have planned effects on real questions, is whether the fluctuations in our economic system are best described by a model in which prices clear markets at every instant or by one in which market disequilibria persist over months or even years."

The problem with the disequilibrium models is whether the assumption of simultaneous existence of idle men and idle capacity holds true for long; idle men exist, but the existence of competitive idle capacity for a long time is doubtful or still to be verified (unless economic policy is completely irrational).

15 Applicability of macroeconomic equilibrium models to disequilibrium situations: the Austrian school

(i) Introduction

The Austrian school always questioned the validity of neo-classical hypotheses of perfectly competitive markets and market clearance prices, the assumption of perfect knowledge, aggregation of economic variables and the lack of the role of expectations and virtually didn't accept the concept of macroeconomics. Hayek showed that social allocation of resources efficiently is not possible. *Schumpeter ridiculed the standard competitive models;* however, attempts to replace the unrealistic competitive model with *more realistic monopolistic competition* model, in 1930s and 1940s failed. Analysis of "interaction of various macro variables, without any examination of the micro-under pinnings of these variables", e.g. examining the impact of *changes in money supply* without considering their structural consequences (through *changes in relative prices)* are held responsible for "persistent mismanagement by governmental monetary authorities", resulting in series of "inflationary booms followed by bouts of depressions." "Keynesian policies are not only inadequate to ensure stability, but have in fact been to blame for its disappearance". Hence "for market capitalism to work smoothly and effectively in the coordination of the plans of market participants, a *reasonably stable monetary framework* is an important requirement" (Kirzner, 1981).

(ii) Macroeconomic models in disequilibrium situations

Now the need for providing micro foundations for macroeconomics is almost universally accepted, by recognizing the importance of market processes during disequilibrium (the nature of competitive market processes), the role of uncertainty and individual expectations in market responses to macro policy, and the search for information ("the subtle processes of spontaneous learning made possible by market interaction under imperfect knowledge") and integrating them into the neoclassical elaborate equilibrium models. What is needed is to "perceive the market economy as an interlocking array of individual decisions", and to recognize that "decisions at the level of production are inextricably linked with expected decisions of resource suppliers and prospective consumers", and to reconstruct economic theory under these premises (Krizner, 1981).

Austrian economists who emphasize the importance of dynamic competition, over the neo-classical concept of static competition (acceptance of dynamic competition necessitates violation of static perfect competition conditions), consider that anti-trust policy ("the sheer size is per se anti-competitive", and "the presence of any discretion to a firm, with respect to prices" is anti-competitive) "has seriously threatened the efficiency and vitality of American industry", and that government regulations have eroded *freedom of entry* which is of critical importance for dynamic competition (Kirzner, 1981).

Along these lines it can be argued that, monopolies with regulation, long-term growth and technological improvement (dynamic competition) viewpoints are preferable to breaking-up monopolies through de-regulation or privatization, creating duplicative, costly artificial, competitors (which eventually results in higher prices being charged to consumers, colluding oligopolies, and less R&D expenditure). Mergers and formation of cartels, in areas where major technological improvements have ended, will only lead to higher prices being charged to consumers; in case of declining industries, facing foreign competition, scaling down operations or phasing them out (when resources released could be employed elsewhere) or formation of a monopoly with regulation and with foreign competition (if viable then) are better options than allowing mergers or cartel arrangements with deregulation. Freedom of entry is essential for (static) competition as well and hence should not be barred by rigid government regulations; however, deregulation rhetoric, in developing countries have created and in reforming socialist countries will create a parasitic informal sector just in order to avoid health and safety regulations and taxation laws, at the expense of formal sector. In the reforming socialist countries, however, freedom of entry and reducing regulations to the bare minimum are essential from viewpoint of creating private business sector, formal or informal; because informal sector is the training ground for potential entrepreneurs.

The fundamental premises of the Austrian school are basically true and reflect microeconomic realities and market processes; however, the hypothesis that "market prices at any given time are sure to be disequilibrium prices" (Kirzner, 1981, p. 119), cannot be true always, in particular when price and monetary stability exist; and under such conditions, even when true, can not be significantly different from the equilibrium levels.

In the present reforming socialist countries, with internal and external disequilibria and open and/or repressed inflation and market imperfections, standard competitive models (econometric or abstract mathematical models) cannot explain the real world, as the Austrian school also correctly asserts. Commander and Coricelli (1992) also observe that *the partially reformed socialist economies* have features similar to market economies with *few producers and sticky prices.* Socialist economies are *characterized by major disequilibria.*

Under 'the suggested method,' macroeconomic estimates are based on decisions (simulations) of enterprises, taking into account market conditions facing them and world prices (which plus tariff, will set the ceiling for price increases) and given price, wage etc. stability. Aggregation is made by adding up enterprise figures and since a program properly designed employing the method would attain internal and external equilibrium, fiscal balance, relative price, wage and exchange rate stability immediately and simultaneously, the likelihood of any disequilibrium is small.

(iii) Causes of stagflation and sticky prices

Monopolistic competition condition prevailing in national economies can be used, without employing a formal model, to analyze some macroeconomic controversies.

Stagflation phenomenon, effects of inflationary expansion (beyond the full capacity output level) and sticky prices and wages can rather be explained by imperfect competition conditions in factor and product markets, than by money illusion, rational expectations, etc. Sticky prices are not observed in perfectly competitive markets, namely prices of agricultural produce, raw materials and minerals fluctuate daily according to supply and demand conditions. Decline in demand automatically translates into lower market price and hence lower output; and similarly increased demand leads to both rise in price and output. Even in this case of output expansion beyond full-capacity level, output reverts to potential level and price increase remains.

Whereas in markets with imperfect competition, increased demand, depending on current market conditions (cost backlog-accumulated cost increases not passed on prices, profit maximization situation, possible reaction of the public, etc.) might just lead to price increase at fixed output level, as microeconomic theory and practice suggest. Similarly decreased demand, depending on profit maximization behavior, might just lead to an equilibrium at the same price level with lower output. The share of imperfect markets in the national economy increased in post-war period with technological advances, new products protected under patent rights, ineffective anti-trust regulations, mergers and creation of conglomerates, product differentiation and brand names, increased opportunities of using mass media for advertising in lieu of price/quality competition, organizational inefficiencies (firms minimizing unit costs for a given output level; i.e. what Harvey Leibenstein (1981) terms as X-inefficiency), powerful labor unions, creation of trading blocs (particularly EEC and the communist bloc) and protection of declining industries, and hence the likelihood of stagflation.

Hence, the solution to stagflation is not increased demand, but increased competition, including effective competition from imports; neither supply-side economics remedies or Phillips trade-off models can work. Privatization of monopolies and de-regulation of natural monopolies (which will hinder technological advance and also lead to collusion) also increased monopolistic competition.

16 Chaotic systems

(i) Theory

In line with recent developments, one can argue that the *classical linear dynamic systems* are no longer valid in modern complex economies, rather nonlinear dynamic models might represent better the real world and *nonlinear growth systems* might behave in a *chaotic manner,* e.g. might produce successively steady growth, then regular cycles and then irregular fluctuations that never repeat themselves, and all these although deterministic, can not always be predicted neither by mathematical models, nor by past observations; and small differences in initial conditions might generate completely different growth paths, through the system's capacity to magnify small differences.

And thus *positive-feedback loops* develop, which magnify initial divergence from equilibrium rather than damp it. In fact, some individual markets like financial markets and dollarization, can better be described by non-linear, even chaotic systems with positive-feed back loops. Many markets, particularly commodity markets, however, are dominated by negative-feedback systems, where divergencies from the equilibrium level are dampened over time (see, e.g. Lipsey et al. pp. 812-14).

On the other hand, large systems describing economic growth in an economy, containing a large number of individual markets and involving invention, innovation and diffusion of knowledge, may be described by *nonlinear dynamic equations, positive-feedback loops, occasional chaotic behavior, and decision making with bounded rationality* (Lipsey, et al, p. 814). High-or hyper-inflation economies in transition, such as the reforming socialist economies, particularly employing 'big bang' approach, with all markets in disequilibrium by large margins, are doomed to fall in this category; hence under present policies and practices, they can never achieve equilibrium. 'The suggested method', starting with as little disequilibrium as possible, might help in this respect.

(ii) Practice: reform program in Russia

The standard reform plan is a five-point strategy, moving rapidly on all fronts: (i) macroeconomic stabilization, providing both the budget is nearly balanced and a tight control over credit is imposed; (ii) liberalization of the prices of most goods; (iii) current account convertibility of currency; (iv) privatization; and (v) the creation of a social safety net; and simultaneously putting in place the legal framework for a market economy (Fischer, 1992).

Simply addressing stabilization is insufficient, because transformation is profoundly structural in nature, and problems faced by the these economies are all interconnected; e.g., "privatization attempts foundering because of valuing enterprises when oil is selling for a nickel a barrel." Privatization, stabilization and liberalization, all must be completed as soon as possible, since maintaining the momentum of reform is a crucial problem. A safety net and Western political and economic support are essential (Fischer, 1992).

William Nordhaus points out that, while general strategies are possible, but no routine approach exist for the Russian transformation; because *chaotic systems become increasingly divergent from one another as they evolve.* Standard stabilization policies independent of economic, social, and political conditions are not appropriate. Nordhaus observes that the Russian government has followed the IMF prescription faithfully. Prices have been liberalized, free entry into virtually every area exists now and Russia has become *the only major country in the world that has no duties on imports,* and shops are stocked with goods as a result of the price decontrol. Michael Bruno noted that "a range of micro problems have beset the transition in most Eastern European economies, however, the problems are even worse in the former Soviet Union" because of conflicts among the republics on issues like internal payments arrangements (Fischer, 1992).

(iii) Sequencing reforms in Russia

Fischer (1992) notes:

> The Russian government started its reforms by *liberalizing prices*-well before it had any assurance that fiscal and monetary policy were consistent with *macroeconomic stability.* The normal prescription is first or simultaneously to establish macroeconomic control and then to liberalize prices. However, that prescription applies to countries where most resources are allocated through *functioning markets* and where price liberalization means removing incomplete price controls and reducing tariffs; this was not the situation in Russia. There *the choice was between liberalizing prices and risking hyperinflation* or maintaining price controls and exacerbating *shortages.*

This choice however was to a great extent between *hidden and open inflation,* since a growing proportion of transactions were being conducted in black markets. Also the government taking a radical and virtually irreversible step, has given the Western aid donors the long-called-for signal, in view of "unavailability of external resources to help finance the budget and stabilize the currency". Fischer sees difficulty with this strategy since it requires doing everything at once (Fischer,1992).

The actual outcome, however, shows that the choice was not between open and hidden inflation, but in fact between hyperinflation and shortages; and resulting hyperinflation rendering both ruble and market signals useless, is self-defeating the very aim of price liberalization and market reform. (Because in hyperinflation conditions one can not claim that there is a well-functioning market mechanism and price signals are useful for planning future.)

On the other hand *the suggested method*, will provide proper guidance and reliable estimates, even under hyperinflation conditions, because the assumption of macroeconomic stability (reducing inflation to reasonable levels) could safely be made and enterprises on the basis of market experience gained, can provide quite good estimates required by the methodology.

Fischer (1992) observes that although the Russian Government has moved quickly to liberalize prices, it has moved slowly, if at all, on other fronts. Particularly "fiscal consolidation and tightening of monetary and credit policy" have not materialized. It has reduced the budget deficit by more than 10% of GDP, by cutting subsidies, defense expenditures and investment spending; but has not been successful in collecting taxes, despite a 28% general sales tax. Revenues have lagged behind estimates because of the decline in exports, exemption of food from tax and poor tax collection. A 40% export tax on oil is planned. Because of the weakness of tax administration the new tax system has to be simple and enforceable, with penalties for tax evasion, *otherwise Russia is bound to descend into the Latin American trap, "where no one pays taxes, no one is punished, the budget is chronically in deficit, and inflation is perennial"* (Fischer, 1992) It should be noted that the overly high rate of sales tax effectively precludes its collection.

17 General conclusion

It is surprising to observe in the last 20-30 years, new theories are implemented with a view to ironing out cyclical fluctuations, reducing unemployment and promoting economic growth, without even theoretically considering their full impacts, nor simulating their possible outcomes (even though overly sophisticated large econometric models are available). This assertion is proven, because otherwise these policies would not have failed such disastrously worldwide. Many policy recipes based on these false, failed theories and premises are still widely in circulation and under implementation. Theoretical exercises based on these fashionable theories are still carried out. Review of literature on transformation economics revealed many examples of these.

Conventional economic theory both neo-Keynesian and neo-classical is either based on false assumptions and/or policy recommendations derived from them are not shown to achieve objectives claimed in theory or practice. Obvious facts are either ignored or obvious effects of policy recipes are overlooked. Neo-classical assumption of near-perfect competition in all markets is obviously wrong. Neo-Keynesians, while admitting rigidities in labor and commodities markets, still recommend demand management policies; whereas it is obvious that expansionary demand management policies would rather lead to price increase than output response, in imperfect competition markets with inflationary tendencies. (Keynesians argue just the opposite, i.e., that under imperfect competion conditions, the Phillips curve trade-off is assured and the aggregate demand increase will only result in output increase without any price effect.)

Neo-classicals, while rightly asserting the importance of monetary stability and placing inflation control over employment creation objective, undermine the very aim of price stability by suggesting supply-side incentives and jeopardize economic growth objective through budgetary deficits, eliminating public saving, crowding-out effects, increasing consumption at the expense of saving and investment virtually.

Free markets are essential, but they are destined to generate economic fluctuations as shown by numerous business cycle theories and empirically verified. Built-in stabilizers are inadequate to eliminate business cycles. Discretionary policies, on the other hand, are bound to generate their own cycles. In basically weak economies (low saving propensity and slow investment growth), every recovery policy period is followed by contractionary policies.

Possibly flexible exchange rate system, removing the BOP constraint imposed on policymakers and ensuing fiscal and monetary discipline under the fixed exchange system, also contributed to this outcome (increase in consumption propensity and lower economic growth rate).

For sustained steady growth in a market economy, adequate public saving, investment and expenditures of developmental nature are essential. The objective still is to have a small, efficient and effective public administrative machinery and reduce public consumption (except that of developmental nature) and bureaucracy, and create gainful employment. It should be noted that every inessential job created in the public sector destroys several gainful jobs in the private sector.

However, the government should spend sufficient sums on human resource development on current and capital account (education, health, science and art), which is crucial for future economic growth. They should support all research and development expenditures of the economy, provide adequate and efficient infrastructure, and in the developing world invest, preferably on a joint-venture basis, in new industries, high-technology industries and giant capital projects (where private initiative and capital become inadequate). All this should be carried out with price stability and observing the fiscal balance or with minimum budgetary deficit, ensuring that no crowding-out of private investment occurs, domestic investments increase and the economic return on public sector projects is strongly positive. This is not a blank check to weak and corrupt governments, because they are bound to misuse and abuse this opportunity for public expenditure and but they any way could not raise the additional tax revenue required to finance such programs. Under the conditions prevailing worldwide, for economic growth and increased employment, a small but efficient, honest and powerful administrative machinery is a prerequisite.

Such a program could raise both domestic saving and investment, provide a minimum but steady economic growth emanating from the public sector in price stability, which would encourage private initiative and investment also by raising hopes of people and expectations of business for the future.

Chapter 21

Phillips curve trade-off

Phillips curve trade-off

1 The Phillips curve analysis in the reforming socialist countries

(i) Phillips curve

The Phillips curve is an inverse relationship between the rate of unemployment and the rate of increase in money wages; as the rate of unemployment decreases, wage inflation increases. The Phillips curve aims at analyzing effects of unemployment on wage costs, while the economy (economic output) fluctuates around its potential level.

The Phillips curve was claimed to have cleared "a logical paradox in theory and a disturbing actuality in the real world", namely "persisting (and even rising) rates of unemployment and a rising price level", a situation which neoclassical monetarists and neoclassical Keynesians alike could not explain. Paul Samuelson had declared that "the Phillips curve is one of the most important concepts of our times." Solow pointed out that "what Phillips found was really pretty astonishing. The simple bivariate relation, relating only one real and one nominal variable, held up very well over a very long time during which the nature of British industry and labor changed drastically." "It did not appear to be a short-run transient affair." "It seemed to say quite clearly that the rate of wage inflation-and probably, therefore, the rate of price inflation-was a smooth function of the tightness of the aggregate economy" (Bell, 1981 pp. 66-67).

Policy *prescription supposedly implied* by the Phillips curve, i.e. trade-off between wage (price) inflation and unemployment was widely used in the 1960s and 1970s in the developing world (some countries, e.g. Turkey and Latin

American countries, still have faith on the long-run Phillips curve and continued the same policy in the 1980s and 1990s) and in a few developed countries.

The Phillips curve solution to unemployment i.e. trade-off between wage (price) inflation and unemployment, in fact, does not exist at all (as now empirically verified and universally accepted for the long run) and the short-run temporary expansion of output by an inflationary expansion above the potential (full employment) level could be explained by the standard Keynesian analysis of aggregate demand shock; which is bound to end up with output reversal (decline to the potential level) and price increase.

Under rational expectation approach, even a short-run Phillips curve does not exist (Frisch, 1986, p. 33). In late 1960's and in early 1970's it was observed that the Phillips curves seemed to have gone flat, implying the trade-offs are not favorable and vanishing (Bell, 1981, pp. 66-69). Arrow (1981) observes that "as the era of general price stability gave way to rising prices, the inadequacies of" the Phillips "formulation became empirically evident. It appears that rising prices themselves cause an increase in wages."

In inflationary conditions with material input, foreign exchange, etc. shortages and rising inflationary expectations which prevail in some reforming socialist countries, an aggregate demand shock, would cause prices of goods, inputs and factors increase simultaneously and due to the subsequent matching aggregate supply shock (shift of the curve), only the price level will increase without any output response (increase). This is now the standard analysis of a fully anticipated demand shock.

Phillips empirically established a stable relationship between the rate of changes of wages and the level of unemployment, which can be described as *'measurement without theory'* in the sense of T. Koopmans. Phillips using the 1861-1913 British data found a non-linear, negative correlation between these two variables, which could explain the relationship (between the two variables) during the 1913-1957 period as well. Phillips observed "that wages remain stationary when the rate of unemployment is 5.5%" and concluded that "money wages rise somewhat faster as the rate of unemployment decreases and somewhat slower as the rate of unemployment increases" (Frisch, *ibid.*, pp. 36, 33-34), i.e. asymmetry in the speed of adjustment.

The theory for this relationship came later by Lipsey, who linked his theory of labor market to the Phillips curve through two functions: (a) a positive relationship between the excess demand for labor and the change in money wages, and (b) a negative relationship between the excess demand for labor and the rate of unemployment, which was considered an innovation in economic theory (Frisch, 1986, pp. 36-41, Bell, 1981). P. Samuelson and R. Solow modified the Phillips curve so that "it represented a relationship between the rate of inflation and the rate of unemployment, instead of between the rate of change in money wages and the rate of unemployment, as had been the case", and recommended it to policy makers "as an instrument that would allow them to formulate policy programs with alternative combinations of unemployment and inflation rates". Thus policy makers had a "menu of choice between different degrees of unemployment and price stability" (Frisch, 1986, pp. 36-43).

Let w= rate of change of money wages (wage inflation), u= rate of unemployment, p= rate of price inflation, p*= rate of expected inflation, x=excess demand for labor defined as between the vacancy rate and unemployment rate and λ=the rate of growth in labor productivity.

Then the alternative Phillips curve expressions and their policy prescriptions, (choice menus) can be written as (Frisch, 1986) follows:

the Original Phillips curve:

(1) $w= f(u^{-1})$

The Phillips - Lipsey excess-demand model:

(2) $w= g(x)$, $x = h(u^{-1})$, $w=f(u^{-1})$

The Samuelson-Solow modification of the Phillips curve: (under mark-up pricing rule)

(3) $p=g(w,\lambda)$, $w=h(p^*, u^{-1}, \lambda)$, $p=f(p^*,u^{-1},\lambda)$

All these equations are written in functional form, because the causal relation is in the direction indicated by the function concerned. Unemployment rate or the excess demand for labor, basically determines the wage rate; hence increase in labor demand or decline in labor supply (due to emigration) would lead to a higher wage level and vice versa, which is in accordance with the labor market equilibrium and economic theory; and causal relationship is correct.

(ii) Policy implications and reality

Whereas in all policy recipes derived from these functions, causal relationship is reversed by employing the inverse function, which even if exists mathematically, economically does not make sense, although theoretical rationale of the inverse function is attempted (e.g. by Friedman), they are not convincing, and this subject is taken up thoroughly later. But as Arrow (1981) succinctly asserts, the Phillips formulation is inadequate and "rising prices themselves cause increase in wages". And hence, the causal relationship implied by the inverse function is wrong. Because the policy prescriptions are of the following form:

(4) $u^{-1}= \phi (w)$, $u^{-1}=\varphi(p)$

For example, Samuelson and Solow interpreted the Phillips curve as a technical relationship and, suggested its use as an instrument of economic policy, since each point along the curve can be interpreted as a possible economic policy program. There is a trade-off between the rates of inflation and unemployment, in the sense that one can purchase less inflation through more unemployment or less unemployment through higher inflation.

The causal relationship in eqs. (4) is economically wrong, because higher wages do not increase the labor demand and employment, on the contrary reduce the labor demand and employment ceteris paribus. This issue is taken up below. Policy recommendations derived from the Phillips curve analysis is overstretching the argument beyond reason, and are unjustifiable inference.

Another aspect of the Phillips curve analysis concerns output and employment cost of stabilization policies (through fiscal and/or monetary contraction); experience shows that if appropriate policies are enforced effectively, about in a year output and price stabilization could be achieved (Turkey, 1946 and 1961), or hyperinflation/high inflation could be stopped very quickly, if at all (Taiwan 1952, Austria 1923, Poland 1924, Germany 1924, Hungary 1925 and 1946/47, Mexico, Chile and Israel during the 1980s, (Vegh, 1992)), or ensuing recession is not as severe and persistent as Keynesians predict and wage cuts are preferred to unemployment (US, early 1980s).

On the other hand, with half-hearted measures (floating exchange rate, or anchoring exchange rate, liberalizing foreign trade and reducing tariffs, lifting exchange control, without establishing fiscal and monetary discipline) and/or supply-side economics (tax cuts, investment incentives and grants) and/or faith on the Phillips trade-offs inflation becomes high and chronic (Turkey 1969-1993).

In the reforming socialist countries, the temporary output losses and downward pressure on prices (recessionary impact) of tight monetary and fiscal policies through the aggregate demand shock generated, would help with the restructuring process of enterprises, which is also pointed out by e.g. by Gomulka (1992); and this policy is superior to the unfair competition exercised to the same end through the wasteful underdevalued exchange rate (Poland, 1990 and 1991). If coupled with a realistic exchange rate, exercise of fiscal and monetary discipline, is the best means of restructuring. And as observed in the US (early 1980s) and in Poland (in 1991: Gomulka, 1992), workers agree to wage cuts when faced with the alternative of job losses, which speeds up the downward adjustment process (shift of the aggregate supply curve).

On the other hand expansionary policies, in the reforming countries, would lead to more price/wage increases than output response, more increase in imports than in domestic output, shortages of foreign exchange and material inputs which would further exacerbate price/wage inflation and disrupt production activities. Expansionary policies, if accompanied by an overvalued currency, produce the most damaging effects.

2 The original Phillips curve, its extension and a critique

(i) The original curve

Phillips studied the empirical relation between nominal wages and unemployment; unemployment stood proxy for output gaps, since very little data was available then on output gaps. Nevertheless "he thought that unemployment provided a better measure of demand pressures in the labor market than did output gaps". A recessionary gap is associated with high unemployment which leads to slow decrease in wages and an inflationary gap which corresponds to low unemployment rate is associated with increase in wages (Lipsey et al, 1990, pp. 580-81).

Solow wrote: "Phillips was comparing *rate of changes of wages, a nominal quantity,* with the percentage of labor force out of work, a real quantity", "... the rate of *wage inflation*-and *probably, therefore the rate of price inflation*- was a smooth function of the tightness of the aggregate economy" (Bell, 1981, pp. 66-67).

The main issue with the original Phillips curve is that, if the change in nominal wages is the dependent (endogenous) variable of a specification for regression analysis, then the possible explanatory variables should have included (i) productivity increase of labor and technological change, (ii) inflation rate, (iii)change in output and employment as the main indicator of labor demand, and (iv) change in labor supply and its components (new entrants, immigration, emigration, etc.). Omitting all other variables and basing the analysis only on rate of unemployment, which would rather explain real wages and employing a single equation bivariate relation could not be considered appropriate.

In fact, over the 1861-1957 period in the UK, wage increases were about 2% above price increases, which is explained by productivity increase (Sloman, 1991, p. 521). *Hence price and productivity increases could possibly explain better money wage increases over the period and then there would exist no Phillips curve at all.*

(ii) Sticky wages

Phillips curve allowed to drop the 'uncomfortable' assumption "that money wages were rigidly fixed and neither rose nor fell as national income varied." "The Phillips curve relationship between money wages and national income determines, in conjunction with productivity changes, the speed at which the short run aggregate supply curve shifts" (Lipsey, et al, 1990, p. 581). However, it is a fact that *not only wages, but even prices are sticky downward* and as noted above *price and productivity changes perhaps could better explain nominal wage changes.* In Turkey, during 1980s despite sustained inflation, all sorts of generous supply-side measures and declining trend of real wages over the period, employment has hardly increased (from April 1989 to April 1992, employment increased by 0.8% p.a. and the official estimate of unemployment remained unchanged at 15.9%).

This result is due to following three reasons, which also repudiate the existence of any Phillips curve:

(a) It is assumed that firms increase their profits by supplying more goods when the real wage declines or given the nominal wage, firms supply more output if prices are higher. Whereas, in output and even employment decisions, importance of wage cost becomes negligible in high-inflation countries without indexation and/or powerful labor unions, with worsening of income distribution. Prices of other inputs, foreign exchange and interest rates tend to have dominating effect on production and investment decisions, as the share of wages in unit costs becomes negligible.

(b) With wage indexation, advantage from real wage decline vanishes. In fact, the cost of living adjustments clause is included in majority of labor union contracts in the US (Dornbusch and Fischer, 1990, p. 520). In high-inflation economies wages generally are indexed to the price level, i.e. adjusted for past price increases.

(c) With sustained high inflation not only income distribution, but efficient allocation of resources is also distorted; uncertainty increases; real interest rates become exorbitant due to high risk premium and high statutory reserve requirements for commercial banks; speculative and short-term investment increase at the expense of productive and long-term investments; a bias is introduced in the calculation of profits and interest income leading to over estimation of them an thus increasing consumption through disinvestment and dissaving; capital outflow increases; tax evasion accelerates; dominance of seller's market conditions and frequent price increases cause inefficiency, waste and increased consumption in firms and households; implementation of investment projects are overly delayed because of cost increases and legal disputes; discipline, productivity and efficiency of labor in general decline along with decreasing real wages; small-and medium- scale enterprises facing difficulties in sales and financing reduce their investments; while low-and middle-income groups dissave, high income group increases luxurious consumption and expenditure on foreign goods, services and assets; etc. All this, increases waste and consumption and reduces saving, productive investment and gainful employment, and the BOP crisis is always imminent.

(iii) Extension to long-term and the role of expectations

> Phillips was interested in studying the short-run behavior of an economy subjected to cyclical fluctuations. ... Others, however, treated the curve as establishing a long-term trade-off between inflation and unemployment.
>
> In the 1960s Phillips curves were fitted to the data for many countries, and governments made decisions about where they wished to be on the trade-off between inflation and unemployment. Then, in the late 1960s, in country after country, the rate of wage and price inflation associated with any given level of unemployment began to rise. Instead of being stable, the Phillips curves were shifting upward. The explanation lay primarily in a shifting relationship between the pressure of demand and wage increases due to expectations (Lipsey, et al, 1990, p. 726).

The *Keynesian model* implies a trade-off between inflation and unemployment, and the Phillips curve implied by the Keynesian model is downward sloping in the short-run, and vertical in the long-run. The long-run Phillips curve, when expected inflation has time to adjust to the actual inflation rate, i.e. when inflation is fully anticipated, is vertical (Froyen, 1986, pp. 307-308).

In the Keynesian model, as in Friedman's explanation, employment increases because the increase in price lowers the real wage and increases the demand for labor. The increase in price is not perceived by the labor suppliers as a fall in the real wage (Froyen, 1986, p.308).

It was gradually understood that the original Phillips curve took into account only the influence of demand on wages and left out the influence of inflationary expectations. The expectations-augmented Phillips curve, shows a vertical shift upward, compared with the original Phillips curve, by an amount equal to the expected inflation rate. This upward shift measured at potential income or natural unemployment level shows the amount of wage increase to occur even "when there is neither excess demand nor excess supply pressure in labor markets" (Lipsey, et al, 1990. p. 726).

The actual wage increase will exceed the expected inflation, when there is inflationary gap, and will be less than it, when there is recessionary gap. Hence the actual rate of inflation will exceed the expected rate, when there is an inflationary gap. When a certain inflation rate is expected, people will demand the increase in wages just to hold their labor supply at the level indicated by the original Phillips curve (Lipsey, et al, 1990, pp. 726-727).

(iv) Position of Phillips curve

The position of the Phillips curve and hence its shifts are dependent on

(a) Cost-push factors such as labor union power or supply shocks (sharp increases in world commodity prices),

(b) expectations of inflation, and

(c) demand shifts among sectors, importance of sector-specific factors and degree of labor mobility.

Insistence on Phillips trade-offs, with policy changes over time focusing on unemployment, then on inflation and later inflationary expectations catching up, will cause Phillips curve shift and produce Phillips loops.

The position of the Phillips curve was relatively stable over the 1861-1957 period, implying that non-demand factors, such as frictional and structural unemployment, cost-push, structural and expectations-generated inflation had changed little; because the position of the Phillips curve was determined by these non-demand factors.

Whereas from 1966 on the Phillips curve has been shifting upward in the UK and in the Western world (Sloman, 1991, pp. 522-23). The fact that Phillips had found that the curve was relatively stable over time, suggested that changes in inflation and unemployment were due to changes in aggregate demand, rather than to changes in non-demand factors.

Keynesians in the UK. claim that the Phillips curve has shifted to the right in the late 1960s and early 1970s, as a result of cost-push factors, namely increased exercise of monopoly power at home and abroad. Growing industrial unrest (increased number of strikes), growing concentration of monopoly power in industry (large number of mergers and take-overs), and a supply shock through dramatic oil and commodity price increases during the said period, led to cost-push pressures and stagflation. Keynesian remedy was some form of prices and incomes policy to shift the Phillips curve back to its original position.

It should be pointed out that prices and incomes policy, scrupulously exercised in the US in the 1970s and in the UK during the 1950s, 1960s and 1970s could only delay some price increases; without eliminating excess demand and excessive monetary expansion, inflation component of stagflation could never be removed and stagnation also remains with price and income controls. Keynesians also accept that *growth in equilibrium unemployment* also led to the rightward shift in the Phillips curve.

It is claimed that, "over time the vertical Phillips curve has moved to the right both in the UK and throughout the developed world. Natural (equilibrium) unemployment had increased, in the UK from around 1.5% of the labor force in the 1960s to around 6-8% in the 1980s. This was due to increased frictional and structural problems caused by the growth of union power and generous unemployment benefits which reduce the incentive to get a job". Average unemployment during 1984-88 was 10.2% (Sloman, 1991, pp. 554-55, 523). "Keynesians and monetarists alike argue that reductions in unemployment below the natural unemployment level can only be brought about by improved factor mobility or other structural policies." (Sloman, 1991, p. 555).

(v) Phillips curve and adaptive/rational expectations

The moderate monetarists, under the *adaptive expectations* (based on past prices, lagged adjustment of price expectations) assumption predict both price and output increases in the short run, in response to aggregate demand increase exceeding the natural level of employment.

Under *rational expectations* assumption (the new classical theory), expectations adjust immediately to aggregate demand change, and hence output and employment remain at equilibrium levels, even in the short-run and only prices change. It is not possible to keep output and employment above the natural level by systematic use of demand management policy. Monetary policy should be used to control inflation; fiscal and monetary policy can not be used to increase output and employment. Deflationary policy will not reduce output and employment, because output and employment will remain at the natural level. Increase in unemployment is due to shifts in the natural rate of unemployment. New classical school, however, rely on supply-side measures.

(vi) US experience during 1981-1985

In 1981, when the US launched monetary restraint to check entrenched inflation of 1970s, neo-Keynesians expected a stagflation phase of 5-10 years, monetarists of 2 years, and rational expectationists of immediate adjustment to full employment equilibrium. Inflation fell from 12.4% in 1980 to 8.9% in 1981 and to 3.9% in 1982; but unemployment rose to 10.9% at the beginning of 1983 (Lipsey, et al, 1984, pp. 711-12).

After the 1981-82 recession, the 1983 recovery in the US was the result of expansionary fiscal policy which promoted faster economic growth and tight monetary policy which contributed to lower domestic inflation and higher interest rates which in turn led to large capital inflow and appreciation of dollar. The appreciation of the dollar during 1980-85 in turn contributed to the reduced inflation rate by making imports and imported raw materials cheaper, and increased foreign competition faced by import substitution industries, like cars and steel (Froyen, 1986, pp. 542-43, 538).

The results of the 1979-82 US stabilization program (which "took effect most seriously in 1982", according to Dornbusch and Fischer, 1990, p.535) show that neither Keynesians nor rational expectationists predicted correctly the outcome. The fact that disinflation was not free of cost, with GDP declines of 0.2% in 1980 and 2.6% in 1982, and 11% unemployment rate in early 1983, disproved the rational expectations hypothesis. The fact that the two-digit inflation of 1979-81 period ended in 1982 (with 3% inflation in 1983), and that recovery started in 1983 with 7% GDP growth in 1984, showed that Keynesians were not right either.

Despite the fact that the 1979-82 disinflation program is not termed gradual by Dornbusch and Fischer (1990, p. 536), it was in fact a gradual program; it virtually did not aim at ending the inflation abruptly and did not either, because despite the fact that the monetary policy was tight, with real balances declining successively 3 years (1979-81), fiscal policy was expansionary with the government budgetary deficits on current account (except for 1979) and overall budget deficits 3% of GDP or higher after 1979 and also because the program was not credible (expectations of reduced inflation was not incorporated into wage and other long-term contracts, as noted by Dornbusch and Fischer, *ibid*, p. 538).

More serious blow, however, was dealt with to the supply-side economics with this experience of Reagonomics (tax cuts and no new taxes). Because supply-side measures produced perverse results; net private saving and domestic saving and net investment recording historical low levels in the 1980s, in the postwar era (Table 22.1). These results are interesting, because in developing countries generous supply-side incentives (like on-the-spot privatizations in developing countries and in some former socialist countries during the communist rule, e.g. in the former Soviet Union) are mingled with fraud and shady deals and rather are means of corruption and swindling Treasury funds and property; hence their experience and evidence might not be considered conclusive, in this respect.

(vii) Century-long time series analyses

Time series analyses of a very long time (e.g. a century) and cross-section analyses comprising many countries, lumping together data, which reflect both movements along demand and supply curves (or their variants) and shifts of them, and disregarding special circumstances prevailing then or in the countries concerned, treating them all in the same manner, using the same functional relationship (even when dummy variables or other methods are used to remedy these complications in a crude manner) are not justifiable, particularly without separately analyzing the critical years or sample segments (when irregular movements or jumps are observed in the relationship under investigation) and without finding out which extraneous factors played a role and treating them under the law of large numbers could not be accepted as the correct methodology. One cannot accept a theoretically wrong hypothesis, because it is empirically verified in this manner. In case of time series analysis of century-long data or cross-country study covering 30-40 countries, additional investigation and study of the said extraneous factors or special circumstances are practically impossible; and hence validity of the results of analysis is questionable.

Table 22.1
Net saving and investment in the US
(percentage of GNP)

	Net Private Saving	Net Domestic Saving	Net Investment
1950-59	7.5	7.4	7.5
1960-69	8.1	7.9	7.9
1970-79	8.1	7.1	6.9
1980-88	5.6	3.1	6.1
1988	4.6	2.8	4.7

Source: Dornbusch and Fischer, 1990, p. 618

E.g., Phillips, finding that the position of the curve was relatively stable over the 1861-1957 period, judged that non-demand factors had not changed over this period. Whereas there was about 2% p.a. productivity increase, and also emigration to dominions which might not have even been evenly distributed during the said period. In lieu of investigating the roles of non-demand factors, inference of these from a simple relationship encompassing (lumping together) effects of several variables, could not be considered scientific. Instead, analyzing and ascertaining that factors, other than inflation and monetary factors, did not affect nominal wage changes over the century would have been required and was a prerequisite for establishing the validity of the original Phillips curve discovery.

3 Does the Phillips curve and trade-off exist at all?

There is no convincing argument for the existence of the reverse causal relationship (inverse function) indicated by the Phillips curve, i.e., for higher money wages leading to higher employment even in labor-surplus countries (definitely not in labor-shortage countries, where the curve was first discovered).

Some economists argue that when aggregate demand increases relative to potential output, inflation rate rises and unemployment (particularly frictional unemployment falls, because workers suffering from money illusion, readily accept jobs when money wages are increasing (see, e.g., Sloman,. 1991, p. 522). Whereas, it is observed that even in a labor-surplus country like Turkey, with relatively high illiteracy rate, even unorganized labor does enter into wage contracts on the basis of real wages, not money wages, and declining real wages over the last two decades, has led to increased mobility and emigration of skilled labor abroad. Even those employed at lower real wages than expected, cost more to employers in terms of low productivity, poor quality of job done, absenteeism, moonlighting, etc.

A more thorough reasoning for the Phillips curve runs as follows: Labor supply will increase in the short-run because of higher money wages offered (ex ante or expected real wage is higher) and labor demand increases because of the expected fall in the ex post level of the actual real wage paid by the employer. "Consequently, unemployment can be pushed below the natural rate." Friedman in the "Role of Monetary Policy"(1) explains:

> Because selling prices of products typically respond to an unanticipated rise in nominal demand faster than prices of factors of production, real wages received have gone down-though real wages anticipated by employees went up, since employees implicitly evaluated the wages offered at the earlier price level. Indeed, the simultaneous fall ex post in real wages to employers and rise ex ante to employees is what enabled employment to increase. But the decline ex post in real wages will soon come to affect anticipations.... Employees will start to demand higher nominal wages for the future. 'Market' unemployment is below the natural level. There is an excess demand for labor so real wages will tend to rise toward their initial level (Froyen, 1986, p. 300).

Firstly, this explanation by Friedman is contradicted by empirical evidence, because real wages do not change over the business cycle.

---

(1) American Economic Review, March 1968, pp. 1-17.

According to the neoclassical theory, the real wage would be high in recessions and low in booms. Empirical evidence shows that wages and employment are independent over the cycle; i.e. the real wage is independent of the level of employment. "Constancy of the real wage is a reasonable approximation to actual wage behavior"; the real wages does not move much over the cycle, in contradiction to the neoclassical labor demand function, which implies that "the real wage would be higher in recessions than in booms"; the real wage is constant as a result of markup pricing and employment changes with aggregate demand. The demand for labor shifts as aggregate demand shifts (Dornbush and Fischer, pp. 490, 691). Since constancy of real wages and its effect on their profit rates should be well-known by employers, they would not interpret a nominal wage increase as an indication of real wage decline.

Secondly, this reasoning by Friedman, is not convincing, because if the perfectly competitive markets assumption is not made, main effect of an unanticipated demand shock is not through its relative price effect (as explained by Friedman), but through its demand (nominal income increase) effect, in other words increase in aggregate demand arising from fiscal and monetary expansion could lead to higher output and employment, if any, before its price effects materialize. Here a distinction has to be made between competitive and imperfect competition markets. Output response to demand increase will be automatic in imperfect competition markets (particularly with saucer-shaped cost curves); but in perfectly competitive markets, however, without a price increase output can not increase. Since the market for food and basic necessities is competitive worldwide, workers will notice price increases quite early.

When price effects emerge, not only output prices but input prices also will rise, and at this instance the same temporary labor which was fooled into accepting employment at lower real wages, apprehending price increases, will withdraw its labor supply; and firms noticing input price increases and that demand increase for their output is not a real demand increase, but nominal one only, will lower their production, particularly those in imperfectly competitive markets. In imperfect competition markets, where holding some idle capacity is a profit maximization strategy, firms will not readily increase employment, and after observing input price increases and that the demand increase is a nominal one, will shift the saucer-shaped cost curves up and lower output to its initial level. Despite all these facts, if lagged wage adjustment constitute a significant cost advantage to an industry (labor intensive with a high wage cost component in manufacturing cost), output and employment would increase in the industry, if extra labor could be hired, which is not very likely. Hence Friedman's reasoning is not valid in this case.

If in the economy the forces of competition are strong enough, as assumed by the modern classical economists, then price increases will emerge right away before any output response, and it will be immediately observed that the demand increase is a nominal one. The cost advantage through lagged adjustment of wages might lead to output increase in sectors where this lag entails a significant profitability increase, until wages catch up. This will call for a two-digit inflation rate, because to alter output and employment decisions, a significant cost advantage must appear. Even then, many firms would not change output since cost advantage for them would be slight; and in many cases of output increase, it would be rather through overtime, redeployment of existing labor force and similar arrangements than by hiring extra labor, if the industry were at competitive equilibrium to begin with (at potential output level), as assumed by modern classical economists. Only marginal firms, having idle capacity would increase output and employment, if they could hire extra labor, in an economy where labor is scarce, real wages are declining and workers have already noticed this fact, in view of rising price level. As a consequence, bulk of increased demand will go to price increases; and in the second round to maintain the same output and employment level, a higher rate of inflation and a bigger dose of demand shock would be required. Could creation of some temporary jobs at this huge cost, be considered a sensible policy?

In persistent inflationary economies, output and employment effects of new demand shocks would be nil. For different kinds of demand shocks and market structures response of firms will differ and this subject is taken up later.

A contractionary demand shock, applied after an expansionary demand shock has run out its effects and when the economic output is at its potential level, would not cause output and employment losses, if implemented by means of a comprehensive, consistent, well-publicized and convincing stabilization program. Such a program would stop inflation overnight or in a very short time, simply by ending excessive fiscal and monetary expansion, if put into effect with resolution and vigor; and this is the only feasible option. On the other hand, a partial, inconsistent and phased (stretched over 2-3 years) stabilization program could never succeed, as ample empirical evidence corroborates, and would lead to bankruptcies, foreclosed mortgages, output and employment losses, and investment declines. In this case there exists a Phillips curve and its trade-off. Hence the Phillips curve and its trade-off exists, when governments are committed to irrational, insensible policies.

In case of partial, phased stabilization programs, price inflation, cost-push pressures, inevitable new demand shocks would continue and would be exacerbated by external and extraneous shocks and conflicting policies (contraction and expansion would co-exist) and a stagflation would be unavoidable. Under perfect competition assumption, marginal firms would be hit hard by declining demand and profits and credit squeeze, and by rising real wages and interest cost. Output and employment losses are inevitable, particularly when firms and plants are closed down, and ongoing investment projects are suspended or abandoned. As noted already, a resolute and powerful government could avoid this chaos and clean up this mess, an along with wipe out the Phillips curve trade-off by drastic and quick action; many governments, however, could not do it, because of the all-powerful inflation lobby representing internal and external vested interest groups.

4 Lucas supply curve

Imperfect information, on the part of workers on prices and real wages, is exaggerated to explain sticky wages and prices by neoclassical school as well, as can be observed from following explanation of output increase as nominal wages rise.

The Lucas supply curve yields real output increase as a result of increase in the stock of money, because of information problem. As a result of the imperfect information of workers about prices, and the full knowledge of firms of the aggregate price level, rise in the price level leads to an increase in the level of employment and output. Firms increase their supply of output, when the real wage declines or given the nominal wage, if prices rise. Workers increase their supply of services, when nominal wages rise, because they would not know whether the increase in labor demand is due to increase in the aggregate demand and the aggregate price level (in these cases they would not increase their labor supply) or a relative shift in demand; and suspecting the latter, might well increase labor supply. Under rational expectations hypothesis, unemployed worker for a new job, take the job if nominal wage is higher, since workers are unaware that price level is rising (Dornbusch and Fischer, 1990, pp. 244-48, 255). The imperfect information assumption in this last case is most inappropriate, since unemployed would know more about prices and the cost of living than the wage level, since he has to sustain his living.

Regarding the assumptions of the Lucas supply curve on workers' and firms' response to rising prices and wages, one notes following observations and empirical evidence: “Since the real wages change very little over the business cycle”, workers do not work more in booms in response to higher wages; “constancy of the real wage is a reasonable approximation to actual wage behavior”, under the markup pricing rule the real wage becomes constant and employment changes with aggregate demand; over the business cycle, large movements in output occur with small movements in real wages (Dornbusch and Fischer, 1990, pp. 691-92). All this shows that, not changes in the nominal or real wages but demand for output matters in the short run, and that demand for labor, not the supply of labor determines employment and output.

Moreover, the empirical evidence does not support the view that only unanticipated monetary expansions (monetary surprises) affect output or that systematic monetary policy does not affect output (*ibid*, p. 690).

Explanation of the latter fact is as follows: Every monetary expansion (systematic or surprise-type) automatically influences output in competitive markets, where every increase in the price of output (nominal or real) cause output increase in the short run, as explained above.

5 Phillips curve under incorrect expectations

Under the rational expectations hypothesis, if people's expectations are incorrect, when aggregate demand increases above the equilibrium level, then firms will increase output, underpredicting the rate of inflation, believing that real demand has risen; and the demand for labor also will tend to increase. Workers also believing real wages will be higher, will supply more labor.

However, in the second round, either under adaptive expectations (unless inflation is sustained) or incorrect expectations (this time overpredicting inflation), output, demand for labor and labor supply will decline through the reverse process; i.e. firms believing that relative price of their products has fallen, will decrease output and employment; and workers believing that real wage is lower than it really is, will decrease labor supply. This is because it is irrational to make systematic errors.

The argument that sticky wages and prices preclude immediate adjustment to demand shocks by firms and labor, and hence lead to temporary shortage or surplus of labor and goods, overlooks crucial aspect of the adjustment mechanism: The argument runs as follows: Since collective wage negotiations determine the wage rate at least for a year, wages cannot be corrected until next negotiation and hence an unanticipated aggregate demand shock will not fully feed into inflation in the meantime. Similarly in imperfectly competitive goods markets, prices are changed infrequently because of saucer-shaped variable cost curves, high cost of changing price list, and in order to collude with other firms and maintain a good public image, etc. The lag in implementing wage and price changes impede inflation to work out its effects fully in the meantime, and cause a temporary shortage of labor and goods, and as a consequence rise in output and employment. In similar fashion, an unanticipated decline in aggregate demand, cause a temporary surplus of labor and goods, and a reduction in output and employment, until wages and prices are adjusted downwards. Under the strict new classical assumptions, wages and prices are completely flexible and hence there is always equilibrium (see, e.g., Sloman, 1991, p. 801).

The latter strict new classical assumptions do not hold true, because perfect flexibility of wages and prices, and immediate adjustment to aggregate demand changes through price and wage changes, perfect information and zero forecasting errors are unrealistic assumptions, as explained above and particularly in the cases cited.

Regarding the former analysis of lagged adjustments and resulting surplus or shortage of labor and commodities, the overlooked fact is that quantities of supply and demand are changed while prices and wages remain unchanged, but not in the direction cited. When workers apprehend that negotiated wages have declined in real terms more than their expectations as a consequence of unanticipated inflation rise, labor supply will decline, in the same manner as labor supply has increased when workers believed that rise in money wages represented a real rise in wages (through reversal of the expectations process and its symmetric opposite effects on labor supply); i.e., the same workers, who offered their services when money wages rose, will withdraw their services now. Hence there is no possibility for employment to increase.

Firms, which do not adjust their prices frequently, have more options under the same circumstances. They could and would increase their prices higher than justified by real cost and demand increases in the past price period, to take care of any eventuality, exigency that may arise until the next pricing phase and the fact that price adjustment in between is costly and embarrassing. This is a behavior casually observed in sustained inflation economies and is rational.

Secondly, firms observing that relative prices have changed to the disadvantage of them in the current price period, in lieu of increasing their supply or running down inventories, they would rather withhold their supply, built up stocks and create a relative scarcity of their products to prepare ground for a hefty increase in their prices in the next adjustment. This behavior is also casually observed in sustained inflation economies, and is rational. Because increasing sales, in view of rising input costs, declining real prices of products and declining profit margin is irrational. Hence there would not be any change in output and demand for labor (employment) as demand increases in response to a decrease in the relative price of product.

Similarly when an unanticipated decline in aggregate demand occurs and real prices and wages increase unexpectedly and as a consequence a temporary surplus of labor and goods emerges, a rational firm, in lieu of reducing output and laying off redundant workers (which is a costly and painful exercise itself), would rather reduce its prices which would restore demand and to tackle with the reduced profit margin due to high wage costs, could renegotiate wages and workers, under the threat of losing their jobs would rather accept lower wages, as they did in the early 1980s in the US. Or the firm after lowering its prices could well decide to absorb the extra wage cost element, depending on circumstances, in order to keep its market share, and considering also that it will re-hire the same workers when real wages decline to their normal level. The firm might take this opportunity to get rid of inefficient workers, but then it will shortly have to restore employment and output.

Moreover reducing output and employment in the face of unanticipated demand fall assumes closed economy and no competition in oligopolistic markets, whereas even colluding oligopolistic firms would undercut competitors when opportunities arise. This situation gives a good opportunity to do so, particularly for the firm which successfully re-negotiated the new wage level. In an open economy, overpriced products would invite foreign competition and import penetration into the market will increase and a rational firm has to protect its market share against such eventuality.

6 Empirical evidence for the Phillips curve trade-off

Empirical evidence showing that in the short-run an increase in the money stock affects primarily output and has little effect on inflation (prices or wages) is considered as solid support for the short-term Phillips curve. E.g. the Data Resources Inc. macroeconometric model for the US economy shows that 0.5% monetary expansion (in real balances) would at the beginning cause output to rise with almost no impact on prices; "only after a year does output start falling back as prices increases build up and bring real balances back down: but even after l6 quarters or 4 years, output is still above its initial level and prices have not risen by a full percentage point". This is considered as empirical evidence for the Phillips curve trade-off, since due to gradual adjustment of wages (sticky wages), a monetary expansion had a lasting effect on output and employment (Dornbusch and Fischer, l990, pp. 480-8l). Following comments can be made on these views:

(i) The fact that real money balances have increased to affect output, but not prices, by itself shows that price increases have lagged behind and expansion policy has been successful, which may be because inflation was not anticipated, or the economy was growing in real terms any way; otherwise despite nominal monetary expansion, real money balances might not have increased; and analysis based on ex post data may not reveal the cause of output growth. If the economy is growing strongly, then money supply and real balances are bound to increase. The experience in the UK in late l980s show that, in modern economies it is difficult to control money supply, even when the authorities are strenuously struggling to achieve it.

(ii) An econometric model will yield results according to behavioral relationships postulated; the fact that these regression equations are found statistically significant does not alter this fact (another behavior pattern specified might well be found statistically verified). Hence simulations from an econometric or macroeconomic model cannot substitute more direct empirical evidence.

(iii) The fact that real money balance increase affects output rather than prices, does not prove that the causal relationship is through the Phillips curve trade-off. Because the causal link could well be directly via excess demand, not through lagging wages. It is implausible, firms responding to about 0.5% increase in demand (price increase estimated after 4 years was still less than 1%) and implicit 0.15% (2) cost advantage arising from assumed lagged wage increase by hiring extra labor to be fired soon.

(iv) In the competitive markets, if there is no price increase, there would be no supply increase. Only in imperfectly competitive markets supply will increase without price increase in response to demand increase.

Following empirical findings and observations, are crucial in winding up this issue: Large movements in output occur with small movements in real wages over business cycles; during booms employment is high and conversely in recessions. Moreover the empirical evidence does not support the view that the intertemporal substitution of leisure explains the fact that small changes in wages can cause large output effects in the cycle. Workers do not work more in booms because of higher wages, since "constancy of the real wage is a reasonable approximation to actual wage behavior" and under the markup pricing rule the real wage becomes constant and employment changes with aggregate demand (Dornbusch and Fischer, 1990, pp. 691-92). Hence, the explanation for workers' and firms' behaviors in response to price and wage inflation supporting the Phillips trade-off is not valid. Labor supply responds to nominal wage increase not because workers are ignorant of the real wage level and firms do not increase output and employment because of the wrongly assumed increase in their expected, profitability through lag in wage adjustments, since real wages are constant anyway in a business cycle and the assumed cost advantage and profitability increase, if any, is of minor significance; one concludes that labor supply increases if labor demand rises and output/employment increases only in response to the aggregate demand increase. Particularly, in inflationary conditions, changes in prices and availability of critical inputs, imported materials and spare parts, high interest cost, expected change in the exchange rate, credit squeeze, possible labor strife, degree of capacity utilization and increasing uncertainty in general, might outweigh any cost advantage arising from lagged adjustment of wages and even expanding sales prospects.

Some regression equations are estimated for the US, Korea and Japan, to find out whether annual changes in real GDP have responded positively or negatively, if at all, to annual price (hence wage) inflation and fiscal expansion

---

(2) Assuming 30% wage cost in the total cost of output and, 0.5% price increase and no increase in the wage rate in the first year.

(government budgetary deficit). Data used are appended to Chapter 22. This is a direct test of both the short-term Phillips curve trade-off (short-term, since no lagged effect is assumed in the specifications)[3] and crowding-out effects of budgetary deficits.

This simple analysis does not prove any theory, but disproves the generally acknowledged beneficial effects on growth of budgetary deficits (or tax cuts for the US) and existence of any Phillips trade-off. Negative coefficients obtained for price inflation and government budgetary deficit indicate that these two factors rather reduce the growth rate of economic output. F-tests show that estimated regression coefficients are different from zero at 5% significance level, except for eqs (1) and (4). The standard errors of coefficients are shown in parentheses below the coefficients.

The US: 1972-1992:

(1) $Y= 7.092 - 0.476\,P - 0.480\,D$ (R=0.476)

(2) $Y= 4.424 - 0.297\,P - 0.894\,\Delta D$ (R=0.597)

Korea: 1972-1983: (Two-digit inflation period)

(3) $\Delta Y = - \underset{}{0.109} \underset{(0.755)}{-1.123\,\Delta D} - \underset{(0.135)}{0.399\,\Delta P}$ (R=0.781)

$F_{2,9}=7.04$; only coefficient of ΔP is significant at 1% level.

Korea: 1971-1990:

(4) $Y = 10.128 - 1.133\,D$ (R=0.3826), $F_{1,18} = 3.09$

(5) $Y = 11.178 - 0.214\,P$ (R=0.462), $F_{1,18} = 4.88$

Japan: 1970-1990:

(6) $Y= 7.788 - \underset{(0.1696)}{0.501\,D} - \underset{(0.0796)}{0.173\,P}$ (R=0.600)

$F_{2,18}= 5.06$; coefficient of D is significant at 1% level and that of P at 5% level. Where, Y= annual growth rate (%) of real GDP, P= rate of annual inflation (consumer price index, (%), D= Government budgetary deficit as percentage of GDP, Δ takes first differences of variables.

---

(3) Although in eq. (3), P_t implies existence of $-P_{t-1}$, since its coefficient turned out to be negative, effect of P_{t-1} on Y_t is positive, whereas the long-term Philips trade-off is zero, if not negative.

7 Keynesian labor market assumptions and reality

Keynesian labor market theory neatly explains Phillips curve trade-off under a basic assumption, which claims that labor bargains in terms of the money wage or expected real wage, and act accordingly. Even when labor supply increases in response to increase in the expected real wage, labor supply will not shrink when the expected real wage does not materialize due to ensuing price inflation. Whereas in reality, those workers who joined the active labor force in response to rising expected real wages, will withdraw their labor, when they apprehend that real wages have not increased.

Under the neo-Keynesian theory; labor supply depends on the current money wage and the expectation of the price level (price expectations are backward looking and adjust slowly, hence price expectations do not change in line with the current economic situation); i.e. labor supply depends on the expected real wage, which is constant in the short-run, and hence the labor supply curve is fixed in the short run. Whereas labor demand depends on the real wage and firms can forecast correctly future prices and their relative prices. With the fixed labor supply curve, an increase in the price level will shift the labor demand curve to the right along the supply curve, yielding a higher employment level and money wages.

The pitfalls of this analysis, other than related to the labor supply, which is already noted, are on the labor demand side. Firms will not readily hire extra labor in response to a temporary demand increase, to fire them after a short while; which will create many complications (extra help is not hired as readily as ordering extra supplies and it is a costly exercise). Moreover reaction of firms to temporary demand increase will depend on the current economic situation and specific conditions the firm live in. However, in countries like Turkey and even the US, where there is a secondary labor market, this is possible.

In the US there is a secondary labor market for nonskilled workers to meet high levels of demand. Peter Doeringer and Michael Piore argue that due to the instability of aggregate demand, firms employ temporary labor and resort to subcontracting on the secondary labor market when demand is high. If demand were high and stable, then firms would have more incentive to create stable jobs (which carry job security) for their entire workforce (Dornbush and Fischer, 1990, p. 563).

In Turkey reliance on the secondary labor market and subcontracting, in the form of underground economy (not correctly recorded and reported) is a permanent phenomenon. Persistent high inflation and resulting continuous uncertainty regarding economic and business prospects, overly demanding labor legislation and high rates of payroll and withholding taxes (about 60%) might explain it.

If the economy is in a recession, then slacks exists in firms and a temporary demand increase will be met by running down already high-level inventories, increasing rate of utilization of existing workforce, considering also that firms are under profit squeeze and trying to minimize costs. Firms will not hire back workers previously laid off, unless they are definitely sure of full recovery of the economy, nor will invest in plant and machinery, unless they estimate a permanent demand increase or a technological breakthrough is involved. One should also consider the fact that declining industries, increased import penetration and previous overheating (full-capacity operation) of the economy had caused the recession Efficient firms will be operating at near capacity even in a recession (exporting the surplus), hence they will not have the spare capacity to utilize by hiring more labor. And these firms will be in a better position to judge the temporary nature of demand increase and act accordingly.

As a consequence a temporary demand increase, even it leads to output expansion, it is least likely that this will entail employment increase.

Moreover Keynesian labor demand function, assuming a price increase automatically leading to increased demand for labor oversimplifies the real world. For many products, the share of labor cost in prices is minimal, hence decline in real wages will not affect output and employment decisions.

In labor-intensive industries like textile, construction, domestic services and service sector in general, where labor cost constitute a significant part in the cost of output, and output and employment could easily expand or contract in response to demand variations, without requiring significant capital investment, several factors (based on casual observations in the developing countries) preclude realization of Keynesian assumptions. Labor unions are least powerful in those sectors and workers are paid at or below the minimum wage level. Women and child labor (except for construction) and unskilled labor are dominant in these sectors. However in construction and service sectors, the wage level is automatically adjusted (almost indexed) to price increases, even in the labor-surplus economies, and wage contracts are very short-term nature, even on a daily basis sometimes. Hence money illusion assumption on the part of workers is irrelevant. And as a consequence employers do not enjoy a relative price advantage (a decline in real wages) when price inflation occurs.

In the textile sector a minimum real wage is paid to maintain the required labor supply (contracts also are on a short-term basis) which does not change over time with inflation. Hence price inflation could affect neither the labor supply nor demand. The limiting factor to growth of the industry, is not cost disadvantage arising from labor cost which is anyway at the rock-bottom level, but mainly external demand for the product. Moreover with accelerating inflation and resulting deterioration in income distribution, the domestic demand for the product might decline, even through it is a basic necessity next to food, which in turn might lead to output and employment losses, unless export increase makes good the shortfall. In the construction sector as well, with accelerating inflation, skyrocketing costs slow down demand for housing construction and building construction investments, and cause considerable delays in the completion of projects.

Hence in all these labor-intensive sectors, experience in developing countries shows that, labor supply and demand will not be affected by price inflation, and output and employment will not increase as a result; on the contrary in the textile and construction sectors, sustained inflation might cause output and employment declines. Output and employment of these sectors hinge on the real demand for output. Similarly the demand for service sectors' output of non-luxury types declines under high-inflation conditions as a consequence of worsening of already inequitable distribution of income.

This Keynesian analysis of labor market focuses on price increase aspect of aggregate demand shock; whereas an unanticipated inflation brought about by gradual banking credit and monetary expansion, (along with sustained economic growth), unnoticed by the public, will first lead to demand increase. And if caught unawares, as happened in Turkey in the late 1960s and early 1970s, will lead to output expansion as well. In markets of imperfect-competition structure and with saucer-shaped cost curves, this kind of demand increase would lead to output increase without any price change. Whereas in competitive markets, output increase could materialize only after price increase and hence, both output and price increases would result in.

Another version of demand shock, as frequently experienced in Turkey, is in the form of an increase in the civil service pay financed through monetary expansion, introduction of VAT or excise tax increase, increase in oil prices, increase in prices of goods produced by public enterprises or a sizeable boost in agricultural support prices, all of which immediately lead to widespread, some of them chain-reaction type price increases and are followed by accommodating monetary expansion. Except for those cases where tax revenue increase is entailed, there is no countervailing effect to fiscal and monetary expansion and inflationary process accelerates as a consequence. On the basis of Turkish experiences in the 1970s and 1980s, on can maintain that, unless the economy is in a deep recession (which is very exceptional for a developing economy, which is always on the verge of inflation) and required capital inflow from abroad in the form of cash loans or program credits materializes, this type demand shock ends up mainly in price all of increases. Wage increases for the public enterprise sector's workers are also immediately passed on to the prices of products produced by the enterprises concerned. This exercise has become a regular routine in Turkey under continuous high inflation (at 60-80% p.a.) but without indexation, in the last two decades. This exercise has not changed income distribution in favor of public sector employees or farmers, and has not even prevented the worsening of income distribution in time.

In wage settlements past experiences will matter if wage increases have failed to keep up with price increases (as in Turkey during the last two decades) and backward-looking behavior or inertia based on past experience will dominate expectations of workers. Wage settlements will have a catch-up component. This whole exercise, which appears irrational if viewed from a long-term perspective, could have been averted by means of indexation on a monthly basis of wages and other fixed payments and prices; and then forward-looking expectations would have dominated collective bargaining, which could well aim at stopping inflation for good in a sound economic stabilization program. Moreover such a strategy, would have been to the advantage of labor (even when inflation could not be stopped), by preventing the declining trend of real wages.

8 Effects of wage increase and decrease in labor shortage and labor-surplus countries

Response of firms and labor to increased nominal wages will change depending on the cause of the wage increase and equilibrium in the labor market.

In countries where labor is a scarce factor, and wages are on the rise because of emigration or rapid economic growth, participation rate into labor supply might increase with consequent increase in employment. And the wage increase has to be a real one. In the long run, however, with increased application of labor saving technology and investments, employment might decline, unless rapid growth in economic output continues.

In labor-shortage countries, productivity increase would lead to a rise in the nominal and real wage level, increased labor supply and employment. Productivity increase due to labor-saving technology, however, would lead to real wage increase, but not employment increase, by itself.

The effect of increase in nominal and real wages stemming from increased protection of industry might or might not lead to output and employment increase depending on whether the affected sectors are growth, mature or declining industries. Resultant higher overall wage level in the economy, however, would reduce output and employment in sectors not protected or not efficient/profitable sufficiently. Overall effect might well be a decline in employment through reduced demand for labor and increased use of labor-saving technology.

Increase in nominal wages arising from rising labor-union power, would lead to a rise in real wages, to lower employment and to adoption labor-saving technology in the long-run.

A lagged increase in nominal and real wages following a price inflation, would lead to an increase in labor supply and employment, if the previous price inflation had caused a decline in labor supply.

An increase in nominal wages due to a rise in the minimum wage level, if not accompanied by price inflation, would lower labor demand and employment, and if accompanied by price inflation (through accommodating monetary expansion) would not lead to increased labor supply, unless Keynesian money illusion prevails. Otherwise, labor supply and employment might increase in the short run.

As a consequence of all this, the long-term inverse relationship observed by Phillips between changes in the nominal wage level and the unemployment rate should rather be result of all other factors, like emigration, fast economic growth, productivity increase, but wage inflation.

Nominal wage rise would lead to increased labor supply, hence employment, only when workers act under money illusion, but even then a rebound is bound to occur when workers perceive the decline in real wages; and this short-term effect is a once-and-for-all one and under sustained inflation, money illusion will evaporate and employment will not change even temporarily. Without analyzing the causes of nominal wage increases in the course of a century, attributing all increases to wage inflation, as the Phillips-curve analysis entails is misleading and a gross generalization.

So far we have focused on increased labor supply responding to higher wages in a labor-shortage economy. Response of enterprises to higher nominal wages in such an economy would per se be reduced demand for labor. Firms facing a demand shock and an accompanying wage inflation would not alter their output and employment, since relative prices and real magnitudes have not changed. If an unanticipated wage inflation is the case (the very case studied by Phillips), there is no reason for firms to judge this as a mere nominal increase beforehand as supposed by the Phillips curve analysis; on the contrary, at the beginning, they will judge this increase as a real one and will tend to reduce their demand for labor.

On the other hand, *decline in nominal wages* might arise from decline in economic growth and hence demand for labor, increased labor supply due to immigration or demographic factors, tight monetary policy, increased foreign competition due to opening up the economy (lowering tariffs, removing import restrictions, etc.), breaking up the labor-union power, etc. In all these cases, except for the tight monetary policy, real wages also would decline for sure. And due to decline in real wages, labor demand would increase, except for the case of declining economic growth, and as a consequence employment would increase. One should also note that, workers would accept lower money and real wages, when there exists the threat of unemployment, as occurred in the US in the early 1980s and it seems to happen in Japan always at the firm level.

In case of the increase in labor supply due to immigration, which in turn might be the result of either increased labor demand or too high real wages, lower money and real wages would materialize at least in some sectors (like labor-intensive ones) and in certain labor categories (un- and semi-skilled, new entrants, juniors, women) and increased employment would result in either case. It is also a mistake to analyze on the basis of the average wage level, while nominal and real wages of labor with seniority and skilled category, and of protected, privileged and priority sectors might move not in line with those of others.

In case of increased labor supply due to demographic factors, real wages have to decline (nominal wages, as well, if monetary expansion does no take place) in order to attain full employment, in the short term.

In case of declining wages due to tight monetary policy following an inflationary period, in the short run decline in employment will occur as output decreases to the potential level, however with economic recovery thereafter employment will increase.

Whereas, declining real wages arising from breaking up labor union monopoly, would lead to higher employment level; as well in the case of reduced real wages resulting from increased import penetration into high-wage sectors (while increased exposure to foreign competition *per se* might lead to decline in output and employment on impact).

One can conclude that declining nominal an real wages under ceteris paribus assumption would lead to increased employment, contradicting the Phillips curve hypothesis.

One last comment is related to the degree of perfect information assumption on the part of employers. Neo-Keynesians would assume that any and every employer would correctly estimate and distinguish whether the change in nominal wages is due to monetary factors or to real factors and react differently and correctly accordingly. But in case of a nominal wage change resulting from a simultaneous combination of real and nominal factors, to assume that every employer would be able to separate different components and respond to real and nominal parts differently is well beyond the reason.

9 Conclusion

In theory and practice there exists no meaningful Phillips curve or its trade-off. The futility of the Phillips trade-off attempts, i.e. creating jobs and incomes by inflationary expansionary policies could also be understood better by considering many other factors than inflationary or recessionary gaps which are always at work in the modern economies to create inflationary pressure. These are expectational inflation (expected increase in costs), agricultural crop failures, changes in indirect taxes and tax rates, ever-increasing government expenditures, increase in imported inflation, frequent exchange rate changes under a flexible exchange rate system, wage increases and other random supply shocks. In such a framework, adding the Phillips trade-off on top of these factors only exacerbates the inflation problem and becomes a useless and harmful exercise. Looking from this angle, it is obvious that at least one policy instrument, namely monetary policy, the most powerful in this respect, should be geared to price stability.

Keynesians, however, acknowledging these facts still argue for expansionary policy to deal with stagflation. Their argument runs as follows: From the mid-1970s onwards, excess demand was confined to certain sectors. Downward stickiness of wages and prices, the increasing concentration of economic power in large multinational companies and large trade unions and the large oil price increases of 1973/74 and 1978/79 created cost-push pressures. Under pessimistic expectations of lower sales, firms reduced production, investment and employment. All this does not represent a short-term difficulty that markets will soon correct. Hence a deliberate policy of reflation is called for. The counter argument runs as follows: Under the circumstances, there is no guarantee that reflation and/or regional policie should increase output (since the long-run Phillips curve is vertical), but increase inflationary pressure through monetary expansion involved and pricing policies of oligopolistic firms with market power.

Turkish experience in 1980s onwards, with overgenerous general, selective and regional policies of reflation, all sorts of export and investment incentives, open and disguised capital grants, soft loans, subsidized inputs, etc. have accelerated inflation (and increased unemployment) than economic growth. An increase in private and foreign business investments in plant and machinery has not even made up the decline in productive investments also resulting from a deliberate policy of curtailing productive investments of public enterprises, and productive investments declined absolutely and relatively.

Chapter 22

A review of country experiences

A review of country experiences

In this chapter the experiences of the industrialized countries and of fast- and slow-growing developing countries, in the last two decades, with the Phillips curve trade-off, supply-side economics, crowding-out effect, and saving, investment and economic growth performances are reviewed.

The aim is not to prove any theory or model, but rather call in question the validity of certain (nowadays) conventional economic models and assumptions. It is not a comprehensive, exhaustive study; it rather aims at to test certain aspects of conventional theories and to raise evidence (even though circumstantial) against them and air some views in support of their critics.

The aim of the following exercises should not be construed as an attempt to analyze economies or problems of the industrialized West; even though some views are aired, on the basis of certain evidence and apparent causes of some problems; the main purpose is to compare policies and performance of the West with the Far Eastern countries and to see whether policies prescribed for the developing countries (e.g. Turkey) based on the US model can assist their growth and unemployment problems and also to find out whether reform programs underway in the former socialist countries employing the US model (open economy and privatization of monopolies) could succeed. It is observed that open economy and deregulated monopolies have caused some problems (unemployment, low growth and investment rates) even in the US (where the economy is in the best position to cope with all these problems, since it is the most dynamic, technologically and organizationally most advanced, endowed with ample capital, human resources and most competitive markets); hence other countries in adopting the US model should exercise extreme caution. It seems that a virtually open economy regime adopted by Poland and Russia would create problems.

1 Economic basis of regression analysis

Employing regression analysis, hypotheses about the Phillips curve trade-off and crowding out effect of fiscal expansion are tested. The wage-Phillips curve can be expressed as

(1) $$w = \lambda (Y_t - Y^*)$$

where $w = [(W_t - W_{t-1})/W_t]$ denotes wage inflation, W_t= nominal wage in year t, Y_t = actual output, Y^*= potential output and subscript t shows time (year).

The price -Phillips curve is

(2) $$p = \lambda(Y_t - Y^*)$$

where $p = [(P_t - P_{t-1})/P_{t-1}]$ denotes the rate of price inflation and P_t= consumer price index (CPI). Eq (2) is derived from the dynamic aggregate supply curve:

(3) $$P_t = P_{t-1} [1+ \lambda (Y_t - Y^*)]$$

The dynamic aggregate demand curve is given by

(4) $$Y_t = Y_{t-1} + \phi (m-p)$$

where Φ= money multiplier effect, m= the growth rate of the nominal money stock, and hence m - p= the rate of change of real balances (Dornbusch and Fischer, 1990, pp. 490, 514, 522-23).

Two assumptions are made:

(i) The actual output in previous year is at its potential level, i.e., $Y_{t-1} = Y^*$; this value is plugged in eq (2). Reasons for this assumption are already well explained earlier.

(ii) In an industrialized economy, the change in real balances in the long run can not exceed the real increase in output (y); i.e.,

(5) $$m - p = y$$

this is substituted in eq (4).

From the quantity theory of money one can write

(6) $$p = m - y - v$$

where $y = [(Y_t - Y_{t-1})/Y_{t-1}]$ denotes the growth rate of output and v denotes percentage change in velocity of money. If velocity is constant in the long run, then eq (6) reduces to eq (5).

Monetarists claim that velocity changes are not significant. Dornbusch and Fischer maintain that, "there is no economic rule that says velocity in the long run tends to be constant" However, in fact, in the US and in many other countries, velocity was constant in the long run. (during 1960s, 1970s, and 1980s). In all these countries, the causal link between money growth and inflation holds, after allowing for output growth. Although velocity changes in the short run and rise in interest rates raises velocity even in the long run, velocity empirically was found constant in the long run (Dornbusch and Fischer, 1990, pp. 644-647). On these grounds (since the past data is analyzed, eq (5) is written. Making the substitutions, and writing $\Delta Y = Y_t - Y_{t-1}$, the aggregate supply function, eq (2) reduces to

(7) $$p = \lambda \Delta Y$$

and the aggregate demand function, eq. (4) reduces to

(8) $$\Delta Y = \Phi y$$

Writing ex post equilibrium of aggregate demand and supply, by plugging eq (8) in eq (7), one gets

(9) $$y = \frac{1}{\lambda\phi} p$$

Eq (9) is estimated by least squares, to test the original version of the Phillips curve trade- off; a positive coefficient for p should be estimated since $\lambda, \phi > o$, if the Phillips-curve trade-off hypothesis holds true. A low coefficient of determination estimated for regression, will also suggest rejection of the Phillips curve hypothesis, since a small part of variation of dependent variable y will be explained by the independent variable p. Dornbusch and Fischer (1990, pp. 518-519) claim that "in the short run, with a given expected rate of inflation, higher inflation rates are accompanied by higher output; in the long run, with expected rate of inflation equal to the actual rate, the level of output is independent of the inflation rate".

The second version of regression analysis aims at estimating the crowding-out effect of fiscal expansion, along with the Phillips curve trade-off. The aggregate supply function is the same as eq. (7):

(10) $$p = \gamma . \Delta Y$$

the aggregate demand function is

(11) $$Y = \gamma\,\bar{A} + \gamma\,\frac{b}{h}\frac{M}{P} + \gamma\,b\,p$$

based on an IS curve Y = α (Ā - b r), where Ā autonomous part of aggregate demand, α= multiplier, r= the real interest rate and an LM curve

$$i = \frac{1}{h}\left(k\,Y - \frac{M}{P}\right)$$

where i= nominal interest rate (i = r + p), M= nominal stock of money;k,h,b>o;

$$\gamma = \frac{\alpha\,h}{h + k\,\alpha\,b}$$; γ is fiscal multiplier and money

multiplier $= \gamma\,\frac{b}{h}$

(Dornbusch and Fischer 1990, pp. 544-46). Total differentiation of eq (11) yields:

(12) $$d\,Y = \gamma\,.d\,\bar{A} + \gamma\,\frac{b}{h}\frac{M}{P}\,(m - p) + \gamma\,b.d\,p$$

or omitting the last term,

(13) $$\Delta\,Y = \gamma\,.\,\Delta\,\bar{A} + \phi\,\frac{M}{P}\,(m - p)$$

(where $\phi = \gamma\,\frac{b}{h}$ money multiplier), writing y=m-p and $\Delta Y = Y_t - Y_{t-1}$ as above and $\Delta\,\bar{A} = D$ = government budgetary deficit, $\beta = \phi\,\frac{M}{P}$ (were M and P takes the values of the first year, (13) reduces to

(14) $$\Delta\,Y = \gamma\,D + \beta\,y$$

Equating ΔY values of the aggregate supply (eq:10) and the aggregate demand functions (eq:14), one obtains

(15) $$y = \frac{1}{\lambda\beta}\,p - \frac{\gamma}{\beta}\,D$$

Since data for government budgetary deficits in constant prices (D) are not available, in regressions D/Y series instead are used as independent variable to indicate fiscal expansion, ($\sigma D/Y$ denotes the impact on demand of fiscal expansion):

$$(16) \qquad y = \frac{1}{\lambda\beta} p - \sigma \left(\frac{D}{Y}\right)$$

Since $\lambda, \beta, \sigma > o$, the coefficient of p should be positive if the Phillips curve hypothesis holds true and the coefficient of D/Y should be negative if budgetary deficits have crowded out private investment.

With this equation, economic growth is tried to be explained by monetary policy (price inflation or stability) and fiscal policy (budgetary deficit); hence low coefficients of determination are expected, since the two independent variables could only explain part of variation in y. Because other factors, such as capacity creation (investment), export growth, technological advance and human capital formation, etc. promote economic growth and might explain it better.

The third version of regression equations is based on the expectations-augmented Phillips curve, which yields the following dynamic aggregate supply curve (the expectations-augmented aggregate supply curve):

$$(17) \qquad p = p^e + \lambda\,(Y - Y^*)$$

where p^e is the expected inflation rate.

The dynamic aggregate demand function might either be eq (14) or one derived from eq (12), i.e.:

$$(18) \qquad \Delta Y = \gamma D + \beta y + \gamma b.\,\Delta p$$

in eq (17) assuming, adaptive expectations and setting $p^e = p_{t-1}$ and $Y^* = Y_{t-1}$ one gets

$$(19) \qquad \Delta p = \lambda . \Delta Y$$

Equating ΔY in eq (19) with that in eq (14) or (18), one obtains (also substituting D/Y for D) eq (20) and (21) respectively.

$$(20) \qquad y = \frac{1}{\lambda\beta} \Delta p - \frac{\sigma}{\beta} \left(\frac{D}{Y}\right)$$

The coefficient of Δp should be positive, if the Phillips trade-off exists and that of (D/Y) negative, since $\lambda, \beta, \sigma > o$.

$$(21) \qquad y = \left(\frac{1}{\lambda} - \gamma\, b\right)\frac{\Delta p}{\beta} - \frac{\sigma}{\beta} \cdot \frac{D}{Y}$$

In analyzing effects of budgetary deficit on the average saving and investment propensity (defined as percentage of GDP), following type of functional relationship is assumed: Let $\bar{S}, \bar{Y}$,& $\bar{D}$ stand for absolute levels of domestic saving, GDP and budgetary deficit at constant prices respectively:

$$(22) \qquad \bar{S} = a + b\bar{Y} + c\Delta\bar{Y} + e\bar{D}$$

where $\bar{D}$ stands proxy for interest rate factor (and for availability of investible funds, in case of investment function) and c.Δ $\bar{Y}$ term takes care of fluctuations in marginal saving propensity due to sharp rises or declines in real income. Dividing through by $\bar{Y}$; and letting S and D denote saving and deficit as percentages of GDP respectively and Y denote growth rate of GDP= $\Delta\bar{Y}/\bar{Y}$,

$$(23) \qquad S = (a/\bar{Y}) + b + c\,Y + e\,D$$

is obtained. Constant term of regression (b), represent the marginal propensity to save out of GDP. Since $(1/\bar{Y})$ and $Y=\Delta/\bar{Y}/\bar{Y}$ are related, in order to avoid multicollinearity, and possible serial correlation, one should leave out either $a/\bar{Y}$ or cY term in the regression. Since a is negative, with steady increase in $\bar{Y}$, S has to increase; whereas, e.g. for the US, S estimated in relation to the disposable income fluctuated (Dornbush and Fischer, 1990, p.300) in 1960s and 1970s and showed steady decline in 1980s (from 7.5% in 1981 to 3.2% in 1987 and consumption as a percentage of the disposable income increased from 90% in 1981 to 94% in 1987. Hence to take care of these fluctuations, rather cY term is included in regressions.

It turns out that the budgetary deficit on current account (D*), is a more powerful indicator of the crowding-out effect on domestic saving, investment and economic growth.

Dornbusch and Fischer (1990, pp. 155-57) claim that, given saving, an increase in the government budget deficit must lower investment; but with extra government spending income rises and hence saving as well, as a consequence interest rates do not rise enough to curb investment; and then there need not be a decline in investment equal to the budgetary deficit. In particular, in an economy with unemployment, output also increases and with monetizing of budget deficits (monetary accommodation), interest rates do not rise at all and no crowding-out occurs. In a fully employed economy, however, crowding- out occurs and monetizing budget deficits may cause inflation. Since the industrialized economies in the 1970s and 1980s could be characterized by high unemployment levels, if the Dornbusch-Fischer hypothesis is correct, no crowding-out effect on saving, investment and economic growth should be estimated in regression analyses.

In analyzing effects of budgetary deficit and price inflation on the average investment propensity, I, (defined as percentage of GDP), the specification is obtained as follows: Let $\bar{I}$ = value of investment, then by the acceleration principle, $\bar{I} = \beta.\Delta\bar{Y}$; and replacement investments (since $\bar{I}$ is defined as gross domestic investment) can be approximated by $\alpha\,\bar{Y}$, and $\bar{D}$ (value of budgetary deficit) stands proxy for interest rate effect and $P\bar{Y}$ for increase in interest rate due to risk factor (in inflationary conditions), where P=the rate of inflation; then

(24) $$\bar{I} = \alpha\,\bar{Y} + \beta\,.\,\Delta\,\overline{Y} + \gamma\,\bar{D} + \pi\,P\,\bar{Y}$$

and dividing by $\bar{Y}$

(25) $$I = \alpha + \beta\,Y + \gamma\,D + \pi\,P$$

A similar alternative expression for S could also be obtained. Alternatively writing

(26) $$\bar{S} = A\,\bar{Y}^{\beta}\,\bar{D}^{\gamma}\,\bar{P}^{\pi}$$

where $\bar{P}$ (price index) stands proxy for risk factor in interest rate during persistent inflation and $\bar{D}$ reflect the crowding-out (interest rate) effect and disappearance or diminution of public saving. Taking logarithm of both sides and differentiating with respect to time and writing for discrete changes and denoting growth rates of D and S, D_r (= $\Delta\bar{D}/\bar{D}$) and S_r respectively one obtains:

(27) $$S_r = \beta Y + \gamma D_r + \pi P$$

which could also be employed in regression analysis.

2 Experience of the UK

(i) Description of performance

In the UK, in the 1980s, investment as a ratio of GDP declined by 3 percentage points compared with the 1968-79 period, and was always significantly lower than those of Germany and Japan (Table 22.2).

"A poor investment record may be in large part be due to managerial inertia and union restrictive practices," and/or to low potential return on investment (Sloman, 1991, p. 849).

According to Sloman, "this low level of investment has been a major reason for UK's poor growth performance". As a result, widening technological gap emerged between the UK and its major competitors, such as Japan and Germany. "In many industries the UK's productivity lags well behind" its competitors. "This, in turn, is reflected in the poor quality and high cost of many UK products. The fact that wages in the UK have been lower than in competing countries has not been sufficient to offset this disadvantage. As a result there has been a growing import penetration of the UK market. Imports of manufactured goods have grown more rapidly than UK manufactured exports" and as a consequence the origin of modern industry, the UK has become a net importer of manufactured goods in recent years (Sloman, 1991, p. 841).

Table 22.2
Gross fixed capital formation as percentage of GDP: 1960-1989 (averages) in the UK, West Germany and Japan

Years	UK	W.Germany	Japan
1960-67	17.7	25.2	31.0
1968-73	19.1	24.4	34.6
1974-79	19.3	20.8	31.8
1980-84	16.3	21.1	29.6
1985-89	16.3	19.1	30.1

Source: Sloman, 1991, p. 841

There are three vicious circles involved (Sloman, pp. 841-42):

(i) "Low investment leads to low productivity, low quality and hence a lack of competitiveness of UK goods". This leads to trade deficit and then deflationary policies with higher interest rates, which in turn leads to low investment.

(ii) Low investment leads to low growth of profits, which in turn leads to low investment.

(iii) Low investment leads to low productivity growth, which leads to low growth in wages, and union pressure for higher wages causes cost push inflation, which calls for deflationary policies, which in turn increases uncertainty and lower profits for firms, and this leads to low investment.

De-industrialization occurred in the UK. "Not only has the competitiveness of UK industry declined, but industrial production in the UK has grown much more slowly than in other industrialized countries." Manufacturing industry hardly grew at all during 1970-1989. "Manufacturing output in the UK in 1986 was only 1% higher than in 1970, whereas in the developed world as a whole it was 50% higher" (Sloman, 1991, p. 842).

North-Sea oil (which in 1985 contributed 16 billion pounds to the value of exports), leading to strong anti-inflationary policies resulted in high interest and exchange rates, which reduced competitiveness of UK exports abroad;

> [i.e. North Sea oil] effectively crowded-out traditional UK exports, [in the early part of the 1980s and oil revenue] rather than being used to pay for more imports of capital goods... to refurbish UK industry,... was used to soften the blow of deflationary policies by helping to keep taxes low... Critics of the Thatcher government argue that North Sea oil revenues should have been spend on long-term investment in the export and import-substituting industries and on improving the nation's infrastructure (Sloman, 1991, p. 843).

In the UK a long-term trend of decline in the average propensity to save is clearly discerned over the 1983-1989 period, which urged the government to introduce in the 1990/91 budget the Tax Exempt Special Savings Accounts to encourage private savings (Sloman, 1991, p. 589). Such measures could bring in only minor results and are definitely not cost-effective and worth-the-while. (A similar scheme is implemented in the US and is going to be implemented in Turkey.)

Table 22.3 describes the relationships between inflation, unemployment and economic growth in the UK over the last three decades.

Table 22.3
UK macroeconomics indicators: 1959-1988
(percentages)

Period	Average Annual Increase in Retail Prices	Unemployment Rate	Average Annual Growth Rate of real GDP	Accumulated Current Account Balance (Billion pounds sterling)
1959-63	2.3	1.9	3.5	0.15
1964-68	4.1	1.9	3.2	-0.95
1969-73	8.7	3.0	3.4	1.52
1974-78	22.1	4.3	1.2	-0.41
1979-83	14.0	8.1	0.8	17.97
1984-88	4.7	10.2	3.6	-11.77

Source: Sloman, 1991, p. 523

From this Table the following observations can be made:

(i) Even before the oil price shock, during the 1969-73 period, rise in the inflation rate (from 4% to 9% resulted in a higher unemployment rate (from 2% to 3%), contradicting the Phillips curve hypothesis.

(ii) Two-digit inflation periods (1974-78 and 1979-83) are associated with low growth rate (1%, versus 3.5% average growth rate in one-digit inflation periods) contradicting the price inflation- real output trade- off hypothesis.

(iii) After the chronic two-digit inflation period, when relative price stability was achieved (5% during 1984-88), (at the cost of increased current account deficit, despite North Sea oil receipts), real income growth rate was restored to 3.5%.

(iv) Increase in unemployment rate is a secular phenomenon, not cyclical, since it showed a steadily increasing trend over the 1959-1988 period (from 2% to 10%).

All this shows that the Phillips trade-off not only does not exist, but that policies based on this hypothesis resulted in higher inflation and lower growth, and the rising trend of unemployment was not influenced by such policies.

(ii) Empirical evidence on Phillips trade-off and crowding-out effect

The relationship between unemployment and inflation rates turned out to be the reverse of what conventionally assumed, although the correlation coefficient of regression equation has become weaker, when 1980s are included in the regression. However, in the UK, where the Phillips curve was discovered, it seems the curve not shifted upward but vanished and reverse relationship became valid after its discovery. Following regression eqs. have been obtained for various periods.

(1) 1959-1973 : P = -6.300 + 5 U (R=0.956)
(2) 1959-1977 : P = -8.701 + 6.146 U (R=0.989)
(3) 1959-1980 : P = -2.469 + 3.522 U (R=0.844)
(4) 1959-1986 : P = +7.081 + 0.207 U (R=0.141)
(5) 1959-1989 : P = 7.227 + 0.127 U (R=0.094)

where P= annual inflation rate and U= unemployment rate (data used are in Table 22.4).

Table 22.4
Inflation, unemployment and economic growth
US, UK, Japan and Germany:1978-1989 (percentages)

	No of Years	Inflation Rate (P)	Unemploy - ment Rate (U)	(ΔU)	Economic Growth Rate (Y)	Budgetary Deficit* (Percent of GDP) (D)
US						
1972-77	6	7.0	-	-	2.0	2.3
1978-80	3	9.7	6.3	-	2.5	2.4
1981-83	3	6.6	8.8	2.5	1.0	4.2
1984-86	3	3.3	7.1	-1.7	4.2	5.1
1987-89	3	3.7	5.6	-1.5	3.7	3.1
1990-92	3	4.2	-	-	0.6	4.8

Table 22.4 (Continued)
Inflation, unemployment and economic growth
US, UK, Japan and Germany:1978-1989 (percentages)

UK

1959-63	5	2.3	1.9	-	3.5	-
1964-68	5	4.1	1.9	0	3.2	-
1969-73	5	8.7	3.0	1.1	3.4	0.7
1974-77	4 1	8.2	4.3	1.3	0.7	5.3
1978-80	3 1	3.2	5.8	1.5	1.4	5.2
1981-83	3	8.4	11.2	5.4	1.3	4.2
1984-86	3	4.8	11.4	0.2	3.1	2.8
1987-89	3	5.7	8.3	-3.1	3.7	-1.6

Japan

1970-73	4	7.6	-	-	7.7	0.7
1974-77	4 1	3.1	-	-	2.7	5.0
1978-80	3	5.1	2.1	-	4.9	7.3
1981-83	3	3.2	2.4	0.3	3.4	6.6
1984-86	3	1.6	2.6	0.2	4.1	5.2
1987-89	3	1.2	2.5	- 0.1	5.2	3.0
1990		3.0	-	-	5.2	1.6

W.Germany

1971-73	3	6.0	-		4.0	-1.0
1974-77	4	5.2	-		1.8	2.3
1978-80	3	4.1	3.2	-	2.9	2.0
1981-83	3	5.0	7.7	4.5	0.3	2.1
1984-86	3	1.4	6.9	- 0.8	2.5	1.3
1987-89	3	1.4	6.0	- 0.9	2.8	1.0
1990-91	2	3.1	-		4.3	2.1

*Minus (-) sign indicates budgetary surplus.
Source: Sloman, 1991, p. 5, 523; IBRD, World Tables

In these regressions grouped data are used because they were available.[1] Following points should be noted in this context. As heteroscedasticity does not occur in time series analyses, there is no need to use weighted least squares. Estimation is based on group means, taking into account the number of observations in each group and the fact that there will be small loss of efficiency by grouping if variation of the values of independent variables within each group is small, compared with the variation of group means around the overall mean (and that in this respect it does not matter whether the groups contain the same number of observations or not).[2]

These results clearly show that high price (and hence wage) inflation is associated with high unemployment. Similar results could readily be obtained from Table 22.4 for the UK, by calculating the original Phillips curve-trade off, i.e. price inflation occurred per unit employment rate change (P/ΔU) for each subperiod during 1959-86, when inflation was on the rise or above 8% annual level. Trade-off between inflation and unemployment was positive and the range of P/ΔU was between 1.6-fold and 24 times and it averaged(weighted) during the 1969-86 period 11 -fold (Table 22.5) and increased inflation led to higher unemployment.

Table 22.5
The UK Phillips curve trade-offs

	P	ΔP	ΔU	P/ ΔU	ΔU/ΔP
1964-68	4.1	1.8	0.0	+ ∞	0.0
1969-73	8.7	4.6	1.1	7.91	0.24
1974-77	18.2	9.5	1.3	14.00	0.14
1978-80	13.2	- 5.0	1.5	8.80	- 0.30
1981-83	8.4	- 4.8	5.4	1.56	- 0.13
1984-86	4.8	-3.6	0.2	24.00	-0.06
1987-89	5.7	0.9	- 3.1	-1.84	-3.44

Source: Table 22.4

(1) To this author.

(2) Jan Kmenta, "Elements of Econometrics", Macmillan, New York, 1986, pp.366-373; Pindyck & Rubinfeld, "Econometric Models & Economic Forecasts", McGraw-Hill, 1981, p. 141.

These effects on prices and hence wages, in lieu of output, are stronger, when systematic expansionary policies against unemployment and stagflation are pursued as in the late 1960s and 1970s, i.e. they could not be the result of unemployment, but reflect the perverse effects of policies applied to cure unemployment. Negative trade-off could occur only when relative price stability is achieved (1987-89 period). It can be concluded that the original Phillips curve trade-off would be attained only in economies with relative price stability; and in high-inflation economies the trade-off is positive.

However, it is not certain that the rise in unemployment level in the early 1980s is due to disinflation and to the Phillips trade-off (rather de-industrialization and increased import penetration might be its cause) or the decline during 1987-89 is brought about by reflation policy, rather it might due to genuine economic growth engendered by price and economic stability, as evidenced by steady rise in domestic investment (as percentage of GDP), from 17% in 1986 to 21% in 1989 (Table 22.6). Whereas it is certain that during 1964-80, inflationary expansion was ineffective in preventing unemployment increase.

Moreover, unemployment cost of gradual inflation reduction, i.e. increase in U per unit P decrease ($\Delta U/\Delta P$), during 1978-86 was high only during 1981-83, when the move was from two-digit inflation to single-digit level; otherwise, i.e. changes within 2-digit or single-digit ranges, cost 0.1-0.3 U increase per unit P decline.

In these regressions, price increase stood proxy for wage increase due to data availability.(3) It should be recalled that even in the US, where labor unions are not powerful, price and wage controls strictly exercised in the early 1970s, could only check price increases, but were ineffective in curbing wage increases. This empirical evidence both refutes the basic presumption of the Phillips curve (the delayed response of wages to price inflation (4) and justifies the use of price inflation as a proxy for wage inflation. The low correlation coefficients of these regressions, however, clearly show inadequacy of the original Phillips curve specification; because other factors than the unemployment level play a role and often dominate in nominal wage and price formation; unemployment level and expected inflation rate could explain only part of variation.

As a consequence new regressions are run to explain the unemployment level (U), by means of annual price inflation rate (P) and real output growth (Y=annual growth rate of real GDP):

---

(3) To this author.

(4) Özmucur (1987) for OECD countries established that in the 1968-73 period, wage adjustments do not lag behind, but precede and exceed price changes.

1959-1973: (annual average inflation rate was 5%)

(6) $U = -2.519 + 0.1897\ P + 1.1379\ Y$ (R=1.0)

1959-1977: (annual average inflation rate: 7.8%)

(7) $U = 0.567 + 0.196\ P + 0.214\ Y$ (R=0.994)

1959-1980: (annual average inflation rate 8.5%, 1974-80 average 16%)

(8) $U = 3.197 + 0.124\ P - 0.439\ Y$ (R=0.854)

1959-1983: (average annual inflation rate 8.5%, the 1980-83 rate declined from 13.2% to 8.4%)

(9) $U = 16.643 - 0.445\ P - 3.607\ Y$ (R=0.794)

1959-1986:(inflation rate declined, the average 1981-86 rate was 6.6%)

(10) $U = 18.186 - 0.540\ P - 3.557\ Y$ (R=0.556)

1959-1989: (the 1981-89 average inflation rate 6.3%)

(11)	U= 13.839 -	0.348 P -	2.232 Y	(R=0.3785)
		(0.223)	(1.0258)	
t - statistic:		(1.558)	(2.176);	

$F_{2,28}=2.34$; Correlation (P,Y)= $r_{PY} = -0.8461$.

(Although F statistic indicates that regression equation (11) not significant at 5% level, coefficient of Y is significant at 5% level and that of P at 20% level). Figures in parentheses below coefficients show their standard errors. Grouped data of Table 22.4 are used in these regressions.

These regressions (although some coefficients are not significant) suggest that, when the inflation rate is rising (1959-1980), inflation causes U to rise. During this period, even real output growth also led to U increase, possibly through wage inflation leading to labor-saving technology. After relative price stability was achieved, (1981-1989 period), an increase in average inflation and real income growth reduced the unemployment level.

One concludes that by systematic inflationary policy, with a view to reducing unemployment, one ends up in a situation where not only price/ wage inflation increases unemployment, but even real output growth achieved thereby increases unemployment, possibly because of replacement of labor-intensive methods, plants and industries by capital-intensive, labor-saving methods, plants and industries. With achievement of price stability, both inflation and real output growth reduce unemployment; however, inflation still reduces output growth; hence direct effect of inflation on unemployment should be weighed against its adverse effect on and through output. E.g. 1% increase in the price level reduces the unemployment rate by 0.35% by eq (11), but reduces real economic growth rate by 0.06% by employing the 1970-1989 regression (eq. 12) below, and hence through output (Y) effect increases unemployment by 0.13% (0.06 x 2.23), and net effect is 0.22% reduction in U; however, using the 1981-89 regression (eq. 14) increase in U through Y effect is 2.92% (1.31 x 2.23) and net effect is 2.57% increase in U.

Table 22.6
UK data
(as percentage of GDP, unless specified otherwise)

Year	Budget Deficit* Overall (D)	Budget Deficit* on Current Account (D*)	Annual Real GDP Growth Rate(%) (Y)	Gross Domestic Investment (I)	Gross Domestic Saving (S)
1981	4.8	2.4	- 9.9	15.1	18.0
1982	3.4	0.4	1.5	15.7	17.6
1983	4.4	1.0	3.7	16.5	17.4
1984	3.2	1.1	2.2	17.4	17.0
1985	2.9	- 0.1	3.5	17.2	18.3
1986	2.4	0.03	4.0	17.1	16.5
1987	0.7	- 0.7	4.8	18.0	16.9
1988	- 1.5	- 3.1	4.0	20.1	16.5
1989	- 0.8	- 3.1	2.3	20.6	16.8

(*) Minus (-) sign indicates surplus
Source: *World Tables*, IBRD

In order to analyze effects of price inflation and crowding-out (of budgetary deficits) on economic growth, following regression eqs. have been obtained. In eq (10), it was already observed that, price increase reduces economic growth rate, since Cor(P,Y)=-0.846. Moreover visual inspection of time series (Table 22.6) shows that declining budgetary deficits immediately lead to higher economic growth (in 1982, 1985, 1986 and 1987). Since budgetary surpluses in late 1980s were spent on consumption, they have not brought about economic growth.

1970-1989:

(12) $Y = 4.6297 - 0.3740\,D - 0.0594\,P$ (R = 0.292)

$F_{2,17} = 0.791$. Regression eq. is not significant.

1970-1983: High inflation and large budgetary deficits, except for 1970-72 period.

(13) $Y = 5.33 - 0.6056\,D - 0.0284\,P - 0.0284\,P$ (R = 0.281)

1981-1989: Average annual inflation rate 6.3% and average annual GDP growth rate 1.9%.

(14)	$Y = 9.818 -$	$0.7459\,D^* -$	$1.3064\,P$	(R = 0.9235)
		(0.3474)	(0.2380)	
t-statistic:		(2.1473)	(5.489)	

$F_{2,6} = 17.375$. Coefficient of D* significant at 10% level, that of P at 1%. Cor (D*,P) = $r_{D^*,P} = 0.307$, $r_{D^*,Y} = -0.602$, $r_{P,Y} = 0.162$.

Where D= government budgetary deficit as percentage of GDP, and D*= government budgetary deficit on current account, also as percent of GDP.

All of these eqs show that both budgetary deficit and inflation reduce economic growth, and even in a period of price stability (1981-89), these effects prevail, become more powerful and are statistically significant.

Regarding crowding-out effect on gross domestic saving and gross domestic investment, the following regression equations are obtained, for the *1981-89 period.* (S=gross domestic saving, I=gross domestic investment, D=government budget deficit, D*= budget deficit on current account, all as percentage of GDP and Y= annual growth rate of real GDP.)

(15) $S = 17.322 + 0.1572\, D^* - 0.0354\, Y$ (R = 0.623)

$F_{2,6} = 1.90$, regression equation is not significant.

(16) $I = 17.307 - 0.9327\, D^* - 0.0004\, Y$ (R = 0.942)

		(0.1406)	(0.0577)
t-stat		(6.63)	(0.007)

Coefficient of D* significant at 1% level; that of Y not significant . $F_{2,6} = 23.56$, $r_{D^*Y} = 0.5465$.

(17) $I = 19.077 - 0.744\, D + 0.032\, Y$ (R = 0.943)

		(0.11.05)	(0.0545)
t-stat		(6.73)	-

Coefficient of D is significant at 1% ; $r_{DY} = -0.483$.

Under Thatcherism, while gross domestic saving declined by about 1 percentage point from 1981 to 1989, and gross domestic investment increased from 15% in 1981 to 21% in 1989 (Table 22.6), crowding-out effect of budget deficits still checked investment growth.

3 Grouped data

(i) Grouped data of the US, UK, Japan and Germany

Estimation of the original version of the price-Phillips curve from the grouped data of the US, the UK, Germany and Japan (Table 22.4) has yielded following very poor results, which imply that the unemployment rate has no effect on the inflation rate. In evaluating the very low coefficients of determination, one should note that by grouping data, correlation coefficient increases, i.e. by going "from individual observations to group means the value of R^2 tends to increase".(5) Very low values of R^2 obtained, despite the overestimation inherent in the estimation procedure, suggest that the original Phillips curve hypothesis does not hold true,(6) at all. (U=the unemployment rate, P= the inflation rate, N=sample size). Moreover, if unemployment has any effect on inflation, it is in the direction of increasing it.

US: 1978-1989 : (N=12)

(5) J. Kmenta, "Elements of Econometrics", 1986, p. 372.

(6) *ibid*, p. 372.

(1A) $P = 4.109 + 0.247\ U$ ($R^2 = 0.013,$)

US (1972-92), and UK (1959-89) : (N:43)

(1B) $P = 6.923 + 0.062\ U$ ($R^2 = 0.002$)

US and Germany (1978-1989) and UK (1959-89) : (N = 55)

(1C) $P = 6.132 + 0.033\ U$ ($R^2=0.0004$)

US, Germany and Japan (1978-89) and UK (1959-89) : (N = 67)

(1D) $P = 4.5028 + 0.2270\ U$ ($R^2 = 0.0236$)

UK: 1959-1989 : (N = 31)

(IE) $P = 7.227 + 0.127\ U$ ($R^2 = 0.0898$)

Using data of Table 22.4, following additional regressions are obtained: (where U= unemployment rate, P= annual price inflation, Y=annual growth rate of real income)

UK (1959-89) and US (1978-89) :

(2A) $U = 12.24 - 0.289\ P - 1.644\ Y$ ($R = 0.380$)

UK (1959-89), US (1978-89) and Germany (1978-89):

(2B) $U = 9.79 - 0.163\ P - 1.168\ Y$ ($R = 0.377$)

UK(1959-89) and US, Germany, Japan (1979-89):

(3)	U = 9.98 -	0.149 P -	1.3715 Y	(R = 0.499)
		(0.0908)	(0.3059)	
t-stat		(1.641)	(4.483)	

$F_{2,64} = 10.64$; $r_{PY} = -0.607$; coefficient of P significant at 5% that of Y at 1%.

UK, US, Germany and Japan (1978-89):

(4)	U = 9.25 +	0.0532 P -	1.1548 Y	(R = 0.575)
		(0.1273)	(0.3007)	

t-stat (0.418) (3.840)

$F_{2,45} = 11.11$, $r_{PY} = -0.532$, $r_{UP} = 0.347$, $r_{UY} = -0.573$.

Coefficient of Y significant at 1%, that of P not significant.

In all of these equations but the last one (which covers the same period for all countries), although the sign of P indicates the existence of long-term Phillips curve, these coefficients are not significant in general; moreover explanation of U by explanatory variables is not satisfactory. As explained in chapter 21, many other factors influence the level of unemployment than price inflation; in fact the coefficient of Y is significant at 1%.

(ii) Germany, Japan and the US: 1978-1989

Following regressions are obtained for Germany, Japan and the US for the 1978-89 period, from the grouped data of Table 22.4.

Germany: 1978-89 : Average annual inflation rate= 3.5%.

$$(5)\ U = 13.434 - \underset{(0.0238)}{1.018\,P} - \underset{(0.0360)}{2.0967\,Y} \qquad (R = 0.9984)$$

t-statistic: (42.773) (58.242)

The coefficients of P and Y are significant at 0% level; $r_{P,Y} = -0.6548$.

Japan: 1978-89 : Average annual inflation rate = 2.8%

$$(6)\quad U = 3.057 - \underset{(0.0053)}{0.1167\,P} - \underset{(0.01159)}{0.0757\,Y} \qquad (R = 0.9895)$$

t-stat: (21.993) (6.531)

The coefficients of P and Y are significant at 1% level; $r_{PY} = -0.00062$.

US: 1978-89 : Average annual inflation rate= 5.8%.

$$(7)\quad U = 11.3045 - \underset{(0.10274)}{0.2525\,P} - \underset{(0.21435)}{1.0117\,Y} \qquad (R = 0.821)$$

t-stat : (2.458) (4.72)

The coefficient of P significant at 5%, that of Y at 1% ; $r_{PY} = -0.63$.

Constants of regression, except for Germany, reflect roughly the average rate of unemployment during the period covered. In a sense, these results indicate the existence of the Phillips curve trade-off, when the inflation rate is low and the country does not have the overhang of an inflationary past. In

Germany, where the annual inflation rate had not exceeded the ceiling of 7% in the last two decades (Table 22.7), the trade-off is strongest (1% price increase leads to 1% decline in the rate of unemployment) and weakest in Japan, where in the 1970s the annual inflation rate averaged 9% and was at 2 - digit level in 3 years. It is weak in the US, which again had 3 years of two-digit inflation rate and the annual inflation rate averaged 8.8% during 1973-1982.

Moreover, this favorable effect on output of inflationary expansion could well be explained by temporary doses of inflationary expansion of aggregate demand within relative price stability under the (classical) Keynesian theory, in lieu of the Phillips curve hypothesis, as pointed out in chapter 21. Furthermore, in evaluating the effect of P on U, one should also consider the negative effect of P on Y, since correlation between P an Y is negative in both the US and Germany. Even in Japan 1% increase in the inflation rate decreases GDP growth rate by 0.17%. (Eq 15 of section 4 below).

(iii) Economic basis for regression equations

Let Y= absolute value of real output, X= absolute value of nominal output, and P = price index, then

(8) $Y = X/P$

and its total differentiation yields:

$$dY = \frac{X}{P}\left(\frac{dX}{X} - \frac{dP}{P}\right)$$

Writing growth rates as $y = dY/Y$, $x = dX/X$ and $p = dP/P$ and dividing by $Y = X/P$ yields

(9) $y = x - p$ or $x = y + p$

If the aggregate demand increase is perceived as inflationary completely, then there will be no output response and $x = p$.

Let increase in labor demand as a proportion of labor supply be $v=ex$, and the unemployment rate=u, i.e. $-\Delta u = v$, then

(10) $-\Delta u = ey + ep$

If in year (t-1), u = o, then for year t, eq (10) becomes (Japanese case)

(11) $-u = ey + ep$

Eqs (10) or (11) could be employed in regression. Alternatively, by writing for year t:

(12) $\Delta X = \Delta Y + \Delta P$

where ΔP = inflationary component of the aggregate demand increase, with X = Y in year (t-1). Dividing by X:

$$\frac{\Delta X}{X} = \frac{\Delta Y}{Y} + \frac{\Delta P}{X}$$

(13) $x = y + p$

where p is the rate of increase of GDP deflator. While ΔY will definitely lead to employment increase, ΔP will generate employment depending on whether inflation is anticipated or not, and on varying degree of response of economic agents. Hence one can write

(14) $-\Delta u = v = \alpha y + \beta p$

This equation can be estimated by regression.

(iv) Price-inflation Phillips curves for the UK, Japan, Germany and the US

Using grouped data of Table 22.4 following regressions are obtained:

The UK : 1964-1989 : (N=26)

(15) Δu = 8. 8.826 -	0.2831 P	-2.1896 Y
	(0.1455)	(0.6217)
t-stat :	(1.946)	(3.522)
SIG	(0.10)	(0.01)

$R^2 = 0.529$, $F = 12.94$, $r_{PY} = -0.827$, SER = 1.542.

where Δu= change in the unemployment rate, P= rate of price inflation, Y= the GDP growth rate, SIG= two-tail significance level, SER= the standard error of regression.

Japan : 1981-1989: (N=9)

(16) $\Delta u = 1.527 - 0.0676\ P - 0.2973\ Y$ ($R^2 = 1.00$)

Germany: 1981-1989 : (N=9)

(17) $\Delta u = -1.743 + 1.2685\ P - 0.3333\ Y$ ($R^2 = 1.00$)

The US : 1981-1989 : (N=9)

(18) $\Delta u = -26.3 + 3.9459\ P + 2.7568\ Y$ ($R^2 = 1.00$)

Surprisingly perfect fit is obtained for Japan, Germany and the US, also because of the use of grouped data. The results show that there is no universal Phillips curve rule. In Japan and the UK, the trade-off is of negative sign but of insignificant magnitude; whereas in Germany and the US, the trade-off is positive and substantial, i.e. price inflation increases unemployment.

(v) Effects of price inflation and the budgetary deficit on the growth rate of economic output

Regressions run using the grouped data of Table 22.4 to determine the effects of price inflation (P) and the government budgetary deficit (D) on the GDP growth rate (Y), show that both factors reduce economic growth rate; and some estimated coefficients are highly significant, particularly that of D in eq (20), of P in eq (21) . (D is expressed as percentage of GDP and N=sample size).

US and UK: N = 42

(19) $Y = 4.05 - 0.1147\ P - 0.2763\ D$ ($R^2 = 0.470$)

US, UK, Germany : N = 63

(20)	Y = 3.57 -	0.0772 P	- 0.2760 D	($R^2 = 0.345$)
		(0.03364)	(0.07279)	
t-stat		(2.295)	(3.792)	

Coefficient of P significant at 5% level, that of D at 1% ; Cor (P,D)= r_{PD} = 0.4096, r_{YP} = - 0.4369, r_{YD} = - 0.5373.

US, UK, Germany and Japan : N=84

(21)	Y = 4.15 -	0.1235 P -	0.1354 D	(R^2 = 0.1414)
		(0.04295)	(0.08286)	
t-stat		(2.875)	(1.634)	

$F_{2,81}$ = 6.5896 (regression equation significant at 1% ; coefficient of P significant at 1% and that of D at 20% ; r_{PD}= 0.2101, r_{PY}= -0.3368, r_{DY} = - 0.2294.

(vi) Final note on the original Phillips curve

Over the 100 years Phillips studied, increase in nominal wages might be the result of (i) past (ex post) inflation, (ii) expected inflation, (iii) increase in labor productivity due to technological change or capital accumulation (increased capital intensity), (iv) decline in labor supply arising from demographic factors or emigration.

If wages increased to make good decline in real wages, due to past inflation and if no further inflation (demand shock) is planned, then employers will not increase employment, because increase in wages is a real increase.

During a period of continuos technological change and innovation, despite rising real wage level, increased international competitive power, would enable increase in exports, output and employment, (which might as well accompanied by some monetary expansion and some wage inflation due to buoyant labor demand), hence increase in nominal wages due to productivity increase (which has nothing to do with wage inflation or lagged effect or anticipated effect of price inflation in the-Phillips-trade- off sense) would be inversely related to declining unemployment. In this case observed superficial relationship, would disguise the real causal relationship.

If emigration increased during a certain period, because of increasing unemployment or expanding frontiers (increased opportunities abroad, in colonies or in the US), real wages in the UK might have increased due to decline in labor supply ; if, however, productivity increase were not involved, output and employment might have declined due to increased unit costs. Then observed inverse relationship would still appear, if tight monetary and fiscal measures led to some fall in nominal wages. Again, observed relationship would conceal real causal link.

Recapitulating, change in nominal wages could stem from (i) inflation, (ii)technological change and productivity increase, (iii) change in labor supply, (iv) change in labor demand. There might be cases where technological change and productivity increase not leading to change in employment, e.g. if new labor-saving technology, while increasing investment and output displaces same number of labor as jobs created, then employment remains unchanged. Of these explanatory factors (for change in nominal wages), past inflation and technology change have nothing to do with unemployment level; or unemployment can't stand proxy for these factors, as Phillips postulated.

A more meaningful regression could have been run, or should be tried, if not for the full period covered by Phillips, for part of period, using changes in real wages, employing some measure, even crude, of price inflation. Moreover another (parallel) regression of employment on wage differentials should have been run using the original Phillips data. This specification, would have eliminated the effects of labor supply changes (due to extraneous factors) on wage changes, and at the same time would have served the purpose directly (since the main purpose of Philips curve analysis eventually turned out to be explanation of change in employment or its rate by wage changes). Comparison of the two regression eqs. might have clarified certain problems.

In view of downward stickiness of wages, nominal wage level has a increasing trend element which might not be eliminated even when taking the first differences. This increasing trend will be the other explanatory factor for wage changes, other than unemployment; and a specification encompassing a trend element should have been employed using the original Phillips data.

In view of globalization and internationalization of capital, labor and product markets, albeit not perfect but much more increased trade flows (increased share of foreign trade in every economy, an increasing secular trend of trade flows, increased international competition in many commodity and manufacturing markets), virtually free movement of short-term and long-term capital worldwide, and increased international mobility of labor (legal or illegal immigration) across national borders, it is much more likely that factor and goods markets are in equilibrium, temporary shortages or surpluses in certain markets will be eliminated by countervailing movements; and markets will move toward competitive equilibrium unless destabilizing monetary and fiscal policy measures disturb equilibrating mechanism (e.g. inflationary remedies to stagflation situations further weakens international competitiveness, comparative advantage of troubled sectors) and otherwise output will normally be at internationally competitive potential levels.

4 Performances of Germany and Japan after the oil-price shock, experiments with the Phillips curve trade-off and crowding-out effect

(i) Germany

Germany achieved 2.65% average annual GDP growth rate during the 1970-91 period, while the consumer price index (CPI) showed 3.85% increase p.a. During the first oil-price shock, Germany even managed to reduce the inflation rate throughout and recording a slight decline in GDP in 1975; the second oil-price shock and the worldwide recession caused GDP to decline to an annual average rate of 0.9% during 1980-83 (Table 22.7), while the unemployment rate jumped from 3.2% in 1978-80 to 7.7% in 1981-83 and thereafter only declined slightly in the decade (Table 22.4). The apparent reason for rise in unemployment might appear as the sound monetary policy being pursued (not indulging in the inflationary luxury of the Phillips curve trade-off); however the real reason is the secular decline in domestic investment from 26% in 1950-73, to 20% in 1980s and rise in government consumption; although domestic saving didn't decline as much over the period (Table 22.8).

Following the oil price shock, there occurred a general decline in economic growth rates, saving and investment rates and increase in capital-output ratios in industrialized countries, except Korea (details of which will be taken up later). Regarding the world-wide rise in capital-output ratios following reasons could be suggested or views could be *aired:*(i) New relative prices called for additional investment for adjustment to the new economic order and made some of the existing capital stock useless or obsolete. (ii) World-wide lower growth rates of economic output, entailing lower growth rates for real exports and real aggregate demand, reduced profitability and productivity (in terms of value-added generation) of investment; (in turn, low rates of return on capital reduced investment). (iii) Possibly relative (real) prices of investment goods also increased, because they are energy-intensive, and development and application of new technologies are more costly. (iv) Emergence of new industrial competitors in Far East and Latin America, reduced capacity utilization of the existing capital stock in the industrialized countries. The situation was exacerbated in some countries like Germany and the US in the 1980s, by too much reliance on monetary policy (interest rate) to maintain price and exchange rate stability (tight monetary policy) and inadequacy of fiscal instruments to support stability and economic growth. (In the US, because the fiscal policy was completely expansionary, domestic savings also declined dramatically, whereas in Germany savings declined less, also because in the late 1980s Germany partly used fiscal policy (Table 22.9) to redress the situation.)

Budgetary deficits and inflation in Germany possibly have not promoted economic growth. It may be observed from Table 22.7 that the highest budgetary deficit (overall and on current account) led to highest GDP decline (1975), declining deficit led to higher growth (1976) and overall budgetary surplus caused high-rate economic growth (1970-73). Following regressions have been obtained: (Y= GDP growth rate, D = overall government budgetary deficit as percentage of GDP, $\bar{D}$ = budgetary surplus on current account as percentage of GDP, P=price inflation ; I =gross domestic investment and S=gross domestic saving, both as percentages of GDP).

1971-1991:

(1) $Y = 4{,}28 - 5.595\, D - 0.246\, P$ (R = 0.446)

$F_{2;18} = 2.23$; regression equation not significant

1971-1985:

(2) $Y = 5.83 - 0.816\, D - 0.529\, P$ (R = 0.583)

$F_{2,12} = 3.09$; regression not significant at 5% level.

1971-1990:

(3) $Y= 3.02 + 0.726\, \bar{D} - 0.328\, P$ (R = 0.493)

$F_{2,17} = 2{,}725$; regression not significant.

Regression equations are not significant, however, the effect of price inflation,if any, on the GDP growth rate is negative.Regression results for domestic saving and investment are better.

1981-1990:

(4)	S = 23.43 -	0.805 D +	0.790 Y	(R = 0.907)
		(0.4657)	(0.1727)	
t-stat:		(1.728)	(4.575)	

The coefficient of D significant at 20% level, that of Y at 1% ; r_{DY}=-0.4885.

1981-1991:

(5)	$S =$ 21.69 +	0.110 D +	1.055 Y		($R^2 = 0.721$)
	(1.266)	(0.5865)	(0.2398)		($\overline{R}^2$=0.652)
t-stat:	(17.13)	(0.187)	(4.40)		

F= 10.35, standard error of the regression (SER) = 1.248.
The coefficient of D not significant, that of Y significant at 0.2% level.

(6) $S =$	50.57 -	0.2285 D -	0.0209 Y -	0.5136 $(1/\overline{Y})$
	(2.507)	(0.1424)	(0.1089)	(0.0443)
t-stat:	(20.17)	(-1.605)	(-0.192)	(-11.6)
2-tail significance level	(0.0)	(0.153)	(0.853)	(0.0)

$R2 = 0.986$, $\overline{R}^2 = 0.980$, SER = 0.297, F = 167.07, DW = 2.906,

where $(1/\overline{Y})$ is the inverse of the value of GDP at 1987 prices x 10^5.

(7) $S =$	50.58 -	0.136 D -	0.0387 Y -	0.512 $(1/\overline{Y})$ -	0.0657 P
	(2.499)	(0.1683)	(0.1099)	(0.0441)	(0.0642)
t-stat	(20.24)	(-0.809)	(-0.352)	(-11.61)	(-1.02)
significance level	(0.0)	(0.45)	(0.74)	(0.0)	(0.35)

R^2=0.988, $\overline{R}^2$=0.980, SER 0.296 DW= 2.91, F= 126,40

(8)	$S =$ 21.79 +	0.228 D +	1.029 Y -	0.0844 P
	(1.39)	(0.742)	(0.270)	(0.288)
t-stat:	(15.68)	(0.307)	(3.816)	(-0.293)
significance level	(0.0)	(0.768)	(0.007)	(0.778)

$R^2 = 0.725$, $\overline{R}^2$ =0.607, SER=1.326 DW= 1.33, F=6.14

(9)	$S=$ 49.81 -	0.125 D -	0.0621 P -	0.4994 $(1/\overline{Y})$
	(1.125)	(0.155)	(0.0593)	(0.0226)
t-stat	(44.26)	(-0.809)	(-1.047)	(-22.11)
significance level	(0.0)	(0.445)	(0.33)	(0.0)

R^2= 0.988, $\overline{R}^2$=0.983, SER= 0.276 DW= 2.776, F= 192.59

Including 1991 (estimate) in regressions has worsened results, as well as including both Y and $(1/\overline{Y})$, serial correlation and changing signs of D (multicollinearity) occur, marginal saving propensity rises to 50% (constant term), although the correlation coefficient has increased. Eq (4) is considered better, which implies that budgetary deficit reduces domestic saving. Moreover using $\overline{D}$, in lieu of D would have yielded better results.

For explanations of domestic investment following regression equations are obtained.

1981-1991:

(10)	I =	18.432 +	0.1474 D +	0.3766 Y +	0.2673 P
		(0.3296)	(0.1758)	(0.0639)	(0.0683)
t-stat:		(55.93)	(0.8382)	(5.8897)	(3.915)
significance level		(0.0)	(0.43)	(0.001)	(0.006)

$R^2 = 0.862$, $\overline{R}^2 = 0.803$, F = 14.62, SER=2.7899.

(11)	I =	18.588 +	0.3736 Y +	0.2983 P
		(0.2672)	(0.0626)	(0.0563)
t-stat		(69.55)	(5.964)	(5.299)
significance level		(0.0)	(0.0)	(0.001)

$R^2 = 0.8486$, $\overline{R}^2 = 0.8107$, SER = 0.308, DW= 2.512, F=22.42.

(12)	I =19.71 +	0.5093 D +	0.2588 Y -	0.01697 $(1/\overline{Y})$
	(4.73)	(0.2687)	(0.2054)	(0.0835)
t-stat	(4.167)	(1.895)	(1.260)	(-0.203)
significance level	(0.004)	(0.10)	(0.248)	(0.845)

$R^2 = 0.564$, $\overline{R}^2 = 0.3767$, F = 3.01, DW = 1.83, SER = 0.560.

(13)	I= 18.76 +	0.520 D +	0.294 Y	(R^2=0.561)
	(0.533)	(0.2468)	(0.1009)	($\overline{R}^2$=0.451)
t-stat:	(35.20)	(2.109)	(2.917)	
significance level	(0.0)	(0.068)	(0.019)	

F= 5.11, DW= 1.823, SER=0.525, r_{DY} = - 0.294.

(14)	I =	19.645 +	0.132 D +	0.3316 Y -	0.0216 $(1/\overline{Y})$	+0.268 P
		(2.826)	(0.1903)	(0.1243)	(0.0499)	(0.0726)
t-stat:		(6.952)	(0.694)	(2.668)	(-0.433)	(3.690)
significance level :		(0.0)	(0.51)	(0.037)	(0.68)	(0.01)

$R^2 = 0.867$, $\overline{R}^2 = 0.778$, SER=0.334, DW= 2.93, F= 9.74.

Again inclusion of $(1/\overline{Y})$ only increases the coefficient of determination; but the quality of regression coefficient estimates deteriorates. On the basis of eqs. 11 and 13, one can suggest that in Germany budgetary deficit and price inflation induce increase in investment; this exceptional result must be due to very low rates of inflation and budget deficit prevailing in this country. Paradoxically or as might be expected, with price stability, moderate budgetary deficits and conservative policies, moderate monetary and fiscal expansion might promote investment growth, along with price increase. However, even in Germany, effect of budget deficit and price inflation on domestic saving is negative, as well as on economic output (tentative result).

(ii) Japan

Table 22.10 shows that low budgetary deficits (less than 1% of GDP) are associated with GDP growth rates above 7% (1970-73) and high monetization rates (14% growth rate for real balances). Excessively high budgetary deficits (6% of GDP) coupled with high inflation rates lead to low growth rates for GDP (3.5%, during 1974-83) and for real money stock (4%). High budget deficit (4% of GDP), if coupled with low inflation rates (less than 2%), GDP growth of 4.5% and real growth rate of 7% for monetary stock could be achieved (1984-90).

Table 22.10
Japan: government budgetary deficit and related variables (percentages)

	Budgetary Deficit (As Percentage growth of GDP)	Average Annual average rate of real GDP	Average Annual increase Inflation Rate	Average Annual in real Stock of Money
1970-73	0.7	7.7	7.6	14.3*
1974-83	6.1	3.5	7.8	4.4
1984-90	3.7	4.6	1.6	7.2
1970-90	4.3	4.6	5.7	6.9

* 1971-73
Source: *World Tables*, IBRD, International Financial Statistics (IFS), IMF

Japan recorded a decline in GDP only in 1974 (by 0.7%)over the 1970-90 period. In 1974 real money stock also declined by 7.2% and the inflation rate was 23%. Except for 1974, the oil-price shocks did not affect economic performance as in other oil- importing countries (except Korea). Japan got over the 1974 oil price shock by reducing the growth rate of nominal money supply from 20% in 1973 to 14% in 1974 and thereafter increasing it by 10-16% p.a.

over the 1975-81 period. The average annual inflation rate was 7.1% during the period (7.7% in 1980) (Table 22.7).

Japan increased budgetary deficit during 1974-83 period and then reduced it during 1984-90 period; results of this fiscal policy change indicate that (Table 22.7) with increased budgetary deficit, growth rates of economic output and real money balances decreased; whereas with declining budgetary deficit (and its crowding-out effects), GDP growth rate and monetization rate (increase in real monetary stock) increased and inflation rate declined. Effects of crowding-out year to year could not be discerned over the period; however, there is a direct inverse relationship between the budgetary current account deficit and GDP growth rate over the 1981-1990 period; while current account deficit increased over 1981-83 and 1989, GDP growth rate declined every year along with it and while the deficit declined over 1984-1990, GDP growth rate increased every year along with it (in 1984, 1985,1987, 1988 and 1990). Herein a simple analysis is made to determine whether budgetary deficits are conducive to economic growth in the short run. The significance and direction of the crowding-out effect will depend on the size of public debt stock (in relation to GDP), size of real money balances, business cycle position(in a deep recession budgetary deficit will help recovery), current inflation and interest rates, saving propensities, nature of budgetary deficit (on the current account or overall), etc. Hence scientific analysis of short-term crowding-out effects, would require quarterly econometric model.

Domestic saving propensity declined along with increasing budgetary deficit; as percentage of GDP, average domestic saving declined form 38.9% during 1965-73 to 33.9% during 1970-81 and to 30.8% during 1981-83, and increased to 32.3% during 1984-90, showing a steadily declining trend during 1981-83 (from 31.9% in 1981 to 29.8% in 1983) and a steadily increasing trend during 1984-90 (from 30.8% in 1984 to 33.9 in 1990), (Table 22.11).

Table 22.11
Japan: macroeconomic data
(as percentage of GDP)

	Budget Deficit	Budget deficit on current A/c	Gross Domestic saving	Gross Domestic Investment	Real GDP Growth Rate%
1981	6.5	2.8	31.9	31.1	3.6
1982	6.5	3.1	30.7	29.9	3.2
1983	6.7	3.4	29.8	28.1	2.7
1984	5.8	2.8	30.8	28.1	4.3
1985	4.9	2.2	31.5	28.2	5.0
1986	4.8	2.2	31.8	27.8	2.6
1987	3.5	0.7	31.8	28.7	4.4
1988	2.6	0.2	32.9	30.6	6.2
1989	2.9	0.7	33.1	31.7	4.8
1990	1.6	0.0	33.9	33.2	5.2

Source: World Tables, IBRD

Successful Japanese and Korean experiences with the oil-price shock clearly indicate that, the k-percent rule of monetarism is not a good rule. Had Japan sustained previous 20-25% monetary growth rate (of 1971-73) in 1974, it would have had a higher inflation rate and recovery would not have materialized in 1975, since adjustment would have taken longer.

Following regression equations are obtained for Japan, using data of Table 22.7, (Y=GDP growth rate, P=the inflation rate, N=sample size; S=domestic saving, I=domestic investment, D=government budgetary deficit, $\bar{D}$ = budget deficit on current account, all as percentages of GDP):

1970-1990 : N=21

(15)	Y=7.788 -	0.501 D -	0.173 P	(R=0.60)
		(0.1696)	(0.0796)	
t-stat:		(2.954)	(2.173)	

$F_{2,18}$=5.06 (regression eq. significant at 5% level); the coefficient of D significant at 1%, that of P at 5% ; r_{DP}= - 0.210.

1981-1990: N=20

(16)	S = 33.47 -	0.8672	$\bar{D}$ - 0.0196 Y	(R=0.8896)
		(0.2308)	(0.2539)	

Coefficient of $\bar{D}$ significant at 1% level, coefficient of Y not significant ; $r_{DY}= - 0.774$.

19811990:

(17) $I= 31.28 - 0.499\, D + 0.177\, Y$ (R=0.581)

$F_{2,7}=1.78$; regression equation is not significant.

Regression results suggest that in Japan, budgetary deficit reduces economic growth rate and domestic investments ; inflation reduces growth rate of GDP; current budget deficit reduces domestic saving.

The problem with the Japanese economy in the last two decades is its low economic growth rate, associated with a rise in private consumption (6 percentage points above the 1965-70 level in the 1980s) and a secular decline (7 percentage points) both in domestic saving and domestic investment over the same period, coupled with a rise in marginal capital-output ratio from 3.5 to 7 over the same period. If these trends are not checked, lower growth prospects are forecast; however, saving and investment started to increase from 1988 onwards (Table 22.12).

5 Miracles of Taiwan and Korea

Taiwan realized the crucial transformation during 1962-73 (and particularly during 1968-73) by raising domestic saving ratio (to GDP) from 13% to 34%, by cutting down private consumption ratio from 68% to 50% and during 1962-72 period, average inflation rate was only 2.9%. Although it might seem that the initial impetus was given by domestic investment, whose ratio to GDP rose from 20% in 1960 to 25% in 1967; the crucial factor obviously was domestic saving and the most crucial period was 1968-73, when domestic saving ratio jumped from 23% to 34%, while domestic investment ratio was stable at 25% (Table 22.13). Over the 1965-73 period, average annual GNP growth rate was 10.4% (Table 22.14). These figures completely repudiate any practical value of the Phillips curve analysis and show the futility of any such endeavor, particularly for developing or semi-industrialized countries. Taiwan also managed very low marginal capital-output ratios. (Due to data availability, only 1950-73 period of the Taiwanese experience could be covered.)

This Taiwanese miracle can be contrasted with the so-called 'Özal Miracle' in Turkey in the 1980s when the average private consumption ratio was 70%, domestic saving ratio was 19.5%, domestic investment ratio 22.5%, average annual GDP growth rate 4.5%, average annual inflation rate 56% and marginal capital-output ratio 5 (GNP per capita $1,370 in 1989(7)) during 1980-1992.

(7) According to World Development Report, IBRD, 1991, pp. 204-205.

Table 22.13
Taiwan: macroeconomic parameters: 1950-1973
(as percentage of GDP, unless specified otherwise)

	Private Consumption	General Government Consumption	Gross Domestic Saving	Gross Domestic Investment	CPI Increase (%)
1950	71.3	18.4	10.3	14.9	-
1955	72.1	18.9	9.0	13.3	-
1960	68.5	18.8	12.7	20.1	-
1961	68.7	18.5	12.8	19.9	7.8
1962	68.2	19.2	12.6	19.0	2.4
1963	64.7	18.2	17.1	16.7	2.1
1964	63.9	16.5	19.6	19.2	0.2
1965	63.4	16.8	19.8	23.1	0.0
1966	60.5	17.2	22.3	23.1	2.0
1967	59.4	17.2	23.4	25.2	3.3
1968	59.3	17.7	23.0	25.6	6.3
1969	57.3	18.3	24.3	25.2	5.0
1970	54.2	19.7	26.2	26.2	3.7
1971	53.6	17.6	28.7	26.1	2.5
1972	52.0	16.6	31.5	24.7	4.9
1973	50.4	15.9	33.7	25.2	13.1

Source: World Tables, IBRD

Table 22.14
Taiwan: macroeconomic data
(ratios and growth rates, in percentages)

Average Annual Growth Rate at Constant Prices	1950-60	1960-73	1965-73
GNP at market prices	8.4	10.1	10.4
GDP at market prices	8.4	10.1	10.3
Private Consumption	8.1	7.9	7.3
General Government Consumption	8.2	5.8	6.8
Gross Domestic Saving	-	173*	19.7
Gross Domestic Investment	14.3	15.2	13.5
Consumer Price Index annual average increase	-	3.3	4.7
As Percentage of GDP			
Private Consumption	70.7	57.2	55.2
General Government Consumption	19.1	17.5	17.3
Gross Domestic Investment	16.9	24.1	25.1
Gross Domestic Saving	10.2	25.3	27.5
Marginal Capital-Output Ratio	2.01	2.50	2.67

(*) Implied growth rate (see: Table 22.25)
Source: World Tables, IBRD

Korean transformation started in the 1960s; during 1960-73 (compared with 1950-60) average private consumption ratio (to GDP) declined from 85% to 74%, average domestic saving ratio jumped from 2% to 16%, domestic investment from 11% to 24% and GDP growth rate from 5% to 9.5%. During 1970-81 private consumption ratio, on the average, further declined to 64% and domestic saving ratio increased to 24%, domestic investment to 29% and 9% GDP growth was achieved. In 1980s improvements further continued; and during 1986-91, private consumption ratio averaged 53.5%, domestic saving 36%, domestic investment 34% and 8.8% average annual GDP growth rate was achieved (Table 22.15). Korean inflation record is not as good as that of Taiwan; but in 1980s (1981-91), average inflation rate was 7% (1986-91 rate 6%) and annual inflation rate didn't reach 30% and during the two-digit inflation period (1970-81), it averaged 16.6%. There is no doubt that with high GDP growth rates, some bottlenecks and sectoral demand pressures could develop and result in higher inflation rates. Even these, however, could and should be avoided by means of careful macroeconomic demand management and indicative economic planning (unless external factors dominate) as Taiwanese experience, and Korean experience after 1982 suggests (Table 22.16). Korean marginal capital-output ratio was 3.5 during 1981-91 and contrasts sharply with the Turkish figure 5. Korea reached a threshold in 1976 with saving and investment ratios of 24%, and breakthrough occurred in 1984 when domestic saving and investment ratios equaled 30% and private consumption ratio fell to 60%; in 1991 investment ratio was 39%, saving ratio 36% and private consumption ratio 53% (Table 22.16).

In *Korea* during 1970-80, when budgetary deficit was 2% or higher (of GDP), growth rate declined (1972, 1974, 1975) and when the deficit was less than 2%, two-digit growth rates were achieved (1971, 1973, 1976, 1977, 1978; even in 1979 increased deficit, although it was less than 2% of GDP led to decline in the GDP growth rate); the only exception was 1980, when the inflation rate reached a peak (29%) and budgetary surplus led to the only GDP decline (3%) over two decades (1971 - 1990), (Table 22.17).

In 1980s as well, all two - digit GDP growth rates were coincided with large (and rising) budget surpluses on current account (1983, 1987 and 1988). It might be argued that this is the chicken-egg situation, arising from the built-in stabilization mechanism of the fiscal system. However, in many countries, without a sound fiscal administration and management system, and conservative fiscal policy stance or practice, planned or unanticipated budgetary surpluses are always spent, even overspent; and even in Korea when rise in current budget surplus didn't lead to a reduction in overall budget deficit, GDP growth rate was not two-digit (1981, 1979 and 1975) and lower than the previous year (except for 1981).

Korea increasing nominal money supply by 33 and 34% respectively in 1972 and 1973 (real money stock by 20 and 30% respectively), met the oil price shocks by reducing growth rate of nominal money supply to 22 and 26% respectively in 1974 and 1975 (real money balances declined only in 1974, (by 1.9%) and inflation rate was 25% in both 1974 and 1975 (up from 3% in 1973). Nominal money supply continued to increase by 25-38% p.a. over 1976-81, monetization also increased at high rates during 1976-78, annual price increases exceeding 18% during 1979-81 coincided with lower GDP growth rates.

Average annual inflation (consumer price index) and real GDP growth rates over the last four decades are shown in Table 22.18.

Table 22.18
Average annual inflation and economic growth rates in Korea (percentages)

	1950-60	1960-73	1965-73	1974-82	1983-92
Inflation rate	52.3	12.7	11.1	18.8	4.5
GDP growth rate	5.1	9.5	10.9	7.8	9.0

It is clearly observed that lower inflation rates are associated with higher GDP growth rates, and vice versa.

The following regression equations are obtained for Korea: (where Y=GDP growth rate,%; S= gross domestic saving, I=gross domestic investment, D=overall budgetary deficit, $\overline{D}$= budgetary surplus on current account, D*= accumulated overall budgetary deficits, all as percentages of GDP; Y*= real GDP index (1970=1.0), P= consumer price index increase,%):

1971-1990: (N:10)

(1) $Y= 11.1789 - 0.124\ P$ (R=0.462)

$F_{1,18}$= 4.885; regression eq. significant at 5%.

(2) $Y= 10.128 - 1.133\ D$ (R=0.383)

$F_{1,18}$= 3.09; regression not significant.

1971-1989:

(3) $Y=11.189 - 0.214\ P$ (R=0.462)

1971-1991:

(3A) $Y= 11.134 - 0.213\ P$ (R=0.460)

1971-1984: (Inflationary Period)

(4) $Y= 8.665 - 0.924\ \Delta D - 0.152\ \Delta P$ (R=0.568)

1972-1983: (Inflationary Period), (N=12)

(5) $\Delta Y= -0.109 - 1.123\ \Delta D - 0.399\ \Delta P$ (R=0.781)

	(0.755)	(0.135)
t-stat:	(1.487)	(2.948)

$F_{2,9}$= 7.04, regression significant at 5% level; coefficient of ΔP significant at 1% level; $r_{\Delta D, \Delta P}$= 0.405.

These equations suggest that inflation rate and budgetary deficit ratio (or increase in these rates and ratios) adversely affect GDP growth (or change in it).

1970-1990:

(6) $S = 30.51 - 3.1305\ D$ (R=0.562)

(7) $S = 16.23 + 3.327\ \bar{D}$ (R=0.392)

1970-1989:

(8) $S = 13.13 + 4.112\ \bar{D}$ (R=0.496)

1971-1991:

(9) $S = 12.41 - \underset{(0.490)}{0.239\ D} + \underset{(0.563)}{5.634\ Y^*}$ (R=0.944)

cor (D,Y*)= r_{DY^*}= - 0.558)

These equations suggest that budgetary deficit (D) reduces saving rate and current budget surplus ($\bar{D}$) increases it.

1970-1990:

(10) $I = 22.64 + 1.776\ \bar{D}$ (R=0.37)

1970-1989:

(11) $I = 20.08 + 2.424\ \bar{D}$ (R=0.566)

1970-1990: (N=21)

(12) $I = 19.63 + 0.680\ D + 2.944\ Y^*$ (R=0.82)

	D	Y*
	(0.480)	(0.490)
t-stat:	(1.417)	(6.008)

r_{D,Y^*}= -0.542; coefficient of Y* significant at 1% level, that of D at 20%.

1970-1989:

(13) $I = 22.265 + 0.167\ D^* + 1.094\ Y^*$ (R=0.762)

1970-1990:

(14) $I = 21.477 + 0.074\ D^* + 2.076\ Y^*$ (R=0.804)

It seems that budgetary deficit, current budget surplus and accumulated budget deficit, all had favorable (positive) effect on investment ratio in Korea; however, the quality of estimates is not good (e.g. addition of 1990 observations in regression produces dramatic shifts in coefficients-eqs. 13 and 14, which implies multicollinearity).

6 The US experience

In the US, macroeconomic ratios deteriorated after the oil price shock, particularly in 1980s with Reaganomics; during 1986-92 (compared to 1965-73), private consumption ratio (to GDP) rose to 68% (from 62%), total consumption ratio increased 2 percentage points, despite 4 percentage points decline in government consumption, although domestic investment ratio declined only 1 percentage point to 17%; however 1991 and 1992 domestic saving and investment ratios recorded historical lows (15%) since 1950 (Table 22.19). To judge these record lows, one should note that business fixed investment component only averaged 11% of GNP over the 1970-84 period in the US (Froyen, 1986, p. 386).

Over the 1982-1992 period, budgetary deficits were also high (Table 22.7). In 1980's, after the public debt stock became large, it seems budgetary deficits adversely affected GDP growth rate (except for in 1983-end of recession and 1989): Considering only years when overall deficit far exceeds current deficit (which reflects automatic stabilization effect), which implies fiscal expansion has taken place, one observes that, when overall deficit increases growth rate declines (1982, 1985, 1990 and 1991), when deficit declines growth rate increases (1984) or becomes steady (1987), when current budget deficit increases growth rate declines (1986 and 1988), and recently when budget deficit exceeds 4%, fiscal expansion does not help much with recovery from stagnation (1990-1992).

Regression results for the US are shown below:

(Where D= government budget deficit, $\bar{D}$= current budget deficit, D*= accumulated budget deficit, all as percentage of GDP; S,I,Y,P as defined above); data used are in Tables 22.7 and 22.19.

1972 -1992:

(1) $Y = 7.09 - 0.476\ P - 0.480\ D$ (R=0.476)

F= 2.64; regression eq. not significant.

(2) $Y = 4.42 - 0.297\,P - 0.894\,\Delta D,$ (R=0.597)

$F_{2,18}= 4.98$; regression eq. significant at 5%.

1972-1991:

(3) $Y = 4.55 - 0.311\,P - 0.877\,\Delta D$ (R=0.60)

$F_{2,17}= 4.78$, regression significant at 5%.

These eqs. may suggest that price inflation (P) and budgetary deficit, D, (particularly increase in it, ΔD) do not increase GDP growth rate (Y), possibly reduce it.

1972-1992:

(4) $S = 19.73 - 0.728\,D$ (R=0.657)

$F_{1,19}= 14.45$, regression significant at 1%.

(5) $S = 19.34 + 0.050\,Y - 0.610\,D$ (R=0.545)

	(0.1268)	(0.2104)
t-stat:	(0.394)	(2.900)

$F_{2,18}= 3.80$, regression significant at 5%; Coefficient of D significant at 1%; $r_{DY}=0.067$

1972-1990: (N=19)

(6) $S = 18.75 + 0.035\,Y - 0.850\,\bar{D}$ (R=0.78)

	(0.0974)	(0.1635)
t-stat:	(0.359)	(5.199)

$F_{2,16}= 12.42$, regression significant at 1%; coefficient of $\bar{D}$ significant at 1%; $r_{DY}=0.25$.

(7) $S = 18.82 - 0.835\,\bar{D}$ (R=0.778)

$F_{1,17}= 26{,}05$, regression significant at 1%;

These equations suggest that budgetary deficit and budget deficit on current account adversely affects domestic saving.

1972-1992: (N=21)

(8) $I = 19.20 - 0.369\,D$ (R=0.417)

$F_{1,19} = 4.00$; regression not significant.

(9) $I = 18.599 + 0.283\,Y - 0.400\,D$ (R=0.674)

		Y	D
		(0.0881)	(0.1462)
t-stat:		(3.211)	(2.735)

$F_{2,18} = 7.49$, regression significant at 1%;

Coefficient of D significant at 2%, that of Y at 1%; $r_{YD} = 0.067$. This equation implies that the accelerator (acceleration coefficient) is equal to 0.283 and the marginal capital-output ratio is 3.53; whereas the ratio calculated in Table:22.25 for this period was about 6.5.

(10) $I = 17.84 + 0.608\,Y - 0.065\,D^*$ (R=0.578)

$F_{2,18} = 4.51$, regression at significant at 1%;

1972-1990:

(11) $I = 18.465 - 0.139\,\bar{D}$ (R=0.209)

1979-1992: (N=14)

(12) $I = 20.24 + 1.056\,Y - 0.130\,D^*$ (R=0.711)

	Y	D^*
	(0.383)	(0.05196)
t-stat:	(2.757)	(2.502)

$F_{2,11} = 5.628$, regression significant at 5%; coefficients of Y and D* significant at 5% ; $r_{YD^*} = 0.0415$.

These eqs. imply that budgetary deficit (overall, on current account or accumulated), reduces domestic investment, or does not increase it.

In conclusion it is better to relate some observations made by Hall and Blanchard regarding the 1990-1991 recession, which are in line with the general thinking in this book regarding neoclassical models and the appraisal of the US economy in the last two decades made herein so far. Hall (1993) concludes that "established [neoclassical] models are unhelpful in understanding [the 1990 recession], and probably most of its predecessors", because "small events can have large consequences". Consumer and business behavior reflect cascading of negative responses. Consumer spending on durables has not picked up; "in spite of low interest rates, firms cut all forms of investment"; "as usual, in a recession, firms cut production by more than their sales fell, making up the differences from inventories"; "little of this falls into the type of behavior predicted by neoclassical models". As a consequence Hall concludes that new models (in which small events can have large consequences) are called for, "rather than the established neoclassical models".

However, the problem with the US economy is not only new models with better predictive power, but also change in the monetary and fiscal policy presently based on false premises of established economic models (neoclassical or neo-Keynesian does not matter) and restore consumer and business confidence in stability and economic growth prospects of the economy by means of sound monetary and fiscal policy, like one recommended in this book. That is, in lieu of ever-changing cyclical monetary and fiscal policy, a stable monetary and fiscal policy geared to price stability and based on balanced budget in principle, aiming at steady economic growth by means of higher saving and investment rates.

In fact, Blanchard (1993) observes that "in contrast to earlier recessions, the decline in confidence was largely prior to (and much stronger than would have been predicted by) either the decline of leading indicators or commercial forecasts of the recession;" and that consumer confidence after having dropped, remained very low in the following two years, "much lower than would have been predicted on basis of historical relations with aggregate variables." This is because drop in confidence of public regarding management of the economy accumulates in geometric progression and this tendency can't be broken, unless by a drastic change in policies, prospects of continuous growth (in lieu of a cyclical recovery) are firmly established.

7 Experiences of other countries

(i) Ireland

Ireland experienced two-digit inflation during 1973-1983; average annual rates of inflation and GDP growth are shown in Table 22.20.

Table 22.20
Ireland: average annual growth rates of real GDP and CPI (percentages)

	1950-60	1960-70	1970-81	1965-70	1965-73	1973-83	1984-90
Real GDP	1.5	4.2	4.0	4.3	4.8	4.6	4.2
CPI	3.8	3.8	15.1	5.6	7.0	15.3	4.4

Source: World Tables, IBRD

Definitions of symbols in regression equations in this section are as follows: Y= GDP growth rate, P=inflation rate (CPI increase); as percentages of GDP: D= budgetary deficit, S=gross domestic saving, I=gross domestic investment; Y*= value of GDP at constant 1987 prices.

Following regression eqs. are obtained: (Data from Table 22.21)

1971-1988:

(1)	Y= 6.85 -	0.274 D	(R^2=0.07, $\bar{R}^2$=0.012)
	(2.699)	(0.249)	F= 1.21, DW=1.78
t-stat	(2.538)	(-1.102)	
2 tail significance level:	(0.022)	(0.287)	

1972-1988:

(2) Y= 9.60 - 0.501 D (R^2=0.215)

(3) Y= 4.16 + 0.0857 P (R^2=0.001)

1971-1990:

(4) Y= 4.64 - 0.0345 P (R^2=0.00476)

1971-1988:

(5)	Y= 3.714 +	0.0236 P	(R^2= 0.002)
	(1.697)	(0.1305)	
2-tail significance level:	(0.044)	(0.859)	

(6)	$Y = 6.803$	$+ 0.1424 P$	$- 0.4283 D$	
	(2.709)	(0.1511)	(0.2985)	
t-stat	(2.511)	(0.942)	(-1.434)	
2-tail significance level	(0.024)	(0.361)	(0.172)	

$R^2 = 0.1224$, $\bar{R}^2 = 0.005$, SER= 3.1, D-W= 1.91, F= 1.046.

1972-1988:

(7)	$Y = 5.032$	$- 0.301 D$	$+ 0.181 P$
	(2.223)	(0.273)	(0.155)
t-stat:	(2.264)	(-1.1913)	(1.1635)
2-tail significance level	(0.039)	(0.288)	(0.263)

$R^2 = 0.093$, $\bar{R}^2 = 0.027$, SER= 3.18, D-W= 1.91 F= 0.777.

Although fit of regressions is not good, these regressions suggest that the effect of price inflation on GDP growth rate is either almost nil (eqs: 3,4,5) or very small (10% inflation increases GDP by 1.4%; eq 6); whereas 1% budgetary deficit reduces GDP growth by 0.3-0.5%.

1971-1988: (N=18)

(8) $S = 18.8765 + 0.0570 Y$ ($R^2 = 0.0032$)

Correlation between S and Y is very weak; in an inflationary economy savings are rather influenced by changes in inflation.

(9)	$S = 23.4122 +$	$0.0769 D$	$- 0.4400 P$	($R = 0.7993$)
		(0.1808)	(0.09151)	
t-stat		(0.4253)	(4.808)	

Coefficient of P significant at 1% level, that of D not significant, $r_{DP} = 0.548$.

1971-1988:
(Y^*= GDP at constant 1987 prices x 10^5 in millions of Irish Pounds)

(10)	$S = 24.790$	$- 0.982 (1/Y^*)$	$+ 0.14416 Y$
	(3.3063)	(0.51699)	(0.2386)
t-stat	(7.498)	(-1.8996)	(0.604)
2- tail significance level:	(0.0)	(0.077)	(0.555)

$R^2 = 0.1959$ $\bar{R}^2 = 0.088$ F= 1.827, D-W= 0.716, SER= 3.022

1971-1988:

$$(11) \quad S = 38.4365 - 1.7377\,(1/Y^*) + 0.0116\,Y - 0.7965\,D$$

	(4.131)	(0.41115)	(0.17185)	(0.19886)
t-stat:	(9.304)	(-4.226)	(0.0676)	(-4.005)
2-tail significance level:	(0.0)	(0.001)	(0.947)	(0.001):

$R^2 = 0.6253$, $\bar{R}^2 = 0.54499$, SER= 2,1355, D-W= 1.35, F= 7.787

$$(12) \quad S = 31.113 - 0.9578\,(1/Y^*) + 0.0939\,Y - 0.2863\,P - 0.28275\,D$$

	(5.0075)	(0.5147)	(0.1577)	(0.1328)	(0.2969)
t-stat:	(6.123)	(-1.8607)	(0.595)	(-2.156)	(-0.952)
2 tail signifi cance level:	(0.0)	(0.086)	(0.562)	(0.050)	(0.358)

$R^2 = 0.724$, $\bar{R}^2 = 0.639$, SER=1.902, DW= 1.424 F= 8.525

$$(13) \quad S = 26.793 - 0.5858\,(1/Y^*) + 0.1398\,Y - 0.3878\,P$$

	(2.1135)	(0.3342)	(0.1497)	(0.0789)
t-stat:	(12.677)	(-1.753)	(0.934)	(-4.9118)
2 tail signifi cance level:	(0.0)	(0.101)	(0.366)	(0.0)

These regressions suggest that price inflation reduced saving ratio by a multiple of 0.4 (eqs: 9 and 13) and budgetary deficit by a multiple of 0.8 (eq:11).

(ii) Luxembourg

Luxembourg which seems to pursue a conservative fiscal policy with budgetary surpluses mostly, recorded economic growth rates at most 3% or decline when budgetary surplus was 2% or less of GDP in 9 cases out of 19 observations (1971, 1975, 1976, 1977, 1979, 1980, 1981, 1982, 1983; exception: 1972) and recorded growth rates exceeding 3% when budgetary surplus (D) exceeded 2% of GDP in 7 cases (1973, 1974, 1978, 1984, 1986, 1988 and 1989; except for 1985 and 1987); average growth rate during the 1971-1989 period was 3.1%. The conservative fiscal policy paid off and GDP declined only in 1975 and 1981 (slightly) over the period and the average rate of inflation was 5.7%. (Table 22.22). The rule for Luxembourg turns out to be as follows: if budgetary surplus exceeds 2% of GDP, economic growth rate is likely to exceed 3%. The following regressions are obtained: (2-T SIG= 2-tail significance level,%; D= Budgetary surplus, as a percentage of GDP):

1971-1989: (N=19; average annual GDP growth rate=3.1%)

(14)	S= 18.41 +	0.979 P +	1.068 Y+	0.433 D
	(3.76)	(0.4399)	(0.3949)	(0.4348)
t-stat:	(4.891)	(2.226)	(2.7054)	(0.9961)
2-tail significance level:	(0.0)	(0.042)	(0.016)	(0.335)

R^2= 0.393 $\bar{R}^2$=0.271, SER=4.726, DW= 0.553, F-stat= 3.236.

(15)	Y= 5.083 -	0.4175 P +	0.1508 D
	(2.016)	(0.2582)	(0.2727)
t-stat:	(2.522)	(-1.6167)	(0.553)
2-tail significance level:	(0.023)	(0.125)	(0.588)

R^2= 0.246, $\bar{R}^2$= 0.152, SER= 2.992, DW= 1.827.

Regressions suggest that the effect of budgetary surplus (D), on GDP growth rate (Y) and saving ratio (S) is not negative (if not positive); whereas the effect of inflation on Y is definitely negative, but on domestic saving (S) is positive. It may be concluded that, in an open economy with conservative fiscal policy and price stability record, monetary expansion (price inflation) at times, might increase saving ratio (at a multiple of 0.98), but reduces GDP growth rate (at a multiple of 0.42).

(iii) Belgium

The price and GDP growth record for Belgium is shown in Table 22.22.

Table 22.22
Belgium: inflation and GDP annual growth rates (percentages)

	1950-60	1960-70	1965-70	1965-73	1970-81	1980-90
GDP, Real	2.2	4.7	4.8	5.0	3.0	2.2
CPI	1.9	3.2	3.6	4.0	7.8	4.8
Wholesale price index	1.0	1.9	2.3	2.8	5.6	-

Source: World Tables, IBRD

In Belgium, where monetary policy seems to have been less liberal than the fiscal policy, judging from the 6% inflation record over 1971-1990 period, as against 7.3% budgetary deficit (D, budgetary deficit ratio to GDP averaged 12% during 1981-86 period ; (Table 22.21; while budgetary deficit reduced both GDP growth (Y) and domestic saving ratio (S) for sure; price inflation reduced Y with 85% probability and did not promote its growth. Regressions are shown below (Data in Table 22.21).

1971-1989: (N=19)

(16)	Y= 6.66 -	0.195 P -	0.383 D
	(1.408)	(0.130)	(0.1264)
t-stat:	(4.729)	(-1.499)	(-3.029))
2-tail significance level:	(0.0)	(0.153)	(0.008)

R^2= 0.389 $\bar{R}^2$=0.312, SER=1.804, DW= 2.873, F-stat= 5.087.

(17)	S= 25.894 +	0.0184 P +	0.2542 Y -	0.7675 D
	(1.264)	(0.0804)	(0.1448)	(0.0918)
t-stat:	(20.49)	(0.229)	(1.755)	(-8.352)
2-tail signifi cance level:	(0.0)	(0.822)	(0.100)	(0.0)

R^2= 0.906, $\bar{R}^2$=0.888, SER=1.045, DW= 1.524, F-stat= 48.352.

(iv) Austria

During the 1970-1990 period, Austria always achieved price stability (never had two-digit inflation), oil-price shocks did not shatter this record (the luxury of Phillips curve trade-off was not indulged). However more expansionary fiscal policy during the 1980s (budgetary deficit averaged 4.6% during 1980-1990, as against 0.8% during 1970-74) seems to have caused the average annual GDP growth rate (Y) to decline from 5% during 1970-74 to 2.3% during 1980-90, and the average domestic saving ratio (to GDP; S) to decline from 30.9% to 24.9% over the same period (Tables: 22.23 and 22.21).

Table 22.23
Austria: budgetary deficit and domestic saving ratios to GDP and GDP growth rate (percentages)

	Budgetary Deficit (D)	GDP Growth Rate(Y)	Domestic Saving Ratio(S)
1970-74	0.8	5.0	30.9
1975-90	4.5	2.4	25.2
1980-90	4.6	2.3	24.9

From regression eqs. 17, 18 and 19 given below, it may be inferred that the budgetary deficit reduces both the GDP growth rate (Y) and saving ratio, substantially; the effect of inflation on Y is also negative with 85% probability.

1971-1990: (N=20)

(18)	Y=	8.346 -	0.342 P -	0.975 D
		(2.339)	(0.2256)	(0.3607)
t-stat:		(3.568)	(-1.516)	(-2.704)
2-tail significance level:		(0.003)	(0.149)	(0.016)

R^2= 0.317, $\bar{R}^2$=0.231, SER=1.737, DW= 2.304, F-stat= 3.71.

(19)	S=	29.92 +	0.0827 P +	0.2288 Y -	1.116 D
		(1.896)	(0.1458)	(0.1512)	(0.263)
t-stat:		(15.786)	(0.567)	(1.513)	(-4.655)
2-tail significance level:		(0.0)	(0.579)	(0.151)	(0.0)

R^2= 0.840, $\bar{R}^2$=0.809, SER=1.051, DW= 1.662, F-stat= 26.37.

(v) Conclusions for small, open economies

The experiences of Ireland, Luxembourg, Belgium and Austria, in 1970-1990 period, suggest that the effect of price inflation (P) on GDP growth (Y) is either negative or nil; whereas the budgetary deficit reduces both GDP growth rate, and domestic saving ratio (S). Hence, for a small, open economy one can conclude that the Phillips curve does not exist and budgetary deficits have adverse effects both on Y and S.

Frisch (1983, p.182) on the basis of the following regression equation for Sweden (1958-73) estimated by Calmfor, and a similar result obtained for

Austria by himself, claims that "for small countries such as Austria or Sweden, the hypothesis for the existence of a long-run Phillips curve might not be rejected."

$$W= 6.25 + 0.08\ (V-U) + 0.31\ \pi_{t-1} + 0.18\ (\pi_t+\lambda)$$

t-stat: (3.53) (2.44)
$R^2= 0.7$, DW= 1.98

Where W= the rate of increase in money wages of international sector, π= domestic inflation rate of international sector= the rate of international inflation, λ= the percent change of labor productivity in the international sector, V-U= the difference between the number of vacancies and the number of unemployed. "The equation suggests that in the long run only half [0.31 + 0.18 = 0.49] of a change in the international rate of inflation π is transmitted to the rate of change of money wages". "In this case an increase in inflation produces not merely a temporary employment effect but a permanent reduction in the rate of unemployment" (Frisch, 1983, p.182).

Although coefficients of independent variables are significant, large constant term (which takes care of influence of other variables excluded from regression) possibly makes the largest part of explanation.

A threshold level for consumption, saving, investment ratios to GDP or GDP growth and unemployment rate is normal, but a 6% threshold level for wage (hence price) inflation in a small, open economy of an industrialized country, during the 1958-73 period could not be considered reasonable. Because even $\lambda=\pi=U-V=0$, this equation suggests 6.25% increase in Swedish money wages p.a., because of unknown reasons (built- in inflation bias). Practical relative significance or importance of the coefficient of (V-U) variable could not be ascertained, since magnitudes of these variables are not indicated. Supposing vacancy and unemployment numbers are denominated in 1,000 workers, then 25,000 increase in the number of vacancies will push the money wage level by 2 percentage points (=25x0.08), while a simultaneous world inflation of 6% would add up 3 percentage points and 2.5% labor productivity increase 0.45 percentage points and as a consequence money wages would increase by 11.7% (=6.25+ 2 +3 + 0.45). The Phillips curve trade-off would explain only 17% of change in money wages, while unknown factors would explain 53%. In conclusion, in lieu of estimating the existence of the Phillips-curve trade-off in a roundabout manner, direct estimation of the effects of price inflation on growth, saving and investment is considered a better approach.

Another observation regarding the interpretation of the study by Calmfor (Frisch, *ibid*, pp. 175-86) is that, it is not legitimate to treat an inflationary process generated by world inflation in a small, open economy, which implies change in relative (real) prices (terms of trade) in favor of tradeables sectors (and hence a real increase in aggregate demand), as a domestic inflation generated to reduce unemployment, whereby relative prices do not change (the very premises on which the Phillips curve trade-off is built) and then to show it as empirical evidence for the existence of the Phillips curve.

(vi) France

It seems France was conservative in the fiscal policy (an average budgetary deficit to GDP ratio of 1.7% over the 1972-90 period); however monetary policy was liberal and allowed inflation rates of about 10% or above during 1975-83 period (Table 22.21).

Regression results given below (where D denotes budgetary surplus) suggest that price inflation (P) adversely affects GDP growth (Y); but the effect of budgetary deficit (-D) on both Y and S (saving ratio) is much more important and also negative.

1972-1990: (N=19)

(20) Y=	4.813 -	0.1707 P +	0.5765 D
	(0.732)	(0.0672)	(0.1961)
t-stat:	(6.572)	(-2.539)	(2.939)
2-tail significance level	(0.0)	(0.022)	(0.010)

R^2= 0.442, $\bar{R}^2$=0.373, SER=1.074, DW= 2.681, F-stat= 6.35.

(21) S=	23.369 +	0.1540 P +	0.3165 Y +	1.526 D
	(2.133)	(0.221)	(0.3786)	(0.3686)
t-stat:	(10.954)	(1.277)	(0.836)	(4.139)
2-tail significance level	(0.0)	(0.021)	(0.416)	(0.001)

R^2= 0.718, $\bar{R}^2$=0.662, SER= 1.626 DW= 1.762, F-stat= 12.755

Most of the explanation is made by the constant term in eq. (21) ; coefficients of P and Y are not significant at 5% ; inclusion of (1/Y*) might improve results.

(vii) Italy

The post oil-crisis era Italian economy had higher inflation rates (P) and budgetary deficits (D), than the French economy (Table 22.21). Regression results suggest that the effect of budgetary deficit on GDP growth rate (Y) is negative (significance at 2%); and the effect of inflation on Y is negative (significance level 37%) and on the saving ratio (S) it is positive (significance 0.1%).

1972-1990: (N=18)

(22) Y=	11.738 -	0.0904 P +	0.6612 D
	(3.451)	(0.09805)	(0.2572)
t-stat:	(3.40)	(-0.922)	(-2.571)
2-tail significance level:	(0.004)	(0.371)	(0.021)

R^2= 0.310 $\bar{R}^2$=0.218, SER=2.169, DW= 1.662, F-stat= 3.374.

(23) S=	18.967 +	0.2320 P +	0.4195 Y +	0.02825 D
	(2.512)	(0.0551)	(0.1412)	(0.16887)
t-stat:	(7.550)	(4.208)	(2.970)	(0.167)
2-tail significance level:	(0.0)	(0.001)	(0.010)	(0.870)

R^2= 0.673 $\bar{R}^2$=0.602, SER=1.186 DW= 1.122, F-stat= 9.589.

(viii) Australia

The Australian data clearly show that with increased inflation (P), GDP growth rate declined (1970-81) and with decrease in the inflation rate, GDP growth increased (1960-70 and 1980-90). (Table 22.21). In fact, regression eq. (24) also confirms this view. Budgetary deficit (D) increases Y (significance 6.4%), but reduces saving ratio (S; significance 16.4%). Regression equations:

1971-1990: (N=20)

(24) Y=	5.459 -	0.3315 P +	0.5124 D
	(1.359)	(0.1443)	(0.2586)
t-stat:	(4.016)	(-2.296)	(1.981)
2-tail significance level:	(0.001)	(0.035)	(0.064)

R^2= 0.301, $\bar{R}^2$=0.219, SER=1.83 DW= 2.373, F-stat= 3.663.

(25) S =	20.577 +	0.1923 P +	0.5926 Y -	0.3929 D
	(1.7827)	(0.1552)	(0.2278)	(0.2695)
t-stat:	(11.543)	(1.239)	(2.601)	(-1.457)
2-tail significance level:	(0.0)	(0.233)	(0.019)	(0.164)

R^2= 0.302, $\bar{R}^2$=0.171, SER=1.723 DW= 0.733, F-stat= 2.306.

8 Conclusions on country experiences regarding Phillips curve and crowding-out

From regression equations run for several countries it has been observed that the Phillips curve trade-off, not only does not exist, but rather its reverse holds true; i.e. price inflation does not lead to economic output increase but decline. Inflation also adversely affects domestic savings, and in many countries domestic investments as well. These adverse effects develop as follows: Sustained inflation increasing uncertainty, causing difficulties in forecasting future, increasing nominal and real interest rates (due to risk factor and crowding-out effect of government budgetary deficits, which always accompanies persistent inflation) curbs domestic investments (particularly productive ones). Sustained inflation increases consumption and waste because of (a) overestimation of real incomes and profits; (b) reduction in efficiency and increasing waste in enterprise sector due to rising prices of output and nominal profits, and prevailing buoyancy. While cautious entrepreneurs refrain from investment, because of uncertainty; many less careful entrepreneurs launch unviable new ventures, many of which remain unfinished due to cost increases, imminent credit squeeze, etc. (c) Rising prices tempt households and firms to make unnecessary purchases, anticipating new price increases, with a view to pre-emptying them. (d) Rise in default on credits and bad debts by households and firms. Domestic savings decline not only because of increase in consumption and waste (of income and capital, as well), but also because of increasing public sector deficit, which means decline in public savings. Moreover capital outflow and dollarization increase with persistent high inflation. Economic growth rate declines also because of less productive public sector investment pre-empts private investment through crowding-out.

Budgetary deficit is a simpler and better indicator of crowding-out than changes in interest rate resulting from this effect, because of frequent variations of interest rate within a year, sometimes divergent movements of short-term and long-term lending and deposit rates in a year, and many frequent interventions into interest rates through monetary or exchange rate policy changes and on different considerations (effects on investment and output growth, on debt service burden on the government budget, short-term capital movements); as against all this, the budgetary deficit is an unwavering indicator of crowding out. The existence of a Phillips curve in the countries reviewed is not traced, in general ; on the contrary the effect of price inflation on GDP growth rate, saving and investment ratios is rather negative; the crowding-out effect of budget deficits on investment and adverse effect of budgetary deficits on saving and GDP growth rate are detected, and these effects are in general substantial.

9 An overview of the performance of the industrialized countries over the last four decades

(i) Introduction

In all the four industrialized countries (Germany, Japan, the UK and the US), an increasing trend of private consumption ratio (to GDP), except for the UK, and declining trend of domestic savings and of domestic investment (except for the UK) are discernible during the 1981-90 period, compared with the 1965-73 period (Table 22.24). Details of change in expenditure structures of the countries and their marginal capital-output ratios are in Table 22.25.

Decline in the Japanese GDP growth rate, after 1973, seems to stem from the rise in private consumption, the decline in domestic saving and investment, and a dramatic rise in the marginal capital-output ratio from 3.5 to 7. In case of Germany, the increase in government consumption, the decline in domestic investment and a substantial rise in the marginal capital-output ratio (from 6 to 9) was crucial. In the UK, while private consumption increased, domestic saving and investment declined in 1981-90, compared with 1970-81; however, marginal capital-output ratio declined from 11 to 7. In the US, the rise in private consumption was dramatic, in 1981-90 over 1970-81, domestic saving and investment, as well, declined and the marginal capital-output ratio increased (Table 22.25).

Overall marginal capital-output ratios could increase because of following factors: (i) increase in infrastructure investments, (ii) underutilization of installed capacities due to recession (iii) output losses due to increased foreign competition, (iv) unviable, in- efficient investment projects undertaken, (v) reduced growth potential or reduction in the overall competitive power of the economy.

(ii) The US experience

Over the 1962-74 period private consumption as a percentage of GDP was stable at 63-62%, with public consumption at 19-21% and total consumption at 82-83%, and 2 percentage point increase in public consumption during 1967-72 period (to 21%) was largely achieved by reducing private consumption from 63% to 61%, and also by reducing gross domestic saving rate from 18 to 17% (and gross national saving rate from 19% to 18), (Table:22.19).

During 1973-80, reduction in public consumption from 21% to 18% led to a large private consumption increase (from 62% to 65%) and a significant saving increase (gross domestic saving rose from 17% in 1968-72 to 20% in 1977-79), gross domestic investment, however, did not change as a consequence, in fact it was stable at 18-19% during the 1962-1979 period (Table 22.19).

An economic crisis period started in the 1980s, with rising and high private consumption (main motivating power of recoveries, rising from 64% in 1979 to 69% in 1992), declining domestic saving from 20% in 1979 to 15% in 1992 and domestic investment declining from 19% to 15% over the same period (Table 22.29).

It seems Reaganomics did not manage to reduce government consumption significantly (17% in 1979, 18% during 1982-85 and 16% after 1988), but managed to increase total consumption from 81% in 1979 to 85% from 1983 on (Table 22.29). Much worse, the recovery in 1987-89 did not indicate a significant investment recovery and in ensuing stagnation years, a big decline in investment occurred; it seems recoveries are weaker and recessions deeper. One can argue that in recessions decline in investment and saving is normal, even as a percentage of GDP; however, in the 1960s and 1970s variations from year to year were slight and there were no such long-term increasing or declining trends.

(iii) Growth potential of the industrialized countries

In order to show the significance of these data on growth potential/prospects, a simpler version of Samuelson's classic multiplier-acceleration interaction model is employed to study the time path of income growth using the most recent basic data of the four countries. (8) Data used and results obtained are shown in Table 22.26. The model is solved for t=2 (year); the time horizon is short-run, since after recovery, contractionary forces immediately set in through tighter monetary policy, etc.; G_o value *and implied* I_o value are based on Y_o=100.

---

(8) The model is $I_t = \alpha(Y_t - Y_{t-1})$, $C_t = \gamma Y_t$ and $Y_t = C_t + I_t + G_o$, where Y_t= GDP, C_t= private consumption, I_t= investment, G_o= general government consumption and α = marginal capital-output ratio, γ = private consumption to GDP ratio; whose solution is

$$Y_t = \frac{G_o}{1-\gamma} + \left[Y_o - \frac{G_o}{1-\gamma}\right]\left[\frac{\alpha}{\alpha+\gamma-1}\right]^{-t}$$

Table 22.26
Results of multiplier-acceleration interaction model for the US, the UK, Japan and West Germany

Parameter or variable	the	US	the UK	Japan	Germany
	1992	1965-73	1990	1990	1981-90
α	6.5	5	6.8 (1970-81)	7 (1981-90)	9
γ	0.69	0.62	0.63	0.57	0.56
G_0	16	20	20	10	20
I_0	15	18	19	33	20
Estimated GDP growth at year t (%)	5.0	8.1	5.4	10.4	5.75
Actual average annual GDP growth rate (1978-89) (%)	2.85	--	2.4	4.4	2.1
Growth rate estimate based on (I_0/α)	2.3	--	2.8	4.7	2.2

In this manner, the (expenditure) structure of the economy determines its growth potential and estimated growth rates are wide of the actuals; (Table 22.26) because estimated figures show the potential long-term growth rates, where as the actuals reflect frequent policy reversals, stop-go process and short-sighted (not growth-oriented) policies pursued.

One can argue that this is very simplistic analysis of very complicated economies and the recommended solution might not work. It is a acknowledged that the analysis is simple and even a curve is not fitted; it however, exposes the basic weaknesses and worsening trends, particularly of the US economy; that the saving accumulation and capital formation is insufficient to create the productive capacity required for generating adequate (sustainable) economic growth and gainful employment; more sophisticated analyses would not change this finding; and it is obvious that anticyclical remedies would not work; a long-term growth initiative (a major saving/investment drive) is called for.

Absence of investment recovery, despite the historically record level (low) interest rates, might suggest that government expenditure increase by deficit financing is appropriate. Inadequate response of output, investment and consumer housing credit demand to low interest rates, however, rather reflect pessimistic expectations regarding the economic prospects and lack of positive initiative on the side of government. It looks as though the confidence of businesses and households in the strength of the economy, economic prospects and in the economic leadership of the government has weakened. This is also because of frequent policy reversals and changes in the economic theories adopted and applied. Expectations of a weak recovery and ensuing inflationary pressure would generate this type of response.

If the government launched an expansion program (for infrastructure investment and the new Marshall Plan) financed by sound means, based on long-term strong recovery prospects, with accompanying measures to cut down consumption (mainly expenditure type taxation and gradually reducing supply side measures and incentives) business investments would respond positively. Many economic problems and complications of the past two decades are created by policy reversals and application of novel, untested (in general wrong) theories or policies.

(iv) Saving investment dilemma and a lesson from the Far East

If the industrialized world could grow at a steady 4-5% rate, then it would solve its equilibrium unemployment problem, and also provide adequate capital injection to developing and reforming countries. In this context, foreign aid could play a pivotal role, financed by increased taxation.

The argument that problem with the industrial world was not saving shortage, but lack of investment opportunities in many instances is short-sighted; surplus saving could be invested in infrastructure and human capital formation or exported. While consumption-induced growth is short-lived, saving/investment-induced growth is perpetual. Capital outflow, would both induce export-induced growth and provide steady income on investment abroad (i.e. saving surplus, even if it did not lead to GDP increase, would increase GNP definitely).

It could be concluded that of the saving/investment relationship "what induces economic growth" is not a chicken-and-egg issue, both generates economic growth and surplus domestic saving could be invested abroad. Denison and Chung (1976) and Dornbusch and Park (1987) studies identified increased supply of skilled labor, increased capital accumulation, technological improvement and economies of scale as explanatory factors for high economic growth rates of Japan and Korea. In case of Korea, Dornbusch and Park found that increased capital stock and a large pool of skilled labor and employment of imported advanced technology enabled exporting manufacturing sector expand and be competitive despite relatively rising average wage costs (relative unit labor costs), and still much lower productivity in Japan and Korea than in the US, also thanks to an undervalued exchange rate. Labor productivity and unit labor costs do matter, but in a market economy in the final analysis, financial and economic return to capital (profitability and marginal output-capital ratios) decides.

When the performance of the Western economies during the last two decades are compared with the Japanese and Korean performances, striking differences are found in capital accumulation and consumption versus growth-oriented policies (through indicative economic planning). Long-term policies overwhelmed short-term considerations; nevertheless short-term stability was also achieved automatically.

The lesson from the Far Eastern experience is that, by concentration on and preoccupation with the short-run, the economy even in short-term could not stabilize; whereas by focusing on the long-term, short-term problems are as well resolved as a side product. (One should not lose sight of forest but for trees). However, at this moment, ideological considerations step in: can't market solve everything? The economy, however requires undogmatic and pragmatic approach.

The Turkish experience also suggests the same lesson: In the 1960s when long-term growth with monetary and fiscal discipline, in a mixed-and relatively open economy, under indicative economic planning was the objective, about 7% p. GNP growth was easily achieved with price stability (inflation rate less than 5%) and with little external borrowing. Whereas during 1980-1992, when the American economic model, with an open economy and completely free capital movements was adopted, 4.5% annual economic growth was hardly achieved with record level of foreign borrowing (external debt approaching $70 billion at end 1992) and soaring unemployment, the advent of a de-industrialization trend before the country became industrialized, plus 60-80% inflation p.a.. As in the US, virtually permanent unemployment problem (5 million open, 5 million disguised unemployment) is termed as structural unemployment and treated as a short-term problem and experiments are made with expansionary cyclical policies, supply-side measures and increased infrastructure and housing investments.

(v) Conclusions

As noted earlier, new anti-cyclical theories, stagflation theories, etc. developed in the US or the UK are adopted on face value and widely exercised in the developing world. Therefore it is worth- while to look into the US and the UK economic problem from long-term (growth) aspect, as compared with the two successful economies Japan and West Germany during the 1970-1990 period and also check roughly validity of these theories and their implications (implementation results). Simple analysis based on saving, consumption and investment propensities and capital-output ratios show that the problems with the US and UK economies are a long-term increasing trend of private consumption propensity and a corresponding declining trend in saving and investment propensity. Also, high and rising capital-output ratios, partly the consequence of short-sighted anti-cyclical fiscal and monetary policies pursued with a persistent inflationary bias, and a strong crowding-out effect in the US in the 1980s.

Whereas in Japan and West Germany, saving and growth-oriented policies enabled sustained economic growth and a high saving/ investment level. However, in Japan, as well, saving propensity declined from 39% in 1965-73 to 32% in 1981-90 (34% in 1990) mainly as a consequence of increase in private consumption propensity (out of GDP) from 52% in to 59% over the same periods; which indicates a need for extra saving effort to participate in the new Marshall plan. (However, in 1990, the 1970-81 average, 57%, was attained. Details are in Table 22.25). Japan has the advantage of a small and efficient government, with current government expenditures less than 10% of GDP versus 20% in the UK and very low capital-output ratio (3.5 during 1960-73). Capital-output ratio increased dramatically during 1970-81, possibly due to catch-up with the infrastructure backlog.

Over the 1965-1990 period, long-term increasing trends are observed in private and total consumption both in Japan and the US; long-term declining trends in gross domestic savings and gross domestic investment are visible in Japan and West Germany. Long-term stability in private and total consumption is achieved in West Germany and the UK. In the US, although government consumption declined 4 percentage points over the 1965-1992, total consumption increased 3 percentage points, and as a consequence gross domestic savings also declined. The UK maintained stability in these propensities. One discerns following facts, taking into account also the inflation record and balance on current BOP account:

(a) Japan has really reflated, as indicated by increase in private and total consumption.

(b) West Germany's saving and investment capacity and growth potential have declined; which explains increase in unemployment (3% in 1978-80 to 6% in 1987-89).

(c) Japan and Germany achieving lower inflation rates than the UK and the US (Japan's growth rate also was higher) realized sizable surpluses on the current account of BOP.

(d) The UK set its macro balances all right, including relative price stability, balance on the current account of BOP and somewhat higher growth rate, but unemployment remained very high and investment have not increased. Thatcherist policies have not solved basic weaknesses of the UK economy, on the contrary they started a more destabilizing and dangerous trend, de-industrialization.

(e) Experimenting with novel theories and 'quick fix' anticyclical policies (treating the economy as a laboratory, as in the US and Turkey), without appreciating their full implications has disastrous consequences. In the US the size of government is reduced with consequent decline in public services and infrastructure, but domestic saving and investment have also declined, because private consumption has increased much faster; no doubt unemployment record has not improved over the period.

(f) The basic weaknesses of the UK and US economies are their low saving and investment capacities and growth potentials, half of those of Japan; and the crucial variables have not changed in the UK and got worse in the US over the period. It seems Germany also on way to join this club, particularly after the unification.

(g) The US economy is in a much worse shape with mounting external and public debt ($3,062 billion by Sept.1992), domestic saving and investment ratios being declined from the average 20% in the 1950-70 period to 15% in 1992.

(h) The solution to the basic problem is reducing private consumption by appropriate taxation and channel the additional revenue to investments and to financing the new Marshall plan.

(i) The best policy against stagflation is to increase competition in oligopolistic markets and convert monopolistic attitudes to competitive behavior (marginal cost pricing) by a tax credit mechanism, when the economy is in a genuine stagflation. Conventional expansionary fiscal and monetary policies are bound to dissipate (not concentrate on sectors which need expansionary effects), lead to price increases than output response, in imperfect competition markets. The classical remedy for monopoly, i.e. giving subsidy for increased output and levying a surcharge on excess profits may prove to be the real cure.

Modalities of the proposal could be worked out; but basically it might operate as follows: In a stagflation, crucial stagnating industries (car manufacture, construction, steel industry, etc.) would be established output benchmarks, by firms, production levels exceeding these limits would be granted tax credit based on per unit output, which would entitle reduction in income/ company tax payable when profits are restored. Tax credit will be financed by an excess profit tax (collected even during recessions, excluding firms with ongoing investment in plant and machinery in a suitable manner) on sectors where oligopolistic market structure exists (excluding dynamic, high-technology or new growth industries). Industries issuing tax credit could be assisted in the arrangement of access to banking credits in financing the output or inventory increase concerned. The proposal would not be inflationary, since outlays will be matched by excess profit tax revenue, which will be collected in advance (estimated long-term surplus should be earmarked for investment, private or public). Economic reasoning for the proposal will be taken up elsewhere. Such a measure has advantage over the classical expansionary policies, because if it is not effective, it will not leave behind any damaging effect like accelerated inflation.

10 Turkish experience

Except for the decline achieved in 1960s (from 76% of 1950s to 70%), private consumption propensity (out of GDP) did not decline in Turkey; the annual average of general government consumption ratio declined from 12% in 1962-68 to 10% in 1980s, despite a bloated public service in the meantime, by means of a substantial decline in real civil service pay. The average annual gross domestic saving rising from 13% in 1950s to 18.5% in 1970s, rose only to 19.5% in 1980s. The gross domestic investment ratio (to GDP), showed sharp increases, from 15% in 1950s, to 20% in 1960s and to 25% in 1970s, but declined to 22.5% in 1980s. The average annual GNP growth rate, increasing from 6% in 1950s to 6.5-7% in 1960- 73 period, declined to 4.5% in 1980-92. Most dramatic increases were in the marginal capital-output ratio which rose from 3 in the 1960s and 1970s, to 5 in 1980-1992 and in the inflation rate, whose annual average declined from 9.2% in 1950s to 3.7% in 1960s (1962-68 rate was 3.5%) shot up to 33% in 1970s and 56% in 1980-92 and 67% in 1988-1992. (Tables 22.27 - 22.28) As a consequence of high-inflation without indexation for more than two decades, Turkey from income distribution viewpoint became one of the worst countries in the world.

Turkey in 1950s attempted to develop without an economic plan and proper macroeconomic management (in the first half of 1950s the economy was open, in the second half completely closed with rigid price control). In 1960s, indicative economic planing aiming at 7% GNP growth rate, within price stability was successfully exercised (with extra tax effort and fiscal and monetary discipline, the economy was relatively open). In 1970s, particularly in the second half, economy became virtually closed and an overambitious development plan aiming at 8.5% annual GNP growth rate was implemented without raising domestic saving by proper measures and monetary and fiscal discipline was virtually abandoned. The 1980s could be characterized by open economy and consumption-induced growth strategy e.g. in 1984 private consumption ratio shot up to 76%, increased competition from imports to manufacturing and agricultural sectors, de-industrialization, excessive rise in particularly short-and medium-term and total 0, large budget and BOP deficits, poor macroeconomic management, complete lack of monetary and fiscal discipline (hundreds of funds established outside the proper budgeting and public accounting and auditing systems), excessive supply side incentives to all kinds of economic activities (without proper benefit-cost analysis of their effects) which led to corruption of great proportions, decline in the share of public investment in productive sectors. Despite some privatization, however, the share of state-ownership in the economy have not declined because of rescue operations of bankrupt private companies and banks. The share of state banks dramatically increased which became the major accumulator of bad debts and lender of unreturning loans).

It should be noted that the Turkish national accounts, being estimated for four decades by production approach only, are not quite reliable (Tables: 22.27 - 22.32). On top of this, frequent major revisions are made in them in late 1980s and recently (affecting figures 20-30 years back), without explanation; even consumer price indices are revised backward. Therefore old figures are used, whenever available.

The 1923-1939 era was a period of reconstruction after 7 years of war and occupation; rapid industrialization (modern industries started in textile, cement, sugar refining, copper smelting, steel mill, armament, glass, etc. successfully) and agricultural development, under complete monetary and fiscal discipline (balanced budgets). Heavy investments in industry, human resource development, railroads and ports, banking, public administration were made; a small but efficient and incorruptible government machinery was set up; railroads and public utilities were nationalized; external debt taken over from the Ottoman Empire was repaid timely and no external aid was received. Public enterprises played a dominant role in the development of economic sectors, where the private initiative was not forthcoming or interested. State entrepreneurship, was not considered as a matter of ideology, but of pragmatism. During 1923-1939, GNP increase averaged 7.9% p.a., while price level (GNP deflator) declined by 1.1% p.a. on the average. GNP per capita increased by 5.6% p.a. on the average during 1928-39, while price level (GNP deflator) declined by 3.5% p.a. on the average (average annual GNP growth rate during this period was 7.7%). The economy was open with moderate tariff protection. (Table 22.31) These phenomena show that (i) prices are not sticky downward (particularly in competitive markets); (ii) there was no Phillips curve.

During the World War II period (1940-1945), general mobilization and increase in defense expenditures and strategic stocks led to labor shortage in the economy, (particularly in agriculture) and large budgetary deficits (despite a wealth tax imposed) and soaring inflation (24.2% p.a. CPI increase) and as a consequence GNP declined by 6.6% p.a. on the average. There were shortages of many goods, inputs and spare parts. Black market activity was high in basic foodstuffs and necessities which were rationed and whose prices were controlled.

During the immediate postwar era (1946-53), 11% GNP growth p.a. was recorded (8.3% annual per capita GNP growth) with 2% inflation rate p.a. on the average. In 1946, a major devaluation of the currency (of 35.5%) was managed with 4.3% consumer price index increase and 32% increase in GNP in 1946 and 6.6% decline in CPI index and 4.2% GNP growth in 1947. This episode shows that (i) a major supply shock like currency devaluation if well-organized and implemented within monetary and fiscal discipline, would not necessarily lead to large price increases and output decline, (ii) the Phillips curve trade-off was rather operative in the reverse direction.

In 1954-59 period, inflationary financing of development was opted, with closed economy and strict price and exchange control and without economic and financial planning; 4.6% average annual GNP growth and 15.3% annual average inflation rate resulted in (Table 22.31).

In the 1960s both economic growth (6.2% p.a. average) and price stability (3.3% average inflation rate) was achieved (Table 22.27) under indicative planning, relatively open economy, with monetary and fiscal discipline.

In 1970s Turkey again opted for inflationary financing of development to speed up growth under indicative economic planning; as a result in the 1970s inflation rate of course increased (average 33% p.a.) and marginal capital-output ratio almost doubled (rose from 2.9 in 1960s to 4.8), but GNP growth rate declined instead to 5.4% (Table 22.27) Turkey in mid-1970s, increased its GNP growth rate target from 7% to 8.5% to catch up with the Western Europe; (i) without increasing its domestic saving rate, but with the blessing of the Phillips curve trade-off, (ii) by borrowing short-term externally through various innovations, like convertible Turkish lira accounts, which entitled depositors immediate medium-term Turkish lira credits at subsidized interest rates and exchange-rate guarantee for short- and medium-term foreign loans obtained by the private sector, etc., (iii) by providing tax relief and generous incentives for all kinds of investments and many economic activities. As expected, not GDP but prices shot up! Although growth rates of about 8% were achieved for three years and gross domestic investment increased (its ratio to GDP averaged 25.5% in 1977-80), GDP growth rate averaged 1.6% p.a. (implying a marginal capital-output ratio of 15.9), as inflation rate averaged 62.8% during 1977-1980.

In mid-1977 foreign exchange reserves of the central bank were exhausted and an acute shortage of foreign exchange prevailed thereafter (during 1977-1980). The private sector was compelled to procure its foreign exchange requirements from whatever source possible, but neither the exchange control was lifted, nor virtually permitted foreign exchange transactions were legalized. The exchange rate also was not pegged at a realistic level and real interest rates (both deposit and lending) were grossly negative. During the 1974-80 period, the GDP growth rate averaged only 4.7% (implying a marginal capital-output ratio of 5.2), against the aimed at 8.5% whereas the 7% realistic growth rate could easily have been achieved with or without some extra taxation and saving effort. This experience shows both dangers of overambitious growth rate targets and futility and uselessness of the Phillips-curve hypothesis in developing countries.

It is the privilege of a country to opt for sound monetary and fiscal policy or fashionable approach; however in case of Turkey, the issue is clear-cut, Turkey recorded much higher growth rates and borrowed much less externally, when price stability was maintained. (Experimenting with novel theories is both futile and wasteful.)

The multiplier-accelerator model when applied to the Turkish data yields a growth potential of 13.3% for 1960-73 (α=3, γ=0.7, G_o=0.13) as against 6.3% actual GDP growth; 13.4% for 1962-68 (α=2.8, γ=0.72 and G_o =0.12), as against 6.5% achieved and 8.8% for 1980-1992 (α=5, γ=0.7 and G_o=0.1) versus 4.5% actual growth.

Regressions obtained for Turkey are given below:

1952-69:

(1)	Y= 6.04195 -	0.0330 P	R^2=0.0046
	(1.2888)	(0.1216)	F=0.074

(Where Y=GNP growth rate, P=CPI increase)

Neither regression, nor coefficient of P is significant; this result implies that inflation does not affect economic growth; if there is any effect, it is negative. (Data of table 22.29 are used.)

(2) Y=	7.520 -	0.21924 PW	(R^2=0.1137)
	(1.488)	(0.15302)	($\bar{R}^2$=0.0583)
t-stat:	(5.05)	(-1.433)	DW=2.332
2-T-SIG	(0.0)	(0.171)	SER=3.73

Where PW= Wholesale price index increase ; SIG=2 tail significance level (data from Table 22.29). Price increase reduces GNP growth rate with 83% of probability. SER=Standard error of regression.

(3) Y=	-45.214 +	0.7182C -	0.2911 PW	(R2= 0.181)
	(47.525)	(0.647)	(0.1651)	($\bar{R}^2$ = 0.0718)
t- stat:	(-0.951)	(1.110)	(-1.763)	
SIG:	(0.356)	(0.284)	(0.098)	(F=1.657)

D-W= 2.14, SER=3.704. Where C= private consumption as percentage of GNP.

(4)	Y= -12.295+	0.353C	-0.398	FI-0.288PW
	(89.72)	(1.067)	(0.9096)	(0.16997)
t-stat:	(-0.137)	(0.330)	(-0.437)	(-1.692)

R^2= 0.192 $\bar{R}^2$=0.0189), SER=3.808 D-W=2.223;
F = 1.109; coefficient of PW is significant at 11.3%. Where FI= gross fixed domestic investment, as percentage of GNP.

(5)	Y= 0.103 C	-0.2332PW	(R^2=0.136)
	(0.02005)	(0.1530)	($\bar{R}^2$=0.077)
t-stat=	(5.137)	(-1.5235)	(F =2.424)

D-W=2.318; SER=3.693; coefficient of PW is significant at 15%.

(6)	Y= 17.237	- 0.6332 FI	-0.2719 PW
	(8.564)	(0.5497)	(0.1582)
t-stat	(2.012)	(-1.152)	(-1.718)
SIG	(0.062)	(0.267)	(0.106)

R^2= (0.062) $\bar{R}^2$= 0.077, F-stat=1.711, DW=2.322, SER=3.693.
Where FI= gross fixed domestic investment, as percentage of GNP.

1924-1992:

(7)	Y= 6.342	- 0.0557 P,	(R^2=0.0297)
	(1.1108)	(0.03889)	($\bar{R}^2$=0.0152)
t-stat	(5.789)	(-1.433)	F =20.5
SIGN	(0.0)	(0.157)	DW =2.202

SER= 7.650; P= annual change in GNP deflator (1924-1938), CPI-Ankara (1939-1951), wholesale price index (1952-69), CPI (1970-92) ; Y= annual change in GNP (1924-1969; 1991-92), in GDP (1970-1990). Data of Table 22.31 used.

1924-38:

(8)	Y= 7.9667	+ 0.0354 P	(R^2=0.00167)
	(2.9156)	(0.2404)	($\bar{R}^2$=-0.075)
t-stat:	(2.732)	(0.147)	(F =0.021)

D-W= 2.82, Y= GNP growth rate, P= annual change in GNP deflator.

1924-51 :

(9)	Y= 5.526	- 0.1148 P	(R^2= 0.0288)
	(2.330)	(0.1307)	($\bar{R}^2$=-0.00855)
t-stat:	(2.372)	(-0.878)	F= 0.771
SIG:	(0.05)	(0.50)	

Y=GNP growth rate; P=annual change in GNP deflator: 1924-1938 and CPI-Ankara: 1939-1951.

1970-90:

(Y=GDP growth rate; P=CPI increase, D=Budgetary deficit as percentage of GDP, DS=Budgetary Surplus on Current Account, percentage of GDP)

(10)	Y= 6.904	-0.0507 P	(R^2=0.1825)
	(1.1384)	(0.0246)	($\bar{R}^2$=0.1394)
t-stat:	(6.064)	(-2.059)	
SIG	(0.0)	(0.053)	
D-W=	1.387,	SER=2.969, F-stat=4.240	

(11)	Y= 6.6546	-0.0550 P	+ 0.1105 D
	(1.3862)	(0.0283)	(0.3322)
t-stat	(4.8007)	(-1.941)	(0.3327)
SIG	(0.0)	(0.068)	(0.743)

R^2= 0.1875, $\bar{R}^2$=0.0972, SER=3.04, D-W=1.405, F= 2.076.

(12) Y=	7.3206	-0.0554 P	- 0.1204 DS
	(1.460)	(0.0270)	(0.2554)
t-stat=	(5.013	(-2.048)	(-0.472)
SIG	(0.0)	(0.055)	(0.643)

R^2=0.1924, $\bar{R}^2$= 0.1027, SER=3.03, F= 2.145, D-W=1.508.

In all of these eqs., the coefficient of P, when significant at 20% level or less, is negative (eqs:2,3,4,5,6,7,10,11 and 12), except for eq (8), in which regression, is not significant and the coefficient of P is significant at 15% level.

For *private consumption* ratio to GDP, (C), the following regressions are obtained:

1952-1969:
(Y=GNP growth rate, P= wholesale price index increase [8]

(13)	C=	73.245 +	0.0541 Y +	0.0884 P,	(R^2=0.224)
		(0.711)	(0.0895)	(0.0436)	($\bar{R}^2$=0.120)
t-stat		(103.017)	(0.6041)	(2.0258)	F=2.16
SIG		(0.0)	(0.555)	(0.061)	SER=0.756
					DW=0.756

1970-1990:

(Y=GDP growth rate; DS= budgetary surplus on current account, as percentage of GDP.)

(14)	C=	67.677 +	0.476 Y +	0.0511 DS
		(1.414)	(0.2219)	(0.234)
t-stat		(47.85)	(2.146)	(0.218)
SIG		(0.0)	(0.046)	(0.83)

R^2=0.2055; $\bar{R}_2$=0.1173; SER=2.968; F-stat=2.329; DW=0.732.

(15) C=	70.229 -	0.03676 P +	0.2848 Y
	(2.4468)	(0.03138)	(0.2694)
t-stat:	(28.7)	(-1.17)	(1.057)
SIG=	(0.0)	(0.257)	(0.304)

R^2=0.2599, $\bar{R}^2$= 0.2864, F=3.16, D-W=0.94.

(16)	C=	73.4439 -	0.0684 P -	0.228 DS
		(1.5777)	(0.02826)	(0.2559)
t-stat:		(46.552)	(-2.419)	(-0.891)
SIG:		(0.0)	(0.026)	(0.385)

R^2= 0.2471, $\bar{R}^2$=0.1635, F=2.954, D-W= 1.098, SER= 2.889.

(17)	C=	71.31	-0.0484P +	0.2252 Y -	0.1469 DS
		(3.24)	(0.0389)	(0.2977)	(0.2803)
t-stat:		(22.005)	(-1.242)	(0.7565)	(-0.524)
SIG:		(0.0)	(0.231)	(0.460)	(0.607)

R^2=0.2716, $\bar{R}^2$=0.1431, SER=2.924, D-W=0.967, F-stat=2.113.

---

(8) From a previous study, it was judged that during 1952-69 period, the wholesale price index was a better indicator of price changes than the consumer price indices in Turkey (Hüsnü Kızılyallı, "Türk Ekonomisindeki Gelişmelerin Parasal Faktörlerle Açıklanması (Explanation of Turkish Economic Development by Monetary Factors): 1946-1974", Boğaziçi Üniversitesi, Istanbul, 1978.

Price increases, during 1952-69, increased private consumption (eq.13); however, during 1970-90, price inflation reduced consumption (eq.16). Over this period income distribution became more inequitable and consumption of durables and imported goods increased.

Regressions obtained for *gross fixed domestic investment* (FI, as percentage of GNP or GDP) are shown below:

1952-1969:

(Y= GNP growth rate, FI=gross fixed domestic investment as percentage of GNP, P= Ankara CPI increase, PW= wholesale price index increase.)

(18)	FI=	15.65 -	0.0799 Y -	0.0672 P	(R^2=0.1219)
		(0.853)	(0.10736)	(0.0523)	($\bar{R}^2$=0.0048)
t-stat:		(18.353)	(-0.74457)	(-1.2835)	
SIG:		(0.0)	(0.468)	(0.219)	

DW= 0.5, SER=1.698, F-stat= 1.040.

(19)	FI=	16.312 -	0.1283 Y -	0.1113 PW	(R^2=0.158)
		(1.0685)	(0.1114)	(0.0724)	(adjusted $\bar{R}^2$=0.0457)
t-stat:		(15.266)	(-1.1518	(-1.5366)	
SIG:		(0.0)	(0.267)	(0.145)	

SER= 1.6627, D-W=0.390, F-stat=1.407

1970-90:

(P=CPI increase; Y= GDP growth rate; DS=budgetary surplus on current account as percentage of GDP.)

(20)	FI=	20.541 +	0.0148 P -	0.1223 DS
		(1.3149)	(0.02355)	(0.2113)
t-stat:		(15.62)	(0.63)	(-0.573)

R^2=0.069, $\bar{R}^2$=0.069.

(21)	FI=	18.843 +	0.0315 P +	0.1494 Y
		(2.051)	(0.0263)	(0.2258)
t-stat:		(9.189)	(1.199)	(0.662)
SIG=		(0.0)	(0.246)	(0.516)

$\bar{R}^2$= -0.0285, R^2= 0.0743, F=0.722, D-W=0.830.

During 1952-69 price increases adversely affected fixed investment at 15% level of significance (eq: 19); in 1970-90, prices increases had a slight favorable effect on fixed investment (eq.21).

Regression eqs for *gross domestic investment*, as a percentage of GDP, (I) for the *1970-1990 period,* give quite a good fit. (Where, P=CPI increase; Y=GDP growth rate; D= budgetary deficit, as percentage of GDP; DS= current budgetary surplus, as percentage of GDP.) In all eqs, the coefficient of P is positive and statistically significant; P affects I by a multiple of 0.13-0.18, hence inflationary expansion to promote domestic investment is not worth the while; moreover effect of P on Y is negative, as verified earlier. The coefficient of D is also positive, but statistically not significant; whereas the coefficient of DS is positive, significant in both senses, in fact dominant next to that of Y (since DS increases I by a multiple of 0.85, while Y increases by multiple of 0.92; eq.22). The positive effect of P on I, can be explained, by incentives virtually indexed to inflation. In the high-inflation economy of 1970-1990, the real value of incentives increases as inflation accelerates, e.g. real present value of interest payments and principal repayment of low fixed-interest-rate loans declines as inflation rate increases. Hence inflation encourages investments entitled to incentives, but effect on the total domestic investment is not significant.

1970-1990:

(22)	I=	8.469 +	0.1797 P +	0.91897 Y +	0.8589 DS
		(2.684)	(0.03564)	(0.2799)	(0.30518)
t-stat:		(3.155)	(5.0423)	(3.283)	(2.814)
SIG:		(0.006)	(0.0)	(0.004)	(0.012)

R^2= 0.6224 ; $\bar{R}^2$=0.5557 ; SER=3.5997 ; F-statistic=9.340 ; DW=1.803

(23)	I=	16.973 +	0.0857 P +	0.3597 D
		(2.2229)	(0.0454)	(0.5328)
t-stat:		(7.635)	(1.8874)	(0.6752)
SIG:		(0.0)	(0.075)	(0.508)

R^2= 0.2664), $\bar{R}^2$=0.1849, SER=4.8761, D-W=1.618, F=3.268.

(24)	I=	11.535 +	0.1306 P +	0.8171 Y +	0.2694 D
		(2.972)	(0.04421)	(0.3347)	(0.472)
t-stat:		(3.881)	(2.954)	(2.441)	(0.5694)
SIG:		(0.001)	(0.009)	(0.026)	(0.577)

R^2= 0.457, $\bar{R}^2$=0.361, SER=4.317, D-W=1.655, F=4.766.

1970-1990:

(25) I=	12.041 +	0.1418 P +	0.83195 Y	
	(2.783)	(0.0388)	(0.3273)	
t-stat:	(4.326)	(3.652)	(2.542)	
SIG:	(0.0)	(0.002)	(0.020)	

R^2= 0.4465, $\bar{R}^2$=0.385, SER=4.235, D-W=1.722, F-stat=7.26.

Regression eqs.for *gross domestic saving* (S) are given below:

1952-1969:

(Y=GNP growth rate; P= Ankara CPI increase; PW=wholesale price index increase; S=gross domestic saving, as percentage of GNP.)

(26) S=	13.305 -	0.124 Y -	0.0375 P
	(1.223)	(0.141)	(0.0689)
t-stat:	(11.85)	(-0.877)	(-0.545)

R^2=0.063, $\bar{R}^2$=-0.062, F=0.50, DW=0.178, SER=2.235.

(27) S=	13.125 -	0.1248 Y -	0.0115 PW
	(1.450)	(0.1512)	(0.0983)
t-stat:	(9.05)	(-0.825)	(-0.117)

R^2=0.045, $\bar{R}^2$=-0.082, F-stat=0.355, DW=0.17, SER=2.256.

For the 1952-69 period, the fit of regression eqs is not good; the effect of PW on S in negative (the coefficient is significant at 12%). In the 1970-90 period, price inflation increased S (the coefficient is reliable at 99%), slightly.

1970-90:

(Y=GDP growth rate; D and DS budgetary deficit and current budgetary surplus respectively, both as percentage of GDP.)

(28) S=	9.843 +	0.1252 P +	0.4598 Y +	0.2643 D
	(3.025)	(0.0450)	(0.3406)	(0.4816)
t-stat:	(3.254)	(2.782)	(1.3498)	(0.4816)
SIG=	(0.005)	(0.013)	(0.195)	(0.590)

R^2=0.4084, $\bar{R}^2$=0.3040, SER=4.394, F-stat=3.912, D-W=1.587.

(29)	S=	8.6198 +	0.1544 P +	0.5163 Y +	0.4134 DS
		(3.1855)	(0.0423)	(0.3322)	(0.3622)
t-stat:		(2.706)	(3.651)	(1.554)	(1.141)
SIG:		(0.015)	(0.002)	(0.139)	(0.270)

R^2=0.4408, $\bar{R}^2$=0.3421, SER=4.2720, D-W=1.526, F=4.467.

(30)	S=	10.3389 +	0.13620 P +	0.4744 Y
		(2.8305)	(0.0395)	(0.3329)
t-stat:		(3.653)	(3.449)	(1.425)
SIG:		(0.002)	(0.003)	(0.171)

R^2=0.3979 ; $\bar{R}^2$=0.3310 ; F=5.948, D-W=1.627, SER=4.308.

Regressions for *gross national saving* ratio to GDP (SN), suggest that, price increase (P) had a slight increasing effect on SN (eqs. 31, 32 and 33).

1970-1990:

(31)	SN=	17.941 +	0.049 P +	0.027 DS
		(1.370)	(0.0245)	(0.222)
t-stat:		(13.094)	(1.998)	(0.123)
SIG:		(0.0)	(0.061)	(0.903)

R^2= 0.2096, $\bar{R}^2$=0.1218, SER=2.508, D-W=0.966, F =2.387.

(32)	SN=	18.947 +	0.0396 P -	0.1062 Y -	0.0108 DS
		(2.8475)	(0.0342)	(0.2615)	(0.246)

(33)	SN=	18.867 +	0.0405 P -	0.1018 Y
		(2.133)	(0.0274)	(0.2349)
t-stat:		(8.845)	(1.479)	(-0.433)
SIG:		(0.0)	(0.156)	(0.670)

F= 2.496, D-W=0.8956, SER=2.497 R^2=0.217, $\bar{R}^2$=0.130

Özmucur (1987) had found that the inflation rate has to be lowered for an increase in the saving rate for Turkey (1969-1973) and for OECD countries Özmucur (1987) had found that the inflation rate has to be lowered for an increase in the saving rate for Turkey (1969-1973) and for OECD countries. (1968-1973), because wage adjustment do not lag behind, on the contrary exceed price changes. For the 1952-69 period, a similar result was estimated for Turkey when there was low-inflation or price stability.

Özmucur's study and other similar studies (Thirlwall, Woodfield and McDonald models) being based on Kaldor or Pasinetti saving functions, make the simplifying assumption that the saving rate is determined by the saving propensities of capitalistic and working classes and shares of profits and wages in national income (Özmucur, *ibid*); whereas the saving propensities (at least in Turkey) of farmers, rentier class and proprietors, professionals, small businessmen, speculators, mafia class, earners of illegal or illicit incomes, bribes, etc. economic agents of underground economy, rural migrants, and in rural and urban areas, differ sharply from those of standard capitalist and working class and among themselves. Moreover, with low-or high-inflation and free capital movements and dollarization in 1980s, part of domestic or national savings might be transferred abroad and then measurement error steps in (because if saving figures are estimated as residuals or on the basis of savings estimates in the country, then under-or over-estimation will be made); on top of this, in Turkey national accounts data could only be construed as rough estimates, since estimates obtained under production approach are not checked by estimates made either under expenditure or income approach. Under such circumstances, whether estimating the effect of inflation on savings in a roundabout manner, under broad assumptions and employing sophisticated economic models is superior to the direct estimation method used herein, is an open question.

Conclusions

Turkey achieved highest economic growth rates under price stability (1923-1939, 1946-1953, 1960s); under inflationary conditions economic growth rate declined (1940-1945, 1954-1959, 1970s and 1980s) and marginal capital-output ratio increased with high-inflation (1970-1981, 1980-1992). The trade-off between price inflation and economic growth is definitely negative. While price inflation increased private consumption during 1952-1969, in 1970-1990 reduced it, but not significantly. During 1952-1969, price increases reduced domestic fixed investments, and increased it slightly in 1970-1990. Price inflation increased domestic investment slightly in 1970-1990, (possibly due to the inflation-indexed incentive mechanism), but the favorable effect of current budget surplus is considerable. During 1970-90, price inflation increased domestic and national savings marginally.

It seems that the high inflation in Turkey over the last two decades has not brought about any beneficial lasting effect. Its long-lasting effects have been (i) change in income distribution, wiping out middle income class, (ii) huge increase in external indebtedness, (iii) dollarization, (iv) decline in productive investments and advent of de-industrialization, (v) big rise in the unemployment level, and (vi) decline in the efficiency of public administration and a rise in corruption.

While in the rest of the world, populist leftist governments prefer the Phillips curve trade-off, ironically in Turkey, rightist governments favor inflationary development.

Table 22.7
Macro data of the US, UK, Japan, Korea and Germany (as percentage of GDP, unless specified otherwise)
United States

	Budget Deficit		Net government borrowing	Real GDP growth rate (%)	Consumer price index increase (%)
	Total	On current account			
1970	-	-	-	0.5	-
1971	-	-	-	3.2	4.1
1972	1.6	0.6	-	5.1	3.4
1973	1.2	0.2	-	4.8	6.3
1974	0.3	-0.7	-	-0.9	11.0
1975	3.5	1.7	-	-1.2	9.0
1976	4.4	2.4	-	4,9	5.9
1977	2.7	0.9	-	4.4	6.4
1978	2.8	0.4	-	5.1	7.7
1979	1.5	-0.6	-	2.0	11.1
1980	2.9	0.5	-	-0.2	13.6
1981	2.6	0.2	-	2.3	10.2
1982	4.0	2.0	-	-2.	6.3
1983	6.0	4.6	-	3.7	3.2
1984	4.8	3.4	-	7.1	4.3
1985	5.4	3.5	-	3.8	3.5
1986	5.1	3.9	5.5	3.2	1.9
1987	3.3	2.3	3.3	3.1	3.7
1988	3.2	2.1	3.3	3.9	4.0
1989	2.8	1.7	2.7	2.5	4.8
1990	4.0	2.2	4.0	0.8	5.4
1991	4.8	..	4.9	-1.2	4.3
1992	5.6	..	3.6(+)	2.1	3.0

Table 22.7 (continued)
United Kingdom

	Budget Total	Deficit on Current Account	Real GDP Growth Rate (%)	Retail Price Index Increase (%)
1970	-1.7	-	2.5	6.3
1971	0.7	-	8.3	9.4
1972	2.6	-	7.5	7.3
1973	3.4	-	5.1	9.1
1974	4.5	-	-2.2	16.0
1975	7.4	-	-0.9	24.2
1976	5.8	-	3.1	16.5
1977	3.4	-	2.7	15.9
1978	5.2	-	3.6	8.3
1979	5.7	-	2.9	13.4
1980	4.6	-	9.1	18.0
1981	4.8	2.4	-9.9	11.9
1982	3.4	0.4	1.5	8.6
1983	4.4	1.0	3.7	4.6
1984	3.2	1.1	2.2	5.0
1985	2.9	-0.1	3.5	6.1
1986	2.4	0.03	4.0	3.4
1987	0.7	-0.7	4.8	4.2
1988	-1.5	-3.1	4.0	4.9
1989	-0.8	-3.1	2.3	7.8
1990	..	..	0.8	9.5
1991	..	..	..	..
1992	..	..	..	..

Table 22.7 (continued)
Japan

	Increase in Real Money Supply (%)	Budget Deficit	Budget Deficit on Current Account	Real GDP Growth Rate (%)	Consumer Price Index Increase (%)
1970	-	0.1	-	10.4	7.5
1971	16.5	0.5	-	4.3	6.3
1972	18.9	1.9	-	8.3	4.9
1973	7.5	0.3	-	7.8	11.7
1974	-7.2	2.5	-	-0.7	23.0
1975	4.4	5.2	-	2.8	11.7
1976	5.4	5.7	-	4.2	9.4
1977	4.6	6.4	-	4.6	8.3
1978	9.3	7.5	-	4.9	4.2
1979	7.2	7.4	-	5.6	3.7
1980	2.2	7.0	-	3.6	7.7
1981	6.4	6.5	2.8	3.6	5.0
1982	6.2	6.5	3.1	3.2	2.8
1983	5.9	6.7	3.4	2.7	1.8
1984	.1	5.8	2.8	4.3	2.3
1985	6.6	4.9	2.2	5.0	2.1
1986	8.6	4.8	2.2	2.6	0.6
1987	9.1	3.5	0.7	4.4	0.1
1988	8.4	2.6	0.2	6.2	0.7
1989	9.3	2.9	0.7	4.8	2.3
1990	3.6	1.6	-	5.2	3.0
1991	-	-	-	-	-
1992	-	-	-	-	-
Average					

Remark: Minus (-) sign indicates budgetary surplus
Source: IBRD, World Development Reports, World Tables
IMF, International Financial statistics (IFS)

Table 22.7 (continued)

Korea

	Overal Budget Deficit	Real GDP Growth Rate (%)	Consumer Price Index Increase (%)
1970	0.8	-	-
1971	0.3	10.0	13.4
1972	3.8	5.8	11.2
1973	0.5	15.2	3.2
1974	2.2	8.9	24.7
1975	2.0	7.7	25.2
1976	1.4	13.5	15.2
1977	1.8	11.0	10.0
1978	1.2	10.9	14.6
1979	1.7	7.4	18.2
1980	2.2	-3.3	28.8
1981	3.3	6.9	21.3
1982	3.0	7.4	10.9
1983	1.0	12.1	3.4
1984	1.2	9.2	2.3
1985	1.2	6.9	2.4
1986	0.1	5.4	2.8
1987	-0.4	12.0	3.0
1988	-1.6	11.5	7.2
1989	-0.2	6.2	5.6
1990	0.6	9.2	8.6
1991	-	8.4	9.7
1992	-	-	6.2

Remark: Minus (-) sign indicates budgetary surplus
Source: IBRD, World Development Reports, World Tables
IMF, International Financial statistics (IFS)

Table 22.7 (continued)
Germany

	Budget Deficit	Budget Surplus on Current Account	Real GDP Growth Rate (%)	CPI Index Increase (%)
1970	-1.0	3.25	6.0	-
1971	-0.9	3.54	2.9	5.4
1972	-0.7	2.81	4.1	5.5
1973	-1.4	3.82	4.9	7.0
1974	0.7	2.05	0.3	6.9
1975	3.6	-1.03	-1.4	5.9
1976	2.8	-0.13	5.3	4.4
1977	2.1	0.33	2.9	3.7
1978	2.1	0.28	3.0	2.6
1979	2.0	0.44	4.1	4.1
1980	1.8	0.70	1.1	5.5
1981	2.4	0.06	0.2	6.3
1982	2.0	0.31	-0.9	5.2
1983	2.0	0.26	1.5	3.4
1984	1.8	0.45	2.8	2.3
1985	1.1	1.13	1.9	2.3
1986	0.9	1.13	2.2	-0.1
1987	1.1	0.65	1.4	0.2
1988	1.7	-0.13	3.5	1.3
1989	0.2	1.51	4.1	2.8
1990	1.6	0.68	4.9	2.7
1991	2.6	-	3.6	3.5
1992	-	-	-	-
Average			2.7	3.9

Remark: Minus (-) sign indicates budgetary surplus
Source: IBRD, World Development Reports, World Tables
IMF, International Financial statistics (IFS)

Table 22.8
West Germany macroeconomic data
(1973 GNP per capita $5,320)

As Percentages of GDP	1950-60	1960-70	1965-70	1965-73	1970-81	1981-91
Private Consumption	58.5	56.0	55.2	54.8	54.9	56.0
General GovernmentConsumption	13.6	15.3	16.1	16.6	19.5	19.7
Gross Domestic Investment	26.1	26.4	26.7	26.4	23.6	20.3
Gross Domestic Saving	27.9	28.7	28.7	28.6	25.6	24.3
Average Annual Growth Rate						
(%, at Constant Prices)						
GNP at Market Prices	8.7	4.4	4.6	4.7	2.6	-
GDP at Market Prices	8.7	4.4	4.6	4.6	2.6	2.3
Private Consumption	8.6	4.6	4.7	4.7	2.8	-
General Government Consumption	5.9	4.1	4.0	4.0	3.5	-
Gross Domestic Investment	10.5	4.1	4.6	4.8	1.3	-12.0*
Marginal Capital-OutputRatio Estimate	3.0	6.0	5.8	5.7	9.1	8.8

*Implied growth rate (see Table: 27)
Source:World Tables, IBRD

Table 22.9
West Germany: macroeconomic coefficients
(as percent of GDP, unless specified otherwise)

	1981	1982	1983	1984	1985	1986	1987	1988	1989	1990	1991	1981-1991 Avarege
Private consumption	57.6	57.7	57.5	57.2	56.9	55.5	55.7	54.9	54.9	54.6	54.4	56.0
General government consumption	20.7	20.6	20.2	20.0	20.1	19.9	20.0	19.7	18.8	18.4	17.9	19.7
Total consumption	78.3	78.3	77.7	77.2	77.0	75.4	75.7	74.6	73.7	73.0	72.3	75.7
Gross domestic investment	20.9	19.4	20.3	20.3	19.6	19.6	19.4	20.0	20.9	21.1	21.3	20.3
Gross domestic saving	21.7	21.8	22.3	22.8	23.1	24.7	24.4	25.3	26.3	27.0	27.7	24.3
GDP growth rate (%)	0.2	-0.9	1.5	2.8	1.9	2.2	1.4	3.5	4.1	4.9	3.6	2.3
Consumer price increase (%)	6.3	5.2	3.4	2.3	2.3	-0.1	0.2	1.3	2.8	2.7	3.5	-

Source: World Tables, IBRD; IFS, IMF

Table 22.12
Japan: macroeconomic data
(1973 GNP per capita $3,630)

As Percentages of GDP:	1950-60	1960-70	1965-70	1965-73	1970-81	1981-90
Private Consumtion	62.0	55.5	52.8	52.4	56.6	58.6
General Government Consumption	8.7	7.7	8.7	8.7	9.5	9.6
Gross Domestic Investment	28.9	36.0	37.3	37.4	33.3	29.7
Gross Domestic Saving	29.3	36.8	38.5	38.9	33.9	31.8
Average Annual Growth Rate (%, at Constant Prices)						
GNP at Market Prices	6.3	10.4	10.5	10.8	4.6	-
GDP at Market Prices	6.4	10.4	10.5	10.8	4.5	4.2
Private Consumption	6.8	9.0	8.7	8.7	4.2	-
General Government Consumption	1.6	6.2	6.8	7.0	4.5	-
Gros Domestic Investment	10.4	14.6	13.2	13.8	3.1	-7.1*
Marginal Capital-Output Ratio Estimate	4.52	3.46	3.55	3.46	12.81	7.07

* Implied annual growth rate (See, Table 22.25)
Source: World Tables, IBRD

Table 22.15
Korea: macroeconomic ratios and growth rates (percentages)

Average Annual Growth Rate at Constant Prices	950-60	1960-73	965-73	1960-70	1970-81	1981-91	1981-85	1986-91
GNP at market prices	5.0	9.4	10.7	8.7	8.7	-	-	-
GDP at market prices	5.1	9.5	10.9	8.6	9.0	8.7	8.5	8.8
Private Consumption	5.8	7.7	9.0	7.0	7.1	-3.0*	4.1*	-12.9*
General Govern.Cons.	3.0	6.6	8.3	5.5	7.8	-1.6*	1.0*	3.8*
Gross Domestic Invest.	0.0	19.8	18.4	23.6	12.1	15.4*	7.8*	26.7*
Gross Domestic Saving	-	616*	-	475*	109*	44.3*	23.6*	41.7*
As percentage of GDP								
Private Consumption	84.8	73.6	72.6	76.8	64.0	57.1	61.4	53.5
General Govern.Cons.	12.8	10.7	10.7	10.5	11.6	10.5	10.8	10.3
Gross Domestic Inv.	11.4	23.9	24.8	23.2	29.4	31.2	29.2	34.0
Gross Domestic Saving	2.4	15.7	16.7	12.7	24.4	32.4	27.8	36.2
Consumer Price Index annual average increase	52.3	12.7	11.1	14.5	16.6	7.0	8.1	6.2
Marginal Capital Output-Ratio	2.24	2.52	2.28	2.70	3.27	3.59	3.44	3.86

(*) implied growth rate (see: Table 22.25)

Source: *World Tables*, IBRD

Table 22.16
Korea: macroeconomic data
(as percentage of GDP, unless specified otherwise)

	Private Consumption	General Government	Gross Domestic Investment (*)	Gross Domestic Saving	Real GDP Growth Rate (%)	CPI Increase (%)
1970	-	-	24.9	15.0	-	-
1971	-	-	22.4	14.8	10.0	13.4
1972	-	-	20.3	16.1	5.8	11.2
1973	-	-	23.0	21.6	15.2	3.2
1974	-	-	25.4	20.6	8.9	24.7
1975	-	-	24.9	18.5	7.7	25.2
1976	-	-	24.0	24.1	13.5	15.2
1977	-	-	26.9	27.5	11.0	10.0
1978	-	-	30.9	28.5	10.9	14.6
1979	-	-	32.6	28.2	7.4	18.2
1980	-	-	32.1	24.3	-3.3	28.8
1981	63.9	11.6	29.5	24.5	6.9	21.3
1982	62.5	11.5	28.6	26.0	7.4	10.9
1983	61.0	10.7	28.8	28.3	12.1	3.4
1984	60.1	10.0	29.8	29.9	9.2	2.3
1985	59.4	10.1	29.2	30.5	6.9	2.4
1986	56.0	10.1	28.4	34.0	5.4	2.8
1987	53.5	9.9	29.5	36.6	12.0	3.0
1988	51.9	9.8	30.6	38.3	11.5	7.2
1989	53.9	10.5	33.3	35.6	6.2	5.6
1990	53.2	10.6	36.9	36.2	9.2	8.6
1991	52.7	10.8	39.1	36.4	8.4	9.7
1970-80 average	-	-	26.1	21.8	8.7	16.5
1981-85 average	61.4	10.8	29.2	27.8	8.5	8.1
1981-91 average	57.1	10.5	31.2	32.4	8.7	7.0
1986-91 average	53.5	10.3	34.0	36.2	8.8	6.2

(*) 1970-1980 Gross fixed investment

Source: World Tables, IBRD; IFS, IMF

Table 22.17
Korea: macroeconomic data (as percentage of GDP)

	Overall Budgetary Deficit or Surplus (-)		Current Budget Surplus	Accumulated Budgetary Deficit	Gross Domestic Saving	Gross Domestic Investment		Real GDP Growth Rate(%)	Real GDP Index		Consumer Price Index Increase (%)
	(D)	DD	($\bar{D}$)	(D*)	(S)	(I)	DY	(Y)	(Y*)	DP	(P)
1970	0.8	-	4.0	0.8	15.0	24.9	-	-	-	1.0	14.5(+)
1971	0.3	-0.5	3.4	1.1	14.8	22.4	-	1.0	1.1	-1.1	13.4
1972	3.8	3.5	1.0	4.9	16.1	20.3	-4.2	5.8	1.164	-2.2	11.2
1973	0.5	-3.3	1.9	5.4	21.6	23.0	9.4	15.2	1.341	-8.0	3.2
1974	2.2	1.7	1.7	7.6	20.6	25.4	-6.3	8.9	1.46	21.5	24.7
1975	2.0	-0.2	2.9	9.6	18.5	24.9	-1.2	7.7	1.572	0.5	25.2
1976	1.4	-0.6	3.7	11.0	24.1	24.0	5.8	13.5	1.785	-10	15.2
1977	1.8	0.4	3.2	12.8	27.5	26.9	-2.5	11.0	1.981	-5.2	10.0
1978	1.2	-0.6	3.7	14.0	28.5	30.9	-0.1	10.9	2.197	4.6	14.6
1979	1.7	0.5	3.8	15.7	28.2	32.6	-3.5	7.4	2.360	3.6	18.2
1980	2.2	0.5	2.9	17.9	24.3	32.1	-10.7	-3.3	2.282	10.6	28.8
1981	3.3	1.1	3.4	21.2	24.5	29.5	10.2	6.9	2.439	-7.5	21.3
1982	3.0	-0.3	2.9	24.2	26.0	28.6	0.5	7.4	2.620	-10.4	10.9
1983	1.0	-2.0	3.6	25.2	28.3	28.8	4.7	12.1	2.937	-7.5	3.4
1984	1.2	0.2	3.2	26.4	29.9	29.8	-2.9	9.2	3.207	-1.1	2.3
1985	1.2	0.0	2.7	27.6	30.5	29.2	-2.3	6.9	3.428	0.1	2.4
1986	0.1	-1.1	3.1	27.7	34.0	28.4	-1.5	5.4	3.613	0.4	2.8
1987	-0.4	-0.5	3.9	27.3	36.6	29.5	6.6	12.0	4.047	0.2	3.0
1988	-1.6	-1.2	4.5	25.7	38.3	30.6	-0.5	11.5	4.512	4.2	7.2
1989	-0.2	1.4	3.8	25.5	35.6	33.3	-5.3	6.2	4.792	-1.6	5.6
1990	0.6	0.8	2.3	26.1	36.2	36.9	3.0	9.2	5.233	3.0	8.6

Remark: Gross fixed investment for the 1970-80 period
(+) 1960-70 average

Source: *World Tables,* IBRD

Table 22.19
US macroeconomic parameters
(as percentage of GDP)

	1950	1955	1960	1961	1962	1963	1964	1965	1966	1967	1968	1969
Private Consumption	67	63	64	64	63	63	63	63	62	61.5	62	62
General Government Consumption	12	17	18	19	19	19	19	18	19	21	21	21
Total Consumption	79	80	82	83	82	82	82	81	81	82	83	83
Gross Domestic Investment	21	20	18	17	18	18	18	19	19	17.5	18	18
Gross Domestic Saving	21	20	18	17	18	18	18	19	19	18	17	17
Gross National Saving	-	-	18	18	19	19	19	20	19	18	18	18
Private Saving	-	-	14.5	15	15	15	15.5	15.5	16	17	15	14
Public Saving	-	-	4	3	3	4	3.5	4.0	4	1.5	3	4

	1970	1971	1972	1973	1974	1975	1976	1977	1978	1979	1980	
Private Consumption	62	62	62	62	63	64	64	64	63	64	65	-
General Government Consumption	21	21	21	20	18	19	19	18	17.5	17	18	-
Total Consumption	83	83	83	82	81	83	82.5	82	81	81	83	-
Gross Domestic Investment	17	18	18	19	19	17	17.5	18	19	19	17	-
Gross Domestic Saving	17	17	17	18	19	17	18	20	20.5	20	18	-
Gross National Saving	17	18	18	19	20	18.5	19	19.5	20.5	21	19	-
Private Saving	14.5	16	15	14	-	-	-	-	-	-	-	-
Public Saving	3	2	3	5	-	-	-	-	-	-	-	-

Table 22.19 (continued)

	1981	1982	1983	1984	1985	1986	1987	1988	1989	1990	1991	1992
Private Consumption	63.5	66	66	65	66	67	67	67	67	68	68.5	69
General Government Consumption	17.5	18	18	18	18	17	17	16.5	16	16	17	16
Total Consumption	81	84	85	83	84	84	84	84	83	84	85	85
Gross Domestic Investment	20	17	17	20	19	19	18	18	18	17	15	15
Gross Domestic Saving	19	16	15	17	16	16	16	16	17	16	15	15
Gross National Saving	21	18	17	18	17	17	16	15	16	15	-	-
Government Budget* Deficit (-)	-0.2	-2.0	-5	-3	-3.5	-5.5	3.3	-3.3	-2.7	-4.0	-4.9	-3.6+
GDP growth rate (constant prices)	2.3	-2.6	3.7	7.1	3.8	3.2	3.1	3.9	2.5	0.8	-1.2	2.1
Consumer Price Increase	10.2	6.3	3.2	4.3	3.5	1.9	3.7	4.0	4.8	5.4	4.3	3.0

Remark: Gross Domestic Saving and Gross National Saving defined as in Table 22.25
(*)1986 on, Net Government borrowing
(+) implied by the public debt figure, Sept.1992
Sources: World Tables, IBRD; IFS, IMF

Table 22.21
Macroeconomic data
1. Ireland

	Budgetary Deficit (-) (As Percentage of GDP) (D)	Annual Growth Rate of GDP (Y)	Annual Increase CPI (%) (P)	Gross Domestic Saving (% of GDP) (S)
1970	-5.5	-	-	-
1971	-5.3	0.0	9.0	16.73
1972	-5.6	5.4	8.9	19.71
1973	-6.8	12.1	11.6	19.99
1974	-12.0	4.3	16.7	14.40
1975	-12.4	5.7	21.0	17.27
1976	-10.1	1.4	18.1	17.45
1977	-9.4	8.2	13.4	18.8
1978	-11.4	7.2	7.7	19.12
1979	-11.9	3.1	13.3	16.61
1980	-13.1	3.1	18.3	14.35
1981	-14.6	3.3	20.4	14.16
1982	-14.8	2.3	17.1	20.44
1983	-12.5	-0.2	10.4	21.03
1984	-10.7	4.3	8.6	22.48
1985	-11.7	3.1	5.4	21.87
1986	-11.2	-0.7	3.9	21.32
1987	-9.6	4.7	3.1	23.04
1988	-4.7	4.5	2.2	25.1
1989	-	6.4	4.0	-
1990	-	7.1	3.4	-

Table 22.21 (continued)

2. Luxembourg

	Budgetary Surplus (as % of GDP) (D)	Real GDP Increase (%) (Y)	CPI Increase (%) (P)	Gross Domestic Saving (as % of GDP) (S)
1970	1.9	-	-	39.0
1971	2.0	2.4	4.6	33.5
1972	1.5	6.8	5.1	34.7
1973	2.8	8.4	6.4	39.8
1974	4.3	4.2	9.4	42.4
1975	1.2	-6.5	10.7	27.3
1976	0.3	2.6	9.7	28.7
1977	0.7	1.6	6.7	24.6
1978	3.4	4.1	3.1	26.4
1979	-0.2	2.3	4.6	28.5
1980	1.3	0.9	6.3	24.6
1981	-2.1	-0.5	8.1	21.7
1982	0.7	1.1	9.4	23.3
1983	-2.0	3.0	8.6	24.6
1984	5.3	6.1	5.6	26.5
1985	10.4	2.9	4.1	25.5
1986	7.3	4.9	0.3	27.8
1987	3.5	2.7	-0.1	24.0
1988	3.1	5.5	1.5	25.4
1989	3.3	6.3	3.3	28.7
1990	-	2.3	3.7	26.6

Table 22.21 (continued)

3. Belgium

	Budgetary Deficit (%) of GDP (D)	Real GDP Growth (%) (Y)	CPI Increase (%) (P)	Gross Domestic Saving (as % of GDP) (S)
1970	1.7	-	-	26.7
1971	2.9	3.7	4.4	25.6
1972	4.4	5.3	5.4	25.3
1973	3.5	5.9	7.0	24.9
1974	2.3	4.1	12.8	25.5
1975	4.8	-1.5	12.6	22.3
1976	5.7	5.6	9.3	22.6
1977	6.0	0.5	7.0	21.3
1978	7.0	2.7	4.5	21.0
1979	7.8	2.1	4.5	19.6
1980	8.2	4.3	6.6	19.3
1981	12.5	-1.0	7.7	16.2
1982	11.1	1.5	8.7	12.4
1983	12.5	0.4	7.7	17.3
1984	13.5	2.1	6.3	18.1
1985	11.4	0.8	4.9	17.4
1986	9.9	1.5	1.3	19.1
1987	7.6	2.2	1.5	19.3
1988	6.6	4.9	1.2	21.6
1989	6.3	3.6	3.1	23.2
1990	-	3.8	3.5	23.8
Average annual rate	7.3	2.63	6.0	21.1

Table 22.21 (continued)
4. Austria

A. Annual growth rates and ratios

	CPI Increase (%) (P)	Budgetary Deficit (% GDP) (D)	Real GDP Growth (%) (Y)	Gross Domestic Saving (% GDP) (S)
1970	-	0.5	-	30.7
1971	4.6	-0.1	4.9	30.4
1972	6.4	0.2	6.2	31.2
1973	7.6	1.6	5.0	31.2
1974	9.4	1.6	3.9	30.8
1975	8.4	4.0	-0.4	26.6
1976	7.3	4.7	4.6	25.8
1977	5.5	3.8	4.4	25.2
1978	3.6	4.1	0.1	26.0
1979	3.8	3.8	4.7	26.2
1980	6.3	3.4	2.9	26.5
1981	6.8	3.1	-0.4	25.0
1982	5.4	4.8	1.2	24.6
1983	3.4	6.0	1.9	23.3
1984	5.7	4.6	1.4	24.0
1985	3.2	4.7	2.5	23.6
1986	1.6	5.9	1.2	24.4
1987	1.4	5.5	1.7	24.5
1988	1.9	5.0	4.0	25.2
1989	2.6	3.8	3.7	26.0
1990	3.3	4.3	4.9	26.6

B: Average annual growth (%) rates for periods (%)

	1950-60	1960-70	1970-81	1980-90
	-	-	-	-
GDP Real	6.0	4.6	3.5	2.3
Wholesale price index	4.8	2.5	5.5	-
CPI	5.3	3.5	6.5	3.8

Table 22.21 (continued)

5. France

A. Annual growth rates and ratios

	Overall Budgetary Deficit (-) (% of GDP)	Real GDP Growth (%) (Y)	CPI Increase (%) (P)	Gross Domestic Saving (% GDP) (S)
1970	-	-	-	27.4
1971	-	3.9	5.9	27.3
1972	0.7	3.7	6.0	27.4
1973	0.4	4.7	7.5	28.1
1974	0.4	2.5	13.6	27.1
1975	-2.6	-0.8	11.7	24.7
1976	-1.0	4.4	9.6	24.7
1977	-1.2	2.1	9.5	24.6
1978	-1.4	3.4	8.9	24.5
1979	-1.5	3.2	10.9	24.3
1980	-0.1	1.3	13.3	23.0
1981	-2.3	1.2	13.4	20.9
1982	-3.4	2.4	11.8	20.0
1983	-3.5	0.7	9.6	19.7
1984	-2.7	1.5	7.5	19.6
1985	-2.7	1.8	5.7	19.5
1986	-3.4	2.4	2.5	20.7
1987	-1.2	2.2	3.3	20.3
1988	-2.3	3.8	2.7	21.2
1989	-1.9	3.6	3.5	22.0
1990	-2.2	2.6	3.4	21.6
Average Annual Rate	-1.7	-	-	23.3

B. Average annual growth rates for periods (%)

	1950-60	1960-70	1970-81	1965-70	1965-73	1980-90
GDP Real	4.5	5.5	3.3	5.8	5.8	2.1
CPI	5.6	3.8	10.1	4.3	5.1	7.0
Wholesale price index	4.8	2.3	8.4	3.3	4.6	-

Table 22.21 (continued)

6. Italy

A. Macroeconomic data:

	Budgetary Deficit (% of GDP) (D)	CPI Increase (%) (P)	Real GDP Increase (%) (Y)	Gross Domestic Saving (as % of GDP) (S)
1970	-	-	-	27.5
1971	-	4.7	1.4	25.6
1972	-	5.3	2.5	24.8
1973	8.7	11.4	7.3	25.1
1974	9.9	18.6	5.4	26.0
1975	15.5	17.3	-2.8	23.9
1976	11.3	16.6	6.5	25.8
1977	11.4	18.2	3.3	26.0
1978	8.3	12.4	3.6	26.4
1979	8.9	14.6	6.0	25.8
1980	10.7	21.3	4.3	24.3
1981	11.2	19.5	0.5	22.8
1982	9.9	16.5	0.1	22.4
1983	11.3	14.8	1.0	22.5
1984	13.1	10.7	2.7	22.7
1985	13.4	9.2	2.6	22.1
1986	14.2	5.9	2.9	22.5
1987	14.9	4.7	3.1	21.7
1988	10.6	5.1	4.1	21.7
1989	10.5	6.3	3.0	21.2
1990	10.3	6.4	2.0	20.8

B. Average annual growth rates (%):

	1950-60	1960-70	1970-81	1965-70	1965-73	1980-90
GDP Real	5.7	5.5	2.9	5.0	4.9	2.4
CPI	3.0	4.0	14.9	4.2	4.1	10.9

Table 22.21 (continued)

7. Australia

A. Macro data

	Grosss Domestic Savings (% GDP) (S)	CPI Increase (%) (P)	Annual Real GDP Growth (%) (Y)	Government Budget Deficit (% GDP)(D)
1970	27.2	-	-	0.7
1971	26.9	6.2	5.1	0.2
1972	27.6	5.8	4.3	-0.3
1973	26.3	9.3	4.0	0.8
1974	24.6	15.1	1.9	0.4
1975	24.6	15.1	2.9	3.2
1976	24.6	13.7	2.9	4.1
1977	22.3	12.3	0.9	2.8
1978	24.2	7.8	5.3	3.0
1979	24.9	9.1	1.9	2.5
1980	23.7	10.1	3.1	1.5
1981	23.6	9.7	2.6	0.7
1982	20.3	11.3	-2.2	0.3
1983	22.2	10.1	6.5	2.4
1984	22.0	3.9	5.0	3.7
1985	22.2	6.7	3.9	2.8
1986	21.8	9.1	2.8	2.2
1987	22.8	8.5	4.6	1.1
1988	23.9	7.2	3.6	-0.4
1989	23.3	7.6	3.6	-1.4
1990	21.2	7.3	-0.9	-1.8

B. Average annual growth rates (9):

	1950-60	1960-70	1970-81	1965-70	1965-73	1980-90
GDP	3.9	5.6	2.8	5.1	5.0	3.0
CPI	6.0	2.5	11.1	3.3	4.3	8.3

Source: World Tables, IBRD

Table 22.24
Macroeconomic parameters of the West
(as percentages of GDP)

	Japan		West Germany		U.K.		US		
	1965-73	1981-90	1965-73	1981-90	1965-73	1981-90	1965-73	1981-90	1992
Private Consumption	52	59	55	56	62	62	62	66	69
Government Consumption	9	10	17	20	20	21	20	18	16
Total Consumption	61	68	71	76	82	83	82	84	85
Gross Domestic Saving	39	32	29	24	18	17	18	16	15
Gross Domestic Investment	37	30	26	20	18	18	18	18	15

Source: Details in Table 22.19

Table 22.25
Macroeconomic parameters
1. Japan

As Percentage of GDP	1950-60	1960-70	1965-73	1970-81	1981-90	1990	1990
Private Consumption	62.0	55.5	52.4	56.6	58.6	57.1	–
General Government Consumption	8.7	7.7	8.7	9.5	9.6	9.0	–
Gross Domestic Investment	28.9	36.0	37.4	33.3	29.7	33.2	–
Total Consumption	70.7	63.2	61.1	66.1	68.2	66.1	–
Gross Domestic Saving	29.3	36.8	38.9	33.9	31.8	33.9	–
Average Annual Growth Rate							
(at constant Prices)							
GNP at market Prices	6.3	10.4	10.8	2.6	–	–	–
GDP " " "	6.4	10.4	0.8	2.6	4.2	5.6	5.6
Private Consumption	6.8	9.0	8.7	2.8	7.9*	4.5*	0.2+
General Government Consumption	1.6	6.2	7.0	3.5	5.3*	4.4*	-3.3+
Gross Domestic Investment	10.4	14.6	13.8	1.3	-7.1*	10.6*	18.5+
Marginal Capital-Output Ratio	4.52	3.46	3.46	12.81	7.07	–	–

Table 22.25 (continued)
2. West Germany

As Percentage of GDP	1950-60	1960-70	1965-73	1970-81	1981-90	1986-91	1991	1991
Private Consumption	58.5	56.0	54.8	54.9	56.2	55.0	54.4	–
General Government	13.6	15.3	16.6	19.5	19.8	19.1	17.9	–
Consumption Total Consumption	72.1	71.3	71.4	74.4	76.0	74.1	72.3	–
Gross Domestic Saving	27.9	28.7	28.6	25.6	23.9	25.9	27.7	–
Gross Domestic Investment	26.1	26.4	26.4	23.6	20.1	20.4	21.3	–
Average Annual Growth Rate								
(at constant Prices)								
GNP at market prices	8.7	4.4	4.7	2.6	–	–	–	–
GDP " "	8.7	4.4	4.6	2.6	2.2	3.3	3.6	3.6
Private Consumption	8.6	4.6	4.7	2.8	4.6*	–	3.2*	-0.9+
General Government Consumption	5.9	4.1	4.0	3.5	3.8*	–	-2.9*	-7.7+
Gross domestic Investment	10.5	4.1	4.8	1.3	-13.0*	–	4.6*	12.6+
Marginal Capital-Output Ratio	3.00	6.00	5.74	9.08	9.14	6.18	–	–

Table 22.25 (continued)

3. United Kingdom

As Percentage of GDP	1950-60	1960-70	1965-73	1970-81	1981-90	1990	1990
Private Consumption	67.1	63.9	61.9	60.2	62.0	63.4	–
General Government Consumption	17.4	17.2	20.4	20.6	20.8	19.9	–
Total Consumption	84.5	81.1	82.3	80.8	82.8	83.3	–
Gross Domestic Saving	15.5	18.9	17.7	19.2	17.2	16.7	–
Gross Domestic Investment	16.8	19.1	18.0	18.5	17.7	19.0	–
Average Annual Growth Rate							
(at consant prices)							
GNP at market prices	2.3	2.9	2.7	1.7	–	–	–
GDP " " "	2.4	2.9	2.5	1.7	2.6	0.8	0.8
Private Consumption	3.0	2.4	2.8	1.6	5.7*	0.2*	4.9+
General Government Consumption	-0.2	2.2	1.9	2.3	3.6*	3.4*	3.6+
Gross Domestic Investment	6.4	5.1	1.9	0.0	-1.8*	-7.0*	11.3+
Marginal Capital-Output Ratio	7.00	6.59	7.60	10.88	6.81	–	–

Table 22.25 (continued)

4. United States

As Percentage of GDP	1950-60	1960-70	1965-73	1970-81	1981-90	1986-92	1986	1992	1992
Private Consumption	64.2	62.3	61.9	63.6	66.1	67.7	66.8	68.9	–
General GovernmentConsumption	15.3	18.3	20.4	18.1	18.2	16.6	16.9	16.2	–
Total Consumption	79.5	80.6	82.3	81.7	84.3	84.2	83.7	85.1	–
Gross Domestic Saving	20.5	19.4	17.7	18.3	15.7	15.8	16.3	14.9	–
Gross Domestic Investment	19.9	18.9	18.0	19.0	17.8	17.2	19.2	15.4	–
Average Annual Growth Rate									
(at consant prices)									
GNP at Market Prices	3.2	4.3	3.6	3.0	–	–	–	–	–
GDP " " "	3.2	4.3	3.5	2.9	2.8	2.1	3.2	2.1	2.1
Private Consumption	3.5	4.4	4.0	3.2	6.8*	4.7+	4.4*	6.6+	10.9**
General Government Consumption	5.3	4.2	2.5	2.0	3.4*	-7.9+	-5.2*	-10.1+	-6.6**
Gross Domestic Investment	2.0	5.0	3.5	1.9	-3.7*	-6.1+	6.0*	-15.9+	-23.4**
Marginal Capital-Output Ratio	6.22	4.39	5.14	6.55	6.40	8.35	–	–	–

Table 22.25 (continued)

Remarks:

Gross domestic saving defined as GDP minus total consumption.

Gross national saving defined as gross domestic saving plus netfactorincome and current transfers from abroad.

Marginal capital-output ratioestimated by $\frac{I/Y}{\Delta Y/Y}$ where I= pross domesticinvestmen and Y=GDP.

*Implied annual rate of increase calculated as , e.g.

$$\frac{\Delta I}{I_{t-1}} = \frac{(1+r)\,(I/Y)_t - (I/Y)_{t-1}}{(I/Y)_{t-1}}$$

wherer is the GDP growth rate.

** Base period is 1981.

+Base period is year 1985.

Sources: World Tables, IBRD;
International Financial Statistic, IMF, March 1993

Table 22.27
Turkey: macroeconomic data (percentage)

As Percentage of GDP	1950-60	1960-73	1965-73	1965-80	1962-68	1960-70	1970-81	1980-90	1980-92
Private Consumption	76.0	70.6	69.7	–	72.1	72.9	69.3	70.2	70.2
General Government Consumption	10.8	12.7	13.0	–	12.0	12.1	12.2	10.4	10.3
Gross Domestic Investment	14.9	19.5	20.1	20.1	18.3	17.1	24.7	22.6	22.7
Gross Domestic Saving	13.2	16.7	17.3	–	–	15.0	18.5	19.4	19.5
Consumer Price Index annual average increase	9.2	6.2	8.6	23.9	3.5	3.7	32.9	53.1	55.6
Average Annual Growth Rate at Constant Prices									
GNP at Market Prices	6.2	6.6	7.1	–	6.4	6.2	5.4	4.8	4.5
GDP at Market Prices	6.3	6.3	6.6	6.2	6.5	6.0	5.3	4.8	4.5
Private Consumption	6.3	5.0	5.7	–	–	5.1	3.8	–	–
General Government Consumption	5.8	9.0	9.9	–	–	6.7	6.4	–	–
Gross Domestic Investment	6.0	9.5	8.0	–	–	8.8	7.7	–	–
Gross Domestic Saving	–	34.5*	–	–	–	21.4*	29.7*	–	–
Marginal Capital-Output Ratio	2.4	3.1	3.0	3.2	2.8	2.9	4.8	4.7	5.0

Source: IBRD Tables, 1976, p.235; 1984, p.185
Main Economic Indicators, State Planning Organization, Ankara
National income of Turkey: 1938, 1948-70, State Institute of Statistics (SIS), 1971
Statistical indicators: 1923-1991, SIS, 1993

Table 22.28
Turkey: macroeconomic data (percentage)

As Percentage of GDP	1950	1955	1960	1961	1962	1963	1964	1965	1966	1967	1968	1969
Private Consumption	78.4	74.1	76.8	76.3	75.5	74.8	72.9	71.6	70.8	69.7	69.5	69.5
General Government	12.4	11.9	10.2	11.2	11.9	11.5	12.0	12.5	12.0	12.3	12.1	12.3
Consumption Gross	10.3	16.6	15.3	15.3	16.4	18.0	16.9	17.4	19.7	19.4	20.6	20.6
Domestic Investment												
Gross Domestic	9.2	14.0	13.0	12.5	12.6	13.7	15.1	15.9	17.2	18.0	18.4	18.2
Saving												
Gross National Saving	–	–	12.3	11.8	12.1	13.5	14.8	16.3	17.9	18.3	18.7	18.9
Gross Public Saving	–	–	–	–	4.2	5.8	4.8	5.1	5.5	7.6	7.2	7.9
Gross Private Saving	–	–	–	–	7.9	7.8	10.1	11.2	12.4	10.7	11.5	11.0
Annual Growth Rate												
GDP	–	–	3.4	1.2	5.6	9.1	5.5	2.8	11.2	4.7	6.8	5.2
Retail Price Index	–	–	2.3	-0.7	2.6	3.1	1.7	5.9	4.4	6.7	0.4	6.5
GNP	–	–	–	1.2	5.6	9.4	5.3	3.4	9.7	4.4	6.8	5.3

Table 22.28
(continued)

As Percentages of GDP	1970	1971	1972	1973	1974	1975	1976	1977	1978	1979	1980	1981
Private Consumption	68.1	70.4	70.8	68.2	74.6	72.5	71.6	69.9	65.9	64.6	69.2	70.4
General Government Consumption	12.8	14.1	13.6	13.2	11.5	12.3	12.7	13.4	13.5	13.6	12.6	10.9
Gross Domestic Investment	22.2	20.3	20.4	19.5	20.6	23.7	22.9	24.9	24.6	25.9	26.4	24.5
Gross Domestic Saving	19.1	15.5	15.6	18.6	13.9	15.2	17.4	17.8	21.8	23.8	20.7	20.9
Gross National Saving	20.7	18.6	19.1	23.5	–	–	–	–	–	–	–	–
-Public Saving	8.3	7.5	–	–	–	–	–	–	–	–	–	–
-Private Saving	12.5	11.1	–	–	–	–	–	–	–	–	–	–
Annual Growth Rate												
GDP	4.9	9.1	6.6	6.4	8.5	8.9	8.7	4.3	3.8	-0.9	-0.7	4.4
Retail Price Index	8.1	16.3	12.9	16.6	18.7	20.1	15.3	28.4	49.5	56.5	116.6	35.9
GNP	5.7	11.2	6.5	8.5	7.4	8.0	7.9	3.9	2.9	-0.4	-1.1	4.2

Table 22.28
(continued)

As Percentages of GDP	1981	1982	1983	1984	1985	1986	1987	1988	1989	1990	1991*	1992*
Private Consumption	70.4	71.8	74.6	75.6	73.6	69.6	67.5	65.2	66.7	67.6	68.5	71.9
General Government Consumption	10.9	10.9	10.2	9.1	8.6	8.9	9.1	8.7	11.6	14.1	9.5	9.2
Gross Domestic Investment	22.0	20.6	19.6	19.5	21.0	24.4	25.4	24.0	22.7	23.1	23.7	22.6
Gross Domestic Saving	16.7	17.3	15.3	15.3	17.8	21.5	23.4	26.1	21.7	18.3	22.0	18.9
Annual Growth Rate												
GDP	4.2	4.9	3.8	5.9	5.1	8.3	7.5	3.7	1.3	9.1	–	–
Retail Price Index	35.9	27.1	30.9	48.5	50.4	37.0	39.6	71.7	63.7	62.2	68.7	70.1
GNP	3.7	4.5	3.8	5.9	5.5	7.8	7.7	3.4	2.1	9.6	0.3	5.4

(*) Refers to GNP
Source: World Tables, IBRD; Statistical Indicators: 1923-1991
SIS National income of Turkey: 1938, 1948-1970, SIS, 1971
Main Economic Indicators, SPO, Ankara

Table 22.29

Turkey: macroeconomic data used in regressions

	Percentage			As Percentage of GNP					
	CPI Annual increase (P)	Real GNP Growth Rate (Y)	Whole-Sale Price Increase (PW)	Private Consumption (C)	General Government Consumption	Gross Domestic Saving (S)	Gross Fixed Invesment (FI)	Invesment in Machinery and Equipment	Total Consumption
1939	2.5	6.9	–	–	–	–	–	–	–
1940	9.4	-4.9	–	–	–	–	–	–	–
1941	16.6	-10.3	–	–	–	–	–	–	–
1942	68.7	5.6	–	–	–	–	–	–	–
1943	37.2	-9.8	–	–	–	–	–	–	–
1944	8.1	-5.1	–	–	–	–	–	–	–
1945	5.3	-15.3	–	–	–	–	–	–	–
1946	4.3	31.9	–	–	–	–	–	–	–
1947	-6.6	4.2	–	–	–	–	–	–	–
1948	5.4	–	3.1	–	–	–	–	–	–
1949	6.4	-5.0	12.6	–	–	–	–	–	–
1950	-3.0	9.4	-10.2	–	–	–	–	–	–
1951	2.5	12.8	6.9	–	–	–	–	–	–
1952	4.5	11.9	0.8	74.5	16.6	8.9	12.6	5.1	91.0
1953	2.9	11.2	2.2	76.0	14.5	9.5	12.1	3.9	90.5
1954	7.7	-3.0	10.5	73.9	14.5	11.6	14.5	3.9	88.4
1955	18.6	7.9	7.6	73.7	14.6	11.7	14.4	3.9	88.3
1956	2.7	3.2	16.8	74.0	13.3	12.7	13.8	3.7	87.3
1957	13.5	7.8	18.5	76.0	12.0	11.9	12.8	2.8	88.1
1958	20.5	4.5	15.1	76.5	11.6	11.9	12.7	3.5	88.1
1959	28.5	4.1	19.5	76.5	12.5	11.0	14.0	4.8	89.0
1960	2.3	3.4	5.2	75.3	12.8	12.0	14.7	5.3	88.0
1961	-0.7	2.0	3.0	74.3	14.1	11.6	14.6	5.4	88.4
1950-60 Average	9.2	6.7	–	–	–	–	–	–	–

Table 22.29 (continued)

(Percentages)

					As Percentage of GNP				
	CPI Annual Increase (P)	Real GNP Growth Rate (Y)	Real GDP Growth Rate	Goverment Budget Wholesale Price Index Increase (PW)	Private Consumption	General Government Consumption	Gross Domestic Saving	Gross Fixed Domestic Investment	Investment in Machinery and Equipment
1962	2.6	6.2	5.6	5.6	74.3	14.8	10.4	14.4	5.7
1963	3.1	9.7	9.1	4.3	75.5	14.3	10.1	14.6	5.1
1964	1.7	4.1	5.5	1.2	73.5	14.3	12.2	15.8	4.3
1965	5.9	3.1	2.8	8.1	72.3	14.1	13.6	14.7	4.1
1966	4.4	12.0	11.2	4.8	72.6	13.0	14.4	16.2	5.1
1967	6.7	4.2	4.7	7.6	72.7	11.9	15.5	16.6	5.1
1968	0.4	6.7	6.8	3.2	72.3	11.7	16.0	17.8	5.6
1969	6.5	5.4	5.2	7.2	71.8	11.6	16.6	18.2	5.2

Table 22.29 (continued)
(Percentages)

				As Percentage of GNP						
				Goverment Budget						
	CPI Annual Increase	Real GDP Growth Rate	Real GNP Growth Rate	Overall Deficit	Current Account Surplus	Gross Domestic Saving	Gross Domestic Investment	Private Consumption	General Government Consumption	Total Consumption
1970	8.1	4.9	5,6	2.7	4.1	18.7	19.8	70.0	12.9	82.9
1971	16.3	9.1	10.7	3.2	3.7	16.9	17.8	72.7	13.4	86.1
1972	12.9	6.6	7.6	2.2	5.2	19.0	19.0	71.3	13.4	84.7
1973	16.6	6.4	5.5	1.7	3.7	21.2	18.9	70.7	13.0	83.7
1974	18.7	8.5	7.4	1.7	3.4	18.2	20.6	74.6	11.5	86.1
1975	20.1	8.9	8.0	1.3	5.2	18.4	23.7	72.5	12.3	84.8
1976	15.3	8.7	7.9	2.0	5.0	17.4	22.9	71.6	12.7	84.3
1977	28.4	4.3	3.9	6.1	2.7	17.8	24.9	69.9	13.4	83.3
1978	49.5	3.3	2.9	4.3	3.4	21.8	24.6	65.9	13.5	79.4
1979	56.5	-0.9	-0.4	6.4	2.9	23.8	25.9	64.6	13.6	78.2
1980	116.6	-0.7	-1.1	3.7	3.1	20.7	26.4	69.2	12.6	81.8
1981	35.9	4.4	4.2	1.8	5.8	20.9	24.5	70.4	10.9	81.3
1970-81 Average	–	5.0	5.2	–	–	–	22.4	70.3	–	–

Table 22.29 (continued)

(Percentages)

			Government Budget		As Percentage of GNP			
	CPI Annual Increase	Real GDP Growth Rate	Overall Deficit	Current Account Surplus	Private Consump-tion	General Govern. Consumption	Gross Domestic Investment	Gross National Saving
1981	35.9	4.2	1.8	5.8	70.4	10.9	24.5	21.1
1982	27.1	4.9	–	–	71.8	10.9	20.6	18.6
1983	30.9	3.8	4.2	3.0	74.6	10.2	19.6	15.4
1984	48.5	5.9	10.0	-4.3	75.6	9.1	19.5	16.2
1985	50.4	5.1	7.4	-2.9	73.6	8.6	21.0	18.6
1986	37.0	8.3	3.6	0.5	69.6	8.9	24.4	21.6
1987	39.6	7.5	4.5	-0.5	67.5	9.1	25.4	23.8
1988	71.7	3.7	4.0	-0.8	65.2	8.7	24.0	25.8
1989	63.7	1.3	4.6	-1.6	66.7	11.6	22.7	23.5
1990	62.2	9.1	4.2	-1.2	67.6	14.1	23.1	19.6
1991*	68.7	0.3	–	–	68.5	9.5	23.7	–
1992*	70.1	5.4	–	–	71.9	9.2	22.6	–
Average: 1980-90	–	–	–	–	70.2	10.4	–	–
Average: 1980-92	–	–	–	–	70.2	10.3	–	–

Table 22.30 Turkish macro data

	As Percentage of GDP				As Percent		As Percentage of GNP			
									Government Budget	
	Gross Fixed Invest- (FI)	Gross Domestic Investment (I)	Gross Domestic Saving (S)	Gross National Saving (SN)	Real GDP Growth Rate (Y)	CPI Increase (P)	Private Consumption (C)	Total Consump-tion	Overall Deficit (D)	Current Account Surplus (DS)
1950	–	10.3	10.3	–	9.4	-3.0	–	90.8	–	–
1955	14.4	16.6	12.6	–	7.9	18.6	–	86.0	–	–
1960	14.7	15.3	13.0	12.3	3.4	2.3	–	87.0	–	–
1961	14.6	15.3	12.5	11.8	1.2	-0.7	–	87.5	–	–
1962	14.4	16.4	12.6	12.1	5.6	2.6	–	87.4	–	–
1963	14.6	18.0	13.7	13.5	9.1	3.1	–	86.3	–	–
1964	15.8	16.9	15.1	14.8	5.5	1.7	–	84.5	–	–
1965	14.7	17.4	15.9	16.3	2.8	5.9	–	84.1	–	–
1966	16.2	19.7	17.2	17.9	11.2	4.4	–	82.8	–	–
1967	16.6	19.4	18.0	18.3	4.7	6.7	–	82.0	–	–
1968	17.8	20.6	18.4	18.7	6.8	0.4	–	81.6	–	–
1969	18.2	20.6	18.2	18.9	5.2	6.5	–	81.8	–	–
1970	18.5	22.2	19.1	20.7	4.9	8.1	70.0	80.9	2.7	4.1
1971	17.1	20.3	15.5	18.6	9.1	16.3	72.7	84.5	3.2	3.7
1972	20.3	20.4	15.6	19.1	6.6	12.9	71.3	84.4	2.2	5.2
1973	20.0	19.5	18.6	23.5	6.4	16.6	70.7	81.4	1.7	3.7
1974	18.5	20.6	13.9	18.4	8.5	18.7	74.6	86.1	1.7	3.4
1975	20.8	23.7	15.2	18.8	8.9	20.1	72.5	84.8	1.3	5.2
1976	23.2	22.9	17.4	17.7	7.9	15.3	71.6	84.3	2.0	5.0
1977	24.4	24.9	17.8	18.0	3.9	28.4	69.9	83.3	6.1	2.7
1978	22.0	24.6	21.8	22.1	2.9	49.5	65.9	79.4	4.3	3.4
1979	20.8	25.9	23.8	23.9	-0.4	56.5	64.6	78.2	6.4	2.9
1980	20.0	26.4	20.7	20.9	-1.1	116.6	69.2	81.8	3.7	3.1
1981	19.3	24.5	20.9	21.1	4.2	35.9	70.4	81.3	1.8	5.8
1970-81 Average	--	--	–	–	5.0	32.9	–	–	3.1	4.0
1960-70 Average	–	–	–	–	5.5	3.7	–	–	--	--
1962-68 Average	–	–	–	–	6.5	3.5	–	–	--	--

Table 22.30 (continued)

	As Percentage of GDP				As Percent		As Percentage of GNP			
									Government Budget	
	Gross Fixed Investment (FI)	Gross Domestic Investment (I)	Gross National Saving (SN)	Gross Domestic Saving (S)	Real GDP (%) Growth Rate (Y)	CPI Increase (%) (P)	Private Consumption (C)	Total Consumption	Overall-Deficit (D)	Current Account Surplus (DS)
1981+	19.3	22.0	18.6	16.7	4.2	35.9	70.4	81.3	1.8	5.8
1982	19.1	20.6	18.6	17.3	4.9	27.1	71.8	82.7	–	–
1983	18.5	19.6	15.4	15.3	3.8	30.9	74.6	84.8	4.2	3.0
1984	18.1	19.5	16.2	15.3	5.9	48.5	75.6	84.7	10.0	-4.3
1985	20.2	21.0	18.6	17.8	5.1	50.4	73.6	82.2	7.4	-2.9
1986	24.0	24.4	21.6	21.5	8.3	37.0	69.6	78.5	3.2	0.6
1987	25.5	25.4	23.8	23.4	7.5	39.6	67.5	76.6	4.0	-0.2
1988	24.0	24.0	25.8	26.1	3.7	71.7	65.2	73.9	3.8	-0.4
1989	22.8	22.7	23.5	21.7	1.3	63.7	66.7	78.3	4.5	-1.1
1990	21.5	23.1	19.6	18.3	9.1	62.2	67.6	81.7	4.2	-1.4
1991*	24.1	23.7	–	–	0.3	68.7	68.5	78.0	–	–
1992*	23.1	22.6	–	–	5.4	70.1	71.9	81.1	–	–
1980-90 Average	21.2	22.6	20.3	19.4	4.8	53.1	–	80.6	4.7	0.2
1980-92 Average	21.6	22.7	–	–	4.5	55.6	–	80.4	–	–

(*) GNP or percentage of GNP

(+) New series

Source: World Tables, IBRD; *Statistical Indicators:* 1923-1991, SIS, Ankara 1993 Main Economic Indicators, State Planning Organization, Ankara

Table 22.31
Turkey: macroeconomic data
(as percent, unless specified otherwise)

	Increase in GNP Deflator (P)	GNP Deflator (1968=100)	GNP Growth Rate (at Constant Prices)	GNP Per Capita Growth Rate (Constant Prices)	Ankara Consumer Price Index (Annual Change)
1923	--	8	--	--	–
1924	12.5	9	14.8	--	–
1925	11.1	10	12.9	--	–
1926	-10.0	9	18.2	--	–
1927	11.1	10	-12.8	--	–
1928	0.0	10	11.0	8.7	–
1929	0.0	10	21.6	19.2	–
1930	-20.0	8	2.2	0.0	–
1931	-25.0	6	8.7	6.7	–
1932	0.0	6	-10.7	-12.8	–
1933	-16.7	5	15.8	13.5	–
1934	0	5	6.0	3.8	–
1935	0	5	-3.0	-5.1	–
1936	20.0	6	23.2	21.1	–
1937	0.0	6	1.5	-0.2	–
1938	0.0	6	9.5	7.7	–
1939	0.0	6	6.9	4.2	2.5
1940	16.7	7	-4.9	-6.8	9.4
1941	42.9	10	-10.3	-11.6	16.6
1942	90.0	19	5.6	4.6	68.7
1943	68.4	32	-9.8	-10.8	37.2
1944	-25.0	24	-5.1	-5.9	8.1
1945	0.0	24	-15.3	-16.1	5.3
1946	-8.3	22	31.9	29.2	4.3
1947	9.1	24	4.2	1.9	-6.6

Table 22.31
(continued)

	GNP Deflator (1968=100)	Change in Constant GNP at Market Prices (*)	GNP Growth Rate (at Constant Prices)	GNP Per Capita Growth Rate (Constant Prices)	Ankara Consumer Price Index (Annual Change)
1948	26	--	–	–	5.4
1949	26	--	-5.0	-7.0	6.4
1950	25	--	9.4	6.9	-3.0
1951	27	--	12.8	10.0	2.5
1952	28	--	11.9	8.8	4.5
1953	29	11.1	11.2	8.2	2.9
Annual Average (1946-53)	–	--	10.9	8.3	2.0
1954	30	-9.1	-3.0	-5.6	7.7
1955	34	7.6	7.9	5.0	18.6
1956	38	6.8	3.2	0.7	2.7
1957	47	6.3	7.8	4.4	13.5
1958	53	11.8	4.5	1.6	20.5
1959	64	4.3	4.1	1.1	28.5
1960	66	2.4	3.4	0.5	2.3
Average 1954-60	13.1	4.3	4.0	1.1	13.4

Table 22.31
(continued)

	GNP Deflator (1968=100)	Change in Constant GNP at Market Prices (*)	GNP Growth Rate (at Constant prices)	GNP Per Capita Growth Rate (Real)	Ankara CPI Annual Change
1961	69	0.6	2.0	-0.6	-0.7
1962	75	6.4	6.2	3.6	2.6
1963	79	7.7	9.7	7.0	3.1
1964	81	4.9	4.1	1.5	1.7
1965	85	4.5	3.1	0.6	5.9
1966	90	10.3	12.0	9.2	4.4
1967	96	6.1	4.2	1.6	6.7
1968	100	6.7	–	–	0.4
1969	108	6.3	4.5	1.9	6.5
Average 1961-69	–	5.9	5.7	3.1	3.4
1970	117	5.7	4.8	2.2	8.1
1971	137	--	7.3	4.7	16.3
1972	151	--	9.6	6.9	12.9

Table 22.31
(continued)

	GNP Growth Rate (Real)	GNP Per Capita Growth Rate	Ankara CPI annual increase	İstanbul CPI Increase
1973	5.1	2.5	16.6	15.4
1974	3.7	1.1	18.7	15.9
1975	6.3	3.6	20.1	19.2
1976	9.3	7.1	15.3	17.3
Average 1970-76	6.6	4.0	15.4	--
1977	3.0	0.9	28.4	27.1
1978	1.4	-0.7	49.5	45.3
1979	-0.7	-2.7	56.5	58.7
1980	-2.3	-4.3	116.6	110.2
Average 1970-80	4.3	1.9	32.6	--
1981	5.3	2.8	35.9	36.6
1982	3.7	1.2	27.1	30.9
1983	4.6	2.0	30.9	29.1
1984	7.8	5.1	48.5	--
1985	4.5	1.9	50.4	48.4
1986	7.5	5.2	37.0	34.8
1987	9.3	7.0	39.6	41.0
1988	1.5	-0.6	71.7	72.9
1989	0.9	-1.3	63.7	59.4
1990	9.7	7.3	62.2	59.3
1991	0.3	-1.8	68.7	67.1
Average 1981-91	5.0	2.6	48. 7	--

(*) *Source: National Income,* 1938, 1948-1970, SIS, 1971
Source: SIS *Statistical Indicators,* 1923-1991, 1993

Table 22.32
Turkey: expenditure on GNP: 1952-1969
(as percentage of GNP)

Year	Private Consumption	General Goverment Consumption	Total Consumption	Domestic Saving	Gross Domestic Fixed Capital Formation		Real GNP Growth (%)	Ankara CPI Increase (%)
					Total	of which Machinery and Equipment		
1952	74.5	16.6	91.1	8.9	12.6	5.1	11.9	4.5
1953	76.0	14.5	90.5	9.5	12.1	3.9	11.1	2.9
1954	73.9	14.5	88.4	11.6	14.5	3.9	-9.1	7.7
1955	73.7	14.6	88.3	11.7	14.4	3.9	7.6	18.6
1956	74.0	13.3	87.3	12.7	13.8	3.7	6.8	2.7
1957	76.0	12.0	88.1	11.9	12.8	2.8	6.3	13.5
1958	76.5	11.6	88.1	11.9	12.7	3.5	11.8	20.5
1959	76.5	12.5	89.0	11.0	14.0	4.8	4.3	28.5
Average 1952-59	75.1	13.7	88.85	–	13.4	3.95	–	–
1960	75.3	12.8	88.0	12.0	14.7	5.3	2.4	2.3
1961	74.3	14.1	88.4	11.6	14.6	5.4	0.6	-0.7
1962	74.8	14.8	89.6	10.4	14.4	5.7	6.4	2.6
1963	75.5	14.3	89.9	10.1	14.6	5.1	7.7	3.1
1964	73.5	14.3	87.8	12.2	15.8	4.3	4.9	1.7
1965	72.3	14.1	86.4	13.6	14.7	4.1	4.5	5.9
1966	72.6	13.0	85.6	14.4	16.2	5.1	10.3	4.4
1967	72.7	11.9	84.5	15.5	16.6	5.1	6.1	6.7
1968	72.3	11.7	84.0	16.0	17.8	5.6	6.7	0.4
1969	71.8	11.6	83.4	16.6	18.2	5.2	6.3	6.5
Average 1960-69	73.5	13.3	86.8	–	15.8	5.1	–	–

Source: National Income of Turkey: 1938, 1948-1970, SIS, 1971

References

Alexeev, Michael (1992),"Saving Behavior and Soviet Reform", *Contemporary Policy Issues*, July 1992: pp. 39-48.

Arrow, Kenneth J, (1981), "Real and Nominal Magnitudes in Economics", in *Bell* (1981), pp. 139-150.

Bardhan, Pranab and John E.Roemer (1992), "Market Socialism: A Case for Rejuvenation", *The Journal of Economic Perspectives*, Summer 1992: pp. 101-116.

Bell, Daniel (1981), "Models and Reality in Economic Discourse", in Bell&Kristol (editors), *The Crisis in Economic Theory,* New York, pp. 46-80.

Bell, Daniel&Irwing Kristol (1981), editors, *The Crisis in Economic Theory,* Basic Books, Inc., New York.

Berend, Ivan T. (1990), *The Hungarian Economic Reforms 1953-1988,* Cambridge: Cambridge Univ. Press, 1990.

Bienkowski, Wojciech, (1992), "The Bermuda Triangle: Why Self- Governed Firms Work for Their Own Destruction", *Journal of Comparative Economics* 16, 1992, pp. 750-762.

Blanchard, O., R.Dornbusch, P.Krugman, R.Layard and L.Summers (1991), *Reform in Eastern Europe*, MIT Press, Cambridge, MA.

Blanchard, Olivier (1993), "Consumption and the Recession of 1990-1991", *American Economic Review (AER), Papers & Proceedings, May 1993*, pp. 270-274.

Bolton, P. and Roland, G. (1992), "Privatization Policies in Central and Eastern Europe", *Economic Policy*, October 1992: pp. 275-309.

Bonin, John, P., (1992), "Privatization and Efficient Contracts: The Workers' Stake in the Transition", *Journal of Comparative Economics*, 16, 1992. pp. 716-732.

Bowles, Paul and Gordon White, (1992), "The Dilemmas of Market Socialism: Capital Market Reform in China- Part I: Bonds", *The Journal of Development Studies,* April 1992; 363- 385.

Brainard, William C. and George L.Perry, (1992), "Editors' Summary", *Brookings Papers on Economic Activity*: 1, 1992, pp. ix-xxxii.

Braeutgam, Ronald and John Panzar, (1993), "Effects of the Change from Rate-of-Return to Price-Cap Regulation", *AER, Papers & Proceedings, May 1993*, pp. 191-198.

Bresnahan, Timothy and Valerie Ramey, (1993) "Segment Shifts and Capacity Utilization in the US Automobile Industry", *American Economic Review, Papers&Proceedings, May 1993*, pp. 213-218.

Brus, W. and K.Laski, (1989), *From Marx to the Market: Socialism in Search of an Economic System*, Oxford Univ. Press, Oxford.

Brus, W., and Laski, (1969), "The Law of Value and the Problem of Allocation in Socialism", in *On Political Economy and Econometrics: Essays in Honour of Oskar Lange*, Pergamon Press, Warzsawa, 1969.

Byrd, William A. (1991), *The Market Mechanism and Economic Reforms in China*, Armonk, N.Y., Sharpe.

Calvo, Guillermo A. and Fabrizio Coricelli (1992), "Stagflationary Effects of Stabilization Programs in Reforming Socialist Countries: Enterprise-Side and Household-Side Factors", *The World Bank Economic Review* Jan. 1992; 71-90.

Carlin, W. and C.Mayer (1992), "Restructuring Enterprises in Eastern Europe", *Economic Policy*; October 1992: 311-352.

Cichocki, K., (1979) "A Mechanism for Allocation of Resources at the National level" in Janssen et al. (1979).

Çiller, Tansu and Hüsnü Kızılyallı (1987) *Dış Borçlar: Tahmin ve Analiz (Turkish External Indebtedness: Analysis and Projections)*, TUSIAD, Istanbul.

Charemza, Wojeiech, (1987), "Maximum Likelihood Methods of Estimation for Disequilibrium Models in a Centrally Planned Economy", *Economics of Planning*, Vol. 21, Nos 2-3, 1987.

Claus, B. and H.H. Taake (1992), "GDR Development Policies in Retrospect," *Economics: Recent German Studies*, Vol. 46, Tubingen, 1992, pp. 89-101.

Commander, Simon (1992), "Inflation and the Transition to a Market Economy: An Overview", *The World Bank Economic Review*, Jan. 1992; 3-12.

Commander, Simon and Fabrizio Corricelli (1992), "Price-Wage Dynamics and Inflation in Socialist Economies: Empirical Models for Hungary and Poland", *The World Bank Economic Review*, Jan. 1992; 33-53.

Cottarelli, Carlo and Mario I. Blejer, (1992), "Forced Saving and Repressed Inflation in the Soviet Union, 1986-90", *IMF Staff Papers*, June 1992, pp. 256-286.

Dembinski, Pawel H., (1991), (translated by Kevin Cook), *The Logic of the Planned Economy: the Seeds of the Collapse*, New York: Oxford Univ. Press.

Denison, E.F. and W.K.Chung, (1976), *How Japan's Economy Grew So Fast: The Sources of Postwar Expansion,* Brookings Institutions, Washington, DC.

Xu, Dianqing., Shenliand Deng and Gene Gruver (1992), "The Application of the Leontief Input-Output Matrix in the Transition Process", *Economic System Research*, Vol.4, No.1, 1992.

Dinopoulos, Elias and Timothy D.Lane (1992), "Market Liberalization Policies in a Reforming Socialist Economy", *IMF Staff Papers*, Sept. 1992, pp. 465-494.

Dornbusch, R. and Y.C. Park, (1987), "Korean Growth Policy", *Brookings Paper on Economic Activity.*

Dornbusch, Rudiger and Stanley Fischer, (1990), *Macroeconomics*, McGraw-Hill.

Dornbusch, Rudiger and Holger Wolf (1992), "Economic Transition in Eastern Germany", *Brooking Papers on Economic Activity*; 1: 1992, pp. 235-272.

Dornbusch, Rudiger (1992), "Lessons from Experiences with High Inflation", *The World Bank Economic Review*, January 1992.

Feldstein and Horioka, (1980), "Domestic Savings and International Capital Flows", *Economic Journal*, 1980, Vol: 90. pp. 314-29.

Fischer, Stanley (1992), "Stabilization and Economic Reform in Russia", *Brooking Papers on Economic Activity*, 1: 1992, pp. 77-126; and "Editors' Summary", pp. xvi-xxi.

Frisch, Helmut (1986), *Theories of Inflation*, Cambridge Univ. Press, 1986.

Froyen, Richard T., (1986), *Macroeconomics: Theories and Policies*, 2nd edition, MacMillan, NewYork.

Geron, Leonard, (1990), *Soviet Foreign Economic Policy under Perestroika*, London.

Le Grand, Julian and Saul Estrin (1989), (editors), *Market Socialism*, Oxford: Clarendon.

Gomulka, S. and Polonsky, A. (1990), (editors), *Polish Paradoxes*, London: Routledge.

Gomulka, Stanislav (1992), "Polish Economic Reform, 1990-91: Principles and Outcomes", *Cambridge Journal of Economics*, Sept. 1992: pp. 355-72.

Guidotti, Pablo E. and Carlos A. Rodriguez (1992), "Dollarization in Latin America: Gresham's Law in Reverse?", *IMF Staff Papers*, September 1992, pp. 518-544.

Hahn, Frank (1981), "General Equilibrium Theory", in Bell, Daniel and Irving Kristol (editors), *The Crisis in Economic Theory*, Basic Books, Inc., New York, 1981, pp. 123-138.

Hall, Bronwyn (1993), "The Stock Market's Valuation of R & D Investment during the 1980s", *AER, Papers and Proceedings,* May 1993, pp. 259-264.
Hall, Robert E., (1993), "Macro Theory and the Recession of 1990-1991", *American Economic Review, Papers and Proceedings*, May 1993; pp. 275-279.
Hansen, Bent, (1958), *The Economic Theory of Fiscal Policy*, Harvard University Press, Cambridge, Mass.
Hare, Paul (1987), "Supply Multipliers in a Centrally Planned Economy with a Private Sector", *Economics of Planning*, Vol. 21, Nos. 2-3, 1987, pp. 53-61.
Hardy, Daniel C. (1992), "Soft Budget Constraints, Firm Commitments, and the Social Safety Net", *IMF Staff Papers*, June 1992, pp. 310-329.
Hausman, Jerry, Timothy Tardiff and Alexander Belifante, (1993), "The Effects of the Breakup of AT&T on Telephone Penetration in the United States", *AER, Papers and Proceedings, May 1993*, pp. 178-184.
Hill, Malcolm R., (1991), *Soviet Advanced Manufacturing Technology and Western Export Controls*, Aldershot.
Hillman, Arye L. (1992), "Progress with Privatization", *Journal of Comparative Economics*, 16, 1992, pp. 733-744.
Horn, G.A., W. Scheremet and R. Zwiener, (1992), "Domestic and International Macroeconomic Effects of German Economic and Monetary Union", *Journal of Forecasting*, Aug. 1992, pp. 459-90.
Zhou, Huizhong, (1992), "An Explanation of Coexistence of Taut Planning and Hidden Reserves in Centrally Planned Economies", *Journal of Comparative Economics*, Sept. 1992, pp. 456-478.
IGEL, (1992), The Investigate Group on Enterprise Loses, "A Comprehensive Report on Investigation into Losses among Industrial Enterprises", *Chinese Economic Studies*, Fall, 1992, pp. 6-46.
Janssen, J.M.L, L.F. Pau and A.Straszak, (1979), *Models and Decision Making in National Economies*, North Holland, 1979.
Jones, Antony and William Moskoff (1991), *Ko-ops: the Rebirth of Enterpreneurship in Soviet Union*, Bloomington, Indiana Univ. Press.
Juselius, Katarina, (1992), "Domestic and Foreign Effects on Prices in an Open Economy: The Case of Denmark", *Journal of Policy Modeling*, 14(4), 1992, pp. 401-428.
Kang, Myoung, Kyu and Keun Lee, (1992), "Industrial Systems and Reform in North Korea: A Comparison with China", *World Development*, 1992, Vol. 20, No.7, pp. 947-958.
Kirzner, Israel M., (1981) "The Austrian Perspective on the Crisis", in *The Crisis in Economic Theory*, by Bell and Cristol (editors) New York: Basic Books, 1981, pp. 111-122.

Kızılyallı, Hüsnü (1989), "An Appraisal of the Turkish Economic Policy and Performance during 1980s and Notes on Economic Development", *Yapı Kredi Economic Review*, Istanbul, April 1989, Vol. III, No.3, pp. 3-37.

Kızılyallı, Hüsnü (1990), *Use of Inter-Regional Input-Output Models in Economic Analysis, Economic Development Planning and Project Appraisal*, Development Bank of Southern Africa, Midrand, Johannesburg (mimeograph), (to be published by the Boğaziçi University, Istanbul).

Kornai, J. (1990), *The Road to a Free Economy*, Norton Press, New York.

Koves, A. and Marer, P (1991), editors, *Foreign Trade Liberalization: Transformations in Socialist and Market Economies*, Boulder, 1991.

Kuyvenhoven, A. (1978), *Planning with the Semi-Input-Output Method*, Leiden, Martinus Nijhoff.

Lange, Oscar (1938), *On the Economic Theory of Socialism*, Minneapolis: University of Minnesota Press.

Lange, Oscar (1970), *Introduction to Economic Cybernetics* Pergamon Press, Polish Scientific Publishers, Warzawa, 1970.

Lange, Oscar (1971), *Optimal Decisions: Principles of Programming*, Pergamon Press, Warsaw.

Leibenstein, Harvey (1981), "Microeconomics and X-Efficiency Theory: If there is no Crisis, there ought to be", in *The Crisis in Economic Theory*, by Bell and Kristol (editors): New York: Basic Books, 1981, pp. 97-110.

Leitzel, Jim (1992),"Western Aid and Economic Reform in the Former Soviet Union", *The World Economy*, May 1992:357-374

Liberman, E.G., (1966), *Profitability of Socialist Enterprises*, in Sharpe (editor), (1966/A).

Lipsey, Richard, Peter Steiner and Douglas Purvis, (1984), *Economics,* Harper International.

Lipsey, R., P.O. Steiner, D.D. Purvis and P.N. Courant, (1990), *Economics*, Harper and Row.

Lipton D. and J.Sachs (1990). "Privatization in Eastern Europe: the Case of Poland", *Brookings Papers on Economic Activity.*

Little, I.M.D. and J.A. Mirrlees (1977), *Project Appraisal and Planning for Developing Countries*, Heinemann, London (reprinted 1977).

Maksimovic, I.M., (1969), "Professor Oskar Lange on Economic Theory of Socialism and Yugoslav Economic Thinking", in Brus and Laski editors, *On Political Economy and Econometrics: Essays in Honour of Oskar Lange*, Pergamon Press, Warzsawa, 1969.

Mansfield, Edwin (1990), *Managerial Economics*, W.W. Norton and Co., New York.

Mayshar, Joram and Gary Solon (1993), "Shift Work and the Business Cycle", *AER, Papers and Proceedings*, May 1993, pp. 224-228.

Megna, Pamela and Mark Klock, (1993), "The Impact of Intangible Capital on Tobin's q in the Semiconductor Industry", *AER, Papers and Proceedings*, May 1993, pp. 265-269.

Merridale, Catherine and Chris Ward (editors), (1991), *Perestroika:The Historical Perspective*, London

Mieszczankowki, M. (1969), "On the Control of Production and Investment in Socialism", in Brus and Laski, *On Political Economy and Econometrics: Essays in Honour of Oskar Lange*, Pergamon Press, Warzsawa, 1969.

Minshan, Zhao, Wen Lie, Liu Heng and Jing Guiliang (1992), "Causal Factors of Losses in Industrial Enterprises Doing Independent Accounting and Suggested Countermeasures", *Chinese Economic Studies*, Fall 1992: 47-55

Nemchinov, V.S., (1964), *The Use of Mathematics in Economics*, The MIT Press, Cambridge, 1964.

Nemchinov, V.S., (1962), "The Plan Target and Material Incentive", *Pravda*, Sept. 21, 1962, in (Sharpe, 1966/A).

Newbery, David, M. and Paul Kattuman (1992), "Market Concentration and Competition in Eastern Europe", *The World Economy*, May 1992: 315-333.

Nuti, D.M. (1989), "Remonetisation and Capital Markets in the Reform of Centrally Planned Economies", *European Economic Review*, Vol. 33, No. 2/3: 427-438.

Osband, Kent (1992/A), "Economic Crisis in a Shortage Economy", *Journal of Political Economy*, 1992, Vol. 100, no.4, pp. 673-690.

Osband, Kent (1992/B), "Index Number Biases During Price Liberalization", *IMF Staff Papers*, June 1992, pp. 287-309.

Özmucur, Süleyman, (1987), "On the Relation between Savings, Distribution, Growth and Inflation", *Journal of Economics and Administrative Studies*, Boğaziçi University, Istanbul, Winter 1987, pp. 67-86.

Özmucur, Süleyman and E.Özötün (1990), "Türkiye Ekonomisindeki Yapısal Değişiklikler", *Boğaziçi Üniversitesi Ekonomi ve İdari Bilimler Dergisi*, Kış 1990, pp. 161-65.

Parkin, Victor (1991), *Chronic Inflation in an Industrialising Economy: The Brazilian Experience*, London: Cambridge Univ. Press.

Pfefferman, Guy and Andrea Madarassy (1993), *Trends in Private Investment in Developing Countries*, IFC, World Bank, as quoted in World Bank News, Jan. 22, 1993.

R.Pohl, D.Vesper and R.Zwiener, (1990), "Macroeconomic Effects of German Monetary, Economic and Social Union", *Economic Bulletin*, 1990 Aug.

Poznanski, Kazimierz Z., (1992), "Privatisation of the Polish Economy: Problems of Transition", *Soviet Studies*, Vol. 44, No. 4, 1992.

Prime, Penelope B. (1992), "Industry's Response to Market Liberalization in China: Evidence from Jiangsu Province", *Economic Development and Cultural Change*, Oct. 1992, Vol. 41, No. 1, pp. 27-50.

Pronk, J.P. and E.J. Schereuel (1969), "Some Reflections on the Effectiveness of Projects Versus Plan Aid", in H.C. Bos (editor), "Towards Balanced International Growth: Essays Presented to J.Tinbergen", North-Holland,1969, pp. 283-307.

Rollo, J.M.C. and J. Stern, (1992), "Growth and Trade Prospects for Central and Eastern Europe", *The World Economy*, pp. 645-668.

Sachs, J. (1991), "Comparing Economic Reform in Latin America and Eastern Europe", *Hicks Lecture*, Oxford University, March 1991.

Şenesen, Ümit (1990), "Türkiye Ekonomisinde Dışalıma Bağımlılık", *Boğaziçi Üniversitesi Ekonomi ve İdari Bilimler Dergisi*, Kış 1990, pp. 115-139.

Senik-Leygonie, Claudia and Gordon Hughes (1992), "The Break-up of the Soviet Union: Industrial Profitability and Trade among the Former Soviet Republics", *Economic Policy*, October 1992: 353-386.

Shapiro, Matthew (1993), "Cyclical Productivity and the Workweek of Capital", *AER, Papers and Proceedings*, May 1993, pp. 229-233.

Sharpe, M.E. (editor), (1966/A), *The Liberman Discussion: A New Phase in Soviet Economic Thought*, White Plains, New York, Iasp, 1966.

Sharpe, Myron E. (editor), (1966/B), "Planning, Profit and Incentives in the USSR", Vol. II., *Reform of Soviet Economic Management*, Iasp, White Plains, New York, 1966: Problem of Planned Price Formation (A Symposium).

Shiller, Robert J., Maxim Boycko and Vladimir Korobov, (1992), "Hunting for Homo-Sovieticus: Situational versus Attitudinal Factors in Economic Behavior", *Brookings Papers on Economic Activity*, 1: 1992, pp. 127-194.

Simon, Gerhard, (1991), *Nationalism and Policy toward the Nationalities in the Soviet Union: From Totalitarian Dictatorship to Post-Stalinist Society*, translated by Forsters, Boulder, Westview Press.

Sloman, John, (1991), *Economics*, Harvester Wheatsheaf/ Prentice Hall, London.

Qun, Son, Lian Zhiming, Wang Donjiang, Liu Wen and Lu Guorong, (1992), "Analysis of Losses Incurred by State-Owned Industrial Enterprises Included in the State Budget and Proposed Countermeasures", *Chinese Economic Studies*, Fall 1992: 56-87.

Stockman, Alan C. (1988), "Real Business Cycle Theory: A Guide, an Evaluation, and New Directions", *Federal Reserve Bank of Cleveland Monthly Review*, 1988, pp. 24-47.

Sutela, Pekka, (1991), *Economic Thought and Economic Reform in the Soviet Union*, Cambridge Univ. Press.

Taylor, William and Lester Taylor (1993), "Postdivestiture Long-Distance Competition in the United States", *AER, Papers and Proceedings*, May 1993, pp. 185-190.

Terrel, Katherine (1992), "Productivity of Western and Domestic Capital in Polish Industry", *Journal of Comparative Economics*, Sept. 1992, pp. 494-
Tinbergen, J. *Development Planning*, McGraw-Hill, New York, 1967.
UNIDO, (1972), "Guidelines for Project Evaluation" by Dasgupta, Marglin and Sen, UN, New York.
Vegh, Carlos A. (1992), "Stopping High Inflation", *IMF Staff Papers*, Sept. 1992, pp. 626-695.
Welfe, Wladyslaw, Jan Gajda and Elzbieta Zoltowska, (1992), "On the Methodology of Constructing Large Econometric Models of an East European Economy (Poland): A Comment", *Economic Modelling*, April 1992: 137-145.
White, Stephen (1991), *Gorbachev and After,* Cambridge Univ Press.
World Bank, (1992/A) (1992), *China: Reform and the Role of the Plan in the 1990s: A World Bank Country Study*, Washington, DC.
World Bank, (1992/B), *Food and Agricultural Policy Reforms in the former USSR*, Washington, DC.
World Bank, (1992/C), *Foreign Direct Investment in the States of the Former USSR*, Washington, DC.
World Bank, (1992/D), *Trade and Payments Arrangements for States of the Former USSR*, by David Tarr and Constantine Michalopoulos, Washington, DC.
World Bank, (1992/E), *Russian Economic Reform: Crossing the Threshold of Structural Change*, Washington, DC.
World Bank, (1992/F), *Income Transfers and the Social Safety Net in Russia*, by Nicholas Barr, Washington, DC.
World Bank, (1992/G), *The CMEA System of Trade and Payments*, by Martin Schrenk, Washington, DC.
World Bank, (1992/H), *Proposals for Post-CMEA Trade and Payments Arrangements*, by David Tarr, Washington, DC.
World Bank, (1992/J), *How Changes in the Former CMEA Area may Affect International Trade in Manufactures*, Washington, DC.
World Bank, (1992/K), *European Integration and Trade with the Developing World*, Washington, DC.
Yeldan, Erinç (1990), 'İhracata Yönelik Sanayileşme ve Bölüşüm-Uyumsuz Büyüme: Türkiye 1980-1989', *Boğaziçi Üniversitesi Ekonomi ve İdari Bilimler Dergisi*, Kış 1990, pp. 332-33.
Zielinski, (1969), *The Consumption Model and Means of its Implementation*, in Brus and Laski, 1969.

Index